Reprints of Economic Classics

THE WAYS AND MEANS OF PAYMENT

The WAYS and MEANS of PAYMENT

By

STEPHEN COLWELL

[1859]

REPRINTS OF ECONOMIC CLASSICS

AUGUSTUS M. KELLEY • PUBLISHER
NEW YORK • 1965

LIBRARY OF CONGRESS CATALOGUE CARD NUMBER
65-23212

PRINTED IN THE UNITED STATES OF AMERICA
by SENTRY PRESS, NEW YORK, N. Y. 10019

THE

WAYS AND MEANS

OF

PAYMENT:

A

FULL ANALYSIS

OF

THE CREDIT SYSTEM,

WITH ITS

VARIOUS MODES OF ADJUSTMENT.

BY

STEPHEN COLWELL.

PHILADELPHIA:
J. B. LIPPINCOTT & CO.
1859.

CONTENTS.

PAGE

INTRODUCTION 1

CHAPTER I.

Exchange of commodities an incident of civilized life — Agencies of this exchange not to be confounded with the exchange itself — The fitness of these agencies best determined by treating them as agencies more or less necessary to the main purpose, but not indispensable — Money, and money of account 25

CHAPTER II.

MONEY OF ACCOUNT.

§ 1. The employment of gold and silver involves terms in which to express their value — Mint price and market price — Money of account a necessity 31

§ 2. Idea of value carried in the mind as the idea of weights, measures of length and capacity — The use of money of account is much greater than of money—Often confused in language — Kelly's Cambist — Varieties of moneys of account — Decimal system 35

§ 3. British money of account — The pound sterling — Guinea — Sir Isaac Newton — Lord Liverpool and the system of 1816—Why fractions in weight of coins—Coins adjusted to money of account—"What is a pound?" — Fixed price of precious metals — Influx of gold — Depreciation only postponed — Remedy — Suspension of payments in Great Britain in 1797 46

§ 4. Colonial currency of Canada, and of the thirteen colonies now part of the United States 55

§ 5. Moneys of account in Italy, Germany, &c. — Evils of varied coinage — Coinage implies a previous price — Coins not a measure — Prices in money of account understood instantaneously — Ricardo — Sir James Stewart — Bishop Berkeley — Montesquieu — Money of account, its limits of usefulness — Edinburgh Review 59

Notes to Chapter II.

I. Marquis Garnier and his critic, Letronne.......................... 75

II. Extract from a paper by the author, in the Bankers' Magazine — Prices — British money of account — Locke and Lowndes, and the recoinage controversy of 1695 — Continental currency—Introduction of dollar unit — Robert Morris — Alexander Hamilton............ 77

III. Extract from a paper by the author, in Hunt's Merchants' Magazine — Nature and functions of money of account — Disturbance of prices of precious metals — Legal tender — Depreciation of paper currency — Coinage system of Great Britain...................... 90

CHAPTER III.

GOLD AND SILVER AS MONEY.

§ 1. Gold and silver a common equivalent or medium in the interchange of commodities — Circulation by weight — Not constituted money by coinage, which only facilitates circulation — Diversity of mints, and confusion of coins —Wear and waste — Clipping, filing, sweating and counterfeiting.................................... 101

§ 2. Circulation of the precious metals as money — Commerce depends on coins for so much use as is made of them, and no more — They perform no functions beyond the use we see made of them.... 110

§ 3. Quantity of money required for the business of a country....... 118

CHAPTER IV.

GOLD AND SILVER STANDARD OF PAYMENT.

§ 1. The precious metals neither a measure nor a standard of value — The legal standard of payment— Standard of coinage — Legal tender — Objections to legal price of gold and silver — Earl of Liverpool — Price of gold fixed by authority in Great Britain — Seignorage on coins for retail business —Waste and folly of incessant recoinage — Legal tender at market price safe in large transactions............ 123

§ 2. Coinage — French coinage — Debasement, frauds, disturbed money of account — System of the United States — Act of Congress, 1792, adopting the dollar unit — Price of gold fixed — Results — Act of June, 1834, reducing weight of gold coins — Result — Act of February, 1853 — Silver coinage — Ingots of gold — Export of silver. 137

Notes to Chapter IV.

I. Earl of Liverpool — British system of coinage adopted in 1816.... 146

II. System of coinage in the United States — Double standard — Proposed adoption of single standard of gold, as a remedy for scarcity of silver — Reduction in the value of our silver coins.............. 149

CHAPTER V.

COINS NOT A MODEL CURRENCY.

The actual use of coins measures their importance and power — Modes of payment more efficient — Each to be judged upon its merits — Usages of trade assign to coins their office — Not a model currency — Bear no higher interest than a credit in bank — The British act of 1844, requiring the issues of banks to fluctuate as gold — Sir Robert Peel — Lord Overstone — Col. Torrens — Question one of commerce and payment — Return to hard currency impossible..... 155

CHAPTER VI.

BANKS OF DEPOSIT.

§ 1. Bank of Amsterdam.. 174

§ 2. Bank of Hamburg.. 181

Note to Chapter VI.

Bank of Amsterdam.. 184

CHAPTER VII.

THE CREDIT SYSTEM.

§ 1. Distinction between credit and the credit system — The latter defined — Business of payments separated from the business of distributing commodities — Trade made virtually a barter — Division of labor leads to this — Relations of debtor and creditor mutual, and mainly among the same classes — The fund which pays debts derived from credits the counterpart of debts — Credits as a currency — Convertibility — Blending credits and money — Diversion of credits from their proper functions.................................. 188

§ 2. Books of account... 200

CHAPTER VIII.

COMMERCIAL SECURITIES.

§ 1. Promissory notes and bills of exchange, their efficiency as means of payment — As evidences of debt, they aid in separating the business of trade from that of payments—Dealers in exchange—Bankers—Concentration of debts and credits—Balances—Use of notes and bills in Lancashire, England, and in the United States — Limits of use in payments — Mutual debts and set-off.......................... 205

§ 2. Foreign exchange a means of payment — Complicated with coinage and its evils, and with increased transactions of domestic trade— Processes of foreign payments readily perceived — Imports — Exports — Dealers in exchange and bankers — Payments, where to be made — Rate of exchange — Circuitous exchange — Fluctuations in exchange — Economy of payment increases trade................ 212

§ 3. Fallacy of making foreign exchange a criterion of domestic currency—Foreign exchange simply the process of paying and receiving debts of foreign trade — The medium employed has its proper agency — So with payments of domestic trade — Neither should guide nor control the other — Payments as distinct as the trade to which they belong — Long-continued adverse foreign exchange of American colonies, and its results.............................. 221

Note to Chapter VIII.

Foreign exchange, its relations with banks — Export of specie — Contraction of our currency — Resident agents of foreign merchants and manufacturers, their influence on foreign exchange and domestic currency.. 228

CHAPTER IX.

BANK-NOTES.

Facility and power of bank-notes—Disadvantages—Issued in exchange for paper of individuals — Convertibility not the basis of bank-notes, but a security against abuses — Inadequacy — Banks, and the restraints imposed upon them — Bank-notes a medium by which commodities pay for commodities—Demand for bank-notes by the debtors of banks, the cause and result — Bank-notes and progress of consumption — Circulation and efficiency — Exchange between banks — Proportion of bank-notes decreasing.............................. 231

CHAPTER X.

DEPOSITS IN BANKS.

A greater facility than bank-notes needful — Banks the reservoir of funds not in actual use — The fund employed in large payments — Credits the fund which pays debts — Depositors employ their credits to pay their debts — The credits will pay the debts — Deposits virtually a system of accounts kept by the banks for their customers — Indebtedness chiefly mutual, and settled by set-off — Demand for deposits — Circulation — Absorbed by the banks in payments of discounted paper — The banks pay for paper with credits, and receive them in payment.. 241

CHAPTER XI.

CLEARING-HOUSES.

§ 1. The Clearing-house of London — Private bankers — Concentration of payments — Mutual adjustment — Mutuality of debts — Processes at the Clearing-house — Amounts cleared — Bullion Report of 1810 — Sir Henry Thornton — Relations of clearing to commerce — Banks and their customers — Payments of foreign trade — Domestic payments of special districts — The credit system — New channels for the precious metals.......... 252

§ 2. Bank adjustment in the United States — Clearing between the banks — Mutual accounts and correspondence — Domestic exchange — Balances of home trade — Mutual debts the basis of this adjustment — The system of clearing in New England, at the Suffolk Bank of Boston.......... 265

§ 3. Clearing between the banks of Scotland — Balances payable in Exchequer bills, notes of the Bank of England, or gold — Their system of deposit, and its influence upon business — Stimulus to punctuality and industry — Circulation of bank-notes in Scotland — One pound notes.......... 271

CHAPTER XII.

FAIRS.

Commercial Fairs of the 13th, 14th and 15th centuries — Continued on the confines of Asia and Europe—Kiachta—Nijni Novgorod—Kief—Concentration of payments — Fairs of Lyons — Payments of Lyons — The opening — Mode of conducting —Viramen de partie — Setting-off debts — Payment of balances — Results — Rationale — Illustrations — Fairs of Novi and others in Italy chiefly for payments... 275

CHAPTER XIII.

THE BANK OF VENICE.

Bank of Venice — Originated 1171, in a loan to the Republic — Office of transfer — Interest paid — Transfers in payment of commodities and debts — Sums deposited taken by the Republic — In 1423, bills of exchange and payments in gross made only in bank — Premium on bank funds — Circulation — Banco del Giro — Evils of coinage, and severity of laws — Department for deposits repayable on demand and transferable—Its success—Deposits taken by the Government, but repaid — Capital of the Bank — London Encyclopædia corrected — Causes of agio — Precautions against fraud — Concentration of payments at Venice.......... 288

CHAPTER XIV.

THE BANK OF GENOA.

House of St. George, or Bank of Genoa — Contrast in financial systems of Venice and Genoa — Complications of Genoese finance — Security exacted by public creditors — The system of 1302, its officers — Private bankers — Bank in 1407 — Large array of officers — Deferred dividends, or Moneta di Paghe — Famine of 1539 — Deposit system — Bank bills — Price of shares — Money and moneys of account — Advantages of Bank to trade — Processes of the Bank — M. Gautier and M. Coquelin on the moneys of account of the Bank — Carlo Cuneo on the moneys of Genoa.......... 311

Note to Chapter XIV.

Italian writers — Dictionnaire du Commerce, Paris, 1839, corrected... 337

CHAPTER XV.

THE BANK OF ENGLAND.

§ 1. Opinions and projects on credit and currency previous to the Bank of England — Samuel Lambe's plan, 1665 — Evils of the coinage—Dr. Hugh Chamberlain's plan, 1665—Large model of a Bank, 1678 — Bank of Credit, 1682 — Bank of Credit, 1683 — R. Murray's plan, 1695 — J. Asgill's plan, 1696 — Office of credit, 1698......... 339

§ 2. Bank of England chartered in 1694 —William Patterson the projector — Founded on a loan of £1,200,000 at eight per cent.— Opposition and objections — Commenced 1695 — Bank-notes — Advances to government — Recoinage — Rate of discount — Business of the Bank — Deposits — Bank bills — Credit — Goldsmiths robbed by Charles II. — Safety of deposits — Use of deposits — Bank bills payable on demand — Bills of exchange and promissory notes on time — Convertibility — Bank-notes not substitutes for specie, but for commercial paper: should fluctuate with this paper, and not with coin — Concentration of payments in London.......... 352

§ 3. Bank of England's credits in account — Deposit of bank-notes — Conversion of individual paper into bank-notes — Bank issues credits, and receives credits in payment — Credits wrongly blended with deposits — Open credits payable on demand hazardous — Objections — Credits payable on demand abolishes time on bills of exchange and promissory notes — Mingling credit and money — Consequences — Real nature of credits in account — Expand with trade, diminish with it — Not money — Payment by bank credits not dependent on money — Not a question of convertibility........ 379

§ 4. Bank of England suspension from 1797 to 1822 — Order of Privy Council — Opposition — Terms of suspension — Extensions — Progress of the country during suspension — Dissatisfaction — Lord King — Convertibility — Processes of payment the same during suspension as before — Bank issues and the commodities of trade — The credit system — Controversy as to depreciation during suspension — Bullion Report, 1810 — Bullionists and anti-Bullionists — Tooke's History of Prices — Prices of gold and silver, and amount of circulation, from 1797 to 1821 394

CHAPTER XVI.

THE BANKS OF SCOTLAND.

The Bank of Scotland chartered, 1695 — John Holland's account — Contrast with Bank of England — Founders of the Scottish Bank avoid relations with Government — Object, economy of money — Bank-notes — Trouble with Royal Bank — Suspension — Modes of relief — Identified with masses, by receiving small deposits on interest — Forty banks, 340 branches — Harmony — English prejudices, Scotch scorn — Cash credits a principal feature — Contrasts with English system — Scotch system equally effective, and safer — Bank failures few, and not disastrous — Suspension of 1797 in England without effect in Scotland — Reports to the House of Lords and to the Commons, 1826 — System not cordially approved in England — One-pound notes — Discussions — Sir Walter Scott's level of gold — Modes of regarding the subject in England and Scotland—Scotch Banks the pride of the people —W. Chambers' distrust, with explanations 407

Note to Chapter XVI.

Regulations for exchange of Scotch Bankers' notes 442

CHAPTER XVII.

BANKS OF THE UNITED STATES.

§ 1. Banks are agencies of payment—Discussions and different views —Banks are dealers in credits — General waiver of legal currency— Paying fund from the proceeds of discounted notes — Banks absorb their own issues — Process exemplified — Demand for bank currency makes it good — Commodities of trade held by debtors to banks — Sold to pay the banks — Bank currency the medium — Commodities the basis ; individual and bank paper mere securities and means of adjustment—Circulation and deposits of New York banks in 1857— Daily payments — Banks of the United States pay and are paid in their own currency, and thus furnish a safe medium for circulation — Mutual debts 444

§ 2. Bank-notes not money, but promissory notes of banks—Perform the functions of money — Deposits are so employed, but are not money—Both substituted by banks for notes of individuals — Banks make securities of paper, not money — Convertibility of bank-notes does not make them money; it is a mere check on the banks — Gold and silver not the basis of bank issues; these are based on paper discounted by the banks, and this paper is based on the commodities for which it is given — Convertibility an inadequate check — Employed with fatal effect against those who rely upon it — It abolishes time on commercial paper.................................. 459

§ 3. Bank issues and agency the chief actual medium of payment — New York banks in 1857 — Contraction of currency — Fund used to pay debts —Process of paying continuous —City banks and country banks — The former chief agents in payments — Demand for specie — Panics — Results — Banks increase, despite abuses of banking—Effects of rapid contractions of currency—What is called specie payments — Banks at the mercy of the mob — Men of business at the mercy of banks.. 475

§ 4. Public right to the facilities afforded by banks — Contractions of the currency, and results —Remedies —Discounts, proceeds payable at a future day in money, but receivable at all times for debts to banks — Deposits payable at a future day, but receivable in bank for debts — Bank-notes payable at a day future, but receivable for debts — Long credits an element of disturbance in the credit system — Diversion of funds of the credit system from their proper channels — Country banks — Their business of a different nature — Present banking system not adapted to it........................... 489

CHAPTER XVIII.

INTEREST.

Distinction between prices of precious metals and interest, or the price payable for the use of them — The price of each fixed by the State—Evasion — Fluctuations in price of gold and silver not coincident with rates of interest — High interest makes no demand for coins — Demand for facilities of credit system determines the rate of interest — High interest does not arise from scarcity of that for which interest is paid, but from fears of banks and capitalists — Usury laws should not apply to paper of the credit system—Amount paid yearly in the United States for interest — Objections — Interest a part of the expense of commercial adjustment — Not a question of money, but of dispensing with money — Economy of interest practicable in England and the United States. 509

CHAPTER XIX.

PRICES.

§ 1. Complexity of the subject — Market value expressed in money of account — Money is for payment — Prices, sales and payments distinct things — Elements of prices — Influence of interests and passions — Necessity of purchasing — Necessity of selling—Fashion and fancy — Plenty and scarcity — Demand and supply — Monopolies — Commercial legislation — Duties — Speculation—Cost of production — Prices in great marts of trade........................ 521

§ 2. Effect upon prices of quantity of money—Theory of Montesquieu acceded to by Hume, Locke, and Harris; denied by Sir James Stewart, Adam Smith, Lauderdale, Malthus, Ricardo, Torrens, M'Culloch — James Mill — Prices not expressed in coins, but in money of account—Wholesale mainly control retail prices—Lauderdale — Malthus — Torrens — M'Culloch — Conflict of opinions — Marquis Garnier — Adam Smith — Ganihl — Humboldt's proportion of gold to silver—Jacob on precious metals — Rise of prices not in proportion to the increase of money—Arthur Young's inquiry into the progressive value of money—Tables of prices in Spain—Beawes — Prices of wheat in France.................................... 538

§ 3. Effects of bank currency upon prices — Increase of wealth in Great Britain in 18th century — Advance in prices increases currency — Power of purchasing depends not upon money, but upon personal confidence — High confidence leads to speculation — Lord Overstone — Tooke's History of Prices — His examination before the Secret Committee of 1832—Evidence on prices before Parliamentary committees of 1832 and 1840 — Influx of gold from California and Australia — Comparison of currencies in United States in 1848 and 1856 — Prices the scale by which products of labor are exchanged—Justice to labor determined by what men can purchase, not by the price they pay.. 564

CHAPTER XX.

PUBLIC PAYMENTS.

§ 1. Processes of receiving and paying — British Exchequer, its practice—Exchequer bills introduced by Earl of Halifax — British revenue always anticipated — Floating debt a saving of interest — Exchequer bills suited to a certain class of lenders — Quantity carefully gauged to the demand —Wisely managed by the Bank of England—Advantage of disbursing revenue before its receipt, thus furnishing the currency in which the revenue is paid — Amount of Exchequer bills issued — Reduction of circulation by sale of Exchequer bills — Rate of interest — The Exchequer and the Bank — British system in contrast with that of the United States........................ 577

§ 2. Financial system of France — Count Mollien and Marquis D'Audiffret — Harmony and subordination of the system — Outline — Relations with domestic exchange — Special distribution of public funds — Money in treasury shortest time possible — Economy of new system — Commission on transfers — D'Audiffret — Money advanced on public account — Firmness of the system — France first appreciates relations of public finance with trade and industry — Perils of credit lessened by this system — Want of details — Contrast with system of United States.......... 594

§ 3. Treasury of the United States — Act of Congress, 1846 — Paper currency the usage of the country — Departure from usage — Effect upon banks — Advance of interest — Increase of private banks — Economy of the system — The remedy a step towards banking — Domestic exchange and the treasury — Centre of operations of treasury and domestic exchanges in New York — Transmission of funds to and from New York — Paper operations of treasury — Present system and the public creditors — Indirect taxation and California gold favored the Independent Treasury....................... 605

Note.—Extracts from Reports of Secretaries of Treasury, Mr. Meredith and Mr. Guthrie, on the subject of Independent Treasury, and also from Report of Mr. Casey, Treasurer.......................... 613

§ 4. Independent Treasury a result of financial difficulties — State banks — Currency of government paper and specie — Opposition to banks and paper currency — Bank of France — Banks not to be crushed, but replaced — Financial system of the act of 1846 — Treasury notes payable on demand without interest, and at six and twelve months with interest — French loans of 1854–5 —Whole loan offered by people in France out of Paris — Board of Treasurers — Principles restricting the issue of treasury notes — Lenders of money, their relations with the treasury — Offices in Washington and New York — Connection of treasury with domestic exchange — Friction — A remedy required, and co-operation of the treasury — A national institution to form point of contact between the treasury and the domestic exchange.................................. 621

Note.—Mr. Guthrie's remarks on banking system of United States.... 626

INTRODUCTION.

We propose to offer here, in as condensed form as practicable, what may be considered as the leading positions of this volume. A statement of this kind will enable every reader to glance more readily over those portions of the work of most interest to himself. It is taken for granted, that whilst there are so many conflicting opinions on the subject of money, currency, banking and credit — that whilst both theory and practice remain in doubt and dispute, and no authority high enough to settle these differences has yet appeared — there is room for the labors of those who may wish to furnish materials for the final adjustment of many vexed questions. It is further assumed that writers treating of these subjects have paid too little attention to the fact, that whatever concerns money, currency, banking and credit, must be considered as strictly subordinate to commerce, of which they are merely agents; this cannot be overlooked, in any aspect in which these topics may be considered, without hazard of error.

The chief inquiry is not, What is the power of money? or, What is the use of money? or, What can be substituted for money? The inquiry which we prosecute, to ascertain the nature and doctrine of money, is, What is commerce, and what is the nature of the agency of money in its affairs? Money, with all its substitutes, is only one of many agents of trade, and, like many others, it is a pure matter of discretion and convenience how far it may be employed. Warehouses and ships are very needful and much used agencies of commerce; but a great business may, upon occasion, be done without them. It is with money, as with every other expensive agency of commerce, a question not how much it can be used, but how far it can be dispensed with. It has always been, and must always be, a chief consideration of the practical merchant, to ascertain to what extent his business can be conducted without so expensive an agent as money. By the progress of civilization, commercial integrity and Christian virtue, it is now possible to carry on immense operations in trade and manufactures without any aid from money; excepting the merest retail business, not one per cent. of the payments of Great Britain and the United States are made in real money.

The main subject of this volume is not, therefore, money, but payments. The inquiry before us has been, not the nature and use of money, but how are the payments or adjustments of commerce effected, whether by money or otherwise. The object has not been to bring forward new doctrines, or to propose reforms, but to attempt a very ample and thorough analysis of the present modes of employing money and credit in the current business of industry and trade. We have supposed that the best preparation for reforms and improvements would be a perfect understanding of the present system, in its various forms. Any suggestion in these pages which may seem to go beyond this, is made with the greatest diffidence, and more by way of contrast or illustration than as advice or doctrine.

It has long appeared to us a grave mistake in those who have treated of money, that they leave out of view money of account, without a due understanding of which, as an agency of commerce, much confusion must reign in the minds of all who approach the study of money or currency. Gold and silver are commodities of great value in small compass, selected for coinage, and made the legal standard of payment; money of account is the language in which prices are expressed, and books of account are kept. A merchant may, in a few minutes, cast his eye over a hundred entries in his journal, in which the sums debited for goods sold may run, in various fractionary sums, from ten to a thousand dollars. He sees at a glance, and understands at what rates the goods were sold. But if the exact sum in coins corresponding to each entry was placed opposite to the entry, instead of the appropriate figures, it might require hours or days to ascertain, by counting and examining the coins, what is otherwise understood in a few minutes. So, likewise, naming prices in money of account is quickly done, and instantly understood; but making payments in coins is necessarily a slow operation. We distinguish, then, between the term money, as applied to giving prices, to keeping books of account, to expressing sums on the face of promissory notes, bills of exchange, and other securities, and the term money, as applied to coins used in making a payment; and this distinction we hold to be so important, that the subject cannot be well understood without it. To some it may appear as if we had labored this point at needless length, and with unnecessary minuteness; but regarding it as the key to many difficulties of finance, and considering the neglect of the subject hitherto, we have thought it better to be profuse of illustration, than to fail of our object in securing for money of account its true position in the consideration of the subject.

People may change their coins once a month; but they scarce change a money of account in half a century. In many of the more retired portions of the older States of the Union, the people still reckon by the colonial currencies of pounds, shillings and pence, as they existed in each of the respective colonies before the era of our independence. The use of a money of account is a mental operation, and is a characteristic of every civilized people. The same mental habit is applied to the use of weights and measures, which makes it extremely difficult to change even what is obviously absurd; people prefer denominations to which they are accustomed, even when inconvenient, to those which are more simple, but which need the familiarity of habit to make them appreciated.

We have, therefore, treated money of account as a leading element of the subject. It is the language of prices, of books of account, of price-currents; it is the mode of expression employed in all money securities, to denote the amount for which they are given; and, in fine, it is the very language of finance. To leave money of account out, when the whole subject of currency, banking and credit is involved, is like leaving arithmetic out of mathematics. It is for want of attention to the real agency of money of account, that such expressions as the "power of money" are often used, when only the power of credit is intended. When a merchant inquires the price of a hundred bags of coffee, learns the rate, and makes the purchase, giving his note for the amount, money has exercised neither power nor influence in the transaction. It was the power of credit which made the purchase, and the power of money of account which enabled the parties to understand each other, make the transaction, and take the note for the amount of the purchase. The greatest power in the commercial world is commercial integrity, and the confidence or credit which it inspires. This is the power which moves nine-tenths of the commodities found in the channels of trade and industry.

Money, by which we intend coins of gold or silver, is neither a standard of value, a measure of value, nor a representative of value.

The precious metals are commodities of value, and do not, of course, lose that quality, though they gain another, by being coined. They become, by coinage and the law of legal tender, a standard of payment. Every man may, by law, claim payment in coins; that is, for any commodity previously sold, for any debt due, every person may exact the expressed equivalent in the commodity of gold and silver assayed and coined at the mint in denominations agreeing with the money of account. All debts are thus payable; and it is only because the parties agree to other modes of payment, that all debts are not thus paid.

There are many obstacles to the use of coins in large transactions, besides their great cost; among these, the risks of theft and robbery, and the care and anxiety which these hazards impose, the danger of counterfeits, the rapid wear and deterioration of coins, the frauds of clipping, punching, sweating, and many others, which are regarded as severe grievances and trials in all countries where an exclusively metallic currency has long prevailed. All these combined have produced a constant effort to escape the employment of coins in large transactions. Gold and silver coins have not lost their interest in the eyes of men; they are still the standard of payment, and universally an acceptable medium of exchange; but they are far from being the universally employed medium of exchange. The men of trade and industry, who but receive money in large amounts to pass it off in the same way, are more concerned to escape trouble, risk and expense in the matter of payment, than anxious to employ only gold and silver which have passed through the mint.

At the present time, then, the precious metals are employed only as the standard of payment, or legal tender, to be appealed to in case of disagreement, a very rare occurrence; as the medium of the merest retail trade; as a reserve or security for their issues, by banks of circulation; and as the medium of paying balances of trade, both foreign and domestic. All these together make not five per cent. of the operations of industry and trade in this country, or in Great Britain. We cannot adopt any safer criterion of the actual power of the precious metals as money, than what we see; their importance and use is precisely what we know to be done with them; nothing more. All the rest is accomplished by means of credit, and the many processes of the credit system.

It must be a great and mischievous fallacy, then, to regard gold and silver coins as a sort of model medium of exchange, to the characteristics and incidents of which all other modes of interchange must be made to correspond. This is nothing less than an attempt to fasten upon industry and commerce the very shackles and inconveniences which they have long been struggling to cast away. There are many ways of making payments without using coins, each of which may stand for what it is worth, and be employed according as it may be available, without being tortured to work as coins would have worked, if they had been employed. When two men of bnsiness deal largely together, keeping the record in their books of account, which once in three months are balanced, and the mutual debts thus paid without any use of coins, there is no possible sense in which the mutual payment thus effected could be made more effectual by any reference to coins, than by this simple and economical method of balancing the sums of the various entries, debts and credits, expressed in money of account, the one against the other. This mode of payment needs no aid in theory, in practice, or by analogy, from any employment of coins; but this mode of payment is one of the main devices of the credit system. As the debts of men of business find their way into the banks, so do their credits; and the functions of the banks, stripped of their many complications, consist chiefly in balancing and thus extinguishing the debts and credits of their customers.

There is no ground, we think, for the doctrine that the incidents and characteristics which attend a currency of gold and silver should be imitated, or even referred to, in the processes of the credit system, much less be regarded as laws. All are equally agents or processes of commerce, and must be considered and judged upon their respective merits, and be employed according to the opinions and sound discretion of the parties concerned. Coins become indispensable only when claimed as a legal right.

The real origin of the deposit banks, such as Amsterdam and Hamburg, was the worn and deteriorated state of the coinage, which, at that time, was a grievance of a magnitude which only those familiar with the commercial history of that period can realize. This evil is only less now, because the circulation of coins is nearly dispensed with. These deposit banks proved to be more useful than their projectors anticipated. The circulation of the ownership of the coins was found to be much more rapid and easy than the circulation of the coins. The wear and tear was saved, and they were more efficient in bank than out of it. And it was ultimately revealed at Amsterdam, that the transfers and payments at the bank could proceed for scores of years after the specie had been removed. This, however, should have been well understood from the first establishment of the bank; for, while the ownership of the deposits was changing every day, no one had an opportunity of verifying the fact of the amount being actually in the bank. Every man who accepted a credit in the bank took it upon his confidence in its administration. The money system, to this extent, thus resolved itself, by a sort of necessity, into a credit system.

The credit system was, in fact, a growth (*ex necessitate rei*) of necessity. It was indispensable to the advance of civilization and industry; it grew with the progress of commercial punctuality and integrity; it now flourishes only in this soil, and cannot be destroyed where it finds this aliment of its growth. It sent forth many vigorous shoots, in various countries, long before it attained its present magnitude and wide extension. The payments at the fairs so prevalent in Europe during the middle ages, some of which continue even down to our time, were, to a large extent, made by setting-off debts against debts. Men learned to pay their debts with their credits; and this mode of payment only disappeared as the progress of the credit system, and the growth of cities, absorbed both the business and the payments of the fairs. These payments at the fairs revealed that the best fund with which to pay debts is debts. Every debt implying a credit, no one could better employ his credits than in paying his debts. This required no money, and was, therefore, not only economical, but free from innumerable risks and troubles inseparably connected with payments in money.

The Banks of Venice and Genoa were both remarkable forerunners of the credit system, and beautiful examples of its economy and power. The political and commercial importance of these two great republics were, in a great measure, owing to their respective banks, the oldest and most important of which we have any account. The lessons taught by these institutions have no doubt entered largely into the progress of the credit system, as now developed; but we strongly insist that the study of the system of these two banks is yet necessary to any thorough comprehension of the power of credit, and of what is necessary to an enlarged and efficient financial system.

The capital of the Bank of Venice consisted of a debt due by the republic to its citizens. The government took the money, and gave in its place an inscription on the books of the bank for the amount, bearing interest. The government returned the money immediately into the channels of circulation among its citizens, whilst the lenders of the money circulated the debt as a deposit in the bank. All the large payments of this great commercial city were, for many centuries, paid in this fund, and the gold and silver coins were released for the purposes of the retail trade, the payment of foreign debts, and the foreign expenditures of the republic. The government of Venice dealt faithfully with these holders of stock in the bank, not only paying the interest punctually, but redeeming any amount which seemed superfluous, or beyond the demand of the public. This policy not only kept the bank fund at par with specie, but more than twenty per cent. above it. The bank was always open to further loans to the government, when such investment was in demand. The capital of the bank fluctuated in amount according to the wants of the people, and not according to the wants of the public treasury.

The Bank of Venice performed its functions for over five hundred years, with an uniformity of success, and immunity from censure or complaint, which no other currency has enjoyed for a tithe of that period. During that time of vast commerce and immense public expenditure, the republic had incessant trouble with their own and foreign coinage, and very many stringent regulations were made and enforced, to cure evils and prevent abuses; but we have no record of abuses on the part of the bank, or of injuries inflicted by it upon the people.

Believing that the commercial fairs of Europe, and the Banks of Venice and Genoa, were capable of imparting historical lessons not yet properly appreciated, we have brought them more prominently before the reader than has been done in any work upon money or currency. We have, in later times, achieved a method of clearing debts between banks; but a lesson may be learned from the payments at the fairs, of successful clearing between individuals. There is no reason, in theory or in practice, why clearing may not, to a considerable extent, be practised between individuals mutually indebted. The history of these fairs furnishes abundant exemplification of this most economical and effective of all the modes of payment.

The history of these celebrated banks furnishes other lessons which will richly repay the most careful attention. They demonstrated the efficacy of circulating deposits as a means of payment, and that the deposits were just as effective when they consisted of a debt due from the government, as if they were gold or silver; and they showed that it was possible to keep the amount of this public debt, as held by the depositors in the banks, within a range of amount which not only prevented depreciation, but kept the deposits always from fifteen to thirty per cent. above gold and silver.

The distinction between credit — the confidence which men place in each other, and which induces them to defer the day of payment for goods purchased — and the credit system has not, in our view, been sufficiently observed. The credit system springs from credit; there could be no credit system without the exercise of that confidence which accepts a future instead of a present payment. The two processes are, however, wholly different; credit refers to confidence, and to the postponement of payment; the credit system refers chiefly to the mode of payment. It is that system by which the payments for commodities are separated from the transactions to which they belong, and made a separate business. More than nine-tenths of all the payments of industry and trade are effected through the processes of the credit system. The payments thus made are in no degree connected with, nor dependent upon any reference to, or any employment of the precious metals. The credit system is that by which men set-off the debts which others owe them against those which they owe to others. This, of all modes of payment, involves the least risk, and is the most effective, satisfactory and economical. No currency can be more suited to pay a man with than that which he has issued himself. It is that which the credit system employs; and it may be added, that this system keeps books of account for those who avail themselves of it, in which they take credit for what others owe them, and are debited with what they owe others.

The magnitude and complication of the credit system conceal its details, and render it, as a whole, difficult of comprehension. It is only by severe and continued analysis that the processes of this vast system of payments can be even partially displayed to the view of the reader.

Books of account may be regarded as one of its most effective agencies. The merchant who debits a manufacturer five thousand dollars for raw materials in the course of six months, and gives him credit for finished goods to the amount of seven thousand dollars in the same period, is very willing to unite with his customer in discharging ten thousand dollars of this debt by balancing the account between them, leaving only two thousand to be paid otherwise than by the balance. The merchant and his customer each receive payment of five thousand dollars without money or currency. Each is paid with the debt he owes; the book is the evidence of the debts, and the balancing is the act of payment.

The issue of promissory notes by each of these parties for the five thousand dollars does not alter the nature of the transaction, but only the mode of payment. The notes, instead of the books, become evidences of debt; and if the notes are exchanged directly, no other payment is necessary. If the merchant finds it for his interest to negotiate the note held by him, the complication commences. But the debts to be paid are not increased; the real nature of the business remains the same; the parties have only changed. The merchant receives the amount payable to him from the person to whom he negotiated the note; and with the amount so received he can pay the note given by him to his customer; and this customer can, with the amount so received, pay the amount of his note negotiated by the merchant. It is the same when both parties negotiate the notes they take; both remain debtors for the notes they gave, and both receive the amount needful to pay, from the parties to whom they transfer the notes. It is thus with all who give and take notes in the course of their business; they use the notes they receive to effect the payment of the notes they give; and it is the same with bills of exchange.

To effect this, further complications and devices become necessary. A class of men is formed, who make it their business to deal in these securities, or evidences of debt. If a banker or broker purchases the two notes given by the merchant and his customer, it is obvious that both receive the means from him to pay the notes of which he has become holder and owner. The process of payment between them will be very simple, if the banker merely give each of the two parties credit on his books for the proceeds of the notes purchased of them. Their respective checks on these credits pay off the whole indebtedness, except the interest deducted for the time the notes had to run, which interest they must pay in other funds.

Banks become, in this way, substantially book-keepers for their customers. They discount promissory notes and bills of exchange at their instance, giving them credit in account for the proceeds; the banks can well afford to take checks upon these proceeds in payment, because they give nothing else for the paper; and every check given in payment reduces the liability of the bank to that amount. The customers of the banks are indebted in large amounts for notes given, and are creditors in large amounts for notes received; the notes are all either discounted by the banks, or placed in them for collection; and the banks thus represent both creditors and debtors. So far as the banks have issued bank-notes, or given credit for promissory notes and bills of exchange, they can receive them in payment, for it is their own currency. Their liabilities to the public are for bank-notes, and credits on deposit; and the return of these in payment is a redemption, to that extent, of their liability.

The books of the banks furnish, thus, a mode of adjustment by which the customers are enabled to apply their credits to the payment of their debts. The profit or commission of the banks is the interest for the time the discounted notes have to run. Promissory notes placed in the banks for collection are usually paid in the same way: the banks can afford to take their own currency for these also, because it is, to that extent, a further redemption of their debt to the public. So far as the indebtedness of the customers of the banks is mutual, it is readily extinguished, for to that amount the debtors hold credits sufficient to make their payments. Every one who has a balance to pay, must do it, of course, to the satisfaction of the bank. It is by the operation of this process that the discharge of much the largest portion of the debts annually paid in the United States is effected.

This process continues with a regular step, because the notes held by the banks mature day by day, and must be met; the proper fund to pay them is that which the banks gave for them, and this is not only the most abundant, but the most accessible. The demand for this fund is, therefore, as strong and constant as the necessity of paying commercial paper at maturity. In becoming chief creditors of the men of business, the banks issue a currency which would not otherwise exist, and which becomes a medium specially adapted, in quantity and kind, to pay every debt due to them. The debts payable at the banks are the proper absorbents of the currency issued by the banks. This currency is good, and attains circulation because it is in demand, not only by all the debtors of the banks, but by all who are their debtors. Such a large and constant demand, in fact, makes this currency available to a very wide extent.

The debtors of the banks become such by giving promissory notes for commodities of trade in general use; and they stand ready to receive for these commodities that bank currency which will pay their debts. The tendency of this currency is, therefore, and should be, to flow back to the banks in extinguishment of debts there payable.

In this, as in many other things, where the largest advantage is found, there is found also the greatest danger of abuse. The great demand for this currency, arising from the urgent necessity under which debtors to the banks are placed, of paying their notes as they mature, invests the bank currency with the full power of money; for that which will pay such a vast amount of debt is needed by so many, that it will purchase whatever can be obtained for money. The banks seem thus to have it in their power to manufacture money, and they are importuned to lend this currency as if it were money. Their power of safely issuing it is limited strictly to the demands of those who require it to pay debts maturing in the banks. It can only be good when the debtors of the banks are able to purchase it from the hands of the public, and when they do so purchase it to pay their debts in bank. It is not money; it has only this function of paying debts in bank, and circulating as a substitute for money, under the stimulus of the demand for it by the debtors of the banks.

The banks have, however, at various times and places, fallen largely into the error of lending their currency as money; and there have been many occasions and periods when their debtors became unable to return it to the banks; and then it was often found that the promises of the bank were worth not so much as the paper on which they were printed. No more of this currency can be issued safely than the banks can find not merely safe men to borrow, but men who have something with which they can actually redeem it from the hands of the public, and restore it to the issuers. If the circulation is not kept active by the demand of the debtors, and if they do not return it at as rapid a rate as that at which it is issued, payment will be demanded of the banks at a rate with which they cannot possibly comply. This abuse of issuing currency without due precaution, and in amounts wholly unjustifiable, is the most common, and one of the worst abuses of banking; and it occurs from ignorance far more frequently than from fraud.

The remedy for these evils which has been most relied on, is that of placing the banks under stringent obligations to pay their currency on demand in specie. This would be a complete remedy, if compliance were possible; but that is not the case — far from it. It involves a stock of the precious metals in the country equal to the deposits and circulation of the banks, and applicable to this purpose of remaining in the banks as a security for their issues. Security, absolute security, should be required of the banks; but it is surely an error to assume that the security must be gold or silver. There are many ways of securing debts, but gold and silver are rarely thought of as security; yet it is required of the banks to three times the quantity in the country. The banks are required to hold this security for public benefit, which involves two great absurdities; one, that the banks should bind themselves to perform an impossibility; the other, that they should be the holders of the security on which the public is to rely.

The fact that bank currency can, to a certain extent, perform the functions of money is only incidental; it is not its office, nor special purpose. Because its special use, however, gives it this power, and therefore opens a wide door of temptation to abuses and over-issue, security becomes necessary not only as a restraint, but to make good losses and damage. This security should, therefore, not only be such as can be given, but such as would be always safe and available; and the banks should not be the holders of it.

The exaction of payment on demand by the banks in coins for all their issues, is not only a demand with which they cannot comply, but it has served further to obliterate the distinction between bank issues and money. So long as no demand is made upon the banks, it is assumed that their issues are convertible at the will of the holder. They obtain, by this means, a higher credit and wider circulation; and that is looked upon as money which is, by theory, convertible, and which is assumed to be so in practice. The temptation to both banks and borrowers is thus increased, and the volume of bank issues swelled, until a collapse becomes inevitable. As the special function of bank currency is to pay debts to the banks, the rule of issue should be not what they can put into circulation, whether deposits or notes, but what they can recall by the payments of their debtors; for if they do not return the notes, the banks can never redeem them.

In all the processes of industry and commerce, there is probably no absurdity tolerated equal to that practised by the banks, of discounting the paper of their customers running from two to six months, and giving their bank-notes or credits payable on demand in coins. The persons who give these notes take from two to six months to arrange for their payment; the banks intervene, abolish the credit which the course of trade dictated to the parties, and become responsible for the whole instanter.

The banks of the United States incur this liability every year, to the extent of not less than $3,000,000,000, and are at no time free from a demand for less than $500,000,000 in specie, a quantity more than double that in the country, and tenfold that held by the banks. There is no conceivable plan by which the banks could fulfil this engagement. It would be impossible for the drawers of the paper thus taken by the banks to anticipate the maturity of their obligations, and pay them in coins; any law framed to enforce such anticipation would be regarded as the height of absurdity and injustice. It is this fearful blunder which has made banks of circulation the terror of many minds, and the object of such prejudice and reproach as scarcely has a parallel. Whilst they fulfil their legitimate functions of purchasing individual paper with their own currency, and receiving that currency again in payment, their usefulness is admitted and extolled; but whenever the sole test of their soundness is applied, and payment in coins for their issues is demanded, they have no choice but to be ruined, or to ruin their customers. They cannot pay their notes and deposits in gold or silver, and must suspend, or commence a contraction of the currency which works a public injury many times greater than the capital of the banks concerned; it not only ruins individuals, but causes the sacrifice of a vast amount of property, and works a still greater loss by depreciation.

If this test of paying all liabilities on demand were applied to the richest firms in the nation, they would all fail. That the banks undertake thus to pay does not alleviate the absurdity; for, on the one hand, they should not be permitted to undertake an impossibility; and on the other, no reliance should be placed upon a security absolutely unavailable.

We impose upon the banks, as a test of their solidity, a condition which, when the time of trial arrives, becomes a scourge to the whole community in which they are situate. It is a test which enables the banks to resist the fulfilment of their engagements by inflicting a grievous calamity upon the public. When called upon to pay on demand, they resist it with all the powers of attack and defence they can wield; and they claim to be sound, not unfrequently, because they have hurt the public more than the public has damaged them.

In place of this dangerous condition, the banks should be required to give ample security for both their notes and deposits, and that security should be lodged with the State; they should be required, under severe penalties, to keep their issues at par with specie. Their notes and deposits should, at all times, be receivable for any debts due to them, or payable at their counters; but they should not be bound to pay specie in any other way than it is payable by their customers; that is, at the maturity of the paper discounted or purchased by them. If the individual paper taken by the banks averages two months to maturity, then their customers have these two months in which to employ the bank-notes and deposits issued to them in payment of their debts in and out of bank; and during that period of adjustment, the banks should be exempt from any demand for specie upon their issues so employed, both because they are performing a legitimate office for which they are specially adapted, and from which they could not be withdrawn without serious evil; and because the credit on the paper for which they were exchanged is not expired. The claims of the banks on the public ought to proceed *pari passu* with the claims of the public on the banks.

On this principle, the issues of the banks would be absorbed in payment of debts due to them. If not so absorbed, the banks should only receive in payment that which will redeem them when presented. Whatever liabilities of the bank are not thus redeemed, should be amply covered by available security.

The practice of paying or extinguishing debts by the process of clearing, now becoming so common among the banks, is not new. Three centuries ago, a very large proportion of the payments of central Europe were made in that way. Then it was effected, on a large scale, between individuals; now it is wholly confined to the banks. Then it was the chief mode of accomplishing the vast payments arising from the trade of the multitudinous fairs of that period; and it so continued, until other modes of commerce supplanted that of the fairs. The clearing at the fairs was simply a process of setting-off debts against debts — the same, in effect, as balancing book accounts. A. said to B., you owe me a thousand florins; pay that amount for me to C., to whom I am in debt. This being done, A. is acquitted, and thus the process goes on. It is obvious that the final balances, among hundreds assembled for that purpose, may be reached by setting-off mutual debts, and drawing verbally on each other at sight, where the process involves more than two persons, and thus continuing to pay, until the result is reached of those who have more coming to them than they had to pay, and of those who had more to pay than they had due to them. The conclusion of the whole was, that the balances to pay were the exact amount of those to receive.

The mode of payment which had most prominence in large transactions, after clearing began to lose its importance with the decay of the fairs, was that of circulation. This was practised not only at the great Banks of Venice and Genoa, but also at the deposit banks which succeeded them. The same money in a bank, or the same credits upon the books of a bank, was by this method kept circulating or passing from person to person, accomplishing a continued circle of payments. Its effectiveness did not come to an end, for it moved in a circle embracing nearly the same parties, gradually passing from the men of one generation to those of another. This circulation is still in full vigor in the Bank of Hamburg, and other survivors of the deposit banks of the seventeenth century; but it has no counterpart in our more modern institutions. The deposits in our banks are the proceeds of discounted commercial paper. The credits issued by the banks, of which these deposits are composed, are absorbed and wholly extinguished whenever they are paid to the banks. Their place is supplied continually by new discounts and new credits.

This mode of payment by circulation of the same money, or the same fund, as, for instance, national debt, differs from clearing. In the former, it passes from hand to hand, performing all the payments its successive owners can effect with it. If these owners were seated at one table, they could circulate a sum in coins from hand to hand to the same effect, and see the money before them at the same time. But if seated at the same table, they could extinguish a large portion of their debts by simply exhibiting their claims, and balancing or clearing them, so far as mutual, and by verbal transfers, as in the fairs, until the final balances were reached, seldom over five per cent. on the amount paid.

Clearing is, beyond all question, the simplest, the most economical, and when applicable, the most efficient of all modes of paying debts. It is precisely analogous to balancing accounts. Parties who are in business relations arrange to ascertain daily, or at convenient times, the state of their mutual claims; and having verified, extinguish them by set-off. The banks of New York extinguished among themselves in that way, in 1857, upwards of $7,000,000,000, or upwards of $20,000,000 each day, upon which the daily balances did not exceed five per cent. This enormous sum is cleared in New York alone, without the use of any currency or medium of payment whatever. It is done by evidences of debt bearing the items of mutual claim, by a statement of the amounts, and by the processes of a balance.

The banks in other cities avail themselves also of the economy and facility of this process. These clearing establishments have been gradually improving their methods, and we believe there is yet room for progress in that respect, not only as between banks, but that the same principles and processes are susceptible of many applications between individuals. This would not only be an advantage to those who may adopt them, but would exert considerable influence in reducing friction in the operation of the money and credit systems. A comprehensive treatise on this subject, in which the subject should be thoroughly treated in reference to its possible applications to clearing between individuals, would be an important addition to commercial literature. The fact that those who give credit to the greatest extent take it from others most liberally, and that the object of such persons is to apply their credits to pay their debts, furnishes sufficient ground upon which to build such an inquiry.

The subject of interest has engaged our attention upon only two or three points. Interest is almost exclusively considered in the light of a charge for the use of money. No adequate explanation of the term interest, as now very generally employed, can be given from that point of view. Strictly speaking, very little money is lent upon interest; there is probably, in the United States, ten times as much interest paid as there is money lent upon interest. We do not regard the proceeds of discounted notes, whether they take the shape of bank-notes or bank deposits, as money. They are merely the credits or securities of the bank substituted for those of individuals. Yet these bank-notes, but more especially the deposits, are really the chief medium of payment. The fund upon which interest is chiefly paid, is that which stands in the banks under the name of deposits. The two great items of interest paid in this country are the deduction made from notes and bills of exchange sold or discounted, and loans of amounts deposited in the banks, the proceeds of discounted paper.

Gold and silver are seldom lent upon interest; they are never sought for as a medium of payment, because a check upon a bank is preferred. Gold will command no higher rate of interest than a credit in bank. When interest has advanced even one or two hundred per cent., there is no corresponding advance in the precious metals. The current rate of interest depends upon the facility of obtaining the needful supply of that fund which is usually employed in paying debts. It is not the plenty or scarcity of this fund which determines the rate of interest, so much as the disposition of the holders. The fluctuations in its amount do not correspond with the fluctuations of interest. It often happens that the deposits in the banks are largest when the rate of interest is highest.

There are many speculations about the level of the precious metals, about money flowing to one country and from another: this flux and reflux, when applied to problems of interest, furnish no light. Within the range of trade, foreign or domestic, the precious metals receive little impulse in any direction from the rate of interest; nor do they exert upon it any appreciable influence, except so far as the loss of specie by the banks may lead to a contraction of the currency.

We have discussed the topic of prices more elaborately, perhaps, than was necessary for our purpose, which was chiefly to show that the relation between the quantity of money, or currency, and prices was not, by any means, so close as many have supposed. The notion long prevalent, that prices were exactly adjusted to the quantity of currency, is shown to have been long since exploded. Among the innumerable influences which go to determine the general range and fluctuation of prices, the quantity of money or currency is found to be one of the least effective.

This subject is specially important as bearing upon the results of fluctuations in the issues of banks. Besides the fact, that quantity of currency has less effect upon prices than is generally supposed, it is to be taken into account that, for all the currency issued by the banks, there is a special and constant demand from the debtors of the banks, which prevents it from having as much influence as it might otherwise have. The debtors of the banks having in their possession the whole range of commodities to which prices apply, are offering them for this currency, to secure it for their constantly recurring payments. Their constantly maturing obligations do not permit them to hold out for extra prices.

We have dwelt at some length upon the subject of public payments, with the view of turning the minds of financial inquirers to a topic which has received too little attention. Public taxation has been largely discussed in many countries; but the mere question of the best mode of effecting public payments has not received the consideration it deserves. The history of productive industry and trade shows that, for the last six hundred years, where civilization has been highest, efforts to improve the modes of payment have been incessant and most successful. From the origin of the Bank of Venice to the present day, in Europe, there has been no rest from attempts to facilitate payments, and economize the means and methods of payment. The motives which have so long and so continuously operated on the ranks of industry and of trade must have been not only strong, but well founded.

That which has so constantly occupied the minds of men of business cannot be beneath notice of governments, under the same circumstances. If the annual receipts into the treasury of France are $300,000,000; if the annual receipts into that of Great Britain are $260,000,000; and if, in the United States, the treasury annually receives $75,000,000, the mere method of receiving and disbursing these vast revenues must become an important consideration — very important, if we take the conduct of the most intelligent men of business, for ages past, as a criterion. This importance refers to the people from whom the revenues are collected, as well as to those to whom they are paid, and to the government itself, in regard to the facility and economy of its financial operations.

A financial system should be specially adapted to the habits and customs of the people for whom it is designed. No government can long depart from the usages of its people, or disregard their modes of business, without paying some penalty, soon or late, for the mistake. We regard the present mode of administering the treasury of the United States as involving this error. The habit of the people to employ paper currency and credit wherever they are applicable, is almost universal. This use would be still more general and uniform, but for restrictive laws, which the abuses of banking have provoked. In the face of this custom of the country, the public treasury has rejected the use of paper currency altogether, and reserves for itself an exclusive currency of gold and silver. This policy has had, during nearly its whole existence, the extraordinary support of the California gold-mines, and has not, therefore, developed fully the harsh and evil tendencies with which it is fraught. The day is approaching when this system, if continued in its present shape, will create a financial disturbance great enough to shake the industry of the country to its centre, and endanger any administration which may attempt to uphold it.

We have compared our exclusive system, as administered under the act of 1846, with the financial systems of France and Great Britain, and find nothing in either to justify or encourage us in continuing a scheme of finance so fraught with peril to the interests of labor and trade. We refer to the manner in which that act has been carried out, not to its provisions as they stand in the statute book. Our system assumes at once the attitude of being independent of the people and the commercial institutions of the country. It has been very aptly called the Independent Treasury, for it admits no sympathy and no relations with the business or the interests of the people. In Great Britain, the Exchequer leans upon the Bank of England, the greatest commercial institution of the country; and in this way a sympathy between the movements of the Exchequer, or public treasury, is established, which runs through and tempers, if it does not control its whole operations.[1] Besides

[1] The following account, given by the "Economist," No. 799, of December, 1858, page 1400, a commercial journal of the highest character, published in London, shows how carefully the authorities of the Exchequer look to the interests and convenience of those from whom the revenue is collected. Complaints had been made of the trouble and risk of attending to pay duties, even in notes of the Bank of England.

"At length, in 1854, the treasury, of its own accord, devised a scheme of which, as it has been in practice now nearly four years, the success and efficiency have been fully tested.

"In the year 1857, the net amount of customs duty received in the port of London was £11,495,322, being, in round figures, about half of the whole amount collected within the United Kingdom. This sum was made up of 158,843 payments, at the rate of 514 in number, and amounting to £37,210 daily. That was the case that had to be dealt with. The treasury adopted two plans, either of which was within the reach of all traders alike. 1. The one plan provided for the receipt of the checks of private traders, drawn upon such bankers as would comply with certain regulations made with a view to the security and convenience of the customs department. According to those arrangements, a check being presented at the custom-house in payment of duties, was received by the proper officer, and the necessary entries for the ultimate delivery of the goods were proceeded with; every hour a clerk was despatched with the checks which had been received within the hour to the various bankers upon whom they were drawn, who placed their mark upon them, which made them payable by the Bank of England, where they were charged to the different bankers' accounts. The clerk then returned to the custom-house with the

this, the Exchequer is a constant borrower from the people, to the extent of nearly the whole annual revenue upon Exchequer bills. It borrows, in anticipation of the public revenue, from those who lend voluntarily upon short loans, and is thus enabled to disburse the revenue previous to its receipt. This is a great accommodation to a large class of lenders, who are pleased to have an opportunity of realizing interest upon short loans, and upon such undoubted security; this class are thus kept in constant relations with the government, and are prompt to supply the treasury with any required

---

checks so marked; the goods were cleared and delivered; and the whole checks of the day paid to the public account at the Bank of England at the close of the day, where they were adjusted to the various accounts to which they applied. By this means a merchant had the check system, and all the security attaching to it, extended to the payment of duties, while the Crown ran no risk. 2. The other plan consisted of an arrangement with the Bank of England, by which a special description of bank-note should be made to be used exclusively for customs duties, and to be received at the bank only from the customs department. They are denominated customs checks. The different bankers receive them from the Bank of England as they do their own notes; and supply their customers with them as they are required for the specific purpose of paying duties. By this means all risk of theft and fraud is avoided. To all intents, they are bank-notes, but to be used only for a specific object, and useless for any other.

"The utility of these arrangements is now seen by the great extent to which merchants have used them. In the last year, the payments of customs duties were made in the following way:—

100,781	payments in cash	£3,320,492
35,317	" by traders' checks	3,563,966
22,745	" by customs special notes	4.610,864
Total payments... 158,843	Total amount	£11,495,322

Therefore, of £11,495,322, the total amount of payments, only £3,320,492 was made in cash under the old plan; while £8,174,799 was made in the two new modes of checks and special bank-notes. And even those payments which continue to be made in cash, consist of the smallest sums, as the *number* of payments made in this way, and representing the smaller sum named, is no less than 100,781; while the number representing the larger sum is only 58,062. The average amount of the payments in cash is £32 19*s.*; while the average in traders' checks is £101 3*s.* 4*d.*, and in special bank-notes, £204 8*s.* 2*d.*

"But the convenience and security which are gained by the merchant by this system, great as they are, do not constitute all the advantages which it affords. It effects a great reduction in the currency. But for it, the sum of £8,174,799 of bank-notes, issued under the limit of the act of 1844, would have been required in 1857 more than were actually used."

assistance in financial emergencies. The creditors of the public derive even more advantage from this mode of disbursement in anticipation; for the Exchequer being always ready to pay, the whole payments of the annual expenditure are made not only with more regularity, but probably weeks, if not months, in advance of what would otherwise be the time.

The present financial system of France, the result of a reform which has been in progress under the auspices of men of great ability and experience for more than thirty years, is perhaps, in many aspects, the most perfect of any now extant. It has rescued the finances of France not only from the greatest confusion and embarrassment, but has placed them in a more enviable position than those of any country in Europe. To the astonishment of the capitalists of Europe, the government of France was able to borrow, in 1855, for the expenditure of the war in the Crimea, upwards of $250,000,000, without resorting to the city of Paris, or capitalists out of France. Not only so, but the sum actually offered in the departments out of Paris was $332,000,000. This offer to the government was from 360,000 persons in the interior of France, very few of whom would have been lenders to the public but for the very excellent financial system which now prevails in that empire.

In Great Britain and France, large use is made of treasury notes, called, in the one, Exchequer bills, and in the other, Bons du Tresor. In both countries, the ministers of finance are permanently authorized to issue them upon certain principles, and under specific regulations. In England, the Exchequer bills are issued and managed with a skill and success which nothing of the kind can surpass. In neither country has there been an over-issue of these treasury securities, for more than a generation past. In Prussia, a treasury currency in denominations as low as five dollars has been issued, for that length of time, and no abuse has occurred.[1] It is very true, that the over-issues of the assignats during the French Revolution, of the continental paper currency during the American Revolution, and the later over-issues in Russia and Austria, are well calculated to create distrust in the minds of all whose attention is turned to the use of a

[1] The Prussian government is so careful of the credit and stability of this emission of currency from the public treasury, that it redeems promptly every counterfeit brought to the public offices. By this wise policy, it obtains the earliest information of the existence of counterfeits, and is thus able promptly to follow offenders. Of course, this greatly increases confidence in the currency.

paper currency for public purposes. But as this whole matter resolves itself into questions of knowledge, official integrity, and financial skill, it should not be summarily dismissed, unless it is conceded that these requisites are beyond the reach of our government. When we remember the fact, that a bank can, with its own notes, or credits on its books, purchase commercial paper to the amount of millions of dollars, and that it can take its own notes and issues in payment of this commercial paper as it matures, thus providing a special currency for this purpose, and saving the use of millions of money — when we know that many nations could pay the entire national expenditure in treasury notes, and that they could, of course, afford to take such notes in payment of all dues at their public treasuries, we should hesitate to give up the problem of a government currency as impossible to solve.

The truth is, not only can it be solved, but it is of much easier solution than many others which constantly engage the attention of men in authority. The order, subordination and numerous checks which now characterize our treasury department, are a far greater triumph of financial skill and good administration than would be the successful employment of treasury notes as a currency. Of course, such an issue by the treasury could only be upon a well-devised plan, and well-settled principles, to be as faithfully observed as are the present processes of the many functionaries of the Treasury Department.

The leading principle of every such emission of paper, as well as that of the banks, is to issue only so much as will return in the regular course of the business in which the issue is made. It is not, and should not be, the issue of so much as will not probably be returned for payment, but the issue of so much as will inevitably return in payment to the issuer. Whatever amount the return payments to the issuer will absorb, is a safe emission; beyond that, all is unsafe. The Treasury of the United States could, in any year, issue one-fourth the amount of the estimated income in treasury notes; the next year, one-half; the following year, three-fourths; and by the experience gained in three years, the officers entrusted with this duty could manage such emission without danger of over-issue. If the public would not readily receive them, they should not be issued at all; if they should fall below par, immediate measures should be taken, at any cost, to recall them in such quantities as would restore them to perfect equality with gold.

The suggestions made in the chapter on public payments are chiefly intended to stimulate inquiry, and secure the attention of men whose experience in financial affairs, and general knowledge of business, may enable them to throw some light on the interesting questions involved in the whole subject.

Although it has not been our design to propose reforms, or even to give intimations of that kind, we cannot forbear introducing here a further remark on the subject of bank deposits. In our large cities these are of great amount, and upon their management depends very largely the state of the currency throughout the whole country. If city banks are constrained at any time, by a demand for the precious metals, to contract their issues, and to withhold the customary facilities of banking by refusing to discount commercial securities, the contraction of currency which ensues becomes an occasion of loss and damage often tenfold greater than the amount of specie involved in the demand. A contraction of currency by the banks in New York soon extends its baleful influences throughout the whole land. The mischief becomes vastly disproportioned to its cause. It is in view of the magnitude of this evil, and of its frequent and inevitable occurrence, that we make a suggestion, dictated more by a desire to save the community from harm, than to save the banks from any liability for specie to which they are justly exposed. The banks should be even more desirous to prevent these evils than to protect their reserve of coins and bullion.

The danger of the city banks, which drives them to the measure of contracting the currency as a defence, arises mainly from liability to pay their deposits on demand in specie. Now, however great may be the difficulty of changing our present banking system, so far as bank-notes are concerned, it does not extend to deposits. These belong to the customers of the banks, residing for the most part in their vicinity, whose chief business with the banks is, through them, to apply their credits to the payment of their debts. This is mainly done by the proceeds of discounted notes, with an average of more than two months to run. The banks may propose to this large class, that the proceeds of discounts shall only be entered to their credit, payable in legal currency when the discounted paper matures, but receivable as now at all the banks for every debt payable there. This would ensure the deposits, for every legitimate purpose to which they are applicable, ample circulation; indeed, they would be no less current and acceptable than they are at present. They could, with equal effectiveness, fill every proper function to which they are adapted. They would cease to be an object of overwhelming alarm whenever a demand for the precious metals occurred; the banks could, therefore, in the face of such a demand, continue their discounts, and supply the usual facilities of payment, knowing that the constant progress of payments to them would absorb all these issues of credit before specie could be demanded for them.

Some modification of this plan might certainly be arranged by men with clear views of the subject, and sufficient experience in banking; the effect of which would be to place the city banks upon a safer basis than they have ever yet rested on, and to take away from them all pretext for those sudden contractions of currency, which, whilst they are a scourge to industry and trade, make the banks themselves constant objects of reproach and detestation to a large class of the community.

There is nothing in the law of legal tender to prevent this. The banks now agree to pay the proceeds of discounted notes on demand, and of course that law places them under the obligation of paying in gold or silver. But on the plan proposed, the banks would only agree to pay the proceeds at maturity of the discounted paper, with the additional stipulation that these credits would be receivable in all payments to the banks. Under such an arrangement the banks would, at all ordinary times, treat these deposits precisely as they do now; but in case of a demand for specie for exportation, they could choose between contracting the currency and refusing to pay specie, except under the terms of their contract with their depositors.[1]

The order in which we have presented the subjects of this volume seems to us the logical one; but we have no doubt there are many who will be more inclined to look first at what is advanced on the subject of the credit system. This will naturally be the case with those who are already familiar with the subject. All such may commence their examination at the seventh chapter, turning to the previous chapters only as they may find occasion, from the tenor of the matters discussed.

---

[1] A memorandum somewhat in this form might be prefixed to each bank book:

"The proceeds of all notes discounted for C. D. shall be placed to his credit, payable in gold or silver to the said C. D. at the maturity of the notes discounted; but subject, in whole or in part, to the check of C. D. in payment of any debt due to the bank, or for the purpose of transferring the same to any other bank or person."

THE

WAYS AND MEANS OF PAYMENT.

CHAPTER I.

Exchange of commodities an incident of civilized life — The agencies by which this exchange is effected must not be confounded with the exchange itself — The fitness and use of these agencies can be best determined by treating them as agencies more or less necessary to the main purpose — Money, and money of account.

In civilized life the industry of men is so largely developed and subdivided, as to involve an incessant exchange of commodities and services. Civilized men require food and clothing of great variety in form, substance and preparation. Their dwellings and furniture are equally varied, and demand for their production an equally varied and subdivided industry. Intellectual, moral and religious wants and exigencies engage also a large force of subdivided labor. In this division of labor, there is one large class employed in producing and preparing food; another in producing and preparing raiment; another in building; another in furnishing buildings; and another in the labor of ministering to intellectual, civil, moral and religious wants: each of these large divisions is again subdivided into lesser classes; and these again by innumerable ramifications and divisions, until each person is reached in his separate individuality. The whole labor of society is thus apportioned among all its members in that way which the force of circumstances, and their intelligence, has dictated. In every community, much the larger number of persons are mere laborers, and have only their labor to give in exchange for such of the comforts of life as they may require. In every case, however, whether we regard classes or individuals, a continual series of exchanges is involved. The manufacturers of clothing must have food, shelter and furniture; the producers of food must have clothing, shelter and furniture; the builders and furnishers of houses must have food and clothing; those who minister to intellectual, civil, moral and religious wants, need all those things; and the others, in like manner, require their services. Descending to every individual of each class, each person must give his labor, the product of his labor, or the products of the labor of others, in order, with that, to purchase what he requires. Every individual who earns a living, whether by his own labor or that of others, must exchange what he has for that which he wants. Even merchants, whose chief business it is to assist in this great interchange of commodities, exchange, by a continued process, their old stock of goods for a new one. The progress of industry and society is thus mainly characterized by a constant series of exchanges, in which every individual takes, directly or indirectly, an interested part. The manufacturer who produces, by the labor of others, goods to the value of half a million yearly, exchanges these goods for the raw materials and labor which enable him, in a succeeding year, to produce a like amount. The professional man, the artist, or the laborer, exchange the exercise of their learning, skill or labor for what they want, consume or enjoy.

The reader may develop more fully, and dwell upon these great features of industry and civilization, viewing them thus apart from the mere agencies by which this vast interchange is effected. It is not difficult to distinguish between the thing to be done, between the exchange thus accomplished, and the means by which it is done. One large and important class of society is composed of the various agents engaged in the process of this interchange as their business or profession: merchants, with their attendants, bankers, brokers, clerks, transporters, and the laborers connected with them, constitute that class in every country. But other agencies are also prominent, such as ships, boats, canals, railways, warehouses, shops, books of account, and money. None of these are essential to the idea of an exchange. They are facilities, agencies, aids more or less desirable or indispensable, according to circumstances. Men who are near to each other may effect their exchanges without the aid of merchant, broker, ship or carriage. They may, by means of books of account and mutual charges and credits, wholly dispense with money. The intervention of money has, in no small degree, blinded men to the distinction between the exchanges of industrial life and the means or agencies by which they are accomplished. This agency of money, although one of the most important, and doubtless one of the oldest and most expensive, is, however, very far from being an indispensable concomitant of an exchange of other commodities. The advantage of a common medium of real value, for which men could safely sell any commodity they had, and with it as readily purchase any they required, cannot easily be over-stated. Money, however, is not of the essence of an exchange, but only an agent to be employed when some advantage is to be gained by resorting to it, of facility, security or otherwise. When a man sells an hundred bushels of wheat for $150, and with that money purchases three tons of iron, the transaction is an exchange of the wheat for the iron. The money employed is as much an agent, as the wagon used to transport the wheat and the iron. The exchange could have been made without it, but it was used because the parties found it more convenient or advantageous to do so. Even when money is employed, its real value as an equivalent is not an essential ingredient of the exchange. If, unknown to one or both parties, the money employed is counterfeit and worthless, the exchange of the wheat for the iron is none the less perfect and satisfactory to all parties; and the counterfeit money may continue to circulate, and be the medium or agent in many such exchanges, before it is discovered.[1] All these exchanges will be as perfect as if effected with good money. This does not prove that when money is used as equivalent, it should not be really

[1] A counterfeit dollar may be the agent of a hundred exchanges, and only the value of the dollar be lost by one person, in whose hands it is detected. A large quantity of false money is always in circulation.

what it purports to be; it only shows that exchanges of commodities may be effected without a real equivalent as a medium. Wheat, in the case above, pays for the iron; the commodities exchanged are the compensation, or payment, for each other. Thus, in the course of the year, a man exchanges the commodities he makes, or has for sale, for those which he requires; that is the main feature and object of his business. The professional man, and he who ministers to intellectual, civil, moral and religious wants, exchanges his services for that which he consumes or requires. These multifarious exchanges are effected with or without money, or other ordinary agency of exchanges; their beneficial results do not depend upon the manner in which they are effected. The exchange of the commodities being the object, every advantage, facility, security and economy would be resorted to in accomplishing that object.

We thus insist upon keeping the object, and the means or agencies of effecting it, separate and distinct, as necessary to attaining clear views of the whole subject. As economy, facility and security are to be consulted in the thing to be done, it is necessary to keep the agencies, in all cases, in a subservient position, to be employed or not, to be changed and modified or not, exactly as the main object dictates.

Although our design, at present, is to treat of only one class of the agencies in effecting this great interchange of commodities and services, that which relates to commercial payments, including money and all its substitutes and modifications, we hold it to be specially important to a true comprehension of the subject that the agent, whatever it may be, should always be treated as subordinate to the object which is accomplished by it. Money, in all its forms and modifications, is to be employed or not, and to a greater or lesser amount, as circumstances, commercial skill and convenience require; always considering, first, the exchanges to be effected, and next, the means of effecting them. This is the channel which men pursue in the actual progress of business, and it is that which will conduct us, with proper discrimination, to the clearest views of the subject.

But another distinction is equally to be marked and kept up

in the mind by those who would attain to clear conceptions on the subject of money. We refer to the distinction between the precious metals, as a common equivalent, and coins from a public mint. It should be understood that it is not coinage which converts the precious metals into money. They would be used as such were there no coins, as is the case in China. Coinage does not give the precious metals a value which they had not before. It is not in the power of any nation to regulate the price of gold or silver; this price must depend on circumstances which no nation can control. But though coinage is not that which gives their value or price to gold or silver, it is that which prepares it properly for the purposes of a medium of exchange. In all the large payments in which gold is now employed, it would be used in the shape of bars, if not in that of coins. In the case of such payments, the mint needs only to prepare bars of fine gold or silver, of some uniform standard or quality, in order that, in paying, only the weight would have to be verified or ascertained. Gold and silver may then answer all the purposes of money, without being coined; for retail purposes, and small payments, the coinage affords a facility or convenience which is fully appreciated and admitted on all hands. But the coins, as such, do not constitute the money. The coins have a uniform shape, weight and quality, or standard, and in this consists their character. Prices are not expressed in coins; that is, coins are not exhibited to express, signify or mark the price of any commodity. There is a mode of expressing prices or amounts, which is perfectly intelligible, in which coins are not employed.

The sums written in books of account, and upon the face of promissory notes and bills of exchange, are not indebted for their definite meaning to coins or coinage. Previous to our adoption of the dollar as the unit of our money of account, all prices were expressed, and books were kept, in pounds, shillings and pence, which had no corresponding coin; so, also, were promissory notes and money securities expressed. These denominations were the money of account of that day, as the dollar is at present. It is well known, as we shall remark more fully hereafter, that these terms had a different significance in Massachusetts,

New York and Pennsylvania. In each of these the unit had a different value or power, which was perfectly understood by the people in those different States; although in neither was there, or had there ever been, any coin corresponding with these various units. Men can carry in their minds a unit of value, as they can carry the idea of a foot, a yard, a mile, or an acre; or of a pound, an ounce, or pennyweight. The physician writes his prescription in ounces, drachms and scruples, in matters requiring the utmost accuracy, and involving life or death. He has, of course, in his mind the most definite and accurate idea of the quantities of the various ingredients to be compounded. But when the prescription comes to be made up, the apothecary must apply the measure or the scales, or he cannot accurately realize the idea of the physician. It is the same with the money of account. It is so universally in use, that everybody is as familiar with its meaning as the physician is with the apothecaries' weight. All prices, and all amounts, are expressed in it; but when a payment is to be made in gold or silver, the scales must be applied, or coin produced, of which the value as expressed in the money of account is known.

Money of account will be the subject of special treatment in the following chapter.

CHAPTER II.

§ 1. *People employing gold and silver have terms in which to express their value — Mint price and market price — Money of account a necessity.*

BEFORE treating specially of the use of gold and silver as money, it will be of advantage to notice and understand the mode of expressing prices, keeping accounts, and stating amounts, which has prevailed among all civilized people, and still prevails. People who have attained to the use of weights and measures, and arithmetic, employ a money of account, in which they state prices, sums and accounts. It is not a mechanical process by which other articles are compared by weight or bulk with gold or silver. It is an arithmetical process, by which, with the aid of some unit of value, taking its origin from a coin or special weight of gold or silver, the value of such coin or weight being fixed in the mind by constant use for a time, becomes a unit, readily borne in the mind, susceptible of being readily added, multiplied or divided by a combination with numerals. There is no nation far enough advanced to employ arithmetic which does not attach a specific value to both gold and silver, and which has not some terms in which to express that value. In the first stage of using the precious metals as a medium of exchange, they are given in exchange for commodities according to the estimate the parties to the exchange make at the time. With the progress of intelligence and arithmetic, people begin to place a general price on the precious metals, as well as upon other things. Every article which is the subject of exchange, becomes the subject of price, and by help of these prices the parties make their sales and payments. The price or value of gold or silver ceases to be what the party possessing them, at his caprice, puts upon them; their price becomes even better known, generally, than that of any other articles; and it is by this price that they are paid or delivered. This fact is obscured and hidden from popular view by the custom of governments fixing a price upon the precious metals for the purposes of coinage. It is thus overlooked too often, that the price at the mint is founded on the market price; the people at large having no occasion to discuss the prices of gold and silver as they do of other articles, the impression prevails that the price of gold and silver is merely an affair of the mint and public authority. It is important, however, and should not be forgotten, that gold and silver are just as much the subject of price as other things, though obscured by coinage and legal enactments. This is familiarly known to dealers in coins and bullion, and to intelligent merchants and bankers; though all such are not equally aware how much they are indebted to the money of account for the facility with which they make their varied computations, and varied transactions, without any aid from coins.

The formation of a money of account among people capable of employing one, is not only an universal mental proclivity, it is a mercantile necessity. It would be literally impossible, in the present state of coinage, to continue for any considerable time to express prices and large sums by the number of coins which would be equivalent to the price or amount. The same effort of mind necessary to remember the value of a coin thus named to express a price or an amount, is sufficient to enable persons to carry the memory of that value in the mind, and use it with the same effect, abstractly, as if referring to the coin. Every coin or weight, of gold or silver, used for any long period as the means of expressing prices or amounts, becomes the unit of a money of account, and is used abstractly and arithmetically. It becomes quite as capable of expressing changes in the value of the precious metals, as of any other articles; for it remains fixed at the value at which it passed into the money of account. It is then employed in expressing the prices of thousands of articles, and for stating all possible sums in the way of computations, accounts and financial adjustments. Being so variously and constantly employed by such multitudes, it attains permanency; being, like the mast of a ship, held by stays and checks innumerable on every side.

The value of the unit, or beginning point, being once firmly fixed in men's minds by constant use, remains there wholly independent of subsequent changes of price which may affect the specific article from which it took its rise. Thus, if it sprung from a coin, or a certain quantity of gold or silver, it becomes afterwards so independent of these as to be quite capable of expressing the changing prices of that or any other coin. It is, then, a matter of fact that all commercial people keep their accounts, compute money, and express prices, by the use of a money of account. The naming a price with them is not naming a coin, or any specific quantity of gold or silver; but it is the employment of the denominations of the money of account, which all understand to express a price. There is scarcely any mental operation more generally and constantly in exercise, than that which is used to fix and express prices. All classes of men have more or less occasion to be familiar with it.

The distinction between money and money of account is not apprehended and kept before the mind with equal facility, by all persons, on the first attempt. If the subject is new to the party making the effort, it will require some earnest attention and patient discrimination. Molière, in one of his comedies, introduces a character who, entering upon the education suitable for a gentleman late in life, finds, to his great surprise and pleasure, that he had been speaking prose all his life without a master. So many have to learn that they have been long employing a money of account, without being aware of the acquisition they had made. Even in those times and countries where money circulated by weight, or in uncoined pieces, there must have been some mode of expressing the value of silver by weight, or of the "pieces" which were cut to a particular weight, and passed as "pieces of silver." Whether bar, piece or shekel, the parties dealing had some way of expressing the value of the precious metals. A people who have arrived at such a degree of civilization as to receive and deliver gold and silver by weight, and to employ arithmetic in the computations connected with such transactions, must be supposed, as we have said, to have some idea of the value of the various quantities of gold or silver which the scales and weights might specify. If a piece of gold were cut from a bar, and found to be of a particular weight, they attached a particular value to so much gold. They did not merely say a shekel gold is worth a shekel of gold, but they attached a price to so much gold as weighed a shekel; and they had some terms in which to express it. If one said to another, I will give you a shekel of silver for an article, the party addressed had two mental processes to go through before he could understand the offer; he had to recall to mind how much gold was the weight of a shekel, and next, what was the value of that much gold. One of these processes involved an abstract quantity, and the other an abstract value. So easily does the mind master these abstractions, that men retain the ideas of weights and values in their minds as readily as they do the power or significance of numbers. Values and quantities have, from the very dawn of civilization, been as readily retained as any of the processes of arithmetic, and they are now as familiar as the multiplication table.

If we suppose the pieces of silver mentioned in the New Testament were of unequal and undetermined weight, we may imagine them to have been offered for what they might happen to be worth; as if the party offering should say, here are thirty pieces of silver: you see them: will you take them for the service we ask? In such an offer, no money of account would be employed. It would be an offer of a quantity of silver to be judged of by sight. But if the thirty pieces of silver were coins, or quantities known and familiar by constant use, their value or price would occur to the mind the moment they were recognized; and in every civilized country there is, and always has been, a mode of expressing and writing down the value, which is thus readily perceived and understood; and this is the money of account. If one person say to another, I will give you these 100 Spanish dollars now before me for your horse, money of account is not necessarily involved; it is the specific offer of the 100 silver coins for the horse. Yet, if the party to whom the offer is made makes any valuation of the 100 Spanish dollars, he can only do it by means of a money of account. If the offer is merely of 100 dollars for the horse, the value or price is expressed in money of account; the payment is to be arranged afterwards, either by a promissory note, or bank-notes, or five $20 gold pieces, or twenty $5 gold pieces, or 200 half dollars. So if, in the United States, one person says to another, "I will give you these 50 British sovereigns, or these 50 French Napoleons, or these 100 five franc pieces, for any commodity," it would be understood to be the offer of a specific article: it would be regarded, not as an offer of money, but of the particular coins mentioned, whether worth more or less. The party accepting such an offer would accept the thing offered. But an offer of 100 dollars, only implies that the payment is to be satisfactory, and if not, the person to whom payment is to be made has the power of exacting it in such coins as the laws have made a legal tender.

§ 2. *Idea of value carried in the mind as the idea of weights, measures of length and capacity — The use of a money is much greater than of money — Often confused in language — Kelly's Cambist quoted — Varieties of moneys of account — British decimal system.*

The idea of a certain value, which of course had its origin in an actual comparison, or perfect familiarity, with some material article, is as easy to fix and carry in the mind as the idea of weight or quantity. As physicians carry in their minds, with perfect certainty and facility, the idea of the weights and quantities involved in ounces, scruples and drachms, and prescribe compounds of medicines requiring the utmost nicety and caution, by their knowledge of these quantities, without scales or weights: so it is with pounds, tons, bushels, yards, feet and inches; these terms carry to the minds of those most familiar with them, perfectly definite ideas, independent of any actual use of weights and measures. They use them constantly, well understanding each other in reference to quantities, not only without the weights and measures, but without any access to them. So men speak of values and prices, perfectly comprehending each other, although they may have no means, nor any occasion for payment.

It is as easy to carry the idea of the value expressed by a pound sterling, a franc, or a dollar, in the mind, as the quantity expressed by a ton, a pound, a bushel, or a foot. The truth is, that there is so much occasion to name prices, or express values, that almost every individual of a community, however insignificant he may be, becomes perfectly familiar with the money of account. It is more used than any reference to weights and measures. After all, none of these ideas cost the mind more effort than that of carrying the value or power of the Arabic numerals. It is no greater effort of mind to understand what is meant by ninety-nine bushels, than to understand what is intended by ninety-nine men. Quantities and values can be made the subject of conversation, of estimate, of contracts, of statistical tables, and of innumerable modes of expression, without any production of the article spoken of, or of the weights, scales, measures or coins by which quantities are actually defined, or payments actually made. It is well it is so, for it would be very inconvenient to produce a pound weight, or a dollar in coin, to explain our meaning when a pound or dollar is mentioned, not to speak of tons and miles.

The value of the unit of a money of account is, in fact, so fastened on men's minds, that it may be said there is nothing they know better, and nothing, so far as their mental habits are concerned, which is so little likely to change. If no attack were made upon this mental habit in Great Britain, the people of that country would continue to keep accounts, compute and express prices, in pounds, shillings and pence for ages to come, even if no sovereigns, or pounds or shillings, were known among their coins. Though flooded with all the coins of the world, they would promptly and readily express the value of every coin in pounds, shillings and pence. It is the money of account of England which at this moment performs the great function of expressing all prices there, whether of stocks, or coins, or bullion, or bank-notes, or merchandize. It is not the gold sovereign, nor the silver shilling, nor the copper penny, which is used to measure the values of these innumerable things; it is the scale of the money of account existing in all men's minds, and applicable to every article alike, which is employed to express every possible price and variation of price.

So, in the United States, our money of account, the dollar and its cents, or hundred equal parts, is used to express every possible price, and change of price, of every article. If bullion rises in price, silver dollars may be quoted at $1.05, or $1.10; or, if it falls in value, they may be quoted at .97, .98 or .99; and depreciated bank-notes are readily valued at any part of a dollar, from one cent to ninety-nine. When English sovereigns or shillings are paid away here, they are not paid as pounds or shillings, but are valued in our money of account at whatever their price for the time being may be.

In every country, when all the transactions by book accounts, all the purchases upon credit and for paper-money, all the computations by money, and all the conversation about prices are taken into account, it will be found that all these taken together immeasurably exceed all the transactions in actual money of gold or silver. It is by no means surprising, then, that the mental operations by which all the vast transactions by books of account, all sales on credit or for bank-notes, all this continual fixing and naming of prices, is carried on, should become the law of reckoning, to which every description of money itself should in the end become subject. Such is indeed the fact, as the actual state of things in every country proves, and this has always been known to intelligent accountants and cambists. It has been prominent in the guide-books of merchants and bankers, but has not been so familiar to statesmen, political economists, and theoretical writers on money.[1] But even where the special functions of

[1] The want of clear views of the nature and functions of money of account is strikingly exhibited in the following passage from a work of the late Leon Faucher: — "The effective money in the middle ages varying constantly, and being at the mercy of every prince, to be altered at his will, they devised a money of account, a sort of abstract or fictitious unit, which might remain relatively invariable in the midst of monetary fluctuations caused by the unskilfulness or the bad faith of governments, and the custom is preserved in some States to this day." — *Sur L'Or et Sur L'Argent, page* 5.

This is written by one who was recently, and at the time of his de-money of account have been understood, there has not been sufficient attention given to exhibit the actual relations between money of account and money of gold and silver; and yet neither can be fully understood until both are understood. We frequently find them utterly confounded, and the attributes of each referred to the other. There is, however, no difficulty in keeping their offices and functions separate, when the distinction is kept in view.

The value of an article, or of a fixed quantity of goods, is expressed instantaneously in money of account. The merchant who says his cloth is worth a dollar a yard, is understood without producing either a dollar or a yard-stick. When a sale actually takes place, and payment is to be made, then gold or silver, and weights or measures, become necessary. If the money laid down is in coins corresponding in denominations with the money of account, it appears to favor the idea that the article sold was measured by the coins. But if payment is made in the precious metals by weight, or in coins not corresponding with the money of account, then the agency of the money of account is called in to express the price of the bullion by weight, or of each coin: so that the transaction is completed by the employment of money of account in fixing the price of the merchandize, in adding the sum of various articles and their prices together, to ascertain the whole amount of the sale, and in fixing or expressing the value of every coin offered in payment. In many large establishments for the sale of merchandize, salesmen are employed in making sales of vast quantities of goods, with the prices of which, in all quantities and varieties, they are perfectly familiar, actually spending the most of their time in naming and discussing them; but few of these salesmen, however adroit, can tell the

---

cease, a minister of finance, and certainly a man of ability. He was employing the money of account of France every day, he was familiar with it, he would have been utterly at a loss without it, yet he accounted it as a barbarous relic of the dark ages. It is like an atmosphere to finance; it is the very language of financiers; they can neither think nor communicate their ideas without it; yet its agency and use is alleged to have belonged to the middle ages!

price of gold or silver by the pound, ounce or pennyweight, or the value of any coin of those metals, except a few domestic coins. When large payments, therefore, are made in bullion or mixed coins, the receiving these is referred to another clerk, who knows both their quality and price.

Any one who will take the trouble to recall to his mind the course of such transactions will perceive that money of gold or silver is not employed as a measure, even when it is used in payment, which is very rare in large transactions. The precious metals as frequently require measurement or estimation as the articles for which they are given in payment. It is no more difficult to express the true value of coins or bullion than of any other article of value. Their chief advantage lies in their safety and convenience as a medium of exchange — an imperishable equivalent in retail dealing, so important to every condition and class of men — and not in the fact that they can be or are used as actual measures or standards. They are standards of coinage, not of price or value. The term standard of value cannot be too strongly condemned. As a matter of fact, gold and silver are employed only as standards of payment in the current transactions of commerce. The invariable formation of a money of account, which, while the precious metals, or some substitute, remain the medium of exchange, or the instrument of payment, becomes the medium of comparison, the expression of equivalents, the language of prices, obviates equally all need of a measure or standard of value for any article which has any price. By aid of this mode of expressing prices, the largest transactions can be instantly accomplished, and notes or checks given in payment, without the aid or presence of coins or bullion, or any thought of or reference to them, and without the knowledge necessary to make the payment in coins or bullion.[1]

---

[1] We refer the reader, for some illustrations of this subject, to "Kelly's Cambist,"[1] a work of admitted authority, founded upon information obtained with great labor and expense, in which the author was aided by the

[1] The Universal Cambist and Commercial Instructor, being a full and accurate Treatise on the Exchanges, Coins, Weights and Measures of all dealing Nations. By P. Kelly, LL.D. 2 vols. 4to.

The moneys of account of France, England, and the United States are as completely established, and their functions as com-

---

British government. Although, on the subject for which we refer to this useful book, we find much confusion of terms, and great need of more discrimination, yet there are facts enough to guide the reader to very certain conclusions, and clear views. He distinguishes money into *real* and *imaginary;* the real are coins, bank-notes, &c.; the imaginary, "also called ideal moneys, are not represented by any coin, but are used in keeping accounts. They are understood to have had their foundation in real coins or weights, which were the original units adopted as the measures of value, and which have been continued under the same denominations, notwithstanding the changes that may have taken place in their intrinsic value."— "Although moneys of account be not represented by real coins, yet their intrinsic value may be determined by their known relation or proportion to certain coins." — "Moneys of account may be considered with respect to coins as weights and measures, with respect to goods; or as a mathematical scale, with respect to maps, lines, or other geometrical figures. Thus they serve as standards of the value both of merchandize and the precious metals themselves. It should, however, be remarked, that moneys of account, though they are uniform as a scale of divisions and proportions, yet they fluctuate in their intrinsic value with the fluctuation of the coins which they measure or represent." The terms standard of value, measures of value, intrinsic value, and representation, as applied to moneys of account, is open to strong objection; but the meaning of the author, on the whole, is sufficiently obvious.

Moneys of account have "their foundation in real coins or weights;" and they often remain unchanged, although the coin or weight on which they are founded may have undergone many changes. When once well established, they become capable of expressing the prices of both goods and the precious metals. By their *intrinsic value* he means the value of the unit represented in the precious metals. Moneys of account do change with the gradual changes in the value of coins, if the denominations of the coins are the same with those of the money of account; because the mass of the people in whose minds the money of account is fixed, fail to distinguish between them when both are called by the same names. But when the money of account does not correspond with any coin, it does not fluctuate, nor even tend to fluctuate, with the precious metals or coins; but remains steady, and quite capable of marking and expressing the variations in the value of coins and bullion. The "Cambist"[1] furnishes "a Table of moneys of account," of which it is remarked, "that some of these are real coins, the value of which may be computed from the mint regulations, or from assays; but when they are imaginary moneys, which is generally the case, their

[1] Vol. II., page 148. Edition of 1835.

pletely performed, as elsewhere; although the franc, the sovereign or pound, and the dollar coins, agree with the unit of the money of account. To understand the system of money in any country, the first requisite is to know in what terms or denominations accounts are kept, prices fixed and expressed, and all the dealings of the people carried on; this, whatever it may be, and whether any coins correspond or not, is the money of account of that country. The chief difficulty in understanding the subject of moneys of account and coinage, is the blending them or not keeping them wholly apart as distinct things. It will be found, as a matter of fact, that in every country the money of account is used to express the value of coins, and that coins do not serve essentially to give effect to the money of account. Where there is a coin corresponding with the unit of the money of account, it is true it presents the value which the other expresses. It is proper, in England, to say that the coin called a sovereign is worth a pound sterling; but it is not proper to say that a pound sterling is worth a sovereign.[1] The pound is the unit of the British money of account, and it is employed not only to express the value of the sovereign, but the value or price of every other coin or quantity of gold over that amount. There is a money of account in Great Britain, based on the shilling, which is seldom employed beyond the value of three or four pounds; prices are frequently expressed in shillings, from one to sixty or eighty, but seldom beyond that amount, though there

---

value must be found by their established proportion to real coins." This table sets forth over one hundred and twenty different moneys of account, and exhibits the fact that several countries have more than one, and some as many as five; a fact which is a proof that past monetary revolutions are not only productive of misfortune and damage at the time, but of enduring evil and inconvenience afterwards. A want of precision in the language of the author, on the subject of moneys of account, is apparent through the whole work; and yet a little attention only is requisite to comprehend his statements. It is only needful, for this purpose, to remember that the money of account is not only as operative, but as necessary, to commercial dealing, where the coins correspond with it, as where they do not.

[1] The sovereign is a recent coin, and when first issued was made to conform to the minutest fraction in the pound of the money of account. See infra, Chapter 4.

is no difficulty in understanding those who express prices in shillings to any amount not too large to be converted, mentally and instantly, into pounds. This double money of account is an argument, in England, for the adoption of the decimal system, which furnishes a relation between the unit of the money of account and its parts, much more easily carried in the mind than that used in the British system of money. It would be much easier to apprehend the value of any part of a pound expressed in hundredths, than in shillings and pence; and this perfect facility of perceiving the relation of all the parts of the unit to the unit itself, saves the formation and use of a subsidiary money of account, like that of the shilling. In the United States we express many prices in cents, but we always perceive the relation of the number of cents to the dollar; and, in fact, the common mode of writing cents is fractionally as $\frac{20}{100}$, instead of 20 cents.[1]

[1] The confusion which reigns in the minds of many men, as to the existence and functions of a money of account, is strikingly illustrated in the discussions now pending in England on the adoption of a decimal system. While many understand its true idea and use, and intelligently explain the difficulties and nature of the proposed change; others, for want of this correct conception, carry confusion into the whole discussion by speaking only of coinage. Some of the reformers absurdly proposed changing the unit of their money of account, the pound sterling. A greater mischief can scarcely be conceived; certainly a more needless evil could not be inflicted on the country. Pounds are already counted decimally; it is only the parts or fractions of a pound to which the reform applies. It is, in fact, the shilling money of account which is to be changed. The coinage part of the question is comparatively of little importance. To change the money of account of a nation like Great Britain is indeed a serious affair, and demands the utmost caution and investigation. The best mode of effecting this change, as it strikes us, is that which has in part received the approval of Parliament, the British public, and the greater number of those who have written on the subject.[1] This preserves the pound unit of account, without displacing the shilling as a coin. It involves the lowering the copper coinage four per cent., which, in practice, would not be found to work injuriously. The mint would take the old copper coins at a premium of four per cent., payable in the new issue. The dealers would give as much for the old coins as ever they did,

[1] The *pound* and *mil* system, in which 1000 mils make a pound. The copper coinage is lowered four per cent., which makes mils and farthings equivalents.

When it was recently proposed, in England, to adopt a decimal system, dispensing with the pound as the unit of the money

---

because they could be reimbursed by the change into new coinage. The British system virtually includes four moneys of account; one with the pound unit already counted decimally; one with the shilling unit; one with the penny unit; and another with the farthing. The change proposed is to dispense with the three latter, and have them absorbed in the first. In fact, it will be found not to be a question of coinage, except the copper money, but a question of the mental habits of the people.

In spite of all that can be done, the people of Great Britain will reckon by shillings for at least a half century to come. This, however, will not disturb the adoption, nor prevent the success, of the proposed money of account. It is now seventy years since the decimal system of this country was legally adopted; and, during all that time, the Spanish coins, halves, quarters, eighths and sixteenths of a dollar, have circulated concurrently with our decimal coinage. They have, doubtless, obstructed in some degree the complete adoption of the decimal money of account in the expression of prices and sums under one dollar. But for the last forty years prices under one dollar have been expressed, if not exclusively in cents, at least with equal facility, and to a much greater extent, in cents than in the terms of the Spanish coin. Both are yet employed, and both generally understood. The term shilling, in the State of New York, maintains its place fully, as it corresponds with the Spanish eighth; but the elevenpenny-bit of Pennsylvania, and the nine-pence of Massachusetts and Virginia, representing the same amount, or 12½ cents of our decimal system, have nearly disappeared. These Spanish coins, which for fifty years greatly outnumbered our decimal coinage, were readily valued in our money of account, and the gain over the old system has been immense. The difficulty, in England, is really less than we have had to encounter. The money of account founded upon the pound unit can be introduced in far less time than it required to introduce the system of the United States, because the pound unit is retained. Here it is given up for the dollar. There the shilling may, and should be, retained as a coin; and will not only prevent confusion in the minds of those who cannot at first understand the nature or the reason of the change, but greatly aid and facilitate the progress of the measure. The shilling bears the same relation to the pound that a half dime does to a dollar in the United States: or, one-twentieth of a pound. While the people are learning the new system, the old coins which form a part of it will enable them to avail themselves of the old system, until they become equally familiar with the new.

The merchants, bankers, brokers, and dealers in bullion, can exercise the most effective influence in introducing the new money of account. Let prices be named both ways; let bills be made out with the sums expressed

of account, Professor Airey, who was examined by the Parliamentary committee on the subject, said: — "I can scarcely con-

---

both ways, for which the stationery should be prepared, and paper properly ruled. This part of the business expert tradesmen, bankers and clerks will master in a fortnight. Their customers, or most of them, must, however, be dealt with in pounds, shillings and pence for many years. For in this money of account will the greater number continue to think, long after the account-books of the government, of the banks, and the principal merchants, are kept by the new system. The books of the Bank of England might be all safely opened upon the new system within a year, or less, from the time the measure was resolved upon; and so of all other large establishments. But cashiers, tellers, and others in like positions, would be obliged to be equally familiar with both systems, and to be able to translate sums instantaneously from one to the other. Great advantage would be gained very soon; but the entire and universal adoption of the new money of account could not have place for from twenty to fifty years. The inconveniences of this gradual progress would not be equal, as a whole, to those of the present system. It would, in fact, be a measure completely successful for those persons and institutions who most require and need the change.

It is a happy circumstance for the success of this measure, that so little change in the coinage is required. None would, indeed, be far better than too much. It would be highly useful, it seems to us, to have the new pieces of the same value as the shilling and sixpence, having the same impression coined, with the addition in figures of their value in the new money of account. Every shilling and sixpence would be a lesson, and an aid to the memory. With this addition there would be less objection to the old crowns and half crowns, than to any possible new coins.

Of the other plans of introducing the decimal system of money into Great Britain which have been proposed, none appear to us so safe and desirable as the one already approved by the House of Commons. Many of them betray a total misconception of the whole subject, and deserve not a moment's consideration. The attempt at a universal system of coinage entertained by some is only a little less visionary than an universal language. Changing coins does not change moneys of account. Governments may order new coins, but the people will not always reckon by them. The best devised system of universal coinage could not, with all the power of modern European governments, be forced upon the people in a century, if at all. As with coins, so with weights and measures. They cannot be changed upon the ground of general conformity, because the inconvenience of the change will endure for a whole generation of those who are asked to make it. The weights and measures in general use are so fixed, as to their meaning, in the minds of the people, that any proposal of change alarms them, or, if it causes no alarm, it will not be received. The French system of weights and

ceive it possible, except by the most violent and offensive measures, to change the principal money of account from its present value of the pound sterling. Every estimation of large, and even of very moderate sums, is formed by the pound. I do not attach great importance to such things as the national debt, or the rental of the country; but the price and rental of private estates, the salaries of officers, the annual wages of servants — in larger matters, the expense of constructing a railway, or sailing a ship — all are estimated by pounds. An alteration of the value of the pound would unhinge every estimate and contract in England. I say, advisedly, every contract for the shilling is inseparably connected with the pound; and every contract which is not ostensibly made by the pound, is made by the shilling."[1]

It is remarked by Dr. Bowring, in his instructive little work on the decimal system, that, "To the pound sterling the most distinct and definite ideas attach, whether on large or small amounts. Mention a pound, five pounds, ten pounds, fifty pounds, a hundred pounds, a thousand pounds, ten thousand pounds, and your meaning is comprehended by everybody."[2]

Every one is acquainted with a large class of prices, and knows a great number of articles which can be purchased for a pound, for five or for ten pounds; the wages of a man for a year, the price of a horse, the rent of a farm, the cost of a cottage or first-class dwelling, the value of a ship, the cost of a steam engine: all such valuations are carried in the mind, and are

---

measures, so much boasted, has made its way only very gradually in France. It is even yet but partially adopted, and is now admitted to have defects which should be corrected before it extends further. It could not have passed so extensively into use, if it had not been originated at a time when change was the order of the day; when all old things, and old institutions, were under the process of being exploded, reformed or modified.

The French system could not be forced upon Germany, nor Great Britain, nor upon the United States. Those who are laboring for the desirable object of an universal system of coins, and weights and measures, must fail of success, because the complications and difficulties to be overcome are equally beyond the reach of science, authority and individual enterprise.

[1] Minutes of Evidence on Decimal System, page 30. Bowring's Decimal System.

[2] The Decimal System, by Sir John Bowring, page 104.

expressed in money of account. In naming such prices, or expressing such estimates, those who use them have no reference to any quantity of gold or silver; for, among those who thus freely speak of prices, few could tell, or without help ascertain, the value of a quantity of the precious metals corresponding to any large sum named by them. If the owner of a cottage, valued by him at a thousand pounds, were to have gold to that amount laid before him in payment, he would be utterly at a loss as to its real value. If the amount were in sovereigns, he could count them; and as each sovereign bears the mint certificate that it contains gold to the value of a pound, he would take the 1000 sovereigns for £1000, not on his own knowledge, but on the faith of the public coinage. The estimate of the article is made in pounds, and the price is perfectly understood by both buyer and seller, whether payment is made at the time or not. If made in gold bullion, it would be carried to a dealer in bullion to be weighed and valued; if in sovereigns, they would be received, not because the receiver knew either the genuineness of the gold, or that the coins contained the requisite quantity of gold to be equal to a pound, but they would be received solely on the faith of the impression on the coin indicating both quantity and quality.

§ 3. *British money of account — The pound sterling — Guinea — Sir Isaac Newton — Earl Liverpool — System of* 1816 *— Why fractions in weight of coins — Coins are adjusted to money of account — "What is a pound?" — Fixed price of precious metals — Influx of gold — Depreciation postponed, but yet to come — Remedy — Suspension of payments in Great Britain, in* 1797.

In further illustration of the subject, we shall notice specially some of the more noted moneys of account, and such as may appear best fitted to explain their nature and functions. The British money of account derives its terms from the fact that English coinage was founded upon the pound of silver, out of which was coined twenty shillings. Since that time, the money of account for expressing large sums has been the pound unit, for small sums, the shilling; but owing to various abuses of the coinage, and other facts which we cannot recount here, the pound of silver which at first was coined into twenty, is now coined into sixty-six shillings. The money of account of England has passed through just so many changes as have concurred to bring down the pound of the former money of account, expressing the equivalent of a pound of silver, to the pound of the present money of account, which is not equivalent to the third of a pound of silver. At this point it has remained unchanged for more than a century. From the reign of Charles II. until the year 1816, when the sovereigns were coined, the pound sterling had no corresponding piece in the coinage. The guinea was intended as a coin to be of the value of a pound, but not having been correctly adjusted, its greater value was at once shown by its price expressed in the money of account; and the price of gold fluctuating, it varied correspondingly in price until the year 1717, when it was fixed by Sir Isaac Newton at twenty-one shillings, at which rate it has remained under regulation of the mint.

In 1816, under the advice of the Earl of Liverpool, and in pursuance of his elaborate report,[1] gold was adopted as the legal tender of Great Britain, and a coinage of sovereigns ordered. In making this important change, if it had been regarded merely as a matter of coinage, it can hardly be conceived that the weight for this new coin would have been fixed at five pennyweights, three grains and $\frac{171}{623}$ of a grain. We ask, for the sake of those to whom the idea of a money of account is not familiar, why this special quantity of gold, involving so minute a fraction, was to constitute the sovereign, which was to be thereafter the most important coin of Great Britain? Coins are easily made of any

[1] Letter to the King on the coinage of the Realm. 4to, London, 1805. This very elaborate report, in which there is much to admire and to learn, exhibits, however, that confusion of ideas and expression which characterize all writings on money by authors who know nothing of, or who disregard the money of account. The eighth, ninth and tenth pages of this celebrated document furnish abundant proof of the difficulties encountered by those who endeavor so to define money in coins as to include all the functions of a money of account. The introduction of the money of account removes all the difficulties so strongly felt by the Earl of Liverpool.

Notes of the Bank of England were then, and have been ever since, a legal tender in England.

weight, and they are readily changed. Why did the British government determine to coin $46\frac{29}{40}$ sovereigns from a pound of gold? Why admit such fractions into their coinage? Why not make the coins even parts of a pound, so that every one might know the quantity of gold in his coins, as well as the value? The reason was, that the British government having resolved that the pound sterling should be represented in the coinage, there could be no discretion as to the quantity of gold in the sovereign, for the value of a pound sterling was well known to all the people, and had remained unchanged for more than a century, and, but for unwise legislation, or want of legislative care, would remain far more steady, and freer from fluctuations, than gold or silver. The sovereign was then necessarily made to weigh 5 dwts. $3\frac{171}{623}$ grains, that it might represent the British unit of money of account; that is, it was made the equivalent of a value known and fixed before.[1] The British government did not create or enact the money of account; it grew up with the progress of the nation, and although it had undergone mutations under abusive regulations, yet it remained unchanged from

[1] The Franc of France weighs (silver)............. 76.5 grains.
Napoleon, " " (gold)............... 99.2 "
Sovereign, England, " " .... 122.5 "
Shilling, " " (silver)............. 86.5 "
Dollar, U. States, " " .... 412.5 "
Eagle, " " (gold)............... 258. "

The coins here mentioned, and all others, are accurately adjusted in weight to the unit of the respective moneys of account they represent. The money of account is not changed to suit the coins, but the latter to represent the former. Where this adjustment is not correct, as was the case with our gold coins before 1834, the coins will not circulate. If coins are undervalued in the money of account, they will be melted or exported; if overvalued, they will be refused. The adjustment of the coin to the unit of the money, or the part it purports to represent, must be correct to the minutest fraction. This is because coins are made a legal tender. Bars of gold or silver of any size may circulate by weight at the market price. Coinage, with a law making the coins a legal tender, is fixing the price by law of the precious metals, and is open to serious objections when applied to larger sums. All that a government can do, in the way of fixing this price, is to force creditors to take them at the price fixed.

the time it ceased to be improperly tampered with and abused. This the government, in the measure of 1816, wisely chose to respect.

It was a prominent feature of this measure, that it fixed the price of gold. The British pound would have remained steady, and capable of expressing, by its fractions, every variation in the price of gold; but the emission of a coin as the equivalent of a pound made it difficult for any but dealers in bullion to tell when gold changed in value. Two things, essentially distinct, were thus blended in the minds of the mass of the people; dealers in bullion alone could detect changes in the value of gold, but the people could not distinguish between the pound of the money of account and the sovereign.[1] This difficulty was increased,

---

[1] "If we have attained a clear conception of the functions of the money of account, we are able to answer the question, WHAT IS A POUND? by simply replying, that *it is the unit of the money of account of Great Britain.* The value of that unit, or its power, everybody in that country knows. The statute which fixes the mint price of gold in England is an application of the money of account by Parliament to the article of gold; and it really no more changes the nature of the money of account, when applied by law to express the value of an ounce of gold, than if a merchant had so used it. The price of an ounce of gold is declared, by statute, to be permanently at £3 17*s.* 10½*d.*, and the Bank of England is required to purchase it from all who offer, at £3 17*s.* 9*d.* Although the effect of thus declaring permanently the value of gold may confuse the minds of many, and lead them to infer that the ounce of gold is the £3 17*s.* 10½*d.*, it does not remain the less true that it is a simple expression of value, and that the ounce of gold and the £3 17*s.* 10½*d.* are not convertible terms, because the latter expresses the value of the former. It may be asked, what did £3 17*s.* 10½*d.* mean before it was used by the statute to denote the value of an ounce of gold? Did not people understand, by £3 17*s.* 10½*d.*, the same thing after its use in the statute as before? And how many thousands reckon familiarly in pounds, shillings, and pence, who know nothing about the mint price of gold.

"If a British statute, or proclamation, declares the gold Napoleon of France to be worth 15*s.* 10½*d.*, that is not merely declaring the Napoleon to be worth its weight in gold, it is the expression of the value in English money of account; it is not the same as if it had declared that the Napoleon, weighing ninety-nine grains and two-tenths, is equal in value to ninety-nine grains and two-tenths of gold. Such a declaration as this would only be intelligible to those familiar with the process of weighing gold. To say that a Napoleon is worth 15*s.* 10½*d.* is perfectly intelligible to every

and the confusion confirmed, by the enactment making sovereigns a legal tender for debts, at the rate of a pound sterling; this was fixing the price of gold by law, and fastening the money of account to gold, whatever might be its fluctuations. When this was done, the mint price of gold was £3 17*s.* 10½*d.*; and this became, under that enactment, thenceforward the fixed price of gold in Great Britain, at which all persons were compelled to receive it in payment. Whatever may be said of the policy of fixing the price of any article, even that designated for money by law, it cannot be questioned that it was a false step to endanger the steadiness of the money of account by fastening it to any coin or quantity of gold. The function of money of account being to express and register values or prices, whatever tended to confuse its operation, change its power, or render its expressions less intelligible or less reliable, was surely to be avoided. Such a measure, if gold remained unchanged in value, could have no other ill effect than preventing people from apprehending clearly the distinction between the unit of the money of

---

English ear; but if you were to ask the exact weight in gold which would be equivalent to 15*s.* 10½*d.*, not one person in a thousand could reply without a calculation, or consulting some authority.

"In England, gold is the only legal tender for sums over forty shillings. If you enter a warehouse in London, and ask the price of any number of articles over that sum, the salesman will inform you instantly; but if you ask him how much gold you shall weigh him for any article, he cannot answer.

"When the English farmer asks fifty shillings a quarter for his wheat, does he measure the value by a mental reference to fifty shillings, or to two-and-a-half sovereigns in gold? Or does he, on the instant, think of either silver or gold? Does he think of anything beyond expressing a price? And did he not, with equal readiness, give the rate before the mint price of gold was fixed as at present? If, as some say, the naming a price is strictly a comparison of the article priced with its equivalent in the gold standard, why is wheat continually quoted in shillings, of which there is no equivalent in gold, instead of in pounds and fractions? Why say fifty shillings, instead of £2 10*s.*? If the process of naming a price was strictly a comparison with gold, the mind would naturally cling to the pound or sovereign, and its fractions, especially where there are equivalents in gold, and say two-and-a-half sovereigns." — *Merchant's Magazine, April,* 1852, *by the author of this volume.*

account and the sovereign, or gold bullion. But if the recent influx of gold had been accompanied by the fall in the price of that metal, which the extraordinary quantity seemed to warrant, then the confusion which must have befallen the money system of Great Britain would have been disastrous beyond estimate or conjecture. The evil, though alleviated, is greater than is now suspected. It is strange that it does not create more apprehension. Great Britain has bound all her subjects to receive 5 dwts. and $3\frac{171}{263}$ grains in payment of a pound sterling. The immense pecuniary transactions of that country with all the world tends to uphold the price of gold when it exhibits a tendency to sink. The flow of gold from all the world to England has been seen, and the current of silver from England has not been less visible. The depreciation must proceed to a serious extent before its effects become clearly revealed or appreciated. The evil must, by its own nature, enhance itself; for the depreciation being more clearly perceived elsewhere, the gold would increase in its flow to the point of over-valuation. Each step of this depreciation would affect every pecuniary transaction of the country, and constitute an attack on the national money of account, in which all prices, rents, wages, salaries, taxes, and securities for money, are expressed. The magnitude of such an evil is wholly beyond estimate. That Great Britain has not already suffered more from this source is one of the most extraordinary things in the history of commerce; for no sane man would have supposed that such an influx of gold could take place, as has occurred within five years, without a heavy depreciation. The causes which have delayed this depreciation are, many of them, now well understood. Among them are usually mentioned as prominent, an immense displacement of silver by the export to the East, caused in part by revolutionary movements in China; contemplated rebellion in British India; short crops; the increase of enterprise and manufacturing industry on the continent of Europe; together with an immense absorption of capital in the construction of railroads; these, added to the war with Russia, produced a demand for gold which no previous combination of circumstances ever equalled.

We can scarcely doubt that the depreciation of gold has only been postponed, and that it cannot be avoided, whether it is to take place by a process so slow as to be perceptible only to those who will be shrewd enough to take full advantage, or whether it occur so rapidly that none may escape its consequences. But whether slow or quick, it cannot occur without much evil to Great Britain and the United States. There is no excuse for encountering such a mischief without preventive measures. The difficulty in providing a remedy is only that which arises from the coinage, and that presents an obstacle only in reference to the merest retail business. Great Britain has only to adopt the same principle and practice in regard to gold that has long prevailed in reference to silver. Let gold above five sovereigns, or some other suitable amount, be a tender only at the market price. The regulation of the United States, on the occasion of the great influx of gold, was precisely that which it ought not to have been. Gold should not have been made a legal tender in sums above twenty, or thirty, or fifty dollars, except at the market price, which will be familiar to all when it is permitted to find its own range like other commodities.

If this were so, every fall of gold would be at once marked on the money of account. An ounce of gold would be quoted in London at £3 17*s.* 10½*d.*, or at £3 17*s.* 5*d.*, £3 17*s.* 0*d.*, £3 10*s.* 0*d.*, £3 0*s.* 0*d.*, according to its market price. Every contract for money in the nation would remain intact, and every debt paid in gold would be paid only at the market price. The sovereigns, and other gold coins and bars, would be public certificates of the quantity and quality of the gold in them, but would be received only at their current value. No confusion or mischief could follow this repeal, to be compared with that which may be feared if a heavy depreciation in gold should occur.

The government, by the adoption of the gold standard in 1816, the coinage of sovereigns, and making gold a legal tender at a fixed rate, endangered the money of account, and placed its very existence on the hazard of the value of gold remaining unchanged. No possible improvement in the coinage of a country could compensate for the mischiefs of a ruined or confused money of account. It is true that such mischiefs have, in past times, been often inflicted upon nations; but the real history of these evils is yet to be written, and their magnitude to be appreciated. New coins are frequently introduced with impunity; and, great as the evil of an over multiplication of coins has been in many parts of the world, it does not compare with the evils involved in an unsettled or broken-down money of account.

The period of the suspension of specie payments by the Bank of England, from 1797 to 1822, furnishes a fit illustration of the functions of a money of account. This period included the wars of the French Revolution and of Napoleon, and the three years of war between Great Britain and the United States. The commercial payments of Great Britain were, during that period, effected almost entirely by means of credit: gold was so much in request for military purposes, that it became an article of merchandize in constant demand, at a high price, in England for shipment to the continent. The daily transactions of men involving the whole business of the country, the payment of taxes and wages, the sale of goods, the whole movement of income and expenditure, and the internal exchanges of the country, were carried on by substitutes for money, or by the various devices of credit. During this long period of paper currency, the money of account fulfilled its functions with a steadiness surprising to those who understood not its nature. All the contracts of Great Britain involving price and payment were made in the language of the money of account. For more than a score of years it was the medium of expressing the prices of all commodities, and all services. It was equally so before 1797 and since 1822; but when there is a currency of gold or silver, or a paper currency, that is convertible, it is difficult for many to separate the office of a money of account from that of coins. It is so fixed in their minds, that gold and silver are the practical measures of value, that there is no place in their conception for the existence or movement of a money of account. It seems strange, however, that any one, during this period of suspension of specie payments in Great Britain, could have failed to see the working of the money of account. Gold and silver, during all that period, ceased to be employed as money in large transactions: no man sold his goods, or rendered his services, with the expectation of payment in coins or bullion.

Few people in Great Britain, in that day, knew the exact price of gold, and no one hesitated an instant in affixing his price to other articles in pounds, shillings and pence. Nor did the dealer in coins and bullion hesitate in naming their price in these denominations. During all that period it was the sole medium of valuation, the sole medium of expressing or fixing prices. Business men, in those days, did not refer to the precious metals in their ordinary transactions. The charges in their books of account, and the sums expressed in their bills of exchange and promissory notes, were stated in the money of account; but they were, neither by law nor by custom, payable in coins or bullion. As a matter of fact, the demand for gold for exportation so increased its value, that it was sold at times as high as 100 shillings the ounce, instead of 77 shillings and 10½ pence, the mint price. The proof that this was no depreciation of the paper currency, as some contended, is, that the fluctuations of silver did not correspond, either in time or rate, with those of gold.[1]

There is no adequate proof that general prices in England indicated any depreciation of the paper of the bank. It was never quoted as below par. The high price of gold was the only real ground for alleging a depreciation of the paper. Yet this fluctuation in the price of gold had occurred frequently before the suspension by the bank in 1797.[2]

It is impossible, then, to refuse to the money of account of Great Britain the credit of having, during the important period of British history between 1797 and 1822, fulfilled the great office of serving as the medium by which the people measured or expressed the prices or values of all commodities and services in all private and all public transactions. It is equally true that it had done so before, and has done so ever since. During that time they were always conversant with money of account, but very little with coins. It was no more evident, however, during that time than since, that the fixing a price and expressing it in money of account is one thing, and payment is another and quite a different thing.

In many of the recent discussions in regard to the adoption of a decimal system, the importance of the British money of account is not only fully acknowledged, both by writers and by the eminent men who were examined before the Parliamentary committee, but the necessity of preserving it intact is strongly urged. Now, if thus important, where is the treatise or work in which the nature and functions of a money of account are developed? Where, in what book, or from what authority, are we to learn the doctrines of this very important agent in commercial transactions?

---

[1] See within, the closing paragraphs in the Chapter on the Bank of England.

[2] Gold was quoted, at the dates affixed, as follows: —

1783, March	81*s*. 9*d*. per ounce.	The mint price being			77*s*.	10½*d*.
1783, May	82*s*. 3*d*.	"	"	"	"	"
1792, May to Sept.	81*s*.	"	"	"	"	"
1795–6	85*s*. 86*s*. 88*s*. per ounce.	"		"	"	"

If changes of temperature can be measured and expressed by the degrees of a thermometer; if the pressure of the atmosphere can be, in like manner, expressed by the scale of a barometer; if places on the surface of the earth can be indicated by lines of latitude and longitude; if men understand each other when they speak of a foot, a yard, a pound, an ounce, or an acre; and if these modes of expressing temperature, pressure, locality, length, weight, &c., can be carried in men's minds, and employed constantly and intelligently to express definite ideas, how is it that we have been so slow to apprehend that prices or values may be expressed in a similar way? How is it that men can carry in their minds distinct and definite ideas of pounds, yards, feet and acres; that they can make estimates, sales and contracts, involving immense weight in pounds, and vast lengths in yards, and large surfaces in acres or feet, without any application of scales or yard-sticks, if they cannot carry in their minds definite ideas of pounds, yards and feet? It would be a vain attempt for government to replace these ideal methods for others substituted by authority. The old thermometers, barometers, degrees of latitude, pounds, yards and feet would maintain their empire over the minds of men once fully accustomed to them, for whole generations.

§ 4. *Colonial currency of Canada, and of the thirteen colonies now of the United States.*

The continued existence of the money of account in the British colonies of North America furnishes an apt illustration of the nature and working of the ideal scale by which men make computations, and express prices. The money of account is the same, in terms or denominations, as that of England, though not the same in meaning. The pound unit of Canada does not express the same value as the pound sterling. It is not now, and never was, represented by any coin of gold or silver. The people of these British colonies receive and pay out the coins of England and France, the United States, and other countries, always estimating their value or price in their own money of account. They have their own banking system, and their own bank-notes issued in sums expressed in their own money of account. So, also, are expressed the prices of all articles of merchandize; and all their domestic money transactions are effected in like manner. If the tenacity of those people for their money of account had not been great, it could not have been maintained thus unchanged for over half a century under the circumstances of their intimate relations with, and dependence on, the government of Great Britain. All the officers and soldiers of the army who go out from the parent country, and all the emigrants, carry with them their habit of using the British money of account: there must be incessant occasion, throughout these colonies, of comparing these two moneys of account; so much so, that very many of the people must be as familiar with the British money of account as their own. The inconvenience of this difference must be very great for the British government and its officials, as well as for the colonial governments and people. The temptation of the Imperial government to make the colonial money of account conform to that of Great Britain must be very great; yet, in the face of all these circumstances, this colonial money of account maintains its sway in the habits and minds of the people. We are not minutely acquainted with its history. The latest authority in our hands gives its value as one-tenth less than sterling; that is, £100 colonial is equal to £90 sterling. It would be interesting to learn whether this colonial money of account has undergone any change within the last fifty years. It is quite probable that fluctuations have taken place in the price of the precious metals in these colonies, owing specially to an unfavorable exchange creating a demand for specie for exportation. Such occasions, by showing an increased price of the coins in circulation, might to some appear like a change in the value of the money unit; whilst, in fact, they would only prove a local demand for the coins or bullion, and an enhanced price. But what it is desirable to know is, whether the Canadian pound, or unit of account, has undergone change in its power or value during the last fifty years, as the same is employed by the mass of the people.

British North America furnishes another remarkable instance of persevering adhesion to a money of account. The French inhabitants of Lower Canada cling to the old mode of computation which prevailed in France a century ago, when their ancestors emigrated thither. Despite their long subjection to British authority, to their being long surrounded by a larger population using another money of account, they cling to the denominations of *livres, sous* and *deniers*. This is a continuation of the old French money of account, in which the French Canadians yet express all their prices, and by which they express the value of all the coins in circulation.

The habits of these Canadians afford, then, plain proof that men do not measure the value of goods by means of gold or silver, or their substitutes, bank-notes; and that they do it by means of a money of account, which is employed not only there, but in all civilized countries, to express the price as well of goods as of money itself. We think it will be found that the French Canadian money of account has undergone no change in its power or value for a whole century.[1]

At the time of the separation of the United States from Great Britain, the money of account of all the colonies was expressed in pounds, shillings and pence; but these terms had very different significations in the various colonies. The term or unit pound, in the following named colonies, is expressed as below in our present money of account. No one of these units corresponded to the pound sterling — that of South Carolina being nearest.

£1, New England and Virginia.........	is equal to	$3.33,	or 6*s.*	to the dollar.
" New York and North Carolina......	"	$2.50,	or 8*s.* "	"
" Pennsylvania and Middle States....	"	$2.66,	or 7*s.* 6*d.* "	"
" South Carolina.........................	"	$4.28,	or 4*s.* 8*d.* "	"

Whoever will take the trouble to trace the history of these various and differing moneys of account, will find that coinage, or the regulations of mints, had little to do with it. The variations originated in part from the same, and in part from different causes. Whilst, in England and France, and other European countries, the fall in the value of the unit of the money of account was caused, generally and mainly, by abusive and fraudulent regulations of the coinage, in these colonies this departure in various degrees from the pound sterling proceeded from the monetary struggles arising from over-importation, a consequent

---

[1] As a specimen of the manner in which the prices of various coins were expressed in the moneys of account of the British Provinces of North America: —

Coins.	Nova Scotia, Halifax.			Lower Canada.			Upper Canada.			Pr. Edward's I.		
	£	s.	d.	£	s.	d.	£	s.	d.	£	s.	d.
British Guinea.......	1	3	4	1	3	5	1	5	6	—	—	—
" Sovereign...	1	5	0	—	—	—	1	4	4	1	10	—
American Eagle.....	2	10	—	—	—	—	—	—	—	3	2	6
British Crown........	—	—	—	—	5	6	—	6	0	—	7	6
" Shilling......	—	—	—	—	1	1	—	1	3	—	1	6
American Dollar ...	—	5	0	—	5	0	—	6	0	—	6	3
French Crown.......	—	5	5	—	5	6	—	—	—	—	—	—
" Five Franc.	—	4	7	—	4	8	—	—	—	—	—	—

Martin's British Colonies, page 229, and Appendix, page 53.

The units of the moneys of account of some of the British Islands are as follows: —

Jamaica.....................	£1 sterling equals	£1 8*s.*	or 6*s.* 8*d.*	to the dollar.
Barbadoes..................	"	"	£1 7*s.*	or 6*s.* 3*d.* "	"
Windward Islands.......	"	"	£1 15*s.*	or 8*s.* 3*d.* "	"
Leeward Islands.........	"	"	£2 0*s.*	or 9*s.* 0*d.* "	"

long-continued unfavorable exchange, and from a depreciated paper currency. The different circumstances of different colonies led to varying results; but, when the advance of industry and domestic trade had secured greater prosperity, and a more settled policy, these various moneys of account became fixed. There never had been any coinage to correspond with, or sustain any of them. The coins in circulation were almost exclusively Spanish; there could be no pretence that these moneys of account corresponded with or represented any coins or system of coinage, or that they were in the slightest degree supported by coins or coinage. Every coin in circulation was as much the subject of price estimated in these moneys of account, as a bushel of wheat, or a barrel of flour. All prices in each colony, and subsequently in each State, were expressed in the pounds, shillings and pence of that locality. The people measured not values by coins, but they expressed the known value of coins like other ascertained quantities, by their own money of account. These varied moneys of account were adhered to, from mental habit, for thirty to fifty years after our present simple decimal system was adopted. It is no uncommon thing now, in the interior of Virginia and Massachusetts, to hear people express prices in the old money of account. In New York the term shilling prevails yet, as it agrees with the Spanish subdivision of the dollar adopted as the unit of our national money of account. It was a common practice for merchants, for twenty years after the adoption of the dollar unit, to keep their books in the pounds, shillings and pence, with blank columns, in which, at their leisure, they converted their first entries into dollars and cents. For though merchants and professed accountants became familiar with dollars and cents, they were obliged to deal with the people in pounds, shillings and pence. It is true the value of the dollar was well known to the men of that day, but it was known only as the value of other things; it had no place in the minds of the people as the unit of a money of account. For them, prices expressed in dollars would have to be converted into pounds, shillings and pence. In the latter terms they instantly understood prices in all their relations; but prices expressed in dollars, or in sterling money, involved a calculation. Notwithstanding the simplicity of the dollar unit, and the extreme inconvenience of the differing moneys of account in the different States, seventy years, or two generations, have passed since the change was made, and yet traces of the old habits of reckoning are to be met with in all the old States. If any man finds himself unable to comprehend the working of a money of account, and its firm hold on the minds of people, let him study these moneys of account of the Atlantic States of North America.

§ 5. *Moneys of account in Italy, Germany, &c.—Evils of varied coinage—Coinage implies a previous price—Coins not a measure—Prices in money of account understood instantaneously—Ricardo—Sir James Stewart—Bishop Berkeley—Montesquieu—Money of account to be taken as it is, and its limits of usefulness studied—Edinburgh Review.*

We have abstained from entering at large into any notice of the moneys of account of various European countries, which, though full of instruction, are so complicated with questions of banking and coinage as to be less easily understood. The small extent of the separate countries of Germany and Italy, and the consequent multiplication of contiguous mints and varied coinage, and the blending in the circulation of so many different coins, early begot an amount of vexation and loss in money transactions, which people only bore because a remedy seemed hopeless. The evil, instead of diminishing, only increased with the lapse of time; for every effort of reform, and every application of remedy, only enhanced the mischief. It is easy to see, however, through the endless mazes of this varied coinage, that the evil would have been insufferable but for the facility afforded by moneys of account in valuing and computing the numberless coins which went to make up the circulation in many parts of Europe. It is true that this facility was somewhat diminished by the formation, in many countries, of several different moneys of account. Some coins were computed in one money of account, and some in another. In some countries one money of account was appropriated to bills of exchange, and another was used in the bank accounts.

People who were flooded with such a varied coinage as that which prevails in Germany and Italy, were often reduced to the patriarchal mode of making payments by aid of the scales. The method subsequently adopted to escape these evils was to publish tables of the various coins in circulation, with their value in the most used money of account of the country where the table was constructed. Such a table is that made by Sir Isaac Newton in 1719, a copy of which is found in the second volume of Kelly's Cambist (page 154); several such tables, of recent date, are found in the same volume, in the pages succeeding. These statements show that there were thirty gold coins called ducats, some twenty-five of which were from different mints, with wholly different impressions, and scarcely any two of which were of the same value. There were twenty-three gold coins called pistoles, from nineteen different mints, of differing values and impressions. No less than fifty-one silver coins, called rix dollars, were in circulation from about twenty different mints, and of varying value. We might adduce many such cases, to show how very complicated and vexatious is the general coinage of Europe. But the real extent of the evil cannot be conjectured from such instances, even if we had space to continue them. To know these coins, and deal in them, becomes a special branch of the business of private bankers, who of course must have a compensation for their skill and trouble. Many of the continental public banks had their origin mainly in this difficulty. To scrutinize, count and pay over these coins became such a burden, that it was assigned as among the chief reasons for the establishment of the banks of Amsterdam and Hamburg. Those who carefully examine the mode of proceeding by merchants and bankers through all this labyrinth of moneys, will find that it was only mastered by the mental habit of subjecting all these coins to the valuation of one or more moneys of account. It is no great difficulty for men much accustomed to deal in money to master several different moneys of account, and employ them mentally with equal facility. There are many men who, from their peculiar position in business, can apply with equal readiness the moneys of account of England, France and the United States. Time and opportunity may give this facility to any person; but, unaccustomed to other moneys of account than their own, the most expert arithmeticians of either of these countries will always be found converting the money of both the others into their own, as a means of ascertaining its meaning or value. An Englishman, simple as the French system is, always mentally converts every sum and price named to him in France into his complicated denominations of pounds, shillings and pence, before it presents to his mind a full idea of the value expressed. So, indeed, must the traveller from France do in the United States, although familiar with a decimal system similar to our own. The price of a horse, or a coat, in dollars does not instantly convey to his mind the value named; it must be turned into francs.

All modern coinage implies some previous mode of expressing value or prices. It will be seen that the coins are always made to correspond with the denominations of this mode of expression. When the English sovereign was first coined in 1816, it was made to contain so much gold as was equivalent to a pound sterling. And so it will be found that coins are always made to correspond not specially with a previous weight or coin, but always with the money of account. This will be shown more fully hereafter. Coinage, as now conducted at modern mints, is not only in accordance with the prevailing money of account, but subservient to it. A certain weight of gold or silver has its price expressed in some particular denomination of the money of account. Three things are expressed in a coin, weight, quality, and price or value. Its weight is ascertained by actual application of the balance in the mint; its quality, or standard of fineness, is also fixed by law and the workmanship of the mint; its price is also fixed by law before it is coined. It is made to correspond to some previous rule in all these respects. It is not, therefore, a measure or criterion of value; but an article prepared by the mint, and vouched by the public authorities as of a proper weight and quality to be employed in payment at a particular price. It is a commodity commonly used in payment, and approved for that purpose, which is brought to one common standard of quality, and divided into pieces accurately weighed, and of such size and weight as will be convenient for use, reckoning and circulation. If these coins were in occasional use among savages for the purposes of exchange, they would probably compare every article with the coin, and among them coins would be a kind of measure of value. In civilized life, coins are not measures of value, but special quantities of gold or silver weighed, certified by the impression received at the mint, and adjusted by the weight given to them to a particular price expressed in the money of account. The gold and silver thus prepared has given to it every possible advantage as a medium of payment. As a general equivalent, no commodity has ever been preferred, and none is likely to be preferred. We therefore count coins, we pay in coins, but we do not express prices nor keep books in coins.[1] All our computations of money, all our conversation about the market value of merchandize, all the sums named in reference to real estate or public revenue, all the sums expressed in bills of exchange — all these, as we have said, are stated in money of account. If one person say to another, I will give you $10,000 for your house, he to whom the offer is made knows instantly the import of the offer; but if, instead of this, he places before him a large cask of dollars, and says, I will give you these, it may require two or three days' time to ascertain how much is offered. So any one understands, in an instant, what value is intended by $100; but it may require many minutes to count and scrutinize $100 in coins. In analogy with the mental process which is applied to all measures and weights when they are merely spoken of and not actually used, men employ a money of account to express prices. It is only arithmetic, with a value affixed to the unit or number one, which is to

---

[1] "A coin is merely a piece of metal, of known weight and fineness." — "It has been said to be both a sign and measure of value; in truth, it is neither." — "It is equally incorrect to call money a measure of value. Gold and silver do not measure the value of commodities more than the latter measure the value of gold and silver. When one commodity is exchanged for another, each measures the value of the other." — *Encycl. Britt., article "Money," by J. R. M'Culloch.*

Mr. M'Culloch and others have thus clearly taken away the old measure, without bringing forward the real agent in fixing prices. It is money of account which makes of the exchanges of civilized people a real barter; it registers prices and amounts, and the credit system effects the payments. Commodity, in fact, pays for commodity. This is explained as we advance.

accompany all subsequent numbers and combinations in proportion to the number of units expressed. Fractions and decimal parts are expressed as in all other cases.

"During the discussion of the bullion question," says Mr. Ricardo, "it was most justly contended, that a currency, to be perfect, should be absolutely invariable in value."

"But it was said, too, that ours had become such a currency by the bank restriction bill; for by that we had wisely discarded gold and silver as the standard of our money; and, in fact, that a one pound note did not and ought not to vary with a given quantity of gold more than with a given quantity of any other commodity. This idea of a currency without a specific standard was, I believe, first advanced by Sir James Stewart; but no one has been able to offer any test by which we could ascertain the uniformity in the value of a money so constituted."[1]

This shows that even Mr. Ricardo, who must have known what was meant by a money of account, could not embrace its functions in his view of money in general. Sir James Stewart, in whose works we first find distinctly set forth the existence and uses of a money of account, did not speak of it nor propose it as a currency; he did not regard it as money. We give his own words: —

"Money which I call of account is no more than a scale of equal parts, invented for measuring the respective value of things vendible.

"Money of account is, therefore, quite a different thing from money coin, and might exist although there was no such thing in the world as any substance which could become an adequate and proportional equivalent for every commodity.

"Money of account performs the same office, with regard to the value of things, that degrees, minutes, seconds, &c., do with regard to angles, or as scales do to geographical maps, or to plans of any kind.

"In all these inventions there is some denominative taken for the unit.

"In angles it is the degree; in geography it is the mile; in plans, foot, yard; in money it is the pound, livre, florin, &c.

"The degree has no determinate length, so neither has that part of the scale upon plans or maps which marks the unit; the usefulness of all those being solely confined to the marking of proportions.

---

[1] Proposals for an Economical and Secure Currency, Section II.

"Just so, the unit in money can have no invariable determinate proportion to any part of value; that is to say, it cannot be fixed in perpetuity to any particular quantity of gold or silver, or any other commodity.

"The value of commodities depending upon circumstances relative to themselves, their value ought to be considered as changing with respect to one another only; consequently, anything which troubles or perplexes the ascertaining these changes of proportion by the means of a general determinate and invariable scale, must be hurtful to trade; and this is the infallible consequence of every vice in the policy of money or coin.

"Money, as has been said, is an ideal scale of equal parts. If it be demanded, what ought to be the standard value of one part? I answer by putting another question: what is the standard length of a degree, a minute, or a second? None; and there is no necessity of any other than what, by convention, mankind think fit to give.

"The first step being perfectly arbitrary, people may adjust one or more of those parts to a precise quantity of the precious metals; and so soon as this is done, and that money becomes realized, as it were, in gold and silver, then it acquires a new definition; it then becomes the price, as well as the measure of value.

"It does not follow, from this adjusting of the metals to the scale of value, that they themselves should therefore become the scale."

Sir James Stewart then refers to the bank money of Amsterdam, and the African custom, mentioned by Montesquieu, as perfect exemplifications of a money of account. "A florin banco has a more determinate value than a pound of fine gold or silver; this bank money stands invariable like a rock in the sea."—*Sir James Stewart's Political Economy, B.* 3, *ch.* 1, *vol. i.,* 4*th ed., p.* 526.

Now, whatever may be the imperfections of this statement, by Sir James Stewart, of the nature of a money of account, Mr. Ricardo should have seen that he did not propose "a currency without a specific standard." He did not propose a currency of any kind; for a currency is something which passes as a medium of exchange, and a money of account is something which every one must carry in his mind as he does his knowledge of words and arithmetic.

"It has long been obvious to observing men that there was something more in the nature and functions of money than was exhibited in the mere coinage of the precious metals, and that many false measures and notions were prevalent in consequence. To some it appeared clear that any substance whatever might serve for money, if men were only agreed to receive it as such. Hence, probably, the Carthaginian attempt at money of leather, and the Chinese paper-money. Those who saw clearly that money performed a certain circle of operations, returning to perform them again and again, were struck with the constantly repeated routine in which money appeared to circulate. This subject was occasionally adverted to long before it was ever seriously taken up. Bishop Berkeley, in his 'Querist,' was one of those who first intimated the distinction between money and money of account. In his 23d query he asks: 'Whether money is to be considered as having an intrinsic value, or as being a commodity, a standard, a measure, or a pledge, as is variously suggested by writers? And whether the true idea of money, as such, be not altogether of a ticket or counter?' Query 25: 'Whether the terms crown, livre, pound sterling, &c., are not to be considered as exponents or denominations' (see, also, the 24th query); 'and whether gold, silver and paper are not tickets or counters for reckoning,' &c. Query 26: 'Whether the denominations being retained, although the bullion were gone, things might not, nevertheless, be rated, bought and sold, industry promoted, and a circulation of commerce maintained?' Query 35: 'Whether power to command the industry of others be not real wealth? and whether money be not, in truth, tickets or tokens for conveying and recording such power, and whether it be of great consequence what materials the tickets are made of?'

"It is evident the Bishop saw dimly the value and functions of a money of account, but that he did not perceive the nature and use of a coinage, or the importance of the precious metals as a universal equivalent. Thus it is, that while some have looked at the money of account, they lose sight of the importance of coins, or the regular mode of authenticating the pieces of gold and silver, which are used sometimes for payment; whilst those who regard the latter too narrowly, are not able to comprehend that money of account in which all men name their prices, and keep their accounts.

"Montesquieu, in the 3d chapter of the 22d book of the 'Spirit of Laws,' treats expressly of ideal money: 'There are real and ideal moneys: civilized people, who all use ideal money, do so because they have converted their real into ideal money. Those who at first had a real money find that by fraud, or by act of the government, a part of the metal which should be contained in a coin is withheld, abstracted, and the piece thus reduced is still called by its former name.' He saw clearly that men reckoned by a money of account, but imagined it was only because the coin had been altered. The truth is, however, that the temptation to alter the coin arose, as we shall explain, from the fact that a gain could be made by using the terms of the money of account to keep up the deception of the debased coin. That which was called a shilling, was still called a shilling, although reduced in quantity and value; but the idea of the value of a shilling being firmly fixed in the minds of the many would be applied, by reason of the name, to the debased coin. And the evil of these changes induces the author of the 'Spirit of Laws' to discourage the use of ideal money. In the 8th chapter of the same book he tells us, that 'the blacks on the coast of Africa have a sign of value without money, purely ideal. A certain article is worth three macutes, another six, another ten macutes. That is the same as if they said simply 3, 6, 10. The price is fixed and expressed by comparison of commodity with commodity, for there is no money in particular, but every portion of goods is money, or means of payment, compared with others.'" — *From an article, by the author of this volume, in the "Bankers' Magazine," of July*, 1857.

The power and functions of a money of account are of great importance; but we must take the money of account for what it is, and for nothing else. We may trace its history, study its applications, and consider its range of power and usefulness; but we cannot deny its existence, nor shut our eyes to the fact that its use is as universal, as it is unavoidable, among all civilized people. It is a very proper and natural inquiry how far a money of account may be relied upon for uniformity and permanence. Since men will estimate and count by an ideal scale, it becomes important to learn all that can be known of this important mental process. What are its advantages and disadvantages? Does the unit of the money of account vary under slight, or only under extraordinary influences? What kind of influences seem most to affect it? These, and other like questions, may well demand consideration; but no one can any more be held responsible for the defects of a money of account, than can any one claim merit for it as an invention of his own. Sir James Stewart was not the inventor of that which had been in use in all ages; and it was not incumbent on him "to offer any test by which could be ascertained the uniformity in the value of a money so constituted." Few men were better fitted to judge of the uniformity of a money of account than Mr. Ricardo, if he had applied himself to that particular point.[1]

---

[1] "It is clearly necessary, therefore, to have a mode of expressing values, which is as applicable to every change in the value of the precious metals as to any other commodity. This is what they have in China, and what they had in Venice, and what they have in Hamburg, and in every commercial community, where their coins do not correspond with the money of account. It is what they have even where this correspondence exists, but with such confusion of ideas as greatly impairs the advantage. Merchants, bankers and capitalists can readily apply the usual money of account to bullion; and the price-currents give constantly the price of gold and silver in bars by the ounce, and of doubloons and dollars. But the mass of

§ 6. *Moneys of account, how formed, preserved, disturbed and destroyed.*

The agency of moneys of account being acknowledged, it becomes a matter of interest to consider how they are formed, preserved inviolate, and disturbed or destroyed. Hitherto, whilst

---

the people are prone, in Great Britain, to look upon the precious metals, and pounds and shillings, as the same thing. It is, however, none the less true, that the course of dealing converts any system of coinage into a money of account used in all the price-lists, and in all sales. Men familiar with prices soon learn to carry the prices of hundreds of articles in their memories, with all the fluctuations that are constantly taking place; and this they do not accomplish by keeping in their minds a distinct idea of the quantity of gold or silver which may be the equivalent of each price, for of these quantities they may have no correct conception at all. However it may be done, whether by mere force of memory or practice, or by the aid of association, it is true that men in business carry a vast amount of details about prices in their minds, who know very little of anything about gold and silver coins or bullion. It is, hence, always the tendency of commerce to create a strict money of account, especially among those who have most to do with trade, and most familiarity with prices. This would be at once seen and credited, were no coins circulated; but it is no less true where it cannot readily be detected, than where it is evident in the business of every day. The occasions in which prices are named, discussed and fixed, are vastly more numerous than those in which any actual or veritable measurement of the value of any article is made in gold or silver; so much more so, that those whose occupations lead them incessantly to the consideration of prices, find it much easier to carry money of account in their heads than money of coins in their hands.

"Mr. Locke has said, men do not contract for denominations, not having noted that they contract by them; and the writer of an article in the 'Edinburgh Review' for October, 1808, says that 'Abstract ideas are of no use in going to market.' Mr. Locke has been frequently refuted and contradicted in reference to some of his positions about money; and the author of the article in the 'Review' has been handled with masterly severity and power by the writer of the book reviewed.[1] The author of the 'Review' has used this flippant expression as an argument; and it is clear enough, from a survey of the entire article, that his conceptions and practical knowledge of the whole subject were far too confused to enable him to escape from fallacies even as glaring as that. He quotes with equal readiness to support

[1] "Essay on Money and Exchange," by Thomas Smith, 8vo. page 231: London, 1807. "The Bullion Question Impartially Discussed: an Address to the Editors of Ed. Review," by Thomas Smith: London, 1812.

the subjects of money, coinage, coins, the precious metals, currency, and banking, have been treated at great length, but little attention has been given to moneys of account, and still less to

---

his positions, that which is directly against, as that which sustains them. He neither comprehends the work reviewed, nor the authors whose works he quotes. This is not for want of ability, but for want of sufficient previous knowledge of commerce and the use of money. He would have found it very difficult to give a philosophical reply to the question, With what kind of money did Englishmen pay their debts from 1797 to 1822, during the period of suspension? His position, that 'nothing can measure value but value itself,' would hardly be a satisfactory response. He could not fairly rid himself of the interrogatory, as he does of the African custom of reckoning, by an imaginary standard of *bars* (originating from bars of iron); 'When the Africans estimate the value of a purchase in bars of iron, they have not, in general, the bars to give for it; they have only some other kind of goods, and their purchases and sales are mere barter, though they estimate the value of the commodities given and received by comparing them with bars of iron. When the Europeans, however, make their estimates by comparison with ascertained quantities of gold and silver, *they have the gold and silver ready* to give for the commodity which is the object of the purchase.' This was a monstrous assumption for an Englishman to make in 1808, even for the sake of argument. That it was done in pure simplicity is evident from the following sentence: 'The convenience of this is very great.' Notwithstanding this convenience, it is probable that not one pound sterling in one thousand of this convenience was used in payment for commodities during the quarter of a century of suspension. And from 1822 to this day, but a very small proportion of such payments have been made in the convenient shape of coins. What, then, did Englishmen use to make their purchases? A more intimate knowledge of the laws of trade would have taught the reviewer, that the transactions of English commerce might be resolved into barter as justly as those of Africa. He would have found it difficult to explain, on his principles, why counterfeit coins and notes are just as efficient and convenient, until discovered, as the genuine; the whole loss falling upon those in whose hands they are detected, although purchases may have been made with them to thousands of times their nominal value. The mind of the reviewer was thrown into a perfect chaos, by assuming that what Mr. Smith called a standard unit of the money of account was meant as a standard of value. He floundered in this misunderstanding, without reaching a single clear conception of the subject strictly under review. Money of account is not a standard of value, it is an *expression of value* or price; by aid of arithmetic and men's mental faculties, it becomes, so long as undisturbed, the surest and most reliable expression of prices or values. There can be no standard of value in the sense in

the manner of their formation, preservation and destruction. We cannot leave the subject without adverting to these topics.

From what we have presented to the reader, it will have been seen that when any special coin, or weight of gold or silver, or any other article of value, has been employed for a time as an equivalent, or in payment for things purchased, people assume the value of the article in question as the unit of a money of account, and employ it, with the aid of arithmetic, to express prices. The more active the dealings of a people, the quicker they fix in their minds the unit from which proceeds a money of account. This is fastened upon the minds of the masses by incessant use; few habits, mental or bodily, are more constantly in use than the fixing and expression of prices. This unit of the money of account becomes familiar to every one; and being

---

which the term is sometimes employed; the right use of the term, as applied to the precious metals, is the standard of coinage."—*Article in the "Banker's Magazine," by the author of this volume, July*, 1857.

The examination of this subject was not without profit to the reviewer. He took up his pen to ridicule and crush Mr. Smith, and his idea of a money of account. He did not spare any weapon used by reviewers; and after having, as he complacently supposed, destroyed all Mr Smith's claims, he very coolly puts forth the very opinion the review is written to controvert. He ridiculed Mr. Smith out of his shoes, and deliberately and gravely steps into them, and thus delivers himself to his readers:—

"Next we account, *by means of money*. Now, what is the operation of accounting? We first state, in denominations of money, the value of any article, or accumulation of articles; and this statement we can manage in various ways. We can add to it another similar statement, or we can subtract it; we can multiply it; we can divide it, and discover various relations which it bears to other statements. In all these operations the terms pounds, shillings and pence exactly resemble algebraic symbols, and the letters *x*, *y*, *z*, might be employed for them. Operations of account, therefore, are undoubtedly carried on by abstract terms or symbols, and *it is impossible it should be otherwise*." — *Edinburgh Review, October*, 1808.

Th. Smith, Wilson, and others, who, during the period of the British suspension, advocated the agency of money of account, committed the serious mistake of applying the terms, *standard* and *currency*, to mere money of account. It was an error to speak of a "standard unit," and still worse of "abstract currency." The reviewer expresses the true agency of the money of account.

employed daily and hourly in reference to thousands of articles of value, it cannot change unless some unfavorable influence is brought to bear upon it. That which is committed to the memories of the people of a whole nation—that which they are repeating constantly, and multitudes do little else from morning to night, cannot be forgotten, and cannot easily change. Any tendency to change in one locality would be checked by another. If undisturbed, we see no reason to believe that the dollar, the unit of our money of account, would change in a thousand years. Some moneys of account are known to have remained unchanged for hundreds of years, one of which was the money of the Bank of Venice. Whenever the business of a people continues uninterrupted, their money of account must continue unchanged, if not purposely or insidiously, directly or indirectly, attacked. Its principle and working being understood, public authority may be employed to protect it from attack or unfavorable influences. Legislation cannot suddenly create moneys of account; it may unsettle and destroy those which long use has established, or it may defend them, and when it is expedient to change, provide that it may be done with the least possible injury to the innumerable interests affected.

There are many ways in which moneys of account become unsettled or destroyed. If the money unit has a coin to correspond with it, the correspondence is of course a fact familiar to every one. This is the case with our dollar coin, and our dollar unit. If we had no dollar coin, the people would have equal facility in the use of their money of account; but as we have one, the fact of their being of equal value is by all taken for granted. Now, if gold should very gradually fall in value, and if the gold dollar coin continued in circulation for a considerable length of time, a gradual accommodation of the money of account to the coin might take place. But such changes being always sooner perceived, and better understood, by dealers in coins and bullion, never take place but at immense loss and disadvantage to the bulk of the people; because the prevailing systems of coinage conceal the market price of the precious metals from all but those initiated in the mysteries of the bullion market. Of course this cause of change is much more effective where the coin is made a legal tender for the amount of the money unit. If, in such case, the coin falls in value, the law still makes it good for the discharge of the same amount as before the depreciation. This conceals the fact of depreciation, and the unit of the money of account is betrayed into gradual conformity with a coin which has really lost its value, and is reduced in its power of purchase. This occurred in many instances after the discovery of America, and the influx of silver, which was a result.

"The want of a clear conception of the existence and functions of a money of account has beclouded nearly all the legislation, and all the speculations on the subject of money, during the last century and a half. We shall have occasion to note how much it was needed in the English controversies during the period of the bank restriction. It is strange, indeed, that what was so well understood at Venice, and familiar there for centuries to her merchants who traded throughout the world, should not have been more generally comprehended elsewhere. At Venice there was a money of account which had no coins to correspond, and nearly all the payments of that great city were made in bank credits as expressed in that money of account. This was so, also, in other countries.

"It is true that kings and ministers were not without some knowledge on this subject. All the attempts to make advantage by debasing the coins, or raising their value, proceeded from some knowledge of the agency of money of account. These attempts were made in the expectation that the habits of the people, in expressing values by the usual money of account, would lead them to continue to estimate coins of the same name, at the same value, after a part of their proper quantity or quality had been abstracted. This kind of swindling was employed to rob the people for centuries, with very considerable success, though not always equal to the expectations of the perpetrators. The fraud did not consist in *merely* making the coins lighter; that could readily be detected, and its consequences avoided; but it consisted in calling that a crown, shilling or franc, which no longer contained the same quantity of silver which coins of these names had formerly contained. When the prices of all commodities were expressed in these denominations, they could not all readily be changed, and contracts would continue to be made for some time before prices would be adjusted to the change. The money of account would continue to operate unchanged long enough to give rapacious rulers some advantage of their operation. But the effect of names, and the new coin being a legal tender, would finally break up the money of account, and compel a new adjustment, or scale of prices. So long as the coins were named by the denominations by which prices were expressed, so long every change in the quantity or quality of metal in these coins, connected with their being made a legal tender, broke up and destroyed, soon or late, the existing money of account. This tampering with, disturbing, and occasionally wholly destroying the adjustment of prices, as expressed in the money of account, was an intense evil inflicted for ages upon the various countries of Europe. It could not, however, have been accomplished so successfully if the nature of the mischief had been understood. The mystery which shrouded the subject of money enabled each perpetrator of this fraud to offer plausible arguments which the people could not successfully refute, even if not convinced. Large capitalists generally shared the profits of these financial operations, whatever pains were taken to reserve the whole to the administration.

"In Venice, where the money of account was undisturbed for upwards of five hundred years, and was the medium in which the value stated in bills of exchange and bank credits were expressed, the chief payments during all that time were made in *bank credits*, bearing a premium of twenty per cent. over the precious metals. Any attempt by the Venetian government to debase the coin would have been futile and ineffectual, unless the bank had been at the same time destroyed, and the money of account broken up. Many changes were made in the coins of Venice, but their true value, in every instance, was at once marked by their value in the bank money.

"The various debasements in England consisted in, from time to time, increasing the number of shillings coined from a pound of silver. In 1066, one tower pound of silver was coined into 20 shillings; by the year 1464, six debasements had increased the number to 37*s.* 6*d.* In 1527, the pound Troy of silver was coined into 45 shillings; two changes carried the number, by the year 1601, to 62 shillings. It is now at 66 shillings. Now, the mere reducing the weight of a coin ought not to be considered a debasement, any more than issuing half crowns instead of crowns. It was the very fact that the public had the comparative value of the shilling clearly in view, that made it profitable to call a less weight of silver by the name of a shilling. If a piece of silver weighing 20 dwts. had been reduced to 19 dwts., it would have been estimated accordingly. But the shilling, as a term of comparison, was applied to a thousand commodities of trade."—*Bankers' Magazine, July*, 1857. *Article by the author of this volume.*

The livre of France was reduced from a pound of silver to very little more than the hundredth part of a pound. In many countries the reduction was still greater. In all the countries where the unit of the money of account originated from the use of the pound of silver in coinage, it would, but for the debasement of the coins, have remained until this day unchanged. Let any one look into the history of one of these violent changes, and he will see what a struggle it is for a people suddenly to change their money of account, and what confusion takes place at such a time in all transactions of money and commerce.

A money of account may also become unsettled or destroyed, and a new one originated, by the depreciation of a paper currency issued in correspondence with the unit of a money of account. This, however, is not so apt to occur, unless the paper currency is a legal tender for debts, or where some special government or bank paper composes the whole, or nearly the whole, circulation. If such paper gradually falls in value to a fixed depreciation, it gives rise to a money of account corresponding to it; and if sales be made by that money of account, and payment be made in coin, the latter is valued in the money of account high enough to cover the depreciation. Many instances of this are met with in Europe; and remarkable cases are found in Austria and Russia. It was urged, as we have already noticed, by many in England, that the notes of the Bank of England were depreciated, during the suspension of specie payments, precisely in proportion to the enhanced price of gold. If this had been so, the English money of account would have been changed in the same proportion; that is, above ten per cent. That appeared to be so to those who could not conceive that gold could rise in value sufficiently to account for all that difference; but it was denied by those who could not believe that ten per cent. had been added to the nominal value of everything in Great Britain except gold. It cannot be denied, however, that if the Bank of England had not, in that important crisis, been managed with signal wisdom and skill; and if the government, in that time of great expenditure, had not acted towards the bank with equal prudence and forbearance, the notes would have depreciated to a much greater extent than ten per cent. It may be questioned whether any instance of like good management on the part of bank directors, and like forbearance on the part of a needy government, can be found. England thus saved her money of account, and avoided immense derangement of the pecuniary concerns of the people.

The history of the suspension of the Bank of England for twenty-five years is probably, taken in all its bearings, one of the most instructive portions of the history of money.[1] The undeniable fact that all the dealings of that period of foreign war, and increased commerce and industry, were carried on in the language of the English money of account; and that nearly the whole of the payments were made in irredeemable bank-notes, and in checks upon banks not paying gold or silver, cannot be explained but by the agency of money of account, and its important subserviency to the credit system.

CONCLUDING REMARKS.

The reader is specially desired to notice that we are not, in this, bringing forward or recommending any new mode of reckoning or computation. We simply assert the matter of fact, that all prices, all books of account, all statements of sums of money, all bills of exchange and promissory notes, and all bank-notes, are expressed in money of account. All that is said or done with reference to money, where neither gold nor silver, nor other medium, is employed, is merely a use of money of account. If this be a fact in the mental habits of all civilized people, as we not only aver it to be, but that it cannot be otherwise, it is important to comprehend all its uses. We must accept the fact, if it be one, together with all its inevitable and all its proper consequences. The conclusions to be drawn from this fact are a separate consideration. There may be differences of opinion as to the deductions which may be drawn from, or the uses which may be made of it; but whatever these may be, we must not shut our eyes to a fact so important, the proof of which is so obvious and so indisputable, and the influences of which are in constant and active operation, whether we notice them or not.

---

[1] See ante, page 52, and closing pages of Chapter on Bank of England.

NOTES TO CHAPTER II.

I.

MARQUIS GARNIER AND HIS CRITIC, LETRONNE.

No writer, so far as we know, has apprehended more clearly the nature of a money of account, than the Marquis Garnier, who, in 1817, read to the French Academy of Inscriptions and Belles-Lettres a memoir upon the values of moneys of account among the nations of antiquity. He published afterwards, in 1819, a "History of Money from the highest antiquity to the reign of Charlemagne." The latter work contains a chapter on Moneys of account, which embraces the substance of the previous memoir. This learned writer ascertained, in the course of his investigations, that it was impossible to comprehend the ancient writers when they spoke of money, or to arrive at any sound conclusions in transferring the money of ancient times into modern money, without resorting to the distinction between coins and money of account. We know that the money of many modern nations cannot be properly appreciated without a due knowledge of their money of account; and can, therefore, readily admit that such knowledge is equally important in the just appreciation of ancient moneys. Without entering into this question, or vouching for the conclusions reached by Germain Garnier, we give his clear definition of money of account:—

"We distinguish then," he says, "two kinds of money—real money, or coins, and money of account, which is the expression of values, or the specification of prices. The valuation of merchandize made by the seller, the offer made by the purchaser, the accounts, the promises to pay, the stipulations of hiring, quotations of stocks, and the rents of farms, all that in every transaction precedes the act of payment, must be carried on by means of money of account. Real money only intervenes for actual payments."—"The elements of which a money of account are made up consist, properly speaking, of arithmetical quantities, which can be mentally multiplied and divided."—"Real moneys consist of coins of metal, of which the form, material, impress and appearance may be readily changed, without occasioning the slightest derangement in the daily dealings of society, or in agreements and contracts already made."—"But as to money of account which has no determined form, being in its nature incorporeal, it is one of the institutions to which people are most strongly and constantly attached by the powerful influences upon the mind of a habit incessantly applied to the highest interests of common life. The denominations of the money of account, the order and proportion of its divisions, assume at length an invariable character, and remain the same during the lapse of ages, to such an extent, indeed, that only more powerful influences, or great political events, can effect any change. The value of this money of account would have been not less steady and unchanging than its denominations and subdivisions, if the injustice and rapacity of governments had not frequently employed them to cheat their creditors and defraud the people, by adopting the expedient of lessening the value of coins. The people, not aware of the change in the coins, would continue for some time to estimate them in their money of account at the same price for which they passed before the debasement, and at which obligations and contracts were previously made. But every alteration in money of account has been regarded as a public calamity, as a source of disorders, public and private; and it has always awakened among a people a general discontent. On the contrary, changes in the impression or the forms or denominations of coins is a common event, inflicting no injury upon any interest, and offending against no established habits of the people."[1]

This is a clear view of the nature of money of account, as well as of the distinction between it and coins, or real money. His success in applying this distinction to ancient moneys has been disputed by Letronne, who, whatever may have been his other qualifications, as a critic of Garnier, furnishes no evidence in his work of his knowledge of that distinction.[2] The difficulties which surround that subject are, perhaps, greater than any with which adepts in ancient history have had to grapple. It is very certain that the distinction taken by Garnier, above quoted, could not but be a great assistance in historical researches touching values; and that no man can understand the subject of money, ancient or modern, who does not comprehend the nature of a money of account.

We would not undertake to decide upon the point in dispute between Garnier and Letronne. It requires something more than a full appreciation of a money of account to decide upon the real value of ancient moneys: on the other hand, it may be well doubted whether any man is capable of adequately mastering the subject, who does not fully understand what is meant by a money of account. We fear that Letronne labored under this disadvantage. He speaks of ideal moneys, but in no place exhibits any real comprehension of a money of account. He professes to meet Marquis Garnier on the ground of facts alone. We enter not into the issue between them here; the reasoning of both appears to be often inconclusive. Garnier adopts the idea that there was a general money of account prevailing extensively among the civilized nations of antiquity. Modern

[1] "Histoire de la Monnaie," par Marquis Garnier. Tome i, pp. 72 to 76.

[2] "Considerations sur l'evaluation des Monnaies Grecques et Romaine," &c. 4to, Paris, 1817.

experience tends to contradict this, as every modern nation has its own money of account, and many have several. One of the proofs to which he appeals as evidence of this, is the fact that Jacob sent money by his sons to purchase corn in Egypt, which money was received and valued, as he supposed, by a common money of account. Now it does not follow, by any means, that because Jacob's money was received by the officers of Egypt, it was estimated by the money of account used by Jacob himself. British sovereigns may be paid for any article in France, but would always be estimated and reckoned as so many francs. As people think in their vernacular language, so they always estimate and deal in their own money of account.

Letronne, referring to the instance of Jacob's money being received in Egypt, very correctly says it was received by weight; and from this he very incorrectly infers that there could have been no common money of account in the case. This plainly evinces that he did not understand the real nature of money of account. It is not probable that any people ever weighed gold or silver in payment, who had not a money of account, in which they expressed the price or value of the different quantities. In China, and in many other countries, gold and silver pass only by weight, but its value is always expressed in money of account. Whether the people of Mesopotamia, where Jacob dwelt, and the people of Egypt, used the same money of account, cannot be ascertained from the fact that Jacob's money passed in Egypt. All money of gold or silver will pass in China by weight: so, doubtless, the money of all the world would have purchased corn in Egypt, being paid by weight. The "four hundred shekels of silver" *weighed* by Abraham, in payment to Ephron for the cave of Machpelah, was "current (money) with the merchant."

II.

EXTRACTS

From an Article in the "Bankers' Magazine," of New York, in the July and August Nos. of 1857, *by the Author of this Volume.*

MONEY OF ACCOUNT.

"INQUIRING prices, and fixing them, occupy a large portion of the time and attention of all men in trade, and not a little of many others whose only connection with business is to purchase for the supply of their own wants. The conversation and discussion on the subject of prices, where no sale or transaction takes place, greatly exceeds, perhaps ten-fold, that which results in a change of property. The minds of a large proportion of the people in all thriving business communities become familiar with the prices of a certain range of articles which they have most occasion to purchase or sell. They keep pace with the fluctuations, and are well advised when they are asked, more or less, for any given commodities. These respective or comparative prices are readily borne in mind. Housekeepers well know the comparative rates of coffee, tea, sugar, rice, pepper, and other things which go to swell the household expenses. They know that a pound of beef is worth more than a pound of bread, and that a pound of butter is worth more than one of beef; and not only so, but they know it accurately and independently of any actual purchase; they know it without actually naming any price in money for each article. This idea of the comparative price of these articles is carried in their minds with perfect facility. And although, for facility and perfect convenience, these prices are expressed in money, yet any one familiar with prices could readily say a pound of rice is worth two pounds of flour, a pound of beef is worth four of flour, a pound of tea is worth eight of coffee, a bushel of wheat is worth two of potatoes, and very many could run round a whole range of comparisons, showing a definite and precise idea of the respective prices of the articles named.

"In all business transactions, prices are fixed and expressed in money of account. It forms the universal medium of estimate and comparison. Money of account may either correspond with the current coins or not. In England, all valuations are made in the terms *pounds*, *shillings*, *pence and farthings*, and occasionally in *guineas*. The coins correspond; that is, in naming a pound, you express a sum or value which has an equivalent in the sovereign; the shilling of account has its equivalent in the coined shilling, and so of the penny. In the United States, the money of account is expressed in dollars and cents, and the coins correspond. In many countries, however, the money of account and coins do not correspond. In China, prices are expressed in tales, mace and candarines; and accounts are so kept, and evidences of debt are written in the same way; so that these denominations are the money of account. Coins are not used in China. Gold and silver are largely used in payments and mercantile transactions, but always by weight, being valued like other commodities in the money of account—the value or price fluctuating according to the plenty or scarcity, the rate of exchange, the degree of fineness, and other causes. There is a very great diversity in Europe in the moneys of account and coins; in many places there are various modes of keeping accounts, and various systems of coins, and no agreement among them; in some there is a partial agreement. In Gibraltar, accounts are kept in dollars, which express a value equal to about two-thirds of our dollar, and without any corresponding coin. [See 'Kelly's Cambist,' 'Grund's Merchant's Assistant,' and other similar works; 'Austria, Venice, Genoa.'] In making a price, it is first, by inveterate habit, stated in the old way, and then converted, if necessary, into the new, as men sometimes think in one language and express themselves in another. So if, in Great Britain, sovereigns and shillings were wholly withdrawn from circulation, and Spanish or French coins substituted, the people would continue to think and value in pounds, shillings and pence until some powerful disturbing cause broke down the habit. It is more than half a century since the present admirable metrical system of weights and measures was adopted in France, with all the advantage of a decimal system; yet the mass of the people continue to think and estimate under the imperfect and complicated systems which had been long in possession of the public mind. The idea of a specific value and quantity once lodged in the mind, and familiarized by daily and constant use, will be as difficult to eradicate as one's native language. We may learn a new language, but we cannot easily forget that in which we have chiefly conversed from childhood, and in which we must continue to shape our ideas long after we may begin to express them in another. There are great numbers of business men familiar with the prices of a large number of the commodities of trade, engaged in daily discussing them, making sales and purchases, or quite competent to make them, yet, when produced and exhibited, wholly unable to recognise the quantities of which they speak, or to specify the quantity of gold or silver which is the equivalent of the prices they so fluently quote. They can tell you the price of a ton of iron, a hundred weight of sugar, or a barrel of flour; but they might be wholly unable to tell whether a lot of iron contained one or five tons, whether a lot of sugar contained one or five cwts., or whether a barrel of flour contained one or five hundred pounds. Nor could they tell the weight or size of the quantities of gold or silver which would be equivalent to the prices named. The editor of a price-current, who is constantly conversant with prices of almost the whole range of commerce, and quite able, from his familiarity with prices, to buy and sell, may be wholly ignorant of coins, of the mode of weighing the precious metals, or any other commodity. When coins are wholly, and for a long period, banished from circulation, men find no difficulty in naming prices and proceeding with the whole business of trade. In the United States, gold and silver are the only legal tender in payment of debts, and yet not one thousand dollars of debt in a thousand millions is paid in those metals. Men must, therefore, be much more familiar with prices, and with money of account, than they are with the precious metals.

"When a price is fixed, in the ordinary course of dealing, the naming such a price is not the same thing as holding up to the party to whom it is named a quantity of gold or silver of equivalent value. When a barrel of flour is said to be worth five dollars, the party fixing that price does not mean the *quantity* of gold in a half eagle, or of silver in five dollars, for that quantity he does not know. He uses the same expression he would use if he were asked the value of the half eagle, 'five dollars.' So if, in England, an article is said to be worth fifty-five shillings, neither party forms any idea of the quantity of gold equivalent to that amount, although payment cannot be made in silver beyond forty shillings. So, during our

Revolutionary War, when for many years there was only a paper circulation, prices were expressed in the various currencies of the different colonies, and very few indeed could have been guided by the quantity of gold or silver equivalent to any price expressed in their pounds, shillings and pence.

"It is evident, therefore, that money of account is the medium in which prices are quoted and expressed in all countries. It is capable of measuring, comparing and stating values to the utmost extent of the requirements of trade. Much confusion of ideas has arisen from blending the functions of coin with those of money of account, in legislation, in works on the subject of money, and in conversation. It is unfortunate for clear views on this subject, that the money of account has not, in all countries, as in China, been kept wholly distinct from the coins.

"The errors prevalent on this subject are very distinctly exemplified by Mr. Locke, in his tract on money, published in the controversy on the recoinage in England, at the close of the 17th century. The great philosopher had no conception of the real functions of a money of account. He tells us that 'Men, in their bargains, contract not for denominations or sounds, but for the intrinsic value, which is for the quantity of silver by public authority warranted to be in pieces of such denominations; and it is by having a greater quantity of silver that men thrive and grow richer, and not by having a greater number of denominations, which, when they come to have need of their money, will prove but empty sounds, if they do not carry with them the real quantity of silver expected.'[1] Again: 'The yard or quart men measure by, may rest indifferently in the buyers or sellers, or a third person's hands, it matters not whose it is. But it is not so in silver. It is the thing bargained for, as well as the measure of the bargain; and, in commerce, passes from the buyer to the seller, as being in such a quantity equivalent to the thing sold; and so it not only measures the value of the commodity to which it is applied, but is given in exchange for it. But this it does only by its quantity, and nothing else. For it must be remembered that silver is the *instrument* as well as *measure* of commerce. And every one desiring to get as much as he can of it for any commodity he sells, it is by the *quantity* of silver he gets for it in exchange, and by nothing else, that he measures the value of the commodity he sells.' (Page 4, 5, *idem.*)

"As the arguments and authority of Mr. Locke are greatly relied upon in the controversy which has been waged on this subject, it may be proper to state his views still more fully. After having insisted upon silver as the proper standard of value, and urged his objections to the double standard, he adds: '*One metal*, therefore, alone can be the money of account and contract, and the measure of commerce in any country. The fittest for this

---

[1] Page 9 of Locke's Tract. "Further Considerations on raising value of Money," 2d ed., 1695.

use is silver. It is enough that the world has agreed in it, and made it their *common money;* and, as the Indians rightly call it, *measure*, all other metals, gold as well as lead, are but commodities.'[1]

"If these misconceptions were not still frequently reiterated, it would scarcely seem necessary to refute them, as that was done at the time of their publication, and has been frequently since. In Mr. Locke's day, silver was the common medium of payment in small transactions, and he was not familiar with the modes of payment in the large operations of trade. He could not distinguish between the shilling of account and the shilling of silver. Even in the 17th century, before the Bank of England emitted a paper currency, a large portion of the great payments of commerce were effected in various other ways among merchants, than by the transfer of the precious metals. When Mr. Locke asserted that men did not contract *for* denominations, he simply overlooked the fact that they contracted *by* them. They used denominations continually as a scale, a measure, or an instrument, in all their quotations of price, valuations and bargains, but only used silver and gold when they were actually present, and then as a commodity and an equivalent. Mr. Locke could not foresee that, for nearly a quarter of a century, gold and silver almost disappeared from the circulation of England, and that, during that period, men were so far from always contracting for silver or gold, that no man ever expected to receive any payment in these metals, or either of them. He could not foresee that his descendant, Lord King, would make himself conspicuous as the only man in the nation who insisted on being paid in gold, giving his tenants special notice that their rents could only be discharged in that way. Yet all the business of the trade and revenue of Great Britain, from 1797 to 1822, a period of immense operations in war and commerce, was carried on *by* the aid of the denominations *pounds*, *shillings* and *pence*, and bank-notes. The theory of Mr. Locke must fall to the ground before such an example as this, whatever may have been the efforts of Lord King to uphold it by his individual exertions.[2]

"The controversy in which Mr. Locke launched his "Further Considerations concerning raising the value of Money," would have been of still greater importance if it had resulted in a true solution of the question. It was, however, conducted, though with great ability, under an entire misapprehension, by both parties, of the true issue. The points started excited inquiry and speculation on the subject of money to such an extent, that England, during the last century and a half, has produced more writings on currency, banking and money, than all the world beside. To these may

---

[1] Page 31, *idem.* His views stated shortly at page 22.

[2] Lord King published a pamphlet on the restriction of specie payments by the bank, in 1803, and gave the notice mentioned to his tenants. This occasioned a special act of Parliament, which showed that the ministry of the day understood the subject as little as his lordship.

be added a huge pile of folios emanating from Parliamentary Committees, embodying a mass of valuable facts, evidence and experience. The misconceptions of Mr. Locke and Mr. Lowndes have never yet been cleared up. It was impossible for them ever to coincide, because they regarded the subject from a different point of view, and, of course, with different objects and impressions. A full comprehension of the nature of money of account was needed to enable them to grapple with the real difficulties of the recoinage. That step had become necessary by the miserable state of depreciation into which the coins of the realm had sunk during the last half of the 17th century. Owing to the natural wear, and the frauds by clipping, punching, sweating, and other similar means, the silver coins had depreciated from *five to twenty per cent.*[1] The point to be settled for the action of the government was, whether the new coins should be issued of the original weight, or be made to correspond to their value at the average depreciation. Mr. Locke, who for the want of a merchant's familiarity with the subject of money, could not bring his powers of abstraction to bear, did not conceive of a mere money of account, but involved himself in a labyrinth of fallacies, by treating silver coin as the only possible money. His fundamental positions were in connection with those already cited, that 'Silver is the instrument and measure of commerce in all the civilized and trading parts of the world.' 'The intrinsic value of silver considered as money, is that estimate which common consent has placed on it.' 'That an equal quantity is always of equal value to an equal quantity of silver.'[2] The last position is always true, says Ruding, except in the case of coinage, to which Locke applied it.[3]

"These unsound and oft-refuted positions are sufficiently plausible to influence many minds. The least reflection will satisfy practical men that silver is not the instrument and measure of commerce; it is merely one of the agents sometimes employed in trade, but frequently dispensed with, and never indispensable. The intrinsic value of silver is fixed, like the value of other articles, by the cost of obtaining it, by the demand for it, and by other causes, special and general, applicable to other commodities. An equal quantity of silver is not always at the same price with an equal quantity of silver, because that implies that no change ever takes place in the value of silver, when, at the present time, all merchants know that it does change frequently; and our price-currents chronicle these changes in the price of gold and silver, as they do other changes in price. Entertaining these false notions, Mr. Locke looked upon a crown or five-shilling piece, or a shilling, or a Spanish dollar, as a certain defined quantity of silver, unalterable in value, and inseparable in idea from the silver itself. In his view, goods were only sold for the silver named as the price. He could not

---

[1] "Lowndes," 60, 61. Taylor on "Money System of England," 81.

[2] Pages 1, 2, "Locke's Tract."

[3] Ruding's "Annals of the Coinage," vol. ii. page 42.

understand that dollars could be said to be worth 4*s*. 6*d*., 4*s*. 7*d*., 4*s*. 8*d*., &c., or that crowns could be quoted, in case of a demand for silver in France or Holland, or in case of a high exchange, at 5*s*. 1*d*. or 5*s*. 2*d*., &c. He saw the confusion of terms, but could not understand why $19\frac{3}{10}$ dwts. of uncoined silver should be at a higher price than a crown purporting the same weight; nor why an ounce of silver, at the very time he wrote, was selling at 6*s*. 5*d*., when it ought to be worth only 5*s*. 2*d*., by his doctrine. For, formerly, when the full weight crown was worth only five shillings for the $19\frac{3}{10}$ dwts. of silver it contained, the ounce of silver was only worth 5*s*. 2*d*. Silver had, therefore, apparently risen about 20 per cent. All this, to Mr. Locke's mind, was the merest confusion of terms, wholly unintelligible, the jugglery of agiotage; for with him a dollar was a dollar, a crown a crown, a shilling a shilling, an ounce of silver an ounce, and nothing more or less. He supposed that men's minds had become confused, and that no change had taken place except a depreciation in the defaced and clipt coins. His opponents saw very clearly the apparent change in value. They saw clearly that, as matters then stood, a crown of full weight was worth 6*s*. 3*d*., and not merely 5*s*., as formerly rated. 'That silver in England being grown scarce, is consequently grown dearer. That it is risen in price from 5*s*. 2*d*. to 6*s*. 5*d*. per ounce.'[1] This seemed to them an actual enhancement of price. It was only apparent, however, for no such increase of price had taken place on the continent. The real difficulty in this question, in which both parties were partly right, was that neither understood nor appreciated the nature and functions of a money of account. The coins had, according to the usage of Europe, been made to correspond with the money of account, a correspondence which has produced unnumbered mischiefs, and stood darkly in the way of clear views of the subject of money. As the coins, in the course of half a century, gradually lost value by abrasion or clipping, the money of account followed, with a change which was so gradual that the public took no note of it. Shillings, which had lost a fourth of their weight, were still called shillings; crowns, which had lost a tenth, were still called and treated by the mass of the people as worth five shillings. But when, after 1690, the depreciation had reached an average of 15 per cent., the extent of the evil began to be felt. As soon as silver coins began to be exported, upon an unfavorable exchange, they were treated as bullion, and valued in the money of account of the countries to which they were to be exported according to their actual weight. It was found at once, that while the great mass of the sales and transactions of the country was carried on in the old denominations, and with the imperfect coins, and these old denominations had gradually, in the minds of the mass of the people, kept pace with the coins, the merchants in the foreign trade, familiar with the price of bullion at home and abroad, very clearly saw the change which

[1] "Essay for Amendment of the Silver Coins." Lowndes, page 77.

had taken place; that the coins were worth intrinsically less than formerly, and they gave 6*s.* 3*d.* for a crown of full weight. But Mr. Locke denied that they gave 6*s.* 3*d.*, and insisted that only 5*s.* was given in depreciated coins called 6*s.* 3*d.*, but having only 5*s.* of silver in them. Confusion had invaded the money of account, and men differed about what was meant by five shillings. Mr. Locke insisted that the new crowns should contain the same quantity of silver, $19\frac{3}{10}$ dwts., as formerly, because that quantity was 5*s.*; Mr. Lowndes insisted that that quantity was now worth 6*s.* 3*d.*, that the new crowns should contain only about $15\frac{4}{10}$ dwts., and that the shillings should contain proportionably, that is, one-fifth less than the old coinage, because he clearly saw that the whole range of prices had been fixed in a money of account, which had been formed upon the depreciated coins.

"Mr. Lowndes wished to avoid the mischief of suddenly wresting back the money of account from its present adjustment to its former position: 'By this project, all computations in pounds, shillings and pence used in accounts, and the reckonings by pounds, marks, half marks, practised in the law of England, and in the records, contracts, and other instruments relating thereunto, will be preserved as they ought to be.'[1] All the contracts for many years had been made in the money of account, as it corresponded with the depreciated coins. To require debts thus contracted to be discharged in coins of full weight, or their equivalent, was an injustice the government could not perpetrate; and the coins were called in, imperfect as they were, to be restored in new coins of the old weight. That only met the difficulty to a small extent, because much the largest proportion of the debtors had no coins in their hands to be thus exchanged. They had to sell goods to raise money, and their goods would sell, of course, at a depreciation proportioned to the increased value of the coins. This hardship was strongly urged as an objection, but in vain, as it was resolved by the authorities that the weights of the old coinage must be preserved. They believed in Mr. Locke's idea of an equal quantity of silver being always of equal value. The money of account, as understood and used by the people, was violated, and all recent subsisting contracts were in confusion.

"The true doctrine of money of account applied to the difficulties of that recoinage, upon which we have dwelt at more length, with the view of showing this doctrine more distinctly, would have settled at once the chief part of the dispute, and enabled them to grapple with the real facts, unobscured by a cloud of misconceptions. If the coins had been as Mr. Locke contends they should be, merely weighed pieces of metal of a certain standard quality, the money of account would have kept its original adjustment; and if the ounce of silver, valued at 5*s.* 2*d.*, had lost one-fifth of its weight, it would have been valued at 4*s.* $1\frac{1}{2}$*d.*; and the gradual depreciation would

---

[1] "Lowndes' Essay," &c., page 85. Lowndes was Master of the Mint.

have been so imperceptible in the course of a series of years, as to have fallen with severity upon none. The money of account would have remained intact, measuring and expressing the value of the pieces of silver and gold according to their weight, with the same precision and readiness as other articles. In case of a rise of the precious metals, consequent upon a high exchange, the rise would be at once noted in the money of account without the least confusion in any mind. The ounce of silver which had, at the ordinary exchange, been rated at 5*s.* 2*d.*, could as easily be stated to be worth 5*s.* 3*d.*, 5*s.* 4*d.*, or 5*s.* 10*d.* Under the proper and unobstructed operation of a money of account, the evil could not have taken place: that is, if the weight and quality in the first place had been simply certified by the stamp of the mint, and the price had been left to the course of commerce, there would have been no inducements to clipping or punching, as the amount thus abstracted would have been deducted by the first person to whom it would have been offered; and when the actual wear began to be appreciable, the loss would have been deducted in all large payments. In this way the loss by wear, for twenty, thirty or fifty years, could never be suddenly thrown at once, with all its severity, upon any community; but would be borne, in the lapse of years, by several generations of business men, by such slow degrees as to be imperceptible as a burden. The object of a recoinage would, in such a case, only be to revise the standard of quality, detect adulterations, and by the re-issue of pieces newly weighed and stamped, to save the people the trouble of weighing and assaying. To this, neither Mr. Locke nor Mr. Lowndes, and those agreeing with them, could have made objection, if they had once perceived the efficiency and utility of an undisturbed money of account. It would have explained nearly every point of difference between them, saved the government 10 per cent. on the recoinage, prevented a great amount of injustice to individuals, and preserved the money of account at its then adjustment. It would have pleased Mr. Locke to have the precious metals issued by weight and quality only; and it would have pleased Mr. Lowndes to have retained the significance of pounds, shillings and pence unchanged, as then employed to express the value of all the commodities of trade."

"We may aptly introduce here a passage from a work on 'Coin and Coinage,'[1] which denotes a clearer conception of this subject than any to which it was the fortune of Mr. Locke to attain. 'For all exchange is either by the actual or intellectual valuation of money; that is to say, either the thing is exchanged for money, or, if it be exchanged for another thing, the measure of that exchange is, how much money either of the things exchanged is *conceived* to be worth; and practice hath found out that in value, which geometricians have found out in quantities, that two lines which are equal to a third line, are equal to one another; so the

[1] By Rice Vaughan, page 3. London, 1675.

money is a third line, by which all things are made equal in value.' Money of account is the line or medium of comparison by which values are compared, stated, expressed, and by which parties discharge their debts, by delivering as many goods into the channels of commerce as they take, 'by which all things are made equal.'

"In the controversy which grew out of the famed Bullion Report of 1810, Mr. Huskisson published a pamphlet, 'The Question concerning the Depreciation of the Currency Stated and Examined,' ably sustaining the doctrines of that report, for which he was, as an acting member of the committee, responsible. That dispute was waged among scores of writers on grounds on which it was impossible they could arrive at any just conclusion. One party contended that, owing to the long continued wars of the French Revolution and of Napoleon, the demand for gold on the continent became extraordinary, as on such occasions it always does, and that, in consequence, it had risen in value. The other maintained, that the bank paper, which was the general currency, had depreciated to the extent of the apparent difference between them. Gold was quoted occasionally as high as £5 4*s.* — the usual price being £3 17*s.* 10½*d.* per ounce. The testimony of merchants, taken before the committee, decidedly sustained the views of the first, that gold had risen. But those who, like Locke, were unable to separate the idea of money from gold or silver, concluded that, as an ounce of gold was always equal to itself, it must always be of the same value; and that, as a pound sterling is the '*unambiguous name of a certain quantity of coined gold or silver*,' the paper must have depreciated, as the gold could not rise in value. No force of argument, no array of facts, could move them from this, as they regarded it impregnable ground. It was shown that other articles had not, like gold, risen in comparison with paper; that silver had not; and that parties were in constant pursuit of the gold for exportation. All in vain; for, in the view of the bullionists, a pound denoted a certain quantity of gold; and however much that gold might be in demand, it could never be more valuable than itself. Mr. Huskisson, with far more knowledge of the subject than Mr. Locke, could not escape from the blinding effects of this error. He was met by numerous adversaries, who labored under other errors of doctrine or fact, which left the question still unsettled. They fought the battle, indeed, on a field where it could never be determined. The very fact that such an array of able men applied their powerful minds, and in numerous instances great practical knowledge, to the solution of this question of depreciation, without full success — for it is still a matter of contest — proves there was some lurking misapprehension in the minds of both parties, which kept them from the true point of the controversy. The merchants, who contended that gold had risen in value, and that the bank-notes had not depreciated to the extent of the apparent difference between paper and gold, sustained themselves by an appeal to facts which would have been irresistible, except to those who could not conceive of a difference in value between a pound sterling and a sovereign, between twenty-one shillings and a guinea. It was useless to array facts to prove that two and two did not make four, for as clear as that did the bullionists conceive their position to be.

"In the years 1811 and 1812, two publications appeared, in which the doctrine of money of account, misnamed Abstract Currencies, was applied with much discrimination and clearness to this question.[1] No reader of these works can fail to perceive that the elements introduced by them into the discussion are indispensable to a fair understanding of the subject, and especially to a safe solution. It was shown that gold had risen, and that the money of account, which continued to correspond with the bank paper, measured that rise in value. As soon as the paper ceased to be convertible into gold, it ceased to fluctuate in value with gold, and became a medium of exchange or currency, of which the money of account was the expression. But we can neither quote from the close-woven pages of Mr. Wilson, nor attempt an abstract, as he follows up the thread of fallacy alleged to run through the doctrines and arguments of the bullionists with a steady perseverance, and in such an unbroken chain, that it is difficult to detach a link. No mind open to the truth, and sufficiently disciplined to the labor of close investigation, can read these pages without perceiving that the doctrine of an abstract money of account has found an advocate few would venture to assail, or could hope to overcome. We are not aware that any reply to Mr. Wilson's publications ever appeared.

"We cannot omit, in our mention of those who have supported the true idea of a money of account, a publication which appeared in Philadelphia, in 1832.[2] In this pamphlet the whole subject is ably and fully handled, and, as a single treatise on this subject, is more suited for popular reading than any yet published. In summing up his conclusions at page 62, he lays it down: 'That value in exchange was originally altogether comparative; one article being compared with another. That, to enable this to be done, it was found absolutely necessary to assume an intermediate imaginary point of comparison, and that this point of comparison is to be found in use in all countries.' He says this is used to express the value of coin, as well as of other commodities. He compares it to the assumed point in algebra; to the imaginary points of the north and south poles; to the imaginary line which is drawn for the meridian; to the degrees of latitude and longitude. By these lines ships are guided thousands of miles over a

---

[1] "Defence of Abstract Currencies in reply to the Bullion Report and Mr. Huskisson:" By Gloucester Wilson, Esq., F. R. S. London, 1811. "A Further Defence of Abstract Currencies:" By the same. 1812. Mr. Wilson was a barrister.

[2] From the press of Jesper Harding: 8vo. pp. 76. The copyright is secured by Thomas Smith. The pamphlet is otherwise anonymous, but in the introduction the writer speaks of himself as a foreigner. Can he be the same Thomas Smith whose works on the Theory of Money we have already noticed? Ante, note, page 67.

trackless ocean, and an unerring account of the track is kept; and few ship-owners would be willing to intrust the care of a ship to a master who should declare that he would take no charts to sea, as they were nothing but imaginary lines drawn upon paper.[1]

"We find a clear expression of the doctrine of money of account in a report made to Congress in the session of 1830–1. 'Nations generally establish a measure of value, founded upon an ideal unit or money of account and contract. Coins regulated in conformity to this standard usually compose the metallic currency, and they are generally the only legal tender in payments. The stamp set upon the metal is the seal of the State, certifying as to the fineness and weight of the coin; and the money unit, or its integral parts or multiples, being exhibited in every coin, facilitates enumeration, exchanges and payments,' &c.

"There is a point in the history of our government from which this subject can be studied with advantage. The subject of the establishment of a mint was brought to the notice of Congress as early as 1782, by Robert Morris, 'financier' to the confederation, in a report submitted by him on the 15th of January of that year. This was not acted upon, and the subject was referred to Alexander Hamilton, Secretary of the Treasury, in April, 1790, who submitted an elaborate report on the 28th of January, 1791. These important papers are accompanied by extended notes of Mr. Jefferson, as they are found at large in American State papers, vol. vii., fol. ed., p. 91. No previous coinage of any importance had existed in the colonies; Spanish coins were almost the only kind in circulation; an excessive derangement in the money of account in the different colonies had occurred; and the fact was constantly exhibited of merchants counting by pounds, shillings and pence, and paying in Spanish coins. This was felt to be very inconvenient, after the affairs of the Revolution, and the subsequent intimate connection of the colonies, had blended their business, and increased their mutual trade. The desire for a uniform system became general. It is evident, from the whole tenor of the documents last referred to, that these eminent men understood clearly enough the distinction between the money of account and money in coins. Mr. Morris desired to retain the moneys of account strictly as they then were, and sought a unit for the contemplated coinage, which would be a common divisor for all. This divisor was the 1-440th part of a dollar, of which 24 would be a penny of Georgia, 15 of New York and North Carolina, 20 would be a penny of Virginia and New England, and 16 a penny of Pennsylvania, &c. His coinage was to be founded on this minute unit, as follows: —

---

[1] There is, in all this illustration, the want of a clear statement that the unit must have an ascertained power or value, derived in the first instance from articles used as money, and from that fixed by use in the minds of the people.

10 units	to be equal to		one penny.
10 pence	"	"	one bit.
10 bits	"	"	one dollar.
10 dollars	"	"	one crown.

This dollar would have been two-thirds of the Spanish dollar. Under this coinage, it was supposed the people would continue their old habit of counting and estimating by pounds, shillings and pence, and that the new coins would be valued in the same way as the Spanish coins had long been. Mr. Morris understood the difficulty with which people changed their habits of mental reckoning and fixing prices, and therefore deemed it safer to change the coins than the money of account, even though the systems in the several States were so various. His coins were not only to be paid as equivalents in value, but convenient, in small transactions, as counters or assistants in reckoning, from their decimal subdivision, and from carrying on their face evidence of weight and quality.

"Mr. Hamilton expressly recognises the distinction between the unit of the money of account, which he says, is 'the pound in all the States,' and the 'unit of the coins,' which is 'not so easy to pronounce,' but which he considers to be the dollar. He recommends the adoption of the dollar as the unit of the coins as well as of the money of account, the more especially as the people were prepared for it by the circulation of the Spanish coins, and by many of the financial operations of the Revolution. Mr. Jefferson coincided with the Secretary of the Treasury, and recommended the adoption of the dollar unit, and the coins issued ever since. 'A required condition of the unit is, that its multiples and subdivisions coincide in value with some of the known coins so nearly, that the people may, by a *quick reference in the mind, estimate their value;* and, if this be not attended to, they will be very long in adopting the innovation, if ever they adopt it.'—'*Am. State Pap., Finance,*' vol. vii., p. 105. 'The unit or dollar is a known coin, and the most familiar of all to the minds of the people. It is already adopted, from North to South, and therefore offers itself as a unit already introduced. Our public debt, our requisitions and their apportionments, have given it actual and long possession of the place of unit.'—'*Ibid. Finance,*' vol. iii., p. 105.

"These valuable papers clearly recognise the distinction between the functions of a money of account and a coinage, though, in many respects, there is a want of that precision in their views, which nothing but a long familiarity with the subject could give. Hamilton and Jefferson seem to take it for granted that the coins should correspond with the unit of account. Morris did not deem that necessary, because, undoubtedly, he understood the matter better than either of them. For want of knowing more, however, his plan was certainly inferior, on the whole, to that they proposed. It would have been a happy time to adopt a coinage recommended since and before, by many eminent men. The standard of quality being fixed, the precious metals to be coined into Troy pounds and decimal parts of a pound, ounces and parts of an ounce, and the dollar being adopted as the unit of account, with a decimal subdivision, these pieces of the precious metals would be readily valued in this money, following all these fluctuations. A coinage intended specially for small transactions of half-dollars and under, would have been advisable to be a legal tender, not beyond ten dollars. The fact that the legal tender of gold or silver, in large transactions, is a very rare occurrence — few people having ever seen it resorted to — shows that it should not be the rule, but the subject of exceptional regulation. The precious metals finding their value according to the market, could not disturb the steadfastness of the unit of account, which would perfectly register and express every variation in them."

III.

EXTRACTS

From an Article, by the Author of this Volume, in "Hunt's Merchants' Magazine," of April, 1852.

MONEY OF ACCOUNT—ITS NATURE AND FUNCTIONS.

"When an Englishman visits the continent, he carries in his mind his own money of account, and by its aid values every coin he meets; he expresses that value in the terms which are most familiar to him: thus the foreign price of every article can only be realized when mentally turned into pounds, shillings and pence. The foreign coins he carries in his pocket are all measured in that way, and it will require a long familiarity with foreign prices before he can think in any money of account but his own. The mental operation is similar to what he uses in learning to speak a foreign language; he thinks first in his own what he may express afterwards in a foreign tongue. If the English traveller is familiar with the home prices of articles submitted to him abroad, he will, without hesitation, annex prices to all the foreign goods he sees in English money of account. He does not, in this instance, use his domestic coins as a measure of value; the operation of fixing such prices is not a comparison of his domestic coins with the foreign goods; it is the expression of their value in English money of account.

"During the time of the suspension of payments by the Bank of England, between 1797 and 1822, such was the demand for gold on the continent, for army purposes, that it became, for most of that period, merely an article of commerce, in great demand for export." . . .

It must be perfectly plain to those who are familiar with the history of that period, that if every coin of gold and silver had been swept by the foreign demand from that country, the people would not the less have continued to transact their business and make payments in pounds, shillings and pence. So they would have done, also, if platina had been introduced as a medium of payment. A whole generation of men came into business during this suspension, who were not familiar with coins, and seldom even saw a guinea or a sovereign; yet they never had any difficulty in buying and selling by pounds, shillings and pence. Did they, in every instance, use coin as their measure of value?

"Does the active salesman, who is continually naming prices from morning to night, carry the image of the silver dollar in his mental vision all the time? Suppose, when he pronounces the price of a bale of goods to be two hundred dollars, that amount of silver coins were thrown before his astonished vision, he would be very apt to say: 'Carry them to the bank or the broker; I am no judge of coins; they may be too light, or they may be counterfeit, for aught I know.' The purchaser may reply: 'Take them by weight, and return any that may be condemned as false coins.' But the answer would be, in almost every such instance: 'I know not the value of a pound, ounce, pennyweight, or grain of silver.' Did this merchant measure the value of his goods by coins? Let us suppose this lot of miscellaneous coins to be carried to the counter of a dealer in the precious metals; it will be immediately inspected, classed and valued in dollars, precisely as the merchant valued his goods. Some dollar coins may be worth one dollar, and one, two or three cents; some worth one, two or three cents less than a dollar: the various classes into which they may be assorted will be separately valued, and the whole being added together will make the sum which the broker is willing to give for the lot. It is soon sold and paid for by a check on the bank, which pays the merchant for his goods. Now, was not this parcel of coins valued in the same way as the box of prints, and were not both equally indebted to the efficiency of the money of account?

"If it be alleged that the merchant and broker had each a reference, in their minds, for the purpose of expressing their several valuations, to perfect dollars, we ask how they could thus carry the idea of a dollar so perfectly as to exceed in accuracy the ordinary coins of circulation. If men can carry the value of the perfect coin in their minds, then that is what is called 'imaginary money,' or money of account, by the Cambist.

"Take another case of a bale of goods, priced, sold, and paid for, in what appear to be new and perfect dollars. It would be said, by those who take that view of the subject, that the value of the goods was measured by the coins which were used, as an equivalent in paying for them. But the coins are all counterfeit, and so perfect that they circulate a long time, performing all the functions of money, without injury or loss to any one except those in whose hands the false coins are at last detected. In this instance, every article paid for in these coins would have been valued in false money;

and as every dollar might have been paid a hundred times without injury to any except the last holder, the rather strange conclusion must be drawn, that false coins are equally efficient in measuring value with the genuine. This will hardly be admitted, and we are driven to the conclusion that it is the ideal dollar of our money of account — the value of our money unit clearly understood and firmly settled in the minds of the people — that is applied without hesitation at all times, and by everybody, to measure the value of every article of sale, or susceptible of valuation, whether goods, coins or bullion.

"Our ancestors brought with them to America the English money of account, and their posterity continued thus to employ it until the present system was adopted by our government after the Revolution. But a money of account cannot, even by legislative authority, be created nor destroyed in a day. The English money of account maintained its supremacy in terms, though greatly changed in signification, through a long period, although almost the only coins in circulation were Spanish dollars, and halves, quarters, eighths, and sixteenths." — "It is yet partially used in the interior of Virginia, South Carolina, and perhaps Massachusetts. In New York the term shilling holds its ground generally to this day, owing, in part, to the shilling there corresponding in value with the Spanish eighth of a dollar. These colonial denominations varied so much, that in Massachusetts a half-dollar coin was valued at three shillings; in New York, at four shillings; and in Pennsylvania, at three shillings and ninepence. A merchant of the last-named State was, sixty years since, just as prompt in affixing pricés to his goods as one of the present day; the former could employ the Pennsylvania currency just as readily as he of this day uses dollars and cents. The former had in his mind no *coin* corresponding with his *pound*, his *shilling*, or his *penny*. There was no such coin: nor could he have in his mind, as the measure of value, any corresponding weight of silver or gold, because very few indeed knew the value of either metal by weight. It is impossible to think or say that the merchants of that day measured or estimated the value of their goods by mental or actual reference to coins, for there was then none such, and never had been. This colonial money of account was a purely ideal scale, the power or value of which was fixed in the minds, and its use in the habits of people. What was so long true of our colonial currency, is to this day true of the Canadian money of account, which has no corresponding coin — the British shillings, and Spanish and American coins circulating there, not corresponding with their money unit. It is worthy of remark, too, that the French population of Canada still preserve the money of account which their ancestors brought over with them, and which has long been out of use in France, namely, *livres*, *sous* and *deniers*. There have been no coins corresponding with this unit and its parts to keep up the memory of this money of account, to confirm its use, or to explain its meaning.

"It would be endless to bring illustrations of our meaning from the moneys of account of Europe and Asia, as every country where industry has flourished, or commerce been active, furnishes proof that the same habit of converting the denominations of coins into a mental scale, for comparing and expressing values, prevails everywhere — in China and Persia, and the East Indies — equally as in the more civilized nations of Europe. China has no coinage, and gold and silver are there sold constantly at their market value, and weighed out in payments, the amounts of which are expressed in the money of account.

"But we need not continue these details further, at this stage of our inquiry. It is proper to say that we do not bring forward this use of the money of account as a *standard of value*, or as what some have called an *abstract currency*. It is no standard of value, nor is it a standard of any kind; nor can it, without an abuse of terms, be called a currency. Its use neither dispenses with a standard of coinage, nor with devices for payment, institutions of credit, nor a paper currency. It is the popular expression of value. Coinage furnishes the legal equivalent.

"A money of account, well established in the habits and minds of the people, is a thing of slow growth, and cannot, therefore, be created by law. Our National Legislature enacted that the dollar should be the unit of our money of account, and immediately the public accounts were translated into dollars and cents; but many years elapsed before dollars and cents became, in fact, the money of account — the popular measure, or scale of value, in the sense in which we use the term. If Congress were, by another act, to require that all business should be transacted in francs and centimes, it would require nearly half a century to make the change in the minds of the people. So far as legislation is concerned, such a change could be made in a day; but long familiarity with the terms, in all the circles of industry and the avenues of trade, can only establish the precise power and force of these terms in the minds of the masses.

"If we reflect that the annual product of our industry, agricultural and manufacturing, in the United States, exceeds three thousand millions in value, and that, on the average, these products are sold many times, and that this mighty mass of valuables is, to its whole extent and in all its parts, put at prices fixed in our money of account, and that an incessant valuation is going on in the infinite operations of trade and industry, we must admit that anything which introduces confusion into such an immensity of business must be an incalculable evil. It falls far short of the reality, if we estimate the successive valuations or prices fixed on goods sold and unsold every month, in the United States, at over a thousand millions. A mistake of one per cent. on this vast sum would be a disturbance on the whole to the extent of ten millions. If our government were to require us henceforth to keep our accounts in francs and centimes, making no other change in our money system, the disturbance created would be a matter of inconvenience, the amount of which must be measured by the immense transactions it would affect, and the necessity of converting such an infinity of sums of money from dollars into francs. But the change would not be confined to mere inconvenience, for many of the ignorant, the dull, and the unwary would become the prey of the designing and crafty. There can, of course, be no adequate estimation of the mischiefs which such a change of our money unit would inflict; and surely nothing can justify such legislation, except greater evils were threatened from the other side. The grounds of our national adoption of the dollar unit were not merely its convenience and superiority; for, strong as are these reasons, they might have failed to overcome the opposition to a change; it was the necessity of harmonizing the differences of the money of the several States, which made the adoption of a new unit, which should be common to all the States, a matter of imperative obligation. And the free communication among the States, with different modes of computation, having among them the same legal money unit, was what efficaciously hastened a complete compliance with the law. The new money of account was a language into which all the varying languages of computation could be translated. When men of Massachusetts and Pennsylvania were accounting together, instead of a mutual transfer of their accounts into their respective currencies, they were both changed into federal money, and thus adjusted. The necessity of doing this constantly, among those residing in different States, greatly assisted and hastened that otherwise slow process of displacing one money of account by another. The inconvenience was less felt and complained of, because it was really not so great as that which they endured under the old diversified systems.

Disturbance of the Money of Account by open and by concealed attacks.

"But if the change of a money unit, under the most favorable circumstances, and for the strongest reasons, is productive of so much inconvenience to all, and risk of imposition upon the unskilful and unwary, what must be the effect where the change is not merely from one unit to another, but a concealed or unseen attack upon the unit itself? what the effect, if resulting from the enforcement of such regulations, as tend to change the value of the unit, aud produce confusion in regard to it in the minds of those employing it? Instances of this kind of change are but too familiar to readers of the histories of European countries, in the frauds perpetrated by mistaken or unscrupulous rulers, in the successive debasements of the current coins. In England this has been done until the equivalent of the money unit five hundred years ago, and that of the present day, is as thirty-two to ninety-nine: they coined originally, including the alloy, £1 1*s*. 4*d*. from a pound of silver; since 1816, they coin £3 6*s*. from that quantity of silver. In France, the debasement has proceeded so far as the rate of seventy to one. The evils and losses inflicted upon the respective countries in which these abuses were practised can never be adequately estimated. Measured by the mere inconvenience they imposed, great as that was, no just idea of the mischief could be attained. A more correct estimate may be drawn from the cries of distress which came from all quarters on the occasion of these debasements. Volumes might be filled with the complaints caused by the iniquities of this process of debasement. In France a heavy tax was agreed to be paid on condition the coinage was permitted to remain undisturbed. It is true that, in the periods when these debasements were most resorted to as a means of raising money, neither rulers nor subjects fully understood the true nature of the evil, although its results were felt by those whom they affected, so as to leave no doubt about the injury. The functions of a money of account were not known, as they are not sufficiently appreciated even to this time. The whole of the mischief was, in those cases, imputed to the change of the coinage, because that was the occasion. No debasement, however great or well managed, could much injure those who were knowing enough to detect the fraud, or in a position to discover it. They could readily perceive that the new coin which purported to be a shilling, and which the authorities required to be so called, was in fact worth only ten pence; and they could take their precautions accordingly. But the mass of the people, who could not distinguish the shilling of their money of account from a shilling coin, would continue to count, and fix their prices, and make their sales in the usual shilling of account, and receive payment in the debased coin. Their eyes would only be opened after the fraud was complete, and after the perpetrators had extracted a large sum from the public; and after merchants and bankers, shrewd enough and unscrupulous enough to avail themselves of the opportunity, had levied a tenfold larger sum. This process of breaking up or destroying a money of account is one of fraud and misconception, where all parties to a transaction are ignorant of what has been done; they speak in one language — the law, under which they act, speaks in another; they make their prices by one scale — the law exacts payment by another. Where, as would soon be extensively the case, one party comprehended the change, and the other did not, a direct advantage could be taken to the extent of the depreciation. Such debasements destroyed the money of account, because the base coin was made a legal tender for its nominal amount of valuation in the money of account. The ignorant and unwary were therefore preyed upon until the extent of their losses finally opened their eyes, and the speculation became no longer available. The prices of all articles would become enhanced to the amount of the debasement, and that being the case, a new money of account would gradually be established, as habit rendered the new unit familiar. It must not be overlooked, that the success of this kind of fraud depended on the fact that the money unit in use, where the fraud was attempted, was so firmly fixed in the minds of the people, that they would continue to compute by it after the alteration in the value of the coin. The success of the fraud would come to an end as fast as the new money of account replaced the old one. The law which made the debased coin a tender at its former value would cease to be effective when all prices were fixed by the new scale. It is well known that men of business had such a dread of the confusion, trouble and loss ensuing from a debasement, that they stood aghast at the prospect or mere suspicion of such an event.[1]

Effect of a change in the value of the precious Metals on the Money of Account — Law of legal tender — Depreciation of Paper Currency.

"There is another way in which a monetary unit may be changed, which it is important to consider, and that is, by a change in the value of the precious metals of which the coins most in use are composed. It is by no means a necessary consequence; but unless the danger is seen, and precautions taken, there is always hazard of the money of account being disturbed where the ordinary coins of circulation change their value gradually, and from causes not generally appreciated. This danger is always greater where the name of the money unit is the same with that of the chief coin—as in the case of our two coins, gold and silver, each called a dollar. If the silver in a dollar coin should depreciate by degrees imperceptible to the mass of men, the unit would alter by a change following at a long interval from the depreciation. During this time a harvest of profit would accrue to those who were shrewd enough to perceive the alteration, and fortunate enough to be in a position to avail themselves of it. Its operation would of course be very unequal; the advantage and disadvantage to some might be equal; many might suffer severely without understanding the reason; and some might be profited without knowing how. The whole mass of transactions occurring within the range of this depreciation, the prices fixed upon all commodities for sale, the contracts of sale, the actual payments in coin, the whole position of debtors and creditors, their books of account, evidences of debt and securities of credit, would be more or less affected. There could be no certainty that the parties to these transactions perfectly understood each other. It might very frequently be a matter of accident or chance on whose side the advantage would fall; but it would be very certain that those who understood the process of depreciation would have power to turn the whole event very greatly to their profit.

"We say that the money unit would suffer even where it did not correspond in name with any coin; we mean, of course, where there is a fixed price on the precious metals, and a law of legal tender. Wherever neither of these circumstances exists, as in China, where great fluctuations in the value of gold and silver occur, there such changes have no effect whatever

---

[1] See the note at page 35, "Snelling on the Coins of Great Britain, France, and Ireland."

upon the money of account. In China, the value of gold and silver can always, in any variation, be expressed in *tales*, *mace*, *candarines* and *cash;* and so in England, if the statute making gold a legal tender at £3 17*s*. 10½*d*. were repealed, the value of gold could be expressed under any possible degree of variation in pounds, shillings and pence. So, if our law making gold a legal tender were repealed, we should have no difficulty in expressing its value in dollars and cents, at any possible depreciation to which it might descend under the effect of the influx of that metal from California or Australia. But when the law compels men to take gold at a fixed value, and coins are issued in gold which are made a legal tender at one dollar, five, ten, and twenty dollars, the mass of men will be slow to perceive any depreciation of a coin which the law holds at the same value. They can only discover the change by a long process of selling at the old value, and being paid in the new; whilst very few will enjoy the equivalent advantage of buying by the old scale, and paying by the new.

"The unit of valuation may be disturbed and destroyed by the depreciation of a paper currency which enjoys the whole circulation of a country. If such a currency is once established in the confidence of a community, so as to be received in all business transactions at par with the unit, or as equivalent to coins of known value, it may decrease by such imperceptible degrees, and from such unseen causes, as gradually to cause a general rise of prices corresponding to the stage of depreciation. This of course, destroys that money of account, and gradually substitutes another; but the process is fraught with all the mischiefs and confusion attendant upon a change in the value of gold and silver.

"This was that which was alleged to have taken place in England in the period of suspension of payments by the bank between 1809 and 1815, when at one time, as we have already mentioned, gold reached the very high price of £5 4*s*. And it is still urged by some in that country, that no more unjust nor impolitic legislation ever took place than that which restored the unit of account to its original place compared with gold. But the very heated controversy which took place within the period above-mentioned, is one of those in which the calm observer of later days, looking through a less prejudiced medium, can clearly perceive that there was much truth and error on both sides; and that their differences were of a nature that no element employed in their discussion could enable them properly to reconcile or determine the preponderance. No doubt there was some depreciation of the paper of the Bank of England, but not by any means corresponding to the price of gold, the demand for which was increased, owing to many special causes, but chiefly to the wars raging on the continent. After the battle of Waterloo, as the affairs of the continent gradually resumed a state of quiet, gold fell by degrees to its average market rates.

"If the strenuous efforts which were put forth at the period of this controversy had been in part directed to preserve the money of account intact, rather than to an angry and excited discussion upon the question whether gold had risen or bank-notes had fallen in value, more light would have been shed upon the subject, and more real good accomplished. The publications of this period, and the Parliamentary reports, form the most valuable mine of instruction on the subject of money and credit anywhere extant, but far too voluminous to be more than merely referred to in this connexion.

"The money unit of the American colonies was destroyed and diversified by a process the opposite of the depreciation of the coin. The long continuance of an unfavorable exchange with England in most of the colonies begot a constant and pressing demand for coin as a remittance. The exports of the colonies were insufficient to furnish bills of exchange for adjustment of the large indebtedness to the mother country, created by incessant over-importation. The only possible mode of discharging a large portion of this foreign debt was by the exportation of coin. The demand thus arising continued so long and so urgent, that the value of coins began and continued to enhance, through a long series of years; the scarcity became so great, that the colonists suffered severely for some medium of exchange, and were driven to various strange expedients, and not unfrequently to a state of barter, in which the commodities to be exchanged were valued in the money of account: that is, all payments were made in the commodities exchanged, whilst all prices were fixed in the money of account. During this period, Spanish dollars and fractional coins, under this special demand, rose in value, and increasing prices continued to be expressed in the usual money of account. The dollar, which at first was worth 4*s.* 6*d.*, became worth 5*s.*, 5*s.* 6*d.*, 6*s.*, 6*s.* 6*d.*, 7*s.*, and 7*s.* 6*d.*, in Pennsylvania; and in New York it went to 8*s.* It is true that, in some colonies, this process was complicated with an excessive issue of paper currency. In such cases, it may not be practicable to estimate the respective influences of the unfavorable exchange and consequent demand for coin as an article of export, and that of the over-issue of paper currency; but that both causes had their appropriate result is easily seen, and the more especially as they were not always contemporary. In some of the colonies no paper was issued, and in them the unfavorable exchange destroyed not less effectually the money unit; and in some of the colonies the original money unit was changed before the issue of the paper currency. It should be noted that neither an unfavorable exchange, nor an over-issue of bank-notes necessarily involve the destruction of the money of account. Where there is a regular place for the transaction of exchange, and regular quotations of the rate of exchange made public, there the nature of the demand for coin is at once seen and understood, and the price of coins nearly keeps pace with the price of exchange; both coins and bills of exchange being rated, in the terms of the money of account, at what they were worth. There was no regular price for exchange, nor were there regular dealers in exchange in the early days of our colonial existence; and the mass of the people did not comprehend the true nature of the demand for coin. Hence, as coins almost disappeared from circulation, and as a high nominal price was continually bid for them, the prices of other commodities fell into a state of confusion, and all harmony of adjustment was gone; for few could tell whether prices referred to an equivalent in coins, or an equivalent in other commodities.

"So in the case of paper issues; its depreciation does not necessarily imply injury to the money of account; for where there is good paper with which to make comparison, it may be quoted, paid and received at any rate of discount agreed upon, from 1 to 99 per cent.—a fact familiar to all men of business in the United States.

Glance at the Causes which introduced the present Coinage System of Great Britain.

"Before examining our own system of coinage in reference to modifications which may seem to be advisable in any aspect of the subject, it may be profitable to glance at the steps by which Great Britain was led to adopt the gold standard. Previous to that change, the double standard had prevailed, and for more than a century had been a source of perpetual trouble to individuals, and loss to the nation. The mischief began before the commencement of the eighteenth century, by the rapid disappearance of silver from the circulation. This process was due to many causes, but chiefly to the over-valuation of silver at the mint of France. This carried off all the heavy silver coins, and left those most worn to perform an increased duty in the circulation, whereby they very rapidly became more and more defaced and deficient in weight. The evil became, at last, insufferable, and brought on a discussion, in the reign of William and Mary, as to the best remedy. In this discussion the celebrated John Locke took a conspicuous part. The government—very honestly, as its members thought, but very unwisely, as it has since been regarded—undertook, in the face of this foreign demand for silver, to recoin the whole silver currency, and to make it of full weight, but without due precaution. Whilst this light currency, depreciated in weight from 10 to 25 per cent., passed by tale, it could not be exported, because the over-valuation was not equal to this depreciation. The recoinage increased the evil, for it exactly prepared the coins for exportation, by making them full weight, without increasing their home value as a legal tender. So the mischief continued, in more or less force, throughout the whole of the 18th century. The effect was to introduce gold into circulation in place of the withdrawn silver. The extreme fluctuations of the gold which was thus drawn so largely into the channels of trade, produced great inconvenience, and kept up bitter complaints. So inefficient were the means employed to keep the silver in circulation, all but the worn and light coins being constantly withdrawn and exported, that in 1797 the further coinage of silver was forbidden. A century of experience, and an immense sum wasted in coinage, had sufficed to show that they could not by mere coinage, countervail the laws of trade in bullion. The sum of the matter was, that they over-valued gold in England, and silver in France; and that, by consequence, France could not keep gold, and England could not keep silver. In the progress of the 18th century, the scarcity of silver, with the influx of gold and its variations—the guinea varying in price from thirty to twenty-one shillings and sixpence — completely unsettled the ancient money of account, and formed a new one upon gold: that is, the plenty of gold made the people by degrees more familiar with its value than with the value of silver; and thus a new money of account began to form upon gold. This was perceived as early as 1774, when silver was declared no longer a tender, except by weight, beyond £25."

CHAPTER III.

§ 1. *Gold and silver a common equivalent or medium in the interchange of commodities — Circulation by weight — Not constituted money by coinage, which only facilitates circulation — Diversity of mints, and confusion of coins — Wear and waste — Clipping, filing, sweating and counterfeiting.*

We have been thus full in the treatment of money of account, its nature and functions, that the distinction between it and coins or bullion might not for a moment be lost sight of in the subsequent discussions of this volume. We have seen that the money of account occupies the whole ground of the expression of prices; the whole ground of books of account, so far as prices, amounts or sums of debt or credit are stated in them; the whole ground of the statement of sums or amounts in bonds, notes or bills of exchange, checks, and other securities; the whole ground of financial estimates, statements and computations; in fine, all that relates to money, where actual equivalents are not employed, belongs to the domain of money of account. The formation of a money of account, which invariably occurs among all trading people above the condition of savages, takes away at once from gold or silver, whether coined or weighed, all application or use as a measure of price, or medium of comparison. Among savages, the precious metals are no doubt directly compared with the articles for which they are bartered: with them it is, literally, so much of one thing for so much of another. It is not so in civilized life, where commodities are very seldom sold with any thought of payment being exacted in gold or silver. The money of account not only serves, to this extent, the use of coins or bullion, but it saves even any actual reference to them; it is, therefore, an immense economy in trade. It narrows the use of the precious metals, perhaps, more than any other agency.

It makes the credit system possible. This diminished use of the precious metals indicates vast progress in industry and trade. In the forming stages of society, it may be necessary to employ the precious metals in almost every transaction. As commerce is now carried on in Great Britain, and in the United States, the use of coins or bullion does not extend to the thousandth part in value of the business; but though the proportion in which they are used is so reduced, they are none the less prized, and still remain that common equivalent with which every other commodity can be purchased. Although very little employed in large purchases, because they can be dispensed with, they are the only articles which every one is at all times willing to take. Their chief office is in the payment of balances of trade. When two nations, or two provinces, or districts, or individuals, trade with each other, their mutual debts may be set off against each other, in the ordinary course of business, so far as equal; but the balance either way is payable only in gold or silver, because, where other articles of export fail, these are always acceptable in discharge of any debt, domestic or foreign.

Small as is the proportion of the precious metals to the whole value of commodities exchanged, yet being employed in the retail dealing, and made the only legal tender in payment of debts, their use is not only familiar to the public, but creates a vague impression that all dealings and prices have a strict reference to coins, or specific quantities of gold or silver. We have shown that this is an erroneous impression: they are seldom referred to when the term money is used. Gold and silver are only referred to in dealing, when the actual intention of the parties is to deal in or employ them. Coins cannot perform the functions which are the attributes of a money of account. They are not used for the statement or expression of values. When used in a purchase, or in discharge of a debt, it is an equivalent — as commodities applied to that purpose, the value of which is as necessary to be stated in money of account as that of any other article. The term money has many significations, and of course two that are very different — when applied to money of account, and to coins of gold or silver: in one sense it is used to express values, and to state amounts; and in the other, it is applied to a commodity used in actual purchase, or in actual payments.

It is in the latter sense that we are now to speak of the precious metals; their use as money in no way divests them of their quality of a commodity. A man may invest his fortune, or any portion of it, in land, in cotton, in silk, in gold or silver. Preference for these metals as a common equivalent dates from the earliest records of history, and probably prevailed long before the idea of money was formed. It would be interesting to assemble here all the fragments of history on this subject; but it would not much subserve our purpose. We have abundant proof, in early history, that gold and silver were employed as "money of the merchant;" that they were weighed and passed as current money. Although called money, when thus weighed and passed, it is obvious that the term means no more than that gold and silver were the commodities used to barter or exchange for all other things, and for all services. This gave them the name and office of money; and in this sense there is neither mystery nor difficulty in comprehending the nature of money. The beauty, admirable qualities, and superior convenience of these metals, as embracing great values in small compass, have in all ages recommended them for this purpose. They were employed three thousand years ago as money; they are still so employed. Gold and silver, in the days of the Pharaohs, were weighed as money; they are still weighed as money in China: they are still weighed among us, and in Europe. The fact of their being weighed by public authority, and issued in pieces of convenient size, in no way alters the nature of their function of money, though it doubtless adds vastly to their convenience, and quickens their circulation. Such pieces of money are not received, in payments and purchases, in virtue of their accurate weight, and their bearing the impress of public authority, but because they are gold or silver, certified as to quality and quantity by the impression of the coinage.

Much of the difficulty of understanding the distinction between money of account, and money the medium of exchange, is removed where the medium or money is weighed. Every one, then, knows that he expresses the price of gold or silver by weight, as he expresses the price of other things. There is no complication in the transaction. The articles thus exchanged are examined as to quantity and quality, the respective values computed, and the exchange is made by the arithmetic of the money of account. It is simply the use of gold or silver as articles for which all other things are freely exchanged; and this use is supported both by the market value of the metals, and by the convenience and confidence afforded by coinage. It is probable that the exchangeable value of gold and silver is enhanced by their being employed as a common medium of exchange, thereby increasing the demand for them in proportion to the amount so used. The use made of them as a medium of exchange by no means alters their price or value; it is only one of the many uses to which they are applied. It is obvious that this medium of exchange is an expensive instrument, the gold and silver employed in this way being of no other use. The great value of the instrument imposes a limit upon its use, and prevents it from being employed as much as would otherwise occur. This limit of circulation could not be overcome by increasing the quantity employed as a medium of exchange; because increasing the quantity involved an increase of the expense of interchange of the medium employed, or a depreciation of the medium employed. In no country does the quantity of the precious metals used as money probably exceed one-tenth of the value of the gross annual product of its industry; and in none does it probably exceed one-hundredth part of the whole transferable property of the people. To employ a larger quantity, as a medium of exchange, has not been found advantageous. To avoid increasing this quantity, and even to save the necessity of employing it all, an immense number of devices have been resorted to, with more or less success, the consideration of which will be reached as we proceed.

The first important step, after weighing the precious metals in payment, was coinage, a facility which greatly promoted a rapid circulation of money. In the shape of coins, a given quantity of money could be employed to make ten payments in the time it would before effect one. Coins are not only accurately weighed, but their quality is also accurately tested; the impression on the piece, which makes it a coin, is an official and legal certificate of weight and quality. The gold or silver, then, which, previous to coinage, had to be carefully cut or subdivided and weighed, and carried to a skilful person to ascertain its purity, passes as a coin instantly from hand to hand, without delay or hesitation. Rapid as the circulation to which this facility of coinage has given rise, the exigencies of industry, civilization and commerce soon exceeded its powers. The movement of the products of industry in every civilized community has long since far surpassed any possible circulation of coins. This, of course, stimulates efforts to effect the exchange of goods without the intervention of money. Besides, the system of coinage was found to be susceptible of such abuses, as tended greatly to limit its usefulness and power. Every country had its own mint, and established its own regulations. The weights of different countries did not correspond; and as the coins of each were adjusted by its weights, it became necessary both to weigh and assay coins circulating out of their own territory. The people of each country were familiar only with the values denoted by their own coins, and therefore could not know the standard of weight or purity adopted at other mints than their own; they could not confide in the certificate impressed upon a foreign coin, because they could not understand it. This difficulty, which has greatly obstructed the use of coins in all parts of the world, is also greatly enhanced by changes in weight and standard of quality at all the mints, and by changes in the impressions or appearance of coins. When more than a hundred different mints were issuing new coins to mingle with the old, a confusion supervened which reduced the convenience of coinage, in some cases, below the old mode of weighing. This evil became so intolerable as to beget loud and bitter complaints, and many attempts at reformation, some of which proved only aggravations of the mischief. Many were the suggestions and plans for a general system of coinage for Europe. It may well be doubted whether the vexations and losses incurred by the abuses of coinage in many countries did not far exceed all the disadvantages of being without any. There are now in the vaults of bankers, in Italy and Germany, immense sums in coins which can no longer be circulated, because the people are unwilling to receive them. They belong to a past generation, their weight and quality are unknown to them, and of course their price is not known. These pieces are only used in bags, in the heavy payments between bankers; they have ceased to be applicable to the ordinary circulation, and have lost part of their powers and usefulness.[1]

---

[1] Germany alone had 68 mints, each with its separate coinage and regulations. When all the gold and silver coins, with their subdivisions, from 68 mints were circulating over a territory no larger than Germany, it can readily be conceived what a nuisance this variety became in business. But when this nuisance was enhanced by a due proportion of counterfeits, by the abrasion, clipping, and other deterioration of coins, it can scarcely be imagined how intolerable the burden became. The complaint was loud and bitter, and projects for reform abounded; a system to be uniform not only throughout Germany, but Europe, was earnestly demanded. The same evil induced the establishment of banks of deposit in Holland.

In urging upon the public his proposal of a convention of delegates from the various governments of Europe, to devise a uniform mode and system of coinage, Scaruffi placed before his readers the whole mischief in bold relief. The director of the mint in Reggio, however, could not move the authorities of that day by his logic, nor by his position; and he lacked the power which Napoleon applied to the subject more than two centuries after, when he introduced a uniform coinage into Italy. No sooner had the power of the French Emperor ceased to be felt in Italy, however, than the Pope, and other princes, commenced the old system of multifarious coinage, the evils of which are now seriously felt: "Dont la diversite embarrasse tous les jours, non-seulement les etrangers et les voyageurs mais meme les banquiers et marchands Italiens."

Italy is said to be famous for the worst coins, and the best writers on money. One of the earliest of these was *Scaruffi* ("*Discorso sopra la Moneta*"), published in 1582, and to be found in the second volume of "*Baron Custodi's Collection of the Italian Economists.*" Scaruffi was, for many years, Master of the mint at Reggio. He was so profoundly impressed with the mischiefs of the coinage, that he looked upon it not only as the scourge of Italy, but as "a conflagration which threatened all Europe." Not satisfied with deploring these evils at home, and with suggesting local remedies, he proposed a plan for a uniform and general coinage for all

The complications and perplexities of coinage have long been a serious grievance to the industry of the civilized world — a grievance, in many localities, regarded as intolerable, and only

---

Europe, the coins to be the same in size, weight, and alloy or standard. If this suggestion of Scaruffi's was not adopted, another important one was. He proposed that all manufacturers of plate and jewelry should be compelled, by law, to place their mark on every article manufactured by them, together with a designation of the quality of the metal. This is now the law in most of the countries of Europe, and should be here.

In this age of paper currency, of higher commercial credit, when public opinion is strong enough to restrain men in authority from debasing coin, it is scarcely possible to credit the injury inflicted upon industry and commerce by the diverse coinage of Italy, its alterations, counterfeits and debasements. This combined evil is not only called, as above, a conflagration, but a scourge, a pestilence; it was compared with the contemporaneous famine and pestilence of the 16th and 17th centuries. The aid of Heaven and the Church was invoked by processions, indulgences, &c., to mitigate the *morbus numericus.* The ecclesiastical remedy was not successful.

"L'Italie fut sans contredit la nation qui souffrit le plus de cet excéss si grave. Divisée pour son malheur en tant d'etats divers, le mal semblait multiplier par le nombre de ces gouvernmens." . . . "Ils persistèrant alors dans la stupide determination de laisser l'Italie ce qu'elle était depuis long-temps, une MOSAIQUE de gouvernemens, de lois, de douaines, de *monnaies,*" &c.

In the Papal dominions a custom has prevailed, which adds greatly to the perplexities of those who have to deal in the coins of Italy. Every Pope adopts new devices, and often makes other changes, for the coins to be issued during his Pontificate; and besides this, the interregnum between the demise of one Pope and the election of another, which is often a period of some months, is characterized by a coinage of its own. Between the years 1700 and 1780, there were issued from the mints at Rome 283 different coins, of which 67 were gold. Besides these, other varieties were issued from other mints in the ecclesiastical States, as Boulogne, Ferrara, and Gubbio. [*"Caissier Italien,"* folio 8.]

In the same period, the other mints of Italy were active, and issued, including those of the ecclesiastical estates, not less than 800 varieties of coin, to circulate in the small territory of Italy.

It was felt to be a great relief from this intolerable confusion, when Napoleon introduced a uniform coinage. This blessing was only enjoyed during the ascendency of the French Emperor. As soon as it ended, in 1814, every government of Italy returned to the old system of coinage, and continues it until the present. A traveller may, at any time, obtain a roleau

escaped by the establishment of banks of deposit, or other devices. We refer now only to the multiplicity of coins of different weights and degrees of purity. Of course this evil was immensely increased by the secret debasement of coins practised in a greater or less degree at all mints, until within a very brief period.

But coinage was found to have its difficulties, independent of mere complication and variety of coins and standards. The coins in actual use were found to lose in weight by wear so rapidly, that the smaller sizes, in the course of a few years, deteriorated in weight from ten to twenty per cent. This inevitable process was slow, but sure; the coins of a whole people became so diminished and injured in their own hands, that men of business were afraid to receive them at their nominal value. This deterioration of course obstructed their circulation, and lessened their power and usefulness. Every European country has suffered seriously from this cause.

Another difficulty encountered by coinage, scarcely less than any other, is the facility it gives to counterfeiting, and to frauds upon the genuine coin. Coined money circulates with such rapidity, upon the faith of the public certificate on its face, verifying weight and quality, that counterfeit coins are put in circulation among the people with a success, which makes it a large business wherever coins are extensively employed; and counterfeit coins often continue long to exercise the functions of money,

---

of coins from an Italian banker, which, though of full weight, can only be disposed of at a discount. We said, may obtain; we should rather have said, he will be fortunate if he is not sometimes served in that way.

Those who wish to know more of the evils of Italian coinage and money, may consult the Cambist writers, Commercial Dictionaries, and numismatic authors who treat of the coins of that country. See *Scaruffi, Davanzati*, and other writers, whose works are contained in the collection of *Baron Custodi*, of the "*Economisti Italiani*," in 51 vols. 8vo. See, also, "*Raccolta degli Scrittori delle Moneta d'Italia, Fillipo Argellati;*" "*Storia della Economia Pubblica in Italia, di Conte Pecchio;*" "*Histoire de la Republique de Venise*," tom. iii. 75; "*Caissier Italien*," passim; "*Marperger on Banks*," 1717, 4to, pages 170 to 189, in German.

before they are discovered. In China, the skill of counterfeiters is such, as wholly to prevent the use of coins; and that vast population is — for that reason, it is said — confined to the primitive mode of weighing, in payments, all the gold and silver used in commerce.

Genuine coins are, by fraud, subjected to processes which rob them of a considerable proportion of their value. They are punched; sweated; filed; sawed in two, the interior scooped out, and filled with lead, the sides being then reunited; these, and other modes of making a profit on new coins, have been successfully practised in every country, to a greater or less extent. By these processes, coins are reduced at once, for the profit of the operator, to the lowest value at which they will circulate. They may thus lose, in a day, as much as they would have lost in years of circulation. If these, and other mischiefs attendant upon a large circulation of coins, are not felt to the extent they once were, it is because the circulation of coins is so largely replaced by bank-notes, that false coiners, finding it unprofitable to pursue the business, have turned their attention, with great success, to the production of counterfeit bank-notes. Whenever governments return to a large circulation of coins, false coiners will be found at their old business.[1]

We find, then, in practice, various limitations to the power of the precious metals as money. They must, in the first instance, be weighed and assayed before they are received in payment. If that difficulty be removed by public authority, and pieces be issued ready weighed, of a certain quality or standard, then the changes of weights and standard, the multiplicity of coins consequent upon the great number of mints, the counterfeits and frauds upon the coins, all together make up a

---

[1] When, upon an occasion not very remote, one of the governments of Italy recalled a coin only a few years in circulation, the officers of the mint, not being aware of the danger, found after a short time that they had already redeemed a much larger amount of the specific coin than the mint had issued, and the offerings for redemption were far from growing less. If this test were applied to many coins, it would reveal a quantity of base money of which few have any suspicion.

great obstruction to the continued and increased use of gold and silver as a sole medium of exchange. We shall recur again to the fact, that the great value of these metals makes their use a very expensive method of effecting exchanges.

These difficulties in the use of the precious metals as an instrument of payment, have operated with such effect in the more civilized portions of the world, that only a very small portion of the exchanges of the products of industry are now effected by the actual intervention or presence of either gold or silver. They are now chiefly used in retail dealing, in small transactions, and in paying balances of trade. The great subdivision of which the precious metals are susceptible, specially fits them for the actual payments of the retail trade. Where countries, districts, or individuals have large and continued dealings, by which they in effect exchange goods for goods, a balance may fall either way, for which the goods are not wanted; such balances are with facility discharged by the export of gold or silver. But there is still a natural tendency in the marts of commerce to avoid, in every possible way, the use of so expensive an instrument of trade as gold and silver. The various modes of dispensing with them, and the substitutes employed, will come under our notice hereafter.

§ 2. *Circulation of the precious metals as money — Commerce depends upon coins for so much use as is made of them, and no more — They perform no functions beyond the use we see made of them.*

No term is more common, in treating of money, than circulation. It is applied equally to all its substitutes, as bank-notes, checks, bills of exchange, and promissory notes, and other securities. It is a term founded on well-known facts, and descriptive of well-known tendencies. With the facts and many of the details of circulation, all men of business are more or less familiar; but not many give themselves the trouble to analyze the process, and its results. They know that money goes and comes; that it passes round, and appears to return whence it set out; and that there is a sort of average quantity of money circulating among a certain number of people in a certain district: that if the very same coins do not, year after year, perform the same round, a very considerable proportion will be found in the same track. Few examine minutely the details which give this circular impulse to money, as it moves in the channels of business.

Money being a medium by which men exchange commodities, its movements are wholly controlled by the course of this exchange of commodities. Men exchange the products of their industry, or their professional or intellectual services, or their bodily labor or skill, for other products, or for other services, or labor or skill. This is the object, sum or result of their transactions; but the business is effected by exchanging these things, first for money, and then by exchanging the money for the things required. The money intervenes, and then retires; it is not of the substance of the transaction. If the exchange desired could, with equal convenience, be effected without the aid of money, it would not be employed. No exchange of commodities is, in the result, any the more effective for having been made with money. The farmer who sells a quantity of wheat for $500, taking a parcel of land in payment, and who afterwards purchases agricultural implements, giving the land in payment, has exchanged his wheat for the implements by the medium, not of coins, but of land; but the exchange is equally as effectual and advantageous for him, as if made with coins. The medium employed leaves none of its marks or characteristics on the exchange. It may be a very grave question, in many localities, whether wheat can be more advantageously converted into flour by steam or water-power; but it is of no consequence to those who eat the bread, what medium has been employed in the conversion. So, whatever importance belongs to the subject of money, and other modes of exchange, it in no way affects the validity or usefulness of the exchange, however it may have been accomplished. The first consideration is the desired exchange; the next is, that it should be effected at the least expense, and with the greatest facility possible. Of course so expensive an article as coined money, whatever its merits as a medium of exchange, will not be used when it can be dispensed with; and, as a matter of fact, very few of the exchanges referred to are now made by the intervention of coins. But although these are now so generally dispensed with, yet the mode and causes of the circulation of money, were it invariably used, requires not the less to be better understood.

Every man exchanges that which he has to spare for that which he wants, and others have to spare; and there is scarcely a community, of which the members are not more or less dependent on each other. All are, to some extent, dependent on the farmer, merchant and mechanic; but these are dependent on the physician, lawyer, teacher, and other professional men; and all are, by a complicated but well-understood dependence, linked together. All receive something, directly or indirectly, from the others. Now, if money were used in all this interchange of commodities and services, it would be found to traverse the whole circle of the community; and though it might pass back and forwards many times in the hands of individuals, yet it would have performed a round in the community. The chief transactions of any community are substantially the same every year, or half year; and it would happen that very nearly the same sum, if not the same money, would pass through the same hands every season. Great variations must of course occur, but there would be an approximation to the same results. The farmer, the mechanic, tradesman, manufacturer, and the professional man, would all go through nearly the same round of exchanges, and be ready, with the return of the season, to go through them again. The money would thus have actually been paid for every commodity, and for every service, only as a medium. The substance of the whole would be the transactions or dealings which had taken place between the parties, the money being left wholly out of view. The rapidity of the circulation determines the quantity of money required; and the rapidity of circulation depends on the state of industry, and upon the roads, rivers, cities, and other natural and artificial facilities. But the circulation is mainly and chiefly facilitated by that mutual dependence in a community which springs up when people supply their own wants. The narrower the circle in which money moves, other things being equal, the more exchanges it can effect. If farmers, manufacturers, tradesmen, mechanics, and men of all the various occupations which go to make up a civilized community, are close together, their exchanges, if effected with money, will be rapid in proportion to their vicinity. If we imagine a people wholly isolated, then the circulation among them would be complete; no part of their money would flow into other channels, and no final balance would remain to be settled with any other community.

The regularity of this movement, and the sameness of the result, has suggested to many minds, in every age of the world, that money does not perform its functions by reason of its intrinsic value, but by virtue of this circulation. It appeared to them that if parties were agreed, any other substance would perform the same office as well. The Carthaginians, history informs us, resorted to leather as a material for money; and the Chinese, some eight centuries ago, to paper, not on any principle upon which paper-money is now used, but simply as a material for money, on which could be impressed a certificate of value, for which each piece of leather or paper was to pass. We have no adequate account of the experiment in leather; but the Chinese trial of paper proved as unfortunate as some of the same kind in later times.

It is obvious enough, upon a little consideration, that much of the efficacy of money depends on the fact that it circulates in accordance with the mutual dependence of the people, and with a rapidity proportioned to the smallness of the circle, and to the natural or artificial facilities which exist to aid the transportation of the commodities for which it is used as a medium of interchange. But the regularity of the proceeding in no community is ever so great, that mere counters could be safely substituted for money of intrinsic value, an idea which has haunted men in all ages, and no doubt gave rise to the experiment of the Carthaginians and the Chinese. The idea is, that if men agree what substance they will use for money, as they only receive it to pay it away, it is perfectly indifferent what the material is, so it be convenient. There are insuperable objections to a mere conventional medium of exchange; among these is the wide door it opens to fraud, and the difficulty of restricting its quantity, which is the only means of maintaining its nominal value. If mere counters, without value, would purchase articles of value, counters would be supplied too rapidly. When the medium employed has an intrinsic value corresponding with its nominal price, then the holders are at all times, and under all circumstances, safe at every stage of commercial progress. Let war, revolution, commercial revulsion, or despotic authority bring forth what evils they may, the people have in their hands either their commodities, or their price in the precious metals. It is true that any material employed as money, which all are willing to receive, may with perfect success fulfil all the functions of money for a time; but no means have yet been found to make money, without intrinsic value, adequate to all circumstances and emergencies. Men may, for a while, concur in such experiments, and all may go smoothly for a time; but when large balances, foreign or domestic, are to be paid, when the season of alarm and trouble arrives, the conventional money, which depends on the confidence of an entire community, is stripped in a moment of all its power and usefulness. Counterfeit money may, for a long period undetected, perform all the functions of genuine coins; but the moment its true character becomes known, all its power is gone.

Whilst, therefore, the circulation of money presents some features of regularity which suggest the idea that counters may be substituted for coins, there are accompanying irregularities, unavoidable obstacles, emergencies, accidents and hazards, which make it impossible permanently to substitute mere counters for coins. The devices now employed so extensively under the credit system are not of this kind; they are securities, expressing that a certain amount is to be paid on demand, or at a day fixed. A counter, without intrinsic value, is neither a thing of value, nor a security, nor a claim upon any one. Whenever it is refused, there is an end of it.

We have already noticed the obstacles to rapid circulation, arising from the wearing of coins, from frauds upon the coinage by punching, sweating, splitting, and debasing; but more especially from the immense variety of coins proceeding from scores of different mints. Whatever facility of circulation any people may have by the nature of the country, or whatever artificial facilities might be provided, these obstacles seem to place a limit to a largely increased circulation of coins, which neither power nor ingenuity can overcome. The first remedy resorted to against this evil was only an alleviation. The collection of this multifarious coinage in sacks, duly counted, indorsed, and sealed with the name of some well-known merchant or banker, only made the sack circulate as so much bullion. The coins were no longer useful or convenient, and their circulation as such was, in fact, at an end.

The next great remedy for these obstacles to circulation was the establishment of such banks as those of Amsterdam and Hamburg. These banks received coins on deposit, after carefully ascertaining their value, and placed the amount received to credit of the depositor. The holder of such a deposit transferred his title to the money in the bank, instead of counting and delivering the coins. This method of transfer would have admitted of a circulation more rapid than any attainable by coins at large, had not these banks surrounded the transfers with restrictions and limitations, which greatly reduced their efficacy. In some cases, but one transfer of the same amount was permitted in one day. It is quite obvious that the same sum might be transferred, under very safe regulations, every five or ten minutes during the day. But this process of transferring the title to money is a very different thing from circulating money. It is, in fact, a stoppage of the circulation of coins; the title circulates in their place. The parties to such transfers do not know, nor do they attempt to ascertain, that the equivalent in coin is actually in the bank. These deposit banks were half-way stations between an exclusively hard-money circulation and the credit system. The parties who transferred and received credits in these banks confided in the fact that the money transferred was there. There was an exercise of confidence and mutual faith, without which the bank could not have existed. We shall have occasion to remark that, in the case of the Bank of Amsterdam, that confidence, and the unimpaired usefulness of the bank, continued long after a large portion of the money had been abstracted by the authorities of the city.

Banks of deposit, then, rather mark the limits of the circulation of coins, than constitute its climax. They belong almost as much to the credit system as to the money system, partaking of the characteristics of both. Whilst civilized people have always shown a strong partiality for the precious metals as a medium of exchange, the history of the last four centuries shows that there have been inducements strong enough to suggest and introduce other modes of effecting exchanges. No doubt the expense of gold and silver as a medium of exchange, the annoying difficulties growing out of a multifarious coinage at every mint, the multiplication of mints and coins, the debasement of coins by governments, and their fraudulent deterioration by rogues, contributed at a very early date to drive merchants and men of business to other methods of payment, and to seek another medium of exchange. But these inducements to resort to other modes of payment, influential as they must have been, were by no means the chief reasons why, at the present day, so small a portion of business transactions are effected by the actual employment of the precious metals as money. The partiality for this money is scarcely less than it has ever been. The great fact is, that the increase of industry and production for the last three centuries, the division of labor, and the consequent vast increase in the interchange of commodities, has far transcended any possible circulation of coins as a medium of payment for the whole of these transactions. It may be safely assumed that when other modes of effecting these exchanges were adopted, it had become, if not a necessity, at least a convenience and an economy too considerable to be resisted. It may be asserted, too, very safely, that though the precious metals intervene to such a small extent, in proportion to the whole payments of commerce, yet they are acting now as effectively as ever they did: that the transactions of commerce, which now take place without the intervention of gold or silver, are such as could not take place if dependent for their progress upon actual payments in the precious metals. The exchanges of domestic and foreign commerce, which take place without the actual aid of gold or silver, are essentially the measure of the incapacity of coins to accomplish the commerce of the present day. Gold and silver money have long ceased to be the chief agent in effecting the exchanges of commodities. Their chief employment now is as the small change of retail business, as a means of paying the balances of foreign trade, and as a security for the public in the business of banking. The quantity of coins withdrawn from circulation for this purpose of banking is vastly more than made up by the greater quantity of bank-notes issued, and by the greater rapidity of bank-note circulation over that of coins. Yet if the comparison between what is done with and without the use of coins be enlarged by adding to the circulation of coins that of bank-notes also, it will be found, especially in Great Britain and the United States, that a very small proportion of the whole payments of these conntries is effected in coins and bank-notes, even when taken together.

We are speaking, it will be kept in mind, of the actual use of coins; of what is effected by the actual transfer of gold or silver as money. We yield nothing to the mistaken idea that coins are in some way employed whenever prices are expressed. Believing that the whole subject of expressing prices, naming amounts, writing down the results of sales in books of account, and all similar matters, belong to and are fully explained by the operation of money of account, we refer, in speaking of the agency of coins as a medium of exchange, always to the actual employment of the precious metals. In this restricted sense, every man can for himself determine to what a narrow channel their circulation is now confined, compared with other more effective agencies.

Whatever indefinite ideas some may entertain upon the subject, the real use of coins is merely that in which we see them employed. Though every man may exact payment in coins of all that is due to him; yet this is almost never done. When not so exacted, the payment is made in some other satisfactory way. The Treasury of the United States exacts payments in coins, and the payments are so made. Business is done with coins only when they are present in the transaction, actually paid and received. For so much use as is made of coins is business indebted to them, and no more.

§ 3. *The quantity of money required for the business of a country.*

Few mystifications have been more profound than those which have pervaded speculations on the quantity of money required for the business of a country, and on questions as to the results of an increase or diminution of money. Such inquiries appear, at first view, important; and few of the earlier writers upon money have neglected a subject so inviting as the amount of money needed to make a country prosperous. To men not deeply versed in the details of commerce, there appeared no insurmountable difficulty in the topic. It was long a favorite notion, that the wealth of a nation was measured mainly by its stock of the precious metals; and legislation exhausted itself in the vain attempt to prevent their exportation. That commerce which brought home gold or silver was considered a national blessing; that which carried it off a misfortune. This opinion, which belonged to the mercantile school in political economy, lingers yet in many countries, and in many minds in all countries. The doctrines on the subject of the quantity of money, to which this opinion when it prevailed gave rise, however, continue to be inculcated as earnestly as before, although they lost their chief support when it was admitted to be contrary to sound policy to prohibit the exportation of coin or bullion.

To us it appears that the subject is wholly impracticable, and that no safe conclusions can ever be drawn from such reasonings. The actual quantity of money in a country never has been, and never can be ascertained with sufficient exactness to make it the ground of any safe deduction. The actual sum of money employed by any country in its trade, for any period of time, it is still more impossible to ascertain. And the quantity actually needed in any country for the purposes of its trade, during any certain lapse of time, is still more indeterminate. Of two countries, the annual value of whose commerce is the same, one will require for that commerce a much larger sum than the other. This may depend on the relative extent of their several territories; on the state of their roads and rivers, and other internal communications; on the articles in which they respectively deal; on the size and location of their cities and towns; on the state of their morals; on the nature of their governments; but more especially on the degree or extent to which the credit system, and its various devices to save the use of money, have been adopted.

So it is obvious that in the same country, at different times, varying quantities of money will be required to transact the same amount of business: this may depend on a state of peace or war, on times of tranquillity or public disturbance, on actual or apprehended mischiefs in legislation, and on the state of mercantile confidence. All these are influences, the intensity of which can neither be measured nor estimated. No man, therefore, can say what sum of money is needed in any country, at all times, nor at any time. Whatever conjectures may, even by the most observing and the best informed, be indulged on this subject, cannot form any data worthy of consideration.[1]

If positive quantities are out of our reach, comparative are only less so; it cannot be doubted that there is sometimes more, and sometimes less money; and business men often experience fluctuations of this kind, which make this but too plain. There is no gauge, however, by which we can measure or estimate the extremes of these fluctuations, or mark their intermediate progress. Nor is the public voice always correct in this matter; for very often money is said to be scarce, when its holders are only unwilling to circulate it freely; and often it is said to be plenty, when its circulation is only rapid, or when credit supplies its place. It is often observed that the deposits in the banks are largest at the time when the cry of scarcity is loudest, and smallest when there is no complaint. So that, although there can be no doubt that fluctuations do occur, yet not always at the time, nor in a way to correspond with public opinion.

---

[1] See C. H. Rau, Sect. 266; Storch, vol. iii, note 12.

The alarm produced by fear of invasion, by rebellion, by a commercial crisis, by large failures, and by many events which disturb a commercial atmosphere, often has the effect of producing this apparent scarcity of money. At such moments, money is deemed the most desirable possession; and all who have it pause before they part with it, and retain it if they can. It ceases to circulate freely, and the impression becomes complete that money is scarce. When no disturbing cause is at work, when trade is brisk and confidence high, all are made to feel that money is abundant, because merchandise, at such seasons, is more desirable than money. At such times, too, the devices for saving the use of money are easily kept in operation, and are more effective; money is thus made more abundant for some purposes, by sparing it in others. It seems, then, to be as difficult to ascertain the actual increase or diminution of money which produces fluctuations, as it is to find the actual quantity used or required in any country; and in neither case can any approximation to the truth be near enough to form the basis of sound conclusions. It is certainly better to approach this subject on safer grounds, and to regard it from a point of view which will take in admitted facts.

If fluctuations in amount are injurious, causes and preventives become more pressing inquiries than the actual quantities added or withdrawn. It is the varying, and not the actual quantity which does the mischief. We have not yet, however, arrived upon safe ground. Not being able to ascertain the sum of money which goes to make up a circulation, nor the sums of increase nor decrease which constitute injurious fluctuations, and knowing that other causes, such as those already indicated, produce the same effects as variations in quantity, there must often be danger of mistake in assigning causes, or in proposing remedies. On a subject involving so many combinations as this, those who are most confident should be the most distrusted. In a general treatise, no useful rules can be given for such investigations; the inquirer must painfully and watchfully observe the facts, and on these rest his conclusions.

Whatever progress may hereafter be made in the statistics of money, great uncertainty must still cling to this subject. If the amount of metallic money actually existing in any country could be ascertained with exactness, yet it could never be known how much was hoarded, nor how much was in the hands of those who kept it for months, or years, wholly unemployed. So in regard to paper currency. The amount issued may be told; but how much is in constant use, no one can tell.

If such speculations are worth pursuing, we leave them to those who find in them an importance which does not strike us. Hitherto, all that we have seen on the subject has been unsatisfactory. What we may further say, in reference to the quantity of money in circulation, will be under other heads. The effect of quantity upon prices is a question of the highest import, and must be fairly encountered. So, also, the agency of increased issues upon the value of the currency, upon the exchanges in stimulating over-action in trade. All these are subjects deserving of close attention; but they involve other facts and considerations than those which concern the actual quantity of money, and the problems which they present can never be solved by weighing gold and silver, or numbering bank-notes.

The quantity of coins required by banks to meet their engagements is a special inquiry, and will come within the range of subsequent chapters. It involves special considerations wholly different from the question, what amount of the precious metals, in the shape of coins, it is necessary or expedient to have for the business of a country. The banks have a certain specified duty to perform, and they must form their estimates according to the nature of that duty. But the quantity of metallic money needful in a country is wholly indefinite, and must be left to the results of the spontaneous action of the people, and their government. No such approximation is possible, as that which may be made to the quantity required by the banks. The real subject is trade and business, and the modes of carrying it on: the quantity of money required for this purpose in a year is one of that class of questions which, though asked in advance, must wait the reply which time reveals. It may be interesting to know how many warehouses, how many clerks, how many ships, and how many carts will be employed during the progress of a year in a particular country; but the information is unattainable. There is, besides, such a wide range of management and economy in all these things, that exact quantities and numbers become, in a great degree, unimportant.

CHAPTER IV.

§ 1. *The precious metals neither a measure nor a standard of value — They are the legal standard of payment — The mint has a standard of coinage — Legal tender — Objections to legal price of gold and silver — Earl of Liverpool — Instances of price fixed by authority in Great Britain — Seignorage on coins for retail business — Waste and folly of incessant recoinage — Legal tender at market price the proper rule in large transactions.*

WE have seen that there is a very obvious distinction between price and payment; that prices are named much more frequently than sales take place, or payments are made. If the price is not satisfactory, neither sale nor payment follow. It is only when a transfer of property occurs that payment is required, and that the equivalent employed to effect that purpose is produced. The parties understand each other as fully when the price is named, as when the payment is made. Prices are named upon assumed quantities of the article, to which the price is affixed; this specified quantity must be carried in the mind, as well as the value of the unit of the money of account. Actual weight or measurement by the parties ascertains the quantity of goods; coinage is generally the mode of defining the quantity of the precious metals employed in payment. Men are not always aware that they employ the money of account in stating the value of their own national coins. When a sale to the amount of one hundred dollars occurs, and payment is offered in British sovereigns, their value is stated in accordance with the then ruling price, from $4.80 to $4.90, and the quantity paid is adjusted accordingly: if the payment be made in eagles, the process is the same; the quantity of gold in ten eagles is readily stated at the known price, ten dollars each; but if the eagles are of the old coinage, they may be rated at one dollar and five or six cents.

The precious metals are, in no proper sense, a *measure of value;* they are simply a convenient equivalent, being of very great value in small compass, susceptible of being brought to uniform quality, and of being subdivided into pieces or coins of any required weight. These pieces are not employed as measures; they are never produced to express or ascertain a price, or show what a purchaser or seller would give or take for any article. If this were necessary, the equivalent in coins would have to be laid down in every transaction, that the party to whom an article of merchandise was offered might know its price. When a horse is said to be worth an hundred dollars, the price is better understood than if one hundred dollars in silver or gold coins had been exhibited as the measure of the value. Neither does expressing prices consist in naming coins, or any number of them; for this facility in stating prices is the same, whether, or not, there exist any corresponding coins — as was exhibited in the case of our colonial pounds, shillings and pence.

The same considerations prove that the precious metals are not, strictly speaking, employed as a sign or representative of value. They are neither signs nor representatives, in any practical sense of these words. Such expressions have all sprung from the want of attention to the functions of a money of account.[1]

---

[1] The Earl of Liverpool, in his elaborate "Treatise on the Coins of the Realm," thus sums up the imperfections of coin as a measure of value: —

"1 Coins are an imperfect measure, because they fluctuate in value even when made of one metal only. Neither gold nor silver will now purchase as much of any article as before the discovery of America. As a measure, neither can now be of the same import as formerly.

"2. If coins are made of both metals, they are liable to vary with reference to each other. In the 43d of Elizabeth, fine gold was to fine silver, at the English mint, as 11 to 1. In 1663, it was $14\frac{331}{682}$ to 1. Guineas were then coined as 20 shilling pieces. After many fluctuations, and rising as high as 30 shillings, they were fixed by proclamation at 21 shillings. Fine gold is now [1805] as $15\frac{2859}{13640}$ to 1.

"3. If the sovereign attempts to fix the rate or value at which coins of

Another attribute frequently given to the precious metals is, that they are a *standard of value*. This is equally inaccurate. There may be a common equivalent — an article that is commonly given in exchange for other articles; but there can be no standard of the value of all articles of merchandise. Every commodity may have its standard of quality — a certain grade being assumed, with which all other specimens are to be compared; but no one article can be assumed or regarded as a standard for other things of a totally different kind. Gold cannot, in the mint, be made the standard for silver; nor can silver be made the standard for gold. Much less, taking the whole range of articles of human consumption, can there be any standard of value or price to which all can be referred, or with which all can be compared. The term standard is, then, inaccurately applied, when it is used with any such signification. It is said, for instance, that the standard of Great Britain is gold; and that, until recently, that of France and the United States was the double standard of gold and silver. Standard of what? There can be no such thing as a general standard of value. The term standard, thus used, is a common but ill-chosen expression of the fact, that in Great Britain gold is the standard of payment, and that in France and the United States both gold and silver were the standards of payment; or, to adopt legal language, gold in Great Britain, and gold and silver in France and the United States, were a legal tender in payment of debts. If the term standard is employed at all, it should be standard of payment.

That there should be some legal mode of discharging a debt is the settled policy of modern times. In some countries, gold is made a legal tender, in some silver, and in some both these

---

different metals shall pass, a third imperfection is perceived. Their prices in the market will frequently differ from the rate at which he has valued them in coins; and when coins of two metals are made a legal tender, there will be two measures of property, occasionally differing from each other. The speculator will profit by this, and the debtors will pay debts in the cheapest medium.

"A fourth imperfection is that which arises from gradual wear, which will lead to the melting of heavy coins, and keeping the light only in circulation." — "*Coins of the Realm*," pp. 10, 11, 12.

metals, in discharge of debts. So willing, however, are people to receive payment of what is due to them in the ordinary currency, whatever it may be, that it is very rare to see a formal tender of gold or silver, or to hear of such a demand. Their use among the banks, and in payment of foreign balances, does not proceed from its being a legal tender, but from pure commercial reasons, which would be equally operative, if the law of legal tender did not exist. Gold or silver would seldom be refused in discharge of a debt, even if no law required it. Few, however, will dispute that it is expedient to provide some legal mode of paying a debt, that every man may be able, in some way, to obtain a legal acquittance of his pecuniary obligations, or at least be discharged from liability for subsequent interest, if the creditor refuses to accept the legal medium of payment. It is in this sense that the word standard may be applied to gold and silver, apart from their quality, with some degree of propriety.

Though it is the policy of modern nations to establish a standard of payment, and though gold or silver are the best substances for that purpose, not only by reason of their intrinsic value, but on account of their being so generally and so long used as money, there are objections to *fixing the price* by law at which gold or silver, or both, shall be received in payment of a debt. This has been done in the face of the admitted fact that both the precious metals fluctuate in value. Nothing has contributed more to obscure the subject of money than this fixing by law the price of gold and silver.

No one has placed the argument in favor of the government fixing the price of the precious metals, in a more distinct and forcible form, than the Earl of Liverpool. He quotes Mr. Harris as differing on the point from Mr. Locke: — "He [Mr. Harris] thought that the regulation of the value of coins — that is, the nominal value at which they were to be legal tender — was a subject of too much importance to be entrusted at any time to private judgment; and it is certain that there has generally been a clause in the mint regulations declaring at what nominal rate or value the coins directed to be made should be current. It is, indeed, hardly possible that the people in general, particularly those of an inferior class, should be able to exercise any true judgment on the intrinsic or relative value of the metals of which any coins are composed; and if they were to attempt to exercise such judgment, they would be exposed to perpetual frauds and impositions from money jobbers, and others, who understand the business better than themselves. The practice of all governments, in every age, has coincided with the opinion of Mr. Harris; and experience has evinced the necessity of fixing, by public authority, the rate or value of coins of every denomination permitted to be current as lawful money or legal tender."[1]

This is a distinct assertion of what many deny, that the price of coins under the prevailing systems of coinage is fixed by authority. The reason of this practice of all governments is sound, so far as concerns the classes the Earl of Liverpool would protect. The system of coinage which prevails in England for silver, is a protection to these classes. The same system can be applied, with proper modifications, to gold, and the protection would be equally complete.

The objection that the people, in general, are not able to exercise any true judgment as to the value of the metals, is of no weight; because there is always, and must be, a market price of gold and silver, which does not and cannot depend on the judgment of people, superior or inferior, as to the intrinsic value of these metals. It is a price determined by the course of trade, and the course of procuring the precious metals. The practice of governments, and legislation on this subject, has been too exclusively guided by consideration of the merest retail trade, and should, therefore, have been confined to that business. It is in the power of governments to fix the price of coins, so far as they can be employed in the retail business; but beyond that, no public regulation is needed; and none can definitely fix the price of coins or bullion, for commerce will make its own price. It is true that governments can enforce a law of

---

[1] "Coins of the Realm," page 16.

legal tender, even against the course of commerce and the laws of trade, as to the payment of debts.

This is what is attempted by the prevailing system, which results in one price of the precious metals arising from the trade of particular nations, and of the world; and another price by public authority, according to which debts must be paid, if so demanded. But this demand is almost never made, and so far the law of legal tender is inoperative. In all transactions between the people of different nations, the commercial price of bullion and coins is alone acknowledged. As the people of no class are in the habit of demanding payment in gold or silver at the mint price, it would not disturb them in the least if, in sums over $20, neither coins nor bullion were a tender at any other than the current commercial price. The necessity, then, of fixing the price of coins by public authority is not acknowledged, and does not exist beyond the wants of the merest retail trade. Beyond that it is operative only for mischief, and is practically repudiated by foreign merchants, and by the domestic also, so far as direct dealing in bullion is concerned.

It is evident that the Earl of Liverpool labored under the mistake, that prices are fixed and expressed in coins: if he had not been wrong in this, he would have felt less afraid to leave coins, in large sums at least, to the market rate.

It is in naming the rate at which coins shall pass, that governments place a fixed price upon gold and silver. It is done, in the case of domestic coins, by prescribing very accurately the weight of the coin, to make it correspond in value to some special amount expressed in money of account. In the case of foreign coins, it is done by stating the price directly in the money of account. A very general mistake is involved in this, which may be mentioned here, although it does not concern the present question. It is assumed that the circulation of money, the stating of prices, and the reckoning of accounts, will be facilitated by a correspondence between the coins and the denominations of the money of account. This is only true in the merest retail transactions. In large payments, it has operated unfavorably to the interests of trade, by causing the coins to circulate at their nominal rate, after they began to be seriously deteriorated by wear, and by fraudulent usages. When this takes place, as has frequently been the case, the evil is one which becomes yearly more difficult to cure; and serious disturbance, both of the money of account and of the coinage itself, is the final result, with great national and individual loss. What is needed, in large payments of the precious metals, is not a correspondence with the money of account, but accurate weights, and the proper standard of quality. If gold and silver were duly assayed, and weighed in bars of convenient size, with the proper stamp of the mint, their value could as readily be stated in money of account as if it were in coins, and it could be paid and received much more readily. Large payments in gold are now made, in England, by weight; and the same is true, to a considerable extent, in France and the United States.

The price of the precious metals is fixed, by law, to the minutest possible fraction. The public authority assumes no arbitrary weight for coins, but requires them to correspond in value to some denomination of the money of account. It orders that a certain quantity of gold or silver shall pass for, or be a legal tender for a certain amount. When, for the first time, an English sovereign was coined in 1816, it was required to contain 5 dwts. $3\frac{274}{1000}$ grains of standard gold, or 4 dwts. $17\frac{18}{11214}$ grains of pure gold: that is, that quantity of gold was then declared to be worth a pound sterling. That regulation continues, with slight change, to this day; and the unit of the English money of account is thus unhappily placed at the hazard of every fluctuation in the price of gold.

As the sovereign was intended to be the actual equivalent to the pound sterling, $46\frac{89}{129}$ sovereigns were to be coined from the pound of standard gold. By this method, 5 dwts. $3\frac{274}{1000}$ grains of standard gold were made a legal tender for a debt of one pound sterling, and one pound of gold was made a legal tender for £46 14*s.* 6*d.* This arrangement was made in pursuance of an act of Parliament, and could only be changed by the same authority: until such authority is exerted, the same quantity of gold could be legally tendered only for the same sum, and in greater or less quantities in proportion to the sum to be paid. This is not the same thing as to assert that an ounce of gold, or a pound of gold, is a legal tender for an ounce of gold, or a pound of gold, as must be alleged by those who leave wholly out of view the money of account. There has been no time, in the last five centuries, when the bankers and merchants of the cities of Europe could not at once tell the value of bullion by weight in their respective moneys of account. It has always been so expressed; and the coinage of every country in Europe has, for a longer period than five centuries, been regulated by the money of account of each respectively. We can now readily refer, in various authors, to the price of gold per ounce, or pound, from the year 1350 to the present time. The English sovereign, now the legal equivalent for a pound sterling, is a coin of the recent date of 1816.

For many centuries previous to 1816, the pound sterling of account had no representative in the coin. An attempt was made to furnish one in the guinea. But the price of gold was then too fluctuating, or the quantity of gold it required was not properly adjusted. This coin was quoted at various prices in the money of account, until it was finally fixed, when Sir Isaac Newton was Master of the mint, at twenty-one shillings. It had ranged previously between twenty-two and thirty shillings.

So much does the history of English coinage abound in proof that the government has, for centuries past, fixed the price of the precious metals in coins, that it seems strange it could ever have been denied or doubted. It can be denied by those only who cannot conceive of coins as anything else than a measure of value, not measurable by anything else. Those who cannot conceive of a pound sterling as having any other meaning than twenty silver shillings, or four crown pieces, or a sovereign, in gold; or who cannot conceive of a shilling as having any other significance than the silver that is in a shilling, cannot of course understand how these mint regulations fix the price of gold and silver. A reference to the history of English coinage reveals that the terms, pounds, shillings and pence, have long been employed to express values in a way that shows them to have a meaning wholly independent of coinage. The value denoted by these terms has, in fact, furnished the sole mode of regulating the weight and denominations of the coins.[1]

---

[1] On the 29th of January, 1660, in the reign of Charles II., a royal proclamation was issued, fixing the price at which a variety of foreign coins should be as current as sterling money of England; as follows:—

		Weight.	Price.
Gold.	The Spanish or French Quadruple Pistole...	17 dwts. 8 grs. ...	£3 4*s.* 0*d.*
	Double Gold Ducat..............................	4 " 12 " ...	— 18*s.* 0*d.*
Silver.	Mexican Dollar, or piece of eight............	17 " — " ...	— 4*s.* 9*d.*
	Ducatoon[1]	20 " 16 " ...	— 5*s.* 9*d.*

In the year 1661, in August, another proclamation fixed the rates at which various coins should be current within the realm; as follows:—

The Unite now current at	22*s.* 0*d.*	to be current at		23*s.* 6*d.*
Double Crown "	11*s.* 0*d.*	"	"	11*s.* 9*d.*
Thistle " "	4*s.* 4¾*d.*	"	"	4*s.* 8*d.*[2]

In June, 1683, another proclamation was issued, fixing the price of foreign coins. We give the following as specimens:—

	Weight.	Price.
The Golden Rider....................	6 dwts. 12 grs.	£1 2*s.* 6*d.*
Quadruple Pistole.....................	17 " 4 "	3 10*s.* 3*d.*
Double Pistole.........................	8 " 14 "	1 15*s.* —
Ducat..	2 " 6 "	— 9*s.* —[3]

In 1688, the same coins were, by another proclamation, made current respectively as follows:—£1 4*s.*, £3 16*s.*, £1 18*s.*, and £0 10*s.*

In 1695, Parliament resolved, on the 15th of February, that guineas should not pass above the rate of 28 shillings. In a few weeks afterwards, the rate was lowered, by the same authority, to 26 shillings. In 1698, the House of Commons resolved that "no person shall be obliged to take guineas at 22 shillings a-piece."[4]

In 1717, the price of guineas was declared to be 21 shillings. A proportionable rate was fixed on other gold coins, and they were, for the first time, made a legal tender.[5]

In September, 1737, the following prices were affixed, by royal proclamation, to various coins:—

	Weight.	Price.
Guinea......................................	— dwts. — grs.	£1 2*s.* 9*d.*
Moidore....................................	6 " 22 "	1 9*s.* 3*d.*
Quadruple Pistole.....................	17 " 8 "	3 13*s.* —
Louis d'Or................................	5 " 5 "	1 2*s.* —[6]

---

[1] Ruding's Annals of Coinage, vol. ii. p. 3. [2] Ibid. p. 5. [3] Ibid. p. 19.
[4] Ibid. p. 46. [5] Ibid. p. 66. Lord Liverpool's Coins of the Realm, p. 84.
[6] Ruding's Annals of Coinage, vol. ii. p. 77.

In Great Britain the uniform practice has been, for centuries, to fix the price of coins, both foreign and domestic, by law. The history of British coinage abounds in illustrations of the mischiefs resulting from this policy; and also in proofs that the money of account was employed in the arrangements of the coinage, but without a clear conception of its character and proper functions. The price of all coins, foreign and domestic, was fixed by law; and the weight of coins was made, in the mint, to conform in the minutest fraction to values expressed in

---

In 1770, a new coinage of gold was made, at the rate of $44\frac{1}{2}$ guineas to the pound Troy. And of silver, at the rate of 62 shillings to the pound Troy.[1]

In 1797, a new gold coin was issued, weighing 1 dwt. $19\frac{1460}{10000}$ grains, which was proclaimed current at 7 shillings.[2]

In 1816, it was enacted by Parliament that silver should be coined into 66 shillings to the pound Troy; crowns, half crowns, and sixpences, to be at the same rate. Silver was not then worth 66 shillings the pound, though made a legal tender at that rate. This over-valuation has saved the British silver coinage from exportation, and from the melting pot; whilst its being restricted, as a legal tender, to 40 shillings has prevented any abuse from its being offered in large sums. This coinage was completed in 1817; and, by proclamation of that date, it was ordained that these new coins should, on and after the 13th of February of that year, be lawful money of Great Britain.[3]

On the 1st of July of the same year, a new gold coin was made current by royal proclamation: — "Each piece was to be of the value of 20 shillings, and of the weight of 5 dwts. $3\frac{274}{1000}$ grains; the piece to be called a sovereign, or 20 shilling piece, and to pass and be received as of the value of 20 shillings of lawful money of Great Britain and Ireland, in all payments whatsoever."[4]

In May, 1821, a royal proclamation was issued, repeating the above order as to the value and weight of the sovereign. On the accession of William IV., the value and weight of the gold and silver coinage was again established as above.

On the 8th of July, 1838, in the second year of Victoria, the value and weight of the gold coins were declared to be as follows: — Double sovereigns, 10 dwts. 5 grains; sovereigns, 5 dwts. $2\frac{1}{2}$ grains; half sovereigns, 2 dwts. $13\frac{1}{8}$ grains. This exhibits a slight decrease in weight, the legal price being the same.[5]

---

[1] Ruding's Annals of Coinage, vol. ii. pp. 82–3. [2] Ibid. p. 96.
[3] Ibid. p. 116. [4] Ibid. p. 121. [5] Ibid. p. 132.

money of account. Undoubtedly, the expressions of value thus affixed to specific quantities of gold and silver were regarded as perfectly definite and intelligible. The meaning of the royal proclamations, and acts of Parliament, were fully comprehended, whether they declared a guinea to be of the value of 20, or 21, or 22, or 25, or 30 shillings. The language of the money of account was used, therefore, to mark and designate the legal value of any particular coin. It was, in fact, the only means the public authorities had to make known the value of a coin; for, after coins are once introduced, the people lose the habit of expressing the value of the precious metals by weight. They take the fixed weight in the coins, and the price fixed by law, and thus lose sight of the distinction between coins and money of account.

Whether the original subdivision of the pound of silver, in the English and French coinage, was governed by a money of account then existing, we need not inquire; but it is very certain a money of account proceeded from that coinage. If the coins at first only corresponded with known weights, and if they were passed merely as equivalents, by specific exchange, for other articles, that state of things only lasted until pounds and shillings, or sols, came to be impressed on the public mind as a money of account; and from that time the coins would be, and were really valued in the money of account. All prices thereafter would be expressed in money of account, and coins would be merely pieces of gold or silver, with a public certificate of weight and quality, subject to rise and fall in price as any other commodity: that is, if any change in price or market value took place, the money of account would register it, as in the case of other articles. But if, in this state of things, the government again intervened, and, availing itself of the already formed money of account, decreed that certain coins should be a legal tender at a certain rate or price, then, from that time, the law made those coins receivable for a fixed sum or price, whatever may be their actual value. From that time their variations in market value could only be followed by those skilled in the mysteries of foreign exchange, or who were familiar with the necessary distinctions between coins and money of account. The fact that a coin was made, by law, a tender for the same amount of debt, however its value might change, would have strongly tended to prevent such coin from varying in price. The law in such cases, however, cannot permanently give a value to coins much above the intrinsic worth of the metal contained in them. Every attempt at this has failed. The money of account, in such cases, may be destroyed and reconstructed according to the new coinage; but if not, it will ultimately vindicate its functions, and both mark and express the true value of every coin, whatever the alterations it may have undergone. It is true that a coinage used for the purposes of change may, to a small amount, be sustained by law at a point above its intrinsic value, as is the case now with the English silver coinage, which is a legal tender to the amount of only forty shillings, and of our silver coinage under a dollar. And this may, no doubt, be done in the same way, and for the same purpose, anywhere, if the over-valuation does not exceed the cost of coinage. To this extent only, indeed, can coin be rescued from the laws which govern bullion. Where coin is occasionally employed in the large operations of commerce, it has ever been, and must ever be, mainly regarded as bullion.

The test of exportation must always bring it to its market value as bullion. The moment it becomes, in the course of trade or foreign expenditure, the interest of merchants to export bullion, it must go, and it can only go at its value as bullion. The mints of France, England, and other countries, have been employed for centuries in coining gold and silver, only to find their coins passing from one to the other for recoinage. Immense sums have thus been wasted in the expenses of coinage, for no good end whatever. Coins are only useful in the retail trade, and they can only be retained in circulation by placing upon them the full expense of coinage. It is perfectly right that the retail trade, which requires these coins, should bear the whole expense of coinage; the convenience and advantage of coins in that trade fully justifies a deduction from the coins of the full cost of the labor bestowed upon them. But, in large operations in the precious metals, coins are not needed; and the expense of coinage is, therefore, wholly lost.

In small transactions coins are not only useful, but nearly indispensable; they have, therefore, a special value for that purpose. In large transactions ingots are more convenient than coin, because weighing is less troublesome than counting; because there is less danger of counterfeits; and because there is no complication between the legal and the market price.

It results, from this view of the subject, that coinage should be confined, as nearly as possible, to the amount required for the retail trade; that, to prevent its being melted at home or recoined abroad, the whole expense of coinage should be deducted from the coins; that the legal tender of coins thus overvalued should not exceed a small sum, in coins of silver, and an amount somewhat larger, in coins of gold. This being arranged, both gold and silver, in bars assayed and stamped at the mint, should be a legal tender, at the market price, in payment of all debts. Foreign coins should of course be regarded as bullion, and be a legal tender at the market rate.

With this very simple and natural arrangement, an abundance of coin might at all times be secured for the retail trade; because it would never, in the first instance, be sought for exportation. The precious metals, freed from arbitrary valuations by law, would in all large transactions fall into the regular channels of trade, and become subject to the laws of supply and demand. None of those extraordinary and often mysterious movements in bullion and coin, which now frequently take place, could occur; for the price of gold and silver would be governed constantly by the exigencies of the demand. When required to liquidate a balance of trade, it would be purchased just as bills of exchange are for the same purpose. There is no more reason why he who must remit for goods purchased in foreign countries should have gold or silver at a fixed price, than that he should have flour or cotton, if he find it for his advantage to make his remittances in those commodities. Under such regulations, no country could drain off the precious metals from another, by any device, without paying the price caused by their demand.

The difficulty of ascertaining the price of gold and silver may seem to be a serious objection. All who are familiar with dealings in bullion know that this is in reality no serious difficulty, as nothing is more easily ascertained in trade than the price of bullion; and it would be still more easily known, if all operations in bullion were only at the market price, instead of being complicated with coins upon which the government has placed a fixed price. The fluctuations of bullion, especially in the great marts of foreign trade, would be greater than under the present system, as they should be, for they should obey the law of prices. As no man would be disposed to keep the precious metals idle, because they are unproductive, they would be continually pressing on the market when the demand was small, and prices would recede; so, when the demand was large, buyers would advance the price to obtain the required supply. But these advanced prices would only be paid by those who needed them. All others would be unaffected by the advance. Just as high rates of interest or exchange affect mainly those who borrow money, or purchase bills of exchange. In truth, no difficulty of ascertaining the market price of bullion, if left free to find its own rate, could be compared with the difficulty of adjusting mint prices so as to avoid, at times, the exportation of coins, or their being melted down, if under-valued, or of their being thrown back into the circulation in undue quantities when over-valued. The difficulties of the fixed price of coins have, indeed, exceeded any that could arise under the system proposed: under the system of fixed prices, the whole subject becomes too complicated for the comprehension of any but the shrewdest bankers and dealers in bullion, who become thus enabled to seize upon advantages and profits which do not belong to any regular operation of commerce. When the market price of bullion shall be the law of all its movements, every business man will understand why it goes and why it comes, and may govern himself accordingly, so far as his interests may be involved. There is no more reason, beyond the mere demands of the retail trade, for fixing the price of gold and silver by law, than for fixing the price, in the same way, of bread and meat.

§ 2. *Coinage — French coinage — Debasement, frauds, disturbed money of account — System of the United States — Act of Congress of* 1792, *adopting the dollar unit — Price of gold fixed — Results — Act of June,* 1834, *reducing weight of gold coins — Result — Act of February,* 1853 — *Silver coinage — Ingots of gold — Export of silver.*

We have, for the sake of distinctness, and to avoid confusion, drawn the preceding illustrations chiefly from British coinage and money of account. The lessons to be drawn from those of France are not less instructive. We need not, however, refer to them for the same purpose. The debasement of the coins was carried much farther in France than in England. The coinage and moneys of account, in both countries, began with the pound weight of silver — in France the pound *marc*, and in England the *tower* pound. In France, the livre of 1789 contained only the seventy-eighth part of the original livre of Charlemagne, in the year 800: in England, silver coins which would be the equivalent of the pound unit, or pound sterling, exceed only by a little a quarter of the original quantity.

Such a succession of frauds as this debasement of the French coins implies must have inflicted upon the people a series of losses equal to the devastations of many civil wars. Whatever profit kings or governments may have gained by frauds of this kind, must have been more than equalled by those of bankers and merchants. What the government gained would always, in fact, be the least part of what the people would lose; for, upon such occasions, the sharks found among money-changers seize the occasion to fleece both government and people. Whenever the money of account is disturbed, as it always is when a currency of debased coins is enforced by authority, or, in modern language, made a legal tender, the language of prices becomes so confused, that men no longer understand each other. Very few can so clearly comprehend the actual state of things as to guard their own interests; some there are, however, who, from position and special skill, are always able not only to ward off the mischief, but to make such gains, on occasions of this kind, as no legitimate business ever affords.

What such frauds have done in France, they have done everywhere else. The law of legal tender, or enforced currency, is the basis on which these frauds have rested. Without such aid, they could never have been so largely perpetrated: coins reduced in weight, or with undue portion of alloy, would have found, very soon, their true market value, and been kept to it. A few might be deceived, but the money of account, being undisturbed, would at once serve to mark distinctly, and express openly, the proper price of the altered coin.

All such debasements of coin by authority proceed upon the ground that the government having previously fixed the price of certain quantities or coins of the precious metals by law, it is safe and practicable to make a less quantity bear the same price.

The history of coinage for nearly ten centuries is a history of public frauds and private injuries; of confusion in prices and in moneys of account; of immense gains, as well as losses, by governments, and still heavier losses, without any gains, by the people. These mischiefs may be credited, without hesitation, to the continued effort to maintain a fixed price and forced circulation for coins, and to the fraudulent debasements to which these efforts opened a door, and offered a temptation. This history affords no lessons more worth remembering than that governments should not and cannot fix the price of the precious metals, even in coins, beyond the demand of the retail trade: that there should not be any other price for the precious metals, whether coined or uncoined, in the large transactions of commerce, than that which is made by the law of prices and the course of trade. The history of money shows that few greater grievances can befall a people than a deranged coinage and money of account: few evils have drawn from the masses of a nation more bitter complaints. But for the great advantage of coins in small transactions, it had been far better that no mint had ever existed.

It should not be lost sight of, then, that a fall in the price of gold or silver, where they are made a legal tender at a fixed price, is equivalent to a corresponding debasement of the coins. Although no government may be responsible, the mischiefs are equally great, and fall largely upon the unwary, or those who cannot help themselves. In such cases, also, sharp and skilful dealers in money reap a vast harvest of profits before people at large are on their guard.

The period of public frauds by coinage had nearly elapsed before our nation came into existence. The progress of civilization had put an end to the deliberate issue of counterfeits of their own coins by the governments of Europe. Other modes of extracting money from the people were discovered, more efficient and less disgraceful. But with the frauds the difficulties did not disappear, and these were found to be sufficient to puzzle the shrewdest statesmen of the day. Unfortunately for clear views of the subject, the policy of a fixed price for coins was persevered in with a pertinacity which denoted that it was regarded as the indispensable accompaniment of a sound system of coinage and money. It became a settled opinion, that the system of coinage which was adapted to the merest retail trade would equally suit the larger operations of foreign commerce and wholesale transactions. As well might men have attempted to carry on the transportation by sea and land, which the larger movements of trade involve, in their pockets, as to have resorted to the same medium of exchange, managed in the same way, for the largest and smallest transactions of commerce.

The mischievous absurdity of a fixed price for the coins of a country has never been accepted by merchants and bankers in large transactions, except to take some advantage by it. Fluctuations in the price of the precious metals operating upon coins, as well as bullion, widely and effectively, have too long been a mystery to the people at large. Coinage, without preventing fluctuation, assists in concealing the cause; and fluctuations defy and derange all the nicely-adjusted valuations of the mints of the world, which may one month be correct to the nicest attainable fraction, and in the next be so far wrong as to drive the whole of a coinage of gold or silver out of a country in a few months. Men are lost in conjectures at such movements, when the productions of a score of years of the vast and multifarious machinery of a mint, millions upon millions of exquisitely executed coins, are carried away, and without hesitation consigned to foreign crucibles to be recoined, and not long afterwards subjected to a similar process at another mint. Thus modern mints are kept in constant activity, using each other's finished products as raw material.

In all this policy and its results, the United States have had their full share. The earliest legislation of Congress, on the subject of a mint, was the act of April, 1792. By this act it is established: — "That the money of account of the United States shall be expressed in dollars or units, dimes or tenths, cents or hundredths, and mills or thousandths; a dime being the tenth part of a dollar, a cent the hundredth part of a dollar, &c.; and that all accounts in the public offices, and all proceedings in the courts of the United States, shall be kept and had in conformity to this regulation." [1]

This is, perhaps, the first time that a money of account was ever enacted or established by any public authority, as an act of power. Moneys of account had, in all nations, grown up in the commercial and mental habits of the people. The dollar unit was employed by Spanish nations, to some extent, as a money of account; but it was not that chiefly used. The Spanish dollar, however, was a well-known coin; and the dollar unit was one familiar to many people of the United States before and during our struggle for independence. It was wisely adopted as the unit of our money of account, because of the great diversity of moneys of account prevailing in the States at that time, and the great need of having one uniform system of reckoning and keeping accounts throughout the whole nation. It was wisely chosen, because no other could have been brought into use so soon. It required, however,

---

[1] See Laws of the United States, and History of Mint Regulations, in Adams' Report on Weights and Measures, pp. 143 to 152.

with all this previous familiarity, from twenty-five to forty years to introduce the present system into general use.[1]

The word "dollar" employed as above by the Congress of 1792, and made the unit of our money of account, had a meaning perfectly apprehended at the time. It was not the dollar coin which was made the unit; the word dollar was made the unit, and this unit was made decimally divisible. This word dollar "expressed" a value which was then, as it is now, well understood. It was understood just as the term pound was in Pennsylvania. If Congress had enacted that the term pound, as employed in the currency of Pennsylvania, should be the unit, it would have been perfectly comprehended, though there never had been a coin of silver or gold corresponding to that pound, or half, or quarter, or any decimal part thereof.

This act of Congress provides for a coinage of both silver and gold:—"Dollars, or units, each to be of the value of a Spanish milled dollar, as the same is now current, and to contain $371\frac{4}{16}$ grains of pure, or 416 grains of standard silver." Other silver coins, less than a dollar, to be in proportion. "Eagles each to be of the value of ten dollars, and to contain $247\frac{4}{8}$ grains of pure, or 270 grains of standard gold." Half eagles to be in proportion. This statute then declares and establishes that $371\frac{4}{16}$ grains of pure, and 416 grains of standard silver, shall be current as money at the price of one dollar, the value of the unit of the money of account. Also, that the price of $247\frac{4}{8}$ grains of pure, and 270 grains of standard gold shall be ten dollars, and that the price of half of those quantities shall be five dollars. It further declares:—"That the proportional value of gold to silver, in all coins which shall be current as money within the United States, shall be as fifteen to one, according to quantity in weight of pure gold or pure silver; that is to say, every fifteen pounds of pure silver shall be of equal value, in all payments, with one pound weight of pure gold, and so in proportion."

---

[1] See extracts from "Bankers' Magazine," ante, page 88, for a more full account of the adoption of the dollar unit.

This statute not only fixes and expresses the price of silver and gold coins in the money of account it adopts, but it fixes the exact proportion between gold and silver, and enacts that a pound of gold shall be worth fifteen pounds of silver. In this, Congress acted in accordance with prevalent opinions of that day — opinions not entirely surrendered by many, even to this time. It is obvious, however, that the proportion between gold and silver cannot be settled by any statutory regulation. It must remain subject to the course of trade, and whatsoever else influences the market price of one or the other of these metals. It belongs neither to the authority, nor to the power of any one nation to adjust that proportion by law; nor, indeed, is it in the power of the political authorities of all nations combined to make or enforce any such arbitrary adjustment. The whole subject belongs to trade, and the markets of the world.

The language of the statute to which we have referred, fixing the price of $247\frac{4}{8}$ grains of fine gold at ten dollars, could only be operative in the United States, and even there only to a limited extent; so, also, the provision that the price of $371\frac{4}{16}$ grains of pure silver shall be one dollar. It is true that these fixed prices, taken in connection with the further provision, "That all the gold and silver coins which shall be struck at and issued from said mint shall be a lawful tender in all payments whatsoever, those of full weight according to the respective values hereinbefore declared, and those of less than full weight at values proportionate to their respective weights" — must have been regarded as valid in the United States, to the extent of enabling debtors to discharge debts at those fixed rates of gold and silver. But they could not compel men to accommodate all their prices and dealings to these fixed statutory rates. They were only binding as to debts contracted; and men might, if they chose, refuse to buy or sell on credit with reference to those rates. In all the large operations of commerce and exchange, these statutory prices of gold and silver are disregarded, and that of the public market governs.

The result, after this enactment, proved that the adjustment between gold and silver was wrong, and that the price of gold was fixed at a rate lower than the current price of the market. As a consequence of this legislative error, gold ceased to circulate as money in the United States in any considerable quantities. This continued to be the case down to the year 1834, when the price of gold was corrected. By a statute bearing date the 28th of June, it was declared that the eagle should thenceforth be coined to weigh 258 grains, instead of 270 grains as before, of which 232 grains were to be fine gold, instead of 247½ as before. This statute fixed the price of 232 grains of fine gold at ten dollars, which was an advance upon the former rate of over six and a half per cent.; that is, that proportion of fine gold was, in the coinage of 1834, withdrawn from the ten dollar piece. This rate of gold raised the proportion of gold to silver to about sixteen for one. The provisions of this act were incorporated in that of January 18th, 1837, which is a consolidation of the laws pertaining to the mint. It makes the new gold coins a legal tender for the same sum expressed in the money of account, for which they were a legal tender before the weight was thus reduced.

Under this adjustment, gold and silver coins circulated concurrently for some years, and the coinage of gold was quadrupled. But the mischief of a fixed legal price was again strongly exemplified when the gold began to come in freely from California. The tendency of this large addition to the supply was to reduce the price. Whilst the law affected to hold the price of gold unchanged, the sudden and rapid departure of the silver revealed unmistakeably the fact that gold had fallen in price in the general market, and that it was now over-valued in our coinage. This cause has continued to operate, until all our own silver coins, and all the Mexican, South American and Spanish coins of full weight have been exported. For a time we had no silver coins but the worn foreign and domestic coins, which were deteriorated to the extent of from five to twenty per cent. The foreign deteriorated silver coins had previously almost wholly disappeared; but the departure of the full weight coins speedily brought them again to light.

They became a necessity; but were, nevertheless, such an annoyance as called for another act of Congress.

The act of the 21st of February, 1853, provided for a coinage of half dollars, quarters, dimes and half dimes; it prescribed that the half dollars should be of the weight of 192 grains, instead of the former weight of 206¼ grains, and the lesser coins in that proportion; but it only made these coins a legal tender to the amount of five dollars. This was a withdrawal of more than seven per cent. of the fine metal from the half dollar coin, and the lesser coins; and, in fact, fixed the price of the coins thus affected over seven per cent. higher than their previous legal price. This measure was adopted and carried into effect in time to save the small change of our retail trade from being wholly carried off. The demand for small money has kept these coins up to their nominal value; and their high nominal rate has prevented their being melted down, or exported as bullion. The principle which dictated this successful measure is that which ought to govern the whole policy of coinage, so far as coinage is expedient. Of the great coinage of California gold which has so magnified the operations of our mint of late years, but a small part retains the form and weights of our coins. This wasteful policy has at length in part been abandoned, and gold is now issued in bars or ingots.

The ingots from the mint being all of the same quality or standard, the price depends wholly upon the course of trade. The market price of bullion in England, France and the United States mainly governs all the large operations in the precious metals in these countries. Yet the fixed legal price has, in some conditions of the market rates, a disturbing effect, the extent of which can scarcely be estimated. The vast and extraordinary drain of silver from America and Europe to Asia and Africa, which has been going on for several years, and which is so much lamented by many, could not have taken place but for the policy of the fixed legal price for gold. That gold has depreciated, to some extent, under its extraordinary influx from Australia and California, is just as certain as that the silver has departed, and is departing. But whilst the laws are ineffectual to prevent gold from falling in price or value, they are efficient in enabling the dealers to exchange it for the silver which is exported. So long as the law makes the depreciated gold a legal tender in payment of all debts, so long debtors will use it to pay their debts. A depreciated medium, if it circulates at all times, and especially if it circulates under the sanction of the law, will supersede every better medium. Previous to 1834 we under-rated gold, and we could keep none; now we over-rate gold, and we have nothing else. Thus the rates fixed by law on the precious metals, beyond the demand of the retail trade, are only available for disturbance and evil, and for no good purpose or end.

Under the rule, or policy, of allowing the market price to govern the whole movement of the precious metals, a great displacement, like that of the departure of silver from Europe, could never take place. The price of silver, as compared with gold, would rise according to the demand, so as eventually to check the movement. The two metals, disturbed in their mutual relations, would immediately find a proportion suited to the occasion. If the present policy of the Western powers is persevered in, and if the supply of gold continues unabated, their whole stock of silver must be exported. They will continue to accept gold, which has greatly fallen in value, for their silver at the old rate. It will not be difficult, hereafter, to estimate the loss which this great exchange of silver for gold is entailing upon the countries which are its victims. It cannot but be enormous directly, but, perhaps, indirectly far heavier. If the depreciation of gold continues, the holders of gold will have the whole loss to bear; and as our silver will be gone, we shall be the losers. All the moneys of account, in countries making gold a legal tender, will be changed. The whole range of prices will have to be modified, and immense losses will be sustained upon all the investments payable in dollars, pounds and francs. If this change could be fully appreciated and understood by those whom it may affect, the mischiefs would be less, for much might be done to distribute and equalize the loss.

But heretofore it has been the case that such occasions are seized upon by the knowing ones to enrich themselves at the expense of the community.

NOTE TO CHAPTER IV.

EXTRACTS

From an Article, by the Author of this Volume, in "Hunt's Merchants' Magazine," of April, 1852.

THE EARL OF LIVERPOOL—BRITISH SYSTEM OF COINAGE ADOPTED IN 1816.

"When gold had thus been introduced into general use, it soon presented the difficulty of light coins. It became a regular business with a certain class of dealers in coins, to seize upon the heavy or new coins as fast as they were issued from the mint, by purchasing them at a slight premium, which they recovered, with a fair profit, by abstracting from the heavy coins as much as they safely could, and in that state returning them to circulation. They were always receiving heavy coins, and always paying away light ones: the mint was furnished with abundant employment in recoining the same gold, and the clippers had a regular harvest in their business. The precautions in the recoinage of 1774 in a good degree avoided this evil; and the Earl of Liverpool, to whom the nation was indebted for that measure, appears not to have lost sight of the subject, until, in 1805, he addressed his well-known letter to the King, since called 'A Treatise on the Coins of the Realm.' This is very elaborate in its detail of the facts on which he founded his proposed measure. He admits that the change he advocates should not be made upon slight grounds. It was a change from the double standard to one of gold, with an over-valuation of silver in the coinage, but restricting the amount to be paid in it to forty shillings. Gold coin was to be made a legal tender at the rate of £3 17*s.* 10½*d.* per ounce, and the sovereign, which was to represent the pound, was made to correspond with that rate per ounce. To induce the adoption of this measure, Lord Liverpool drew up his letter, of 236 quarto pages, in which he reviews the whole history of British coinage, and adds an appendix, containing an account of the relative values of gold and silver among the ancient Persians, Greeks, and Romans. This performance is very reliable, as far as the facts and estimates made in it are concerned; but its authority in doctrine has been called in question. He had, however, chiefly in view the adoption of the measure: he did not attempt to produce a general and scientific work upon coinage. He adopts the old notion, that the 'money or coin of a country is the standard measure by which the value of all things bought and sold is regulated and ascertained; and it is in itself, at the same time, the value or equivalent for which goods are exchanged, and in which contracts are generally made payable.' This proposition, so far as money is alleged to be a measure of value, is rejected by M'Culloch, and other noted authorities. The former says: — 'A coin is merely a piece of metal of a known weight and fineness.' — 'It has been said to be both a sign and a measure of value; in truth, it is neither.' — 'It is equally incorrect to call money a measure of value. Gold and silver do not measure the value of commodities more than the latter measures the value of gold and silver. When one commodity is exchanged for another, each measures the value of the other.' — *Encyclo. Britannica, Art. 'Money.'* But whatever objections have been raised against the Earl of Liverpool's definitions, it is conceded that, since his measure was adopted, no proposition should be entertained of another change.

"The Earl of Liverpool having shown that silver was the real or practical standard down to the beginning of the 18th century, alleges that it gradually ceased to be such, and that gold, during that century, became the actual standard. In his language, 'Gold coins are now become, in the opinion and practice of the people, the principal measure of property.'[1] 'And it may therefore be inferred that, in the opinion of the dealers in these precious metals (who must be considered the best judges on a subject of this nature), the gold coin has, in this respect, become the principal measure of property, and, consequently, the instrument of commerce.' He subjoins, 'that the foreign nations who have any intercourse with us, and even those who deal in the precious metals of which our coins are made, concur in this opinion.' At a subsequent page (170), he states this position, and illustrates it at large. 'The gold coins have, in fact, become, for almost a century, the mercantile money of the kingdom.'

"In answer to the objection, 'That, by declaring the gold coin to be at present the principal measure of property, an alteration will be made in all bargains, and in the terms of all covenants and contracts which were concluded when the silver coins were understood to be the principal measure of property,' he admits 'This objection might have some weight, if the change had happened of late years only; but it has been already shown that it has existed, and that all payments have been regulated in conformity to it for almost a century. This objection might also have weight, if this change had been brought about by the authority of government. It has been shown that it was brought about, not by the authority of government, but by the course of events, with the acquiescence, and, I may say, the general consent of the people.' (p. 173.) He dwells upon this gradual adoption of the gold standard by the people, and argues, from a great variety of facts and considerations, that his proposition involved no actual change in

[1] "Treatise on the Coins of the Realm," pp. 139, 145.

the accustomed use of money; that, consequently, contracts could not be affected, the measure being chiefly a legal recognition of existing mercantile usage.

"The Earl of Liverpool, in support of his plan, lays no small stress upon the fact that Great Britain, being the chief commercial mart of the world, it is especially fitting that, while people less rich should retain silver as their standard, a country so important should adopt gold. This idea is repeated, in the course of his work, in a way that shows it was a favorite notion. The glory of a gold medium, however, was fraught with mischief which Great Britain, with all her wealth, could neither wholly prevent nor repel. By the adoption of his plan, the Bank of England was compelled to redeem its notes in gold — a commodity subject to exceeding irregularity of demand, and consequent fluctuation in value. Every war and every commercial crisis on the continent of Europe brought a demand for gold on that bank. Gold being so much more readily transported than silver, every unfavorable balance of trade among neighboring countries might bring a circuitous demand upon an institution which was the only one in Europe compelled to pay in gold at a fixed price. Every unfavorable harvest, and consequent large importation of wheat, entailed a corresponding demand for gold, which could be carried off with facility, when silver might not have been touched. In all such matters of payment, the party receiving makes choice of that which suits him best; and certainly no greater facility can be afforded to a foreign creditor than to pay him in gold, at a fixed rate, from which it cannot rise, however brisk the demand. Thus was the Bank of England made the great depository of gold, to which it flowed from all quarters when not wanted, and from which it was taken to any quarter of the world where there might be any special demand or occasion for it. There could have been no objection to this ebbing and flowing, if the bank had been merely a dealer in gold bullion, buying at a low rate when it was not in demand, and selling at a profit when there was a demand. The bank had no privilege but that of purchasing all that came at £3 17*s.* 9*d.*, and paying to all that demanded at the rate of £3 17*s.* 10½*d. per ounce;* but being the issuer of the principal paper currency of Great Britain, they were bound to redeem (after the resumption of specie payments in 1822) at that price. It was a hazardous experiment to make the Bank of England the only place at which gold could always be had at a fixed price, and to make gold the basis of the English bank-note currency; so that every regular and irregular demand for gold at once affected the condition of the British paper currency, and through it the whole industry and trade of the country, although neither may have had anything to do with the demand for gold. Those who are familiar with the history of that bank, which has, perhaps, been more wisely managed than any similar institution, can readily recall instances when the bank, to save their gold, were obliged to restrict their issues, until distress, injury, and ruin befell thousands upon thousands of people who had no share in the cause of the mischief. For every million of gold that the bank could thus retain in their coffers, they would be compelled to withdraw very many millions of currency from the ordinary channels of business. If this evil is inseparable from a paper currency, it was surely unwise to aggravate it by subjecting the Bank of England to the payment of notes and deposits in that metal which is most easily carried off, and most liable to variable and extraordinary demands; and, moreover, to redeem notes at a fixed rate in an article notoriously fluctuating in its value all over the world. If the bank has been able to struggle through all the commercial storms which have swept over the world since 1822, it is well known at what repeated and immense sacrifices to the nation; and that, upon a recent occasion, to resort to the Bank of France for aid became a matter of necessity. A very large portion of the evils of this struggle would have been saved, if the bank had been allowed the privilege of paying in silver; and still more, if permitted to pay in gold at a market instead of a mint price.

System of coinage in the United States — Double standard — Proposed adoption of single standard of gold, as a remedy for scarcity of silver — Reduction in the value of our silver coins.

"We have already adverted to our adoption of the dollar for a unit of computation and money of account, as a measure justified by the necessity of reconciling the currencies of the different States, and also by the fact of its being already familiar to the minds of the people. In fact, although different moneys of account prevailed in different groups of the States, they were all about equally familiar with the Spanish coin of a dollar, and its parts; and these were the only coins with which they were familiar. They had long estimated in pounds, shillings and pence, and, when they employed them at all, paid in foreign coins. There was, therefore, a very good preparation in the employment of these coins for more than a century by the colonists, for the adoption of the dollar as the money unit. This was done under the confederation, although no mint was established, by act of Congress, until April, 1792. By this statute it was enacted:— 'That the money of account of the United States shall be expressed in dollars or units, dimes or tenths, cents or hundredths, and mills or thousandths.'[1] That the 'dollars or units each be of the value of a Spanish milled dollar, as the same is now current, and to contain $371\frac{4}{16}$ grains of pure, or 416 grains of standard silver.'[2] By the same law the eagle, then first provided for, was to be 'of the value of ten dollars or units, and to contain $247\frac{4}{8}$ grains of pure, and 270 grains of standard gold.' It is now nearly sixty years since the passage of this act, and the dollar coin then ordered and provided for still contains the same quantity of pure silver — $371\frac{1}{4}$ grains — and so far its value remains unchanged. By degrees it has

[1] Section 20. [2] Section 9.

expelled the old moneys of account; it being rather rare, at this day, to hear of pounds, shillings and pence, except in the State of New York, in which the Spanish eighth of a dollar corresponds to the shilling, and the hundredth to the penny. The fact of the people there adhering to the terms shilling and penny, against the usages of the rest of the country, shows with what pertinacity men cling to their money of account. The only alteration which has taken place in our established dollar coin was by the act of Congress of 1834, which directed that 3½ grains of the alloy be withdrawn, reducing its weight from 416 to 412½ grains. The coins of both metals were, by the act of 1792, to be a legal tender; the dollars at 'their current value, and gold at the rate of 24¾ grains for a dollar.' As it almost invariably happens, where the double standard prevails, one of the metals was over-valued, or one was under-valued, as compared with the current market value in commerce. In our case the gold was under-valued, for it never circulated concurrently with silver until after the act of 1834, which raised the mint price of gold over 6½ per cent, by rating $23\frac{22}{100}$ grains of gold at the value of a dollar, instead of 24¾ grains, as fixed by the act of 1792. Even after this increase of 6½ per cent. in the mint price of gold, it failed to become a currency in this country until it began to flow in so rapidly from California, that an actual depreciation of several per cent. took place. The consequence was, that the silver in our banks began to be rapidly shipped off to Europe — a drain which did not cease so long as silver could be obtained. It is, in truth, impossible to adjust the relative value of gold and silver by any legal enactments, in such manner as to overcome the influence of the market rates of those metals. It has long been deemed absurd to fix the prices of other commodities by law; perhaps the time is not distant when it will be regarded as absurd to fix an unchangeable price upon an ounce of gold, as upon a bushel of wheat, or a day's labor.

"The history of commerce certainly discloses that the changes in the value of gold have been remarkable and frequent in all periods of which we have authentic records, and not less so in the last half century. We have already mentioned that, between 1802 and 1810, gold rose to 20 per cent. above the mint price; but we add, to show the superior steadiness of silver, that the variation in price of Spanish dollars at the Bank of England was less than 2 per cent., and in that period the bank purchased to the extent of seventy millions of ounces.

"It has been proposed, for the purpose of remedying the scarcity of silver, which the recent depreciation of gold has withdrawn from circulation, to reduce the weight of standard silver in our dollar from 412½ grains to 384 grains; that is, to take from it $25\frac{65}{100}$ grains of pure silver, thus reducing its intrinsic value 6.91 per cent. It is said this debasement is only to be applied to the fractions of a dollar. It may be that no evil would ensue from such a change, especially if confined to quarters, dimes, and half dimes, and if they were not made a legal tender beyond five, or, at most, ten dollars. The use of these small coins could scarcely impair the dollar unit. But the measure does not appear by any means commensurate with the evil. It would still be found that silver was scarce; and if these debased coins were increased in quantity beyond the mere demand for change, they would depreciate to their bullion value, and become a nuisance.

"It appears more natural, as well as advantageous, to look for the remedy on the side whence the grievance comes. The scarcity of silver has arisen from the depreciation of gold; and that by reason of its abundance, more than from any special demand for silver, or any increase in the value. Instead, therefore, of disturbing our silver coinage, so intimately connected with our money of account, would it not be safer to confine any measure intended to meet the present difficulty to gold, the fall in value of which has occasioned the exportation of our silver? If the matter had been understood in time, a very simple measure would have prevented the shipment of silver. Gold had depreciated, but the legal price remained; and the silver was rapidly carried off before the banks were supplied with gold, and before they were fully aware of the depreciation.

"If, at the moment the silver began to disappear, Congress had intervened, and repealed so much of the act of 1834 as made gold a legal tender at the rate of $23\frac{22}{100}$ grains to the dollar, gold, which was flowing upon us from the Pacific, would have instantly sunk to its market value, and have become the preferable remittance, more especially as Great Britain adheres to a fixed price for gold.

"A fixed relation between gold and silver, an established legal price for both on the assumption that they will not change in their relation to each other, and that the value of each must remain unchanged, is a policy so mistaken, that it should not stand long on any statute-book; but, least of all, should it be upheld in the face of facts which clearly exhibit that one of the precious metals has actually changed its value materially, and must soon, by the inevitable laws of trade, undergo a more important change. It requires no very strong effort of thought to perceive that a people who attempt to uphold the price of a metal which has permanently fallen in value, will be abundantly supplied with the article they continue to overvalue. This very fact destroys what is called the double standard, and substitutes the depreciated single one. If this were the whole mischief, it would be small; but the mass of the people continue to reckon and estimate in the long established money of account, whilst payments, until the proper remedy is applied, continue to be made in the depreciated coin. The double standard may exist for a long time without inflicting any special injury beyond the confusion of ideas which it creates; but when the fluctuation of either metal commences, injustice is flagrant on every side. It is as if the parties in trade were provided with one measure to make their purchases, and another of different capacity by which to make their sales; and this not according to a uniform practice, but according to every man's knowledge, cunning, capacity, and the grade of his morals. The double standard becomes, upon an occasion like the present, when not an intelligent doubt can be entertained of an early depreciation of gold, a positive and impending evil of a magnitude not easily estimated, but which can scarcely be over-rated. As little time as possible should be lost in removing it, because in commerce, as well as in other occupations of life, 'coming events cast their shadows before;' and because, while the shrewd and well-informed will 'stand from under,' and avoid the mischief, the unwary and uninformed will be made to suffer and become the prey of those who can, under cover of law, make a business of fraud.

"The double standard, absurd at all times, and specially objectionable in the anticipation of a considerable decline in the price of gold, is, however, immeasurably less objectionable than the adoption of a single standard of gold in our present circumstances, even when we leave out of view the money of account, and the infinity of commercial considerations connected with it, and regard the change to be made merely in the light of a standard. If it be, as most of the approved writers on money suppose, that prices are strict comparisons with coins — that sales are only made with reference to coins — what must be pronounced of the policy which rejects the metal which is unmoved, and takes that for a standard which is in the very act of going down? With what degree of accuracy can the masses of people in the United States keep pace with the decline which may take place in gold? This decline may, at times, proceed by slow and imperceptible degrees, and at times, according to the accidents or movements of trade, by jerks. In either case, but a very small number of men will be able to appreciate its downward progress. The public will only register it by their losses; and their eyes will only open when it is too late. It is more than probable that the dealers in bullion in London would first perceive and take advantage of every step in this depreciation.

"It would be a misfortune of no small moment if, in place of the double standard, our past system had been the single gold standard, as it is in Great Britain. We should now be trembling with apprehension of the decline of gold, and all the innumerable and injurious results which such a decline in the value of a standard metal imposes. That these apprehensions are now felt in an eminent degree in England, is abundantly plain to all who are observant of financial and pecuniary affairs in that country. Many there know that danger is imminent, and rejoice that the demand for gold on the continent postponed the expected mischief. But the gold is now returning, and the Bank of England is now stocked with it beyond all precedent. This influx upon that bank must continue, unless partially interfered with by wars, or anticipations of wars, on the continent. So long as the bank continues to give, as compelled by law, £3 17*s.* 9*d.* for gold, it will, under the depreciating process, flow there from all quarters of the world, until the government repeals this awkward obligation.

"As this subject is viewed by many of the ablest men in England, it seems surrounded with insuperable difficulties, and impenetrable darkness. And yet, if the doctrine and functions of a money of account were thoroughly studied, the remedy for the whole anticipated evil would be far more simple and easy of accomplishment than many duties the government has to perform. Let the bank be released from the obligation to take gold, and let the mint price be repealed, that gold may take its value in the market with silver. The English money of account will safely and effectually register all prices and values, preserve unchanged all contracts, salaries and annuities, and permit the vast concerns of the British Treasury and British industry and trade to proceed undisturbed in their accustomed channels. It would be necessary to connect this measure, at no distant day, with another for the special protection of the money of account. The responsibility of vigilance, in regard to the money of account, might be placed upon the Chancellor of the Exchequer; constant observation of the value of silver bullion, and proper restraints upon the quantity of bank paper circulation, would keep the money of account unchanged. Experience would show whether this system might not be continued indefinitely, and it would at least afford time to devise other appropriate remedies for the evil. If the money of account could maintain itself unchanged, with an almost exclusive paper circulation, during the first twelve years of the suspension of payments by the bank in 1797, surely the same, and even a much better result, could be obtained by a well-devised measure now, when the bank is able to pay every demand in gold. At all events, those who can repose no confidence in such an arrangement, might feel very safe if their bank paper was kept at par with silver bullion until time had pointed out some better plan. This would not be changing, as some may think, from the gold to the silver standard; it would be simply dispensing with any standard, except the mint standard for coinage. And this, as we contend, is what the mental habits of trading people lead them to do, be the law of the money standard, or standard of payment, what it may.

"It is difficult to conceive how any one could have thought of dispensing with our silver standard, and adopting the single gold standard in the United States, at this moment of expected depreciation of that metal, unless the suggestion came from England. That they may want companions in their trouble is not at all improbable; but that we should volunteer that sacrifice is past comprehension. If England continues, in spite of common sense and commercial prudence, to pay the same price for gold after it begins to depreciate, she will receive it as long as she has anything to give for it, until she is bursting with gold at every pore; and when the plethora can be endured no longer, and the hour of depletion arrives, then a heavy loss will accrue, and ruin will overtake multitudes through its effects upon the Bank of England.

"If the United States should adopt the single gold standard with our present legal or mint price, a portion of that loss would be thrown upon us. It is true, the laws of trade very often obviate, for a time, the natural consequences of unwise legislation, or the most absurd commercial blunders. At the present moment we are under such heavy indebtedness to England for goods imported in excess of the value of our exports, that we have all the advantage of the game in gold. We are paying in a depreciating metal; but our merchants who are trading with California are receiving payment in the same falling commodity, If we adopt the gold standard now, we might not suffer immediate injury, owing to our indebtedness; but we should enter upon a game of agiotage and profit and loss with the Bank of England and the great merchants of London, in which, according to our past experience, we should come out heavy losers. The retention of our double standard, with a fixed price of gold, may involve many and serious mischiefs in our domestic trade, but cannot affect us injuriously in our foreign trade so long as we are indebted abroad, and our banks retain the privilege of paying in gold. In case, however, of a favorable balance with any country in the world, our remittances would all come in the depreciated metal. The further this subject is pursued, the more clearly will it be seen to be the undoubted policy of both England and the United States to repeal the fixed price of gold, and make it a tender only at the market price. This is a favorable time to make the change here, because the market price will not only be maintained during the present adverse exchange with England, but if that exchange continues as now, it would inevitably go above our mint price: that is, while, by the natural course of events, gold would be depreciated from its over-supply, by the state of our indebtedness to England, and the great demand for funds to remit, it might rapidly go to a high premium. It is impossible to say what would have been the price of exchange on England during the past year, if the parties remitting had not been permitted to take gold and silver from the banks at par. Now, if the banks were permitted to pay in gold at the market price, or the same price at which, from time to time, it might be declared to be receivable at the sub-treasuries of the United States, we should be receiving a premium on gold at the moment when it might be intrinsically under par."

CHAPTER V.

§ 1. *The actual use made of coins measures their importance and power — Modes of payment of greater efficiency adopted — Each to be judged upon its own merits — Usages of trade assign to coins their office — Not a model currency — They carry no higher interest than a credit in bank — The British act of* 1844, *requiring the issues of the bank to fluctuate as gold — Sir Robert Peel — Lord Overtom — Col. Torrens — The question one of commerce and payment — Return to hard currency impossible.*

In some respects, the extravagant estimate placed upon gold and silver, in their functions of money, is not too great. As such, they are an universal equivalent. Every article which is for sale can be purchased for gold or silver. This is not true, to the same extent, of any other commodity. They have maintained their place, as the best materials for money and coinage, for thousands of years. It is not wonderful, therefore, that they should be prized as the chief items and emblems of wealth. Their actual employment, to a large extent, in those small dealings which are immediately connected with daily living, and in all the details of food, lodging and raiment, brings their importance and utility home to all who purchase such necessaries at pleasure, as well as to those who, from poverty, do not enjoy that advantage. This, together with the fact that so many make no distinction between money and money of account, creates the impression that, somehow or other, all purchases and payments are indebted for their validity to gold or silver money; that, when not employed in any transaction, they are in some way involved and referred to, is the firm belief of multitudes. This impression can only be wiped off by a full comprehension of the office and functions of a money of account. When this is attained, and when he who examines this subject can fully discriminate between the use of money of account, by which prices are expressed, and the use of coins, by which payments are made, it is not difficult to estimate the real importance of the precious metals employed as a medium of exchange. We are disposed to think that no safer or closer approximation can be made to their importance or value as a currency, than that which is denoted by the actual extent to which they are employed. We do not mean to say that the manner of their use is best, nor whether they may not with advantage be more or less employed; but we mean that the real extent to which they are employed is the truest criterion of their importance and power as a currency. We have seen that more coins are manufactured than are required, and that the chief mints of the world have long been mainly employed in working up the products of other mints. Of course no exact estimate of the amount of coins actually required for the business of a country can be made; but the amount must be exceeded, when large quantities of coin are exported, to be recoined at foreign mints.

We have said that the power and importance of gold and silver, as a medium of exchange, are best measured by their actual employment and agency. We may go further, and say that, in all those transactions of trade, foreign and domestic, in which the precious metals are not employed, they not only exercise no agency whatever, but they are not needed. When we are considering the uses to which the precious metals are put as money, or a medium of exchange, whether coined or uncoined, we should confine our views to their proper range of use. And when we are considering that vastly larger proportion of the payments of trade which are made without any agency, direct or indirect, of gold or silver, we should study the very processes by which these payments are effected. They are as valid, complete and legitimate as are the transactions carried on by means of coins; and, therefore, of so much the greater interest, because that portion of commerce which is effected without the agency of the precious metals, saves the great expense of employing them — an economy which cannot be rated at less than ten times the whole quantity of the precious metals now in use. So far as the exports of a country are made by bills of exchange, and other means, to pay for its imports, so far the payments are as well and effectually made as the small balance either way, which is discharged in gold and silver.

Whatever be the utility and importance of the precious metals as a medium of exchange or an equivalent, their utter insufficiency to accomplish the payments of the present day shows that, though they may never be wholly dispensed with in commerce, their efficacy as means of payment has been so far transcended by other modes, devices and contrivances, that nothing can be more fallacious than to regard them as a model. Wagons, carts and wheelbarrows were once the best vehicles of transportation; and in some places, and for certain uses, they are yet the best; but it would be signally absurd to insist that locomotives should be carefully regulated in their construction, speed and use on the model of wagons and carts of the olden time, or of those which are still in use.

Upon this subject our attention should not, then, be mainly directed to silver and gold, merely because they were the earliest medium of exchange, or the one most highly prized as such, but rather to the object to be effected. We are not bound to employ so expensive a medium, if we can avoid it. In all stages of commerce, we find there has been a constant effort to dispense entirely with the use of the precious metals. The great object of commerce being not merely to obtain and circulate gold and silver, but to effect an exchange of commodities and labor, the interchange which is effected without any medium of intrinsic value must certainly be much more economical than that in which the precious metals must be employed. When the payments of foreign commerce between two nations are effected through mutual bills of exchange, by which the commodities exchanged pay for each other, the dealings between them are as effectual as if carried on at every step by payments in gold or silver. When neighboring tradesmen or merchants deal with each other, it matters not to what amount, debiting in their respective books of account the price of what they sell to each other, their payments are made by simply comparing and balancing accounts. These modes of payment are undoubtedly as effectual, and far more economical and rapid, than if the parties had paid the coin in every transaction. Dealings like these do not require to be governed by rules or considerations which pertain to the circulation of coins. The precious metals, in the shape of coins, are only one of many means of effecting an interchange of commodities; and being far from the most efficient, the mode of their operation should not be the rule when they are not employed. As well might the transportation of goods by camels and carts be made the rule for railroads.

The prices of commerce are all expressed in money of account; bills of sale are all rendered in money of account; bills of exchange, and promissory notes, are for sums expressed in money of account; books are so kept; and all payments, however made, are but the discharge of debts ascertained and expressed in money of account. In all this coins have nothing to do, unless they are used in final payment, which is very rarely the case. Gold and silver being, then, but one of many agencies of commerce, however necessary and desirable in their place, however appropriate that the many questions relating to their use be wisely and skilfully determined, there is no propriety in their being regarded as models or guides to determine questions arising in other modes of payment.

As nearly all the large dealings of commerce are now carried on, and the payments made, without the use of any medium of exchange, or any one without intrinsic value, there is neither reason nor logic in appealing to the doctrine of gold and silver money for instruction or guidance in these large operations. The necessities of commerce have revealed cheaper and more rapid modes of payments. Men have availed themselves of various agencies, explained hereafter, to set off the debts of the people in one country against the debts of the people in the other. If individuals in England owe to individuals in the United States the sum of five millions, and if individuals in the latter owe to individuals in the former five millions, the whole can be settled by bills of exchange, without the slightest obligations to or any use of the precious metals. The merchandise of one country is, by this process, made to pay for the merchandise of the other.

No medium of intrinsic value need intervene. The parties dealing simply ascertain, and keep some evidence of their respective dues, until the account between them can be balanced or set off against each other. In such transactions, there being no need of gold or silver, it would be hard to divine why the shadow should intervene where the substance is not required. We cannot see why, if gold and silver cannot be made to effect the payments of commerce, they should be the basis of rules and regulations for payments in which they have no part.

The progress of business, the usages of commerce, and the requirements of industry, have in fact assigned to the precious metals their true place and office. If we examine the position thus assigned, we find them employed as the small change of the retail trade, as the means of paying balances, and as banking securities. The current payments of business, out of the merest retail trade, are very seldom made in coins or bullion. It is a fact well known in this country, that where notes are issued in sums small enough for the purposes of the retail trade, they invariably supersede the use of coins, even in the retail business. It requires very stringent laws in Pennsylvania to keep out of her circulation the one dollar notes of the surrounding States; and even with the aid of these they are but partially kept away: such is the indifference to coins, in a country where each individual has a legal right to demand payment of every debt due to him in gold or silver. The precious metals, therefore, find no actual preference even in the small payments of the retail trade. Experience has shown the same results, even where the paper thus preferred was inconvertible.

In Great Britain, and in the United States, long periods of time have elapsed, in which payments were almost exclusively made in inconvertible paper currency, or in other devices of the credit system. This was the case in Great Britain in the memorable period between 1797 and 1822; a period of continental war, but of great commercial and industrial prosperity; a period in which the public revenue and productive industry reached a higher point than had ever been attained before. But even since the resumption of specie payments in Great Britain, and in the United States, the payments of commerce are, to a very small extent, made in coins or bullion, though every creditor can legally insist upon such payment. Commerce, then, can be carried on without resort to the precious metals, in case of national emergency; their agency is comparatively small and special, when such emergencies do not exist. In the city and State of New York, nearly the entire domestic circulation down to a dollar is of paper; and so it is throughout the New England States. A very large proportion of their current payments is made in notes under five dollars; and the amount of coins required is only in change for sums under one dollar. They prefer this system, and adhere to it. The Scots are so extremely tenacious of their one pound notes, that they have strenuously resisted repeated efforts of the British Parliament to prohibit the issue of such notes in Scotland.[1] And highly as the English authorities now pride themselves upon the fact of permitting the issue of no bank-notes under five pounds, it is a fact well known, that upon one occasion the Bank of England was saved from suspension, on the occasion of a run upon its specie, by offering to the public one pound notes, a box of which happily remained in the bank, the remnant of former issues. We adduce such facts as these, and many such might be indicated, to show the comparative importance of the precious metals as a means of payment. It is impossible to estimate the exact agency, or comparative efficiency, of any of the various modes of effecting payments. We can only determine their respective usefulness by observing their operation side by side. We cannot but see that, whatever advantages the precious metals have in their intrinsic value, in their superior fitness for coinage, in their being the only legal medium of discharging a debt, in every creditor's having the right to demand them in payment, yet, after all, they are employed to but a very limited extent, and are always displaced by paper whenever it is offered, both for large and in small transactions.

[1] One of these efforts called forth a witty and energetic protestation by Walter Scott, in several long letters under the signature of *Malachi Malagrowther*.

We repeat, then, that there is neither propriety, nor necessity, nor logic, in looking to the doctrine of the precious metals and coinage for rules or regulations in regard to processes of payment, and devices of the credit system, which are wholly independent of the precious metals in their theory, and in their operation. Because gold and silver, one or both, are the safest and best medium for payment of balances, for bank securities, and for legal tender in cases where parties cannot agree, it does not follow that the doctrine and usages which govern payments in the precious metals should be the rule in payments by the credit system.

We may adduce, as further proof that the precious metals occupy no specially important rank in the great business of paying debts, that when the demand for means to pay debts is so urgent that the rate of interest rises from the half of one to one, two or three per cent. per month, the demand in such cases is never for specie or coins, but merely for such funds as are usually employed in payments. Coins or bullion do not fluctuate in value, with the rate of interest; when interest rises one, two or three hundred per cent., coins may not increase in value one per cent. A great demand for the means of paying debts does not imply any increased demand for coins or bullion. When the pressure for money is greatest, and interest at the highest rate, gold or silver coins command no higher interest than a credit in bank. A credit on the books of the Bank of Venice, which was not convertible into specie, but only transferable in payment of debts, always stood at a high premium over current coins. It is evident, then, that the partiality entertained for the precious metals is not strong enough to increase the price or the demand, in times of pressure or scarcity, any more than when money is plenty, and interest low. What is needed, at such times, is not gold nor silver, for upon such occasions they are specially inconvenient, but simply funds which will pay debts, whether bank-notes or bank credits. The most urgent necessity to which the man of business is subject, is that of paying his debts with perfect punctuality; his credit depends upon this. Yet, in his most pressing wants for money, it never occurs to him that coins are any more desirable than anything else that will acquit him of his obligations.

It would seem idle to maintain this point further, by argument or illustration, if men of high position and acute minds had not even recently yielded to the fallacy, that substitutes for money should be regulated so as to operate like a currency wholly of gold or silver. Upon this idea, chiefly, was Sir Robert Peel's bill of 1844, to modify the Bank of England, founded. The bank was allowed, by this bill, to issue notes, to a certain specified amount, on the security of the debt due by the government to the bank. Beyond that sum no further issues were to be made but upon gold actually in the bank; the avowed object being to make the notes fluctuate precisely as a gold currency would fluctuate. The error involved in this measure, and the deceptive reasoning upon which it was based, was strongly urged at the time: experience has equally condemned it since; and it only stands a monument of the difficulty a government finds in retracing a false step.

It will be some gain if the public learn from experiment, that the only connexion which the gold in the Bank of England has with its current operations is as a security to the holder of its notes, and to its depositors. The immense amount of payments effected by the customers of the bank, through its agency, are in no way dependent on the gold in its vaults for their efficacy. The government may limit the business of the bank by reference to the quantity of gold on hand, if the public interest demands it; but it should not propound, as a reason for such limitation, that the movements in the deposits and notes of a bank should correspond with the fluctuations of a currency wholly metallic. This is running the cart against the locomotive, the "ship of the desert" against the steamer of the ocean. A greater amount of payments are made, in the Bank of England, for the benefit of its customers in one week, without touching a penny of its coin, than could be effected by that coin, in its regular movements, in a whole year. The bank, whatever its demerits, or whatever reforms it may need, as an instrument for accomplishing the payments of commerce, is just as much more effective than the coin in its vaults, as a locomotive with its freight train is superior to a man with a wheelbarrow. When it becomes expedient for a steamer at sea to tack and take the same zig-zag course which a sailing vessel is compelled to take, then it may be wise to regulate the movements of the credit system by those of coins and bullion.

The influence of a great and honest statesman was sufficient to carry, against much opposition, a measure destined to be called the greatest mistake of his useful life. We shall not enter into the subject at large here: the whole substance of the positions taken in this volume are opposed to the principles propounded as grounds for the act of 1844.[1]

The advocate of the act of 1844 regards the whole subject of money and credit from a wrong point of view. The real subject is commerce, and the real question is, how the payments of

---

[1] We cannot easily persuade ourselves that this act is really a product of Sir Robert Peel's mind. We rather incline to give the credit to Col. Torrens, who has defended it with ability, and evidently regarded it with the kind of favor which a man bestows upon his own progeny. Col. Torrens speaks thus, in a pamphlet published in 1848: — "These provisions of the act of 1844 were framed in conformity with the following principles," &c. Again: "Such being the principles upon which the act was founded, it became incumbent on *those who were* concerned in framing it," &c. Further: "Upon these grounds the *framers of the act* assumed," &c. It will be observed he does not ascribe the act, or its principles, to Sir Robert Peel; he fully approved the measure, and assumed to know the principles and views of the framers, without any intimation that they were those of the distinguished statesman to whom they are usually ascribed. From such modes of expression, when taken in connexion with the fact, that the act is almost universally ascribed to Peel, we can only draw the inference that Col. Torrens was either the framer, or one of the framers of that act. It may be, after all, that Lord Overstone is entitled to be regarded as the chief adviser of Sir Robert Peel, in reference to this measure. We confess that we should look upon this as extremely improbable if there were no evidence to that effect. Surely, his great practical knowledge, and well-known discrimination, should have protected him from so serious an error, however congenial it may be to a mind like that of Col. Torrens. Whoever may be the real author of this false legislation, we trust he may live to see that even great names cannot perpetuate great mistakes.

commerce can be most effectively and economically accomplished? This question, without reference to its connexion with the Bank of England, had long and constantly been the subject of study upon the part of men of business and of finance. They had, long before the bank was in existence, determined that the precious metals were to be wholly dispensed with in payments, when the payments could be as well effected without them. In this they had succeeded to such an extent, even before the days of banks of circulation, that by far the largest share of the payments were made without any aid from coins.[1] The establishment of the Bank of England did not change the nature of the question, which was still how to economize the use of coins in the payments of trade. This bank, whatever the faults of its constitution, became one of the most efficient agents of commerce ever established; only second, perhaps, to the Bank of Venice: and to the praise of English commercial integrity be it said, that no banking institution was ever, for such a length of time, more honestly and wisely managed. Its proper government has involved more real difficulties than any other bank ever encountered, and it has triumphed over all. Its chief object and business has been to effect payments without the use of coins. It has enabled its customers to make their payments, to the amount of many millions sterling weekly, without the use of either coins or bullion. As a security for these customers, and a convenience, the bank agreed to pay all its own debts upon demand in coin; but this it did upon the presumption that the wants for coin would not exceed its ability to pay, as in ordinary times they do not. Unless some extraordinary emergency occurred to create a special demand for specie, the business of the bank was not conducted with any reference to coins; and proceeded as well, and in the same way, with five millions in coins in the bank, as with fifteen millions. The current payments at the bank, among men of business, are not in the slightest degree facilitated by the coins in its vaults. When, from any unusual circumstance, such a demand

---

[1] See Chapter on "Fairs," infra.

upon the bank for coins occurs as makes it necessary to curtail its accommodations, and thus diminish the amount of its debts payable on demand; this, though it may prove a very great injury and inconvenience to the customers of the bank, cannot alter the nature of their business, nor lessen their need of the usual facilities: the curtailment of which, by the bank, is a measure of defence as between the bank and the public, by which the customers of the bank of course suffer. They still demand the same accommodation from the bank — their business still requires it: the flow of coin from the bank is of no consequence to them, if they can keep up the amount of their deposits for current payments. An extraordinary demand for coins would be of no more importance to them than an unusual demand for coffee or cotton, unless it had the effect of diminishing their accommodations at bank. They would not admit, for a moment, the doctrine that their economical and efficient mode of adjusting mutual demands — the paying their debts by the use of their credits — should depend upon short crops at home, or any special demand for specie abroad, either for rebellion in China, wars in the East Indies, or commercial revulsions anywhere.

They would regard "the natural law of equilibrium, by which the precious metals are distributed throughout the countries of the world,"[1] as an intangible phantom. For men of commerce know that the amount of coined money employed by a people depends mainly upon their mutual confidence, and the extent to which they employ the most approved devices of the credit system. A high state of commercial integrity will dispense with a large proportion of the coin which might be required without it. The merchants of a country in which commercial honor is of a high grade, and in which mutual credit and confidence correspond, would be very slow to admit that their modes of payment — that of applying credits to the payment of debts — should fluctuate in amount, just as the circulation of coins may happen to vary. They would regard as purely visionary the

---

[1] Col. Torrens.

idea of any ebb and flow of gold, regular or irregular, by which their business was to be limited or regulated. It is the accidental circumstance, that the bank pays its debts in gold, which makes it necessary for them to watch the demand for gold, and guard against the contractions of the bank. They do not regulate their business by the movement of gold, but protect themselves against the effects of some of its movements, as they would against any other unfavorable incident.

If the question were merely as to the mode of securing the convertibility of bank-notes, we should, at this stage of our inquiry, have no remarks to make upon the act of 1844; but when the avowed object is to produce a fluctuation in the quantity or amount of bank-notes, similar to what would take place if the coin or bullion were employed in place of the notes, we see that the whole proceeding is founded on a misconception of the separate functions of money, and of the credit system. We have already stated that the chief use of money is in the small operations of the retail trade, in the final distribution of the products of industry, and, with the further aid of bullion, in the payment of balances in the foreign trade of nations, or balances between different districts of the same country. More than ninety-five per cent. of the larger operations, or debts of commerce, are settled and adjusted without resort to the precious metals, which are only used where the modes of the credit system do not apply. If France exports to the amount of a hundred millions to England, and the latter to the amount of ninety-five millions to France, the indebtedness between them, to the amount of ninety-five millions on each part, is adjusted by bills of exchange, and other devices of credit. The precious metals are called in to pay the balance of five millions. There is, indeed, no resemblance between this use of the precious metals and the processes of credit by which this vast indebtedness of one hundred and ninety-five millions would be fully paid and settled. On the contrary, the five millions' worth of gold and silver employed to cover this remaining debt would be merely another commodity exported to bring the transactions between the nations to a balance.

Every medium of exchange, every commercial equivalent, and every mode of payment, is strictly subordinate to the great purposes of commerce. Each must be regarded separately, in reference to its mode of subserving the ends of commerce, its special adaptation, and the means of increasing its efficiency. There is no more reason in mingling book-keeping and coinage, than in mixing together ships and warehouses: all these things are mere agencies of commerce. Each has a special purpose to subserve, and its use should be studied with reference to that purpose. Now, the mode in which coins and bullion are employed, and the extent to which they are used in the current payments of commerce, foreign and domestic, is easily traced and known: in considering their uses, powers and efficiency, we should not lose sight of the facts which thus belong to their use and history. As but a small proportion of the great payments of trade are made in the precious metals, we must constantly distinguish between what is done with, and what is done without them, and regard these distinct methods with equal attention. These modes are so totally different, that a knowledge of the use of coins or bullion is very far from making an adept in the processes of the credit system. The latter are not derived from the former, and must be examined and studied upon different facts, and circumstances as different. When coins or bullion are employed, they are used as an equivalent for the merchandise or articles for which they are given; that is, one article of value is given for another, and the transaction is ended. But the payments of the credit system are effected by devices complicated with various securities, such as bills of exchange, promissory notes, books of account, bank-checks, and many other agencies. By this credit system, the goods sold pay for the goods purchased—all that intervenes being the paper securities which all the buyers and sellers hold as evidence of their claims and transactions. The only link between the money system and the credit system is the money of account, which is a universal accompaniment of the money system, but indispensable to the use of the securities and other devices of the credit system.

The credit system is an incalculable saving in the commerce of the world, because it dispenses with the necessity of employing immense sums in the precious metals. But it does not affect to dispense with them altogether; it leaves all balances to be paid in money. It makes large demands upon the precious metals, to be held as securities for contingent or future payments. The credit system is one thing — the money system is another. Both are agencies of commerce; they operate differently, and must be studied according to their respective modes of operation.

The narrow channel of usefulness in which coins can be employed, now well understood, may be enlarged by discoveries and efforts yet to be made; interest will ever be a sufficient incentive to such progress. As matters now stand, it is more in the natural order of things to consider how to dispense with the precious metals advantageously, in effecting the operations of commerce, than how to employ them. Let us suppose the subject presented in these two points of view to two large consumers of each other's products. If the question between them be how they can effect an exchange of their products with the most economy and advantage, they may devise various modes of doing this, without using money, which is the most expensive of all agents. They may, for instance, simply charge each other with the amount of the respective purchases as they occur. The accounts thus kept may be compared and balanced once a month, or once a year, and the amount resulting either way be carried to a new account, or be paid in gold or silver. If the question, however considered between these parties, be strictly how they can best employ money or coins in their dealings, it will be merely whether the cash shall be paid upon each transaction, or only at agreed intervals. They will not arrive at the economy of doing their business without gold or silver, because they will not be looking for it.

The necessity of properly regulating and restraining the issue of bank paper cannot be controverted; the security required, whether gold, or silver, or something else, should be of a nature to inspire and secure confidence. If gold or silver be the security required, so be it. But it does not follow that the paper must fluctuate in amount as the precious metals would do, if they were the sole medium of payment. Gold and silver being themselves commodities of trade, for which there are various specific uses and demands totally apart from their uses as a medium of commerce, the rule which would withhold bank issues, because the precious metals were in demand, must work directly against the interests of commerce. It would be like the conduct of a commander in the field, who should dismiss his auxiliaries in the same proportion he was losing his own regular forces. It may be necessary for the banks at times, under the present systems of payment, to reduce the issues of their paper when specie is in demand; but this is a measure of safety for the banks, and it is only as a measure of safety that it is enforced. The banks can give no reason why they should reduce their circulation, when the precious metals are being exported, but that their safety requires it. If the banks were able to protect their circulation under such circumstances, it would accord with their own and the public interests to enlarge their circulation when money is thus withdrawn. What, in peculiar circumstances, may be prudent or expedient, should not be converted into a law or rule of public economy, or a principle of banking.

The bank of England may contract its issues when gold is exported, or it may not, according to the circumstances of the case. The discretion of its directors, their knowledge of financial operations and the course of trade, must govern their decision. The bank might be compelled, from motives of caution and safety, to restrict its issues, in the face of a demand for gold from some distant part of the world; but a demand for gold on the other side of the globe is in itself no very good reason why British merchants and manufacturers should be denied their usual bank facilities. The bank, in the circumstances, may not be able to afford them; but that arises from the constitution of the bank, and not from any condition of British trade which would make the withholding of the usual facilities proper. The act of 1844 converts the caution of the Bank of England into a law of trade. If the people of France at any time want more gold in their domestic trade, it forms no sound reason why the people of Great Britain should, on that account, make less use of credit in their domestic trade.

It cannot be said there is even any such analogy or connexion between the mode of payment by the use of the precious metals and the various modes and devices of payment employed in the credit system, that one should be a law or rule for the other. When gold is rapidly leaving England, should men of business then cease proportionably to employ their books of account — should bills of exchange, as a means of adjustment, be less resorted to? The contrary of this is, in fact, the sound rule, and the one to which the intelligence of the people, and the necessity of the case, alike lead. When the quantity of coin diminishes, the resort to other devices of payment increases. During the time of the suspension in England, the payments of trade were not restricted, nor diminished, in proportion to the quantity of specie remaining in the country. The people transacted their business, and made their payments, not by reference to the diminishing stock of the precious metals, but according to the laws of mutual trade. Instead of allowing their business to sink with their stock of gold, they gave it a wonderful development, both in volume and value.

The history of commerce shows, as we have had frequent occasion to remark, that various devices of credit and payment are so many plans to avoid the necessity of employing the precious metals. These devices have been numerous and efficient, in proportion to the progress of trade, and measure that progress with considerable accuracy. They have been, in fact, devices of necessity: the precious metals having been made to perform all that was possible, resort was had to other means of payment to carry on that trade, which would not otherwise have had any existence. Considering the partiality which has always existed for gold and silver, they could never have been so largely dispensed with, without very substantial reasons. The plan of returning wholly to the use of gold and silver, at the present day, for all payments, is therefore plainly impossible on other conditions than reducing commerce to the extent to which it is now carried on by means of coins and bullion. It must be noted, that these are not idle; they are now used constantly, to the extent of their capability. The quantity shut up in banks—a small amount, in proportion to the whole—is all that could be added to the mass in circulation. It will be seen, by a little consideration of what is now done in trade by metallic money, and what by credit and substitutes for money, that a return to the metallic medium would necessarily involve a reduction of commerce to less than a thousandth part of its present importance. The various modes of effecting payments without hard money are the result of more than three centuries of effort and experience. It betrays, then, small acquaintance with the history of commerce, to propose an exclusive use of the precious metals in all transactions of trade.

We have already adverted to some of the evils and vexations of a hard-money currency; we might greatly enlarge upon that topic. It is true that many of the mischiefs which inflicted so much injury, caused so much distress, and drew forth such loud complaints, were the result of abuses, as in fact is the case now with the abuses of credit. But there are objections to an exclusive currency of the precious metals, apart from any abuse sufficient to warrant all the efforts of the last three or four centuries to introduce another system of payment.

One of these is the expense of providing a medium of so great intrinsic value. As the cost of the medium to the transactions effected in a year, so is the annual charge. We have now, in the United States, about $250,000,000 in specie, which we retain at a cost of $15,000,000 yearly, besides the charge for coinage. How much this stock of the precious metals would have to be increased, to perform the business of this country, would be estimated very differently. It would require, probably, all the gold and silver now in use as money in the world, to make the current payments of Great Britain and the United States. But the cost of handling, transporting, counting and guarding such immense quantities of treasure is beyond all calculation. The cost of maintaining such a stock of hard money would be a tax which no modern people would endure for a single year. No effort that the people of the United States could be brought to make would double our present stock. It would be the purchase of a dead or unproductive stock of 250,000,000. Who would be the holders of this unproductive article? If the people had desired any great increase, they would have it now; they are exporting gold by the million weekly. The increased quantity does not enter the channels of circulation, because the people do not desire it. They can, at pleasure, change notes for coins, but they do not; they can exact payment of every debt due to them in coins, but they do not. Whoever supposes this indisposition to hold coin in place of notes or credit, can be overcome by legislation or essay writing, is greatly in error. The resort to credit, as a substitute for money, has steadily increased for more than a century. This progress is now more rapid than ever. It is not measured merely by the number of banks and bankers, but by the manner in which business is transacted with them. There is every indication that this progress is yet to be greater than heretofore, and that the time will never again come when a return to a currency of the precious metals will be among the possible things. The depreciation of these metals has been so great since the discovery of America, that one of the difficulties has increased many fold. It is little thought of now, but the time was when travellers carried coin for their expenses, and families kept it in their houses for the same purpose, that the terror endured from fears of robbery was fully justified by the danger in which every family lived, and every traveller moved. Piracy and robbery, with accompanying murders, for the sake of hard money, were prevalent throughout Europe, and upon all seas.

Now that the custody of large sums of the precious metals is almost exclusively committed to banks and bankers, the danger and the risk of keeping and transporting large sums in the hands of individuals is forgotten, or not appreciated. If such custody were resumed by merchants and capitalists, robbers and pirates would soon resume their vocation. Gold and silver have no ear-marks; there is no valuable possession so easily secreted, and so difficult to follow.

No evil, however, of the days of hard money was more severely felt, none was more fiercely denounced, than the terrible grip of usurers. The power of the money-kings of those times was far beyond any modern experience in that line. Year after year, a storm of indignation burst forth upon the heads of money-lenders; the clergy preached, and wrote, and denounced the extortioners; and nothing kept the Jew from the wrath of the laity, but the strong arm of kings and magistrates, who plundered those who plundered the people; thus transferring the odium to the Jew, whilst the prey came to their pockets.

CHAPTER VI.

BANKS OF DEPOSIT.

§ 1. *Bank of Amsterdam.*

BANKS of deposit, of which that of Amsterdam was the first, seem to occupy an intermediate position between payment in coins or bullion, and payment by the methods of the credit system. The difficulties encountered in the use of coins became so great, as to be deemed very serious grievances. There was continual hazard in keeping and transporting coin, on account of robbers, pirates, dishonest agents, counterfeiting, and the numerous ways of abstracting from coins a portion of their value by plugging, gutting and sweating, besides the gradual wear, which made it impossible for many to protect themselves from loss and risk. These, and similar vexations attending the exclusive use of coins in payment, were so much felt as to produce great and wide-spread complaint throughout all Europe, during the sixteenth, seventeenth and eighteenth centuries. It was felt that some remedy was indispensable. The history of commerce furnishes an account of many of the modes adopted to escape these inconveniences. Some of these will be considered hereafter, as falling under the head of the credit system. The functions of the deposit banks may be regarded as partaking somewhat of that character; but as the payments made by them were, in fact, virtually a mere transfer of the ownership of certain quantities of the precious metals, they belong rather to the class of payments in money. It is true, the parties paying and receiving this title to money do not verify the fact of the money being in the bank. It was believed to be there; and, so long as that belief continued, the payments could proceed. These payments consisted in transferring a title to so much money as purported to be paid; the money remained untouched, and unseen. This change of ownership by transfer of title might have been made available for a very rapid mode of payment; but the whole proceeding was hedged by so many ceremonies, checks and securities, that the deposit banks were never as available as they should and might have been. The regulation, that the same sum could not, unless in very special cases, be transferred twice in the same day, seems absurd to merchants and bankers of the present time. It doubtless added to the treasures of the banks, for it must have required several times as much more money to make the required payments in bank, at the rate of one payment for each amount in a day, than if payments could have been made at pleasure.

The Bank of Amsterdam was established in January, 1609, under the guaranty of the city, and the government of its magistrates. The avowed object was to afford some relief against the intolerable nuisance of worn and defaced coins, which flowed into a great commercial mart like Amsterdam from all the world. The currency made up of these coins had long been at a discount of eight to ten per cent.; and bills of exchange, payable in this currency, were of course at a like discount. The leading measure upon which it was founded, and by virtue of which it had a rapid rise and growth, was that all bills of exchange, for sums over 600 florins, were payable only at the bank. In a city where so many payments were concentrated, this regulation drew daily vast sums to its vaults. Every person who had bills to pay for himself, or others, was obliged to open at once an account in the bank, by depositing the amount of coins or bullion needful to meet his payments. These deposits were scrutinized, tested, valued, and the proceeds carried to the credit of the depositor, less five per cent., besides a charge of ten florins for opening the first account.

As this bank money subsequently bore a premium, the deduction of five per cent. was not a loss. The depositor having received his credit upon the books of the bank, was prepared to transfer the whole, or a part, in payment of bills of exchange, or any other debt. This policy rapidly absorbed the vast sum required to make the daily payments of the city. And as no person was permitted to transfer a deposit or sum on the day it was received, a much larger sum was required to effect those payments, than if the depositors had been allowed to transfer forthwith. The coins and bullion thus deposited were not reclaimable, but, according to the theory of the bank, were locked up for ever. Deposits were safe, in the hands of all holders, from legal seizure and attachment. The bank received money, also, for safe keeping, which was returnable on demand, the depositor paying a small charge for the service. Although it paid no interest for deposits of any kind, it became thus the depository of many people and institutions, who were afraid to keep money in their own possession.

Though the credit given to those opening accounts was less, by five per cent., than the actual deposit, yet this mode of payment was deemed so much more eligible than counting, handling, testing and scrutinizing coins and bullion, the risk was deemed so much less, and the facility so much greater, that the bank deposits attained a permanently higher value than the ordinary currency.

The business of the bank was *to receive*, *to keep* and *to pay*. The payments were made by a transfer from the account of the payer to that of the receiver: this was done by the party transferring, in person, or by his agent specially authorized, and by his delivering to the proper officer of the bank a written order, or check; thus:

Folio 1609.

Messrs. Commissioners of the Bank — Please pay to Isaac Dewitt the sum of One Thousand Florins, Four Sols and Six Deniers.

Amsterdam, 25th March, 1709.

F.1000 4*s*. 6*d*. SAMUEL MOSES.

On presentation of this paper by the drawer, or his special agent, the sum expressed was debited to the drawer, and credited to the party to whom the payment was directed to be made. The amount thus transferred could not be again transferred until the next day, except on a few special occasions. The bank was shut fifteen days in January and July of each year, in which time the books and accounts were all closed, and opened anew. Special scrutiny and comparison was instituted at the opening of the new accounts, to see if the bank statements agreed with those of the depositors. For the three days following the opening of the bank, parties were permitted to transfer amounts received by them, at their pleasure. The bank was open every day, from 7 A. M. to 3 P. M.; but, after 11 A. M., every transfer cost six sols, the charge before that hour being two sols. There were, besides, other charges and fines not material to be detailed. The number in the margin of the check was the folio of the bank book in which the account was kept. The accounts were numbered from *one* onward, and the folio was made to correspond. Each clerk had a specified number of accounts; and when a check was presented to the clerk in charge of the proper folio, he could at once turn to the page, write off the amount, and make the transfer.

The operation of this mode of payment would permanently absorb an amount of the precious metals equal to the largest sum employed at any one period, and of course more than would be required for the average payments. As, according to the theory of the bank, money once deposited was never again restored to circulation, the tendency would have been to swell the bank credits to a larger sum than was required for current payments, and of course to diminish their value. This was met by a policy, on the part of the bank, which overcame that difficulty, and became a source of profit to the bank, and to brokers.

When it was found there were too many bank credits in the market, which was shown by their being freely offered for sale, brokers were employed by the bank to purchase them at four per cent. premium. This practice grew into a regular business: brokers were always furnished with bank credits to sell at five per cent. premium, and with coin to purchase them at four. This kept the price within a range of one per cent., and always at a premium, except on very extraordinary occasions. A desirable equilibrium was thus maintained by a simple contrivance, by which the medium set apart for payment of debts was preserved from diminution, and from irregularity in value.[1]

The bank also received on special deposit any amount of bullion or coin offered; each sum being counted, weighed, and placed in sacks, upon which, if gold, the depositor placed his seal. A receipt (*recipisse*) was given him, in this form: —

Amsterdam, 1 *March*, 1700.

Jean Dewitt has deposited in Bank One Thousand Louis d'Or, at the rate of Ten Florins and Fourteen Sols each, upon condition that he may withdraw them within the space of six months, paying one-quarter per cent., or, in default thereof, that they shall be taken by the Bank at the rate above-named.

Flo. 10.700. N. N.

For the Bank.

The party making this deposit could renew his right to withdraw the identical specie, from six months to six months, paying each time the regular charge of half per cent. for bullion, and a quarter for all coins, except ducatoons, which were charged only one-eighth. The amount of his deposit was immediately carried to his credit in account, and became transferable like other bank credits. The recipisse was also negotiable and marketable, varying in value with the kind of coin or bullion it represented. If not suffered to expire by its limitation of six months, the holder could always withdraw the special deposit it described by returning the recipisse, and transferring an equivalent amount of bank credit. While the credits thus obtained were passing on the books of the bank in the current payments of the day, the recipisse, or right to withdraw the special deposit, was passing from hand to hand among the dealers in coins and bullion.

These bank deposits continued to fulfil their functions with great regularity and effectiveness. In large transactions, such as the payment of bills of exchange, the risk appeared to be reduced to the lowest possible degree, and the immense trouble with coinage was wholly overcome.

---

[1] "Universal Merchant," by Donald Magens. American ed., p. 178, &c. "Stewart's Pol. Econ." vol. ii., p. 292, 4to ed.

The bank received its first serious check in 1672, sixty-three years after its establishment. When the French army had entered the Low Countries, and had taken Utrecht and many other places, an alarm for the safety of the deposits in the Bank of Amsterdam spread over the whole country. The depositors, although not strictly entitled to draw their deposits, in what they deemed the imminent hazard of the bank, demanded coin for their respective credits. The demand was complied with promptly, so long as it continued. Those living at a distance from Amsterdam sold their credit even at a discount of five or six per cent., which was equivalent to a total loss of ten or twelve per cent., as these credits were, at all ordinary times, worth five or six per cent. more than par. The alarm was soon over, and the bank, not having been violated by the French army, was soon again in possession of all its treasures.

There were times, also, when bank credits went above the the usual premium of five per cent. The usual range of these fluctuations was four to six per cent., and furnished a class of brokers, and dealers in coin and bullion, a very profitable business. They were equally ready to serve those who wished to sell or to buy coin or bank credits ; and their operations, as well as those of a similar kind in which the bank was interested, while they tended to increase the number of the fluctuations, kept the price within a narrow range. The dealing in coins, as represented by the recipisses of the bank, could be carried on with very little capital. The holder of a recipisse for 1000 louis d'or might sell the right to receive these coins for 10 florins, and the purchaser could only withdraw them by transferring the equivalent in bank credit.

So the coins or bullion could be deposited, and be used for payment of debts, while the depositor could avail himself of any rise in its value. The recipisses became, therefore, so many footballs for speculation. It was a mode of dealing in the fluctuations of coin, without being obliged to hold the coin. The right to the coin was the subject of their speculative dealing, and not the coin itself. An active competition was easily maintained, in a business requiring no capital. It tended greatly to increase the deposits in the bank.

For almost two centuries the bank enjoyed unimpeached credit, performing all its functions with unceasing steadiness, and greatly to the benefit and commercial prosperity of Amsterdam. The amount of treasure amassed in its vaults has been variously estimated at from five to eighty millions sterling. If ten millions sterling be taken as a safe estimate, and it be assumed that the whole capital was moved only one hundred times in a year, its payments in that time would amount to one thousand millions sterling, or $4,800,000,000. The transfers of this enormous sum were made, during that long period, in unhesitating confidence as to the security of the deposit. The bank permitted no scrutiny into its condition, and rendered no account to the public; but merchants never doubted the validity of a security which was incessantly used in paying debts. In 1790, it was discovered that a large portion of the famous deposit had disappeared fifty years before, and that a gradual diminution had been taking place during that period, until the actual quantity remaining was small indeed. The amount withdrawn had been lent to the East India Company, the Provinces of Holland, and the City of Amsterdam, none of which were in a condition to make instant restitution.[1] The bank failed, because its guardians had been unfaithful to their trust. Before this breach of trust became known, transfers of the abstracted deposits, and payments by them, had been made to the value of hundreds of millions sterling per annum; yet these payments were ever after unquestioned, as to their validity and efficiency. No evil or disadvantage, no check to commerce, was felt until the abstraction was discovered, and the loss fell upon the holders of that moment.

[1] It is marvellous that, with the example of the Bank of Venice before them, the Bank of Amsterdam was not reconstructed upon the principle of transferring public debt.

§ 2. *The Bank of Hamburg.*

The Bank of Hamburg was established in 1619, ten years after that of Amsterdam. The extreme inconvenience of a deteriorated coinage from various mints, of differing standards, compelled the merchants to resort to this mode of relief, availing themselves, however, of the co-operation and guarantee of the city. One of the effects of the circulation of base coin was to produce an unfavorable foreign exchange — a great grievance at a free port like Hamburg. The whole evil was so great, as to evince that the abuses of coinage may be a serious check to trade. The remedy was that previously adopted at Amsterdam, to lock up the coins, and circulate the credit granted for them. The bank at first received on deposit only the rix dollars of the German Empire — a silver coin of approved standard. It was supposed that coins thus deposited in the vaults of the bank would be safe from the whole army of sweaters, pluggers and clippers; that they could not suffer by wear; and that they would be safe from burglars, robbers and pirates. They discovered, in process of time, that there was an insidious mode of attack, from which the bank did not escape, with all their caution. The mint of the Empire issued coins of the same name and apparent value, but of a lower standard than those which the bank had received. These being put into circulation, soon found their way into the bank. Those merchants who were in the secret were able to drive a very successful business by depositing the new, and withdrawing the old coins. Before the mistake was discovered, a large proportion of the new coins had found their way into the bank, to the great dismay of the managers. The new coin was of less value than the old, in the proportion of 516 to 540, or nearly five per cent. less. This produced so great a disturbance, that for a time the bank was shut. The difficulty was adjusted by assuming an average on the above proportion, say 528; and upon this the accounts of all the depositors were adjusted. This marc banco was not represented by any coin; but from that time, in 1770, it has continued to be the unit of the money of account of the bank. At the same time, having had this experience of the danger to be apprehended from mints of a foreign power, it was decided that the bank should receive ingots of silver or coin only as bullion. Every deposit was duly assayed or tested, and the credit on the books given accordingly. The standard adopted was one of alloy to 47 parts fine. The bank money thus established has proved, according to the best authorities, one of the least variable in Europe. For a long period it has stood at a premium above the currency of coins in general circulation, from 20 to 25 per cent. premium. This argues very strongly that, however circulating coins may suit for the purposes of small change in the retail trade, they do not suit for the large operations of banking and foreign exchange. In all operations of foreign exchange, coins can only be regarded and treated as bullion; and large dealers in coins are compelled to be governed by the principles which govern foreign exchange.

The bank is under the government of five directors, two counsellors, two treasurers, and two of the principal magistrates of the city: one of each kind goes out annually. The vaults in which the treasure is placed have each five different locks, and each director holds the key to one of these locks, so that no vault can be opened without the whole five directors being present. No employee of the bank, and no broker, is allowed to open an account; for brokers in Hamburg are not regarded as merchants, and do not enjoy their privileges; only merchants and citizens of Hamburg are permitted to open accounts. A loan office is connected with the bank, which is permitted to lend bank money on pledge of gold, silver and jewels, to the amount of three-fourths of their value. The officers of the bank have the management of the mint, and the coinage of the city.

The credit of this bank has been rarely shaken. It endured a severe trial from the confusion in the coinage above mentioned; it once over-extended its loans on pledges; and it was wholly absorbed by one of Napoleon's Marshals, Davoust, who took all its money for his army. The French government subsequently made restitution, and the bank resumed its position and operations.

The mode of payment at the Bank of Hamburg is substantially the same as that which we have described as having been followed at Amsterdam. The same regulation of one transfer of the same sum daily, unless on special occasions: the same strictness as to the hours of business at the bank — the time of transferring being from 7 to 10 o'clock A. M.; with the permission from 10 to 1 P. M., and from 3 to 5 P. M., by paying for the privilege. The times for inquiring whether transfers had been made were the same, but with a charge if the information was required at the two later periods. These charges were usually compounded with the clerks for a fixed sum, on payment of which information could be had at all hours. These regulations are by no means necessary or incident to such banks. There is no reason why the deposits in such banks could not be transferred by checks as rapidly as the deposits of the Bank of England, or the banks of the United States. And this would be giving to the precious metals all the efficiency, in commercial payments, of which they are susceptible.

The Bank of Hamburg is, to this day, a living, useful and flourishing establishment. It is a proof that, although institutions and devices of credit have long since far outstripped, in effectiveness, any possible application of the precious metals to the business of commercial payments, yet there is no good reason why every proper method should not be adopted, of making coins and bullion available, in the payments of trade, to the utmost extent of which they are susceptible. There can be no doubt that there is room, in every important commercial city in the world, for a bank whose business it should be to receive, hold and allow the transfer of deposits of gold and silver bullion brought to a common standard, or all fine, and without alloy. They could be thus rapidly circulated in payment, and be ready for any emergency or demand.

NOTE TO CHAPTER VI.

THE BANK OF AMSTERDAM.

We have ample accounts of the Bank of Amsterdam. Its central position, in reference to the trade of Europe, gave it great prominence from the time of its establishment, and during all its career of nearly two centuries. The great prosperity of Holland, as commercial agent for other countries, not only increased the business of the bank, but made it more extensively known.

Simple as its constitution was, to many it appeared a mystery; and by merchants only were its real benefits and functions understood. Joseph Marshall, an intelligent English traveller, who visited Amsterdam, and extended his travels over all northern Europe, in 1768, 1769 and 1770, after referring to the great fame of this bank, proceeds:—"Here a natural question may be stated: What is the use of such a bank? The excellence of a bank of circulation is evident at first sight: by circulating paper, they have it in their power to remedy numerous evils, which, in certain situations of affairs, attend a languid circulation of coin. If money is too scarce, such an institution may make it plentiful: and another great utility (at least it has been so esteemed in England) is that of issuing large quantities of paper, to supply the home demand for a currency, while the precious metals are at liberty to go abroad in whatever method, or on whatever business, the merchants may find advisable, in order to increase their commerce and their fortunes at the same time. But, on the contrary, a bank of deposit is not attended with any of these conveniences: circulation is much impeded by it. The circulation of a million of guilders is attended with certain advantages in the United Provinces, by animating industry. Suppose the million is locked up in the bank: it may be said they will still circulate in the books of the bank: true, they circulate at Amsterdam, but nowhere else. Thus the establishment of a bank of deposit has only the effect of fixing a vast portion of all the wealth and trade of a country in one spot; of which Amsterdam, with the worst harbor, yet possessing the most trade of any town in Holland, is a pregnant instance. This local advantage of facilitating circulation in one spot, in prejudice of all others, is surely a partial decision in its favor. In a political point of view, it may be pronounced dangerous to the State. A foreign enemy attacking a town, or a province, is an evil that can be remedied; but what if an invader lays siege to a bank? What ruin and confusion must ensue? Banks of circulation are open to some accidents, but not a twentieth part of those of deposit.

"The treasure of the Bank of Amsterdam is an absolute secret to all, but those who have the government of it. The value has been computed, or rather guessed, at from 20 to 40,000,000 sterling; but naming any particular sum must be, at best, but wild work. It is, however, a very astonishing system of accumulation; for it is a well-known fact, that money once paid and entered in the bank books can never be demanded; and it is a well-known fact, that money is perpetually paid in. Here, therefore, seems to be a constant ingress, but no egress; consequently a treasure which seems constantly to increase." — *Marshall's Travels through Holland, &c.*, vol. i., page 53.

This expresses the opinion entertained by many common observers of the Bank of Amsterdam, but more especially of Englishmen. It is not, then, universally conceded that banks of deposit are safer than those of circulation. On one point which excited the concern of this traveller, Sir James Stewart sheds some light: — "The city of Amsterdam knows, from long experience, the rate of demand for bank money; and it is not to be supposed that, upon any sudden emergency which may heighten that demand for a time, they should be such novices as to increase the credit upon their books so far, as to run any risk of overstocking the market with it." . . . "During my stay in Holland, I was at great pains, to no purpose, to ascertain whether the bank ever issued any part of their credit cash upon such occasions." . . . "The popular opinion is, that coin is taken out for the service of the State: the opinion of many intelligent men is quite contrary." . . . "My opinion is, that every shilling written in the books of the bank is actually locked up, in coin, in the bank repositories. That although, by the regulations of the bank, no coin can be issued to any person who demands it in consequence of his credit in bank, yet I have not the least doubt but *that both the credit written in the books of the bank, and the cash in their repositories which balances it, may suffer alternate augmentations and diminutions, according to the greater or less demand for bank money.*" . . . "There are upon the square before the town-house of Amsterdam, between 10 and 11 in the morning, a number of cashiers, whose business it is to buy and sell bank credit for current coin. They bargain with all those who have occasion either to buy or sell; and, according to the demand for specie or bank credit, the agio rises or sinks: and as these cashiers must constantly gain, whether they furnish bank credit or current coin, since they are never demanders in either operation, it is commonly found that there is in their favor about $\frac{1}{16}$, or perhaps $\frac{1}{8}$ per cent., according to the revolutions of the demand; that is to say, one who would first buy specie, and then sell it, would lose $\frac{1}{8}$, or perhaps but $\frac{1}{16}$, by his operation." . . . "It is a matter of fact, that the bank lends both coin and credit to the brokers, cashiers or lombards, who are constantly on the square before the town-house." . . . "Whenever, therefore, the bank finds that the agio falls too low with respect to coin, and when, in consequence of that, the demand for coin *increases*, then they lend coin out of their repositories to the brokers; and when it rises, they lend credit. This coin the brokers dispose of to those who have bank money, and who want to convert it into coin. They sell the coin for bank credit; the purchaser writes off the transfer in favor of the broker, and he again repays the value of the coin to the bank, by transferring the credit he obtained for the coin in favor of the bank. This done, the bank may expunge this credit from their book, by which means their deposit of coin is diminished, and also a corresponding amount of credit." . . . "If, on the other hand, those who have coin find it will not serve their purpose as well as bank credit; they come with it to the brokers, who sell them bank credit for it: this coin the brokers deliver to the bank, which writes off the credit lent to the broker in favor of him who has paid his coin for it." . . . "It is a curious method of preserving an exact proportion between the coin on deposit, the credit written in their books of transfer, and the demand for bank money." — "*Inquiry into the Principles of Political Economy*," *by Sir James Stewart*, 4to edit., vol. ii., page 298, &c.

"The value of bank money was formerly very uncertain, as the agio often varied from 9 per cent. to par. These variations were partly occasioned by the actual condition of commerce at the respective periods, but chiefly by the schemes of brokers, stock-jobbers, &c. To prevent the possibility of these great variations, the bank came to a resolution, some years since, to sell bank money for currency at 5 per cent., and to buy at 4 per cent. agio; which measure has effectually answered the purpose, by keeping the market price between those extremes." — "*Universal Merchant*," *by D. Magens*, 1753; Phila. edit., 1797, page 180.

Those who wish for further information in relation to the Bank of Amsterdam may consult, among many others, the following works: —

"*A General Treatise of Moneys and Exchanges*," *by A. J.*; 4to: London, 1708, page 351. "*Traité General du Commerce*," *by S. Ricard*, 5th edit., *par N. Struyk:* Amsterdam, 4to, 1732, page 146. The same work enlarged to 3 vols. 4to: Paris, 1799; vol. i. p. 74. "*Guide des Negocians*," *par M. Laurent Lipp: Montpellier*, 1793, 2 vols. 4to; vol. i. p. 63. "*Universal Merchant*," *by D. Magens*, edition of J. Aldrich: Philad,, 1797, page 177. "*Smith's Wealth of Nations*," book iv. chap. iii. "*M'Pherson's Annals of Commerce*," 4 vols. 4to: London, 1805; vol. ii. p. 253.

M'Pherson says: — "The best and most copious account of the Bank of Amsterdam ever published in the English language is that which was communicated by Mr. Hope, of Amsterdam, to Dr. Smith, who has inserted it in his '*Wealth of Nations*.'"

Any one who will take the trouble to compare, will find that Mr. Hope's account is taken from the books above referred to; and although the statement is well drawn up, many important particulars not inserted will be found, by the diligent inquirer, in the works above quoted, as well as in those referred to below: —

"*Cours d'Economie Politique,*" *par Henri Storch,* 4 vols. 8vo: Paris, 1823; vol. iv. page 96 "*Inquiry into the Principles of Political Economy,*" *by Sir James Stewart,* 2 vols. 4to: London, 1768; vol. ii. p. 292. "*Kaufmans-Lexicon,*" *von Carl Gunther Ludovici,* 5 vols. 8vo: Amsterdam: Leipsic, 1768. "*Banken und Munzwesen,*" *von J. G. Busch,* 8vo: Hamburg, 1824, page 169. "*Dictionnaire Universal de Commerce,*" *par Jaques Savary des Bruslons,* 4 vols. folio: Geneva, 1742; Art. "*Banque,*" vol. i. p. 278. "*Kelly's Cambist,*" Art. "*Amsterdam.*" "*Beschreibung der Banquen,*" *von P. J. Marperger,* 4to: Leipsic, 1717, page 119. "*Postlethwaite's Dictionary of Commerce,*" 2 vols. folio. *Sir William Temple's Works,* folio, vol. i. page 32.

THE BANK OF HAMBURG.

Very full details respecting the Bank of Hamburg may be found in the books referred to under the proper heads; but more especially in that of J. G. Busch, translated into French, with the title: "*La Banque de Hambourg rendue facile.*"

CHAPTER VII.

§ 1. *Distinction between credit and the credit system — The latter defined — Involves a separation of the business of payments from the business of distributing commodities, aud makes trade virtually a barter — The great division of labor makes this necessary — Relations of debtor and creditor mutual, and exist mainly among the same classes — The fund out of which debts are paid arises from the credits which are the counterpart of the debts — Circulation of credits as a currency — Convertibility carried too far — Evils of blending credits and money — Diversion of credits from their proper functions — Order of considering this subject.*

Credit, in no one of its meanings, is the same thing as the credit system; the latter implies the former, but the former does not include the latter. Credit refers chiefly to the confidence which dealers repose in each other, and to the consequent postponement of payment upon transactions of sale. When one sells and delivers goods to another, agreeing to receive payment at a future day, that is giving credit upon one side, and taking it upon the other; but this transaction may not fall within the credit system, which imports something more than personal confidence and deferred payment. The credit system is that by which not only personal confidence exists between the parties, inducing them to sell and deliver goods, and defer the payment, but by which the payment is eventually effected, without resort to coin, bullion, or any similar equivalent: it is that by which commodities or services are made to pay for commodities or services: it is a system by which men apply their credits to the extinguishment of their debts. It embraces all the devices by which payments are properly made, without the use of the precious metals, except cases of strict barter.

Under the credit system, no equivalent is given at the time of sale, the payment being postponed for a time definite or indefinite; the payments for commodities are separated from the actual transactions of sale and purchase; the articles of trade are bought and sold, and distributed for consumption at home and abroad — the payments accruing being reserved for a separate and a distinct department of commerce.

This is in direct contrast with the cash or money system, in which every article is either paid for in the precious metals at the time of delivery, or at some time afterwards. These two systems work side by side; and though frequently much blended in operation, the distinction between them is plain enough to be always kept in view. It must, indeed, be strictly regarded by those who would understand the subject of money and credit.

The importance of the credit system may be estimated from the fact, that in Great Britain and the United States more than 95 per cent. in value of all the payments of business and of trade are effected by its means. The credit system is employed with effect wherever civilization extends; and it may be added, in not very far from the proportion in which civilization prevails. It deserves, therefore, not only to be studied, but to be understood in its most simple elements, as well as in its most extensive ramifications.

Next to the industry which is applied to the actual production of the commodities of human use and consumption, the chief business of men in civilized society is to exchange these commodities, one for another. In the subdivision of labor which then takes place, the whole production is so divided that each man, or class of men, makes but one thing, or but the part of one thing. This makes an incessant process of exchange necessary. Each producer, or class of producers, exchanges his particular product for all the variety of articles of food, raiment, &c., which go to make up his or their entire consumption. One great problem of industry is to effect these exchanges with the greatest rapidity, ease, and at the least expense. If article could be exchanged for article, as savages make their exchanges, vast expense would be saved. This, in civilized society, is impossible, because of the variety of products, and the widely separated position of the parties. To effect this exchange, and to secure other important advantages, society has, with the progress of civilization, resolved itself into various classes, which minister, by this subdivision, more effectually to the general interests. One class has charge of civil administration; one of education; one of the public duties of religion; one is made up of physicians; another of lawyers; one is engaged in the fine arts; another in manufactures; another in agriculture; another in commerce, or the distribution of the products of others' industry; and another in the business of payments, as brokers, bankers, and dealers in exchange. All these, and many other classes, require the services or consume the products of each other. They deal with each other as classes, and as individuals. Every individual exchanges his services, or labor, or products, for such of all the others as he requires. This exchange, though often very circuitous, is certain, and occurs as the result of the business of every individual. Whatever the medium of this exchange, whatever transactions intervene, the object of each party is simply to exchange what he has to dispose of, whether services, labor or commodities, for what he wishes to obtain from others. Each individual, in fact, directly or indirectly pays for what he purchases with that which he has to sell. This, as we shall perceive in our further progress, is the true basis of the credit system.

The importance of fully appreciating the functions and agency of the money of account becomes very apparent when we attempt to enter upon the subject of the credit system. In all the transactions of sale taking place under the credit system, the actual use of the precious metals is dispensed with. They are only employed to pay balances of account, and generally only as bullion. It is only in the retail trade that coins are employed in the purchase of goods. The whole expression of prices, all the entries of book-keeping, all statements of amounts in bills of exchange, promissory notes, and other securities, are made in the language of the money of account. All the transactions of trade, foreign and domestic, which are made verbally or on paper, depend therefore on the agency of the money of account. Values are not expressed in coins, but in money of account; the price of coins and bullion are thus stated, and cannot be stated any other way. The language in which prices are expressed is illimitable, as the language in which ideas are expressed. There is no paucity in the language of prices. Some suppose that a strict relation exists between the rate of prices and the quantity of money; this supposition is groundless. There is a mutual dependence between prices and payments: that is, if the medium in which the payments of a country are made becomes very scarce, or if the processes and adjustments by the credit system become disturbed, and thus checked, prices may be affected by the necessities of the holders of commodities, who may be compelled to sacrifice goods to meet their engagements. But these reductions will not so affect the prices of other kinds of commodities, the holders of which may not be under that necessity. The subject of prices will be specially considered hereafter; they will be found to depend far more on other elements, than on the plenty or the scarcity of money.

The credit system could not exist for a day, but by the aid of a money of account. It can dispense with the use of the precious metals to a very great extent; but it cannot operate at all but through the agency of a money of account. During the suspension of specie payments in Great Britain, between 1797 and 1822, the entire payments of the country, in all transactions above the merest retail trade, were made under the operation and by the devices of the credit system. Money was not employed in any large payments. Even balances were paid in notes of the Bank of England, by law a legal tender in payment of all debts.

We have said that the credit system operates by a separation of the payments of business and trade from the transactions which originate the payments. The business proceeds in one channel, and the payments in another. This is one instance, out of many, of that division of labor which is extending to all the employments of society; and in none has it proved more useful or effective than in that of payments. It has introduced an economy which may be said to correspond to the difference between the amount of payments made in money and the amount made by means of credit. It may be doubted whether any saving ever made in the processes of business can be compared with this.

By the agency of money of account all prices and valuations are fixed, expressed verbally, stated in writing, entered in books of account, set forth in promissory notes, bills of exchange, and other securities; all the values or amounts involved are thus stated and preserved for adjustment or future payment. For every article sold upon time a debt and a credit of exactly equal amount are created; there is a debtor and a creditor — the one having to pay the exact sum which the other is to receive. If the debtor can purchase that credit, he becomes both the debtor and creditor, and both debt and credit are extinguished, being merged in the same person. The same extinguishment occurs when some third party assumes the place of the debtor, and also purchases the credit; both debt and credit meet in the same person, and are merged. What is thus true of every case of debt and credit between any two persons who become debtor and creditor, and of a third party who may step in and take the place of both, is true of the whole class of debtors and creditors. To a very large extent they are the same persons, because the persons who take credit largely are the persons who give it largely. The creditors and debtors are, therefore, mainly the same persons. It is among persons who thus mutually occupy the relation of debtor and creditor, that the credit system effects an adjustment or payment without the use of money. The debtor needs only to purchase or redeem the amount of credits which correspond to his debts. As every debtor may be presumed to have incurred his debt in the purchase of some commodity which is to be sold again in the same, or in some other shape — for to this class belongs the largest class of debts and credits — he may be supposed to have the wherewithal to pay his debt. The merchant who purchases goods to sell again, or the manufacturer who purchases raw material for his special branch of industry, may be supposed to have obtained, by incurring the debt, that which, when sold, will be of sufficient value to pay the debt. In their positions it is not necessary that they should sell for only gold or silver. All they need is to become creditors for the amount of the sale, and the credits thus obtained will, by the adjustments of the credit system, pay their debts. So any one who is debtor and creditor to the same amount will be able, by the devices of the credit system, to set one against the other, and be discharged. As the person who sells commodities for gold or silver does not keep these metals, but employs them in turn to purchase what he may require, so he who sells upon a credit, by which another person becomes his debtor in a note or bill of exchange, does not keep these securities, but employs them, or the proceeds of them, to make other purchases or payments. The credit system does not, then, really furnish a substitute for money, so much as a mode of dispensing with it. It is dispensed with at the time a purchase is made, by stating the amount in money of account, and postponing the day of payment; it is dispensed with at the day of payment, because the debt is adjusted or paid by a process which does not require the aid of gold or silver. All business men who avail themselves of the credit system have debts (notes) to pay; the credits (the same notes) made by incurring these debts are the most abundant, as well as the most convenient, and the most easily obtainable medium in which payment can be effected. The debts are all to be paid, and the credits are all to be extinguished; the debtors become the active agents in this. Debtors are under a severe necessity of meeting every payment: no human obligation, however many may be the exceptions, is better observed than the payment of debts, and especially is this the case among those who most employ the credit system. Credit is often said to be money; it is really and practically preferable to money, besides being, as a medium, cheaper; it costs very little more than good faith and good management. He who employs a thousand dollars to make a purchase, has first to purchase or borrow the thousand dollars; whilst he who makes the same purchase upon credit not only purchases without money, but the commodities he purchases will provide the means to pay his debt. The same commodities of trade or industry, on account of which debts are chiefly contracted, being commodities in general demand, will be sufficient to purchase or redeem credits enough to pay the debts contracted in purchasing them.

It will be seen, by this, that the credit system is really a mode of exchanging commodities or services without the intervention of any medium of value. The things to be sold or exchanged are valued in money of account. The person parting with them takes a security for the value, and employs that security in the purchase of other things, or in the payment of debts contracted for them. In short, by the credit system men exchange what they have for what they want; the one pays for the other, according to prices and sums stated in money of account; the payments are made in some of the various ways by which the credit system effects its adjustments. The credit system is, then, a complicated system of accounts between those who avail themselves of it. Whether this system is susceptible of being simplified, and made still more efficient and economical, deserves attention; but our object is first to make its present mode of operation well understood.

The processes of adjustment or payment by the credit system are very various and complicated, and will, therefore, be treated hereafter in some detail. It may tend to clear our conceptions, however, if we consider this system in some of its leading general features. We have already remarked that the trade or business depending on payments proceeds as if they were made — the making and arranging the payments becoming a separate occupation. That this may be done with more efficiency, the whole indebtedness becomes, in fact, a fund for this purpose. At all times there is a large amount, in the aggregate of debts, incurred for goods sold; but this aggregate, however great, agrees precisely with the amount of credits. There is, then, a fund of credits, or credit securities, exactly equal to the amount of the debts. So long as this fund of credits is in the hands of individuals, it is not very active as a medium of payment. But when large sums come to be concentrated in the banks, it becomes an efficient manageable fund for the extinction of debts.

The whole amount of the credits may, in this way, become available as a medium of payment. It is divisible, at a moment's warning, into sums of any amount; and as applicable, in payment of debts, as any other medium could possibly be. As all the debts which originate in the credit system are but the counterparts of the credits, the credits become an article of great demand. Such, indeed, is the magnitude of the transactions carried on by means of the credit system, being more than tenfold all others — and such, of course, the amount of the debts and the number of debtors — that no demand is more active, urgent and constant than the demand of this large class of debtors for these credits, or the means of paying the debts. The debtors are, in fact, the holders of the articles of most general consumption; for, that they might be such holders, they contracted the debts. They are, then, not only under a stringent necessity of obtaining credits to pay their debts, but they have the best means of obtaining them; having for sale, purposely selected, the commodities of daily consumption with the use of which the people cannot dispense. The credits, whatever be the shape they take, whether that of negotiable paper, bank-notes, or bank deposits, become a general instrument of purchase, not because they are money, or representatives of money, but because they are the chief medium for paying debts; and as such are in great demand among those who have incurred debts by the purchase of articles of general consumption. The holders of credits employ them in payments to all classes of society — industrial, professional, mercantile and literary — because all yield commodities or services, and because all are consumers. Credits are thus distributed through a whole community, through all the ramifications which the wants of society can produce; and they flow thence to the hands of those who sell the articles which all classes want and must have. The great routine of the credit system consists in exchanging commodities and services for credits, and then in distributing these credits widely and minutely in society, whence they flow, under the demands of constant consumption, to the holders of the articles of constant use, by whom they are extinguished in payment of their debts. This operation never ceases its movements; new credits and new debts are created every day; old debts and credits are merged, set off, or extinguished every day; and the whole of the intermediate movements are incessantly going on. In all this multifarious business no money is employed, and none is needed, but the money of account, except in small transactions.

It does not follow that there is no longer any office, use, or agency for gold or silver coins. It seems to be a new proof of the convenience and advantage of coins, that they circulate with perfect facility along with the currency of the credit system. Either may at any time be employed, as the convenience or inclinations of the parties may suggest. In retail transactions, nothing yet known can be preferable to coins of silver or gold. In small transactions, as well as in the balances which accrue in large business, it is frequently necessary to use a medium which is at the same time an actual equivalent. The business of the world is so much increased under the impulses and facilities of the credit system, that full employment for the precious metals is found in the payment of the fractions. The credit system pays the millions, the thousands, and the hundreds; gold and silver is employed to pay the tens, and fives, and ones. In many parts of the United States only the fractions under one dollar are paid in coins. It is a matter, certainly, in which people may make their choice. In the United States, the people follow their own inclinations: there is a different law, on the subject of banking, in almost every State. The Constitution of the United States prohibits anything but gold and silver coin being made a legal tender in payment of debts: yet, with this legal right to demand gold or silver coins, not one hundred dollars in one million of the debts over fifty dollars are ever paid or exacted in coin. The people prefer the adjustments of the credit system. In New England, in New York, New Jersey, Delaware, and many other States, they employ notes of denomination as low as one dollar. The saving in this is very great. The expediency is a separate question. It is safe and proper to do so probably just in proportion to the virtue, intelligence and commercial integrity of the people.

We have seen that the real fund employed in the payment of debts is that arising from the transaction of the business by which the debts were created. One circumstance attending this is of very great importance — the fund applicable by the credit system to the payments, is precisely of sufficient amount to pay all the debts, for the credit and debt are counterparts. If not diverted from this, its proper channel, there would rarely be any difficulty in finding means to pay debts. Individuals might have trouble, owing to peculiar circumstances, in meeting payments; but a whole class or body of men could not, unless from other causes, because the fund for payment could never be short, and interest upon credits could never go to a high rate. This suggests that a distinction should be made by law between interest on credits and interest on money.

The blending credits and money, and treating them mainly as identical, has been a fruitful source of error and mischief. This fatal policy has been the parent of more commercial revulsions than all other causes combined; it has ruined millions of men of business in Great Britain and in the United States. The fund of credits is really and properly applicable to the payment of debts of trade incurred in the distribution of the articles of general consumption; that is, to the extinction of both debts and credits — a relation in regard to each transaction only intended to be temporary. Any diversion of credits from the legitimate purpose of paying such debts is hazardous; for, as they amount to the same sum as the debts, there can never be more than enough. This credit system being founded on human confidence, is by its nature, it is true, extremely elastic, and capable of bearing much abuse; yet, for the same reason, it is subject to sudden collapse and utter ruin. Under our present system of credit, a great amount of credits and securities are annually diverted from their legitimate purposes, and employed as money. This abuse is met by a prolongation of the time of adjustment; that is, further time of payment is given to those who are not prepared to meet engagements. This extension of time is often liberally granted for years, but the period is sure to come when creditors must realize their balances; no further time can be given; the only alternative is payment or bankruptcy. Debts are then often spunged; or, rather, a certain number of debtors fail, and never pay, and the equivalent amount of credits become worthless.

The great temptation to this diversion of credits arises from the fact that, by our present system, they are required to be convertible at will into gold or silver. The whole of the credits which are made active — that is, all that are turned into bank-notes or bank deposits — are required to be convertible. In point of fact they are not so convertible, and they cannot possibly be, as they amount at all times to a sum from ten to twenty times greater than any possible amount of gold and silver which would be available for such a purpose. This legal, but not real convertibility of these credits gives them the character, and makes them available to a very great extent as money; it deceives and misleads, without any equivalent benefit. The assumed convertibility does not add, in the least degree, to the efficiency or availability of the credits for the payment of debts, nor does it make such payment any more valid. But for this pretended convertibility, it would be difficult to divert credits largely from their true channels; it is a mischief without any redeeming circumstance.

If it be alleged, in favor of this convertibility, that the promissory notes and bills of exchange are, by law, payable at maturity in gold or silver; that is very true, it may be replied, but it is only at maturity, when no one ever thinks of demanding gold or silver, because payment is just as acceptable and valid in the usual mode. By the course to which we object, the whole amount of these credits is assumed to be convertible at once and continuously; they are thus turned into a *quasi* money, and applied to all manner of purposes to which money is properly applicable. The effect is the same as if promissory notes and bills of exchange, whatever be the time of maturity, were by law made payable at any moment the holder might please to demand the amount in gold or silver.

But we do not intend here to enter into the consideration of the securities proper to be exacted from banks or bankers, who issue bank-notes to serve the purposes of money. We may discuss that hereafter, and in its place.[1] Neither do we now assert that there is any better security for those who are the receivers of bank-notes, than convertibility. What is now suggested is, that we carry convertibility too far when we attempt to make far the larger portion of the great fund of credits convertible, on demand, into gold or silver. This fund, which is nothing else but the evidence of prolonged credits granted in the progress of industry, trade and consumption, and which, through the processes of the credit system, are the appropriate medium for the discharge of corresponding debts, neither the necessities of business, nor the demands of convenience, require to be convertible on demand into gold or silver.

This requirement, as it operates, is one of the most mischievous blunders of modern times. When two merchants keep an account in their respective books against each other, they settle these accounts, adjust the respective debts, and balance or extinguish them, without the idea of convertibility crossing their minds. What two merchants thus do directly for each other, the books of banks and bankers do for the community of business men. On their books these men find themselves charged with their debts, against which they seek to bring their credits, that, meeting on the same books, both debts and credits may be alike extinguished. With this operation convertibility has little to do, and need have nothing. The mischief of this requirement does not spring from the law which makes every debt payable in gold or silver, for that leaves every creditor to accept any mode of payment which he pleases: it is as absurd, however, as if every debtor were placed under the impossible

[1] Considered in the chapter on the Bank of England, and in that on the Banks of the United States.

obligation to keep gold and silver in his possession sufficient to pay, on demand, every debt he owed.

In all ages of the world efforts, more or less successful, have been made to dispense with the precious metals as a very expensive medium of exchange. The success of these experiments has been in proportion to the state of civilization, and the progress of mercantile morality. It would lead us into too great detail to trace the history of these efforts, or even to specify their various kinds. We shall only describe a few of these modes of payment, such as are not only characteristic of others, but effective in themselves. Our object in this will be, not to give a general view of each topic, but merely that aspect of each which relates to payments. Many of these subjects have various bearings, very complicated relations, and diverse points of view. Our attention will be confined to that of payments, or commercial liquidation. These topics may be taken up in the following order: — Books of account, Promissory notes, Bills of exchange, Bank-notes, Bank deposits, and Clearing-houses.

§ 2. *Books of account.*

However numerous the phases of the credit system, it may be regarded as having its best summary in book-keeping. When two persons in business, having frequent dealings with each other, instead of making payment or passing an equivalent at each transaction, simply debit each other in account with the proper amount, their payments are only deferred to a future day. They have separated the business of payment from the transaction which gave rise to the debt. Each receives and enjoys the services or commodities obtained from the other, as his wishes or interests dictate; and each is to make satisfaction, or render an equivalent, at a subsequent time. The main object in view in their business is, therefore, attained by both before any payment is made.

We may suppose the account between a merchant and manufacturer to stand thus, the debt and credit being reversed on their respective books: —

The books of J. Black, at the account of J. White.

Date.	Goods.	Dollars.	Cts.	Date.	Goods.	Dollars.	Cts.
1850, Jan. 1	To mdze....	1000	00	1850, Jan. 5	By mdze....	2200	00
" Feb. 2	"	1100	00	" Feb. 6	"	2100	00
" Mar. 3	"	1200	00	" Mar. 7	"	1950	00
" April 4	"	1300	00	" April 8	"	1800	00
" May 5	"	1400	00	" May 9	"	1750	00
" June 6	"	1500	00	" June 10	"	1600	00
" July 7	"	1600	00	" July 11	"	1500	00
" Aug. 8	"	1700	00	" Aug. 12	"	1400	00
" Sept. 9	"	1800	00	" Sept. 14	"	1250	00
" Oct. 10	"	1900	00	" Oct. 16	"	1100	00
" Nov. 11	"	2000	00	" Nov. 17	"	1050	00
" Dec. 12	"	2100	00	" Dec. 20	"	1000	00
" " 31	To bal. cash	100	00				
		18,700	00			18,700	00

If two persons have dealt thus with each other during a year, their books of account will be a check upon each other; and if both are correct, will exhibit the same result. At the end of the year, it will be found that J. Black has, at various dates, sold goods to J. White to the total amount of $18,600; and that J. White has sold goods, during the same time, to J. Black to the total amount of $18,700. Each of these parties thus received large quantities of goods of great value from the other, without any payment. The books are the evidence of the transaction, and express, in money of account, the value of the goods, or the amount of the mutual indebtedness. When these parties meet at the end of the year, for the settlement of their accounts, they have but to strike a balance, which shows that J. Black has to pay to J. White $100; and this being done, the whole indebtedness of $18,600 on one side, and $18,700 on the other, is fully discharged and paid. The goods delivered by the one have paid for the goods delivered by the other. The $18,600 thus paid by each of the parties is as effectual, satisfactory and legal as the payment of the balance of $100 in coins by J. Black. Transactions of this kind are of constant occurrence in all civilized countries. It cannot be alleged, with any pretence of reason, that the business thus carried on could have been any better done, if each delivery of goods had been paid for at the time in coins. This would have involved the necessity of obtaining and keeping on hand, during all the year, a considerable sum in coins.

If we suppose that, at the time of the adjustment of this account, each party had refused to accept of any payment but gold and silver, the only legal tender in payment of debts, it would have required $37,300 in coins to have paid off the two debts; or if the parties could have so far favored each other, as that one should pay first, then the one who came prepared might at once pay over to the other $18,600, and immediately receive it back.

It is obvious enough that there can be no advantage in one mode of payment over another, so that the party paid is fully satisfied. Every payment in coin involves an outlay of equivalent amount to obtain the quantity necessary. The parties to the account above stated, if their sales had been made in coin as they proceeded, would have been obliged to part with many thousand dollars worth of their goods in the beginning, to obtain the medium of exchange necessary to carry on their subsequent business. This expensive medium is saved in all cases where it is practicable to effect payments by the simple but sure process of setting off debts against debts, and of making commodities sold pay for commodities bought.

The same mode of adjustment is equally applicable where the articles sold and entered in account are coins or bullion. And so of any other indebtedness, whether incurred at the time of the charge, or whether of debts existing before in the same, or any other form.

What is thus stated of two persons keeping mutual accounts is equally true of three or more; their accounts, when properly made up and balanced, display at once the real state of their mutual indebtedness; and each one will be willing to surrender his claims upon others for a similar discharge of his own debts.

To carry the supposition to an extreme for the sake of illustration, each of two parties may purchase or assume all the debts of the other to all persons, and charge these assumptions in their respective accounts. The whole indebtedness thus mutually incurred can be extinguished by the simple process of set-off, except the balance, which may be in favor of one or the other.

It is very obvious that the usefulness of book-keeping, as a mode of extinguishing indebtedness, has never reached its practical limits. In theory all the debts of commerce may be thus set-off or paid, because the debts and credits are exactly equal, and of course would balance each other. But if such a general balance be impracticable, by reason of the complications it involves, it is no objection to employing this agency to its utmost proper limit as the cheapest and safest mode of payment ever devised. It is the chief object of every man of business who avails himself largely of credit, to apply the credits he gives to the payment or extinguishment of those he takes. He would desire nothing better than to be charged, in books of account, with every debt he owes, if, in the same books, he could have credit for the debts or sums due to him. If all business men of a particular locality were to keep their accounts in one set of books, every man would be thus debited and credited, and only their balances would remain to be paid. It is certainly desirable that an agency so effective and safe should be carried to a wider range of operation than has yet been attempted.

This subject deserves the more attention, as many of the processes and devices of the credit system derive their chief efficacy and advantage from the simple methods of book-keeping. The man of trade who asks a bank to discount for him the notes he has taken in business, and give him credit for the proceeds on its books, and who applies the credits thus obtained to pay the notes he has given to others which are presented to him for payment by the same bank, has merely availed himself of the books of the bank, on which he is charged with his debts due to others, and credited with the debts of others payable to him.

What proportion of the whole payments of the credit system is made in this way cannot be estimated, nor even approximated. But it may be said that, in one aspect of the business, the whole operation of the credit system may be resolved into the methods of book-keeping. The grand result of the system, so far as the payments of trade are effected by it, is that the products of industry, and the services and labor of men, are exchanged at prices expressed in money of account; and what men thus give or deliver is made to pay for what they receive. Whatever the complications which intervene, or whatever the machinery employed, it is all resolvable into an adjustment of accounts. It would shed a flood of light on the whole movements of the credit system, if some one would trace out and exhibit distinctly the agency of book accounts in accomplishing that vast sum of payments which are effected without resorting to either coins or bullion. Every bank, banker, broker, and other agent in the business of payments, must rely on books of account to keep up the progress of the business, and insure accuracy. Books of account intervene, therefore, in every step of the great process of adjustment, by which the chief payments of trade are effected.

CHAPTER VIII.

§ 1. *Promissory notes and bills of exchange, their nature and efficiency as instruments of payment — As evidences of debt, they aid in separating the business of trade from that of payments — Negotiation of in payments — Dealers in exchange — Bankers — Concentration of debts and credits — Balances — Use of notes and bills in Lancashire, England, and in the United States — Limits of their use in payments — Mutual debts and set-off.*

A HIGH antiquity is claimed for the use of bills of exchange: though many authorities ascribe their invention to the Jews, who were expelled from France in the years 640 and 1181, and who, taking refuge in Lombardy, were afterwards called Lombards. It is very safe to assign them an ancient date, as their use is so obvious among merchants, that we can scarcely imagine how such a device could be overlooked among men in trade who had learned the art of writing.

Any promise to pay in writing is a promissory note; and any direction in writing to another to pay a sum for the writer is a bill of exchange. A minute history of these forms of security might be very interesting; but our object is merely to show their nature, use and efficiency, rather than to recount their history—a task which belongs to the annals of commerce. For present purposes they may be considered together, distinguishing, as we proceed, their different operation.

Promissory notes and bills of exchange are a part of that system by which the payments of trade are separated, both in time and operation, from the trade in which they originate. They are evidences of the debt consequent upon the transactions which gave rise to them. Their day of payment is appointed on their face; and they move in the channels which conduct them to that mode of liquidation selected by the parties owning them. Their utility is not confined to postponing the day of payment, and affording time for arrangement; they may perform an intermediate office. The seller of goods for a thousand dollars, who takes therefor a bill or note payable in three months, can only realize the money at maturity of the paper; but he can at once purchase commodities to that amount, and transfer the bill or note in payment. He may thus, by the intervention of the paper, exchange goods to the amount of a thousand dollars for goods to that amount; that is, the goods sold will become the payment for the goods purchased. One man of business may say to another, "I have sold to A. B. goods to the value of a thousand dollars; I will order him to pay you that amount in discharge of what I now purchase from you;" and that order in writing would be a bill of exchange: or, he may say, "I will give you, in payment, a written promise to pay which I took from him, and which I will direct him to pay to you;" and that would be negotiating a promissory note, an act equivalent to drawing a bill of exchange, for the negotiator or indorser thereby orders his debtor to pay the amount of the debt to another. Promissory notes and bills of exchange are thus employed to purchase commodities, to be again sold for other notes and bills, which are in their turn employed to purchase other commodities. It is mainly by the primary agency of bills of exchange and promissory notes that the whole mass of goods in commerce are collected, transported, bought and sold, and finally distributed to the ultimate consumers with very little intervention of money in the shape of coins, except for the merest retail operations. This movement owes some of its power and efficiency to the circulation of these bills and notes in actual payment. For he who has received such payment, and with that paper purchases what he requires, has only done what he would have done with the money: he has exchanged the goods he had for those he wanted. The same end is in view, and the same end is thus attained, whether the intervening medium be money, or individual promises to pay. The natural progress of this negotiation would be to concentrate the paper thus issued for goods in the hands of the large dealers, who either become virtually private bankers, or have large operations with those in that business.

The common mode of employing bills of exchange and promissory notes, in commercial places where there are no public banks, is by intervention of private bankers and dealers in exchange. These become purchasers and depositors of nearly all the individual engagements to pay money in circulation. If, for the sake of clearness, we suppose that in any such community all this paper had fallen into the hands of two such bankers or dealers, they would between them hold claims upon all who had issued such paper; that is, all who had to pay money on such liabilities would have to pay it to one or the other of these dealers in paper, or to both of them. All these payers would be also receivers; and they would not only pay as above, but receive through the same two agents of exchange. Such payers and receivers being the business men, are debtors and creditors among themselves: all the money they owe is payable among themselves, all the debts being the equivalent and counterpart of all the credits. The bankers would soon reduce the whole liabilities and credits of their customers to an account between themselves and the balances due their customers. The debts and credits of each individual in trade, so far as these had taken the shape of bills payable, would be brought face to face in their books of account, and there balanced. If these private bankers enjoyed, in an equal degree, the public patronage, their books would not be wide of an even balance. They would, in fact, have assumed the payment of all their customers' debts, in consideration of having assigned to them all their customers' credits; which they could safely do, because credits and debts exactly correspond. The transfer of the whole of the credits absolutely to one man would, in its effects, work a total extinction of the whole: the transfer of the whole to two would only require an adjustment to be made between the two according to the amounts they had respectively received. This discharge of the whole of the debts, by their meeting in the same hands with the whole of the credits, does not so close the matter as to leave nothing further to be done. If every man in trade owes, in notes and bills, precisely the same sum which is owing to him in the same manner, then the meeting of all the debts and credits in the same hands would be an absolute and final discharge of the whole. But as most men in trade make a balance on their bills payable and receivable, favorable or unfavorable, these balances only remain to be adjusted: that is, each individual must receive what is coming to him on his bills receivable more than he has to pay on his bills payable; and each one must pay what he is indebted over the amount of his bills receivable. The sum of these balances is known to be small: men's profits, on the average, bear a small proportion to the whole amount of their transactions.

It was better understood centuries past than it is now, that by such means payments to a vast amount could be effected; better understood, because the complications of trade were fewer then than at present, and the whole operation of the adjustment could be distinctly traced and comprehended by those conversant with business. This mode of liquidation has been practised for ages, not only where greater facilities were wanting, but in Venice, Genoa, Lyons, and Amsterdam, where great facilities were enjoyed, because it was not only consistent with the processes of the great banks and the fairs, but could aid their operation, and receive aid from them. This mode is not less efficient at the present day, as we shall have occasion hereafter to notice.

Very much the largest proportion in value of the transactions of trade, domestic and foreign, is carried on by the issue of promissory notes and bills of exchange. These securities are thus used to postpone the time of payment, to serve as evidence of indebtedness, and to operate as a medium of payment. As every negotiation of such notes or bills effects a payment, their circulation measures the amount of the payments accomplished. In the manufacturing districts of England, especially in Lancashire, enormous sums are annually paid by this kind of circulation. Long lists of names, besides those on the back, are frequently appended to notes and bills there, which show they have paid a debt for every name.

The promissory notes, after performing their round of payments, and effecting a proportionable transfer and exchange of goods, are finally discharged by bank-notes, or checks on the books of a bank, or on the books of individual merchants. The domestic bills of exchange thus used in Lancashire, after undergoing this circulation, are sent to London, where they are payable, and are there extinguished or discharged in some of the banks of that city. It is not our purpose to point out here more than the use which is made of these securities before they mature. Their discharge or payment at maturity will be considered under another head. The sum of the exchanges of goods effected by this kind of circulation in England has been so great as to have attracted special attention and Parliamentary inquiry.[1] In this country this mode of payment is more or less employed throughout its whole extent; but in no part to such an extent as in England. The law, process and effect of this kind of circulation is nearly identical here and there. Undoubtedly, a large amount of goods change hands by this mode of payment every year; but in a widely-scattered population like ours, a limit to this mode of payment is soon encountered in a want of mutual knowledge and confidence. It is thus that a much larger proportion of bank-notes is used here than in England. We cannot, of course, even conjecture the sum of the exchanges of goods effected in the United States by the

[1] One of the witnesses before a Parliamentary committee, in May, 1826, testified that bills of exchange on London, at 60 days were the principal part of the circulating medium in Lancashire. They were issued to as low an amount as £5. They circulated from hand to hand in payment, being indorsed by each party paying them. A witness being asked if he had seen these bills of exchange as low as £10, with 50 or 60 names upon them, he replied: — "Yes, with twice that number. I have seen slips of paper attached to a bill as long as a sheet of paper, and when that was filled, another attached to that."

Another testified before the same committee, that the bills between £10 and £30 constituted four-fifths of the circulation; but that the proportion of the whole of the bills of all amounts to the circulation of bank-notes and coin was 20 to 1. Some bankers estimated that proportion as high as 50 to 1.—*Report of the Lords' Committee on Promissory Notes, &c., printed May 26th*, 1826, pages 183 and 186.

negotiation of bills or notes. It is one of the great elements of commercial adjustment. The payment or extinguishment of these bills here, as in England, is effected generally in the banks, or through facilities furnished by banks.

But however awkward and inconvenient promissory notes and bills of exchange as a medium of payment, when employed specifically for that purpose, they are susceptible of being so managed as to be converted into one of the most convenient, rapid and effective modes of payment yet discovered. A man of business may be the holder, for instance, of $50,000 of such paper in twenty different sums, from $595 to $9595. He may be àble to employ these notes, to some extent, in his large transactions, but meets constant obstacles in the amounts which do not suit, and in the names of drawers and indorsers which may not be sufficiently known. If he carries these notes to a banker of good standing, and obtains a credit on his books for the whole sum less the interest, with the privilege of drawing checks for the amount at his pleasure, it is manifest that he can have nothing more convenient nor effective for the payment of his notes as they mature, or the making any needful purchases for continuance of his business. His twenty notes are, by this process, melted into one fund, which will flow out at his own order, slowly or rapidly, as he may require.

What the bankers do for one man, they do for a whole community of business men. Their books become a vast reservoir of such funds, upon which the owners draw as they have occasion. These reservoirs of funds really represent an amount for which commodities have been sold; the transactions have taken place; the promissory notes are both evidence of the transactions, and securities for the amount of the sales. As men of business give notes as well as take them, and as vastly the largest proportion of the business paper actually represents a mutual indebtedness, the great office of this fund is to enable the parties to pay and extinguish their mutual debts. If one has converted his notes into a credit, at his banker's, of $50,000, and owes $40,000, it merely reduces his credit to $10,000 to pay off his debts. This is not only the best use to make of his credit, but it is indispensable to the progress of business. The transactions of business proceed as this indebtedness is created; the purchases, sales, the production, distribution and consumption involved, all go on under the facilities of the credit system, in the business to which we refer, by the issue of the paper of the parties. The payment of this paper is effected by a series of subsequent transactions, as a separate business. The chief facility by which this payment is accomplished arises from the fact that the debt is mutual. In every million, about nine hundred thousand is strictly mutual, and is susceptible, therefore, of ultimate payment by being balanced on the books of the bankers. The mode in which the balancing process is effected is very obvious, but will be specially explained under the heads of bank deposits and clearing houses. If one man is the holder of more of the paper of others than he has issued to others, another has issued a greater amount than he holds; and of all this variety, the credits of the parties at their bankers is a true reflection. These credits become, then, the expression, in money of account, of what has taken place and is going on in the channels of business in which commodities destined to consumption travel.

The great fund out of which the payments of trade or business is made is the credits granted upon the business or commercial paper. This fund represents commodities sold and to be paid for; the parties who transact the business out of which the fund arises are both creditors and debtors. They are not only willing, but it is their interest to apply their credits to extinguish or pay their debts. No creditor can ask any more effective payment to himself than that which enables him to pay his own debts. If a thousand men in one district have to their credit a million, it is probable they will owe among themselves nine hundred thousand: this sum can be fully and satisfactorily paid by the application of this amount in the credits. Their credit of a million will be reduced to one hundred thousand, and their whole debts as between each other will have been discharged. This payment is of the same nature, though made circuitously, as that which is made directly between two men who, having mutual transactions entered on their books of account, meet, and, so far as the indebtedness is mutual, discharge it by a balance.

In a civilized community, the obligation of a man to pay his debts is so sacred and so pressing, that he can desire no better medium of payment of that which others owe to him, than that which will serve to pay his own debts.

§ 2. *Foreign exchange as a means of payment — Complicated formerly with coinage and its evils — Now with increased transactions of domestic trade — The processes of foreign trade and payments readily perceived — Imports — Exports — Dealers in exchange and bankers — Payments may be made in either country — Rate of exchange — Trade with all nations — Circuitous exchange as effective as direct — Fluctuations in exchange — The economy of this mode of payment increases trade.*

The operation of the exchange between any two or more countries, having a mutual commerce, is effective in accomplishing a very large portion of the payments of that commerce. In reference to foreign trade, nations may be taken separately, and each nation spoken of as debtor for all that its people have imported, and creditor for all that has been exported. The business transactions of any country which lead to the exportation of commodities, are settled and adjusted at home; so, also, of transactions in foreign goods after they arrive; but there remains to be adjusted or paid the debts and credits arising between importers and exporters of the respective countries engaged in mutual trade, together with the debts and credits arising between the respective importers and exporters, and the persons from whom they purchase and to whom they sell. Upon debts and credits in this posture, foreign exchange is brought to bear as a mode of adjustment. The exchange of commodities first takes place, prices and amounts are adjusted, and then comes the affair of payment as a separate business in the hands of different parties, who are devoted to it as an occupation.

Foreign exchange has been long, and is even now by not a few, considered a most complicated and perplexed subject, level only to the comprehension of merchants of great shrewdness and special experience. It was, in former times, mixed up with many difficult problems of coinage; with numerous complex questions arising out of the various debasements of coins and currency, which made it impossible for many to understand its mysteries, and possible for only a very few to master its details. The days of debasement being pretty well spent, the subject of foreign exchange need not now be regarded as so unintelligible and forbidding.

It is not certainly so very hard to conceive of all the debts owing by persons in one country to persons in another, and to persons in all other countries, as being collectively a sum owing by one country to another, or to all other countries. In this view, every commercial country may be regarded as being indebted to each country with which it trades for all it has imported from each. This debt for imports is mutual to the extent of the trade of each with the other. Looking at the foreign trade of each country apart from its details and as a whole, it is much more simple and easy of comprehension than the domestic, which is more difficult to examine in the mass, and to separate from its details. The whole process of foreign and domestic trade is, in fact, perfectly alike; for if the trouble were taken thoroughly to analyze the home trade, it would be found to consist of a series of exports and imports from distinct regions or districts, of which every one may be compared to a separate nation. The small states of Germany, which carry on a foreign trade with each other and the world, are many of them no larger than counties in Pennsylvania. The domestic bills and other devices by which the payments of home trade are effected, perform the same office which is assigned to foreign bills in reference to that trade. In our relations with foreign countries, we have the advantage of well-defined boundaries, and of the custom-house and shipping regulations, to exhibit the amount and value of the trade; also of the fact that foreign payments concentrate largely in agencies separate from those in which our domestic payments are made. It is much easier, therefore, to ascertain the amount of our foreign than of our domestic payments. Besides, the former bear hardly a comparison in amount with the latter. There is, therefore, apart from coinage and its incidents, comparatively little difficulty in this subject of foreign exchange.

In the foreign trade there are two distinct classes of persons whose movements, with those of their various agencies, make up the operations of the foreign exchange. There are those who have exported goods or sent them out of the country, and who are entitled to payment from abroad; and those who have imported goods, or brought them into the country, and who must make payment abroad. If no device of economy, or expedient of convenience were resorted to in making these payments, the debtors abroad and the debtors at home would be obliged to transmit, from their respective countries to the countries of their respective creditors, the aggregate sums equivalent to the whole foreign trade. This would afford the absurd spectacle of a continual movement of the precious metals to effect what the trade itself had effected. It is very apparent that the nation which has, in the aggregate, exported to the value of a hundred millions, and imported to the value of ninety millions, has virtually paid for the imports by the exports. It is only necessary that those who owe the ninety millions for goods imported should pay that sum to those who are creditors for goods exported, and there would remain only ten millions to be otherwise paid. This is, in fact, the process. A class of dealers in exchange, who combine this business often with that of banker, broker or merchant, become purchasers of the bills drawn by the exporters of goods for the proceeds, and the same class become sellers of bills to those who, having imported goods, have remittances to make for them. If the amount exported is an hundred millions, bills to that extent may be drawn and purchased by these dealers; and if imports to the amount of ninety millions have been made, the dealers can sell exchange to that amount; and by this means a hundred and eighty millions of the payments arising out of this foreign commerce will be effected: that is, ninety millions' worth of goods exported will have been set off against ninety millions' worth imported. The main instruments of this payment or adjustment are bills of exchange between the parties engaged in the trade; these bills pass into the hands of those whose business it is to deal in them, and who, by keeping an open credit abroad, are always prepared to draw for sums to suit purchasers. Thus the amount due from individuals in another country becomes a fund upon which bills can be drawn, in sums to suit those who have payments to make there.

As the dealers in exchange have correspondents in many countries, it is of little moment to the progress or the facility of the payment whether the bills drawn for that purpose are all drawn in one or the other, or partly in both countries: the main thing to be effected being merely to balance the accounts so far as equal. This is a matter which proceeds wholly by individual choice and management. In our trade with Europe, the exchange business is chiefly done at home; that is, our exporters generally sell their bills at home, and our importers make their payments by specie exported or bills remitted. The market for the exchange is, then, with us; the barometer of the price of exchange is on our side of the water. The price at which exporters can sell their bills, and at which importers must purchase them, is subject to fluctuations arising from the supply and demand, and from other causes which affect prices generally. It is quite probable that the pressure of the demand is more steady, and that the adequacy of the supply is better known, where the market is chiefly on one side. The agency of the dealers on the other side is to collect the proceeds of the bills drawn upon the exports, and hold them subject to the bills drawn by dealers in exchange in the regular course of their business. On our side the dealers in exchange, whilst employed in purchasing bills for which they pay here, are also engaged in selling bills for which they receive payment here: on the other side their correspondents receive money for the bills remitted to them, and pay it out upon the bills drawn upon them. The operation is clearly, as stated, a mode of applying the goods sent abroad to payment for those brought home.

It is essentially a distinct operation from the home payments. The principle in both is the same, and the processes may occasionally be the same; but they are not the same thing. It is proper that those who export goods should be paid for them, and that those who import should pay for their imports. It is the same with those who buy and sell at home. In both foreign and domestic trade, goods are made to pay for goods; but when goods are exported, they have left the domain of domestic trade, and when goods first arrive, they have not yet entered into the domestic trade.

Those who export cotton, flour, and other commodities, are drawers of bills of exchange for the proceeds of the sales: the importers of foreign goods are purchasers of bills for the cost of such goods; or, if such goods are sent over by the foreign merchants or manufacturers, then they are purchasers of bills to the amount of their sales. The dealings between these parties, and the competition between bankers and brokers who are the intermediate agents in this business, govern the rate of exchange. The standard of coinage in each is the basis of the rate of exchange between any two countries. Between Great Britain and the United States this basis is the quantity of pure gold which, in Great Britain, is the equivalent of the pound sterling—the unit of the money of account there, and the quantity of pure gold which here is the equivalent of our dollar of account; or, taking our dollar coin and the British sovereign as the points of comparison, what is the price or value of each expressed in the money of account of the other. If, for instance, our dollar is worth four shillings and two pence in England, and a sovereign is worth four dollars and eighty-one cents here, the rate of exchange will be founded on this comparison, and will depend for its fluctuations upon the supply of bills and the demand for them, and upon such other influences as affect the price of exchange. A debt in England, although the debtor lives here, is expressed there in pounds, shillings and pence, the English money of account. Bills on England are expressed in English money of account, and must produce, when paid, the amount thus expressed; they are, however, bought and sold here at rates expressed in our money of account.[1]

What has been said of the trade between one country and another, for the sake of distinctness, is equally applicable to the whole foreign commerce of any nation. For by the same process of exchange—of buying bills and selling bills; of receiving the proceeds of bills remitted, and paying the amount of bills drawn—the exports of one nation to all other nations are used to pay for the imports of that nation from all others. As the number increases, the complication increases; but the object—the principle is the same, and the processes have only become more complex. We can readily comprehend how the purchaser of exchange upon one country may extend his business to the purchase of bills upon another, or more countries, or upon all countries. The business of the dealer in exchange being thus extended, he becomes a seller of all that he buys. In this country this dealer may purchase bills on all parts of Europe, and establish a correspondence in every city; or he may remit his bills to one house in London, and supply his customers with bills on London, which make a good remittance to all other places; or he may establish a house or correspondence in Paris, Havre, Hamburg, and Amsterdam, and draw upon all these or more points. The mode of adjusting all the payments of the foreign trade is that which all the parties concerned adopt as the most economical, rapid and convenient. Sometimes payments

---

[1] The mode of quoting exchange on England has absurdly continued the same since the act of Congress of March 2d, 1799, regulating the collection of duties, which then fixed the proportion between the pound sterling and the dollar at $4.44 to £1. This, by various changes in the coinage of the two countries, is now $4.84–5 to £1; but the mode of stating the rate of exchange continues to be the same, and quotes the bill for £1000, which sells for $4845, at 9⅛ per cent. above par. This shows how perseveringly men of business adhere to their modes of computation and expressing prices, but in no way affects the real price of exchange. This absurd custom should be abandoned, as it adds to complications, and tends to prevent the uninitiated from comprehending a subject which is of interest to all.

between particular places are settled in one way, and sometimes in another. He who owes a debt in Amsterdam may remit a bill on London, or Hamburg, or Havre, or direct as special information or circumstances may dictate; or a remittance may pass through several hands before it reaches its destination. The old works on exchange are full of minute and curious expositions on the subject of circuitous exchange.[1] They regarded skill in this art as the merchant's highest attainment. Its whole scope was, however, in not a few respects, better understood centuries ago than at the present time. Foreign exchange was then comparatively of more importance than at this day, when the progress of domestic industry has magnified the home trade of civilized countries vastly beyond the foreign in value and importance. The business of the foreign exchange is merged now in other vast transactions, and in this way it may not enjoy some facilities formerly accorded to it; and it does not stand out so conspicuously as one of the great processes of commerce. We have but to revert to the mode in which bills of exchange were paid at the fairs of Lyons,[2] and other cities and commercial marts, to be made fully sensible how well the subject of exchange was understood in past ages, and how skilfully the mode of adjustment was then adapted to the requirements of commerce. At Novi and Placentia, in Italy, for a long period previous to the eighteenth century, multitudes of merchants congregated every three months, for the mere purpose of liquidating debts; very little trade was carried on at the fairs held in those places, though vast sums were daily discharged by the process of set-off.[3]

Merged, however, as exchange operations are in a mass of great financial, banking and commercial transactions, they may be separated and brought very distinctly under survey by a little attention to the subject. There is due to every country,

[1] A curious diagram may be seen in "Postlethwaite's Dictionary of Commerce," illustrating the results of circuitous and complex operations in foreign exchange. Art. "Exchange."

[2] As may be seen in the chapter on "Fairs," in this volume.

[3] "Robert's Map of Commerce," folio; London; at "Placentia."

from all others, a certain amount in the aggregate; and there is due from each country to all others, in the aggregate, a certain sum. Whatever may be the processes or the complexity of details by which it is effected, it is manifest that, by the use of bills of exchange, the amount which is owing to any country may be applied to the extinguishment or payment of the debt due by that country, so far as it will reach, if not sufficient to cover the whole. The object is the same as in the direct exchange between any two countries; it is that the merchants of any country may apply the debts due to them to payment of the debts due by them. This is the same operation which is effected among individuals by the working of bank deposits, or the circulation of bank-notes; or among the separate districts of the same countries by the accounts of banks with each other, or by the mutual accounts and correspondence of dealers in domestic exchange. The operation to be performed, in paying foreign debts, may be readily comprehended by supposing that each country should send a statement of its claims upon all others to a common place of adjustment. From all these statements a balance-sheet could be framed, showing at one view the debts and credits of each, and the balances, favorable or unfavorable, of each. The whole sum of the indebtedness, except these balances, could of course be discharged upon this balance-sheet. As no such place of adjustment exists, whatever mode of payment comes nearest to this simple plan is likely to be the most convenient and economical. Bills of exchange are certificates or evidences of debt, which fall into the hands of dealers in exchange; and their offices, books of account and mutual correspondence throughout the world, are in the place of a clearing house or office common to all. If all these payments could be concentrated in one office, the whole extent of the business would be at once perceived and appreciated; the amount of the balances to be provided for would be at once ascertained; and measures for payment in the most advantageous mode could be adopted. As the work of adjustment now proceeds, however, in a detached manner, by the drawing and circulation of bills of exchange, it remains long in doubt how the balances will result; and exchange fluctuates in price, because no one can tell what the supply will be in comparison with the demand. This fluctuation in the price of bills is a real obstacle to the progress of adjustment; but it is an obstacle not necessarily belonging to the process of payment. It arises from ignorance of facts which are accessible; from the want of information which is attainable by proper legislation. The mere advance in the price of exchange arising from over-importation, and a consequent short supply of bills, is no evil, but a wholesome regulator of trade. It is a check upon over-trading, a damper upon speculation, and thus a benefit to commerce, although it interposes a difficulty in such payment. Every means should be used to avoid fluctuations arising from uncertainty, from want of correct information — not those which proceed from the greater or less demand or supply of bills.

The use of bills admits an interchange of commodities to the extent of the productive power of nations: the only limitation is, that the interchange must be equal. The goods of one must pay for the goods of the other; and so long as this equality is regarded, no difficulty can occur in the payment. When the equality is violated, and other payment is required than in the usual commodities, then difficulty arises, which will be extreme in proportion as the inequality is great. The efficiency of bills for this mode of setting off debts has been found ample for almost every exigency of trade; they circulate over the widest extent of territory, and from one nation to another, and thus save all necessity for a general congregation of merchants. The great system of payments, by which the exports and imports of a nation are balanced against each other, goes on thoroughly among merchants widely scattered, without personal communication, and without their appreciating the magnitude of the transaction of which their individual concerns form a part.

The examination of tables of exports and imports of the principal commercial countries will reveal at a glance how the mutual accounts are balanced by the paper process, and to what a small amount, comparatively, is the aid of the precious metals brought in requisition. It is true that, in the course of this adjustment, in which such multitudes scattered over a vast space are concerned, many difficulties arise from the varying moneys of account, and regulations of the mints, in those countries in which the goods are valued, from the monopolizing operations of great capitalists, from a spirit of speculation, from a general want of confidence, from the condition of the currency in the countries engaged in the commerce, and from a great variety of other causes; but these impediments are merely the friction of the machinery which continues to accomplish the payments of trade. The fluctuations in the price of bills of exchange thus employed as instruments of adjustment, which attract so much attention, and are so important to certain classes of merchants, are of small consequence comparatively; for when bills are above par, the exporter reaps the profit; and when below par, the importer who is the purchaser enjoys the advantage. At least this is true, except so far as foreigners have not usurped the business of importation.

The great law of trade upon which exchange is based, is an equivalent exchange of commodities: where this fails, exchange ceases. Where the debts are equal, the operations of exchange will balance them: where the equality ceases exchange stops, except so far as it may be prolonged upon the credit of those who deal in it, and a further transfer of commodities, or of money, must take place.

§ 3. *Fallacy of regarding foreign exchange as a criterion of domestic currency — Foreign exchange is simply the process of paying and receiving debts of foreign trade — The medium employed has its proper agency — So with the payments of domestic trade — Neither should guide nor control the other — The payments as distinct as the trade to which they belong Long-continued adverse foreign exchange of American colonies, and its results.*

Among the fallacies which have prevailed at various times in regard to foreign exchange, one of the most absurd and most dangerous has been, that the rate of foreign exchange furnishes a true criterion of the value and quantity of the interior currency. It is, perhaps, not so difficult to imagine how such a notion originated, as it is to tell why it has so long maintained its sway over intelligent minds; for it is still defended by statesmen and authors of high standing in Great Britain. These go so far as to contend that the foreign exchange is the true regulator of the currency of a country; that money or currency should be plenty or scarce, as exchange rules low or high.[1] This is not merely wrong, but it may be asserted that a more unsafe and delusive guide for the regulation of a paper currency cannot be found. The fact that an exportation of specie consequent upon an adverse exchange produces a contraction of currency, and other mischiefs, does not prove the rate of the exchange to be the rule of currency. The exchange is simply the adjustment, by bills of exchange, of the payments arising out of the foreign trade, which in many countries does not reach 1 per cent. of the home trade, and in none does it reach more than 10 or 12 per cent. The payments of the foreign and domestic trade are to be made by those engaged in each; and they are wholly distinct: the payments of the foreign trade may be larger or less, but each must be provided for according to its demands. Over-trading in the home trade produces a high rate of interest; over-trading in imports produces a high rate of exchange. The operation of adjustment by bills is much more effective, because more concentrated, in the foreign trade than in the domestic; so far as they are equivalent, it is setting off the goods exported against those imported, thereby effecting an immense saving of money in the mode of payment, none being used except to discharge balances. The dealers in exchange may be said to be bookkeepers of the foreign trade, who charge the goods exported, and credit those imported, and only pay or demand money upon the balances for or against their own country. In paying these balances only is gold or silver used. In the home trade the domestic currency is largely used, because this trade is more subdivided, more mingled with the retail; because no arrangement for payment by domestic bills of exchange and promissory notes has ever been devised so comprehensive, and yet so simple, as

[1] Torren's Letter to Tooke, 1840, page 20.

the payments by foreign exchange; and finally, because the home trade is of ten times the magnitude of the foreign. To carry on the home trade with advantage, a large amount of currency is required; and bank-notes, and the working of bank deposits, have been found very effective, economical and convenient. They are so readily adapted to all the requirements of business, that they save a resort to many otherwise necessary expedients. The payments in this home trade are thus distinct from those of the foreign; there is no propriety in blending them, and still less in making them dependant upon each other, or in giving one control over the other. There is no necessity that confusion or trouble in the one should produce like results in the other. General causes may operate alike on both; but what specially disturbs the payments of the merchant engaged in foreign trade should not necessarily disturb the payments of the domestic trader, as each class must pay its own debts by that mode of adjustment which is most approved. In all this we refer not to the ability to meet engagements, but to the mere machinery of payment; and we mean that derangement in the machinery of payment used in the foreign trade should not, and does not, necessarily derange the payments of domestic trade, unless some unwise and needless connection is established between them. If the importing merchants of the country have, therefore, in competition with foreigners, imported too many goods, and they find a short supply of foreign bills to make their foreign remittances, that furnishes no sound reason why the merchants and manufacturers of the interior should be embarrassed in their business, or why they should not be supplied with the regular quantity of domestic currency which that business requires. If the importing merchants find themselves under the necessity of taking specie from the banks to complete their payments, that should not abridge the facilities of the domestic merchant.

How, then, has it become a doctrine, that the supply of domestic currency should be regulated by the state of foreign exchange — a doctrine about as well-founded, as that our supply of beef at home should be determined by our supply of pepper from abroad? This strange and erroneous opinion sprung from another doctrine not less false, but more plausible; that foreign exchange is a true index (not of the price, for that would be true, but) of the value of money. Those holding this opinion seem to think that whatever value or price we may place upon our domestic currency, be that what it may, it is brought to an unerring test when it comes to be applied to the purchase of a foreign bill: that is, when we wish to place a sum of money in a foreign country, we must necessarily institute a strict comparison between our domestic currency and the money of the country to which remittance is to be made. This is clearly a mistake, when laid down as a general rule; so, also, is an opinion frequently stated in connection with it, that the rate of exchange is governed by the plenty or scarcity of money. No doubt the supply of money has its influence on foreign exchange; and if all other influences were removed, the rate would depend on the money market. But that which completely destroys both these doctrines is, that the rate of foreign exchange depends mainly on the supply of bills, and the demand for them.[1] This supply depends on the amount of goods exported, and the amount to be remitted for goods imported. These are main elements of the rate of exchange. The quantity of goods exported depends on the state of the markets throughout the world, and the special intelligence, enterprise and activity of those engaged in that trade; the amount of goods imported depends on similar considerations. If large exports make bills plenty, they must be sold at a discount; if large imports make bills in great demand, they must sell at a premium. It is the price of the bill, the paper instrument of exchange, which fluctuates in proportion to the supply and demand; these variations do not indicate the value of money, or its scarcity or plenty; but they mark the current price of the article of remittance.[2] It is the bill of exchange which, in these cases, is bought and sold, and not the money. But this ceases to be the case when the price of bills becomes

---

[1] "Blake on Exchange," page 91. [2] Ibid. pages 32, 33, 60.

so enhanced, that the buyers turn their attention from the purchase of bills to the purchase of coin or bullion. These becoming, then, the special article in demand, at once rise in price; and whilst under this influence, vary in their market value according to the intensity of the demand. Of course the intrinsic value of the precious metals undergoes no change corresponding with these variations. The influence and effect are special and local. It is well known to experienced merchants that, under the operation of a continued demand for the precious metals for remittance, they may reach a very high price in countries where there is no access to banks compelled to deliver them at par. The only check, if the demand continues, is the flowing in of the precious metals for the benefit of the high price. It is often said that exchange cannot rise higher than the cost of remitting the specie; but this is not true, as a general rule, except where there are banks bound to furnish specie on demand. This opinion only took root in England after the establishment of the Bank of England.

In many cases, where the effect of a continued demand for the precious metals for exportation has been most remarkable in its influence upon this price, the operation has been masked by the destruction of the money of account. Our commercial history, previous to the separation from Great Britain, affords many apt illustrations.[1] A long-continued adverse exchange caused gold and silver to be in such constant demand for export to England, that the price of exchange, and of coins or bullion, ranged for a long time, and in many places, from £133 to £175 currency for £100 sterling. This enormous rate was the effect of a continued unfavorable exchange. Other causes operated simultaneously, in some of the colonies, to break up the *money of account*, or establish a depreciation of the colonial currency. These were chiefly the abuse of paper issues: thus, in Massachusetts, the price of exchange reached £1100 for £100; in Rhode Island, £2300 for £100; and in South Carolina, £700

---

[1] "Hays' Negotiator," p. 221. "American Negotiator," vol. iv. "Postlethwaite's Commercial Dictionary," Art. "Currency."

for £100. The price of the Spanish dollar in Massachusetts, in 1749, was sixty shillings; the sterling price was four shillings and eight pence. It was not these vast fluctuations which produced the results we are about to notice, as they were so rapid and extraordinary as to require and to receive legislative correction. But the unfavorable exchange and high price of the precious metals which prevailed extensively and endured for a period of more than half a century, finally broke up and changed the money in which all men reckoned and kept their accounts. We do not say that this was a necessary or proper result, but that it was inevitable, unless the theory of money was better understood, or counteracting measures were adopted. When men were first offered an advance for coins — that is, when five shillings began to be offered for the dollar, that was worth only four shillings and eight pence in England— they would readily see that this was an advance in the price of coins; and it would be equally clear, as the price advanced gradually to seven shillings for the dollar. But when this price remained almost stationary for half a century, the general prices of the country would become fixed or arranged on the depreciated scale. For a long time it might be that prices would be quoted in both ways; that is, for specie and for currency. And so, in fact, they were in every colony; and every purchaser had it in his selection to pay in specie, in currency, or in articles of trade; and the price was according to the payment.[1] By degrees the original price of the dollar was lost sight of in all the dealings in the colonies; the high price at first known to be the result of special demand for exportation, or of a high exchange, from long habit came to be regarded as the regular price; and the general range of the rates of commodities being more commonly quoted in the depreciated scale, the latter became established in all minds as the money of account. The change of the money of account, or scale of reckoning, would be thus complete. It was by this process that the pound, shilling and penny sterling became so changed, that

[1] "Felt's Massachusetts Currency," page 54.

the dollars worth from four shillings six pence to four shillings eight pence, came to be rated in the colonies at six shillings, seven shillings six pence, and eight shillings. Thus, in Virginia, in Pennsylvania, and in New York, a separate and different scale of reckoning was adopted: in the first $\$3\frac{33}{100}$, in the second $\$2\frac{66}{100}$, and in the last $\$2\frac{50}{100}$, became the equivalent of the respective pounds or units of the respective moneys of account; and the prices of all the commodities of trade were adjusted and expressed in these several moneys of account, in proportion to the value expressed by these units.

The rate of exchange is, then, strictly applicable to bills of exchange, and only expresses the price of these commercial instruments of adjustment and remittance; when coin or bullion become the cheaper remittance the rate expresses their local price. Foreign exchange is no criterion, either of the value of money, or of its scarcity or abundance. If money is plenty, when bills are in demand, the rate of exchange may go higher; if scarce, it may restrict the exchange to a lower point than it would reach in a more easy money market. The whole operation of foreign exchange, so far as it belongs to commerce, is an affair of the foreign merchants: it arises out of their business, it is an economical expedient to effect their payments, and is governed in its movement by the varying amount of these payments.

NOTE TO CHAPTER VIII.

Foreign exchange in its relations with our banks — The export of specie, and the contraction of our currency — Resident agents of foreign merchants and manufacturers, and their influence on our foreign exchange and domestic currency.

THE fact that, in Great Britain and in the United States, the exportation of gold produces a contraction of the respective currencies, which, if continued, results in a commercial crisis, is, as we shall see hereafter, a consequence of the special constitution of our respective banking systems. In securing the solidity of our banks, and the convertibility of our paper currency, we have placed them under the necessity of furnishing to the buyers of foreign exchange coins or bullion at par, whenever it becomes their interest to demand them. It becomes their interest to make such demand after every excessive movement in their business. They are chiefly foreigners, and are the more apt to over-trade, and over-stock our markets with foreign goods, because they are imperfectly acquainted with the wants of the people, and the state of our markets. Besides, they are frequently forced to flood our markets, because their own are already filled or broken down, and they prefer to make forced sales, when they are to be made, among us, to making them at home. All such operations, however, must create an extraordinary demand for bills of exchange, a rise in their price, and a consequent demand for the precious metals, which the banks are called upon to supply. Every holder of gold and silver, in such cases, is permitted to ask the highest rate he can obtain for them ; but the banks cannot advance the price, and must furnish all that is required, at the risk of ruin. To save themselves in such emergencies, they must curtail their facilities to the domestic trade, until interest among domestic traders rises three or four hundred per cent., and the fall of prices has inflicted upon the country suffering it a loss of perhaps ten times the whole value of the over-importation which caused it. If no other fault existed in our present banking system than this, not a moment should be lost in finding a remedy. But so false are some of the opinions entertained by writers and public men of high standing, both in the United States and in Great Britain, that they regard every evil arising from the working of the foreign exchange as inevitable. They may be considered as looking at the fluctuations of exchanges as they do at the changes of the weather and the seasons. They must be encountered and endured, and all we can do, as they think, in defence is to look to our clothing and our shelter. They regard the fall in prices consequent upon the contraction of the facilities of the home trade, although inflicting a loss equal to all the specie in the country, as desirable, because the low price of goods may tempt the exporters of the coin to send commodities of trade. They know of but two ways of protecting the banks from the extraordinary demands of importing merchants: the one is to make the paper-money used chiefly by the domestic trader excessively scarce; and the other, to cause a general fall in prices sufficient to cause an increased exportation of goods. If this is not an enormity of mischief and absurdity, it will be needless to seek for one. It is crushing a hundred thousand to save a hundred; it is crushing industry to save commerce; it is crushing him that makes, to save him that carries; it is levying ten per cent. on three thousand millions of home products, to save the importers from paying ten per cent. on three hundred millions of foreign products; sacrificing the value of 300 millions, and ruining thousands of men, to save a few scores of importing merchants the disadvantage of a high rate of exchange. It is in England that the opinions we controvert are most frequently asserted; the act of 1844, in reference to the Bank of England, is expressly founded upon such doctrines. It is not to be supposed they will be without defenders here, and that our commercial legislation will escape the influence of absurdities sustained by such high authority.

There is another abuse of our foreign exchange which has prevailed of late years upon quite a large scale, with results very injurious to the regular course of business. The practice originated in the days when sailing packets required an average of a month to make a passage to Liverpool, and before steamers and telegraphs had lent their aid to commerce, of drawing bills upon European correspondents at sixty days, without interest. This practice, like that of quoting the pound sterling at $4.44, under a law of 1799, is still absurdly continued. Now, when the mails, and parcels, and gold itself, go to Europe in from ten to fifteen days, the continuance of this long exchange has become a source of positive mischief. All who are acquainted with the manner in which the importation of foreign goods is conducted in the United States, know that it has, in a large degree, fallen into the hands of foreign houses. The *ad valorem* system of 1846 has contributed mainly to this. There has long been a disposition, on the part of foreign manufacturers, merchants and speculators, to make our markets the receptacle of the surplus not merely of foreign production, but of all the foreign markets. The temptation was great on two grounds: our people were extravagant consumers, and by sending commodities here they saved their own market from breaking down. When, in addition to this, they were made, by the *ad valorem* appraisement, the valuers of their own goods, they had the strongest inducements to sell goods here not in active demand at home. Double invoices were freely used and tendered, not only to merchants, but to all persons bringing goods from Europe. This system, however, involved some risks, and occasional serious losses, and has been nearly superseded by another system of evasion. The foreign manufacturer now sends here a clerk, or agent, or partner, who becomes forthwith an importing merchant. The goods to be imported are invoiced to him at cost, without any perjury, or other evasion of law. The goods are sold in our market for the highest price which can be obtained; and the whole proceeds, profits and all, less only the expenses of the agent, are remitted to the foreign concern in specie, or by bill, according to the state of the exchange. This system invites large importations, because the foreign manufacturer is virtually the importer; he reaps all the profits, and foreign labor is proportionably encouraged. It brings, also, a much more formidable and serious competition against our manufacturers, because the goods brought here against them are produced where wages, and interest, and many articles of raw materials, are at half, or less than half, the rates prevailing here. The sixty day bills on Europe are found to be a powerful incentive to this anomalous mode of importation. These foreign agents, clerks, or partners become sellers of bills of exchange. For this purpose the foreign house to which they belong has only to introduce them properly, and pay promptly the bills thus drawn. In this way these houses can raise money in New York to any extent necessary, not only for the payment of duties, but also to be remitted in the shape of bills purchased, or specie, to their establishments in Europe, to assist in the manufacture of goods to be sent here. If the specie is sent over, the use of the money is thus obtained for some forty days without interest, and the operation may be repeated, and a large accommodation secured: they find it easier to raise money in the New York market, where interest has ruled from seven to ten per cent., than in Europe, where it has ruled from three to five per cent.

We have reason to believe that this process has carried — and if no change occurs in our policy, must continue to carry — large quantities of the precious metals from the United States. It furnishes a strong motive to remit by specie, instead of by bills of exchange; because the specie, when it arrives, is cash in hand, and not a bill with forty days to run. Thus we often see gold shipped in large sums, when the state of the exchange scarcely seems to justify it. These foreign houses are so many agencies for drawing money from the United States, and transmitting it to Europe to aid in building up establishments there, which, without this help at our expense, have more than power enough over our industry and our laborers. The effect is to raise interest here, and to reduce it there; to disturb our currency, and render their own more safe; to make our money market hard, and their own easy.

Of all this, it is not difficult to see the mischief, the injury sustained by our industry, and by our currency: what is the advantage? We have importing merchants enough to secure us from any want of foreign goods, without this ample license to foreign houses, manufacturers, and merchants. This influx of foreign agencies comes chiefly from France, Germany, and Belgium.

CHAPTER IX.

BANK-NOTES.

The facility and power of bank-notes — Some disadvantages — Properly issued in exchange for the business paper of individuals — Convertibility not the basis of the power of bank-notes, but a security against abuses — Inadequacy as such — Distinction between business of banks and the restraints imposed upon them — Bank-notes a medium by which the commodities of trade pay for commodities — Great demand for bank-notes by the debtors of the banks, the cause and result — Bank-notes represent value of articles of consumption in channels of trade — Received in payment for these articles of necessity as freely as specie — Circulation of, efficiency in that way — Exchange of between the banks operates like tickets — Proportion of bank-notes employed in business decreasing.

PROMISSORY notes, or bills of exchange, depend for their effect in circulation as a medium of payment, upon the credit of the parties —drawers, acceptors and indorsers—whose names are attached. Unless these are widely known, their paper cannot have a large circulation, as scrutiny and inquiry may have to be made with regard to every name. This is a serious check to the circulation of such paper. The credit system has furnished, in the shape of bank-notes, a very efficient and convenient medium of exchange. A bank with large capital and good credit furnishes its own notes at the regular rate of interest, in exchange for those of individuals. The bank-notes being of convenient denominations, in amounts suited to the ordinary transactions of business, large and small, are at once not only more available in payments than promissory notes and bills of exchange, but more so than coins of silver or gold. It cannot be necessary to enlarge upon the facility and efficiency of bank-notes as a medium of payment. It is hardly possible to conceive of any medium more easy to carry or circulate as a substitute for money. The substitution of these in trade for promissory notes, or bills of exchange, proved from the first an immense facility in business. But as bank-notes are attended with many difficulties in regard to hazard of robbery, of fire, of forgery, and insolvency of banks, they do not furnish a satisfactory medium in all respects, and leave much to be desired. Whatever facilities there may be in their use, so many are the obstacles in the way of shaping an adequate banking system, so much difficulty in obtaining proper securities against abuses, so much distrust in the public mind of institutions having the important power of issuing their own notes to be circulated and received as money, that we refrain here from entering into these or any similar topics. Our object now is only to explain how bank-notes are so effective as a means of payment, and how the substitution of the notes of banks for the notes of individuals operates. We assume, then, for the present, that the notes are issued by safe banks in good credit, and doing a legitimate business.

The proper, safe and legitimate business of a bank of circulation is to issue its own notes, either in substitution or in exchange for commercial paper, such as the promissory notes and bills of exchange of individuals. These may not be sufficiently known; their paper is, for the most part, of unsuitable form and amounts, indivisible, and otherwise inconvenient for general circulation. The notes of a bank, on the other hand, are well-known, of convenient amount and form; they are divisible, or at least obtainable in any desired denominations, and are otherwise convenient for constant use in payment of large or small sums. They not only perform all the functions of a currency, or circulating medium, which the individual commercial paper, for which they are substituted, could perform, but many other purposes which it could not; they become, in fact, not merely a substitute for individual paper, but for money itself. It is this latter quality which makes the power of issue so dangerous to the public, and therefore the subject of so much caution on the part of public authorities. It cannot be denied that the power of issuing paper-money, for such in effect is bank-notes, should not be conceded without extraordinary safeguards and precautions. Among these, one of the most stringent and effective is the liability of redeeming all their issues on demand in gold or silver. Even this has not proved effectual, nor prevented frequent abuse. It is left to the public to make the demand or not; if made, it destroys the system; if not made, abuses are not only possible, but continue to occur.

But whilst it is almost universally conceded that, with all its imperfections, the restraint of specie payments is the most reliable and effectual check upon banks of circulation, it must not be regarded as the basis of their efficiency or usefulness when properly conducted. It is a security to the public for their good behavior, a check upon over-action, not a power to maintain movements, or give efficiency to movements otherwise useless. For twenty years and more, the Bank of England paid no specie for its notes; and the question which arose thereupon was not whether the payments of England were not effectually made, during that time, in the notes of the bank, but whether the bank had not abused its privilege by issuing too many notes. So in the United States, during the suspension of specie payments, the trade of the country proceeded; and bank-notes were not less employed in current payments, than when redeemable in specie. The validity of these payments, for the time being, are not called in question; but the people of this country have never been satisfied that such a power can be safely committed to the interested hands of bank directors. The continuance of specie payments is demanded by them as the best guarantee which can be given by banks of circulation. It being important that this distinction be kept in mind by those who would understand the true ground of the success of banks of circulation, as one of the great devices of the credit system, we have placed it thus broadly before the reader. Let him regard the movements of the real business of the bank wholly apart from the restraints and responsibilities under which the bank is placed to keep it from running astray.

We recur, then, to the remark, that the proper business of a bank of circulation is to issue its own notes in place of the actual business paper of individuals. For the latter accommodation, the bank charges interest the same as if it advanced money. We pass over the fact at present, that the banks frequently give, in place of the notes, merely a credit for the amount of the paper discounted on their books, which is to the same effect as if the notes had been received and deposited. The operation of bank deposits in payments will come under separate consideration. We have explained the process by which a payment is made by the negotiation of a promissory note or bill of exchange. The holder of such business paper has sold commodities of trade, for which he received the paper; he purchases other commodities, for which he pays with this same paper. We have stated that this mode of payment is applicable only to a very small range of business, and that its inconveniences led probably to a larger employment of the more convenient and effective medium of bank-notes. If the holder of a promissory note, or bill of exchange, who gave commodities for it, desires to purchase other commodities for the amount or a part of it, he may exchange it for the notes of a bank. If, with these bank-notes, he purchases other commodities, or pays debts for commodities already purchased, it is obvious that he, in substance, exchanges the articles for which he receives the promissory note for those which he purchases with the bank-notes. Thus these paper promises, whether the notes of banks or of individuals, furnish a medium by which men exchange what they have for what they want. It matters not, to men of business, how the final adjustment or discharge of these bank-notes and individual notes is effected, so that they thereby make what they sell pay for what they purchase. It will come in our way to explain fully how this paper adjustment takes place; how this immense amount of bank-notes payable on demand, and these individual notes payable in a few months, all in gold or silver, are all fully paid, discharged and retired without the use of one per cent. of the amount in the precious metals. As this explanation involves other processes not yet touched, we reserve it for a future page, merely insisting here on the superiority of bank-notes, as a medium of exchange, to the business notes of individuals.

The debtors to banks of circulation in any commercial community are under a strong necessity of promptly meeting their engagements: no more imperative motive can be brought to bear upon them than that of preserving their credit, and continuing their business. Ruin, bankruptcy and utter discredit stare every man in the face who falters in the performance of his engagements. Every energy, every effort is put forth for this purpose; no sacrifice of means, of time, of skill, of mental activity, or watchful anxiety, is spared to accomplish punctually the payment of every liability as it matures. This, then, creates a demand for the bank-notes, of proportionate intensity. There are goods offering for sale by those who have debts to pay, which must at all hazards be paid; and these goods must be fully equal in value to the sum of the debts to be paid, because the debts were created by the purchase of the goods: of course, the necessity of realizing in the bank-notes, or what is equivalent, will compel the sellers to be reasonable in their demands. All this merchandise is, therefore, not only applicable to the purpose, but all the holders who are debtors to the bank are so many agents actively employed in the redemption of the bank-notes. It is this imperative demand for the bank-notes, and this extreme necessity of meeting bank liabilities, which sustains so amply the value of the notes of all well-managed banks. A man may reduce his expenses for food and clothing, and wait many days for the gold and silver which he is accustomed to pay for these necessaries; but he cannot postpone a day the payment of his note in bank: there is no one article, then, so indispensable to those who are indebted in banks as bank-notes, or their equivalent. The notes issued by banks, in discount of commercial paper, must correspond as the paper discounted does to the value of the goods for which it was given. It would require all the bank-notes thus issued to purchase the goods, the sale of which created the paper in exchange for which the bank-notes were given. The goods are sufficient to redeem the notes issued upon them, and therefore sufficient to pay or redeem the bank-notes substituted. Apart from the artificial securities required of banks, this is the real basis of bank-notes. They are issued in exchange for individual notes, which are given for the purchase of merchandise; the sale of this merchandise produces the means to redeem the individual notes, or the bank-notes. It is this feature which gives banks of circulation their firmest support. In any commercial community where such banks abound, they hold a very large proportion of the notes given for merchandise, and that merchandise must be the virtual basis on which their issues rest; the holders of merchandise of all descriptions, to suit the demands of necessity or luxury, offer it as freely for the bank-notes as they would for gold or silver, because the bank-notes will pay their debts as effectually as anything else can.

The summary of this process of payment is, that merchants purchase goods, and manufacturers purchase supplies, with their individual notes or bills, which are exchanged for bank-notes; and these bank-notes are either sought after and obtained by the debtors of the bank, to be returned in payment of their liabilities, or they pay the bank in some medium which will redeem the notes. The goods sold create the paper discounted, and sold again they furnish the means to withdraw the paper discounted, and the issues of the bank: or, more generally, the continual operation of trade constantly originates new paper, and thence new issues from the banks, which furnish the medium in which the individual paper is continually paid. The manufacturer, merchant and farmer purchase stock in one period of the year, for which they give their notes, which the holders convert into bank-notes. In another period they sell and create paper, which is applied to meet their engagements. Thus goods are bought and sold, or produced and sold, until the distribution is complete, and merchant and producer have received and issued paper until it is evident, in the regular routine of their business, that it supplies the means of its continuance. Every such business man, in the course of a year, issues his own notes to a certain amount; he receives, also, the notes of others to a certain amount; he requires some facility to set-off the notes he receives against those he has given. The bank furnishes that facility in several ways. The debtor cannot directly exchange the individual notes issued to him for those he issues, but he can convert those he receives into bank-notes, which will be received in payment for, or exchange for his paper. The bank gives nothing but bank-notes, or bank credits, for the paper it discounts; it requires nothing for payment but bank credits, or bank-notes. The debtor does not obtain this facility without paying for it; he must purchase the bank-notes, and he does this not with money or coins necessarily, but with business paper received, perhaps, for the very goods by purchase of which his debt was created. It is thus that the whole body of debtors to the bank are competitors, with all the merchandise in their possession, for the bank-notes in circulation which furnish such a convenient mode of discharging their liabilities. The bank-notes so much in request by the debtors become equally in request by the whole body of consumers who use, employ or consume the goods held and offered for sale by this whole body of debtors. Coins and bullion are received in exchange for these same goods, simply because of their intrinsic value; but as these will go no further, in payment of debts, than the bank-notes, the latter are employed almost exclusively in countries where banks of circulation are found.

This operation of payment is entirely independent of the precious metals; their presence or agency is not in the least needful; they have no part in the transaction. We are not speaking of banking as regulated by law, but merely explaining the process of liquidation, as effected by bank-notes. The usefulness of bank-notes as a medium of payment is not confined to the mere process of liquidation above specified; their efficiency in aid of commerce is, perhaps, greatest by their perfect facility of circulation. In practice they do not pass immediately into the hands of the debtors of the bank, and from them into the bank in payment or liquidation of the notes discounted. They circulate through every channel of trade with a rapidity of movement wholly unattainable by any possible circulation of coins. They are dispersed, by the thousand varieties of expenditure among all classes of the community, to the whole mass of the people in such proportions as the course of trade, salaries, wages, fees, and other modes of income and expenditure, may bring about;

all take them freely in payment, simply because they know they will be as freely received. The only question is, will they pass? Whilst they are performing all this movement, the demand for them by the debtors of the bank, which is urgent and imperious, is operating with incessant and anxious vigor to obtain the quantity of bank-notes necessary to meet their daily maturing engagements. As these engagements, in the first instances, gave origin to the issues of the bank, the amount in circulation is just the amount required. The demand for them is, therefore, equivalent to the whole quantity extant. So long as this demand continues, bank-notes must keep their value, as they are in demand to pay the same amount for which they were issued.

The process by which bank-notes, in themselves of no intrinsic value, effect a payment in this circulation is the same as that which gives efficiency to a payment made by negotiating promissory notes. The miller who sells a lot of flour for bank-notes, and with the same notes purchases wheat, has exchanged his flour for wheat. The merchant who sells goods for bank-notes, and with those notes purchases other goods, has in fact merely changed one lot of goods for another. Thus the bank-notes are a mere medium of exchange. They are received for what is sold only because they will be received for what is purchased. It is not even the solvency of the bank, nor the fact of its redeeming its notes in gold or silver, which gives efficacy to such circulation of notes. The real character of the notes employed in any transaction can seldom be known to the receiver; they may even be spurious, yet the validity of the exchange will be the same. He that sells iron for bank-notes, and with the notes purchases flour, has exchanged his iron for flour, let what may be the character of the notes. To make the transaction complete, it is only necessary that the party receiving the notes for iron should know that they will be received without hesitation for flour. Whatever may be the real value or character of the bank-notes, so long as the parties exchanging merchandise continue to make them the medium, so long will their commerce proceed without hindrance. The exchange of goods, in any particular instance, could not indeed be more effectual if, instead of notes, gold itself had been used. We do not allege that the medium is a matter of indifference, nor recommend that worthless rags should be employed for that purpose; but we show that it is not the genuineness of the notes, nor their convertibility, nor the solvency of their issuers, that gives validity to the sales of which they are the medium. What is necessary to be done to secure the confidence of the public in bank-notes, so that they may the better perform the functions we have described, and prevent the abuse of over-issues by the banks, is matter of separate consideration.

The view which we desire to present here is simply that the exchange of the iron for the flour is not essentially dependent on the actual goodness of the notes used as a medium. The iron may be sold for a promissory note, and that note given for the flour; or, the iron merchant may simply charge the flour merchant in his books for the value of the iron, and be charged himself for the flour; and when these books are settled and balanced, the reciprocal payment will be as effectual as if gold, or silver, or bank-notes, or any other medium had been employed.

In one aspect of this circulation of bank-notes they operate like counters or tickets; they are issued in discount of paper given for goods, they are carried to the vicinity of banks, and paid for goods to persons who deposit them in bank, receiving a credit on the books instead; the banks receiving each other's notes, exchange them, and being thus acquitted of each other, they owe only to their depositors, and this indebtedness to the depositors is liquidated by the deposits being used to pay and withdraw the discounted paper. This is the channel in which a vast portion of the bank-notes run; but they are not confined to this course, and therefore run into a thousand channels, ever varying with the diversities of trade, and the schemes and whims of men.

But useful and efficient as bank-notes are in various ways, one of which — the saving in the wear of coin — we have not mentioned, there is a limit to their power; or, rather, other modes of payment have been devised and extensively employed, of superior efficiency. We find that the circulation of bank-notes in Great Britain, and in this country, has kept pace neither with the increase of banks, nor with the immense enlargement of business. The circulation of notes by the Bank of England reached, for the first time, the sum of twenty millions sterling in 1806. In 1817 it reached twenty-nine and a half millions; but for the whole period the average is but little, if any, above twenty millions. This is remarkable, if the immense progress of Great Britain in commerce, agriculture and manufactures be taken into account. It cannot be doubted that, if bank-notes were employed now as in 1806 and in 1817, it would require forty millions from the Bank of England. The circulation of 1856 averaged about twenty millions. The act of 1844, which was restrictive of the issue of notes, may have tended to keep down the circulation; but the average circulation of the ten years preceding 1844 was considerably under twenty millions. It is obvious, from this, that the proportion of bank-notes employed in Great Britain is decreasing, and has been for fifty years. A comparison of bank returns, in this country, for the last twenty-five years, will exhibit a similar result. As the payments occurring in the business of Great Britain have increased in proportion to the population and productive industry of that country, which have nearly doubled, it is evident that other modes of payment or adjustment have, to a large extent, taken the place of bank-notes. That which has been most extensively employed, and which, to the greatest extent, supplanted the circulation of bank-notes in Great Britain, and in the United States, is bank credits, which operate under the name of bank deposits. A very large proportion of the individual paper of men of business, in the United States, is discounted by the banks without taking the form of bank-notes, or being included in the circulation of the banks. The proceeds of the discounted paper are merely placed to the credit of the party, and take their place as deposits. This form of credit will be next considered.[1]

---

[1] The efficacy and power of bank-notes as a currency will be further dwelt upon in the Chapters upon the Bank of England and the banks of the United States.

CHAPTER X.

DEPOSITS IN BANKS.

A greater facility than bank-notes needful for large operations — Banks become the reservoir of all currency not in actual use for retail trade — This constitutes the great fund employed in large payments — The credits form the fund out of which debts are paid — Each depositor employs his own credits to pay his own debts — All the credits will pay all the debts — The deposits are virtually a system of accounts kept by the banks for their customers — Indebtedness of business chiefly mutual, and settled by set-off — Demand for deposits — Circulation — Absorbed by the banks in payments of discounted paper — The banks give credits on their books for paper, and receive those credits in payment.

THE concentration of payments at the great centres or entrepôts of commerce enables the banks to afford another facility of payment far more effective and important than bank-notes. In the large payments incessantly going on at these points, counting bank-notes would be considered a serious obstruction to business; and keeping them on hand for constant use would be regarded as a needless risk, burden and expense. At such places merchants and others keep open running accounts with one or more banks, depositing bank-notes and money as fast as received to the credit of their accounts; thus making the banks the receptacle or reservoir of all the currency and money not in actual use for the operations of retail trade. The banks, in this way, absorb a very large portion of all the currency in circulation. These deposits in the principal cities greatly exceed in amount the circulation of the banks, and their operation or working is far more efficient and active than that of the bank-notes. One effect is not only to return to the banks immediately all the notes not required for circulation, but to save the issue of immense sums. When individual paper is discounted, the applicant, instead of receiving bank-notes, takes credit for the proceeds in his deposit account, and draws upon this account to meet his maturing payments. The paper discounted is daily falling due, and being paid by checks drawn by the debtors on their bank account. The banks are constantly discounting newly-offered paper, thus keeping up the accounts of the depositors. While these accounts are continually used up and extinguished on one side, they are continually renewed and extended at the other. It is but to a very small extent, probably not one per cent. of their amount, that deposits are made in gold or silver; they consist in part of bank-notes absorbed from the circulation, but chiefly of credits granted upon the discount of commercial paper. The credits thus granted give the option to take bank-notes, if required; and they serve not only to pay debts at the bank at which the account is kept, but at other banks in the vicinity. This of course leads to large transactions among the banks. Individuals find their liabilities scattered through many banks, all which are paid by checks on the bank in which their account is kept, or by bank-notes taken up by check for that purpose. Thus all the discounted paper, and all individual notes deposited with the bank for collection, are paid by the working of these deposits; the bank is paid in its own notes, in a check on itself, by charging the debtor in account, or in the notes of or a check upon another bank. Men of business who keep accounts in bank, are creditor and debtor during the year to nearly the whole extent of their business. They give their individual paper as evidence of debt in their purchases: they take paper from others for the amount of their sales. The banks discount the paper they take, and demand payment of the paper they gave. The banks, in effect, keep a set of books of account for their customers, in which they are credited for what is due them from others, and debited for the amount of their debts. The convenience and advantage of these books may be better understood if we notice that the bank does not merely give its customer a credit for the amount of a bill or note, engaging to return the same bill or note on demand, or the amount when collected. It gives an open credit, which enables the customer to draw as occasion requires for any sum, large or small, within the amount of the credit. In this shape the credits of a customer become perfectly manageable and applicable to the payment of his debts as they mature and are presented. What is done for one, is done for all. The whole amount of the commercial or individual paper discounted at the banks is susceptible of being employed in this very effective way. The banks become so many reservoirs of the means of commercial liquidation. Notes and bills merely lodged for safe-keeping or collection would afford no advantage to be compared with the actual process. By the mode adopted, the whole proceeds of all the commercial paper discounted is constituted a fund, which being drawn upon as required by checks, becomes more convenient and effective than money in discharge of debts. By a single check, the work of a moment, any sum can be instantly paid with its minutest fraction. That which, however, gives real foundation and continuous efficiency to this rapid and easy mode of payment, is, that this great fund mainly belongs to those who are, in fact, creditors and debtors of each other. Each individual is both creditor and debtor; and the chief care of each is so to manage his credits as to make them available in discharge of his debts. This deposit fund is a vast facility for this purpose; it is a safe and good fund for those who use it, because it safely and finally discharges their debts. Gold and silver can do no more. If a merchant owes $100,000 in various sums, upon promissory notes, to divers persons, and if various persons owe him $110,000 upon notes given to him, he can in no way be more safely or legitimately accommodated than by being enabled to apply $100,000 of what is owing to him in discharge of the $100,000 he owes. For this purpose it is obviously not necessary that the amounts to be thus employed should be converted, or even be convertible into money. The banks merely convert it into a fund, upon which the parties concerned can draw. If a merchant, therefore, who has $110,000 to his credit in bank, draws upon this fund for $100,000, and applies it in payment of that amount of debt, he is debited the amount, and his debt is acquitted. The fund for payments thus furnished on the books of the bank is continually replenished by constant streams of fresh business paper, and constantly drawn off and diminished by the amount of debts paid. Its effect is to enable the customers of the banks to set-off their credits against debts with more or less facility, according to the varied circumstances of each case.

The business or commercial paper of a community is thus converted, not into money, but into a fund, the amount of which and all the dealings in it are expressed in money of account. All are willing to receive payment of what is due to them in this fund, because with it each one can pay what he owes to others. No more acceptable medium of payment can be found or produced than that which will pay debts; for, among civilized people, there is no necessity of business more imperious than the payment of debts. No one will trouble himself to exact payment of what is due to him in gold or silver, if he can pay the debt he owes by a check on a banker. No individual can desire a greater facility for payment of his debts than that of applying to that purpose the debts which others owe to him. This involves no employment of the precious metals. The money of account, in which all amounts are expressed, is common to creditors and debtors, and understood by both. What one person can do, in applying his credits to his debts, any number can do. Thus the credits become the fund out of which the debts are paid; but as the operating parties are mainly both debtors and creditors, the whole payment is a mere process of adjustment by which those concerned balance their accounts. It is quite possible, theoretically, to bring the mutual claims of all these persons into a series of accounts with each other in one book, and thus balance them, without checks or money, or any so-called deposit.

The banks keep open accounts with each other, which daily exhibit the operation of these payments. The bank upon which its customers have drawn most largely, whether in notes or checks, will fall in debt to the others accordingly; but each will be able to present claims upon the others in proportion to the amount it has received in checks upon them or their notes. Each will be found to stand, in regard to the others, a debtor and creditor. These amounts are adjusted every day, once in two or three days, or as convenience may dictate: each one has a balance, favorable or unfavorable, with every other; and when their accounts are settled, the whole of these mutual claims, except the balances, are paid and forever extinguished. Banks keeping such mutual accounts soon learn the course of trade, and are able to regulate their business with reference to this mutual indebtedness, so that the balances fluctuate but little, and the amounts to be paid on settlement will rarely exceed five per cent. of the sum paid off. In each bank the same process goes on between individual depositors as among the banks. So far as there are mutual claims among those keeping accounts at the same bank, they will be settled, however complicated, by the working of the deposit account. Each customer of a bank is not only creditor and debtor in certain amounts, with reference to his whole business, but he is debtor and creditor in certain amounts with other customers of the same bank. So far as this mutual indebtedness may exist between the customers of the same bank, their debts will be paid by check on the bank, and what one account gains another loses — the deposits are neither increased nor diminished. The bank is continually granting credits, which go to swell the sum of its deposits; and it is continually receiving payments in these credits, which extinguishes so much as is thus received. As banks receive their own notes in payment of all dues to them, so to the same effect they receive the checks on themselves of any of their depositors. The deposit is very rarely of coin or bullion, or other article of intrinsic value; its circulating value arises from the fact that, like bank-notes, it will make purchases, and pay debts. We have seen that the demand for bank-notes to meet bank engagements, and others as pressing, is stimulated by a necessity the most inexorable — the necessity, among merchants, of punctuality in their payments. To effect their payments, merchants spare no anxieties, labors, nor sacrifices. This is the practical and most powerful support of the issues of banks of circulation; and it applies as strongly to the deposits or credits granted in that shape, as to the notes of a bank — the deposits being far more employed in paying debts than bank-notes. A man may refrain from incurring expenses, to pay which the bank-notes are usually employed; but he cannot refrain from paying his debts, even when he has neither notes nor deposits, unless he is ready to suffer bankruptcy. The checks upon these deposits are, therefore, as good payment as the bank-notes, not because they are, like them, convertible into gold or silver, but because they are, like them, receivable in payment of debts. Nearly the whole of the large purchases of commerce are made upon promises of payment at a future day; whatever is receivable for these payments must be, for the occasion, as desirable as gold or silver; for these can make no more effectual payment, and are far less convenient and safe.

The bank deposits are the grand receptacle of all the funds not needed for immediate use, and of the large sums required for the heavier payments of trade. Being composed chiefly of credits granted upon the discount of commercial paper, they do not spring from gold or silver, they do not turn into gold or silver, they do not represent gold or silver: if they may be said to represent anything, it is the value of the merchandise, the sale of which upon credit has given existence to the mass of both bank-notes and bank credits. The operation of deposits is, like that of bank-notes, both direct and circuitous. The gold or silver which is deposited in banks to credit of him who transfers his ownership by check continues thus to circulate, until the amount or the equivalent is withdrawn or paid to the bank. So the credits granted upon discount of individual notes may be transferred without limit from one to another, each time making a payment, until absorbed by the constantly recurring demand of the bank upon its customers. Nine-tenths of the amount of the deposits in our banks consist of their own notes, and of the credits granted as above; yet all blend into one common mass, and effect the same results as if the whole deposit had been gold or silver.

The successful operation of this most efficient of all the means of payment is not dependent upon the actual employment of the precious metals, coins or bullion. It neither excludes nor requires them. A merchant who pays, in this way, to the amount of half a million yearly, may not, altogether, have deposited a thousand in coins. The amount to his credit is constantly growing by receipts, as well as diminishing by payments. The result at which he aims, and which he effects, is to apply, in the progress of his business, the proceeds of his sales to the payment of his purchases; to set-off his credits against his debts. Where the creditor and debtor are depositors in different banks, the debts are paid with equal facility, their payments merely leaving matter for adjustment between the several banks. If we suppose that all the business men of Philadelphia had deposit accounts in the Bank of North America, when it was the only bank in that city, the adjustments of all would have been completed on the books of that bank. Each depositor would have to pay a certain amount to others in that city, and others in that city would have to pay a certain amount to him: each depositor could have drawn upon his account for money deposited, and for the proceeds of notes discounted, in payment of his debts as they matured. If we suppose that, whilst this was the only bank in the city, there were 1000 persons who were thus creditors to, at least, the average amount of $10,000 each, and debtors to at least the same sum; and that there were 100 persons who were each, in like manner, creditor and debtor to at least the sum of $100,000; and that there were 10 persons each, in like manner, indebted $200,000: the sum of this indebtedness would be $44,000,000: if this amount were run off three times in a year, it would make a total of $132,000,000, or $11,000,000 for each month. Whatever course might be taken in regard to the sums or balances owing beyond this mutual indebtedness, nothing else would be necessary for the extinguishment of this large sum of $11,000,000 each month than drawing and receiving checks, with corresponding entries on the books of the bank. Thus would be extinguished the individual paper discounted by the bank, corresponding with the commercial transactions which had given rise to it. For goods received the depositors had issued their notes, and for goods delivered they had received notes; and all these had been discounted by the bank, and converted into a fund available for the payment of all, because it would be of the very same nature as the debts it would be employed to pay. The bank which would have purchased all these notes merely with credits on its books, would receive these credits in payment when the period of maturity arrived. We may attain, perhaps, a more distinct idea of the effect of the deposit system of payment, if we suppose the merchants in a city without banks to have adopted a mode of payment or adjustment of this kind. Having opened an office, and appointed their agents for its management, they deposited, instead of money or bank-notes, simply their business paper, notes, and bills of exchange, receiving credit for the amount in the books of the office, less the interest till maturity. A fund would be thus constituted of all the commercial paper of the city. When a note or bill matured, the debtor or payer would simply draw his check for the amount to be paid, and thus reduce the sum of his credit so much. If the party paying had not credit on the books to a sufficient amount, he would either borrow from those who had, or pay the deficiency in money. It will be noted that, by this mode of adjustment, the sum applicable for payment would exactly correspond to the amount of the credits granted, less the interest or discount, which would have to be paid in money, or be otherwise arranged. The money paid in by those whose credits were unequal to their debts would go to those whose credits exceeded their debts; and the money paid in as interest, or as the difference between the proceeds of a note and its face, or nominal amount, would belong to the office. Thus this business would close and balance as soon as all the paper matured; or it might be continued at pleasure, the new credits being granted according to the regular progress of business.

We have supposed deposits thus created to be only used in payment of the paper which gave rise to them; but they might be employed for other payments. The demand for them to pay the paper on which they were founded would be urgent, and would proceed from the holders of the goods, the purchase of which gave origin to the paper deposited; and yet there might be intervals, whilst the paper was maturing, in which these deposits could be freely circulated as a currency, by means of checks, throughout a whole commercial community. Their value would be undoubted, because the demand by those under the absolute necessity of obtaining them would ensure their commanding at all times, in any article of trade, their nominal value. These credits would, therefore, circulate just as the deposits of a bank circulate; for if the debtors in these deposit accounts should fail to secure the amount of deposit required to meet their engagements, they must pay in money, and thus furnish the fund to repay the credits or deposits when demanded by those into whose hands the circulation may have carried them.

A very efficient circulation of deposits might be originated and kept up on this plan, upon the basis of commercial paper, continually discharged by payment, and renewed by fresh supplies. To the extent of the direct adjustment or set-off of debts between the parties to such an arrangement — that is, not including the circulation of which we have just spoken — the whole result may be attained by simply opening an account at a suitable office, and charging each accountant with all the notes and bills he is bound to pay, and crediting him with all he produces against others. This would be a direct set-off of each one's credits against his debts, and an exhibit of balances showing what sum each one had to receive or pay. The whole of the equal indebtedness would be extinguished at once, and the amount to be paid on the debtors, balances would be exactly equal to the amount to be received, so that these balances paid in would discharge the whole. The course of trade shows that, in any mercantile community, these balances range between five and ten per cent.; so that, in adjusting an indebtedness of a million, the sum of the balances would range between fifty and a hundred thousand. In the working of the actual deposit accounts of our banks, it is rare that these balances are all withdrawn from bank; they are, in part, lent by the holders to the debtors to meet their deficiencies; or, being allowed to remain, their accumulation enables the bank to extend accommodations to those whose balances are unfavorable. In process of a few months, the balances greatly change; many of the debtors and creditors change places. The system of adjustment just supposed might be continued from month to month, or year to year, the operation of the book entries being sufficient to effect the payments through any number of fluctuations.

The main result of the deposit system, as now managed by our banks, is a mode of keeping the accounts of persons who have large mutual transactions. This will be more apparent, if we suppose another mode of accomplishing the same payments. Let each one who makes a sale of merchandise charge the purchaser with the amount; and when he makes a purchase, let him credit the seller with the amount. If an abstract from all the books of those who would otherwise be the depositors were furnished for the purpose, an account could be stated with each person, showing all his transactions, exhibiting the resulting balances and the amount extinguished among the whole. The promissory notes and bills of exchange usually employed are evidences of debt arising upon sales of merchandise or other transactions; the abstract of entries above supposed would furnish evidence of the same debts, susceptible of payment in the same way.

The actual system of payment now in use in the most commercial nations is that the business of trade — that is, the sales and transfers of merchandise — proceed among merchants according to their convenience, and their opinions of what will best meet the demands of consumers, and promote their own interests. This process of distribution by the merchant to the consumer is based mainly upon the confidence of merchants in each other. The goods are delivered at once — the payment is deferred. The goods proceed by a thousand channels to their final destination — the whole business of payment is reserved to be separately accomplished. These payments are effected by the employment of separate agencies, professions, institutions and hosts of men; as well as by the aid of books of account, promissory notes, bills of exchange, bank-notes, bank deposits, and gold and silver. In this system sometimes one way is best, and sometimes another; sometimes one agency or agent, and sometimes another; sometimes notes, sometimes checks, sometimes gold, and sometimes silver. All these are but various means of attaining an end. The usage is always to employ the easiest and least expensive mode that will be effectual. It happens rarely, perhaps, that the parties paying have their choice of all the various modes of payment; they can choose only among the facilities which may be offered, or may be within their reach.

Looking at the whole process of payment in any commercial country, it presents a mass of details, and a complication of procedure, which defies the hand of analysis, or the eye that would pierce through the whole. It cannot be understood nor described by any direct examination: various attempts to do this have failed, as the innumerable treatises upon money and banking amply prove. Our object has been to show distinctly the end to be accomplished; to exhibit clearly the most effective processes of payment; to show how they operate singly, and in various combinations; and to leave each reader to follow these processes as far and as faithfully as his facilities for information, and his powers of observation, may carry him.

CHAPTER XI.

CLEARING-HOUSES.

§ 1. *The Clearing-house of London — Private bankers of London — Concentration of payments — Mutual adjustment — Clearing-house — Mutuality of debts — Processes and forms at the Clearing-house — Example of clearing — Amounts cleared — Bullion Report of* 1810 — *Sir Henry Thornton — Relations of clearing to commerce — The Banks and their customers — Payments of foreign trade — Domestic payments of special districts — The Credit System — New channels for the precious metals.*

THE vast accumulation of payments in London led the private bankers, in whose hands the business, or a large proportion of the business was concentrated, to adopt a plan for economizing the use of bank-notes, for saving time and trouble, which may fairly claim to be one of the highest exhibitions of the power of the credit system. The country merchants and bankers who made and received their payments in the metropolis, kept their accounts with these private bankers, many of whom had thus committed to their keeping very large sums of money. A great average balance remained in their hands, the use of which was one of their principal sources of profit. As no firm with more than six partners was allowed to issue bank-notes in London, these bankers never felt themselves able to compete with the Bank of England in that department of banking: issuing no notes of their own, they used only those of the Bank of England, when their payments required the use of notes. They all kept accounts with their customers, and immense sums were daily paid by checks and transfers on their books. They paid out, when required, for these checks the notes of the Bank of England; and were, of course, obliged to keep a supply constantly on hand for that purpose. These bankers, besides having to pay out bank-notes on the order of their customers, found themselves daily indebted to each other in immense sums accruing from the system of concentration which has been noted. Each banker was daily receiving from his country correspondents drafts and bills for collection and discount, payable at the counters of other bankers; and all were thus daily subjected to heavy demands from each for the amounts of these drafts and bills.

These mutual demands were greatly increased by the checks and bills and drafts of city customers: so that, each afternoon, every banker was called upon to disburse large sums of bank-notes to every other banker. Payments were to be made and received between more than forty banking establishments; and this process necessarily involved the daily use of very great sums in bank-notes, or the keeping a heavy deposit account with the Bank of England. This would have required, if notes were used, a large proportion of the actual circulation of the bank; and, of course, that these bankers should keep this large amount in that disposable form which would prevent their making any profit upon it. Under such circumstances, it is not surprising that the active minds of the bankers recurred to the mode of payment which we are about to describe. It is not now my purpose to examine the steps by which they perfected the institution of the Clearing-house, but only to exhibit its uses and powers, as a means of payment or liquidation, as managed in the state of perfection to which it has been now brought.

Every man who purchases and sells, who receives payments and makes payments, finds at the end of the year a balance for or against himself on the whole year's transactions, small, however, in comparison with the sum of all his dealings. If he takes credit for all his purchases, and gives it on all his sales, he may apply his credits to his debts, and thus extinguish both; and that would be perfectly practicable, if his purchases and sales are made with the same person. It would be only balancing their books of account. If he deals, however, with a great many different persons, both in purchasing and selling, and gives and takes credit in every transaction, he has only to call in his credits, and with the proceeds pay his debts; but this is impracticable in the complications of business, unless by means of circulating credits, such as bills of exchange, promissory notes, deposit accounts, and bank-notes. The concentration of payments at London arose out of this mutual interchange. Very large sums were to be paid daily, and these daily payments were an adjustment of the accounts between parties who had been both buyers and sellers. One class of merchants have large sums coming to them, but they owe heavy amounts to others; hence an immense accumulation of mutual demands. If all these had met at one banker's, a very large proportion would have been extinguished at once upon his books. Each banker, however, being for the time owner of all committed to his care, the process of adjustment was modified. All mutual claims meeting upon each banker's books were extinguished there, and the bankers became creditors and debtors of each other for all the credits and debts of their customers which had not met and been settled by the parties, creditor and debtor, being customers of the same bank; and this very large indebtedness was that which was intended to be adjusted and paid at the Clearing-house. Its mode of liquidation, however, deserves more particular mention.

In the old post-office building in Lombard-street, London, is, or was, an apartment devoted to the business of the Clearing-house. This establishment is kept up for the benefit, and at the expense, of certain private bankers in the metropolis, who are associated for that purpose. As the institution implies a very considerable degree of mutual confidence, it consists only of such as have chosen to enter into the mutual arrangement.[1] Two inspectors are appointed to preside over the process, to prevent mistakes, and to authorize the payment of balances. Each banker has his drawer or box in the clearing-house, and each one or more clerks, who carry thither, at several stated hours on every day, all the claims which his house, up to that time,

[1] It has recently admitted into its circle many institutions formerly excluded, especially the joint-stock banks.

has on all the rest. The respective clerks, after charging them on their balance-sheets, drop into the drawers of each house all the claims upon it. This process is continued until four o'clock in the afternoon. Then each clerk finishes a balance-sheet, which he had commenced and carried on as the claims were deposited. They are provided with alphabetical printed lists of the clearing bankers, with columns ruled for debtor on the left, and creditor on the right side. Each clerk puts the name of his own house at the top of his sheet, which exhibits, when finished, the balance which his house owes to others, and what others owe to it. The summing up at the foot of the debtor side shows how much his house owes altogether, and that on the creditor side how much all owe to it; and the balance between these totals shows how much his house is to pay or to receive. This amount each clerk is enabled to make up by a constant inspection of the drawer of his house, where he finds the claims against it as they come in. Every bill or check has the name of the banker or firm to which it belongs written across its face, thus indicating to whom the amount must be credited. They keep a minute of the claims upon every house as they deposit the evidences in the drawers, and thus are enabled to make a balance with each, and transfer it to their balance-sheet, by the hour of four o'clock, when no further entries are permitted. They then compare their balances, which must agree, or there is error. If there is a balance due by one house to another, it must, if right, be the very sum which that house claims.

After their balance-sheets are all made up and verified by comparison, the inspectors make up from them a general balance-sheet, by debiting each bank with all it owes, and crediting it with all the others owe to it. The balance to be paid by each bank is placed on the same line with what it owes, in a column on the debtor side: the balance to be received by each bank is placed on the same line with its credits on the creditor side. This general balance-sheet further verifies the individual balance-sheets, as, if all is correct, the sum of the debtor and creditor columns will be equal, and the sum of the balances to be received and paid will be equal. It will show at a glance, too, what each creditor bank is to receive, and each debtor bank to pay. We subjoin a specimen of the general balance-sheets, omitting fractions. In the "Supplement to the Report on Banks of Issue," made in 1841, may be found, at page 320, a table of the daily payments at the Clearing-house for every day of the year 1839. The balances paid in bank-notes for that year averaged about seven per cent. of the whole sum paid.

DEBTORS.		NAMES OF THE BANKERS.	CREDITORS.	
Amounts.	Balances to be paid.		Amounts.	Balances to be received.
£280,000	£20,000	Barclay.............	£260,000	....
80,000	5,000	Barnard............	75,000	....
110,000	10,000	Barnett	100,000	....
50,000	10,000	Bosauquel..........	40,000	....
50,000	5,000	Brown..............	45,000	....
110,000	....	Carries	120,000	£10,000
110,000	....	Dennison	120,000	10,000
50,000	5,000	Fuller...............	45,000	....
280,000	20,000	Glyn.................	260,000	....
100,000	10,000	Hanbury............	90,000	....
110,000	....	Hankey	115,000	5,000
280,000	....	Jones................	300,000	20,000
150,000	....	Lubbock	160,000	10,000
200,000	....	Masterman.........	215,000	15,000
150,000	10,000	Prescott	140,000	....
80,000	....	Price	85,000	5,000
160,000	....	Robarts.............	165,000	5,000
50,000	....	Rogers..............	55,000	5,000
40,000	....	Stevenson..........	45,000	5,000
60,000	....	Spooner............	65,000	5,000
150,000	15,000	Smith...............	135,000	....
80,000	....	Stone	90,000	10,000
60,000	....	Vere.................	65,000	5,000
40,000	....	Weston	45,000	5,000
110,000	10,000	Williams...........	100,000	....
60,000	....	Willis...............	65,000	5,000
£3,000,000	£120,000	....	£3,000,000	£120,000

The balances being all compared and found to agree, each house pays at once into the clearing-house the general balance which it owes; and as the whole sum to be paid must be precisely the sum to be received, any one who owes may pay to any one who is to receive. The sums thus paid are acquitted in notes of the Bank of England, except the fractions of balances under five pounds.

Mr. Thomas, one of the inspectors of the clearing-house, stated before the bullion committee, in 1810, that the average payments effected daily in the establishment amounted to £4,700,000, and that the average daily amount of bank-notes required to pay the balances was £220,000, but sometimes the balances were equal to £500,000. On settling days at the stock exchange, the amount of payments at the clearing-house were stated to reach £14,000,000. If we take the former sum, £4,700,000 ($22,500,000), as the amount more strictly belonging to commerce, we have a weekly payment of $135,000,000, a monthly payment of $586,000,000, and a yearly payment of $7,040,000,000; and all this effected with the use of less than five per cent. of the amount in bank-notes. The Clearing-house had then been in operation for thirty-five years, and during the twelve years before 1810, the immense payments above indicated had been made without the use of gold or silver, or any metallic money of any kind, and by the aid, for payment of balances, of bank-notes not redeemable in coin; of bank-notes not redeemable in anything, and only receivable at the bank whence they were issued in payment of debts, or on deposit. All these great payments were in addition to those effected at the Bank of England, at the counters of the private bankers, and by the aid of bank-notes out of doors in the current payments of trade, and those made on account of the public treasury. It is probable that, in the year 1810, these together exceeded the amount acquitted at the clearing-house many times; perhaps not less than $75,000,000 were then daily paid in London without the use of gold or silver, or bank-notes exchangeable for these metals.

The business of the Clearing-house has not, we believe, increased in proportion with the increase of the general business of England. The deposits of the Bank of England now generally average £20,000,000. If these deposits were moved on the average once in each week, which is not a violent presumption, as immense sums change hands several times in a day, this would make the payments at the bank over £1,040,000,000 for the year. It is, perhaps, equally safe to say that, in all other banks, an equal movement of deposits takes place in the current payments of business; the two sums making the vast amount of £2,080,000,000. This added to the yearly payments of the Clearing-house, makes a total of £3,000,000,000, equal to $1,440,000,000,000. The working of the deposits in Scotland and Ireland would greatly increase this vast aggregate.

The Clearing-house had not been the subject of much remark until the Bullion Committee of 1810 examined one of its inspectors, and devoted a half-page (see page 252) of their report to a statement of his evidence. It has since been noticed by not a few continental writers of repute, and also by many in Great Britain. Previous to that time Henry Thornton, Esq., had spoken of the establishment in a note near the end of the third chapter of his very excellent work on "*Paper Credit*" in which, after a few remarks explaining its mode of operation, he says: "This device, which serves to spare the use of bank-notes, may suggest the practicability of a great variety of contrivances for sparing the use of gold, to which men having confidence in each other would naturally resort, if we could suppose bank paper to be abolished."

How strange, that he who so well understood how and why *paper credit* was substituted for gold and silver in commerce, did not perceive and appreciate more fully the fact that the Clearing-house was an institution founded on the necessity of saving, besides time and trouble, not merely gold, but even currency. Bank-notes, although a vastly more convenient medium of payment than even gold coin, were yet not to be had without an equivalent in value; and it became, in the estimation of bankers and merchants, important to save the use of them. They were an expensive article to keep on hand, and it became needful to ascertain how far they could be dispensed with in payments.

It is far too confined a view of the operations of the Clearing-house to regard them as a mere adjustment between the bankers concerned. The banks no doubt lend their own capital as far as it goes; but their chief business is dealing in the commercial paper of their customers. Every man of business using credit largely finds himself, in its progress, creditor for the paper he takes, and debtor for the paper he gives. If these credits and debts were compared once a month, once in three months, or once a year, there would be found, perhaps, no large balance either way. When such a person sends all his credits to a bank, it is chiefly that he may obtain facilities, in managing these credits, to make them available in paying debts. He appears, therefore, on the books of the bank in which he keeps his account, as a creditor for the amount others owe him; but those who are his creditors for the amount of the paper issued by him have also their accounts in the same bank, or in others. Each individual is able, by these open accounts, in the manner already explained in the chapter on deposits, to apply his credits to the payment of his debts as they mature. If all kept their accounts in the same bank, the credits and debits of all would appear on the same books, and the clearing would be done on these books. But as there are many banks, and the customers divided among them, the banks resort to the expedient of the Clearing-house, which makes them one for the very purpose of which we are speaking. The claims presented by each bank at the office of the Clearing-house are merely the claims of its customers; but these customers are met, at the Clearing-house, with all the claims against them maturing on that day. Thus, every day, the vast multitude of business men who are customers of these clearing banks have, by the operation of this clearing process, their debts and credits balanced and extinguished as effectually as though they had met in the same bank, and on the same books.

By this process the customers of the banks, although they do not pay the notes or paper issued or accepted by them until it matures, are enabled, by the facility afforded by the banks, to anticipate the maturity of the paper which is payable to them. The parties keeping accounts with one of these banks, and having their notes on time discounted, have a fund upon which to draw to meet their payments as they mature. They draw upon the deposit fund — the proceeds of discounted paper — for the amount of these payments, and the bank takes up the matured paper as it appears at the Clearing-house. The bank is reimbursed when the discounted paper is paid in money, or by the return of the credit it gave for the paper. As all these banks are engaged in the same business, and as their customers, whether country banks or individuals, remain very much the same, the result of the whole is that this machinery of banks and bank accounts, and the processes of the Clearing-house, enable their customers one and all to apply their credits to pay their debts, without the intervention of money. To the extent that their customers' credits and debts are equal, they can be paid and extinguished by liquidation, or set-off, in the manner we have described; but so far as any individual has more coming to him than he owes, or owes more than he has coming to him, so far a balance would arise to be settled in money or bank-notes. Of course the sums to be thus paid would together be the very amounts to be received; and the sum of the balances thus due from individuals would be the amount of bank-notes to go each day to the creditor banks. The amount of the daily clearing, then, exhibits the amount to which the mutual claims of all the customers of the banks are equal; and the sum of all the daily balances is the sum of the amounts payable to certain customers of the banks, and the sum of the amounts which certain other customers have to pay. These balances are the only amount which is payable in money at the Clearing-house, and for this payment notes of the Bank of England are always employed. In the year 1839, according to a Parliamentary Report of 1841, the whole amount of the clearings was £954,401,600, or over £3,000,000 for each day; the whole sum of the balances for the year was £66,275,600. The highest sum cleared in any month was £87,610,500 in August, and the lowest £70,833,800 in December. The largest sum of balances was £6,348,500 in January, and the smallest £4,755,000 in December. Thus, for the year 1839, the customers of the Clearing-house paid off debts among themselves to the amount of £954,401,600, a sum far exceeding the national debt of Great Britain, without any use of gold or silver, and with only £66,276,600 in notes of the Bank of England. To the extent of £888,125,000, the debts of these parties were mutual and equal, and the operations of their bank accounts balanced and extinguished them; and to that extent commodities had paid for commodities. The effect was the same as if the same parties had kept the whole accounts on their own books of account, and had balanced them as occasion required.

This clearing operation among the banks is, then, one of the most effective of the various devices of the credit system to economize the use of money: for this vast amount of debt, equal to $4,500,000,000, was paid in a year without the use of a single coin. So far as the Clearing-house operations extend, the result is nearly complete. It is effected through more complications than are absolutely necessary, but the great fact is manifest, that a sum equal to the national debt of Great Britain has been paid, without employing in that payment one pennyworth of gold or silver. This result has been reached by a very simple principle — the making provision for men to apply their credits to the payment of their debts. Unassisted — that is, without some special arrangement for the purpose — men cannot set-off their credits against their debts; but with proper management, it can be done with even more facility than through the London bankers and the Clearing-house. As two men mutually indebted upon book accounts can balance and extinguish their debts, so two men, holders of each other's promissory notes or acceptances, can, so far as they may be equal, off-set them and thereby extinguish so much debt; so two banks, mutually indebted upon the notes of each held by the other, can pay and discharge their respective debts to each other; so can any number of individuals or banks. It is simply needful that persons indebted be provided with a mode of applying their credits to the payment of their debts. This process is susceptible of great variety in the means, and of very wide application. It is upon this principle that the payments of foreign trade have long been effected. If the United States and Great Britain have mutually exported to each other commodities to the value of $100,000,000, the amount is adjusted by the familiar process of bills of exchange. He who has exported commodities to the value of $10,000, is paid when he sells a bill for the amount. The adjustment proceeds afterwards without any further trouble on his part. The bills are concentrated in a few hands in each country. If a house in London purchase in each week a million of dollars of American paper, and a house in New York with which it is in business relations purchases a million of dollars each week in bills on London, it is easy to see that it requires no money to pay to each other the two millions. As business is generally conducted, the bills are forwarded from this country, and the respective claims are balanced and extinguished on the books of the London house.

What is thus done so readily between nations is effected with equal facility between the different parts of the same country, wherever there is a mutual trade. It takes place in the United States between North and South, and East and West, and between our chief commercial and manufacturing cities, to a total amount probably five times greater than the sum of our foreign trade. This great sum, so far as it is equal, is balanced by the processes of our domestic exchange on the books of our banks and brokers. Coin is only used where there are large balances to pay, as in the foreign trade. The large payments of the United States in a year greatly exceed $10,000,000,000, and the balances paid in coin would not ordinarily reach one per cent. of that sum.

The credit system has thus accomplished the great result of separating the actual sale and delivery of commodities — the actual transactions of commerce from the payments. The progress of civilization and private integrity have made this possible; its immense advantage is such as not only to secure its continuance, but to make it a very strong safeguard of commercial honesty. Almost the entire commerce, foreign and domestic, of the whole civilized world is now carried on from day to day, and year to year, with much less, we believe, than one per cent. of the actual values exchanged in coin or bullion. The whole of the prices, sales, bargains, books of account, notes, and bills of exchange, are expressed in money of account; and the whole processes of adjustment by bankers, brokers, and clearing-houses, are all stated and expressed in money of account.

The credit system, then, intervenes with its various devices of books of account, promissory notes, bills of exchange, bank-notes, bank deposits, clearing-houses, &c., to enable the parties who have bought and sold, who are all creditors and all debtors, to liquidate their debts and credits, and thus extinguish them so far as they are equal; that is, where a merchant has to receive, during the year, $200,000, and to pay $190,000, the credit system adjusts the whole sum of $390,000 by paying the $10,000 difference in money, and extinguishing the $380,000 by set-off, or liquidation. The goods which go out of the manufactory or warehouse pay for those which come in. The difference only requires money. To effect the exchange with advantage, laborers, horses, warehouses, wagons, drays, canal-boats, railways, and ships are employed; to effect the payments, gold and silver for the balances, bills of exchange, promissory notes, bank-notes, banks, bankers, and all the devices of books, checks, and clearing or balancing accounts, are requisite.

The economy of these means of making payments is scarce less than that enjoyed by commerce in the means of transportation above mentioned. To make the daily payments of the clearing-houses in gold would require some three or four hundred tellers; in silver, an army of some thousands, with a vast number of drays, carts and laborers for its removal. The cost of keeping on hand such a quantity of the precious metals would be enormous for the interest alone, besides all the extra expense of tellers, clerks, and assistants. To save this, the machinery of credit is put in motion, and payments are effected as we have described. What a nation imports, it pays for by what it exports; what a district receives for its consumption, it pays for by what it furnishes for the consumption of others; and what an individual merchant purchases in the way of his business, he pays for by what he sells in the way of his business. When coined money is used in these transactions, they can only be carried on to the extent that such money can be obtained for the purpose, and with that speed at which money may be made to circulate; but when credit in its various forms is used, then this business finds no limit but the limit of human industry in producing, and human power in transportation and distribution, and human integrity in the subsequent processes of payment.

Such, however, is the magnitude of the transactions of modern commerce, that fuller employment is given to a much larger stock of the precious metals, in paying occasional balances, than was formerly given when a large proportion of the payments were made in coin or bullion. So full is this employment, that it may be said that all the commercial business which is now done without the aid of the precious metals in the payments, is so much of an addition to what would be done if they were exclusively employed.

There cannot be a doubt that new modes of economizing money will yet be devised, and that the power of the credit system will continue to be enlarged, and its processes perfected, until much of the friction which is now felt in the business of payments will be removed. We may hereafter indicate a method of effecting some beneficial improvements in that respect.

It is true that the credit system is not without its difficulties and obstructions; its contrivances have not always been happy; its devices have not always been successful; and the needless friction is sometimes terrible. That, however, is less the fault of the credit system than of those who undertake to point out its laws, and to manage its concerns. It is demonstrable as any problem in mathematics, that if men were as honest as they should be, and as knowing as they might be, a commerce greater than the world has ever seen might be carried on by the sole use of well-devised and well-managed institutions of credit.

We have, however, to regard the subject in its connections with men as we find them now, and as they are likely always to remain; and while imperfection and selfishness are such striking characteristics of humanity, we shall find them displayed in their worst forms in the management of property and credit. The machinery of the credit system can only be so far perfected as the interests of those who employ it will permit.

§ 2. *Clearing between the banks of Scotland — Clearing twice a week — Balances payable in exchequer bills, notes of the Bank of England, or gold — Banks of Scotland — Their system of deposit, and its influence upon business — Stimulus to punctuality and industry — Circulation of bank-notes in Scotland — One pound notes.*

The banks of Scotland have a well-organized system of clearing, or exchanges, among themselves, which takes place twice a week alternately, at the Bank of Scotland and the Royal Bank in Edinburgh. The payments are made in exchequer bills, Bank of England notes, or gold, at the option of the payer; but if these are wanting, in drafts on London at ten days. Exchequer bills are chiefly used, the Bank of England notes being only used to pay the fractional parts of £1000. The sum of £400,000, in exchequer bills, is apportioned among the nine banks associated; and it is agreed that this whole sum shall be kept in the circle, by each one keeping up its proportion of the allotted amount. The process of clearing is simply charging on the clearing-books each bank with its own debts, and crediting it with its own credits. Each has a large amount to pay, and a large amount to receive, and a balance to pay or receive. This clearing includes not only all the mutual claims arising among the banks, by drafts, collection of bills of exchange and promissory notes, deposit receipts, and checks, but also the claims arising to each bank upon the notes of the others received in the course of business.[1] The clearing and payment of the balances completely adjusts all claims twice in each week; the whole mutual indebtedness, however, of the Scotch banks does not enter into this clearing. The banks in any one town or city generally settle among themselves, and give four days' drafts on Edinburgh for the balances which are adjusted at the clearing. This system of clearing is by no means perfect, but it is scrupulously well-managed, and made a most important feature in the wisely-conducted banking system of Scotland. There is no country where there is more reliance upon banks, and none where they have more powerfully stimulated the productive forces of the

[1] II. Report of 1841, Banks of Issue, Interrogatory, 1683.

people. We cannot but remark, that whilst there are strong objections to the theory of the Scotch banks, their constitution secures a very safe and prudent management. In fact, they have been conducted for a century and a half with almost unequalled discretion and success.[1]

The working of the deposits of the Scotch banks is probably not exceeded in efficiency by any equal amount of deposits, and the amount is probably greater than elsewhere in proportion to the capital of the banks. The system of cash credits, one of the chief characteristics of their banking, consists virtually in giving to their customers a certain amount of deposit, upon which they draw at pleasure, and upon the operations of which an interest account is kept. The customer is thus deeply interested to return the amounts drawn by him with as little delay as possible; and the movements of the deposit accounts are, consequently, rapid. The banks in Scotland regulate the amount of these cash credits by the actual business of the country, and by the effect upon their circulation. The bank which perceives increasing indebtedness to other banks, or a great reduction of deposits, is warned to contract operations. So, if the banks collectively find, by their accounts at the clearing, that their general indebtedness is swelling beyond their usual means of payment, they are warned that their customers are over-trading. Whilst the people of Scotland are trading strictly among themselves, and within due bounds, their payments must be susceptible of easy adjustment upon the books of the banks by the circulation of bank-notes, the settlements between banks, and the Edinburgh exchanges. In a wholesome state of trade or production, merchants and producers sell to an amount as great as they purchase; the amount they have to pay is no greater than they have to receive. The bank or cash credits are used in the purchase of goods, which, being sold, furnish the means of repayment. There is no over-trading, financially speaking, among individuals, so long as their

[1] Since the above was written, a most unhappy case of bank failure has occurred at Glasgow. But Scotland has less to answer for, in the way of bank frauds, than any country in the world which has derived so much advantage from banks.

sales are equivalent to their purchases; and the payments to be made through the banks, in such a business, will create no undue indebtedness among the banks. There is, in like manner, no difficulty in the payments of any city or district, so long as its business furnishes claims upon others equivalent to those which are presented against it. If Scotland exports to an amount equal to her imports, there will be no inconvenient payments to be made in London to cover a deficiency. So long as the trade between individuals, districts or cities and Scotland, and between the rest of the world and Scotland, runs nearly even, the banks find their adjustments easy and safe. The safety and efficiency of the Scotch system of banking consists in its exhibiting to its managers the real state of trade, and in its showing clearly the relation between the course of trade and the operations of the banks. The books of the banks keep the accounts of the whole trade of Scotland; each bank represents so many individuals as are its customers, and so far as its customers have mutual dealings with each other, their mutual claims meet and are settled upon the books of the bank; and so far as the claims of its customers lie against those who are customers of other banks, it must present those claims against the bank at which they become payable. So that, in fact, the goods are moved and distributed, and bought and sold in the regular course of trade, as best subserves the interests and wishes of those concerned; the payments are made in the banks by that process of adjustment to which we have adverted. The friction of this machinery of payment is so little, that the progress of industry and production in Scotland, under its favoring assistance, has, during the last century, had no parallel in Europe.

It is a striking feature of the Scotch system, that it not only dispenses with the precious metals to a remarkable degree, as a matter of economy and facility, but also of bank-notes to a very great extent, as other facilities can be found which are superior. It is estimated that the ordinary deposits in the banks in Scotland amount to £30,000,000. If the whole sum is moved but once each week, it effects the enormous sum of £1,560,000,000 of payments in a year. The whole bank-note circulation of

Scotland seldom exceeds £3,500,000, or only one-ninth of the deposits; whilst the circulation of the Bank of England is generally larger than its deposits. The superiority of the Scotch system is fully shown in this double economy of coin and notes. That this economy is the result of their system of management is apparent from the fact that banking is free, and that there was no restriction upon the issue of notes until the Act of 1844, which only restricted them to the amount shown to be required by their business on the average of several years.

In England, coins are used for payments below £5; in Scotland, £1 notes form over two-thirds of their currency; and yet, in Scotland, the whole circulation of notes is not greater, in proportion to the population, than in England. It is now not far from one pound to each person; but if £1 notes were issued in England, it is believed that £30,000,000 would be quickly taken into the circulation, which would make two pounds to each person. It is rather rare to see gold coins in Scotland; their £1 notes almost supply the place of sovereigns. That the people are, in this respect, well satisfied is apparent from the steady determination with which they defend their one-pound currency against the jealous attacks of English currency-mongers.[1]

[1] See the celebrated letters of Walter Scott, on the currency of Scotland, under the *nom du guerre* of Malachi Malagrowther; II. Report of 1841, Banks of Issue, Appendix.

§ 3. *Bank adjustment in the United States — Clearing between the banks in the United States — Mutual accounts and correspondence — Separation of sale and distribution of goods from payments — Domestic exchange — Balances of home trade — The correspondents of banks their mode of clearing — Mutual debts the basis of this adjustment — The system of clearing among the banks of New England at the Suffolk Bank of Boston.*

In the United States, the clearing or liquidation among the banks of all mutual claims, except those arising from their circulation, is mainly accomplished on their ledgers, and by their correspondence.[1] There is a constant necessity for this correspondence, arising from the mutual transmission of drafts, checks, promissory notes, bills of exchange, &c., for collection. Upon these collections a large portion of their mutual demands arise. It cannot be necessary to particularize that every city or district of country, as a whole, must have claims upon others, and must, as a whole, be indebted to others. These mutual demands are entrusted to the banks for collection; or, what is the same in the view now taken, these claims are purchased by the banks, and collected for their own account. In this country these payments are made through the agency of the banks almost wholly; for, when exchange brokers and merchants intervene in the business, they generally employ the banks in some stage of the process. In this way the payments arising upon the trade between the East and the West, the North and the South, and among the great cities on the seaboard, are made upon the books of the banks. Whatever sum is received for account of any bank by another, is credited accordingly, and whatever is drawn for is charged; so every transaction of debtor and creditor is made an item of book account, which runs on from year to year, being balanced as often as necessary to make out the balance-sheet, or state of the bank. So far as the respective charges and credits balance each other, their mutual indebtedness is paid, and the claims held by the customers of the

[1] Since this was written, clearing-houses have been established in Philadelphia and New York, of which some notice will be taken in the Chapter on the Banks of the United States.

one bank against the customers of the other are discharged. The effect is the same as if the accounts had been kept directly between them; the bank has acted as their book-keeper. This adjustment, however, among banks has a wider and more complex operation, as carried on among a number of banks. One bank may have on its books accounts with one hundred other banks, and each of the hundred may have accounts with as many other banks. These circles of banks keeping mutual accounts may be ramified over the whole country, running from the far North to the extreme South, and from the East to the far West. The operation is the same in affording a facility to every creditor to present his claim against his debtor through the banks, and to every debtor to make payment in the same way. The banks in this business may be taken as representing the locality in which they are severally situated, and as holding the credits or claims of their customers upon all, however distant, with whom they dealt: so they respectively stand ready to receive, from their immediate customers, whatever they owe to all others. This is the domestic exchange of the country. The goods have, by the action of merchants and others, been bought, sold, and distributed according to the course of trade, and the demands of consumption; the payments are reserved for the agency of banks or bankers. Each locality, or commercial district, is creditor for what it has sent into the market, and a debtor for what it has purchased. The commercial paper to which this commerce has given rise is remitted to the banks, and thus every bank will take credits for the exports of its district, and apply those credits to meet the claims upon that district for its imports. These domestic payments are, then, effected upon the books of the bank, as already stated; and as such accounts must continue to run, even the balances may remain to be adjusted, from time to time, according to the course of trade, and the corresponding course of payments. These balances may be transferred to any part of the United States by mutual checks, drafts, &c., among the banks; so that a vast adjustment of balances must take place among the banks, besides the accounts to which the immediate transactions of their customers give rise.

This adjustment is readily accomplished by mutual checks, if the trade has been sound and equal; if not, it may be necessary, at some point, to pay ultimate balances in coin. The banks in the West may fall largely in debt to those of the East for goods purchased for Western consumption; but that debt may be paid by drafts of the banks of New Orleans upon the Eastern banks, the market of New Orleans being that at which a large portion of the customers of the Western banks make their chief sales. So the banks of other districts may become indebted in heavy balances to other banks; but they can meet this indebtedness by large credits to which they may be entitled elsewhere.

The result of these bank accounts, and the correspondence by which they are kept up, is the same as if they all had a common clearing-office, at which each should be debited and credited with all they had to pay, and all they had to receive. Each bank account would then be similar to the clearing accounts of each banker at the office in London. The effect of the whole proceeding in our banks is, that the liquidation of the domestic exchanges — the payments resulting from the domestic trade — is accomplished on the bank ledgers, and the balances are distributed according as the parties are entitled. It will be noted that, taking the whole of any series of transactions, the amount to be paid is the same as that to be received; they are, of course, equal. The balances, however, result differently at different times; and there is a continual transfer of funds taking place, by which balances are paid by one party at one time, and received by the same, perhaps, at another. So far, however, as in this business the banks have as much to receive as to pay, their credits are equal to their debits; and their books suffice to effectuate a mutual discharge between them, and a final liquidation among their respective customers.

The banks also keep large deposits with each other, as their position and the nature of the trade among their customers may require. It is, therefore, found to be an advantage for some banks to make actual deposits with others, for which they are credited in account as for sums collected or received in any other way. They also draw and are drawn upon by each other, both for their own adjustments, and at the instance of individuals; all which goes to their respective accounts, and to swell the sum of the domestic exchanges liquidated on the books of the banks. The advantage and facility of this mode of adjustment is greatly increased by other modes of operating between banks at a distance, by which remittances to remote points are made easy and prompt.

It is by these, and similar means, that the payments arising upon the commercial operation of distributing to their proper customers the cotton, sugar, and other products of the South — the pork, beef, tobacco, and others of the West — the manufactured fabrics of the North — and the various articles, manufactured and imported, of the cities of the seaboard, are achieved. These payments are effected neither by gold, nor silver, nor bank-notes. The goods are made to pay for the goods. Money of any kind is not only unnecessary in such operations, but an actual and serious impediment and hindrance. The larger payments are thus made, and with the more facility, because the number engaged is smaller; as the business of distribution widens, and more persons take part, it becomes necessary, under the present system, to make use of bank-notes, and occasionally of coins.

A system of exchanges prevails among the banks of New England, which may be cited as another illustration of the operation of clearing. It is too frequently regarded as merely a mode, on the part of the banks, of redeeming that portion of their circulation which accumulates at Boston. It is, however, a more important arrangement than such a description suggests. Boston being the chief centre of trade for these States, a very large portion of the bank-notes flow into the banks of that city; and it is a great convenience to have these notes redeemed in such manner as to save all expense and time in sending them home to the issuers. That motive was most influential in introducing the plan; and with the country the operating motive in keeping up the process was the security it afforded against over-issues by such banks as were disposed to abuse their powers, and because it further secured to every bank that amount of circulation to which its legitimate business gave it a title. But the effect of the arrangement was more important than this convenience, or this security, indicated. It furnished a knowledge of their respective strength; it gave a steadiness of movement, an increased power of accommodation to the business community, their customers, which was of mighty advantage to the industry and trade of the whole region. This plan originated in an agreement among the banks in Boston, by which a certain sum furnished by the others was lent, free of charge, to the Suffolk Bank; in consideration of which that bank undertook to receive from the others all their country bank-notes, and send them home for payment, or arrange with the issuers for their redemption. The Suffolk Bank succeeded in making an arrangement with the country banks, by which all their indebtedness at Boston is settled at that bank. Of course this involved large operations. The quantity of manufactured goods sent by the interior to Boston is immense; and the value of the cotton, wool, iron, flour, pork, beef, and other domestic products, and of the foreign goods offered for sale at Boston, taken into the country, must also be immense. Very much the largest portion of this trade must be carried on, in the first instance, by the individual paper of the respective purchasers. To a very great extent, the paper given by the merchants of Boston for the products of the interior is set-off, in this adjustment at the Suffolk Bank, against the paper given by the country merchants, manufacturers, and dealers, for their purchases in Boston. However this paper may be negotiated or circulated, both parties rely on the goods they purchase to take up the paper they give for them; and the respective claims are either held by the banks, and balanced on their books, or, if they have been exchanged for bank-notes, these are exchanged. The various banks of Boston, according to their position, and as their convenience or interests may dictate, settle among themselves a vast amount of indebtedness; but all that does not readily come within the scope of these minor adjustments is carried into the great liquidation at the Suffolk Bank. In this way not merely the debts which the country owes to Boston, and those which Boston owes to the country, are settled, but New Haven and Hartford present their claims upon Portsmouth and Bangor at Boston, and so the latter upon the former. The Suffolk Bank not only calls upon others to pay, but must also pay to others. The business is resolved into a general adjustment of accounts. In the long list of banks, each one is debtor and creditor: the list of the debts exactly balances the credits; but separately some fall in debt, and some have balances to receive; and as the balances owing are the same as those to be received, being in fact the same thing, those owing have only to pay into the Suffolk Bank their adverse balances, to be handed over to those holding favorable balances, and the whole liquidation is made.

In this operation, vast as it is, there is only occasional need of gold or silver, and no use made of bank-notes, except to redeem them. In the great and direct movements of domestic exchange, by which cities and districts settle for their mutual purchases, the chief agency is the books of banks, and into these books the whole business finds its way; the operation is completed with but small aid from either coin, bullion or bank-notes. The latter enter more largely into the business, because they are issued for circulation, and are thus used until they arrive in banks which employ them as a set-off against their own. It is not necessary, however, for the successful accomplishment of this business, that the banks which conduct it should be anything else than banks of deposit and discount, without specie, and without the power to issue notes. In this case, the only change in the business would be that the place of the notes would be supplied by checks and drafts. The parties who receive and deposit the notes would draw upon their debtors for the same amount, and receive it through the banks, thereby giving to the deposit banks the same amount of claims upon each other as the notes would give to banks of circulation. It is not intended to say that the notes are not the most convenient, but simply that this great discharge of mutual obligations is not dependent on them for efficacy. Other means of effecting it, with even superior facility and economy, may yet be found.

CHAPTER XII.

FAIRS.

Commercial Fairs — Their agency in commerce — Continued on the confines of Asia and Europe — Kiachta — Nijni Novgorod — Kief — Concentration of payments — Fairs of Lyons — Payments of Lyons — Mode of preparation — The opening — Mode of conducting — Viramen de partie — Setting-off debts—Payment of balances — Results — Rationale — Illustrations — The Fairs of Novi and others in Italy chiefly for the purpose of payments.

THE origin of the fairs,[1] or periodical markets, which for centuries constituted a chief feature of the commerce of Europe and Asia, is of remote antiquity.[2] In the 13th, 14th and 15th centuries, the greater part of the commerce of Europe was accomplished at fairs. Thousands of these markets, shorn of their importance and magnitude, are yet held on those continents;[3]

[1] Fairs are thus defined by Savary:—"A concourse of merchants, of manufacturers, of artizans, of workmen, and of many others of every condition, and of every profession, inhabitants and strangers, who meet every year at a special place, and at a special time; some to bring thither, sell and deliver their goods, manufactures, works, merchandise, and provisions; others to make their purchases, and some solely through curiosity, and for the sake of the amusements generally enjoyed at these sorts of assemblies." —*Dictionnaire du Commerce,* "*Foire.*"

[2] The fairs of Lyons have, according to some French writers, an antiquity as high as the period of Roman domination in Gaul.—*Duchesne, Antiquité des Villes.* A summary of their history may be found in *Encyclo. Methodique Commerce,* vol. ii., page 140.

[3] Not less than 500 are yet enumerated as existing in France, and upwards of 70 in Belgium. It may be said they subsist with diminished importance throughout Europe; they have dwindled most in Great Britain. In many parts of Asia and Africa they remain in full vigor. It is in the memory of many yet living, that fairs were held in this country, especially

those best maintain their importance, whose locality is in Asia, or on the confines of Europe, and among a people whose civilization, industry, and facilities for trade, correspond with the state of Europe in the Middle Ages. The chief part of the commerce between Russia and China is now carried on at the Fair of Kiachta, in Mongolia, on the frontiers of China. The Russians carry to this fair furs, skins, Russia leather, woollen cloths, German and Russian heavy linens, cattle, and the precious metals, which they exchange for tea, silk raw and manufactured, porcelain, sugar, rhubarb, nankins, musk, &c. The Fair of Nijni Novgorod, in Russia, is still the mart of a great trade; its transactions have been estimated by some writers as high as $100,000,000 in the six or eight weeks during which they last. The actual sales, at the Fair of 1849, exceeded $45,000,000. The Fair of Sinigaglia, in Italy, retains also a large trade; the value of its exchanges, as late as 1834, being estimated at $16,000,000. It is very apparent that the concentration of merchandise and merchants which such an immense business implies must afford extraordinary facilities for trade, the making of payments, and indeed all kinds of mutual adjustment.

In many parts of Russia, Poland and Germany, where the facilities of commerce are not even now equal to those of France and Italy two or three hundred years ago, some of the fairs are continued. To those mentioned above may be added that of Kief on the Dneiper, in Russia. Besides its fairs for merchandise, it has an annual assembly for payments, which lasts from the 10th to the 30th of January. In that of 1804, there were present 941 proprietors, 149 merchants, and 144 clerks. The payments of that year, estimated by a duty of a half per cent.

---

in connection with horse-racing; but they never took deep root here. Their existence is considered as an index of the state of civilization; and it is observable that, in those countries where they most flourish at the present day, the state of industry, trade, and the progress in civilization is about that which existed in Europe during the Middle Ages. But that they still flourish in some parts of France is evident from the fact that, in 1833, about 80,000 persons attended the Fair of Beaucaire, and that business was done, on that occasion, to the amount of $30,000,000. They prevail, to some extent, in Mexico.

levied upon them, amounted to 22,659,000 roubles, equal to about $16,994,250. This sum must, of course, have been settled in twenty days.

Merchants found that a very great proportion of their payments could be most conveniently made at certain fairs; and that where it was most convenient for all to pay, it became most desirable for all to receive. Bills of exchange were generally made payable at the various fairs: these were held at intervals of from three to twelve months, and the bills were made payable at the fairs whither the parties generally resorted. A very great concentration of payments consequently took place. In many instances, the payments effected at the fairs vastly exceeded in amount the actual sales of commodities, and became the object of special attention and legislation.

The modes of effecting payments, in the days when fairs were in the height of their importance, were various and multiform in different countries, and even in the same country. If no special modes of payment or adjustment were resorted to for the purpose of saving time and expense, the vicinity of parties brought thus into contact enabled them to give to their goods, and to money, a circulation of tenfold rapidity.

We refer to the methods and processes of the PAYMENTS at Lyons as a specimen and illustration of the mode of adjustment pursued in these commercial assemblages of the Middle Ages.

The fairs at Lyons were among the most important, in their day, of any in Europe. There were held in that city four in each year: Kings, or Epiphany, began in January; Easter in April; August in that month; and All Saints in November; Four "PAYMENTS" were also held, one for each fair. The Epiphany Payments were held in all March; those of Easter, all June; those of August, all September; and those of All Saints, all November. Engagements to a vast amount, arising out of other transactions than those which occurred at the fairs, were made payable, at these Payments, by bills of exchange, book accounts, and otherwise. Those who resorted thither either for the business of merchandise, or for the payments of commerce carried on elsewhere, opened an account in their books with each

Payment by name. This exhibited what sums the accountant had promised to pay, and what sums others had agreed to pay him at each Payment, and the names of the persons, debtors and creditors. The balance of this account showed at once how much each merchant had to pay more than he was to receive, or to receive more than he was to pay, at each Payment. Bills drawn payable at future Payments were expressed thus: "*Pay to A. B. at next Easter Payments,*"&c.; or, if Easter Fair had begun, and it was intended the money should be payable at the Payments of the same fair, it was expressed: "*at the current Easter Payments.*" Much of the business done at the fairs was upon a credit of three or six months, and made payable at the proper Payments. A very large proportion of the sales were for cash; that is, payable at the Payments immediately ensuing the fair. The parties who had made up their accounts for the fair previous to their coming, continued their entries in the same account of their debts and credits, as they multiplied by the transactions of the fair, until it closed. Those parties who could not attend in person, or who preferred it, were allowed to send their accounts, duly authenticated, to be presented by an agent duly authorized.

At this assemblage of all the principal merchants of Lyons, and of those from other parts of France, and from foreign countries, every PAYMENT was opened with ceremony. The *Provost Marchand* came to the exchange with his Register, and six Syndics — two French, two Italians, and two Swiss or Germans — and then, after a short discourse to the assistants, recommending probity in trade, and observance of the laws, customs and usages of the place, the laws, customs and usages were read, and the clerk drew up a *process verbal* of the opening of the Payment.[1]

[1] "It is admirable to see the manner in which the bankers and merchants of Lyons make their acceptances and payments among themselves of the bills of exchange which they draw, and which are remitted to them from every part of Europe, payable at the Payments; for there will be paid sometimes, in two or three hours, a million of livres, without disbursing a penny in money: that is indeed surprising to those who do not know how it is effected. It may not be out of place to explain it here.

The first five days were devoted chiefly to the presentation and acceptance of such bills as were not previously accepted: on the third day, however, a special meeting was held, at which

---

"The opening of every Payment is made on the first day of the month, excepting holy days, for each one of the four annual Payments. During two hours each day set apart for that purpose, is held an assembly of the principal merchants of the place, both French and foreign, in the presence of the Provost of merchants, or, in his absence, before the oldest magistrate present, in which assembly commences the acceptance of bills of exchange payable at the current payment. This continues till the sixth day of the month inclusive, after which the holders of bills may protest them for non-acceptance during the rest of the month.

"Formerly acceptances were made verbally, and not by writing; but the bankers and merchants of Lyons carried a little book called a BILAN, in which to make acceptances. They entered in it all the bills of exchange drawn upon them, and which were presented by those who were the holders. An acceptance was signified by the mark of a cross on the margin of the book in which they had registered the bill, which denoted that the bill was accepted; but if they wished to deliberate whether they would accept the bill or not, they put a letter V on the margin, which signified (*vu*, seen) that it had been presented; and when they refused to accept, they put S. P., which signified (sous protest) that it was under protest; that is to say, that he who was the bearer ought to protest it within three days after the current Payment, that is, on or before the third of the following month.

"But now acceptances are made in writing, in pursuance of the third article of the law of June, 1667, for reasons which will be mentioned in their place.

"On the third day of the month of Payment, they fixed the rate of exchange between Lyons and all foreign places. This was done at a meeting of merchants, foreign and domestic, in presence of the Provost of merchants.

"On the sixth day, the business of payment commenced, and continued until the last day of the month inclusively, after which no entries in their bilans, or book of payments, could be made; and if any were made, they were held to be void according to law.

"The Payments of each day were commenced by the merchants and bearers of bilan in the hall of the exchange, at ten o'clock in the morning, and terminated at half-past eleven, after which hour no further payment was allowed.

"The mode of proceeding was as follows: — The bankers and merchants carried to the exchange their bilan of debit and credit; that is to say, a book in which they had written on one side what was due to them, and upon the other what they owed. They addressed themselves to those to

the rate of exchange between Lyons and all other places in France or abroad was settled and fixed for the current Payments, by a plurality of voices. After the fifth day no more bills could be accepted; and before the meeting of the sixth day, all the accounts for the Payment must be definitely written out and closed. These accounts were termed "BILANS," being not mere loose leaves, but sheets carefully fastened or bound up together. A *balance* once made up and submitted could not be altered; and its proprietor was, by the regulations of the Payments, held responsible for the correctness of his entries. Such was the character of those admitted to these Payments, that a balance stated in this way, says an excellent writer on commerce, who visited Lyons while these fairs were yet in full vigor, "carried, during my residence in that city, as much credit among the merchants of the place as if the same had been done with witnesses by a public notary." Those whose business did not admit their being the bearers of BILANS, were permitted to send in their debts and credits by any broker or banker who would become responsible, by adding them to his own.

All the preliminaries being accomplished, on the morning of the sixth day the bearers of these little books, or prepared state-

---

whom they were in debt, and gave them for debtors one or more of those who owed them a like sum: this debtor, or debtors, being accepted in their place, the substitution was entered in their books, and the debt was regarded as paid. All parties did the same, and so the payments proceeded. At the end of the month, those who owed more than was due to them paid the amount in ready money to the holders of bills who had more coming to them than they owed.

"The bills of exchange payable at the payment, and not paid before the last day of the month inclusively, were to be protested within the three first days of the following month.

"If a banker or merchant accustomed to carry a book at the place of payment meets with no one willing to accept him as a debtor, during the time of payment, he is reputed to have failed. There is no place in the world where merchants are more ready to give credit than at Lyons; so, also, there is no place where payments are more punctually made; for, if the time of payment is permitted to pass one day, the credit of the party is lost, and he is accounted as bankrupt."—*Parfait Negoçiant, par J. Savary*, 4to, 1777; tome i., chap. xii., p. 257.

ments assembled at the exchange as the clock struck ten, and afterwards upon each day not a holy day at the same hour, to be adjourned at precisely half after eleven. In this assembly every one present met his debtors and his creditors, or those who appeared for them. The mode of adjustment adopted was for each one, by inspection of his book, to ascertain in what way he could best apply his credits in discharge of his debts: the usual manner of proceeding was by debtors procuring the assumption of their debts by those who were indebted to them. A. owes B. a thousand, and B. owes C. fifteen hundred. B. asks A. to assume a thousand of his debt to C.: the latter accepts the assumption, and a thousand is thus paid. By comparing books, it is perceived that D. owes a large sum to E., the latter a like sum to F., the latter a like sum to G., the latter a like sum to H.; and all being met, it is agreed that these sums shall be acquitted by a payment from D. directly to H.[1] In all cases these under-

[1] The act of writing off debts, or making these assumptions, was called, technically, a "*viremen de partie,*" a term in much use, and of pregnant meaning, in European commerce a few centuries ago.

"According to article fourth of the law of 1667, the business of transferring, paying or setting-off debts was to commence on the sixth day of every payment; but according to usage, no written entries were made in their books until the sixteenth.

"The *viremens de parties* are transfers, or set-offs, which the bankers and merchants make among themselves, by means of which they pay in a moment considerable sums with little or no money.

"To accomplish easily these payments, or set-offs, the bankers or merchants who frequent the exchange make a "bilan," or statement, for every payment in which they enter to their debit the sums which they owe, and the names of those to whom they are in debt; and to their credit the sums which are due to them, and the names of those who owe them. When they commence paying, they look upon the debtors of the person who owes them as their own debtors, and the creditors of the person to whom they are in debt as their own creditors."

The author here furnishes the model of a transfer, or set-off, which makes the matter no plainer than to say that some two, three or more persons find, by inspection of their books, that they are debtors and creditors of each other in such way that they can, by a transfer, or by assumption, of one of the parties, pay off or extinguish two, three or more debts. It is plain enough that when A. owes B. a sum of money, and B. owes C. the

takings are forthwith entered upon the book in the hands of each, so that the books continue to exhibit the exact progress of the adjustment, and the state of indebtedness up to the close of the payments. It is impossible, by any description, to trace the processes by which parties thus situated could finally reduce their indebtedness to the mere balances which each one had to receive or pay more than he owed, and till it was seen that the balances to be paid were, in the aggregate, the same that were to be received, being in fact the same thing. It is obvious that, so long as any one who owed anything had any amount coming to him, he could apply it to his debt; and the adjustment would only cease when the debtors present had no further credits which they could apply to the further reduction of their indebtedness. They could do nothing more than pay the balances of their several accounts to whomsoever they might have become indebted in the many assumptions which had occurred. In each case this balance would be precisely what the statement exhibited at the beginning; that is, the result would show that each person would have to pay in, at last, the precise sum which his statement showed, at first, he was in debt more than was coming to him; and of course each one having a favorable balance would receive, after his debts were all paid, the sum which, at the first, he knew was coming to him more than he owed. The changes of indebtedness which would take place in the progress of such an adjustment might be many, but the result would be according to

---

same sum, and so on through the alphabet, one payment by A. to C. is enough to discharge the whole, if all are present, consent, and make the proper entries. So, however complicated the indebtedness, the parties could proceed by dividing sums, until all was paid, except the balances.

"According to article eight of the law of 1667, it was necessary that every transfer, or set-off, should be made in the presence of all concerned in it. Every such transaction, after twenty-four hours, becomes irrevocable and binding as any act whatever; and if any party concerned in a transfer is not present at the exchange at the time of the writing, they take care to send him a memorandum of the transaction, and if he keeps silent twenty-four hours, it is regarded as binding, and the debt as paid."—*Banque Rendue Facile aux Principales Nations de l'Europe, par R. P. Girardeau, Negoçiant a Lyon;* 1703, 4to, page 129, also 302.

the original statement. It is clear that, by perseverance and comparison of books, they could not fail of a complete discharge of all the mutual indebtedness, and payment of the balances would close the whole.

The following account of these Payments is from a reliable English writer, who was himself a witness of the process: —

"The sixth day, all the merchants residing upon the place appear in a certain public room, near the Bourse, with their books or bilans, containing both their debits and credits of both open debts and bills of exchange; and these address themselves to one another, and to whom they are indebted, intimating unto them their readiness to transfer parcels, or, as they term it, virer partie, to give for debtor one or more who doth owe and stands indebted to them the like sum or parcel, the which being accepted by the creditors, the sum is respectively registered and noted in the *bilan* aforesaid; and after that time that parcel is understood to be transferred, and remaineth entirely upon the *risgoe*, peril and fortune of the party that did accept the same. And in this manner here I have observed a million of crowns hath in a morning been paid and satisfied, without the disbursement of a denier in money; and, therefore, to this purpose all merchants resident here, or their servants for them, are compelled in this manner to appear with their *bilans*, thus to satisfy accounts with their creditors, and make good their payments, or, in default of their appearance, are, by the custom of the place, declared as bankrupts. And this, in brief, is the remarkable custom of Lyons, in matters of exchanges, upon every Payment."[1]

The parties who, at the opening of the Payments, knew they would have balances to pay or receive, could not anticipate to whom they would, by the result of all the operations, make payments, or from whom they would receive them. These balances to pay or receive being of equal amount, corresponding, of course, in the aggregate to each other, might have been paid in at the office of the exchange, and have been taken by those enti-

[1] "Map of Commerce," by Lewis Roberts, edition of 1700, Chap. 303.

tled to them, and then the result of the adjustment would have been merely a setting-off of mutual debts, without a remainder. At Lyons it required the continuation of this process for several weeks to close up the large transactions of that city, and the merchants who congregated there. No doubt there was much room for the exercise of commercial and arithmetical skill; and as one object was in the view of all, the whole operation was greatly expedited by the efforts of expert, prompt and experienced merchants, who would be present.

To understand more fully the *rationale* of this mode of adjustment, let us examine in what other modes the end could have been attained. If we suppose this assemblage to be seated round a vast table, any one having a sum of 10,000 livres in coins could have paid it to any other to whom he owed that sum, or more; the receiver could, in like manner, have passed it round to any one to whom he was indebted, and so on, each one making the proper entry on his book. This money might thus circulate, until it fell into the hands of some one who had paid all his debts. A further sum might then be started from another quarter, and be circulated with like result. It is obvious that this circulation would not cease until the payments were nearly completed; and a comparatively small sum would, by such circulation, effect the whole adjustment: a sum sufficient to pay the final balances would be ample to pay fifty, or a hundred times the amount, as rapidly as it could be passed round the table.

Another mode would have been to make a common fund of the whole of the claims, each person being entitled to an amount of that fund corresponding to the whole amount of the credits on his book, or "*bilan.*" The payments might then have proceeded by each one drawing checks for the precise amount of his several debts, and delivering them to his creditors. This would have discharged the whole mass of indebtedness, except the balances, in a morning. Or, what would have been shorter still, each one could have delivered simultaneously a release of all claims, except the balances, which their books showed to be payable and receivable by some who had to pay more than they had to receive, or to receive more than they had to pay.

Or, another way. If a clerk had been appointed by consent of all, and a copy of each "*bilan*" furnished to him, he having read them aloud before the whole assemblage, and no objection being made, could have declared the balance as stated, and have received the amount on the spot from those who had balances to pay; and thus proceeding with the whole, each man's debts and credits would have been settled as soon as read. Each one, by inspection of his own statement, could have determined whether the one read was correct, so far as it affected him. When the accounts had been read over, and the balances paid in, the whole business would have been adjusted, and the clerk would have in his hands precisely the sum necessary to pay those who were entitled to receive more than they had to pay. This would have been a safe and rapid way of completing this liquidation. The same thing might have been done in a more formal manner, by taking the copies of the "*bilans*," as delivered in to the clerk, and making up from them a formal account with each individual, as might be done by comparison of all the statements, by which it would be seen if the claims made by each were admitted in all cases by those against whom they were entered. This formal account with each being balanced, would furnish the same result.

The amount of indebtedness thus discharged yearly at the "Payments of Lyons," independent of the balances paid in money, were estimated at from fifty to a hundred millions of crowns. The whole amount of coins required to pay the balances could not possibly exceed a quarter of a million.[1]

There were many fairs which, from their central or convenient situation, were made principal points for this mode of adjusting accounts. Lyons was one of these. At some, as Novi,[2]

---

[1] As late as 1841, business was transacted, at the Fair of Leipsic, to the amount of £4,905,000, and this without including the vast business done in the sale of books. — *Facts and Figures*, page 57.

[2] "Novi is in the Genoese territory, upon the confines of Lombardy. It is there the Fairs of Genoa are generally held, called, however, now the Fairs of Novi. They were formerly held at Bizanzone. At these fairs the chief bankers and merchants of Italy, Lyons, &c., meet for the purpose of

Placentia, and Bolzano, in Italy, scarce any other business was done. Of the former, Postlethwaite gives this account in his "Dictionary of Commerce:" — "Though there resorts here no small concourse of tradesmen, with all sorts of commodities, yet 'tis not that which renders them so considerable, as that the most eminent bankers and merchants from Lyons, Italy, and from some other more remote parts, meet here to settle their affairs, and balance accounts, chiefly in matters of bank and exchange." . . . "This fair being principally for regulating payments four times a year, it might properly be called the transfer fair; for, of the many millions there negotiated in a year, there's not above 100,000 crowns paid in specie." — *Article "Fairs."*

At the present time we have no data from which to estimate, or even approximate the amount of the payments made at the fairs of Europe, in the period of their greatest success. We know that when trade had increased, in certain channels, to such an extent that the fairs no longer sufficed as places of depôt or sale, payments continued for a long time to be chiefly made in them. Those who are curieus on this subject may, in the travels, memoirs and histories of the time, find abundant evidence of the immense agency of these institutions in the promotion of foreign and domestic trade. They will find, also, that the payments made in the precious metals bore a very small proportion to those made in the manner we have indicated.

The usefulness of the fairs arose from the concentration of merchandise and merchants, and the consequent efficiency given, in the first instance, to the circulation of money. This concentration led to the discovery of the system of payments afterwards adopted. This system, doubtless, had its agency in leading

---

making payments and adjusting accounts, especially those which concern banking. Very little other business is done. There are four of these fairs held each year; each lasting eight days, though sometimes the business of the bankers and merchants prolongs that period." — *Traité Generale du Commerce, par Samuel Ricard; 5th edition par N. Struyck;* Amsterdam, 1732, page 337, 4to: and see, at page 595, full instructions for keeping books in reference to the mode of settlement at these fairs.

bankers and merchants to the adoption of a more effective banking system. It taught men not only the mutuality of commerce, which enabled them to set-off mutual debts, but also the use of circulating credits as a medium of exchange, or a means of payment. It set men free from the idea that payments must necessarily be made in money, and convinced them that, however important the precious metals were in occasional emergencies, and however necessary for payment of balances, and for the business of retail trade, they were not only not necessary, but a positive impediment in the large operations of trade. It taught them that mutual confidence, and undeviating punctuality, were the true foundations of that system of exchanging the products of industry with each other, which men call trade.

CHAPTER XIII.

THE BANK OF VENICE.

Bank of Venice — Originated in 1171, *in a loan to the Republic — Office of transfer — Interest promptly paid — Transferred in any amount in payment of commodities and of debts — All sums deposited with the Bank taken by the Republic — In* 1423, *bills of exchange and payments in gross ordered to be made only in bank — Premium on bank funds — Circulation — Banco del Giro — Evils of coinage, and severity of laws respecting it — Department for deposit of money repayable on demand — Deposit transferable — Its success, without injury to the old business — On two occasions these deposits taken by the Government, but repaid — Amount of capital of the Bank — London Encyclopædia cited and corrected — Causes of agio — Precautions against fraud — Great concentration of payments at Venice.*

In the year 1171, a Venetian fleet of a hundred galleys was sent to avenge an outrage perpetrated by the Grecian Emperor, Manuel, upon Venetian merchants in his empire. This fleet humbled his pride, and compelled him to give satisfaction. The contest is memorable for having given origin to the Bank of Venice. "For the republic being oppressed by the charges of the war against the Emperor of the East, and at the same time involved in hostilities with the Emperor of the West, the Duke Vitale Michel II., after having exhausted every other financial resource, was obliged to have recourse to a forced loan from the most opulent citizens, each being required to contribute according to his ability. On this occasion, and by the determination of the Great Council, the office of chamber of loans (LA CAMERA DEGL' IMPRESTITI) was established: the contributors to the loans were made creditors of that office, from which they were to receive an annual interest of four per cent."[1] The Bank of Venice

[1] M'Pherson's Annals of Commerce, vol. i., p. 341. Sanuto; Vite di Duche di Venezia, App. Muratore Script v., xxii. col., p. 502. This is

gradually assumed the form under which it was, for many ages, the admiration of Europe, the chief instrument of Venetian finance, and the chief facility of a commerce, not surpassed by that of any European nation. Its progress and form were, however, clearly that which naturally grew out of the position of the first contributors to the loan. Its origin was not the first occasion in Venice, or elsewhere, where the State became a borrower from its subjects; it may have been the first in which the loan was taken by a regular subscription, and the subscribers became a specially constituted board for their own protection, and the management of the loan.[1] The book in which these loans were inscribed was authenticated by the government, and made evidence of the whole amount of the debt, with the proportion belonging to each subscriber. It was an easy step to commence the transfer of these loans in part, or in whole. The interest was punctually paid by the government into the office, and distributed thence to those who were entitled to it. Facility of transfer, coupled with the security of the State, and regular payment of the interest, seems to have led to a very rapid circulation of this loan.[2] It must have been regarded, at that day, with great favor as a mode of investment, for nothing of similar

---

thought to be the first mention of a rate of interest per cent. Four per cent. was, no doubt, far below the customary charge of that day; but whether foreseen or not, the privileges of the *chamber of loans* soon indemnified these public creditors for this low rate of interest.

[1] "If I mistake not, this bank is also the most ancient establishment of a permanent national debt, or the funding system, which is now carried to such a height in almost every country in Europe." — *M'Pherson's Annals of Commerce*, vol. i., p. 342.

[2] "As the interest of the loan was always punctually paid, every credit inscribed on the book of the chamber of loans might be regarded as a productive capital; and by laws, these inscriptions, or the right of receiving the interest upon them, could be frequently transferred from one citizen to another. This practice, in the course of time, exhibited to all the lenders how very simple and easy was the process of paying and receiving debts among themselves by transfers upon these books; and from the moment that the advantages which commerce might derive from this method of paying debts was perceived, bank money was invented." — *Econ. Politique, par Henri Storch;* vol. iv., p. 95.

convenience and availability has ever been enjoyed, or was then accessible.[1] The creditors, being thus associated, could bring their united influence to bear upon the government, to insure the regular payment of interest, and to obtain such extension of privileges as time and experience showed to be important and valuable. The reimbursement of the loan ceased to be regarded as either necessary or desirable. Every creditor was reimbursed when he transferred his claim on the books of the bank. From being convenient and valuable as an investment readily obtained, and as readily disposed of, it became, by a natural process, a medium of payment in transactions of commerce. That fund, which was desirable to all seeking investment, would be willingly, in many instances, accepted in payment of debts already existing, or for goods just purchased. There is good reason to believe that this fund was largely used in this way for centuries before the final arrangements were made, of which our accounts are more clear. It is not unlikely that irregularities crept into the mercantile usages of the bank; that transfers were made otherwise than in the bank, and perhaps by circulating papers or checks authorizing the bank to make transfers for the amount expressed to bearer. Such a practice, unauthorized by the State, would lead to confusion, to mistakes, to forgery, and litigation. Whatever may have been the malpractices which grew up in the usages of the bank, in the first two hundred and fifty years of its history, it fully vindi-

[1] "There was at Venice that which, more than any previous commercial policy, opened men's eyes to an advantage of great importance, contributing alike to the prosperity of the State, and to the benefit of trade. She was the glorious inventress of the Guarantied Bank [banco garantito], differing both in its operations and by its security from common banks, as much as from those called public banks. For, in the case of the Guarantied Bank, if robbery occurs, if the servants and officials of the bank commit fraud, if the managers administer it badly, the government is held responsible for the whole; no private person suffers any loss. But in the case of other banks, the government is only bound to do justice, by giving all the assistance it can in the discovery and punishment of the criminals, and for the recovery of the loss." — *Broggia Trattate delle Monete,* vol. ii., p. 270, being vol. v. in *Custodi's Collection of the Economisti Italiani.*

cated, in that period, its power and utility as a financial agent of the republic, and its efficiency in promoting the movements of commerce.

There is no question, although we have not the details, that the government had found it perfectly easy to enlarge the amount of the original loan or stock of the bank, as the demand for its funds generally exceeded the supply. All money deposited for the purpose of obtaining a credit in bank was accounted an addition to the original loan, and as such taken into the public treasury as money lent to the State. Every such investment increased the stock of the bank, and replenished the treasury of the republic. If individuals could make purchases and pay debts by transfers in bank, the public treasury could well afford to receive, in payment of its dues, credits in bank, as that would be only equivalent to taking up its own obligations. Thus, the more these credits were employed, the more the demand for them increased, the more rapidly money flowed into the treasury, and the more readily the government could afford to receive payment of its revenues in the funds of the bank.[1]

The way was opened, by the experience of two centuries and

---

[1] "By degrees the government introduced the usage of making certain payments by drawing upon the bank, in place of making them in specie. It commenced by receiving these drafts into the public treasury without hesitation; and when this usage became established, a law was passed, that bills of exchange might be paid in money of the bank, whether foreign or domestic, when drawn for above the sum of three hundred ducats. These drafts could not be refused, unless stipulation had been made to the contrary." — *Daru. de Hist. Venice*, vol. iii., p. 73.

"To give these bank credits great rapidity of circulation, an account of debit and credit was opened with every proprietor, admitting of the prompt transfer of credits; and that these might be readily effected and accepted with safety, it was decreed that they should not be seized in execution for debt, nor be the subject of mortgage." — *Ibid.*, p. 74.

This statement may not be strictly correct, in asserting that the enactment, that all payments not otherwise agreed should be made in bank, was the result of the use which the government had made of the bank. This decree was the result of the efficiency of the bank, as long experienced and admitted, and of the confidence that both the people and the government would derive great advantage from the measure.

a half, for the next chief characteristic of the Bank of Venice. In the year 1423, in the administration of the Doge *Thomas Moncenigo*, it was decreed that all bills of exchange payable in Venice, whether domestic or foreign, should be paid, unless otherwise stipulated and so expressed, in the bank; and that all payments in gross, or in wholesale transactions, should be effected also in bank. This at once brought the mass of the payments of that great commercial city to the bank.[1] Whatever irregularities, and whatever confusion had prevailed, this introduced a uniform and, from long familiarity with the bank, an intelligible system. The endless diversity, and bad condition of the coins circulating in Venice were a sufficient recommendation of the new regulation to all who had not very special reasons, indeed, for disliking it. This measure at once created a great additional demand for the funds of the bank, and brought large sums into the public coffers. The government,

---

[1] "It was established, by a solemn edict of the Republic, that all payments of merchandise in gross, and of bills of exchange, should be made only in bank; and that all debtors should carry their money to the bank, to receive credits in bank therefor; and that creditors should receive payment in bank, by a simple transfer from their debtors. He who was creditor upon the books of the bank became debtor as soon as he had made his transfer, or payment, to another, who became creditor in his place. Thus the parties did but change their position, without its being necessary to make any payment in money (réel et effectif)." — *Savéry's Dict. de Com., Art. "Banque,"* vol. i., p. 277.

"By this means the Republic of Venice, without restricting the course of trade, became the mistress of the money of the people; and without being obliged to resort to extraordinary taxes to sustain the war against the Turks, so long protracted, it drew to the bank, and thence to the public treasury, the sums of which it had need, without resorting to loans, so often prejudicial to commerce. The credit granted by the government on the books of the bank for this money continued to perform the same functions as the money. Although, for distinction, called imaginary money, it was equivalent to real money, since it had the same value. No one believed himself less rich from his money being all in the bank, because, with his credit in the bank, he could obtain money when he wished; whilst the Republic, from this bank, and the credit which it had given it, drew effective succor for its wants, an aid which it never could have received by taxation." — *Parfait Negoçiant*, vol. i., p. 464.

however, no longer paid interest for the sums received from the bank. The funds obtained in this way were brought to the bank for the payment of bills of exchange, and were paid in for that purpose, and not with a view to interest. The rapid succession of payments occurring at a point where all the payments of Venetian commerce were accomplished, made the intervals during which the funds remained in the hands of any one merchant too short to make him solicitous about interest on balances or deposits. As all payments of the kind above designated were, by law, to be made in bank, unless otherwise agreed, and as that mode of payment was far more convenient, it became almost the exclusive usage of trade. All who had engagements to meet, found them in the bank: of course, all such provided the bank funds necessary to meet them, or carried to the bank the amount of coins requisite for the purpose. The government continued to take all money paid in as a consideration for allowing an inscription on the books of the bank to the credit of the depositor. The sums which thus flowed through the bank into the treasury would, with the previous bank funds, make up the quantity needful for the convenient discharge of the commercial payments of Venice. As this amount fluctuated from year to year, and during each year, with the course of commerce, a very effective mode of accommodating the supply of bank funds to the exigencies of the demand came obviously into use. When the payments in bank were heavy, and the bank funds in great demand, money flowed freely into bank, and the credits were proportionably increased. When an occasional demand for the precious metals arose, the holders of bank funds could readily dispose of them at a slight reduction for coins. The purchasers of bank funds were sure of meeting soon a demand for them; for the demand for a medium in which the ever-recurring payments of debts were made so much exceeded in intensity the occasional demand for specie for exportation, or any other use, that during the whole existence of the bank, with very slight exception, the bank fund was at a large premium over coins, so large that it was finally fixed by law at 20 per cent.[1]

[1] A full explanation of the *agio*, or premium of the bank funds, in Venice, will be given infra.

The republic could well afford to maintain a liberal policy towards an institution so important, both as a fiscal and commercial agent. That the inhabitants of Venice were well satisfied, we cannot doubt, as not an objection was ever made to the bank, at least none is extant; neither book, nor speech, nor pamphlet, have we found, in which any merchant or dweller in Venice ever put forth any condemnation of its theory, or its practice. There was no hesitation in carrying money to the bank, so long as it was not doubted that bank funds would purchase specie without loss, whenever it might be needed; and the uniform premium of bank funds settled that point. Under such a system, the regular payments of trade would proceed with a rapidity and economy previously unknown, so far as the history of commerce informs us. In this aspect, it deserves special examination.

"If Jean, Pierre, Claude and Jacques, and consecutively every inhabitant of the same town, had but one banker, who kept an account with each one of them in a register provided for the purpose, this banker could make all their reciprocal payments without moving a cent of their money, since it would suffice simply to write upon his register the receipt from one, and the payment by another; from which would result two things — they would avoid the trouble of receiving and counting money, and the expense of each having a cashier and book-keeper.

"Another respect in which the position of this banker would be advantageous to them would be, that he could put the money of all to good use, without diverting it from its proper destination, or interrupting the progress of their payments, which would be effected there by means of his books. And a third advantage would arise if this same banker would lend the money thus economized to his customers, by which they could augment their trade, both at home and abroad.

"This is what the Republic of Venice happily accomplished by the establishment of its bank, which became a perpetual banker for its inhabitants. It received from them the money previously employed in payment for merchandise in gross, and of bills of exchange; for, by public edict, all payments for merchandise in gross were to be made only in bank. All debtors were obliged, for this purpose, to carry their money to bank, and to receive credit therefor, and all creditors to receive payment there. Every payment was made by a simple transfer of a credit upon the books of the bank from one to another. He who was a creditor upon the book of the bank became debtor as soon as he had assigned to another, who thus became a creditor in his place; and so on, from one to another, the parties simply changing their position of debtor and creditor, without any necessity of a payment in money."[1]

If there were a thousand accounts opened in the bank by the chief men of trade in Venice, they would be found to be all paying as well as receiving, and the sums to be paid would be mainly to each other. There would, therefore, be a vast sum in the aggregate payable yearly by persons in Venice to persons in Venice. If the whole number of such persons be taken by conjecture, as above, at a thousand, then nearly the whole sum owing by all of them would be receivable by all of them. It would, to a large extent, be a mutual debt among the thousand, each one having to pay to others not far from the same amount he was to receive. If the whole sum to be paid and received annually was a hundred and twenty millions, the monthly payment would be ten millions, and the daily over three hundred thousand. The amount of bank funds which would be sufficient to meet such a daily, monthly, or yearly aggregate, experience and time could alone fully teach. It would depend on the rapidity of the movement; on the regularity with which the paper matured; on the degree of confidence subsisting among the parties, which would lead them to favor each other by short loans, from those who could spare for a brief time to those whose receipts did not, for the time, correspond with their payments. The whole fund in the bank would thus move in a circle among its customers, each one receiving and paying yearly according to the extent of his business. The fund would substantially remain, all the time, among the same persons, only varying in the distribution.[2]

---

[1] Parfait Negoçiant, vol. i., p. 463.

[2] It was from this movement in a circle, the efficacy of which was fully perceived in Venice, that the bank took the name by which it was long called in Europe, Banco del Giro. It was seen that each day's business caused the transfer of a large amount of the bank credits, and a corresponding change of ownership; and that this change took place day after day, and yet, at the end of a year of these daily changes, the whole credits belonged to nearly the same persons, though not perhaps in the same proportions. It was as if they were moving in a circle, of which each day was a step; but whether moving slow or fast, they could not go beyond the enclosure.

It is worthy of remark, that this very efficient mode of adjustment discovered and used so largely at this early period in the history of commerce, was not dependent for its efficacy on the guarantee of the republic. That guarantee sprung out of the mode in which the bank originated: this convenient method of liquidation sprung from the use of this new substitute for money.

The facility of payment furnished by the bank, which made it the admiration of Europe, honorable at once to the government and merchants of Venice, and a support to the pride and power of its people, consisted in substituting, as a medium of payment, the debt of the republic for current coin. The coin in circulation in Venice was, in many respects, a nuisance of the most vexatious kind. It consisted not only of the variety which the many mints of Italy at all times afforded, but of that vastly increased variety which had accumulated from the coinage of more than a century. Besides this multiplicity of the new and old coins of Italy, was the coinage of many countries of the far East with which Venice carried on a vast commerce. To make all the payments of the domestic and foreign trade of Venice in these coins, of different degrees of purity, and many of them much deteriorated by wear, required time, patience, and skill, which but few merchants could adequately command.[1] The

---

It was well understood, too, in that day, that if coins had been employed in such an adjustment, they would have performed the same rotary movement, so far as they could be made to effect it.

"Car sans debourser aucune somme, il s'y fait à toute heure des payemens pour les quels il ne faut que changer de nom des parties: de sorte que les sommes y ROULENT *de l'un à l'autre* sans sortir des coffres des Prince, que jouit de ce fond sans payer aucune intèrêt." . . . "On l'appelle *Banco del Giro* à cause de tours perpetuels que l'argent y fait. — *Traite Generale du Commerce, par S. Ricard,* 1732, page 301.

[1] With all the advantages of their bank, the Venetians were extremely careful to restrain abuses of their coinage. Their coins enjoyed a high reputation for purity throughout the world. They punished those who were guilty of infringing the laws for the protection of the coinage with whipping, and other severe penalties. Persons were equally prohibited from paying or receiving coins at a rate more or less than the nominal value. No doubt one effect of this strictness was to promote payments in the bank in a fund which the mischiefs of coinage could not reach.

facility offered by the government, through the bank, saved all this. The government took the coins one time for all, giving therefor a corresponding credit in the bank; and allowed the depositor or lender to transfer this credit claim upon the republic in payment of his debt, in place of transferring or paying over the coin in each payment. Whatever men can employ in payment of debts, they will be willing to receive in payment, and this independent of any legal compulsion.

Experience soon evinced the power and convenience of this mode of payment. These bank credits were divisible to every desirable degree, and they could be transferred with a readiness, speed and safety, beyond all comparison, superior to any mode of paying in coin. The same sum or credit might be kept in

---

Foreign coins were only allowed to be introduced into the city under very special regulations. Dealing in coins by private or public banks was prohibited under severe penalties. All coins to be changed or sold were to be carried to an office opened for the purpose at the mint; the determination of the authorities being to protect the mass of the people from all the evil practices of dealers in coins. All contracts made payable in coins were to be at the rate named in the law. Every tradesman or laborer induced or compelled to take any coin otherwise than at the legal rate, was enjoined to make known the facts to a court of justice, and exhibit the money paid to him; upon which the party paying him this money was not only compelled to give him legal money, but to pay him also twenty-five ducats of a fine.

Every person carrying money into Venice was obliged to submit it to the inspection of a public officer at the mint. Any failure to comply with this involved a forfeiture of the coins so introduced into the country.

Officers from the mint were required to pass daily through the city, visiting especially places of dealing, to give information, to detect offenders, and to see the kind of coins in circulation. These officers were not permitted to receive compensation of any kind, but were to render their services free to the people.

These regulations were printed, and fixed in conspicuous places throughout the city. Informers were not only encouraged, and their names kept secret, but, in many instances, they were largely compensated out of the pockets of the offenders. The severity of these laws is such, in fact, that it is difficult to imagine what could have been the extent of the abuses which made them necessary. For full details, see *Marperger on Banks*, pp. 180 to 189, 4to: *Berschreibung der Banquen, von J. P. Marperger*, Leipsic, 1717.

such rapid circulation, as to effect an amount of payments, in a specified time, far beyond any possible movement of coin. This rapidity became a great economy, for a much less sum of credits was made to effect a given amount of payments with far greater speed than could have been attained with coin. But this economy resulting from increased speed and power of circulation was still more important, arising from the fact that the coins which were deposited as the basis of the credit were very soon again restored to the usual channels of circulation by the payments of government. Thus the coin was not withdrawn from its proper functions, and the credits remained a perpetual fund, to be employed in large payments. This system of payments was so well adapted to the exigencies of commerce, that it was maintained in full vigor, in the great commercial city of Venice, for almost four hundred years. It was an institution or device of the credit system, for by its aid payments were effected, and that to a vast amount annually, without any use of coins or bullion. It only perished when the city itself fell, at the conquest of Italy by Napoleon; but the conqueror carried off no coin, no penny of prey. The credits of the bank were crushed under the rude touch of an invading foe. They were lost to the proprietor, but no equivalent passed into the hands of the destroyers. If the holders of these credits suffered, the invaders were not enriched. In assuming the sovereignty of Venice, the conqueror assumed the right and the duty of making good these bank credits.

In some respects, these bank credits of Venice approximated to the power and convenience of the bank deposits of our day; and, but for certain regulations, they might have been fully as efficient. Some of these regulations will be noticed as we proceed.

Experience finally dictated that the convenience of merchants required a facility, in certain transactions, which the bank as constituted did not afford. This was simply a place of deposit—a bank, or office, in which coins or bullion could be deposited in safety, with the right of withdrawal at pleasure, or of transferring the ownership, if desirable. To meet this requirement, the government established such an institution as a second or coordinate department of the bank. It was provided that money should be received and credited, on the books of this office, to the depositor. This measure was completely successful. The republic having previously kept good faith with its citizens, they did not doubt that the plan of the new establishment would be carried out with equal fidelity.[1]

Those who received money for which they had no immediate use, and foreign merchants making purchases in Venice to carry to their own country, could thus deposit their coins in a safe place, and wait till the course of business determined what mode of disposition would be most beneficial or convenient. Such depositors could not only withdraw their deposit, but could transfer the right to withdraw it, or its equivalent in other coins; so that the funds of this deposit branch were always liable to be withdrawn. It became, of course, the depository for that large amount of money which, in every commercial community, must be kept ready for any occasion which the fluctuations of business, or public affairs, might disclose. Those even who had bills to pay with their money in a short time, making it necessary to carry it into that ancient branch of the bank, from whence it would pass into the public treasury, might prefer retaining it in their power until their payments matured. The convenience of this depository would lead, no doubt, to making many bills of exchange, and other liabilities, payable in coin, which had for a long time, under the law and usages of commerce, been payable in bank funds. Parties contracting previously having the privilege of making debts payable, by so expressing the contract, in coins, preferred omitting that stipulation, as the mode of paying in bank funds was the most advantageous and convenient. But, under the regulation of the new depository, the convenience became equal in each department, and other considerations would

[1] "The necessity which existed, of making occasional payments in money, gave rise to the opening of a cash office (Caisse de Comptant) for those who wished to be paid in coins. Experience proved that this measure did not cause any sensible diminution in the funds of the bank." — *Dict. de Com., par Savary, Article "Banque,"* p. 276.

determine the choice. The success of this depository did not check the flow of money into the public coffers, as the demand had always been greater than the supply of bank funds, and therefore caused no complaint nor disappointment on that ground. It was perfectly apparent that the bank, by this addition, had become a vastly more efficient and useful institution; and the whole policy of the republic shows that the importance of a steadfast and firm support of the bank was perfectly understood. A large amount of specie rapidly accumulated in the depository, which was transferred on its books from one person to another, in the same mode as in the other departments of the bank. It was, therefore, made to perform the adjustments of commerce, so far as applicable, as efficiently as the other, while the fund was constantly at the disposition of its owners. It bore no interest, and was therefore only profitable by the intermediate use thus made of it. The advantage to the holders was, that while they could dispense with keeping coins for occasional employment as such, they could be made available for current payments in the new depository. Of course the amount thus kept would be small, in comparison with that fund which would be employed exclusively in effecting the ever-recurring payments of the great mass of liabilities constantly in course of liquidation. It would also be exceedingly fluctuating, because it would correspond with the changes of trade in each year, and from year to year. In these respects it would simply keep pace with the exigencies of commerce; no external force or power would restrain its limits at one time, and unduly extend them at another. It would be perfectly elastic and impressible to the movements of trade. None of the mischances of commerce could be charged to it, for it simply performed the duty of a depository, and permitted a change of ownership of the sums deposited to any extent desired. It was a servant, not a master. Bound by certain rules, from which it dare not swerve, it exercised no discretion.

It was found, in process of time, that although the amount of the deposit thus made fluctuated largely, yet a great sum remained unmoved by any emergency of business. This was, in part, taken by the government on occasions of pressing need.[1] On two occasions this cash office suspended payments; and on one of these the suspension was continued for several years; yet such was the confidence in the government, and so accustomed were the people to the operations of the older branch, that the transfers of these removed deposits proceeded, during the suspension, as if the specie were still present,[2] the government receiving them in all payments to it; so that, during the period of the suspension, the two departments of the bank were resolved into one, as to their *mode of operation*, the fund in each being equally a public debt, but not of equal value, for the old bank credits maintained their advantage in that respect under all changes. The government seized the first opportunity of enabling the cash-office to resume its payments, and the whole current of this department of the bank fell into its appropriate channels.

The original capital, or subscription, which constituted the bank, is stated to have been 2,000,000 of ducats. In the middle of the 18th century, the amount was estimated at 5,000,000; and towards the end of that century, at the close of its long and

---

[1] "Its credit was so fully established in the end, that although it was well known that the government had withdrawn a portion of the funds of the cash-office upon two occasions of great public necessity, upon which this department of the bank suspended payments (in 1600 and 1717), and although these suspensions were unexpectedly prolonged, the funds of neither branch suffered serious or general discredit. The confidence that the republic would make all right was unshaken. It was believed, too, that the government would at all times take these credits for anything due to the public treasury." — *Daru, Hist. de Venice*, vol. iii., p. 74.

[2] "During the progress of the war against the Turks, the republic having exhausted its treasury, was constrained to suspend payments at this cash-office, which caused some diminution of the credit of the bank; nevertheless, it did not interrupt its regular business. All the evil which it produced was, that those who were afraid resorted to persons who relieved them by giving them ready money for their bank credits, at ten or fifteen per cent. discount. Several years afterwards the republic, upon occasion of a new coinage, returned the money to the cash-office, and restored it to its full functions and high place in public opinion. The credits of this office were soon again at par with the precious metals, and so remained." — *Parfait Negoçiant*, vol. i., p. 464.

and successful career of five hundred years, at 14,000,000 or 15,000,000.[1]

We have no means of determining the actual efficiency of the fund thus employed in the payments of Venice. There does not appear, in the notices of the bank left to us, any limitation to the circulation or transfers of the credits on its books. Every precaution, apparently, was taken to prevent mistakes; and every transfer made by the clerks of the bank, in the presence of the parties, or their agents duly authorized, bore on its face the nature of the transaction.[2] No receipt or voucher was necessary, when a payment was made in bank, as the transfer in payment was regarded as the best evidence, being sufficiently explanatory to show the actual nature and occasion of the payment. It is not improbable that the whole fund of the bank performed payments, in the aggregate, annually to five hundred, and perhaps a thousand-fold the amount.

It does not appear that any tax was imposed upon these bank credits, except a collateral inheritance tax of ten per cent., when the funds of the bank descended, or were devised by a deceased proprietor, to collateral heirs; and a forfeiture, or escheat to the state, of such deposits or funds as belonged to proprietors deceased intestate without heirs. Both these were discontinued as soon as the necessities of the public treasury permitted.

The Bank of Venice enjoyed a reputation, throughout the commercial world, which greatly promoted the success of Vene-

---

[1] Histoire de Venice, par Daru, vol. iii., p. 75.

[2] The mode of making the bank transfers, and specimens of the forms of entries, may be seen in *Postlethwaite's Dictionary, Art.* '*Venice;*' and in the *Encyclopœdia Methodique, Commerce,* vol. i., *Art.* '*Banque.*' The alphabet was subdivided, and each person applied to the book-keeper to whose subdivision the letters of his name assigned him. Every subdivision had two clerks, by whom all transfers and entries were made. The party making a transfer appeared before these two clerks, and dictated the entry or transfer to be made, and both clerks wrote in separate books from that dictation. The entry specified what was paid, whether a bill of exchange, or balance of account, &c., and if a bill, where drawn, or in some way designated the bill. This made the entries on the books of the bank good evidence for all payments, and safe vouchers.

tian trade. It was a tower of financial strength to the republic in her long and expensive wars, and of course contributed no small share to the celebrity of the city, as well as to its power and wealth. That the advantage of such an institution to commerce was early and fully comprehended by the Venetian merchants, is evident from the fact that those engaged in their Eastern trade established a bank in Damascus, of which we only know that it was the repository of great treasure when that city was taken and pillaged by an Eastern conqueror, early in the 15th century.

"This bank was established on such judicious principles, and has been conducted, through the revolution of many centuries, with such prudence, that though the government have twice, since its establishment, made free with its funds, its credit has remained inviolate and unimpeached."[1] This, from the "Annals of Commerce," is one of many loose and imperfect accounts of the Bank of Venice which have long been in circulation, transferred from one work to another, varied and mingled, until it has become a complicated task to extricate the true from the false. One of the more recent of these statements we give entire from the London Encyclopædia, as it furnishes occasion to correct some errors.

"The original subscription fund of the Bank of Venice was 2,000,000 Venetian ducats, equal to £433,333; but by a solemn edict of the Senate, the whole trading community of the republic were compelled to deposit their money in bank, with which a credit was opened equal to the deposit made, which could only be made available for transfer; so that not only the subscribed capital, but also the aggregate amount of the deposits, resolved themselves into a national debt.

"Whether the transfers at the bank, in the early period of its establishment, required personal attendance, as is the case of transferring the national debt-stock at the Bank of England

---

[1] M'Pherson's Annals of Commerce, vol. i., p. 341. It was a part of the fund of the cash-office which was, upon emergency, taken by the government for public use, and subsequently restored. In the mean time, the transfers of the office proceeded as if the specie was still in its vaults. The confidence of the people seems not to have been impaired.

in the present day, or whether effected on written orders corresponding to the checks in the present English practice of banking, does not appear: but be that as it might, derangements in the social economy of the state soon ensued; the agio, or difference between the current money and transferable amounts at the bank, attained the rate of thirty per cent. Yet such was the insidious and illusive nature of the bank system, that the bank increased in popularity in proportion to the extent of the derangement that ensued; the inconvenience frequently occasioned in the minor transactions of commerce, as well as on occasions of citizens or strangers requiring money to defray the expenses of foreign journeys, led, in the course of time, to the bank paying out money. Yet such was the influx of money, which the crusading armaments brought from all parts of Western Europe, that after the system of making payments in money was practised, the deposits always exceeded the demands. At a later period, when the Venetians themselves turned crusaders against the Turks, the subscription fund of the bank was increased to 5,000,000 of ducats, the whole of which was made use of by the Senate to aid them in their operations of warfare; and, as previously stated, throughout the whole period of its career, it was made an instrument of aggression in aid of political aggrandisement: yet such was the fortuity of circumstances, and for several centuries having no rivalry, its integrity does not appear to have been questioned; the derangements occasioned by the fluctuation of the agio led ultimately to an edict of the Senate, fixing it at twenty per cent., at which rate it continued up to the period of the extinction of the republic, in 1797."[1]

It is very clear that that writer did not go far for his information. There is no doubt that the rule of the bank required the presence of the party transferring, either in person or by attorney; and this was carried so far, that no endorsed bills of

---

[1] London Encyclopædia, Art. "Bank." *Laus est ab hoste laudari.* It is apparent that the Encyclopædist knew very little about the Bank of Venice, and that he had not taken the pains to digest what he did know. He had no conception of it as a system, nor of its efficiency as a mode of payment.

exchange were permitted. The payee, or his attorney, could alone receive payment.

The assertion that the whole trading community was compelled to deposit their money in the bank, is a great mistake. After the bank had been in operation more than two centuries, it was ordered that all bills of exchange, and all payments in gross, where parties had not otherwise stipulated, should be paid in bank. The only articles to be exclusively paid for in bank funds were *oil* and *quicksilver*. The rule that bills of exchange, not otherwise expressed, should be thus paid was no doubt complied with, because both convenience and interest dictated it; but as cash payments for merchandise would be made when the contract was made, the payment would be in bank or other funds, as the convenience of the moment might suggest.

It was a great mistake, also, to state "that derangements in the social economy of the state soon ensued; the agio, or difference between the current money and transferable amounts at the bank, attained to thirty per cent." The impression is created here, that derangements in the social economy were caused by the peculiar constitution of the bank, and that the agio of thirty per cent. was unfavorable to the bank; neither of which was the case. There is no evidence extant that the Bank of Venice ever caused any derangements of the social economy. The voice of the best authorities is all the other way. The bank was an advantage to Venice never questioned by those familiar with its usages. The *agio*, instead of being against the bank, was in its favor; its funds rose to thirty per cent. premium over the current coins, and continued to fluctuate near this high rate, until the government, by decree, limited the premium to twenty per cent., at which it continued permanently fixed so long as the bank existed. The ground of this agio is not adequately explained by any one, and was probably inexplicable to the encyclopædist, who evidently looked upon the institution with no friendly eye.

The unit of the money of account of the bank was the ducat. A gold coin of that name had long enjoyed, in Venice, an exemption from the changes so frequent then in coins, and had been held in high repute, far and wide, for its purity. In the money of account formed upon that coin were the books of the bank kept. It was said, by some, that the agio arose in part from the superiority of Venetian ducats to other current coins. But as it was perfectly understood that no coins passed, neither any right to any, on a transfer in the bank, it is impossible to attribute the agio to any such consideration. It is true, however, that the nuisance of multiplied coinage has for centuries been exhibited in Italy in its worst aspect; and the evil was aggravated in Venice by a large admixture of coins which her widely-spread commerce brought from all the world. In Italy, the perplexity caused by multiplicity of coins and moneys of account, as already noticed, reached an alarming extent. In the same city, frequently, there existed among merchants quite a diversity in the moneys of account. It required a person specially skilled to tell the value or price of the various coins passing in trade, expressed frequently in different moneys of account. In some instances, special moneys of account were appropriated to special coins, or special commodities.

Any method which offered an escape from such intricacies, from employing such coins, from the danger of taking counterfeits, and from the risk of keeping money on hand for large payments, could not but be regarded with continued favor. Even at this day, the evils of an over-multiplied coinage press with great severity upon the people of Italy. Large quantities of coins lie, like bullion, in the coffers of the bankers; and when it is necessary to dispose of them in bulk, a close and tedious inspection becomes necessary. In a hundred coins, no five may be found alike. This mischief existed in full force in Venice, and had its due share, no doubt, in creating the *agio*. It is far from adequate, however, to account for the agio of thirty per cent. mentioned above, or the twenty per cent. fixed by law, much less an additional *agio*, to be mentioned hereafter.

To comprehend this extraordinary fact of a credit on the books of a bank, with no money in its vaults, and not bound to make that credit good in later times even by the payment of the interest, or to redeem it in any way, having been for hundreds of years at a high premium over gold and silver, we need only remember that these credits were the funds in which debts were chiefly paid. If credits had been convertible at will into the precious metals, the agio could never have originated, much less attained so high a point; for the moment the holders of credits advanced the price, specie, if a legal tender, would have become the medium of payment, as the cheaper medium. In a commercial community like Venice, as elsewhere, large transactions were nearly all done upon credit. The chief use for money, or bank credits, was not in the purchase of commodities, but in the payment of debts incurred for goods purchased upon credit, or on time. When the republic decreed, in 1423, that bills of exchange, and other large payments, should be paid in bank, unless the parties had otherwise stipulated, it introduced the usage of making nearly all payments there, because parties preferred receiving payment in bank, and in the fund in which they had to pay their debts. There was then probably ten times more demand for bank credits than for coins, which were only required for export, for the retail trade, and for other special but limited uses. The necessity of punctually meeting all commercial engagements was not less in Venice than in New York or Philadelphia. Failure to pay was ruin. The merchant in good credit might purchase at his pleasure upon deferred payments; but the day of payment must arrive, and with it the unavoidable necessity of meeting these liabilities, however thoughtlessly incurred. To this compulsion no resistance could be offered; from this obligation of mercantile punctuality there could be no escape, no evasion. Doubtless merchants in those days pushed their credit, as in later times, and found days of payment days of struggle, anxiety and difficulty, as merchants do now. Bank credits, by the law of the land and their own arrangements, being the only funds in which these constantly maturing, and constantly pressing debts, could be paid, were in a demand proportioned to this urgency. If the same mode of adjusting debts were resorted to now, the result would be, that inconvertible bank credits would go frequently to a high premium over gold and silver. If any one doubt this, let them attempt a solution of the question, Why is it that our gold and silver coins, and bank-notes convertible into them, remain at par, having no greater purchasing power when interest is at two or three per cent. per month, than when it is at half per cent.? It is the demand for money to pay debts which thus advances interest; and this does not affect the value of coins or bank-notes in circulation, because they are not available in the large payments of commerce. It is that fund which circulates in our banks as "deposits," which actually attains the highest rates of interest. This is the fund in which debts are paid, and the daily employment of this fund is an hundred-fold the extent of any use of bank-notes or coins. It is upon this principle that we explain the agio of bank credits at Venice over the current money.

No doubt this premium created surprise, and many, perhaps, looked upon it as unjust; but it was the result of the merchants' own movements. The government did not cause it, nor did the banks. It was, therefore, acquiesced in by the merchants as a result of their own acts in their own business. The government, so far from producing, attempted to limit it to twenty per cent., an attempt which was rendered wholly abortive by the introduction of a *sur agio*, or super-premium, calculated upon the agio and the original sum together. This additional premium ranged at from twenty to thirty per cent. for a long period, and exhibited in its fluctuations partly the pressure for money to pay debts, and partly the current value of the coins which were offered in exchange for bank credits.

The precautions against mistakes and frauds enforced by the government of Venice in the affairs of the bank, far exceed any required by the authorities of the present time, jealous as they are of banks. Not only, as we have seen, was every transfer made in the presence of two book-keepers, who were required to keep separate sets of books, but the bank was shut one day in each week; and four times in a year, each time twenty days. This was to balance and thoroughly supervise the books. During the period when the bank was thus shut, no bill payable in it matured, or, rather, none could be protested until six days after the opening, six days being the grace allowed on bills in Venice.

A custom obtained among merchants, and others, of writing-off or transferring bank credits in blank during the time when the bank was closed. The entries intended to be placed on the books of the bank at the opening, were made by the parties upon books mutually exchanged, or left in the hands of a broker, proper authority being given to make the entries, and the arrangement was completed, except the formal execution on the books of the bank. No doubt this facility was confined to those who entertained for each other great mutual confidence; it may have led to many transfers of the same sum whilst the books were closed, and thus in part have compensated the injury to business caused by shutting the bank.

The great feature of the Bank of Venice — that which required all bills of exchange payable in that great commercial city to be paid at the bank — appeared at first blush to be an arbitrary requirement, if not a most unjust one. It was giving a forced currency to the bank deposits, consisting merely of debts due by the government. It was soon found, however, to work so well in practice, that it brought an immense accession of business to the city, and to the bank. Bills of exchange became of increased use in all the neighboring commerce, and a vast concentration of payments took place at Venice, and in the bank. This increase enlarged the capital of the bank. The money brought in to pay bills was taken by the government as fast as it was received, until the amount of the deposit, or debt of the state, was adequate, by rapid circulation, to the current payments of commerce. This made the bank a great clearing-house, or place of adjustment, for merchants of many countries. Venice was for centuries the greatest entrepôt of commerce in Europe, if not in the world. The chief payments or liquidations of this trade were effected at the bank. As is the case in many great commercial cities of the present day, payments to a great amount were thus effected at Venice upon transactions which had occurred elsewhere. It was found, therefore, then as now in regard to London, Paris, Hamburg and New York, that it was convenient and of advantage to have funds in Venice. The payments of bills required daily such a large sum, that the demand for funds for that purpose was always very great; and where everybody wanted funds, everybody sent them.

The bank became, then, a place of liquidation; merchants made their bills payable at the point where was the greatest concentration of means to pay them, and where it was most for their advantage to receive payment. Those who had occasion for gold or silver, purchased with these deposits what was required; and, with slight exception, for more than four hundred years the precious metals were at a discount, compared with the bank funds — the demand for that which would pay bills of exchange being greater than for gold or silver for any special use to which they could be applied. The great mass of the purchases of commerce were made, in the first instance, by bills of exchange; and the great operation of payments consisted in liquidating these bills. The demand, therefore, for the deposits in which they were paid was as incessant as the movement of commerce itself. These bank deposits circulated on the books of the bank, therefore, precisely in accordance with the movements of trade; and the customers of the bank thus applied these credits, or the debts due to them, to the discharge of the debts they owed.

CHAPTER XIV.

THE BANK OF GENOA.

The House of St. George, or Bank of Genoa — Contrast of the financial systems of Venice and Genoa — Complications of Genoese finance — Security required by public creditors — The system of 1302, *and its officers — Private bankers — The Bank established in* 1407 *— Its large array of officers — Deferred dividends, or Moneta di Paghe — Famine of* 1539 *— Deposit system — Bank bills — Price of shares — Money and moneys of account — Advantages of the Bank to trade — Methods and processes of the Bank — M. Gautier and M. Coquelin on the moneys of account of the Bank — Carlo Cuneo on the moneys of Genoa*

THE finances of Venice and Genoa present a remarkable and instructive contrast. The public loan of Venice, which gave origin to the bank, was forced; but the whole subsequent history of the bank and the public credit is one of entire confidence on the part of the people, and admirable prudence, good faith, and forbearance, on the part of the government. Venice made the public debt the chief currency, or medium of exchange, in all the large operations of trade; and the public debt was wisely kept at that amount which not only preserved its value, but furnished the full quantity of currency required for trade, with the means of increasing or diminishing the amount, according to the proper demand. This mutual confidence and prudent management are creditable alike to the financial skill and intelligence of all concerned. The government enjoyed a loan, free of interest, equal to the whole capital of the bank, without having given any special guarantee, or any evidence of the debt, except an inscription on the books of the bank; the people enjoyed a currency, which for centuries stood at a high premium over gold and silver. The Bank of Venice, and its public finances, commencing in violence, soon settled into a simplicity and regularity of progress, and freedom from undue fluctuation, of which, for such a long period, there is no parallel.

The finances of Genoa, commencing with the 13th century, furnish a history equally remarkable, and perhaps equally instructive, although in many respects in striking contrast. The turbulence of the nobles of Genoa kept the state, for ages, in a condition approaching civil war. In the midst of these violent intestine commotions, the financial system of Genoa had its origin and growth. The public loans were the spontaneous offerings of the lenders, who, though willing to lend, exhibited from the first no confidence in the mere promises or credit of the government, and exacted most rigidly, from time to time, the utmost security and the strongest guarantees the government could give. This policy on the part of the public creditors was continued for more than a century, until the Genoese system of finance became the most complicated, and in many other respects the most extraordinary, of which we have any account. These public creditors became a body of great power and influence, governed by its own laws, enjoying its own magistrates, privileges and rights, wholly independent of the state — in fact, a financial *imperium in imperio.* These privileges were not usurped, but were the result of well-considered concessions, which could not be interfered with by the government, without the violation of many solemn stipulations and oaths of office; and, in fact, they were respected for ages, amidst strifes of party, internal and bloody dissensions and civil wars, occasional foreign domination and mutations of government, which for violence and rapidity have never been exceeded. In the midst of all this tumult and rage of individual contest and civil war, we cannot adopt modern phraseology and say that the public credits of Genoa stood unshaken and unimpaired; but we can say that the public creditors of Genoa held their position and their privileges untouched and perfect. They had no occasion to ask or look to the government, in these troublous times, for the payment of interest. They had provided against that necessity when they lent their money. Every loan was secured by the special assignment, on the part of the government, of taxes, customs, or other revenue, sufficient to pay the interest. This transfer was generally absolute, and was accepted in full of the interest; so that the creditors did not always receive a regular rate of interest, but a dividend according to the product of the security or fund assigned.

A complete survey and reconstruction of the Genoese system of finance took place in 1302. Various departments of inquiry in connection with it were in succession submitted to the consideration of different committees, or commissions, by the Council of the Ancients; reports were made, a long deliberation followed, and finally a law or decree of 271 articles was adopted. We mention this only as evidence of the attention bestowed upon the subject, for we can notice very few of the details of this elaborate system.[1] The public creditors were chiefly known by

---

[1] The organization of the public creditors, if they can strictly be called such who were for the most part purchasers of the public income, consisted in part of the following officers: —

1. Four VISITORS, two nobles and two of the people, over thirty years of age, and holding estates of not less than 300 lires, and not in debt to the state. They remained in office six months, having, before assuming the office, sworn faithfully to fulfil its duties. They had the aid of four notaries, or clerks. It was their duty to scrutinize all accounts of other officers, to require them to account, to receive their oaths of office, to make at the end of the year a report, with a summary of the year's payments and balances. All their documents were to be accompanied by their seal (the face of St. Michael). Every other public officer was prohibited from hindering or interfering with the full exercise of their functions.

2. Two persons, called CONSOLS, had charge of the office of transfer, who had various duties, besides those of seeing to the proper transfer of shares. To these were added, afterwards, two others in the same office, who were called COMFORTERS (Confortators), to whom special duties were assigned. In 1321, four others were assigned to this office, called COUNCILLORS; the whole eight constituting the Council of Transfer.

3. KEY-KEEPERS (Clavigeri) had charge of the treasury, or money on hand, and made all payments in money. Their whole proceedings were subject to a vigorous supervision.

4. The JUDGE (Del Giudice del Capitolo), who had jurisdiction of all questions arising under the collection of the revenue by the public creditors. His acts and decrees were of public validity, and all other courts were obliged to acknowledge their force.

the appellation of COMPERE, or purchasers, for they had in fact purchased certain revenues of the government. The loans were divided into shares of one hundred *lires* each,[1] a few only not being subject to that subdivision, being probably transferable, as at Venice, in sums at the pleasure of the holders.

---

5. The VICARIO was a judge of still higher authority, having criminal as well as civil jurisdiction, in matters of revenue, taxes, fines, &c.

6. Another Judge, holding a special office (Giudice de Calleghe), was required to be selected from twenty of the largest foreign creditors, at a special meeting held for that purpose. When sitting to decide questions to be submitted to him, he was to call to his assistance other creditors, who could then vote with him. No one could be offered as security for a debt, or for the good conduct of officers, who was not first approved by this Judge. The nobles were not received as security.

7. FARMERS of the revenue (Appaltatori). An extensive system of subletting the collection of the taxes, revenues, customs, &c., was adopted. Much of the business of the judges consisted in deciding questions in reference to these farmers, and in enforcing their contracts. The rules under which they acted, and which they were sworn to keep, were very stringent. They were required to make a payment in hand at the time of their contract, and to give security within the first quarter for the full payment, either by an order upon a banker, or by deposit of money or precious stones; and having undertaken a contract, they were not to leave the hall until they had completed the preliminaries. They could not sublet their contracts without due permission. Their payments were to be made in money, or by checks upon the banker who had previously agreed to pay their orders. No debtor in default, no member of the Council of the Ancients, and no Abbate of the people, could become a Farmer of the revenue. Every Farmer in arrear paid five per cent. per month, if in arrear; and if it passed a year, that rate was doubled.

8. PROTECTORS, whose duty it was to watch that all the laws, regulations and contracts respecting the public debt and revenue were duly observed and enforced. It is a prominent feature in all these offices, that the supervision is very much subdivided, and very much separated from the execution of the services, the faithful performance of which they were intended to secure. No doubt the need of so many officers was increased by the fact that many large cities and territories were among the securities which the republic had assigned to the creditors.

[1] The lire of Italy had a similar origin with the French livre, the English pound — that is, a weight. The term is still used in Milan and Genoa. Coins of that name are now of the value of about fourteen cents; but what their value was in the 13th century, is a subject of research.

We might greatly prolong the sketch given in the note, of the offices pertaining to the public finances of Genoa; but it would still fail of placing the whole system before the reader. In addition to the many oaths and securities required of the officers we have named, and their subordinates, the chief officers and councillors of the republic were required to take an oath to observe all laws and contracts touching the rights of the public creditors, and that they would in no manner, directly nor indirectly, interfere with the revenues or income pledged for their payment. No doubt this vast array of officers connected with the public debt, and with salaries depending on the continuance of the system, greatly assisted in giving it strength to resist the shock of warring factions, and the perils of revolution. The parties connected with this system were strong enough to be feared and courted by all sides, and they secured immunity in all circumstances by keeping somewhat aloof from public affairs. The public creditors, or the compere, were, however, very prompt, upon occasions of great public emergency, to come to the aid of the government with large sums of money, and other useful assistance.

The reader will be further impressed with the complication and minuteness of regulation applied in Genoa to this subject, when he learns that the number and kind of books to be kept in these offices were all prescribed, and required to be renewed every year. The books of every year, as soon as closed, passed into another office, out of the hands that kept them. Yet, in the most turbulent population of the Middle Ages, these minute regulations were observed for centuries, and as long as the republic maintained its importance.

There were private bankers of two kinds in Genoa previous to, and after the establishment of the Bank of St. George. One kind confined their business mainly to transactions connected with the public revenue and finance, and to dealing with public officers. The other carried on such general banking business as receiving money on deposit, changing money, lending money, &c. These were placed, by law, under very strict regulations. They were required to take an oath to fulfil faithfully the duties of their profession. They were sworn not to abrade or clip coins, directly nor indirectly, nor to keep young persons in, nor allow hangers-on about, the bank; to write down immediately all money deposited with them, by whom, and to whom and at what time payable; to refuse to exchange false money, and to inform upon all persons offering suspected coins. They were to make known whether the bank was the property of one or many, and if there were partners, to make their names known at the office of a Tribunal of Commerce, before which they were to enter into obligations to comply with the law of banking, and pay all penalties. The name of each partner was to be posted up in the bank, and the amount of his interest.

Early in the 15th century, murmurs arose among the people of Genoa in regard to the financial position of the country. After several years' complaint, a commission, or committee of eight were appointed, in the year 1407, to report a plan of reform. The commissioners were men who enjoyed the confidence of all parties. They found various bodies of compere, or public creditors, each holding their own securities, and making altogether an injurious complication. The commissioners, after consulting with the classes concerned, determined upon paying off the whole public debt, and a resumption of all grants and securities. To effect this, they proposed to issue shares of 100 lires each, in sufficient amount to pay off the whole, so far as the holders could receive payment. To the shares thus issued were added some banking privileges, and they were to be secured by the reassignment, on the part of the republic, of such part of the customs, revenues, taxes and property before held by the compere, as were deemed adequate, to be enjoyed by the House of St. George upon the same terms and privileges, and with the same rights and remedies, which accompanied them in the hands of the compere. The number of shares to be issued were 4767.

The Bank of St. George was established in pursuance of the recommendations of the commission, a further loan was effected by the republic, and the measure appeared to find full favor with the people. The government had, by this measure, succeeded in reducing the interest payable upon the public debt to seven per cent.; any overplus collected from the revenues assigned, were payable to a sinking fund (Code di Redenzione). The creditors had previously realized nearly eight per cent.

The Bank of St. George was as watchful of its special interests as its predecessors, the compere: besides the general provisions by which it enjoyed largely their ancient powers and privileges, it obtained not less than nine further concessions during the first century of its history, and among these a most distinct and full exemption of bank shares and deposits, from all attachment and confiscation for any public or private claims, upon any pretence whatever. The organization or government of the bank became complicated to a degree even far exceeding that of the compere.[1]

---

[1] The government of the Bank consisted —

1. Of a General Council of 480 members, over eighteen years of age, and holders of not less than 10 shares.

2. Eight Protectors, six of whom over thirty, and two over twenty-five years of age, holders of 100 shares.

3. Thirty-two Electors, who were to select the Protectors.

4. Four Proveditors, who had served as Protectors.

5. Eight Procurators, six of whom over thirty, and two over twenty-five years of age, and holders of 40 shares.

6. The Council of 1444, so called from the year in which it was instituted. It consisted of eight members, qualified as the Procurators.

7. Eight Councillors of the Salt Impost, with the same qualifications.

8. Four Sindicators, holders of 40 shares; two of these to be twenty-five, the others to be over twenty-two years of age.

9. The Treasurer-general. He was elected by the Protectors and the Council of 1444. He gave security to the amount of 90,000 lires, besides a deposit of 160. His salary, at first 1660 lires, was finally advanced to 3256, an increased deposit being required. He held his office five years, subject to annual confirmation. He was to be over thirty years of age, and not allowed to be engaged in any other business, public or private. He was to have no interest in any bank, or any concern of bankers, or other persons dealing in money. He could not be a stockholder in St. George, nor have an account current with any officer of the same. He was required to be in his office with his weigher every morning and afternoon, to receive and pay. He could only receive and pay the coins specified as taken by the bank, namely, from the mints of Genoa, Spain, Venice, Florence, and Naples, of the weight and at the price fixed by the Protectors: other money was taken by the government tariff. Biglietti, for dividends, were payable in scudi, at 4.10 lires. Cartulario, or bills for deposit, were payable in the

The rage for system and regulation was carried so far, that when, upon an extraordinary public emergency, the bank made a great effort to assist the republic with money, it resolved to pass three annual payments of interest: very little was left for the future in the arrangement of the business. The three years' interest were each postponed three years, the first year omitted being payable on the fourth year, the second on the fifth, and the third on the sixth. A new account for these deferred dividends was opened with the shareholders, and they were duly credited with each dividend payable at the time fixed. These past dividends soon became as saleable as the shares of the bank, the interest being deducted according to the time they had to run to maturity. In this way the bank received them for all taxes and dues, and the shareholders suffered only the loss of the interest on their dividends, but enjoyed the advantage of a credit for three years' income, which, if need required, they could turn into money at only the discount of current interest Upon the occasion of this measure, the ecclesiastical shareholders alone hesitated to give their consent: they could not, being, we

---

same coin which had been received. All false money was to be cut. The treasury was never to be without the sum of 24,000 lires. The Treasurer kept one of the three keys of the treasury, the Prior another, and the Sindaco of the Compere the third.

All these officials were elected in modes specially set forth, each class by some particular combination of the others held for that purpose. The duties of each class were designated, and special oaths and securities were exacted. Besides the above, were a host of subaltern officers, of greater or less importance, such as Revisors, Fiscal Advocates, Judges, Chancellors, Consultors, &c., to all of whom special duties were assigned.

Oaths, numerous and solemn, were a prominent feature in the government of the bank. They were made upon "the Holy Evangelists (Sacrosanti Evangelj)," and after minutely enumerating the obligations undertaken, ended with, "So help me God, and these Holy Gospels (Cosi m'ajuti e questi santi Evangelj)." There were not only general oaths of office, but special oaths for special duties, as they occurred. Some of these oaths bound the officers to the strictest silence, in reference to the affairs of the bank; and in some cases they were sworn not to make remarks, nor utter doubts, nor in any other way to convey anything, from which conclusions could be drawn respecting the business of the bank.

may suppose, for the most part in the position of trustees, give their assent without wounding their consciences;[1] and application was made by the bank to Pope Calistus III., who kindly authorized the measure, accorded the delay asked for by the bank, and saved the consciences of the hesitating.

This system of deferring dividends for three years, but giving credit for them in advance, was repeated afterwards; and again, for the sake of the ecclesiastics, the aid of the Pope was invoked with success, as appears by a Bull of Sixtus IV., in 1479. Owing to special facilities offered by the bank, these deferred dividends standing on the books to the credit of shareholders became the subject of great traffic. They were much used as a means of purchase and payment, under the name of *Paghe Scritti*, or *Lire di Paghe*, for which there was always a current price, which, in fact, constituted a separate money of account in Genoa. They were received in the bank, upon terms declared in advance every year, as a collateral for money advanced, generally at the rate of seventy-five per cent. of their nominal rate.

In the year 1539 a severe famine occurred, which compelled the government to avail itself largely of the aid of the House of St. George, as it became necessary to commence and prosecute several public works, for the purpose of employing, and in that way feeding, the poor. The advances made by the bank resulted in a new contract[2] with the republic, by which the most of the taxes and customs pledged to the bank were conveyed to it in full property. The arrangement was satisfactory to both parties, and was specially helpful to the bank, by giving increased confidence in its shares, and wider credit to the institution. The ancient privileges were not only retained, but enlarged. No new taxes could be imposed, affecting those assigned to the bank, without its consent. The Doge, the Governors, and their successors, were required every year, at the instance of the officers of the bank, to swear upon the Holy Evangelists to observe all

1 "Erano participi nelle compere molti Ecclesiastici e Corporazione religiose, ne potevansi prendere deliberazione in proposito senza timore di gravare le coscienze." — *Carlo Cuneo*, p. 119.

2 Magno Contratto di Consolidazion.

the covenants and stipulations contained in the new contract, the bank paying into the public treasury, every year, 50,000 lires.

Whatever may have been the precise functions of the House of St. George as a bank, previous to the year 1673, a great change was made at that time. Its shares had, before then, been largely and freely employed in purchases and payments. It had received deposits, and issued bills for them in sums to suit the depositor; and these bills had circulated with great acceptance as a substitute for money. The bank had not, however, become a great commercial agent. In the year 1673, after a period of tranquillity and commercial activity, the city was found to be overflowing with the diverse coinage of Europe, Asia and Africa; the inconvenience became so pressing, as to require a remedy. The government of the bank therefore applied to the republic for an enlargement of its powers and privileges. The application was successful; and, after the example of Venice and Amsterdam, bills of exchange of any amount, payable in Genoa, were made payable at the bank, with all other debts over 100 lires. This concession to the bank was fortified and enforced by heavy penalties. The circulation of the shares, and of the bills of the bank was, by this new regulation, freed from many formalities and delays previously encountered. The presence of a notary was no longer necessary at a transfer of shares or deposits, and the bills were circulated simply by endorsement.

The transfers of shares and deposits soon fell into the simple and easy process observed at Venice. The bills, however, were a feature of banking peculiar to the House of St. George. They were not issued in small amounts, nor in special denominations, but in the handwriting of the officers of the bank, and in sums requested by the depositors, or persons applying. The business of the bank enlarged so rapidly under this policy, that, as some writers express it, four banks of the same kind had to be established to meet the demands of trade. This was merely a division of the customers of the bank, by the alphabet, into four portions, each of which was provided with a separate organization of officers, clerks, books, &c.; so that each of these departments was independent of the other, though all were integral parts of the same institution. The bank soon became widely and favorably known; its possession of immense revenues caused it to be regarded as one of the richest institutions in the world. This, no doubt, increased for a time its commercial power and usefulness.[1]

Some of the modes of transacting business in the bank strongly illustrate the financial caution and skill of the Genoese people. Each of the four departments of the bank in which deposits were received, was attended by two notaries, or clerks, one of whom credited the depositor, and the other charged the treasurer, or cashier, with the sum received; the treasurer entered the amount in the depositor's bank-book, or manual. Here were three checks upon the amount of each deposit. It was not in the power of the two receiving clerks, or notaries, to charge the treasurer with more money than was received, nor was it in their power to give the depositor credit for more or less than was received. There were separate books for the entry of receipts of gold, and of silver. There were three separate treasuries: one for deposits of coin, which were to be returned, on demand, in the very kind deposited; one for a general depository of gold and silver coins at rates fixed by the bank; and another for current coins, at the rates named in the annual table of rates published by the government.

The shares into which the public debt, as held by the bank, was divided, were called "luoghi" (places), being for 100 lires each. They were transferable verbally, in the presence of a notary of the bank, by writing, by will, or by mortgage. These shares circulated freely and extensively in commerce, both in purchase and in payment. They attained a value far above par,

---

[1] The power of the bank no doubt created apprehensions, which sometimes found expression, in despite of its repressive influence. Foglietta, an historian of Genoa, says that this bank "became a body of the richest citizens — a republic more potent and terrible than its mother. It began to be feared that the bank would swallow the republic; that is, that the republic would reappear as a bank, after having been swallowed as a republic." — *Economisti Italiani, Parte Moderna*, vol. viii., p. 360.

and held it for a period of more than two centuries. In an elaborate table,[1] taken from the books of the bank, by Carlo Cuneo, the rate of the dividends is given from the year 1409 to 1800, and the price of the shares, from the year 1559 down to the same year. The shares were at 48, in 1559; in 1582, at 112; in 1606, at 219; in 1621, at 278. This advance was attended with many and wide fluctuations: the rate continued to vary between 140 and 200 down to 1739, after which the quotations are in scudi of 4 lires 4. In 1740, the quotation is 30 scudi, which is still over 25 per cent. above par: the rate fluctuates, down to 1797, between 20 and 34 scudi; in 1798, it is at 8, and in 1800, at 4. The same table furnishes the price of the deferred dividends (valute delle paghe) from 1559 to 1764. They are singularly free from fluctuation. Being much employed as a currency, this steadiness of value must have been a great recommendation.

The money of Genoa, during the period in which the bank flourished, although understood practically by those who were immediately conversant with it, was a mystery which writers of history did not penetrate. The only reliable account of it now is in the works upon exchange, book-keeping, upon the value of coins, such as merchants' guide-books, bankers' assistants — works not rare then, in various forms, from heavy folios and quartos to light books for the hand. When the history of money is properly written, these books must furnish the materials. The occasional references to this subject by historians are, for the most part, wholly unsafe. Such a system of moneys of account, coins and currencies as existed at Genoa could never be understood without special initiation even by contemporaries, much less by those who look back at it from the distance of half a century. It would require far more space than we can give to attempt an exposition of the subject, and far more figures than the reader would care to look at. Such an examination would

---

[1] This table may be found at pages 307 to 311 of "*Debito Pubblico di Genova.*" The abstract was made, the author modestly intimates, "non senza fatica."

not, however, be without its profit to the real student of the theory and usages of the money system.

The currencies of Genoa were of several kinds: —

1. The bank shares, consisting each of 100 lires of the public debt, as held by the bank. It was, in fact, by the constitution of the bank, rendered a bank stock. This circulated with almost as much facility as a bank deposit. It became the foundation of a separate money of account, in which the value of the bank shares were ever after expressed. This money of account became fixed at the point when the shares had risen to a rate about twenty-five per cent. above par. Bank money (valute banco) was then always rated at about twenty-five per cent. above the common currency. The bank shares went up, subsequently, to nearly three hundred per cent. above nominal par, and were quoted accordingly; but the money of account called bank money never varied. It became a reliable register of the values to which, by the custom of merchants, it was applied. It was as readily used to express the value of coins, and other currencies, as it was to state the value of the bank shares. The bank also issued bills in the denominations of this money of account, which served as a currency of the same nature as the shares, but current out of the bank by means of these bills. It is probable they were issued upon the hypothecation of shares, which were redeemable upon the return of the bills. These were used to some extent in the early history of the House of St. George, but were less used when the business of the bank was enlarged; and deposits, with bills issued for them, came into use as a currency.

2. The bank deposits being transferable with facility, were employed largely as a currency in the chief transactions of business. The bank bills issued for deposits were also used extensively as a currency, but to what extent, as compared with the deposits, we are not informed. These deposits and bills represented coins of full weight and value, and were payable on demand in such coins. The coins themselves were not a currency, but an article of merchandise. The madonines of Genoa were probably the only coins taken by their face, without weighing

and assaying; but they were subject to fluctuation in the market, and those who needed them were obliged to pay the current price. Coins of gold and silver, from the mints of Genoa, and coins of gold, from the mints of Spain, Venice, Florence, and Naples, were taken on deposit at a rate fixed by the protectors (officers) of the bank; and other coins at the rate fixed by the tariff of the government. All these were convertible into currency by being deposited at the rates fixed by the bank. A money of account was formed upon these deposits, in which their value or price was regularly expressed: it remained constant, whatever fluctuations occurred in coins or bullion. This money of account, called moneta di permessi, expressed in lires, with that prefix, denoted a value of the lire about fifteen per cent. above ordinary currency. The duties payable at the custom-house, and other public revenues of the bank, were all estimated in this money of account; and the books pertaining to them, and the money in the treasury of the bank, were kept in it.

3. Another currency of Genoa was the deferred dividends of the bank. A credit for these dividends was regularly entered to each shareholder for three years' dividends on each share. The par of these credits was 21 lires for each share. This was subject not only to the discount of interest, but to such further discount as the course of the market might impose. The market value, subject to variation of interest according to time of payment, in 1559, was 14 lires 4s. In the course of a century they rose to 17 lires. They stood subsequently, for a century, at 18 lires. Upon these, as we have already said, a money of account was formed which expressed, in lires di paghe, the varying value of these credits according to the time they were payable, and the state of the demand for them. They were receivable by the bank for all demands, at a rate fixed every year, with deduction of interest according to time. The people of Genoa well understood what was meant, when moneta di paghi was spoken of; and this currency was as acceptable as any other, because it was taken by the bank not only in payment, but as a security, advances at the rate of seventy-five per cent. being made upon it at all times. The bank could always regard it as a favorite cur-

rency, because it was a debt of the bank; and receiving it was extinguishing a debt in advance at a fair rate of discount. Lires di paghe were always above par in the common currency.

4. The common currency of Genoa, in which retail business and many other transactions were carried on, were the usual circulating coins of gold and silver, a large portion of which were much worn by use, or which had suffered from paring, plugging, sweating, and other modes of abstracting from the value of coins. This money had also its separate money of account, called fuori banco, or out-of-bank money. The coins to which it referred were in all states of deterioration, though taken for a time, even after they had lost a part of their weight, at their nominal value. The money of account which supervened upon the use of these abused coins, took a lower standard for the lire than the other currencies. It became, however, a real, though less permanent money of account. In it the prices of retail trade were expressed, and generally all the common transactions of life not connected with the larger movements of trade, or with the bank. It was the ordinary money of account: when the others were used, their specific name was frequently mentioned; and people were generally supposed to express amounts in fuori banco, unless there was something to show the contrary. It in no way appeared on the books of the bank, though no doubt the books of account of the distributing merchants, tradesmen, and shopkeepers, were wholly kept in it. In their books all other currencies were reduced to this money of account.

The advantage of the bank to the commercial community in which it was situated was very much the same which we have already specified in regard to the Banks of Amsterdam, Hamburg, and Venice. We need not repeat the benefits of avoiding hazards and troubles in making the large payments of commerce in coin, nor refer again to the rapid circulation attained by transferring the ownership of coins, instead of the coins themselves, in the payments of trade. We need not even advert at length to the lesson taught by this mode of payment, that it is not essential to a payment that coins or bullion should be seen, handled or touched, to make effective payments; and that, therefore, neither coins nor bullion are of the essence of a payment; and that, however necessary it is that payments should be complete, satisfactory and irreversible, yet these requisites are all fully attainable without actually employing the precious metals in any shape; and that, in fact, abundant employment can always be found for the precious metals, when every device to avoid their use in commerce is exhausted.

The Bank of Venice made one important step in advance of its contemporaries: it circulated the ownership of a claim upon the government, or of coins on deposit; the Bank of Genoa not only circulated both, but first resorted to the use of bank bills. This was not done, it is true, in the improved and convenient forms now in use; they were not issued in denominations of thousands, hundreds, fifties and fives, but merely in such sums as were required by those who took them. They were, besides, only negotiated or passed by endorsement; yet, with all this, it was a long step in advance, and furnished to the commercial community a most effective instrument of payment. We are well informed that the bills issued by the bank were much employed, but cannot now ascertain whether they were issued in small sums. We believe they were chiefly employed in large transactions. A deposit of gold or silver entitled the depositor to a bank-note, or notes, for the sum; the holders of shares in the bank were also entitled to bills, upon some terms not fully explained, but probably constituting a form of circulating the shares out of the bank, which were otherwise only transferable in the bank. Bills were issued upon the deferred dividends, reduced to their value. These several forms of bills performed large service as currency, in connection with the bank shares, and the deposits in the bank. All these were at a large premium over the remaining circulation of coins called fuori banco money.

If the payments of a great commercial city like Genoa had been made in coins, there could have been no escape from the use of mules and carriers, with an army of expert tellers. Various plans of avoiding the risk, trouble, delay and expense thus encountered, had at different periods been adopted: this of bank bills was first resorted to in this instance, and with such success, as to afford great satisfaction. It was found to be a rapid, safe and efficient means of payment. The principle upon which this proceeded was soon understood; it was not essentially different from that which governed other modes of payment. Amounts payable and receivable could only legally be discharged in coins, or other legal currency; but debtors are only anxious to be acquitted of their obligations in any manner that shall be effectual, satisfactory and creditable. They do not necessarily ask or exact payment in coins; they are content to receive what they find others are willing to take. In Genoa, the merchant who had money to receive was quite willing to take bank bills, because those to whom he was under engagements were quite as willing to receive them from him. When a bank bill of 10,000 lires had thus passed into his hands, and from his hands into those of another to whom he was in debt, it had made two payments of that sum, and discharged debts to the amount of 20,000 lires. This was not in virtue of any intrinsic value in the paper bill, but because it had been accepted in payment by one, and received from him in payment by the other. So, if the bill had been an undetected counterfeit, it might have passed through an hundred hands, each time making as perfect a payment, and effecting as complete a discharge of the parties, as by any other means.[1] The process is the same as if each creditor should say to his debtor, at the time of payment: "I will acquit you of the ten thousand you owe me, if you will furnish me the means of discharging that amount which I owe to others." It matters not, to the validity of the payment, whether that debtor delivers to that creditor a bag of coins containing the required quantity,

---

[1] We are very far from thinking that spurious money can make as safe, or as good a currency, as genuine. It is a fact, however, to which we need not shut our eyes, that there is always a considerable amount of counterfeit money in circulation, performing the office of good money. The best coins need to have credit accorded to them, or they cannot circulate as money; if that credit is, from ignorance or mistake, given to bad coins, they will fulfil the functions of money. Coins should be good, that they may deserve and continue to enjoy the credit which is essential to their continued use as coins.

a bank-note of the amount, or a paper giving him a right to a credit with those to whom he is bound to pay a like sum.

The circulation of bank bills was a method in detail, by which those who kept no direct account with each other could set-off their credits against their debts, or apply the one in discharge of the other. Each one who received a bank bill in payment, and had transferred it away in payment, had made an entry on each side of the general account of his debits and credits, and had to that extent balanced the account: every succeeding operation of the same kind was with the same effect, and thus the entries made progress as time elapsed, until the balance remained which would have resulted if the whole proceedings had been a mere act of book-keeping. What was thus done by one, was done by all, and the process of liquidation proceeded as men's liabilities matured. It cannot be questioned that bank-notes have some advantages over transfers of bank credits: they circulate everywhere, and at all times; in bank hours, and out of bank hours, day and night; in country and city, between those who have bank accounts, and those who have none; between the poor and rich, foreigners and citizens, without formality or loss of time, and without intervention of notary, or proof of identity; and of course no medium of exchange, so far as they are applicable, has ever been found more convenient and effectual. The Bank of Genoa, by thus fully exhibiting the advantages of bank-notes, may be considered as the link which connected the deposit banks with those of circulation. The range of usefulness, however, of bank-notes is far less than that of deposits: the convenience of the former, to a certain extent, is undoubted; but the larger payments will always be made by deposits.

Although the House of St. George was inferior, in importance and commercial utility, to the Bank of Venice, it was a vast concern, of great power and wealth, which enjoyed for a long period high confidence in Europe. Genoa was a free port, so called; that is, an entrepôt where goods could be landed, stored, assorted, and reshipped to any part of the world, without paying duties; but all goods passing into consumption in Genoa were subject to duties collected by the bank, which had also the revenue arising from several hundred storage-houses situate within the enclosure of the free port, and other similar perquisites.

The Bank of Venice, resting wholly upon the stability of the republic, and its own good management, had a career of commercial success and high credit of more than five hundred years; but perished utterly with the Venetian government, offering, however, not a penny as a prey to its destroyer. The Bank of Genoa having a vested interest in a large real estate, and in the revenues of the port, survived the shock and the ravages of the French invasion; but shorn of its importance, its credit, and of nearly all its wealth, which became the prey of a French army. If the administration of the House of St. George had been directed chiefly to commercial utility, under wise arrangements, its constitution would have been consistent with great efficiency. It might easily have been placed in the same rank with that of Venice. The exterior circulation of notes issued for deposits was an advantage not enjoyed at Venice. In the latter city, however, the process of adjustment was better understood, and therefore more directly practised. It was carried to the utmost point of commercial convenience, and the resort to payment in coins was only when special reasons made it necessary; as when coins were required for exportation, or in dealing with foreigners, or for the retail trade. In Genoa, the circulation of bank-notes was mainly a mere substitution of the notes for coins, by which, indeed, a greatly increased activity could be given to the circulation; but the coins were lying, in the mean time, unemployed. This bank-note circulation cost the interest of the coins on which it was based. In Venice, the government took the coins brought to the bank, and applied them to the public service, and to that extent lessened the necessity of taxation, and strengthened the state, which was the guarantee of the bank. Both these banks were highly prized in their respective cities, and of great reputation abroad; both maintained their standing and usefulness longer than any other banks have ever done; but in each respect, the Bank of Venice takes precedence.

In an article on banks, in the "Encyclopædia of Law" ("L'Encyclopedie du Droit"), M. Gautier, speaking of banks founded in imitation of that of Venice, remarks, "that in creating them they established for their use a fictitious money, or money of convention, of fixed value, and usually higher than that of the current money in which their payments and receipts were made, and their accounts kept, by means of an agio varying between one and the other."

In remarking upon this, the able author of the article on banks, in the "Dictionary of Political Economy," M. Coquelin asks: "And why this adoption of a fictitious money in the most part of the banks instituted at that period? Is it explained by the circumstance, that the deplorable abuse of debasing coins was then very frequent in most of the States of Europe; and that, however the Republics in which these banks were established had avoided these abuses, by the relative wisdom of their administration, they were yet not safe from the invasion of debased coins thrust upon them from abroad, thus deranging their commercial transactions? It was to give to these transactions a safer basis that the banks adopted an ideal money, which was secure from all alteration.

"When coins of gold or silver were paid into one of these banks, it reduced them of course, after an assay having for its object to show the quantity of fine metal which they contained, into the ideal money of which it had made choice, giving to the coins, however, for greater safety, a value somewhat less than they had in reality.

"This substitution of an ideal money for the current money is, perhaps, the greatest service which these ancient banks of deposit have rendered. By this means they have at least introduced security into their commercial relations, and endowed the cities in which they were situated with a sort of relative credit, very superior to that enjoyed by others. Add to this that, in permitting merchants to effect their payments and their receipts by the simple method of writings, they saved them in a certain degree from the care and expense which ordinarily attend the handling and the transportation of coins. With this exception, they have fulfilled no essential functions which belong to banks, as we regard them at the present day."[1]

These remarks, by writers of high intelligence and authority, furnish striking instances of the confusion which must prevail in the minds of those who treat of money, without duly attending to the distinction between money and money of account. M. Gautier, who was for a time President of the Bank of France, saw clearly that the business of the Bank of Venice was done by means of a money of account, which he calls a fictitious money, or money of convention. He inferred, erroneously, that it was established or agreed upon solely for the purposes of the bank. It was not established by any act or agreement of the state or people; it was not even contemplated, nor thought of; it was the growth of circumstances. In its nature it was not new; for all the coin and money in previous use, and all articles of commerce, had their prices expressed in one or more moneys of account then in use. It being the invariable habit of people familiar with prices, and the expression of values, to fix the denominations in which they are expressed independently of the coins, or other values, from which they take their origin, firmly and fully in their minds, the people of Venice, in a very few months or years, became perfectly familiar with the current value of the deposits of the Bank of Venice. They would soon cease to make any comparison between the denominations in which the value of these deposits were expressed and coins. They would have learned their value, independent of any such comparison. If it happened that nothing in the conduct of the government, or those controlling the bank, disturbed the estimate made of the value of these deposits, the money of account founded upon them would be fixed. While coins without were subject to deterioration in many ways, and to debasement on the part of governments, and therefore to fluctuation in price, the deposits would remain unchanged; and the money of account founded on them would become more firmly fixed in the minds of those who were constantly employing the funds of the bank in their current payments.

---

[1] Dictionnaire de Econ. Politique, Paris, 1852, Art. "Banque."

The explanation of M. Coquelin is still more unfortunate than the position of M. Gautier. It is really very careless, if not extravagant, to say that the chief service rendered by the earlier banks of Europe was the employment of this ideal money (monnaie ideale). It is certainly to the credit of Coquelin, that he perceived and appreciated the use of these moneys of account; but how could he fail to perceive their universal use, if he really understood their application in those banks! The reason he gives why the banks ever resorted to their use is nothing to the purpose.

The bad state of the coins, and the debasements of the coinage by public authority, were inducements to the establishment of the banks, but had nothing special to do with the ideal money, or moneys of account, which grew out of the usages of the banks, and the mental habits of a commercial people. The agency of these moneys of account in the commerce of that period must have struck the mind of Coquelin with great force, to have induced the remark we have cited: it only needed that he should open his eyes a little more, to see that the service rendered by moneys of account in that day have been far transcended by their agency, in later times, in all banks, and in all the transactions of the credit system, of which they are the chief instrument.

To exhibit still more evidently the difficulty of explaining the money of Genoa by those who do not observe the distinction between money and money of account, we subjoin the following long extract from the most elaborate work upon the finances and Bank of Genoa which has come to our hands. We quote from a chapter, the title of which is: "The different kinds of money used at the Bank of St. George."[1]

"In a city like Genoa, essentially addicted to commerce, the increase (l'aumento) to which the effective money was subject, in the progress of years, could not be overlooked in the payment of debts of long standing; and, in fact, we find that a law of the

[1] Memoire Sopra l'antico Debito Pubblico, Mutui, Compere e Banco di S. Giorgio in Genova. Dell Carlo Cuneo. Genova, 1842, 8vo., chap. xxvi., p. 127. The author was Inspector of the Royal Archives.

republic, bearing date 1637, recognizes this obligation in regard to ancient debts.[1] In the Bank of St. George, however, where they were always careful to observe equality and justice in the payment of their dividends, they always calculated the increase which, in the lapse of time, had taken place in the lire gianuina; and, therefore, they always reduced the lire gianuina to the value it had at the time the payment was to be made. In this way, it was found that the hundred lires di numerato, or gianuina, of which the bank share was originally composed, was valued in progress of time at lires 194.4 fuori banco money.[2] Such an increase, however, is not to be confounded with the value of the share in commerce, which, besides the above increase, was greater or less, according to the greater or less credit of the bank in public estimation, as happens now every day with the current price of the public funds.

The moneta di paghe was, in substance, the value of the paghe written in moneta di numerato, reduced as above into moneta fuori banco. It was of somewhat less value than moneta di nu-

---

[1] The increase here intended is not of the quantity of the money, but the price. It is notorious, however, that during the whole of the 15th, 16th and 17th centuries, the value of silver was declining. There was, strictly, no such increase as the words of the author import. He, no doubt, refers to the fact that the money of account had changed, as it did in England, and every European country. The lire of the money of account expressed a less value, in the progress of time, than it had done before. The lire of the money of account in 1550 expressed a very different value from that of 1650. A specific coin or weight of silver was nominally of greater value, because the word lire, in which values were stated, expressed a less value in 1650 than in 1550. So, in England, a shilling once denoted the equivalent of the $\frac{1}{20}$ of a pound of silver; now it only denotes $\frac{1}{66}$ of a pound of silver. The increase spoken of by the author was a depreciation of the money of account consequent upon the abuses of coinage by public authority, by wear of coins, and by frauds, as occurred in France and England.

[2] The author is more happy in stating what was done by the bank in the payment of dividends. The shares consisted originally of 100 lires, as they were coined in 1407. In declaring the dividends two centuries later, they reduced the value of that coin to its true rate or price at the time the dividend was declared. This was done by the money of account used in the bank, which had not followed the fluctuations of the money of account fuori banco.

merato reduced into moneta fuori banco, because, as we have shown, the written paghe did not become numerato until four years; therefore, the written moneta paghe was subject, in commerce, to a discount greater or less, according as the paghe were of the first, second or third year.[1]

"The moneta di banco and fuori banco did not then proceed from any special operation or purpose of the Bank of St. George,[2] but, as we believe, from a continual inspection of the different money-tariffs published by the Magistrates of Money. Their origin seems to have been in this way: —

"The republic, by the above cited law of the 19th of September, 1637, so much extolled by Carli in his great work upon money, legally established, perhaps before any other nation, that as gold and silver coins were subject to a progressive increase in their current value, it was necessary, not to offend justice, that ancient debts should be paid by reducing the value of the money or coins of the time in which the debt was incurred to that of the time in which the payment was made.[3] Hence, the money-

[1] This very obscure explanation could only be comprehended by those who already understood the subject. The fact was, that the constant use of these paghe, or deferred dividends, as a currency, established for them a specific unit, or lire of specific value, which became the basis of a money of account. In this money of account their value or price was always expressed, and they were reduced to other moneys of account, according to the use made of them. If used out of bank, they were turned into money fuori banco; if paid into the bank, on account of revenue, they were converted into moneta di numerato; if employed in the purchase or redemption of bank shares, they would be converted into moneta banco. The value of these paghe, whether of the first, second or third year, was always expressed in their own money of account.

[2] These moneys of account did not proceed from any special plan or intention of the bank; their origin was that slow and silent, but sure operation, by which moneys of account are always formed in a mercantile community, when a new unit of value is used, in which prices are expressed and payments are made. The lire, or scudo, as applied to the bank shares, to bank deposits or coins of full weight (moneta di numerato), to the paghe or deferred dividends, were such new units; and upon each a money of account was formed, in which the books of the bank were kept, each in their respective department.

[3] Here we have a public law of Genoa cited as recognising that gold and

tariffs were specially intended, in Genoa, to give notice every year, or every six months, of the value of the silver scudo at the time in which the publication was made. Prior to 1730 we have not succeeded in finding any money-tariff in which the distinction is made between moneta di banco and moneta fuori banco; but in the said statute we find a statement concerning the money of Genoa, which indicates the value of the scudo from year to year, down to 1681, when it was lires 7.12.

"It seems that, after this period, the Magistrates of Money believed it to be their duty not to permit any increase beyond that rate, since there are extant some decrees made by these magistrates, in which they threaten with the penalties of bankruptcy those who exchange money at a higher rate than that fixed in the tariff; and from 1682 to 1730, we have met with no tariff in which the value of the scudo is placed higher than lires 7.12.

"We cannot state with precision the reason why the Magistrates of Money believed it to be their duty to maintain, for so long a time, the value of the scudo at lires 7.12. We find, how-

silver coins were subject to a progressive increase of value — a statement which can only be true as the price of these metals was expressed in a changing money of account. Carli, the eminent writer on money quoted in this paragraph, supplies a remarkable explanation of this difficulty when treating of the money of Milan. He informs us that the apparent increase of the zecchin of Milan in five centuries, from 1261 to 1750, was as 1 to 14.10: that is, that coin during all that period, of the same weight and standard, was quoted, in 1261, as worth 1 lire; and as worth lires 14.10s. in 1750. He gives, no doubt, the correct explanation. Prices were expressed in lires and denari, or pennies, which was the common money of account. The payments of retail were made in copper and billon, or other base money, or at least to such an extent, that the value of the lire was estimated, by the mass of the people, through this base money. In the five centuries mentioned, the base money was degraded by the government very nearly in the proportion of the apparent increase of the zecchin. Carli says there were many opinions on the subject; but he sustains his own in a way to leave no doubt of his correctness. We believe this is the true explanation for Genoa. The ordinary money of account, in this long series of years, was changed by the degradation of the lower coins, which the people handled most. *Economisti Italiani, Carli*, vol. ii., p. 12. *Custodi's Collection, Modern Part*, vol. xiv.

ever, that these magistrates, in the tariff of the year 1741, perhaps for the first time, distinguished the moneta di banco from the moneta fuori banco, giving to the silver scudo the value of lires 7.12 in moneta di banco, and the value of lires 9.10 in moneta fuori banco.

"From this we believe it may be inferred that the Magistrates of Money fearing, perhaps, that the continued increase in the value of the silver scudo would prove injurious to the Bank of St. George, determined to put an end to that increase by means of their annual tariffs, and to keep it at the rate of lires 7.12. But as the force of circumstances proved stronger than the power of the magistrates, they were obliged to abandon this idea, and to fix the scudo in moneta di banco at lires 7.12, which was the value at which they received and paid it at the Bank of St. George, and in moneta fuori banco at lires 9.10, which was the value in commerce.

"The Bank of St. George, however, in 1751, looking more to its own convenience, and seeing that the difference between the moneta di banco and that of fuori banco had gone up already to a premium of twenty-five per cent., determined that from that year deposits of money should be made in the bank in moneta di banco, at a premium of twenty-five per cent., and that they should be repaid at the same premium.

"The moneta di permesso enjoyed only a premium of fifteen per cent. over moneta di banco, as we find from the tariff of 1755. We cannot give any account of the origin of this money, since precise dates are wanting for that purpose; but as we find in the published tariffs that there were current many scudi much worn, which were permitted to circulate at a value, in moneta fuori banco, less than lires 9.10, it is probable that from this permission the moneta di permesso had its origin.[1]

"We have not intended, by these observations, to furnish any definitive system of the moneys of Genoa, but present them as

[1] It is not material for our purpose to expose the very serious errors in this paragraph. They are so great, as to create the suspicion of a misprint. The next paragraph discloses that the author had no great confidence in this portion of his labors.

our opinions, in the hope of exciting ulterior researches upon this subject; and as a learned lover of the history of his country, George Batta Gandolfo, librarian to the University of Genoa, is collecting precious materials concerning the money of Genoa, with the view of preparing an extensive work, which cannot fail to be of the highest interest, we hope much time will not elapse before we shall have, upon this subject, statements and explanations sufficient to make the whole matter entirely plain."

NOTE TO CHAPTER XIV.

If the work of G. B. Gandolfo has ever seen the light, it has not been our fortune to meet with it. There are, however, materials in abundance within reach of any one desirous of thoroughly understanding the money system of Genoa. They will be found in the works cited ante, pages 186, 187, and in others of like character. From the contemporaneous works on commerce and money, to which the bankers and merchants of that time resorted for guidance, we can now obtain reliable information; and by the study of these merchant's guides, in the order of time, the history of Genoese money may be traced. Italy has furnished, besides, many great works on money, being famous for the worst coins, and the best writers on coinage: among these we refer to some of the more distinguished: Davanzati, Serra, Turbulo, Galliani, Corniani, Scaruffi, Carli, Vasco. A reference to others may be found in the note at page 108.

Although Carlo Cuneo, from whom we have made the long extract at the close of this chapter, has failed in adequate statement and appreciation of the moneys of Genoa, his work, as a whole, is invaluable, and furnishes details which can nowhere else be found, without researches which very few have it in their power to make. The Bank of St. George, doubtless, yet contains all the documents needful to afford materials for its history; but it seems they are guarded with a jealous care, which places them out of the reach of the ordinary inquirer. Cuneo furnishes a reference to his authorities, which shows that his researches were thorough and extensive. The Appendix gives fac-similes of three different forms of the manuscript bank bills issued by the Bank of Genoa.

The following is from a Commercial Dictionary published in Paris: —

"La Banque de Gênes date de 1407. C'était aussi une banque de dépôt, mais établie sur une plus grande échelle que celle de Venise, et qui a obtenu beaucoup plus de célébrité en Europe. Son fonds primitif fut composé de propriétés domaniales, appartenant à l'Etat et administrées par une corporation qui devint plus tard le conseil et le gouvernement de la banque. On peut la considérer comme un grand mont-de-piété commercial destiné à faire des avances aux citoyens, moyennant certaines conditions plus ou moins favorables, selon les circonstances. Elle était administrée avec une extrême sévérité et tout ce que nous savons de son organisation prouve qu'elle fut plutôt une institution financière liée aux intérêts du gouvernement, qu'une caisse ouverte aux besoins des particuliers. Elle reçut un terrible échec lois de l'invasion des Autrichiens vers le milieu du dernier siècle, et elle a cessé d'exister avec la république de Gênes." — "*Dictionnaire du Commerce, Gillaumin & Co.*, Paris, 1839, vol. i., p. 210, Art. "Banque."

This is calculated to mislead. The Bank of Genoa was only on a larger scale, because more connected by its constitution with political affairs. Holding among its guarantees such possessions as Corsica and the Isle of Cyprus, and having, by its large number of officers, a strong voice in the government of Genoa, it drew the attention of all concerned in the public affairs of that city. In commercial power and efficiency it was far inferior to the Bank of Venice. This extract is another illustration of the mistaken notions which prevail, even among well-informed persons, in relation to the Banks of Genoa and Venice.

CHAPTER XV.

THE BANK OF ENGLAND.

§ 1. *Opinions and projects on the subject of credit and currency previous to the charter of the Bank of England — Samuel Lambe's plan,* 1665 — *Evils of the coinage — Dr. Hugh Chamberlain's plan,* 1665 — *Large model of a Bank,* 1678 — *Bank of Credit,* 1682 — *Bank of Credit,* 1683 — *R. Murray's plan,* 1695 — *J. Asgill's plan,* 1696 — *Office of credit,* 1698.

THE insular position of Great Britain preserved the people, in some degree, from some of the mischiefs and vexations of a multitude of mints, and a multifarious coinage. The annals of English commerce show, however, that grievances arising from their coinage, even subsequent to the period of the heptarchy, were by no means insignificant. We might illustrate this by citations from writers of every age from William the Conqueror. Matthew Paris, in his "Chronicles," says that "in those days the money of England was so intolerably abused by detestable clippers and false coiners, that neither the English inhabitants, nor even foreigners, could look upon it without being deeply grieved (*illæso corde*); for it was clipped almost to the innermost ring, and the border of letters either wholly taken away, or very much diminished."[1] — *Ad annum,* 1248, 32 *Henry III.* "*Ipsis quoque diebus Moneta Anglicæ, &c.*" In the reign of Elizabeth, a reform of the coinage, arising from these and similar abuses, was undertaken; and in the "Summarie of Certain Reasons" for the measures then adopted, we are informed that, "for these base monies, there has been carried out of the realme the rich commodities of the same, as wolle, cloth, lead, tinne, leather, tallowe, yea, and all kinds of victual, as corne, salt,

[1] See Diseases of Coin, 1696.

beer, butter, cheese, and such like, so as counterfaieters have, for small summe of monies, carried out six times the value in commodities of the realme."

Among the earliest advocates of banks in England whose works are before us, is Samuel Lambe, a well-known London merchant, who lived in the days of Charles the First, but did not publish the pamphlet we are about to notice until the year 1655, in the time of Cromwell, to whom it is thus addressed: "Seasonable Observations humbly addressed to his Highness the Lord Protector."[1] One of his chief objects is to show the advantage the Dutch people had over England, by reason of their banks: "The benefits they have received by banks are these: By the help thereof they have raised themselves from poor distressed, to high and mighty States. They have increased the general stock of their own country so much, that they can, when they please, ingross the particular commodity of one country, and sell it again at their own price in the same, or another that wants it: they furnish many facilities, as well as profits, in time of war: they have thus grown so strong, that they make peace with other nations on their own terms, as, for instance, Denmark and France: they make war with the English at sea, to whom they there always yielded: they rule over many petty powers in the East Indies."

"The prejudice we receive by banks are these: It brings down the interest of money to three per cent., at which rate men in Holland borrow money, and lend it again in England at six or eight per cent.: they furnish money to make purchases in England at the cheapest seasons of the year, which are again sold ten per cent. cheaper than the regular English merchant can sell them in London." This, Lambe says, the English merchant cannot do for want of capital, and he cannot borrow the money at less than six per cent., besides "procuring and continuance," that is, a commission for obtaining the loan and renewal of it.

---

[1] Trade, Shipping Banks, by Samuel Lambe, 1657.

"The good we may do ourselves by banks, if settled in England, are many, for no nation ever yet made use of them but they flourished and thrived exceedingly: they will by well ordering of them, bring back the gold and silver drained out of this land by the Hollanders' banks: they will increase the stock (capital) of this land: they will increase the fisheries, navigation and shipping: they will increase the revenues and customs: they will wonderfully employ the poor, and increase manufactures and foreign trade: they will increase trade in our plantations, and cause ships to be built in New England as good, or better, than any built in Holland," &c., &c.

His definition of a bank is "A certain number of sufficient men of estates and credits joined together in a joint stock, being, as it were, the general cash-keepers, or treasurers, of that place where they are settled, letting out imaginary money" (credit expressed in money of account) "at interest, at two and a half or three per cent., and making payments thereof by passing each man's account from one to another, with much facility and ease, and saving much trouble in receiving and paying money." He then illustrates, by an example, how a credit thus given may be transferred very many times, and come at last unto the merchant who first issued it, all the debts for which it was transferred being fully paid.

The constitution of Mr. Lambe's proposed bank was peculiar, and illustrates the prevailing opinions on the power and uses of credit. "That the society of good men, or governors, that shall manage the banke be chosen by the several companies of merchants of London, viz.: East India, Turkey, Merchant Adventurers, East Countrey, Muscovia, Greenland, and Guynne Companies," each company choosing two or more, and filling their own vacancies. The persons thus chosen and met together "shall choose to themselves two or more of the ablest merchants that trade chiefly, or altogether, for Spain, and the like who trade for France, Italy and the West Indies, for each place two or more, as shall be thought fitting," &c. "Such a society, knowing most English merchants that trade to all parts, and thereby knowing whom to credit, and by their knowledge will well understand how to govern the banke, and by the help thereof to countermine the Dutch in their designs in any part of the world where they prejudice the English by their bankes." The bank was to be open to receive deposits, which were to be repayable on demand; "interest to be allowed on deposits to the aged and widows"—"imaginary money, or credit, to be let out upon ticket" (that is, subject to transfer) "at two and a half and three per cent." "All bills of exchange to be received and paid in banke. The chosen men may take a house near the Exchange, and set there certain hours every day: that the good men who manage the banke make up their accounts once in every year: that the profits of the banke go to the good men that manage the same, in lieu of their great care and pains," and defraying all charges: a reserve, however, of a portion of the profits to be made to increase the credit and power of the banke: "that the banke also furnish another banke with competent stock, to let out any summe of money under £5, or £10, at reasonable rates; for many poore people are now forced to give intolerable rates, as about 6*d*. per week for the use of 20 shillings."

It is a remarkable feature of this plan of a bank by an intelligent London merchant, that it proposes no capital, nor any fund paid in, by the good men who were to manage and to receive the profits. It does not clearly announce that the deposits were to be lent, as a source of profit; if that were intended, it was evidently not the main object. The chief business of the bank was to consist in the issue of credits, to be circulated or transferred on its books. The person at whose instance such credit was to be issued must, of course, give the bank some security or guarantee adequate to the amount of the credit asked for: this may have been a promissory note, bill of exchange of the applicant, or of some other person, or it may have been gold or silver bullion, or a bond or mortgage. The credit would not have been granted without some sufficient guarantee that it would be redeemed, and the interest paid. As no permanent capital was proposed, it was not intended that the credits issued should be permanent, but that all should be redeemable and extinguishable on the return of the security.

The plan differed, therefore, materially from any of the continental banks. Taking the Banks of Venice and Amsterdam as types of these, it differed from the first, which only circulated on its books the debt of the State; and from the second, which only circulated the ownership of an actual deposit of coin or bullion; whilst the proposed bank was intended only to circulate a credit issued for the occasion upon special security: it was intended merely to be a substitution of the better credit of the bank for the credit of the applicant. If the credit of the bank should not be more available than that of the individual, it would not be applied for, nor would it be received by those who could not use it in payment. This was, then, a bold conception of the power of credit, and contemplated a high state of confidence and unblemished commercial integrity. Mr. Lambe plainly aimed at a procedure like that now carried on by our system of bank deposits. When a note is discounted according to our modern system of banking, a credit is given for the proceeds on the books of the bank; and the credit thus given is transferable at the pleasure of the holder, until extinguished by payment of the security on which it is founded.

The state of the coin in the 17th century forced the whole subject of money and currency very specially upon public attention. A writer, 1696, commences a pamphlet on this topic in these words: "The inconvenience and mischiefs that the currency of clipt and counterfeit money necessarily occasions are so manifest to everybody, that it is as needless to point at any of them as it is impossible to enumerate all. It violates all contracts, and alters the measure of trade, breeding confusion in all commerce," &c.[1]

Some of the bitterest discontents of the English people with which their annals make us familiar, have arisen from the condition of their coinage. Prudential measures were devised by Edward the Sixth, but not fully executed; the reform was left to be more fully carried out by Elizabeth, who took all the credit of having accomplished what Edward could not, and Mary dared

[1] Currency of Clipt Money, 1696.

not do.[1] But crying as this evil of debased and deteriorated coins was in England, it fell far short of the corresponding mischief on the continent, and did not lead to the remedy adopted there, of establishing banks of deposit, in which the coins might be placed once for all out of the reach of the clipper and sweater, not subject to wear, and safe from the debasing schemes of men in power.[2] These banks were multiplied on the continent during the first half of the 17th century. There appears to have been no attempt of the kind made in England during that time. In the latter half of that century, the subject of banks occupied very much of the attention of the English public. A vast number of plans, and projects of banks, were brought before the public. Not one of these, so far as we know, or can learn from a large number of publications of that period now before us, on the subject of money and banks, proposed a bank for the deposit of coins or bullion. They all looked to banks as instruments of credit, the chief advantage of which would be the furnishing some substitute for money — some form of credit to circulate in the place of money. The success of the goldsmiths, and other private bankers of London, in issuing their notes payable to bearer on demand, had been recently remarked, and it had excited the imaginations of men of business as to the power and utility of credit. The goldsmiths not only issued such notes for circulation in place of money, but also bonds, or sealed bills, bearing interest, but payable at a fixed day: these were also employed as a currency. The public mind thus excited on the subject of credit, and teeming with hopes of some great delivery from the evils of the money system, began to bring forth plans of banks, and schemes of credit.

We shall notice a few from publications of that period, of which the author of a "Discourse on Money" says: "I see many printed proposals of banks of a lower rate; projects and funds of gain and security, &c., to adventurers, everywhere pub-

---

[1] Camden, in his life of Elizabeth, thus speaks of this achievement of the Queen: "Magnum sane, memorandum, quod neque Edwardus potuit neque Maria ausa." — Page 61.

[2] Essay on Money and Coins, London, 1757.

lished and pressed on the people." This he afterwards calls "fishing for gudgeons."[1]

"The office of credit, by the use of which none can possibly sustain loss, but every man may certainly receive great gain and wealth, with a plain demonstration how a man may trade for six times his stock, and never be trusted; and that, if generally received, there can afterwards no accident happen to cause a deadness or slowness of trade, except wars, nor need men make any more bad debts"—is the title of a pamphlet by Dr. Hugh Chamberlain, published in 1665. His project is: "Neither bank nor lumbard, because the foundation of credit in bank is money, and here it is goods and merchandise. And for goods received in a lumbard, they deliver out money, and here credit; and yet it is like both; for, after the same manner and limitations, in every respect, as goods are received, stored and preserved in a lumbard, shall they be in this office; and credit shall be delivered out and transferred exactly after the manner as it is in foreign banks." The meaning of this is, that parties making deposits of goods shall, for the value agreed, receive a credit for the amount on the books of the office, transferable in the same manner as at the Banks of Venice or Amsterdam. The object was to make goods a material for deposit, instead of money, as in the banks of the continent at that day, or the proceeds of notes discounted at the present day. The check, or order of transfer, was to be in this form:—

> Gentlemen:—Pray make A. B. creditor for £100, and me debtor for the like sum, for which this shall be your warrant.
>
> To the Society of the Office of Credits.

It was designed that the office should become a great depository of goods, to the mutual advantage of buyers and sellers. Heavy stocks of goods, instead of being in the warehouse of the purchaser, were to be placed in the depositories of the office, where the seller obtained a credit for them, whilst the purchaser could withdraw them as his sales progressed, and only make his

[1] London, 1696, page 141.

payments at the same rate. The whole scheme is developed with ingenuity and earnestness.

In 1678, appeared "Proposals to the King and Parliament of a Large Model of a Bank, Showing how a fund of a bank may be made without much change, or any hazard, that may give out bills of credit to a vast extent, that all Europe will accept of, rather than money, by M. Lewis." His preface says: "All men are satisfied a bank is very advantageous to a nation, &c., &c.; but the great question hath been, how to make a fund that shall be credited by all, without vast quantities of ready cash or bullion to lie dead, which we have not to spare for such a purpose."

The author of the "Large Model" proposes that the whole kingdom shall be divided into three or four hundred precincts, in each of which shall be an officer of the bank, with officers and assistants appointed or elected by the people of the precinct, which was to be responsible for the conduct of these officers, and for the safety of all money deposited with them. This was upon the principle of the English common law, that every hundred was liable to make good any robbery committed within it. It was supposed this would secure competent and faithful officers. These branches, or offices, were to draw upon each other, according to the demands of business, so as to make the domestic exchange as easy as possible, by receiving money at any office, and paying it out at any other office. Bills of credit were, upon demand, to be issued to any requesting them, upon deposit of the equivalent amount in money. These bills were transferable certificates of deposit. But bills of credit were to be issued upon deposit of any other articles of value. The author of this scheme asserts that "a bill of exchange, or a bill of credit, that is transferable upon a good man is as good as money, for money is nothing but a medium of commerce, or security for a while, that when we part with one thing we can spare, we may purchase another thing of the like value." He instances many cases of such bills passing as money in England. "Diverse citizens" bills at this day are accepted as current, though they have no other security but the honesty of the man, and the supposition of an estate; and yet many are glad to leave their money in such hands, without interest, for safety. I heard a person of quality say that he saw the same money transmitted nine times in one morning, by writing of the credit from one to another, and the money in specie was left untouched at last."

The details of this model of a bank are set forth most elaborately, and the whole plan consistently developed, with a great variety of ingenious and instructive illustrations. Among other facts referred to, is one in regard to the Bank of Venice, which we have not met elsewhere. It is well known that the bank money of Venice maintained a value far above specie; and this premium rose so high, as to call for public interposition, which fixed the premium at twenty per cent., and that this was afterwards avoided by a *sur agio*, or a premium on the twenty per cent. Mr. Lewis informs us that a sagacious merchant of Venice suggested a method, at last, by which the difficulty was overcome: Whenever the tendency of the bank money was too strongly upward, the bank tendered the specie itself in payment of credits; that is, the party who expected to receive bank money, or credits, in payment, was paid in specie by the bank; so that he who attended at bank to receive a payment, did not know but that he would receive payment in gold or silver. This method could be brought to bear very effectively upon those who were disposed to monopolize the deposits, or bank money. One chief cause of the premium upon bank credits was, that bills of exchange were payable in them; and men who had bills to pay were obliged to procure bank credits for that purpose. Speculators, however, would be repelled by the plan mentioned by Lewis.

A publication, dated in 1682, bears the title of "Corporation Credit, or a Bank of Credit, made current by common consent in London, more useful and safe than money." This was a proposal addressed to the authorities of that city, referred by them to a committee, upon report of which the plan was approved, and the bank authorized. The plan of working this bank did not differ very much from that of Lambe's, but it required a subscribed and paid-up fund as "a fund or foundation of honor," which might be paid in tin, lead, copper, steel, or iron, raw silk, wool, or cotton, or in brass or iron wyre, linnen cloth or calicoes, or other goods sufficient to raise the money subscribed. Sixteen reasons are given why such a bank would be a public benefit, chiefly referring to the promotion of trade and industry. Five reasons why private interests will be promoted, among which are: "The trouble of counting money may be much avoided; the usual loss by receiving counterfeit and clipt money will be saved; many fruitless journeys for money will be saved," &c.

"The credit here recommended answers all the ends and intents of money, for it will pass as far as it is known, and our money doth no more. So of the sealed bags of money in the East Indies, which pass as far as the East India prince hath credit. This credit is better than money, for it will pass from man to man without any damage to itself, or its possessor; but money occasions great loss of time, as well as trouble, is subject to clipping, counterfeiting and robbery, and is oftentimes the occasion of bloodshed and murder."

"But to further satisfy some men how trade can be driven, commodities bought, and debts paid, without money or specie, besides the indubitable certainty of its being practised in the several foreign banks, I shall form an example or two of the manner and conveniences of it. As, suppose A. oweth B. £100, B. the like to C., C. the like to D., D. the like to E., and E. to F., and F. to G., and G. to H., and H. to I., and I. to A., which if it were possible for them all to know, they might agree upon a meeting, and quit each other by rescounter" (set-off), "and then all are satisfied, without one farthing being paid in specie; where else, for want of this meeting (because each knows but his immediate debtor and creditor, and not the mediate), or for want of ready money, they are all puzzled with debts and credits. If all these debts are to be paid by the circulation of £100 in money, it will be defeated, if any one in the chain is tempted to employ the money otherwise, or if the money is lost or stolen on its passage; neither of which is so likely to happen if credit be employed, which would quickly and surely discharge every debt without risk or loss."

A pamphlet of 1683 thus defines a Bank of Credit: — "It is a fund of goods, or assurances of lands, &c., deposited for the raising of credit thereupon, under the greatest security of constitution and persons that can be devised; upon which fund the depositor is furnished with *bank bills of credit* for supply of his occasions, which will be as useful as money to him." The bank bills of credit were to be issued with every possible security against counterfeits, the precautions being set forth.

"Besides which, two trustees and the storekeeper of the bank out of which the bills shall be issued, do also testifie that the value of the said bills is in the bank: all which officers are upon their oaths, and give good security for the honest discharge of their respective employments, so that no one can hope to make tender of a false or counterfeit bill, or one unduly come to his hands, without being detected; in which respect these bills are better than gold or silver, besides they save charges in carrying, and time in telling and retelling money in payments, and it is easier and safer travelling with them; nor can any of these be fraudulently issued out of the office itself, for they are printed in the bank house, on paper made on purpose," &c.

In the same year, 1683, the Bank of Credit is described and explained in a pamphlet, the author of which regards the subject from the same point of view.

In 1695, appeared "A Proposal for a National Bank, consisting of land, or any other valuable securities or depositums, with a grand cash for the return of money," by Robert Murray. The author dwells at length on the great advantages of the Bank of Amsterdam, which he regards as "incomparably the best and greatest in the world, being built on these three pillars: First, an authentic registry of all receipts and payments above 300 guilders; secondly, the enjoining the payment in bank of all foreign bills of exchange; and thirdly, the city and government undertaking the security of all money paid in bank."

In urging his own plan, he thus speaks of the advantages of banks: — "The great convenience attending banks, and the difficulty of trade where banks are wanting, show their necessity and use in all trading countries. To avoid the trouble of telling, retelling, carrying and recarrying, and the danger and loss of counterfeit money, men are under a sort of necessity to trust their cash in the hands of private bankers and goldsmiths, where public banks are not established; and this they continue to do, notwithstanding the incredible losses often sustained by frequent failures and insolvency of many, to the ruin of those that trust them."

The author declares himself the advocate of public banks under the control of public authorities, and the guarantee of the state. "The bank intended by this proposal is to be under the authority, care, inspection and control of the public magistracy, as most consonant to reason, nature and political economy." The bank was to consist of all things capable of being a fund of credit, as land, ground-rents, &c., and be divided into 10,000 shares, of £100 each, or £1,000,000, payable in ten quarterly instalments; "which sum will be found a stock sufficient to circulate the said credit from time to time issued:" this money to be deposited in the treasury of the City of London, and branches to be established in some fifty of the chief towns of the United Kingdom.

The business proposed for this bank was to make advances upon bank, foreign, inland bills, exchequer tallies, upon goods, upon annuities, and public taxes, such as the poor rates, to honest persons capable of employing their time to good advantage, &c.

In the same year, 1696, was produced "Several assertions proved to create another species of money than gold and silver," by J. Asgill. The first assertion is, "that there is a necessity of creating another kind of money;" the third is, "that all proposals for making bills of credit current money directly, by act of Parliament, can be of no use;" the sixth is, "that securities on land are capable of all the quality of money, and therefore they are capable of being made money, for land is durable and incorruptible, the earth being the great store-house of the world, where all the magazines of life and defence are kept sweet and safe. Such securities are divisible into larger or lesser sums, and capable of having their value stamped on their face, and of being made transferable by delivery."

In 1698, was published "The Constitution of the Office of Land Credit," a project very elaborately developed, by Hugh Chamberling, the author of the pamphlet noticed ante, page 345. This scheme of a bank was brought out under the sanction of lofty names; among the honorary managers are four earls, and many other lords, barons, and gentlemen of repute. It is stated that the projector, Chamberling, had devoted thirty years of his life to this subject. Some of his positions are: "That lands and hands are the material and efficient causes of all true, genuine and natural riches: that credit, rightly founded on land, must evidently be more secure than any other sort of credit: that credit having all essentials of the usual money, and some other additional advantages, wants nothing but a coercion law, enforcing its currency, to enable it to assume the name of money." The form of the institution, its mode of government, the plan of settling the credit or security upon lands, are all minutely set forth.

These notices of projects and schemes of banking some century and a half old are given to the reader without comment, the object being merely to make known the current of opinion at that time. We might enlarge the list, for plans of banks continued to appear for many years after the Bank of England was chartered; but we have, perhaps, more than satisfied the curiosity of the reader. It is evident that great misconceptions prevailed as to the power and real nature of credit; this is manifest in all these plans. The subject was not as well understood as it was upon the continent. It is not for many years after the date of these publications, that we find in England any well-written account of the continental banks or credit system.

§ 2. *The Bank of England chartered in* 1694 — *William Patterson the projector — Founded on a loan to the government of* £1,200,000 *at eight per cent.— Opposition and objections — Commenced business* 1695 — *Powers indefinite — Bank-notes — Advances to government — Recoinage — Rate of discount — Business of the Bank — Use of deposits — Issue of bank bills — Employing its credit — Goldsmiths, or private bankers, robbed by Charles II. — Safety of deposits in Bank of England — Use of deposits by depositors and the Bank — Issue of bank bills payable on demand — Bills of exchange and promissory notes on time — Convertibility — Theory of bank-notes not substitutes for specie, but for commercial paper, and should fluctuate with this paper, and not with coin — Concentration of payments in London.*

The Bank of England owes its origin to one of the most fruitful schemers of the latter half of the 17th century — the same who was the projector of the Bank of Scotland, and the chief promoter of the disastrous enterprise undertaken by the Darien Company, of planting a colony on the Isthmus of Darien.[1]

The charter of this bank was obtained in 1694, in the sixth year of William and Mary. The scheme, which was due to the genius of William Patterson, had been on foot several years, and had been urged on the government with great perseverance. It had to encounter, like other schemes for banks, opposition from various quarters. The tories, who were in opposition to the government, opposed it as likely to be an aid to the administration; the goldsmiths, private bankers and usurers, opposed it as likely to lower the rate of interest, and diminish their profits. The cautious and conservative regarded it as a novelty, fraught with danger to the country; and they prophesied fearful results, if this bank were chartered. Patterson, who well knew the necessities of the government, then engaged in war, and frequently obliged to pay from ten to forty per cent. interest for short loans, in anticipation of the public revenues, had made it a prominent part of his plan to offer the public treasury £1,200,000, at eight per cent. interest.

---

[1] Five vessels, containing this Scotch colony, left the port of Leith in July, 1698; and of 1200 persons who embarked, 30 only remained alive to return the next year.

This was all that secured attention to his project. It was strenuously resisted, both in Privy Council and in Parliament; but finally triumphing over all opposition, the charter of the Bank of England was issued in 1694. Previous to this date, about £500,000 of the stock had been subscribed through the efforts of Michael Godfrey, one of the most active promoters of the enterprise in London. The remaining £700,000 was, after due notice of the opening of the books under the charter, subscribed in ten days.

The bank was not allowed to go into operation without the persevering and determined opposition of the various classes whose interests were opposed to it. There was no evil omen which was not seized upon, and no objection which the most fertile imagination could conjure up, which was not brought to bear against it. It was said that banks could only prosper in republics, and that, if attempted under a monarchy, the monarch would either absorb the bank, or the bank would absorb the monarchy. It was alleged that it would become a monopoly, and engross the whole money of the kingdom; that it would be subservient to the government, and be applied to the worst purposes of arbitrary power; that it would not assist, but weaken commerce, by withdrawing money from trade to apply to stock-jobbing; that it would produce a swarm of stock-jobbers and brokers, to prey upon their fellow-creatures, and corrupt the morals of the nation. It was said, in one of the pamphlets of the day: "That the Bank of England crept into the world, not being in any votes" (proposed laws) "by that name, but in an act granting to their Majesties several duties upon tunnage of ships, beer, ale, &c., for securing certain recompenses to such as should subscribe £1,200,000 on a fund of eight per cent.," &c.

The writer roundly asserts that there were many who, if they had known what kind of bank was wrapped up in that bill, would have been willing to lend the money gratis for several years, to obtain such privileges.

Another opponent admits there was some excuse for establishing the bank, but none for continuing it. "The nation had been for several years engaged in an expensive, hazardous and doubtful war; the government had drained all their projects to raise the necessary supplies; but the credit of the nation sunk, occasioned partly by the divisions of Parliament, the deficiency of the funds, and most unfortunately by the baseness of our coin, so that neither our money nor our credit would pass at market." In this necessity, the author admits the government had no choice but to accept the alternative of a bank. "And when such an enemy was at our doors, it was too favorable an opportunity for such a fort as this to be erected, which, though then designed for our defence, serves now (1707) to overawe us, and has turned its cannon against the state it was built to protect." After indulging in this strain at some length, he proceeds: "We are, God be thanked, greatly recovered from that dangerous crisis, our credit retrieved, our money recoined, great part of our debts paid, and almost all provided for." . . . "We crowd more to get our money into the funds, than heretofore to get it out; and we are freed from any necessity of supporting the wants of the government. It is, therefore, a matter of prudence whether the bank ought to be continued longer."[2] To this continuance the writer opposes all his powers of logic and abuse. His warnings and denunciations are alike terrible. Of the two evils, he thinks the bank far more dangerous than a standing army; that neither should be allowed in time of peace; and that both should be disbanded as soon as the work of war is done. He concludes by exhorting those who have the power, "if they would have their peace and liberties safe, by putting it out of the power of any to molest them, and by keeping their elections free, not to repair this fort (the Bank of England), that overawes them, and by their compassion to the poor tradesmen, and their own interest, *not to establish iniquity by law.*"[1]

This may serve as a specimen of the rhetoric employed against the Bank of England in the first years of its existence. The opposition which began with its birth has followed it down to the present hour. Every recurrence of a renewal of its charter

[1] A Short View of the Dangers and Mischiefs of the Bank of England. London, 1707.

[2] He gives the bank no credit for all this.

brings forth a host of objectors. It is now, however, so thoroughly incorporated with the body politic and financial system of England, that its continuance is not only necessary, but indispensable. To touch it with unskilful hands is hazardous, to shake its credit is ruinous not only to public, but to private interests.

On the 1st of January, 1695, the bank went into operation. Its whole capital, when paid in, and as paid in, was to be lent to the government as a special loan, the interest whereof was secured upon certain specified taxes mentioned in the charter. In addition to the interest of £96,000, the further annual sum of £4000 per annum was allowed to the bank for the management of the loan. "The Governor and Company of the Bank of England had full authority granted them, in whatever concerned "borrowing or receiving moneys, and giving security for the same under their seal; in dealing in bills of exchange, buying or selling bullion, gold or silver; selling any goods, wares or merchandise deposited with them for money lent or advanced on them, and not redeemed at the time agreed, or within three months after; in selling such goods as may be the produce of lands purchased by the bank; in lending or advancing any of the moneys of the corporation; and in taking pawns, or other securities, for the same." From this, it will be apparent that the banking business of the corporation was not very particularly described or specified. The main fact was, that the subscribers to a public loan of £1,200,000 were incorporated as a bank, and left to shape their business, under these general powers, as their interests and the demands of their customers might dictate. Their first object, no doubt, was to invite deposits; and certainly the security of such a large amount of loan to the government was superior to any ever before offered to depositors in England.

The act of incorporation conferred no special power of issuing bank-notes, or other paper, to circulate as money; but this power seems to have been regarded as incident to the corporate powers conferred in the charter. One of the first notices published by the bank, dated 11th February, 1695, was to the effect that three cashiers named in the notice were the only persons authorized by the bank to give notes on behalf of the company either for payment of money or bills; that is, either of the three cashiers, and no other person, were authorized to sign and issue notes, for which the bank was to be accountable. We find very few particulars in regard to the earliest issues of the bank. No notes were at first issued under £20. When the "infant" bank, in 1696, encountered the difficulties of the national recoinage, it for a time suspended payments, and, as a measure of relief, issued bills under seal, bearing six per cent. interest, with which they redeemed the cashiers' notes, which were payable on demand without interest.

That the bank issued these sealed bills and the cashiers' notes freely, is evident from a statement furnished to the House of Commons, dated 10th November, 1696, by which it appeared that there was outstanding sealed bills, £893,800, cashiers' notes, £764,196. The cash then on hand, £35,664, was all they had to meet £1,657,996 of sealed bills and notes. The advances made by the bank had been chiefly to the government, only £231,000 appearing to have been lent to individuals. The government being the chief debtor, was bound to afford the necessary relief in the emergency. This was done by allowing the bank to increase its stock, in payment of which increase a portion of the outstanding liabilities of the bank were absorbed. So great was the financial derangement growing out of the recoinage then in progress, of the embarrassments of the government, and the over-issues of the bank, that the obligations of the public treasury were at a discount of forty or fifty per cent., and bank-notes at twelve to twenty per cent. It is evident that the notes of the bank had for a time been received with great favor, or so large an amount as £1,657,996 could not have been issued in less than two years.

The government had determined upon recoining in full weight a silver currency depreciated 25 per cent. by wear and clipping: the bank continued to issue its bills for this light coin, though obliged to wait the movement of the mint for the new coins.[1]

---

[1] Ante, pp. 80 to 85.

The old coins were, by proclamation, declared uncurrent, and the bank could not obtain new coins from the mint fast enough to meet the demands of a community greatly in need of currency. This contributed much to increase the issue of bank-notes.

The measure of the government brought an addition to the stock of about £1,000,000, and reduced the liabilities of the bank to the same amount. This, with an act of Parliament, containing many provisions favorable to the bank, raised the stock in a few months to 112 per cent., greatly enhanced the price of the government securities, and gave the bank-notes free currency. The bank recovered from its first suspension, by this aid of the government, in a very short time. It must be noted, however, that the aid rendered by the bank to the government was even more important and substantial than that rendered by the latter to the bank.

The charter was not only silent with reference to the issue of notes, but also in regard to the payment of specie. That very important matter was left to be regulated by the general laws of the country. The corporate body could issue notes, and having issued them, it was bound to pay them in lawful money, as other persons and bodies corporate would be bound. No general alarm seems to have been felt on the occasion of this first suspension, and the obligations of the bank seem to have been regarded as safe, though not convertible instantaneously into money.

We have already remarked that the bank was, under the general terms of its charter, left to shape its policy according to the course of business and the dictates of its own interests. To induce deposits, the bank early made a distinction in the rate of discount between its regular customers and all other applicants, of from two and a half to three per cent., the highest rate being six per cent. The first error of the bank, that of lending too freely to the government, had the result, in the end, of establishing its credit the more firmly, for it secured thereby effectually the continued and efficient support of the national treasury; and being thus strongly established, it very rapidly secured the confidence of men of business and wealth. Although specially authorized to receive merchandise and personal property in security for loans, very few of its operations took that direction; its business consisted mainly in dealing in bills of exchange, and other commercial paper, and in receiving deposits.

The bank having nothing in its vaults at the outset but certificates of public debt, to the extent to which the £1,200,000 had been paid up, had only three modes of carrying on banking business open to it.

1. To lend or employ the money deposited by its customers, to the amount it might be safe or expedient to lend or use money which was payable to depositors on demand.

2. To issue bank-notes for circulation as currency, or bonds bearing interest, to be taken by those who desired such security for investments; and to employ the bank-notes, and the money received for bonds, in the purchase of promissory notes and bills of exchange at such rates as would leave a profit to the bank.

3. To employ its credit, which soon attained a high grade, in discounting bills of exchange and promissory notes for its customers, giving them merely a credit in account on the books of the bank for the proceeds of the paper discounted, and allowing the parties obtaining such credits to transfer them, in sums to suit their convenience, to other persons.

The bank, notwithstanding the check it received in the second year of its existence, rose rapidly in importance and in business. It blended at once, in its operations, all the modes of business above specified: but as these modes of banking are essentially distinct operations, even when carried on by the same bank, we shall consider them separately; the more so, as the confusion of terms and ideas resulting from these blended processes of the bank has, from that time to the present, produced a degree of confusion in men's minds, upon the subject of banks of circulation, very unfavorable to clear perceptions on the subjects of money and banking.

The business of receiving, holding and paying out deposits is probably as old as the use of money. It has assumed many different forms in different ages, and among different people; but the business has existed at all times, and in all nations, where gold and silver money were employed. It was always, and is yet, unavoidable. A large portion of those who have occasion to receive money, could not and cannot be judges of the genuineness of coin or bullion; they could not weigh and test it with sufficient accuracy; this, of course, gave rise to a class of men skilled in the precious metals, and with them these metals were deposited for safe-keeping, and convenience of paying. In all ages, the safe-keeping of the precious metals was one of the most difficult exigencies to provide for, and one which created unceasing anxiety. We find mention of bankers in the history of every ancient civilized people, who exercised their functions very much as they do in China at this day. Our Saviour, in one of his parables, makes the lord of the unfaithful servant say: "Wherefore, then, gavest not thou thy money into the bank, that at my coming I might have required mine own with usury."[1] From this, it appears that the bankers of that day were in the habit of paying interest on deposits.

The bankers of England, previous to the charter of the Bank of England, and to a large extent for a long time afterward, were the goldsmiths. Their business made them adepts in bullion and money, and required safe depositories. Very large sums were entrusted to them by the nobility, gentry, and business men of England.[2] But as these private bankers had been, on two occasions, robbed by the monarchs of England, some distrust of their ability to protect money committed to them naturally found a place in the minds of depositors. The Bank of England took, from the beginning, the position of a great and powerful corporation. It commanded at once so high a degree of confidence, as to secure large deposits. One of its first by-

---

[1] Luke, xix. 23.

[2] In the reign of Charles the Second, when the money of the bankers, or goldsmiths, was seized in the exchequer, where it had been deposited for safety, the amount was £1,328,526 — a great sum for those days. Charles the First had seized £200,000, deposited in the mint, in his time. One of the bankers robbed by Charles the Second had £416,724 taken from him.

laws assisted in strengthening this confidence, by requiring that the cash of the corporation should "be carefully kept under three or more locks, the keys whereof shall be kept by such three or more of the Governor, Deputy Governor and Directors as the said Court of Directors shall from time to time empower to keep the same, each of said persons keeping one of said keys."

The keeping of money for a large number of persons, who only draw it as their wants and occasions require, leaves a considerable proportion in the hands of the banker, subject to his disposal, as not at all likely to be called for by the owners. This the banker may lend upon good securities, in the hope that it will not be required, or that, if the whole or a part should be demanded, he will be able, by means of the same securities, to raise the amount demanded. The private bankers of England, and indeed of all Europe, had realized large profits from this allowed trading in money not their own. It was, however, not a very unusual occurrence that, in times of alarm and commercial panic, a run on such bankers took place, and their discredit and ruin followed upon their inability to meet the demands of customers; for they found, by experience, that the season of alarm and distrust which produced the demand for deposits, was one in which they could not realize upon the securities taken for loans. The Bank of England could not, of course, be exempt from this difficulty. It must always have been, and must always be, a business of no little hazard, to lend the money of parties entitled to repayment on demand.

It is urged by some, that all business transactions in which money is involved should be for money in hand; but even if all sales of property were for cash, which never has been the case in any civilized country, and never can be, yet many transactions in credit would take place. All deposits with bankers are credits given to the bank; all loans of money by the bank are transactions of credit, as well as all loans from one individual to another. There never was a civilized country in which such transactions did not take place. Of course, periods of alarm, panic or commercial distrust must occur, from one cause or another; and at such times, neither banks nor individuals can immediately recall the money they have lent or deposited. The history of the Bank of England furnishes many such occasions; but as the bank enjoyed the full confidence and support of the government, it was ever able to bear the pressure of such occasions with less damage than any mere private bankers. No depositor in the Bank of England has, during its existence of one hundred and sixty years, ever lost his deposit. During that time, immense sums deposited with private bankers, and inferior establishments, have been totally lost. It cannot be doubted that the bank, despite the losses incident to lending money, to the temptation of employing too freely the money of its customers, and the sacrifices involved in replacing money upon occasions of panic, has realized large profits from this branch of its business, which has been increasing in magnitude and advantage from the institution of the bank until the present time.

We have thus presented deposits in the single view of their safety, and the advantage of the bank in lending such proportion of them as it may be expedient to employ in that way. And we have only referred to deposits of actual money — that is, of coin or bullion. Other values which are included in deposits, such as bank-notes and bank credits, will be considered hereafter. Our object has been to separate the various functions and processes of the business of the bank, and to give the reader a distinct view of each process, without which he cannot understand the whole when combined.

There is, however, an aspect of deposits of money, which may be deemed equally as important to the bank, and more so to the commercial public, than that which we have presented. The deposits would not reach nearly so large an amount, if they were expected to lie in the bank useless to the depositor. Money is deposited not only for safe-keeping, but for actual and rapid use. The bank allows the deposits to be transferred from one account to another, in as rapid succession as the convenience of the parties may dictate. The circulation of deposits may, by this means, be vastly beyond any possible actual movement of money by counting and delivery out of bank. Without any trammels of counting, weighing, scrutinizing and assaying, such as must take place with coins and bullion, these, when once deposited, may be transferred by check on the books of the bank a hundred times daily, if needful. This may give trouble to the bank, which must have clerks enough to make these transfers, and keep the accounts of all correctly. The operation of these transfers takes nothing from the bank; the money remains; the ownership only changes. The great facility, safety and rapidity of this mode of payment attracts large sums, because the depositors have, in much the largest number of cases, a far more efficient use of their money as it lies in bank, than they would have if it were in their own hands. This use of deposits so swells the amount deposited in bank, as to place a much larger sum at the disposal of the bank for its own profit. Thus the bank could lend a certain proportion of its deposits, and receive interest therefor, at the same time that the owners of the deposits were making the utmost use of their money which could be made under any circumstances.

This mode of payment offered to its customers by the Bank of England was the same which had been enjoyed, to some extent, on the books of the private bankers; but the superior credit of the bank, and the far larger number of its depositors, gave much greater effect to this rapid mode of payment than could take place between the same parties as depositors with different private bankers. This advantage gradually attracted to the bank a large portion of the money of the country, which became available for a mode of payment, the most effective of which it was susceptible. The money deposited was thus made to perform the same duty, in proportion to the amount, as that which was shut up in the Banks of Amsterdam and Hamburg, with this advantage to the depositor, that he could withdraw his deposit at pleasure. The bank deposits became the most popular and safe mode of effecting the larger payments of commerce, foreign and domestic, and they absorbed the amount needful for that purpose. It is obvious that, with the comparatively rapid circulation of deposits, a much less amount would be required for these payments, than if coins had to be employed for that purpose. The deposit system of payments was one not only of great efficiency, but of great economy; it saved probably three-fourths of the money which would be required to make the same amount of payments by the actual counting and delivery of coins; but, in fact, payments could be made ten times faster by deposits than by coins. The money thus economized was lent by the bank to its customers, who would be, in a large degree, the very same who made the deposits. The depositors had, then, not only more effective use of their money as a deposit, but their united deposits placed at the disposal of the bank a large sum to be lent to them for their accommodation.

Another mode of business open to the Bank of England was the issue of bank-notes, or other securities of a similar nature, for which they might find a demand. Bank-notes, properly speaking, were unknown in England at the origin of the bank. The notes of the goldsmiths were regarded in no other light than that of promissory notes of individuals. They never reached that full currency as money to which bank-notes have since attained. The notes of the Bank of England were for a long time, by writers and in public documents, called promissory notes payable on demand, to distinguish them from the usual business notes drawn upon time. As the Bank of England was the first to issue bank-notes, now technically so called, in that country, it may assist our perceptions of the true nature and functions of banks, if we regard them from the point of view taken by the bank, when it first issued a form of security which has since occupied so much of the time and attention of the commercial and political world, and about which opinions have been so divided.

The bank was authorized by its charter to deal in bills of exchange, and as bills were much used in England in the domestic, as well as in the foreign, trade, they were of course early offered to the bank. It would be apparent to the bank, that the amount of foreign and domestic bills was far greater than the money and bullion in the country. The bills of exchange, therefore, offered to the bank a vastly larger opening for business than any possible operations in money or bullion. It became an interesting point to decide in what way the bank could deal in bills of exchange, foreign and domestic, and it may be added promissory notes, with advantage to itself and the public. The subject, as thus presented to them, was much simpler than it is regarded now, when it involves so many complications.

Bills of exchange and promissory notes had then, as now, some time to run before maturity, say an average of three months. During that time, these securities were of no use to the holders, unless they could transfer them in payment of debts, or in the purchase of property. This advantage would be rare, for the amounts would be inconvenient, and the exact standing of the parties not always known. But as these securities, among men of business, make a very large item of their possessions, they would naturally be used in obtaining loans; and so far as the bank had money to lend, it would not only look with favor upon such securities, but would incline to carry its dealings in them far beyond the amount of any money it could command. The obvious suggestion would be, to give the holders of these securities of such inconvenient amounts, and limited credit, the notes, in small amounts or denominations, of the bank itself, payable at the same time. The bank would deem it quite safe to exchange its own promissory notes for approved notes or acceptances of individuals, both payable on the same day; so that, on these transactions, the amount payable by the bank each day would be the same which was payable to the bank. For this exchange of notes, or securities, the bank would of course exact a compensation in the shape of commission, discount or interest. The advantage to the customer of the bank would be obvious; he would receive, for instance, in place of a bill of exchange or promissory note for £180, nine notes of the bank for £20, each of which would be gladly received by all persons in the payment of debts or goods. The inducements to such a business would be quite sufficient to secure its continuance on both sides.

But the Bank of England, on the suggestion of certain bold and ingenious financiers of that day, decided to go a long step farther, and so to increase the inducements on its side as to insure a large business and great favor with the people. It was urged upon the bank, that it might not only issue its notes in small denominations, in exchange for individual commercial paper having some time to run, but that such notes might safely be made payable to the holders, or whoever might present them, on demand. It was alleged, in justification of this bold idea, that these small notes issued by the bank would pass into circulation like money, and thus be dispersed over the kingdom; that they would furnish an immense facility in business, and become almost indispensable in the transactions of domestic trade; that they could not, and would not, therefore, be returned suddenly and in large quantities upon the bank. It was further urged that it would be a very great convenience to the holders of these, if an occasional want of money or coins could be supplied at once by presentation of these notes at the bank; that it would be easy for the bank to supply these occasional wants, and that the doing so would give the notes a currency like money, and a favor with the public far beyond any previous anticipations.

Upon such considerations, the bank decided to issue notes payable to bearer on demand, in exchange for individual paper payable at a future day. The bank thus undertook to perform an impossibility, in the hope that it would not be called upon to redeem the promise, or make the attempt. What the bank could do was to give its own notes, of convenient denominations for circulation, in exchange for individual paper, and payable at the same time; and in doing this alone, the bank could have rendered a great service to the public with small risk. The bank had not the money, and could not, therefore, purchase the paper offered; the notes offered by the bank were not money, though a much better substitute for money than the notes of individuals, which could only circulate to a very limited extent as a medium of payment. The bank issued notes payable to bearer, without endorsement, and this certainly added to the facility and convenience of their passing rapidly from hand to hand as a currency. It departed from sound principles, when it made these notes payable on demand in gold or silver; for it must be contrary to sound principles, to undertake to do what cannot be done. The bank-notes were nothing more, and should not have been held up to the public as anything more, than the mere promissory notes of the bank, convenient in form for circulation among all those who chose to take them, not as money, but as promises to pay money. The promise should have been only such as the bank could perform. Strictly speaking, the bank could only pay in coin when it received in coin. It could exact payment in coin for the note received of every individual only when the note matured, and not before. The accommodation between the bank and its customers was mutual in this exchange of notes; the bank received a profit, and the customer received the bank-notes a better medium of payment, one which would be received out of the bank, as well as in it, in payment of debts, or in the making of purchases. But it should never have been imagined for a moment, that by this process between the bank and its customers they manufactured money. If the notes issued by the bank had been payable in specie only upon the day when the paper taken by the bank was payable, then the bank would receive every day from the public as much as the public could demand from the bank. The bank-notes would, in this case, have served every legitimate purpose which such an instrument could serve. If all the business-paper of England had been thus exchanged for notes of the Bank of England, then all this business-paper could have been paid off and discharged by these bank-notes. This surely was an advantage in itself, and an economy of money very desirable to be achieved. Nothing more than this should ever have been expected of bank-notes.

It is true that bank-notes might have been issned on the basis of specie alone; in that case, the specie should have been kept ready for their redemption, pound for pound. But when the notes of a bank are issued in exchange for the notes of individuals, they should in strictness be payable in gold or silver only when the notes of the individual are so payable. The bank would then either receive its own notes back, or something that would pay them when presented.

If we suppose the Bank of England to have received from its customers individual notes and acceptances to the amount of £5,000,000, at the rate of six per cent. discount, and having an average of two months to run, it would then have issued its own notes to the amount of £4,950,000. The bank would thus have furnished to the many debtors whose paper it held for £5,000,000, a perfectly good paper currency, in which payment of this sum could be made. And these debtors would only have to purchase from the public this £4,950,000 of bank-notes, and carry with them £50,000 in money, to pay off the whole indebtedness of £5,000,000, and be freed from their liabilities. Surely, bank-notes might be employed in this way, without calling them money; and every needful security might be required of a bank against the abuse of this power of issuing bank-notes, without attempting to make them money.

In the case supposed above, the bank, if its issues were payable on demand, would be under an obligation to pay £4,950,000 in coin, on presentation of its notes. But the holders of these notes had not given coin for them, and the notes for which they were given would not be due for an average of two months. The debtors of the bank needed but one per cent. of the amount in money, and the public needed only that the bank-notes would pay all their debts, and make all their purchases. There is no conceivable use of making bank-notes payable on demand, but as a check on over-issues and abuses. The experience of a century and a half in Europe proves that it is no adequate check. Other checks and securities, far more safe and reliable, have been applied, and not nearly so burdensome, to banks. The Bank of England, in the first instance, really offered the security of the public debt; and during its whole history it could always have given, and could now give, that security for its whole circulation, if it were only compelled to pay its notes in specie, *pari passu*, with the payment of the individual paper held by the bank. Every really useful function of a bank-note can be as fully performed by one payable in specie at two, three or four months, as if payable on demand. It is certainly, upon occasion, a convenience to be able to ask for and receive specie on demand; but it is a convenience the public can have no right to expect, as it involves an impossibility. It would be a great convenience for merchants, if they could open their port-folios at any time, take out notes and acceptances, and make demand for the amount in specie; but it is an advantage impossible to be accorded. It is an advantage, in the case of the bank, only maintained for the public at a cost ten times greater than it is worth. This advantage, which the Bank of England only offered, in the first instance, to attract business, and to give currency to their notes, has been paid for since, by the people of England, in a series of pressures, revulsions and currency fluctuations, which have inflicted injuries and losses upon the government and people of Great Britain, in comparison with which the present national debt may be insignificant. It may be said, however, that this system has advantages which go far to counterbalance these evils. But what should be thought of a system of currency which fluctuates between such a height of advantage on the one hand, and such a depth of evil on the other?

The suggestion was discussed very early in the history of the Bank of England, that there was a certain proportion which ought to be preserved between the liabilities on demand and the amount of coin which ought to be kept to meet them; and one-third was often named as a safe proportion. This has often been repeated and relied upon, down to the present time. As a principle, it never deserved a moment's consideration; it could never be anything but a conjecture, and all the history of banking proves it to be utterly fallacious in the hour of trial. The same principle should be applied to the engagements of banks which is applied to the engagements of merchants — what they engage to do, they should be held strictly to perform. If they undertake to pay all their notes on demand in specie, there should be no guessing and no conjecture in the matter, but full and complete preparation to meet the engagement. Dollar for dollar should be the rule, or means to obtain the dollars before they could be demanded.

The error committed by the Bank of England was not in agreeing to pay their notes in specie, but in issuing notes payable on demand; in discounting paper having two, three, four or more months to run, and giving their own notes payable instanter. No financial contrivance can make this possible, and no ingenuity ever gave a sound reason for it. We may imagine that all the commercial paper of Great Britain was discounted at the Bank of England, and the proceeds issued in the shape of bank-notes; we may imagine that these are received by the public as a convenience of the highest order, being the change given by the bank for the very inconvenient paper issued by individuals; but we cannot imagine that the bank could pay on demand, in gold or silver coin, a sum equal to the whole amount of the commercial paper issued by individuals. It would require ten times as much coin to support those bank-notes as it would to pay off the commercial paper in exchange for which they were issued. For a million in coin would, in the course of three months, pay off ten millions as it matured from day to day; but it would require ten millions in coin to discharge ten millions in bank-notes payable on demand.

We are far from contending that the Bank of England should have issued notes not payable at all in gold or silver. The bank should have promised only what it could with certainty perform; that is, to pay the bank-notes at the maturity of the notes for which they were given. There may have been then, and may be yet, serious objections in practice to any mode of issuing bank paper in the rather unusual form of post-notes, maturing on an average of about three months. That, however, is the true theory of bank-notes issued in exchange for the commercial paper of individuals; if a proper effort had been made, practice might long since have formed a sound and available system on this safe basis.

It would be very safe to aver that, upon the system of post-notes issued to meet the maturing of the notes discounted by the bank, the Bank of England would never have suspended payments of specie; and, what is of far greater consequence, the bank would not have been obliged to regulate its issues according to the fluctuating movements of specie; movements which might have their origin in India, or China, or America, and by which the whole interior or domestic business of the country would be ruinously affected, though without any necessary or legitimate connection.

It should be borne in mind, that the great business of domestic and foreign trade is not governed, though it may be affected, by the fluctuations in the supply of the precious metals. The wants of men at home and abroad must be supplied, whether the precious metals are plentiful or scarce. We have shown that the domestic, as well as the foreign, trade is mainly an exchange of commodities; and that the only use made of gold and silver is in the payment of balances, and in the small dealings of the retail trade. It is a false and unsafe principle to assume that promissory notes of banks or individuals must fluctuate in supply as the precious metals fluctuate in quantity. The business, that is, the exchange of its commodities, in no civilized country is accomplished by coin or bullion, and in the present state of productive industry it cannot be so done. The great transactions in commodities by which they are distributed in every country, and between different countries, and thus forwarded for consumption to the retail venders, are carried on, in the first instance, by bills of exchange and promissory notes, the amounts of which are stated in money of account, as were the prices for which the commodities were sold. This business proceeds ordinarily without any reference to the supply of the precious metals. The individual paper issued in these transactions being exchanged for bank-notes, may be thus paid without any use of coins or money, except the balances and the discount paid the bank. The bank-notes should not, then, fluctuate with the supply of the precious metals, but with the business in which they are issued.[1] They are nothing more than a substitute, by the bank, of its own promissory notes for those of individuals, by which the latter are enabled to pay their debts among themselves. If a man of business, who had issued his notes and acceptances for £10,000, found they had been discounted in the Bank of England, and that £9900 of the notes of the bank had been issued in exchange, he could find no better nor safer medium in which to pay his debt to the bank, than these bank-notes, so far as they would reach. He would, therefore, give any commodities he had pur-

---

[1] Ante, pp. 163–4.

chased by this issue of his own paper for £10,000, to procure the bank-notes with which to pay his debts; for the bank-notes are, for his purpose, of equal avail and far greater convenience than coin. If he is a holder of the notes of others for £10,000, he may have them discounted, and thus procure the notes to extinguish his indebtedness; the bank always keeping a sufficient claim on its debtors to redeem all its notes. It is a process by which individuals change their own notes into bank-notes, and with them pay their debts; in other words, a process by which men apply the paper which others owe to them to pay the paper upon which they are indebted to others. In any business community, the parties who issue their own notes largely are the same who receive notes largely from others: thus, when this individual paper is converted into bank-notes, it furnishes a convenient medium for the discharge of these mutual debts; every one being willing to receive, in payment of debts due to him, that which others will take in payment of his debts.

We have already, in the chapter on bank-notes, remarked at some length on their peculiar functions or applications; our object is now only to recall some of these, and to show how bank-notes become the safest medium for paying the promissory notes or acceptances of individuals. A. B. is the creditor of C. D. for £1000, and holds his promissory note, at four months, for that sum: A. B. carries it to the Bank of England, and receives there for it £980 in bank-notes. The bank becomes thus the creditor of C. D. for £1000, and it becomes thus possible for C. D. to pay his debt of £1000 in bank-notes, less the discount. The bank is equally willing and ready to receive its own notes in payment, from every one of whom it is a creditor. It has thus issued a common currency, which all its debtors may take, and return in payment of the debts they owe to the bank. The bank-notes are good, not because the bank has undertaken the impossible task of paying them in specie on demand, but because there is an effective demand for every note issued by the bank, to pay debts due to the bank, and which must be paid at the risk of ruin.

The notes issued by the bank in the purchase of bullion, and on the deposit of coin, rest immediately on that basis of bullion and coin: those issued in exchange for commercial paper rest immediately on that basis. Supposing the notes resting on these different bases to have been distinguishable, the former would return to the bank only when the convenience of the public dictated, or when there was a demand for the bullion or coin for which they were given; the latter would return by necessity, and upon a different principle.

When the bank gave its notes in exchange for commercial securities, it held the person liable, on these securities, for an amount, equal to the discount, greater than its notes emitted. It looked, of course, narrowly at the ability of these parties to meet their engagements at maturity. By the emission of its bills, the bank furnished to the public the very medium of payment which would pay off and finally discharge the commercial paper. According to the course of commerce, the party who purchases merchandise gives his note or bill, payable at a subsequent day, and by consequence such purchaser has at his command merchandise which he estimates at as much and more than the amount of his note or bill. He has the very commodities for which he gave the commercial security taken by the bank in exchange for its notes; these commodities, in his estimation as a merchant or dealer, are, on being sold, sufficient to command a value in money or bank-notes equal to his own liability. He can redeem the notes of the bank issued for his paper, by sale of the same goods which originated his paper. The merchant depends on sales of his goods for means to pay the debts he contracted in their purchase; and the value of commercial securities depends mainly on the certainty and facility with which merchants can convert their goods into the means of paying their liabilities. The bank furnished a facility for such payment which did not before exist; and the goods held by its debtors would be freely offered for its notes, they being as available as money to extinguish indebtedness. The public, by this issue, were furnished with a convenient currency, the real value of which would be fixed by the demand of the debtors of the bank. These could neither doubt nor temporize; they must be prepared, on the day of payment, with either the money or bank-notes. The demand for bank-notes would be urgent and imperious: the alternative would be, the notes, or money, or bankruptcy. This demand, as already observed, would more than equal the amount of the notes in circulation, so that every solvent debtor of the bank would be an agent to give value to its notes, to withdraw them from circulation by offering for them as much as he would for a corresponding amount of gold or silver. There could be no depreciation of the bank issues whilst the external demand equalled the amount issued. If the bank discounted, in a week, a million sterling of commercial securities, all running off in four months, at the rate of six per cent. per annum, and paid out £990,000 in its own notes, the debtors of the million would, within the four months, be compelled to prepare for payment of that amount as it matured; and the holders of the notes would soon perceive the operation of the necessity to which these debtors had subjected themselves. The bank-notes would, accordingly, be held at the same value as coin, because they would pay the same amount of debt. This result would be more perfectly produced by the working of the bank, after it had been long in operation, when the demand for its notes would be increased by the enlarged amounts falling dne, and by its widening circulation, which would carry many notes beyond the reach of the debtor, and thus force him to pay in money some portion of his liabilities.

A merchant may purchase, or not, as he deems most for his interest; he may select his own time for dealing; there is no actual necessity in this part of his business. But having once made his purchase, and given his paper, a necessity from which there can be no escape, nor evasion, is laid upon him to meet his payment. The competition, therefore, among the debtors of the bank, to secure its notes or money, would equal, if not surpass, any other competition in trade. It was this incessant demand, pressed by the very merchants who held goods selected with a view to the wants of the public, which gave to bank-notes the value and efficacy of money. Doubtless, the promise of the bank to pay its notes on demand had weight with some; very few, however, received the notes for the purpose of demanding coin, or because coin could be demanded; they received them because they could be employed with the same effect as money. They were more abundant, convenient and safe; they answered the same purpose, and were therefore preferred. The immediate question with them was, will these notes be received in payment from us, and not as to the ability or willingness of the bank to redeem them. It was nothing to the receiver of the notes what might be the actual condition of the bank, so that the notes would pay like money. Men received money only to pay it away; and when notes were offered as a substitute, they were received only when they could be paid like money. Individuals could not investigate the situation of the bank, but they could easily ascertain whether bank-notes would buy goods, or pay debts.

If the commercial paper discounted by the bank was payable in a short time, the demand for the notes would be proportionably active, as the debtors must be prepared at the day with notes or money. If it happened that a portion of the debtors failed to make good their engagements, and take up their paper, then a corresponding demand for the bank-notes ceased, and a surplus remained in the hands of the public, which must soon or late be presented for payment to the bank, upon which the loss in such cases fell.

It is upon the operation of this active exterior demand for its notes, that the Bank of England has been so eminently successful during its whole existence of one hundred and fifty years, through many severe trials, and one long period in which it did not pay its notes on demand in specie. If the potency of this demand, in sustaining a circulation of bank-notes, were not seen at a glance, it is abundantly proved by the fact that the Bank of England, during this suspension of twenty-five years, maintained a vast circulation not redeemable in specie. Its notes were, during this time, the chief medium of payment. It is well-known that every attempt to obtain such a circulation has failed, unless founded upon a specie basis, or upon an exterior demand equal to the amount of the circulation. The most arbitrary and despotic government has never succeeded in forcing a circulation, and in keeping it at par, in violation of these principles. But we shall revert to this subject again.

We have thought proper to insist upon the efficacy of the demand for bank-notes created by indebtedness to the bank, in supporting a circulation, because many in England supposed that a large portion of the notes of the Bank of England had no other basis than a *promise* to redeem them on demand. The fact that the bank had promised to pay its notes on demand — a promise held out because it was not expected that performance would be exacted — seemed to lead a portion of the public into the belief that in it consisted the whole security and value of the notes. This idea once entertained, continual apprehensions were felt by the timid and distrustful, even whilst the notes were daily fulfilling every function which could be required of them. The bank merely designed to offer a currency which would be adequate to all the ordinary payments, and which would command money whenever, from special circumstances, it might be needed. This it performed for more than a century, but unhappily not without creating the impression that its notes were all based, like the credits of Amsterdam, on an equivalent in specie. And as the holders of the English notes knew that such equivalent never existed in the bank, they supposed themselves called upon to believe that the bank, upon emergency, could procure the coin to redeem its issues. The bank could, it is true, at all periods of its history, have furnished to the holders of its notes as much coin as was really needed for the purposes of domestic or foreign trade. In one condition of commerce, the precious metals would flow into the bank; in another, they would flow out. In all which, the bank was able and bound to accommodate its customers. The goodness of its notes issued for commercial paper would not depend upon these ebbs and flows of specie, but on the solvency of the debtors of the bank; and this solvency would not depend on the amount of specie in the country, or in the bank, but on the means which the debtors held to command the bank-notes.

There was a great difference between furnishing to commerce

all the coin really required for the payment of balances, and converting at once all the issues of the bank into gold or silver. So far as commerce is concerned, the latter was impossible, and wholly unnecessary. Commerce could provide for its own necessities, and would have placed the bank in the proper condition for this purpose; but a panic got up under the idea that bank-notes, to be good, must necessarily be payable on demand, it could neither resist nor allay. There has never been a time, in the history of the Bank of England, when, if a sufficient amount of its notes had been presented to absorb all its specie, the balance in circulation would not have been perfectly safe and good. The question of depreciation is not touched here; its important bearing on this subject will require more than a passing consideration.

Whatever reasons of expediency or sound policy there may have been for requiring a bank to pay its notes in specie, it is no more right to say that the issues of the Bank of England were based upon coin, or a promise to pay in coin, than it was to say that the commercial securities discounted by that bank were founded upon their promise to pay coin. The real basis of the commercial paper was the commodities for which that paper was given; and that basis was not changed or disturbed by the fact that the evidences of debt to which it had given rise were paid, settled, arranged or extinguished in any other way than by payment in coin. A very small part of these evidences would have been paid in coin, if they had not gone into the bank; they must and would have been adjusted in some other way. The same goods which formed the basis of the commercial paper, became the basis of the bank-notes into which that paper was converted; and there was no commercial necessity that the bank-notes should be paid in coin, any more than the commercial securities. There was an advantage in being able to procure coin when specially needed; but a great mischief, in supposing that bank-notes could not be as good as gold, without being convertible instantly into gold; that beef and mutton purchased with bank-notes were not as good as if purchased with silver; and that debts paid with bank-notes were not as fully extinguished as if discharged in gold or silver.

We have said more than belongs to this place, of the nature of the circulation issued by the Bank of England; the chief design now being to point out the mode and facilities of payment afforded by such a circulation, compared with those before enjoyed. It cannot, however, be necessary to speak of the superior conveniences and advantages of bank-notes as a medium of payment. The sturdiest objector to banks does not deny what is so manifest: his objection goes to the risk of loss, the danger of fraud, and the abuses of credit. In all cases, where banks of circulation have been established and conducted with even a moderate degree of prudence and skill, the notes have almost invariably been preferred to gold and silver. There is, in fact, no comparison between bank-notes kept at their proper value and coin as a medium of payment, in regard to convenience, safety and efficiency. We cannot now conceive of any medium of payment intended for general circulation, superior in these respects to bank-notes fully enjoying the public confidence. Greater permanence may yet be given to the paper, and additional safeguards provided by the engraver against forgery; but nothing superior in facility will ever probably come to the aid of commerce.

Those, however, who have adequate ideas of the power of credit, know that bank-notes cannot exhibit the highest stage of its utility. Ever since the establishment of the Bank of England, there has been an increasing tendency in the payments of commerce to concentrate in London. Although the bank had furnished a medium at par with gold in London, and at par, if not worth more, through all the Island, yet the practice commenced, and has continued until this day, of giving notes and bills payable in that city; and of course merchants and dealers received and paid there a large proportion of their credits and debts. Those who had money on hand found it as available in London, and more safe than at home; those who had to pay money could, with credit, more readily obtain it there than at home. But that great city became not only banker for the whole Island, and for the whole British dominions, but for all nations having commerce there. An immense and hitherto unparalleled concentration of payments took place in London. This was in compliance with a law of trade which continually presses upon merchants the necessity of increasing the efficiency, and economizing the means of payment. Great Britain has long been the country which has displayed the proudest triumphs of commercial integrity. All the world has been willing to confide money to the London bankers. It was too obvious to escape the attention of British traders out of that city, that the more the bank-notes and bank credits were concentrated, the more rapidly they could be circulated. A million in the city could perform as many payments in a day, as five millions scattered over the country. The system in the city tended, as we have seen, to resolve itself into the operation of paying by checks, which was safer and more rapid than with notes. There can be no question among those who have examined the subject, that the saving in the use of bank-notes, in time and in trouble, in making the payments of London has been a vast assistance to British commerce. The accumulation of money there has greatly strengthened the bank, and has enabled it more freely to advance to the government, and to merchants, than it could otherwise have done. In regard to the payment of specie, the bank was more in the power of the private bankers and merchants in the metropolis; but they were less dangerous than the same classes in the country. The bank had more command of its circulation than if it had been diffused among the whole population; and could, with greater facility, increase or diminish it as the demands of commerce might require. This system was directly opposed to its interests, so far as it regarded a very great and wide circulation of its notes; but, in many other respects, it promoted the best interests of the bank, of the public treasury, and the kingdom at large. It was found that, in one period of the year, the agricultural counties had a surplus in the hands of their bankers, which could be lent to the manufacturers, whose surplus, in the time of their harvest, could be lent to the aid of the farming interest; and during all the year, these funds were at the command of commerce, when otherwise unemployed.

§ 3. *The Bank of England's credits in account — Deposit of bank-notes — Funds in bank — Conversion of individual paper into bank-notes — The Bank grants credits for private paper, and receives the credits in all payments — The credits wrongly blended with deposits — Open credits payable on demand in specie, hazardous — Objections — Paying credits on demand abolishes time on bills of exchange and promissory notes — Mingling credit and money — Consequences — Real nature of the credits in account — Expand with trade, diminish with it — Not money — Payment by bank credits not dependent on money — Not a question of convertibility.*

We have seen how a bank, with all its capital lent to the government, could do business upon its deposits, and by the issue of bank-notes; it remains to consider how much larger a business than in either of these ways could be done with its credits. The business of granting credits to its customers, in the manner we are about to specify, did not probably occur to the Governor and Company of the Bank of England until after the bank had commenced business. It was rather a result of the two branches of business we have specified, than a forethought. There is no doubt they intended to employ their credit in every proper and available way, but they did not foresee the vast business which would be opened on their books for their own profit, and the advantage of the public, by the mere use of CREDITS IN ACCOUNT.

The progress of their business soon revealed to the bank, that their customers not only needed a place of deposit and security for their coin and bullion, but also for their bank-notes. The deposits of coin, of which we have treated above separately for the sake of distinctness, were swelled by the deposit of large sums in bank-notes. It was soon perceived that a much larger amount of payment was effected by this movement of the deposits, than by the circulation of both bank-notes and coin. The chief demand for means to pay debts was not for bank-notes, or for coins, but for funds in bank; and this demand was early responded to, on the part of the bank, by discounting business-paper, and giving the customer for whom the discount was made, not bank-notes or coin, but simply a credit in his account, which to that amount swelled his deposit. This credit rested on the same basis precisely as that upon which the bank-notes were issued, namely, individual business-paper. By this device the deposits of the bank were increased to a sum far beyond the aggregate of bank-notes and coin on deposit. The bank became, to some extent, a book-keeper for its customers; it gave them a credit for their claims upon others, and charged them with the claims of others upon them. This was the case so far, at least, as the respective claims were discounted; and the bank charged the same commission, or discount, for this credit in account as it did when it advanced or lent coins, or issued bank-notes. This became soon the most important department of the business of the bank, as well as the most profitable; for the keeping these accounts was not so expensive to the bank as issuing its notes.

These credits, as soon as given and entered in the deposit account of a customer, were worked in the same way, and to the same effect, as deposits of coin and bank-notes. No distinction was made in the management, use or efficacy of a deposit, whether it originated in one of these ways or another. The bank, for every amount of credit thus granted, held the corresponding amount of discounted paper. The return of the corresponding amount of credit was all the payment the bank asked for the business-paper it held. The credits were, therefore, as efficacious to discharge a debt in bank as coins or bank-notes. The bank held the individual notes against the credits it granted; it surrendered them on the return of the same amount of credits, or the amount granted for each note or bill, with the amount of the discount in money. The bank liquefied for its customers the inconvenient and unemployed individual paper in their port-folios, and made it available by transfer, in any desired amount, for the payment of debts. A man with £10,000 of private paper, in twenty notes of various amounts, could do little or nothing with them in payment of his own liabilities; but with credits in deposit to the amount of £9900, he could effect any payment or purchase which he could have done with the money.

This would have made a safe and extremely profitable business to the bank; but it involved an onerous obligation, and a heavy risk. The credits were entered in the deposit accounts of the customers, which deposits were made up of bank-notes, bullion and coin, and were, by the practice of the bank, payable on demand in coins. Thus the bank, whilst exchanging a credit on its books for business-paper having several months to run, became liable to pay these credits on demand in coin. This liability became one of great hazard to the bank; for, whilst any run upon it for payment of notes would be gradual, because the notes were always widely circulated, the demand for deposits could be made instantly to a very large amount. The depositors in the bank, from an early period of its existence, have always had it in their power to demand more money from the bank than it could pay, and of course to force it into suspension.

This was not a necessary risk. The credit account should have been purely a credit account, only payable by the bank in money when the paper matured for which the credit was granted. The credit granted by the bank answered every needful purpose, without being payable on demand. The real legitimate operation, whether the bank issued its notes or granted credits, was, that the payment of the discounted paper by the drawers or acceptors should absorb the bank-notes or credits, and return them, or something that would redeem them, to the bank. This routine of operation would end the transactions in each case. The bank, in receiving a promissory note at ninety days, received but a security for a credit granted by one individual to another; for this it exchanged its own credit, which, to make the transaction correspond, should also, so far as it concerned payment in money or coins, have been at ninety days. Nothing more should have been attempted, where nothing more could be accomplished, than to make business or commercial paper available for the purpose of adjustment, payment of debts, or set-off of mutual claims. The bank could spread all a man's credits on its books, and make them available for the payment of his debts. It could render him no greater service; it could neither convert his paper into money, nor lend him the amount in money, nor could it safely agree to pay on demand the credits granted on its books. The promissory notes and acceptances issued in the course of business or time should not have been, by any attempted device of banking, changed into notes or debts payable on demand; it was too hazardous a measure; there was no need for it. It is enough that a safe method had been found of changing these time securities into a shape in which they could be as fully available for their own payment and final discharge, as either gold or silver.

The transfer of credits permitted to the depositors on their written order or check became, in the hands of the great merchants and dealers in commercial securities in London, one of the most effective modes of payment ever employed. It was freed from the forms and precautions which were practised at the continental banks; and any conceivable amount of payments could be made in a morning by the active movement of a comparatively small sum on the books of the bank. At the Bank of Amsterdam, he who received a transfer in bank for payment, could not transfer or pay away the amount thus received until the next day — a precaution which must have checked the circulation of the deposits to a most injurious extent; but for this regulation, it may be presumed that a third of the actual deposits would have fully sufficed to make all the payments of Amsterdam. There was nothing in the constitution of the deposit banks which prevented them from offering the same facilities of transfer as the Bank of England; but when they were established, the minds of merchants had not conceived such a convenience, nor the efficacy of such a rapid circulation. The banks once in operation could not easily, without creating apprehension, make any great change in their mode of conducting business.

It is difficult to imagine any scheme of adjusting the large payments of commerce superior to this. It embraces at once all the efficacy of set-off, and all the convenience of rapid circulation; the advantages of both these processes enter into and form the basis of this successful mode of payment. It is superior to the mere operation of set-off between individuals, because this requires a meeting to adjust accounts; it is superior to the mere circulation of bank-notes, because it is applicable to any fractionary sum; it saves the risk of counterfeits, of theft, and of fire, and all the trouble and time of receiving, counting or locking up notes; and, more than all, it saves the necessity of a deposit of coin. The bank takes all the risk of forgery from its customer, who has only to avoid taking checks from those whose honesty he doubts. The merchant's check-book lies open before him, and his deposits can, by his own hand only, be changed in an instant into that which is as available as money.

No error in practice or principle which can be laid to the charge of the Bank of England, was more full of risk and danger than this undertaking to pay bank credits on demand. It was an engagement useless as a security to the public, because it could not be kept, if performance was demanded, and it was useless, if performance could not be exacted. To make this more plain, let us suppose that a manufacturer or merchant, desirous of making his own paper as available as possible in the furtherance of his business, had issued £1000 in £20 notes, payable in four months; that the drawer of these notes, finding his credit not sufficient to give them proper and useful currency, had carried them to the bank, and proposed to give at the rate of two per cent. on the whole amount, if the bank would endorse them; that, for this commission, or interest, on the notes for the time they had to run, the bank had lent its credit, by endorsing the notes, making them thereby current for all purposes of payment — this would have been all the aid or facility the bank could safely give, by the mere use of its credit. If the bank could not lend the party the money on security of his £20 notes, it could only offer the aid of its credit to make the notes good and available until the day of payment arrived. The bank could not pay the debt of its customer, if it could not lend him the money; the issuer of the notes endorsed by the bank would have been obliged to pay them at maturity, and upon faith of this only could the bank have ventured to endorse them. The bank could not extend its aid to the drawer of the notes beyond their maturity, for that would have been equivalent to paying them. The persons into whose hands these endorsed notes would fall, would expect punctual payment, and the bank or drawer must pay;

but as the bank could only lend credit, it could not pay all the debts of those it could aid with its credit. The bank could not, therefore, extend the aid of its credit beyond the maturity of the notes guaranteed, because that would involve payment by the bank.

But if the bank could not safely assume the debts of its customers, at the maturity of notes endorsed by them, it could not agree to pay these endorsed notes on demand in money. Yet this is the very thing which the bank actually undertook to do; it issued its own notes, payable on demand in gold or silver, in exchange for the notes of merchants and manufacturers, payable in three or four months: that is, the bank discounted notes of its customers to the amount of millions sterling, payable on demand; it virtually made a four months' note payable instanter; it abolished time on notes and bills of exchange, and made them payable on demand, relying on a generous public not to take advantage of the extraordinary offer.

But the bank was still more daring; it discounted notes largely, and carried the amount of the proceeds to the credit of the party, as so much money deposited: that is, in the same column in which the bank gave its customers credit for gold and silver deposits, it gave them credit for the amounts of notes and acceptances having months to run before maturity, and engaged to pay the amount of these securities on demand. It mingled a process of credit with a process of cash, in a mode as absurd in theory as it was dangerous in practice. The men who had given their notes on time had provided for a regular progression of payments, according to the movements of business and the demands of consumption; but the Bank of England virtually abolished the contract of deferred payment between the parties, and became paymaster on demand of debts not due for months, and to an immense amount.

The bank had no warrant, in principle or in practice, for this hazardous engagement. Its only excuse was the same which was given for the issue of bank-notes payable on demand, without the money to pay, namely, that the bank would not be asked to pay them all at one time.

We regard this error of the Bank of England as the parent of the greater portion of the mischiefs and evils for which banks, in more modern times, are answerable. The banks, from that day to this, have continued to issue notes payable on demand, and to grant credits so payable, in exchange for securities payable in from 30 to 120 days. They do this, relying wholly on the forbearance of the public, just as the Bank of England did at first. Sad experience has shown that there are times when the public is not only not forbearing, but when men rush with frantic haste to demand of the bank payment of both notes and deposits. Nearly every bank in existence, conducted on this plan, has, at some period of its history, felt the power and rashness of the public in seasons of commercial panic. The banks lose their power and usefulness at the very moment when the public most needs their assistance. Friends in sunshine, they become enemies in the storm.

This mistaken step of the Bank of England, perpetuated by our modern banks, and producing some of the worst results of modern banking, demands more full explanation of its nature, and the causes of its operating so injuriously. It may be less difficult to comprehend the evil, in its origin in one bank, than in the midst of the complications of thousands of banks.

We have already, in another place, shown what was as true in the 17th century as it is now, that the great operations of industry and trade are nearly altogether carried on by individual credit. Merchandise and raw materials were, at the origin of the Bank of England, as now, purchased and sold for promissory notes and bills of exchange. There was no time when there were not such securities in the hands of individuals, to represent the chief transactions which had taken place in the previous few months. The average credit may have been two, three or four months; but, whatever it was, there were bills of exchange and promissory notes extant, to show that individuals had undertaken to pay every specific sum in a specific time. To some extent, this individual paper was always circulated in purchases and in payments; but its use, in that way, was always limited and inconvenient. It was upon this mass of business-paper, which could not have been, in London, in 1696, less than five millions sterling, that the Bank of England designed to operate. On the continent, many devices were resorted to, as we have seen in the Fairs of Lyons, and the Banks of Venice and Genoa, to enable the parties to such paper, debtor and creditor, to adjust their mutual claims without the necessity of payment in coin. The parties holding this paper were, for the most part, both debtors and creditors; they both received it from others, and gave it to others. With them the great problem was, how to pay with the greatest economy and convenience. What each needed, was some plan by which he could use the notes or bills of exchange he held, to pay or satisfy those which others held against him. This facility had been afforded in England only by private bankers; but when it came to be offered by the Bank of England, on a larger scale, and with greater security, the opportunity was gladly accepted.

He who had liabilities to the amount of £5000 to pay, in any given month, might have promissory notes and acceptances to a much larger amount in his hands, but be wholly unable to apply them, before they had matured, to the payment of his own, which would mature sooner. The bank offered the required facility—a credit on its books for the paper not yet due; upon which credit he was permitted to draw for the amount of each of his maturing liabilities as they became due, transferring so much of his credit, upon every occasion, as would be necessary to extinguish a debt. As the bank dealt with one, so it dealt with all. It liquefied, as it were, upon its books, these promissory notes and acceptances to the amount of millions sterling. In the hands of the holders they were securities, evidences of debt and credit incapable of subdivision, and available, to a very small extent, as a currency or in payment; but, spread as credits on the books of the bank, they became one of the most efficient means of payment or adjustment ever employed. The whole of this individual paper became, on the books of the bank, a fund which could be drawn upon and used in payments to its whole amount. Every man concerned in it would be enabled thus to apply his credits to the payment of his debts. No better payment could be made, and in the case, none more economical. It could be more economical and easy only where men set-off, in comparing their mutual accounts, their charges one against another. The bank provided, in fact, a system by which it kept books of account for parties holding claims upon each other. If the bank gave, on these books, a credit of a million sterling, receiving therefor the paper of parties indebted to that amount, the bank required no better payment than the return of an equivalent amount of credit for each note or acceptance retired.

This whole matter would have been, on the books of the banks, the working of a process of adjustment. It no more required the presence of gold or silver, than it is required by those who balance their book accounts. The money would be required only where the process of set-off or adjustment failed. If any individual could not return the equivalent of his debt in credits granted by the bank, he would have to pay the money: that is, the debtors upon the paper held by the bank would have to redeem the credits granted by the bank in the purchase of the paper, or else pay the money with which the bank could redeem them. This process of adjustment is one which could proceed as steadily on the books of the bank as the progress of industry and trade. Within a certain range it would require no money; that range would depend on the mutuality of business. So far as a customer of the bank had claims upon others which he could apply to the claims upon himself, he would require no money. As with one, so with all; so far as the customers of the bank had claims upon each other, no money would be required for their adjustment. So, as between nations; no money is required for payments, except to pay balances. Doubtless, the fluctuations of trade would have their effect upon this process of adjustment; but, whatever irregularities might arise from this cause, the process would proceed so long as business continued. This process, in fact, could never fail nor be diminished in its efficacy; but would expand when commerce expanded, and contract when commerce contracted. It would operate, in this respect, precisely as it would between those who had been in the habit of dealing largely with each other upon the faith of their respective books of account. If their transactions grew larger, their acccounts would only be longer; and if their mutual business diminished, the accounts would be shorter. In either case, the process of adjustment would be the same, and equally effectual, whether the accounts were long or short, or the amounts great or small.

When the Bank of England undertook, as a means of attracting business, to pay bank-notes and credits in account, issued for individual securities not due, on demand, it was not foreseen what a Pandora's box of evils was being opened, to trouble the commercial world. The bank intended no more than to offer a facility and convenience, which it was believed there would be no temptation to abuse. So far have been the anticipations of the bank from being realized, that, from the very first movement of the bank in this direction, the public seized upon the facility or convenience as being the substance of the transaction, and not, as intended by the bank, as the incident or shadow. The public at once looked upon bank-notes and bank credits, convertible on demand into gold or silver, as money, and not, as devices of the credit system, instruments of adjustment. In this aspect, bank-notes and bank credits were a boon, indeed, to men of business. It was no less than an exchange of their paper, payable some months after date, into that which was payable on demand. Bank-notes and bank credits became cash — looked upon and treated as money. This was entirely changing their character and legitimate use; they should have been regarded as mere instruments of adjustment, having the same effect as books of account. The Bank of England, and all other banks of circulation, have since been held, as a matter of justice to the public, to this convertibility of their credits and their notes; and the important distinction between payments by adjustment, or setting-off debts against debts, and payment in money, has been lost from the mind of the public.

It did not result, in the case of the Bank of England, that this giving bank-notes and bank credits, payable on demand, for the paper not due received from its customers, virtually changed that paper into money. It is true, the bank-notes and bank credits became a currency, with a circulation and powers similar to those of money. Their chief utility or efficacy was not derived from their being payable on demand, but from their use as instruments of adjustment. They had, thenceforward, two characters—the one as a currency, or substitute for money; the other, as a means of adjustment. They were employed in both characters, but without observing the distinction. The operation of adjustment, by which nine-tenths of the debts were actually discharged, was no longer understood; and the whole efficacy of the payments was attributed to the use of bank-notes and bank credits, in their character of money or currency. Without here estimating the increased efficacy thus given to bank-notes and bank credits, we insist that their efficiency was mainly as instruments of adjustment. We have already explained the process. If the bank had received a million sterling of individual paper, maturing in an average of three months, for which it had issued bank-notes to the amount of £985,000, these would be applicable at once to the payment of the individual paper as it matured, not because they were payable on demand, but because they constituted a claim upon the bank, which the bank would promptly redeem by giving up the paper of individuals as it fell due. The bank, in this case, would hold a claim upon certain persons of the public for a million, and certain persons of the public would hold claims upon the bank to the extent of £985,000. The bank would gladly receive this amount of its notes, so far as they would reach, in the payment of the million of securities held by it. Such a transaction between the bank and its customers would require no help of coins or bullion; they would not be needed, and it would not be economical to use them. Although the notes and credits were convertible, they were never for the purpose of such payment converted. The process of adjustment proceeded in the same manner, and to the same extent, as if the bank-notes and bank credits had not been convertible.

We are not discussing the question here, whether such notes as the Bank of England issued should have been payable on demand or not, nor the restraints and securities which should have been placed upon such a power: that is a separate topic. We are considering merely the processes of payment as it may be effected by the notes and upon the books of a bank. We wish to show that the process of adjustment by which men are enabled to apply what others owe to them in satisfaction of what they owe to others — that is, to set-off credits against debts — is in no way dependent upon money. It is a process corresponding precisely to that of balancing accounts, or setting-off mutual debts arising upon books of accounts. This balancing of accounts is in no degree dependent upon any use of money. When parties are willing so to regard them, one debt is as good as another; and, therefore, it is perfectly proper for men to pay debts with debts: and this method is equally effectual and final, whether done by the aid of a bank, or by the aid of books of account.

We are very far from saying that bank-notes or bank credits, payable on demand, should not be paid on demand. Banks, as well as individuals, should be prepared to pay what they engage to pay; they should make no promises which they have not good reason to believe they can fulfil under all circumstances. The Bank of England, however, never was able, and never expected to be able, to pay all its notes and credits, if payment of the whole were demanded. The belief was, that it could pay all that would be demanded; and one of the reasons for promising to pay on demand was, to make the bank-notes and credits a currency so desirable and convenient, that payment of them would not be demanded. We do not here, then, touch the question of the securities which the Bank of England, or any other bank which makes such promises, should give for their performance. We are contending that the system of adjusting mutual debts upon the books of a bank, for which they are admirably adapted, should be allowed to operate by itself upon the principles which belong to it. It needs no aid from gold or silver; and there was no more need of making the items of debt and credit thus adjusted payable in specie on demand, than there was of making every item of a book account payable on demand, before the parties could be allowed to balance their books.

Let us suppose the Bank of England to have had deposited in

their office, for collection, a million sterling of business-paper, having an average of three months to run, and that, upon application of the holders, the whole is discounted and credit given to them respectively for the proceeds upon the books of the bank; and that this credit is given solely for the purpose of paying debts to the bank. It is obvious that every person so credited is at once prepared to transfer to the bank so much of his credit as will satisfy or extinguish his debts to the bank. So far as the parties concerned in this million sterling were mutually indebted, they would be prepared to meet their indebtedness. They would have been thus furnished with the most convenient and effectual mode of payment which can be conceived. Every man thus credited, and against whom the bank held claims, would have it in his power to make his payments without fail as they matured. The effect of this operation would have been very much the same as if the bank had simply charged each customer with his portion of the indebtedness, and credited him with the paper discounted for him. This would have been the substance of the transaction as a whole, and it would have effectually discharged all the mutual indebtedness involved in the million sterling, which would have been, according to the course of business, not less than two-thirds to nine-tenths of the whole.

This very beautiful, effective and simple process of extinguishing debts was complicated, sadly and disastrously, by the ill-considered practice introduced by the Bank of England. It is true that, by means of bank-notes and bank credits, the process of adjustment could go on effectively, whether the notes or credits were payable on demand or not; but the public gradually took up the opinion, that the availability of the bank-notes and bank credits depended upon their convertibility into gold or silver. This was overlooking the whole process of adjustment, the power of which was far greater than any possible employment of gold and silver. The distinction between the agency of coins and the process of adjustment being lost sight of, it was assumed that the precious metals, or money, was the basis of this most effective means of settling debts. The next step was, that bank-notes and bank credits being, by this assumption, based on money, or the precious metals, the issue of bank-notes and bank credits should be strictly regulated by the amount of coins which could be kept on hand to redeem them. It was pretty generally insisted that the Bank of England should keep on hand one-third enough of specie to redeem its notes and credits, on the presumption that more would never be demanded. This doctrine was maintained and pressed upon the bank for more than a century. Its influence, so far as it prevailed, on the minds of the people and the government was, in some respects, extremely injurious to individual and commercial interests. It assumed, as the criterion of the quantity of bank-notes and bank credits to be issued, the quantity of money in a country, instead of the amount of the exchanges of commodities. Manufacturers and merchants purchase and sell commodities, and give and take their own notes in settlement of the amount of debts; and they do this without having one-third, or even one-hundredth, of enough specie on hand to make final payment, and, indeed, without thinking of any payment in specie; for it is the rarest thing in the world for any merchant or manufacturer ever to exact payment of a debt in gold or silver. It is enough for these men, that they can purchase with their own paper, and sell for the paper of others, which can be applied to pay their own.

The business of England in the 17th century, as it is now, was carried on, in its large operations, upon the credit of individuals who issued their own paper for all purchases, and received it for all sales. It is upon the paper thus issued, that the business of banks of circulation is founded. This individual paper is not based upon, nor regulated by, the quantity of money in circulation, nor would there be any propriety in its being so regulated. Before the Bank of England was established, there were always modes of effecting payments of this private paper, to a large extent, without money. The great point aimed at, in regard to payment of this paper, was not to procure money to pay it, but to pay it without resort to gold or silver. The business was not to be regulated by gold and silver, but by the industry and energies of the people, and their facilities for transportation and consumption. The whole exchange of commodities, and their entire distribution, previous to the final operation of the retail trade, move on in the regular channels, whilst the payments are reserved for a special and separate department of business.

As the trade of a country, foreign or domestic, is not dependent upon the precious metals, so neither are the payments. It is obvious to all who know anything of the movements of trade, or the processes of payment in the large way, that neither the one nor the other are carried on by means of gold or silver. Prices are all expressed in money of account; the sums named in bills of exchange, promissory notes, bank-notes and books of account, are all expressed in money of account; finally, all debts and credits are so expressed. What is required, in the processes or machinery of payment, is, that they should be commensurate in power with the work to be done. As so few payments are actually made in gold or silver, it is evident that they are not regarded as adequate to the task to be accomplished. Their agency is now restricted to the retail trade, and to the payment of balances in the foreign and domestic trade. Their use in the banks is purely precautionary, and as a security to the public against over-issue, and for payment of balances between banks. The great payments of trade are not effected, directly nor indirectly, by means of the precious metals. Out of the retail trade, they are mere commodities, the supply and use of which is regulated by the demand for them, and the means of purchasing them. The machinery and processes of payment have very little necessary or actual connection with the precious metals, whether in the shape of coins or bullion.

§ 4. *The Bank of England suspends payments from* 1797 *to* 1822—*Order of suspension by Privy Council—Opposition to the measure—Terms of suspension—Dates of extensions—Position and progress of the country during suspension—Dissatisfaction—Lord King—Convertibility—Efficacy of payments—Processes of payment the same during suspension as before—The real basis of bank issues, the commodities of trade—The credit system—Controversy as to the depreciation of bank-notes during the suspension—Bullion Report of* 1810—*Bullionists and anti-Bullionists—Opinion of Tooke in History of Prices—Table of prices of gold and silver, and amount of circulation, from* 1797 *to* 1821.

We are not assuming to give a history of the Bank of England, nor even the merest sketch, but only such features of its business as may serve to exhibit its agency in the great work of commercial payments. One of the most remarkable events in the history of the bank was its suspension of payment in 1797—a suspension prolonged for upwards of twenty-five years. This suspension itself deserves a history, to which justice has never been done. It was, without doubt, made necessary by the immense advances made to the government during the wars and continental troubles consequent upon the French Revolution. The commercial disturbances of the time were scarcely less than the political, and both operated severely upon the bank. The advances to the government were, however, quadruple the discounts afforded to commerce. This caused inability to furnish the needful facilities to industry and commerce, and increased the distrust which the state of affairs at home and abroad was calculated to awaken. Early in the year 1797, which was the year after the attempted invasion of England, a steady drain carried off the specie from the bank at such a rate, that in February the directors became thoroughly alarmed, and laid the facts before Mr. Pitt. He brought the subject at once before the Privy Council; he had suggested to the authorities of the bank, that it might be expedient for the government to restrain the further payment of specie, to examine carefully the condition of the bank, and to give its notes the benefit of a public guarantee. The Council met on the 25th of February, 1797, and determined, in consequence of the "unusual demands for specie that have been made upon the metropolis, proceeding from unfounded or exaggerated alarms," . . . "that it is indispensably necessary for the public service, that the Directors of the Bank of England should forbear issuing any cash in payment, until the sense of Parliament can be taken on that subject." This mandate of the Privy Council was obeyed, and payments in specie ceased on the 27th of February, 1797.

A large meeting of bankers and merchants of London was held the same day, over which the Mayor presided, at which they resolved unanimously that they would not refuse to take bank-notes in payment of any sums of money to be paid to them, and that they would use their utmost endeavors to make all their payments in the same manner. Some alarm, but no special excitement, ensued among people thus suddenly arrested in their run upon the bank. The Opposition in Parliament did not permit so good an opportunity to pass, without employing this as a weapon against the government. Fox, Sheridan and Pulteney made violent speeches against the bank, and the policy of suspension. Mr. Fox said, "the measure had destroyed the credit of the bank;" that it was equivalent to "seizing the money of individuals." Mr. Sheridan said he "considered it a farce to call that a bank, whose promise to pay on demand was met by another promise to pay at some indefinite period. It was ridiculous to think of placing confidence in paper upon any principle but that of its being paid when it became due." Pulteney submitted to the House of Commons a bill for the erection of a new bank, in case the Bank of England did not pay specie on the 24th of June, 1797, "or within four months from the day of suspension." But this outcry and opposition proved powerless against the exigencies of the time; the bankers, merchants and people supported the government. The policy of non-payment, which at first startled Mr. Pitt, was by him afterwards declared to be, in the peculiar circumstances of necessity in which the government was then placed, like "finding a mountain of gold."

On the 3d of March, 1797, immediately following the suspension, the bank was authorized to issue £1 and £2 notes; and some Spanish dollars were issued for the same purpose of furnishing change. The bank had not for twenty years issued notes under £5. On the 3d of May, the Bank Restriction Act passed, being "An Act for continuing for a limited time the restriction contained in the minute of Council, of the 26th of February, 1797, of payment in cash by the bank." It indemnified the bank for the suspension, prohibited the payment of specie, except for sums under 20 shillings, but allowed depositors of £500 in specie to withdraw three-fourths of the amount. The bank was permitted to advance to the private bankers of London any sum in specie not exceeding, in the whole, £100,000, and £25,000 each to two banks in Scotland. The bank was not to be sued for the non-payment of any note for which they were willing to give other notes; and no person could be held to special bail for any debt, for which he had tendered payment in notes of the Bank of England. This act was to be in force 52 days, until the 24th of June. On the 22d of June, an act was passed, continuing suspension until one month after the commencement of the next session of Parliament. In November, 1797, a third act was passed, continuing the suspension until six months after the end of the war. In 1802, after the truce of Amiens, the restriction was again, by act of Parliament, continued until March, 1803. Two acts passed in 1803, on the subject of the restriction, and the one of December continued it until six weeks after a definitive treaty of peace. This did not occur until 1815, and then another act until 1816, when it was continued to 1818, and thence to July, 1819. It was only continued from this date to February 1st, 1820. This last continuation was contained in Peel's Bill, providing for the resumption of specie payments by degrees, beginning on the 1st of October, 1820, and reaching full payment on the 1st of May, 1823. These continuations by law of the restriction show that the subject was before the people for upwards of twenty-five years.

This was an eventful period of the history of Great Britain, distinguished alike for progress in arts and arms, in industry and commerce. The great agent of British finance, during this long struggle, and this wonderful series of successes, was the

Bank of England. At the date of the suspension, its stock of specie had been reduced to £1,086,000. The country was then apprehensive of an invasion by the hitherto invincible Napoleon, and alarm was prevalent. The war had already proved burdensome, and heavy loans had been negotiated. The revenue of the United Kingdom had grown from £19,258,000 sterling, in 1792, to £23,126,000, in 1797; the public debt of £261,735,000 had about doubled itself at the date of suspension. To give some idea of the difficulties encountered by the nation during the suspension, we furnish the following statements: —

The public revenue, which, as just mentioned, was £23,126,000 in 1797, increased steadily to £72,210,000 in 1815, and stood at £54,282,000 in 1820.

The amount raised by loan and taxation, during that time, was never less in any year than £47,362,000; during nine years it was over £70,000,000; and for the years 1813 and 1814, it was, respectively, £108,397,000 and £105,698,000.

During the suspension, loans were negotiated for the government to the amount of £350,000,000. In January, 1816, the public debt had reached the sum of £885,186,000.

In this trying period, the bank made advances to the government, in anticipation of the public revenues every year, from £10,000,000 to £28,000,000, besides being the chief agent in negotiating and funding over £100,000,000. The specie in the bank increased, in 1798, to nearly £6,000,000; in 1799, it reached £7,564,000. It then decreased, until, in the years 1813, 1814 and 1815, it had fallen to very little over £2,000,000. It fluctuated greatly down to the year of resumption, having been as high as £10,000,000 in 1818, and as low as £4,185,000 in 1819.

The circulation of the bank, in 1796, £10,730,000, had been reduced more than a million before the suspension took place in February, 1797. It was then gradually increased to its maximum of over £27,000,000, from 1815 to 1818; in 1822, the year of full resumption, it was £18,665,000. The deposits of the bank were £4,892,000 in 1797, being then more than a million below the average of the preceding ten years. They fluctuated greatly during the succeeding twenty years, the highest being over £12,000,000 in four different years, and not falling to £6,000,000 until 1820, when they were at £4,094,000. After this, up to the year 1844, they had not reached £14,000,000.

Three millions of acres of land, hitherto unimproved, were inclosed and brought under cultivation during this period of suspension.

In 1801, the quantity of cotton imported was 54,000,000 pounds; in 1822, it was 143,000,000 pounds. The manufactured cotton goods exported in 1801 were of the official value of £7,000,000; in 1822, of £27,000,000.

Between 1797 and 1814, upwards of £37,000,000 of subsidies were paid by Great Britain to her continental allies, for their assistance in the war.

But we need not multiply figures, to show that the period of the suspension of specie payments in Great Britain was one of great progress in wealth, industry, commerce and power, notwithstanding all the disadvantages of an inconvertible paper currency, the vast expenditure of the war, and the great burden of taxation. After speaking of this eventful period of British history, in which the nation surmounted so many difficulties, and finally came off conqueror in a contest with the most powerful and the most skilful commander the world has ever known, a recent historian of the Bank of England says: — "These things are not written to defend, they are only penned to mitigate the wrath which has been poured upon the Bank Restriction Act. Extraordinary events require extraordinary measures; and our history, from 1797 to 1815, is unsurpassed in the annals of nations."[1]

But whatever may be urged by the enemies of the Bank Restriction Act in their "wrath," the friends of commercial credit may well claim that the achievements, during a quarter of a century of suspension, deserve to be faithfully studied and well understood. It is a fact that, during this period, a vast revenue of hundreds of millions of dollars was paid by the people, and hundreds of millions of dollars were raised by public loans every

---

[1] History of the Bank of England, by John Francis, vol. i., p. 252.

year, between 1797 and 1815; that thousands of millions of dollars of commercial debts were paid every year of the suspension, with little or no intervention of the precious metals — facts which deserve a better explanation than has ever been given. If the countless millions of dollars of debts discharged during this quarter of an age of paper money be well and sufficiently paid, it should certainly be understood upon what principles it could be done.

There was, doubtless, in many minds, during all this period of inconvertible bank-notes, a vague feeling that these payments were, after all, indebted for their effectiveness to some secret power of the precious metals. The bank-notes carried on their face a promise to pay a certain number of pounds sterling, and although these pounds were never paid in gold or silver, yet the promise was there, and the promise, for the time, was taken for the performance. The efficacy of current payments was seldom attributed to the working of the credit system, where it belonged; and a few, at least, considered themselves deeply wronged, because they could not, at pleasure, convert their bank-notes into specie. The fact that an intense demand for gold on the continent, arising from the wars and disturbances prevailing there, had enhanced the price of gold everywhere, did not escape the notice of those opposed to a paper currency, and this increased their "wrath." They regarded themselves as injured to the extent of this increased price of gold, upon every pound that passed through their hands. They scouted and despised the very currency by which the business and government of the United Kingdom were carried on, and to which, whatever may have been its faults, the people and government were at that juncture under infinite obligations. One of the most distinguished of these objectors, Lord King, in despite and contempt of the law which gave his tenants the right to pay their rents in bank-notes, served a formal notice upon them to pay their dues in gold. He published a pamphlet overflowing with arguments against the suspension, and with solemn reproof for the wrong done to people who were obliged to receive and pay bank-notes, at par with silver.

We need not explain at length here, what we have so fully explained elsewhere in this volume, that the payments of Great Britain, during the period of suspension, did not derive any part of their efficacy from the precious metals, nor from the promise to pay—a promise not performed, nor intended to be performed. The efficacy of the payments, during a period of suspension, rested upon the same principles which make payments efficacious, when bank-notes and bank credits are convertible. The object of convertibility not being to make payments by notes and checks upon deposits valid, but to be a security against over-issues, and other abuses in banking. The fact that gold or silver can be obtained for notes, adds nothing to the validity of payment in the notes: if the parties concerned are willing to pay and receive notes in payment for goods or debts, it matters not to the validity of the transaction whether the notes are convertible or not. So far as convertibility is concerned, it is a question of public policy; a question whether any bank can, with safety to the public, be permitted to issue notes as currency upon any other security than payment of the notes thus issued in demand in gold or silver. We are not now discussing that subject.

Nearly the whole business of every civilized country, except the merest retail trade, is carried on, in the first instance, upon personal credit. Purchases in the large way are made neither with the precious metals, nor with bank-notes, but upon the security of promissory notes, bills of exchange, and other like securities. These securities, whatever their form, and whatever they promise, are expressed, like the entries in merchants' books, in money of account. They are evidence of the amount of credit, and of course of the amount of debt. The issue of these securities accomplishes a movement of commodities to the value which they represent. The next step, is the payment or discharge of these obligations. The parties who have purchased have the commodities, the parties who have sold have the securities. But the holders of securities are themselves debtors for the amount of other securities issued by them for the purchase of the very goods they sold. Thus a great mass of business men transact a vast amount of business by the issue of their own paper. It becomes a prime object of every one of these men to apply his credits to pay his debts. They all go to the bank, and have their securities converted into bank-notes or bank credits. The bank becomes the holder of the securities for which it has issued notes or credits. The bank gives nothing for these securities but its own paper promises or credits, and these to an amount less the discount. The debtor in any of the securities held by the bank has only to pay the bank in its own issues — the very currency in which the bank paid for the securities. In this way, the whole of the debts can be paid, and the whole of the securities can be discharged and retired by the parties who issued them. There is an indebtedness to the bank to a larger amount than the issues of the bank, and there is a constant daily effective demand for the issues of the bank, whether notes or credits, by parties who must constantly and daily meet their debts maturing in the bank. There is, in commercial countries like Great Britain and the United States, no other article so extensively in demand as bank-notes and bank credits, for the purpose of discharging debts payable in bank. Such debtors never look for gold or silver to pay these debts; it would be utterly in vain.

It is evident, then, that the process of payment is the same, whether the banks are in a state of suspension or not. This process is effective, rapid and economical, because it does not require any aid whatever from the precious metals. The restraints which the law imposes upon banks, and the securities it requires for their good behavior, have nothing to do with the nature and efficacy of the process, further than to secure the faithfulness of the servants, and the proper working of the machinery by which the payments are accomplished.

In reference to the mode and progress of payment during the period of suspension, we have made our remarks general, because they apply to any banks of circulation in a state of suspension, as well as the Bank of England. We have already explained, in the chapter on bank-notes, how they fulfil the functions of a medium of exchange, circulating like money; and in the chapter on deposits we have explained how they were employed in payments. At the hazard of some repetition, we shall add something here.

Notes of the Bank of England bear on their face a certain value, expressed in money of account, and a promise to pay that amount on demand. This promise is not what gives currency and efficacy, for performance is only exacted in times of panic. The real efficacy of the notes proceeds from this, that so large a proportion of business men are either indebted to the bank, or are indebted to those who owe the bank, that the notes are in great demand at the amounts expressed on their face; for this amount they can be used to extinguish debts in the bank as effectually as gold itself. But the notes are not dependent for their currency upon this general demand. There is a special demand of greater potency. The debtors of the bank are not merely men of business, whose paper has been discounted by the bank; they are men of business, who, upon their own credit, and with their own paper, have purchased commodities suitable for general consumption. It is their business thus to purchase and sell, and as a body they hold the chief articles of general and regular consumption. What they have to sell, others are obliged to buy. The bank holds the individual paper with which these commodities were purchased, and the debtors hold the commodities the people want. These debtors of the bank, then, are not the only persons who need the bank-notes with which to pay their debts, but they are the holders of the very articles, for the purchase of which money would otherwise have to be paid. The process, then, is, that men with their individual paper purchase commodities; the bank purchases this individual paper by the issue of its own, or bank-notes; the people among whom these bank-notes circulate, purchase with them the commodities in the hands of the debtors of the bank. The real basis of this issue of bank-notes is the commodities purchased with the discounted individual paper. These commodities are sold to redeem that paper; the people need these articles, and must have them; they do not need gold, and can do wholly without it. The basis of banking, then, is this individual paper, and the basis of this paper is the commodities it purchased. The whole process is carried on by an expression of prices and amounts in money of account. The bank-notes may and do circulate widely among those who do not employ them in the purchase of commodities; but they will constantly and finally tend towards the bank, because this consumption of commodities is a great and never-ceasing operation, and all must contribute to it; the bank-notes must always maintain their value, because so many must have them or money.

If a flour dealer in Liverpool gives his note to B. S. & Co. for £1000 for 1000 barrels of American flour, and B. S. & Co. send that note to the Bank of England for discount, and receive the proceeds in notes of the bank, it is plain, whether the notes thus received, or the notes of a Liverpool bank, are circulated in their place, that an instrument or medium of exchange has been put in circulation that will purchase that flour, whether the notes circulated are at the time payable in gold or not. It is enough for the flour dealer that he can pay his debt, and withdraw his note from the bank, with the bank-notes; and it is enough for the people that they can purchase flour with the bank-notes, on as good terms as with money. The process would be the same, whether the bank was suspended or not.

A dealer in cotton may give his note to an American shipper for £1000 for cotton; the Liverpool dealer may sell it to a Manchester manufacturer, taking his note for £1050; it may be manufactured into a variety of goods, and sold for £1500 to a merchant of London, for which his note is taken. If these individual notes were all discounted at the Bank of England, and the proceeds placed to their credit respectively, it is obvious, without pursuing the cotton further, that the Liverpool dealer would be in funds to pay the £1000 to the importer of the cotton, and the manufacturer would be in funds to pay the £1050 to the dealer; and these payments would neither require gold, nor be less effectual than if made in gold. The substance of the transaction is, that the first purchaser of the cotton paid his debt by selling it, and the manufacturer did the same thing. This is, in fact, the main process of the credit system. Men purchase, and give their promises to pay; they sell, and take promises to pay; the bank enables them to apply those they take in payment of those they have given. Commodities, in the large transactions of business, pay for commodities; and the credit system is that by which the books are kept, the securities taken, and the payments finally adjusted. The currency furnished by the bank affords a facility of constant use and application in the retail business, which is thus connected with the larger transactions: that is, the breaking up the larger notes of the wholesale operations, by exchanging them at bank for notes or deposits, furnishes the currency by which business in detail is carried on with increased facility and despatch.

A very remarkable controversy arose, about midway of the long bank suspension of England. The great demand for gold, for the military expedition of the continent, exhibited itself, in 1810, in an apparent difference between gold and bank-notes, of about 15 to 20 per cent. This was regarded as intolerable by those who were afterwards called Bullionists. The subject was brought before Parliament, and gave rise to the celebrated Bullion Report attributed to Francis Horner and William Huskisson, both young men of eminent abilities and promise, but not so well versed in the subject of banking and finance as some of the merchants and bankers whose opinions they disregarded in their Report. The Report insisted strongly upon the depreciation of bank-notes as the cause of the difference between gold and bank-notes. The subject was ably discussed in the House of Commons. The decision of the House was against the resumption of specie payments. The discussion was continued afterwards for many years, in journals, pamphlets and books, with great earnestness, talent and practical knowledge. It is not even now settled to the satisfaction of all who take an interest in the subject; Bullionists and Anti-bullionists stand, to this day, arrayed against each other, with as little appearance of agreeing as they exhibited forty-five years ago. The question is, in fact, as interesting as it was then, and the discussion as instructive. As usual in such cases, there was much truth and soundness in the statements and arguments on both sides.

On a view of the whole controversy at this remote period, and from this side of the Atlantic, where there has been no excitement on the subject, it strikes us that the advantage in this dispute is with the Anti-bullionists, who insisted that gold had risen in price, and that there was no considerable depreciation of bank-notes. The Bullionists, believing that all prices are expressed in gold, and believing, with Locke, that a pound of gold or silver must always be worth a pound of gold or silver, and that, therefore, the apparent variation in price of gold was, in fact, only a variation in the price of bank-notes, it was only necessary for them to exhibit the table of the prices of gold expressed in paper, to prove their case. From this point men could not be driven, who could not conceive of gold rising and falling in price. They did not know that prices are never expressed either in gold or silver, nor in bank-notes, but always in money of account, which is capable of expressing and registering the fluctuations in the price of gold or silver, as of cotton or wheat. This fact alone disturbs the main position of the Bullionists, and compels them to look elsewhere for the solution of the difficulty. According to their own views, the depreciation of bank-notes should have been expressed in the language of trade, as so many per cent. below par. Instead of this, gold was quoted as the fluctuating article, and this clearly evinced the commercial opinion. We subjoin a table of the prices of gold relied upon to prove the depreciation; and we add, in two other columns, the price of silver, and the quantity of circulating bank-notes. We think the table, thus constructed, proves incontestably that there could have been no such depreciation of bank-notes as has been alleged. All the circumstances show that there was an extraordinary demand for gold; it would have been strange if there had not been; and this table proves it, for there was no such variation in the price of silver. The highest authority in England on the subject of prices,[1] after a careful examination of all the facts, decides that there was no such fluctuation or rise in the price of other articles of commerce, as to

[1] Tooke's History of Prices and of the State of the Circulation from 1793 to 1837, vol. ii., p. 350.

denote any depreciation in bank-notes. This examination extended to over forty different articles, of which tables are given of the prices from 1782 to 1838, and is, probably, as thorough and reliable as any ever constructed.

DATE.	Price of Standard Gold in bars, per oz.			Price of Standard Silver per oz.		CIRCULATION.
	£	s.	d.	s.	d.	£
1797	3	17	6	5	3½	10,394,000
1798	3	17	10½	5	1	12,637,000
1799	3	17	9	5	1	13,174,000
1800	4	5	0	5	1	15,946,000
1801	4	4	0	5	1	15,384,000
1802	4	3	6	5	8¾	16,141,000
1803	4	3	6	5	7½	15,646,000
1804	4	0	0	5	7½	17,110,000
1805	4	0	0	5	9½	17,134,000
1806	4	0	0	5	9½	19,378,000
1807	4	0	0	5	9½	18,314,000
1808	4	0	0	5	8	17,649,000
1809	4	10	0	5	8	19,058,000
1810	4	10	0	5	8	22,906,000
1811	4	15	6	6	2	23,323,000
1812	4	15	0	6	2	23,217,000
1813	4	15	0	6	2	24,019,000
1814	4	19	6	6	4	26,584,000
1815	4	9	0	5	11½	27,254,000
1816	4	0	6	5	4	26,885,000
1817	3	19	6	5	1	28,470,000
1818	3	19	6	5	4½	26,986,000
1819	3	19	6	5	4½	25,139,000
1820	3	17	10½	5	0¾	23,891,000
1821	3	17	10½	4	11¼	22,039,000

CHAPTER XVI.

THE BANKS OF SCOTLAND.

The Bank of Scotland promptly chartered, and its whole plan prescribed in advance — John Holland's account of it — Contrast with the origin of the Bank of England — The founders of the Scottish Bank merchants who avoided relations with the Government — They looked to it as a means of economizing the use of money — Bank-notes — Trouble with the Royal Bank — Suspension — Modes of relief — Little loss of credit — Identified with the mass of the people by receiving small deposits, and paying interest for them — Forty banks, and 340 branches — Harmony of action — English prejudices and Scotch scorn — Cash credits in account a principal feature — Mode of operation — Contrasts with the English system — The Scotch system equally effective, and more safe — Failures of banks few, and not disastrous — Suspension of 1797 in England has no effect in Scotland — Report in the House of Lords, 1826 — Report in the Commons — The system not cordially approved in England — One pound notes — Discussions in England and Scotland — Lessons for England on currency — Sir Walter Scott on the level of gold — Different modes of regarding the subjects in England and Scotland — Scotch Banks the pride of the people — W. Chambers' distrust of the system — Explanations in reply.

THE first public bank in Scotland was established by act of the Scottish Parliament, in 1695, previous to the consolidation of the two governments. It was suggested by the same William Patterson who projected the Bank of England, but seems to have been indebted for its shape and constitution to John Holland, who, with other merchants of London, were participants, with men of capital in Edinburgh, in this enterprise. Its plan was deliberately drawn up in advance, and its privileges and restraints distinctly marked. The Bank of England crawled into existence, being wormed through the English Parliament under cover of an act in reference to "Duties upon the Tonnage of Ships, and upon Beer, Ale and other liquors." The Scotch

Bank had a free birth, and found favor with that class of English merchants who disliked the Bank of England. Holland has given an account of his agency in bringing forth the Bank of Scotland, in a pamphlet bearing this ominous title: — "The Ruine of the Bank of England and all public Credit inevitable," (1715). Holland was only induced to engage in this scheme, by being assured that he could have an "Act of Parliament on his own conditions." The plan drawn up by him has proved the foundation of one of the most successful banking systems which has yet been tried. Prominent among its provisions is the prohibition to lend to the King. The Bank of England originated in a loan of its whole capital to the government, and began its actual business by lending its whole credit in the same way — a measure which resulted in its being made and continued a great financial agent of every administration, from that day forward. Mr. Holland did not appreciate the necessity of such an agent, nor comprehend the propriety of its being associated with a bank, or with the business of banking. The readiness to establish a bank in Scotland is seen in the fact that, whilst in England the shareholders lent the government £1,200,000 for an exclusive monopoly of twelve years, the Bank of Scotland was allowed a monopoly of twenty-one years, without any bonus or favor to the government.

The Bank of England was moulded by those circumstances in which it had its origin, and which accompanied the earlier years of its history. Its whole subsequent history has a double aspect — one, its connection with the government — the other, its relations with commerce and individuals. This double history proves, whatever may be alleged to the contrary, that the uniting these two kinds of business in one great banking business is inconsistent neither with the true system of banking, nor with the true system of finance. That the Bank of England has, in many ways, inflicted its full share of evil upon the people of England is well known, and at times these mischiefs may have been caused by the connection of the bank with the government. But whilst such evils are seen, felt and remembered, the advantages of the connection are neither observed nor understood.[1] The founders of the Bank of Scotland were chiefly merchants, who had their eyes turned exclusively to the advantages of banking for their own class. They were of that class which had so strongly advocated institutions of credit in England, previous to the establishment of the Bank of England. They were men who knew well the functions and practice of the Banks of Venice, Genoa and Amsterdam, and the modes of payment at the Fairs on the continent. They believed in the efficacy, safety and propriety of circulating credit, although their ideas of the mode of carrying it out may have been far from definite or harmonious. They fully understood that, to a certain extent, to be determined in the progress of business, a system of credit could be made to supply absolutely the place of money. They wished to avail themselves of that economical device as far as it was applicable. The object was not to supplant or find a substitute for the precious metals, but simply to effect the ends of trade, to every possible extent, without them, knowing they must intervene and be employed whenever the exigencies of payment required.

The Bank of Scotland issued bank-notes of several denominations, from the beginning of its business, from £100 down to £1, and even less; but as we have already dwelt largely on the functions of that form of currency, and shall have occasion to do so again, in treating of the banks of the United States, we shall make them the occasion of only incidental remark, in speaking of the banks of Scotland. In one aspect of their use in Scotland, the general observations we have made respecting them apply; in another, their use is modified by that peculiar feature of the banks of Scotland which distinguishes them from all others. An exhibition of that feature will show how bank-notes operate or circulate, in reference to it.

The Bank of Scotland, with all the care and skill of its early management, did not escape a signal reverse. Having a monopoly of twenty-one years when established, its directors undertook to extend that monopoly beyond the time, by extinguishing

---

[1] We shall specially advert to this subject in a Chapter on Public Payments.

the Royal Bank of Scotland—a rival which threatened to be of sufficient importance to divide the business of the country with them. This narrow policy was met by a measure, on the part of the Royal Bank, which forced the Bank of Scotland to suspend payments in 1727.[1] Although this was a serious affair for that bank, it was surmounted without any great diminution of its credit or business. The measure of relief from which it derived most benefit shows the confidence of the public. It issued notes payable at six months after date, bearing five per cent. interest, and with these redeemed a portion of its circulation of £5 notes and upwards. This succeeded so well, that it was applied, a few years afterwards, to the notes of £1 and below that amount; and subsequently, upon emergency, it was for a time resorted to by all the banks of Scotland, until it generated abuses, which being the subject of much complaint, the system was abandoned.

Whilst the Bank of England, from its first conception, was identified with the government, the Bank of Scotland, and those which succeeded it, identified themselves with the whole body of the people, from the laborer who could save five pounds to the richest merchants and manufacturers. They became at once, and have continued to be, the savings banks of the poor but industrious classes. The banks paid one per cent. below the current rate of interest for these deposits, and returned them on demand, or according to stipulation. These savings of the poor help largely to make up the vast sum of deposits which characterizes the banks of Scotland. One important result of this has been to give the benefits of these savings to the general cus-

[1] The Royal Bank had obtained the use of £20,000 of public money, which was to be distributed in Scotland. The first use which was made of it was to arrest the jealous career of the Bank of Scotland. From that time to this, the Scotch banks have been noted for harmonious co-operation. It is asserted by some writers of good authority, that this proceeding of the bank was wholly unprovoked, and that it used the public money which good-fortune threw in its way, to humble and injure an institution which had such an advantage of them in credit, and in an established business, that it was thought expedient to bring some discredit upon it, as the best means of gaining business.

tomers of the banks, instead of their being invested in the public debt, or lent upon mortgage, as in England. No doubt this has contributed greatly to that progress in wealth and productive industry which has so much distinguished Scotland for more than a century. It had another good effect, in begetting that care, caution and prudent management for which the banks of Scotland have so well-founded a reputation. This acceptance of small deposits, and paying interest for them, had also the effect of giving the poor a deep concern in the same banks in which were the deposits of the rich, who were owners also of the stock. The interests of both classes were thus bound up in the same banks, subject to the same management and the same vicissitudes. The prosperity of the banks was the security of the poor depositor, and a guarantee of both his interest and his principal. A large circulation was regarded by the poor as not only beneficial, by making currency abundant, but as evidence of the success of the banks. That jealousy of banks so visible both in England and in the United States, does not exist in Scotland; and yet the proportion of banks in Scotland to the population is far less than in England and the United States: far less, if we regard the principal banks; but these have been so favored in Scotland, that 40 banks have been permitted to establish 340 branches: so that Scotland has 380 bank offices for a population of less than 3,000,000; these 380 banks, emanating from only about 40 heads, are not, however, like 380 rival establishments struggling for superiority, and aiming to supplant each other in business, if not to crush each other as competitors. There is a harmony and unity of object among the heads, which is diffused among all the branches, which is seen in the regularity and steadiness of their operations, and which is felt throughout the whole community. No country enjoys a paper currency so free from fluctuations in quantity, as that of Scotland: yet so little are the advantages of the Scotch system known and appreciated elsewhere, that there has been a constant itch in England to reform the banks of Scotland, and bring them nearer to English ideas of currency. The Scotch system is so contrary to the notions prevailing in England upon the subject of money and currency, that some of the statesmen and currency-mongers there endure, with bad grace, the standing refutation which the Scotch banks furnish of their opinions. They regard their success as exceptional and accidental; and, but for personal as well as currency prejudices, they would prefer giving the credit to the good management of the banks, rather than permit any portion of it to stand for the benefit of the system. The English people do not understand the Scotch system, but the Scotch people do understand the English system; and having seen the terrible inflictions it has visited upon England, and from which they are nearly exempt, they return the officious kindness which would disturb their system, operating to their entire satisfaction, and assimilate it to the English system, which is fraught with dangers, and is not even popular at home, with mockery and scorn.[1] The struggles on this subject, in Parliament and out of it, have been many; but in all, the Scots have come off victorious, having, in not a few instances, extorted the admiration of those who, perhaps for the first time, were fully made to understand the effectiveness and safety of Scotch banking.

The chief distinction, however, of the Scottish system of banking is found in the cash credits granted by the bank, and which we designate cash credits in account. These are peculiar to Scotland; and although they do not constitute the chief business of the bank, they no doubt exercise a controlling influence, and give a special character to the whole practice of the Scotch banks. It is estimated that there are twenty thousand of these accounts, covering a sum of five millions sterling. As the actual deposits in the Scotch banks amount to thirty millions sterling, the cash credits bear nominally but a small proportion to this item of deposits. The importance of the cash credits is to be

---

[1] Sir Walter Scott compares this persistent effort to reform the Scotch banks to that of an eccentric but hospitable Scotch laird, who forced the guests who remained with him over-night, to take one of Anderson's pills before retiring — a practice which he had long followed, and which he was determined every one else should follow, who came within reach of his kindness. "*Only one leetle Anderson.*" — *Malachi Malagrowther, Letter I.*, p. 29.

considered with reference to their functions and activity, rather than their amount. A cash credit is an account opened by a bank with a customer for an amount from £100 to £1000, which is placed not to his credit, but at his disposal. The applicant for this accommodation, which is only granted by the directors of the principal bank, is strictly examined as to his business, means and prospects, and the credit is accorded upon his giving two or three sureties in a bond for the amount of the credit. This bond is so drawn, as to cover any liability to the bank for the amount, whether drawn upon the credit as drawer or endorser of bills.[1] No limit is placed to the use of the credit,

---

[1] The form of keeping a cash credit account may be seen at page 76 of the Report from the Lords' Committee, on the circulation of notes under £5, in Scotland and Ireland, printed in April, 1827. The form of the bond is as follows: —

"We, A. B. C. D. and E. F., considering that the bank has agreed to allow us a standing credit to the extent of one thousand pounds sterling upon a cash credit account, to be kept in the name of one of us, the said A. B., in the books of the said bank, and to be operated upon by him, and may also discount or purchase bills, whereon the name of the said A. B., or the firm of any company of which he is a partner, may stand as a drawer, acceptor or endorser, and that upon condition of our granting these presents: *Therefore* we, the said A. B. C. D. and E. F., hereby bind and oblige ourselves, as full debtors and co-obligants, and our respective heirs, executors, and successors whomsoever, all conjunctly and severally, to content and pay to the said bank the foresaid sum of one thousand pounds sterling, or such part or parts thereof as the said A. B., or any person or persons having his letter or other written authority, shall value for or draw out by orders or drafts on the said bank, or its manager, cashier, or any of its officers at Edinburgh, or any of its agents, cashiers, or other officers elsewhere, in virtue of the foresaid credit: and also such sum or sums of money as the said A. B. shall stand engaged for or be indebted, resting or owing to the said bank on account of any bills discounted or held by it, whereon his name as an individual, or the firm of any company of which he is a partner, shall stand as drawer, acceptor, or endorser, or any sum or sums for which he or they shall stand engaged or indebted to the said bank by acceptances, endorsations, letters of credit, guarantees, or in any other manner of way whatsoever, and all or any of which obligations as aforesaid the said bank shall be entitled to place to the debit of the said account and of the obligants hereto, at any time before this bond is discharged and delivered up, and that without intimation to any of the said parties, but not exceeding in

it is terminable, at the pleasure of either party, by payment and discontinuance on the part of the customer, or by withdrawal of the accommodation on the part of the bank. But it is rare

---

all the said principal sum of one thousand pounds sterling, and interest due thereon; and that at any time when the same shall be demanded after three months from the date hereof, together with the legal interest thereof, from the time or times of the respective advances until the same be repaid, with a fifth part more of the said principal sum due of penalty in case of failure. And it is hereby specially conditioned and agreed to, that a stated account, made out from the books of the said bank, and signed by one of its accountants, shall be sufficient to constitute a charge or balance against us and each of us, whereof no suspension shall pass at the instance of any of us, except on consignation only of the sum due thereon. And it is hereby declared that there is nothing hereby meant to supersede or vacate the security which the said bank already holds, or may hold, over any shares of stock of the said bank and profits thereon, belonging or that may belong to any of us for any advances under this bond or otherwise, it being always in the power of the said bank to appropriate or allow of the disposal in any way whatever of all or any of the shares of said stock; and the said parties to this bond hereby declare that they have no lien over the said shares, or any right to insist upon the application of the same to payment of any debts to be hereby contracted. And further, the said parties agree that the obligation hereby come under shall remain in full force in the same manner and to the same extent as if such shares of stock had never belonged to any of the parties hereto, and it being hereby agreed that the said bank may allow credit on the said shares, or the same to be sold, and the price to be paid to the seller, or may apply the same to any other purpose according as it shall deem expedient, being bound in the latter case to account only to the person or persons to whom the shares belonged.

"And further declaring, as the said cash credit account is to be in the name of the said A. B., and he is to conduct the transactions thereon, it is hereby especially provided and agreed to, that all communications on the part of the bank, regarding either the management by him of the accounts or repayment of the balance or balances which may become due thereon, shall or may be made to us, the other parties, through the said A. B., with whom the said bank shall be at liberty to make any arrangements, by affording further opportunities for better management of the accounts according to the rules of the said bank, if deviated from, or in any other way required, or by giving time for repayment of the balance or balances thereof, without any direct application to or concurrence by us the said C. D. and E. F. on the subject, until the said bank shall consider this necessary for a final settlement. And it shall also have the power, without consultation with or consent by us, to compromise with or give time to any of

that a termination takes place, except in the case of persons retiring from business; for the advantage is so great to each of the parties, that both strive to make it mutually beneficial, and to prolong it during a whole business life. A cash credit is a perpetual resource to the holder for any sum within the amount. He draws upon it at any moment, as upon a deposit, for the sum required, and pays interest upon the sums thus drawn, and returns at his convenience any sum in his hands, upon which he receives one per cent. interest less than the rate on sums drawn out. It is the advantage of the holder of the credit to deposit his money as quickly as possible, as a regular interest account is kept with him: he is charged with interest, say at five per cent. upon all he has taken, and credited with interest at four per cent. for all he has deposited. At convenient times, generally twice a year, the account is made up and balanced, and a new account is opened. A credit account in Scotland is, therefore, literally a loan of credit on the part of the bank, which credit is to be paid for in proportion as it is used. When a bill of exchange is discounted by a bank in England, the proceeds are placed to the credit of the person obtaining the discount as so much money, to be drawn for at pleasure; and this is supposed to be discounting business-paper. The cash credit of a

---

the parties on the bills discounted or held by it as aforesaid, we, the said C. D. and E. F. having always full opportunity afforded us by the said bank, whenever we, or either of us, wish and apply for the same, to see any of the transactions and state of the said cash credit account, and other transactions of the said A. B. in which we may be interested by the obligations of this bond; and the said bank shall only be bound to attend to any instructions we may give on the subject in writing, and acknowledged in writing to have been received. It being hereby expressly declared that all the parties to this bond are *pari passu* co-obligants to the said bank; and that all and each of us are equally bound to it, and shall not be entitled to plead that any of us are the cautioners for the other; and we, the said A. B. and E. F. consent to the registration hereof, and of the foresaid stated accounts, in the books of council and session, that letters of horning on six days' charge, and all execution necessary, may pass on a decree to be interponed then and thereto, in form as officers, and for that purpose we constitute, &c. In witness whereof these presents, written upon this sheet of stamped paper, by our procurators, &c."

Scotch bank has no reference to special transactions of business, but is an open credit, to be employed as occasion demands. In England, the bank which deals in promissory notes and bills of exchange, is dealing in paper which represents business transactions which are past; in Scotland, the bank opens credits for its customers, with reference to business which is to come. In Scotland, the banks give their customers a credit which helps their standing, and upon which they can draw for the purpose of payment, whenever there is need. The theory of the English banks is, that the currency must follow, and be controlled in quantity, by the business transactions which go before. The theory of the Scotch banks is, that these business transactions being all managed by men of business, who decide according to the exigencies of industry and trade what will promote their private interest, and meet the wants of the people, it must prove an important aid to men thus engaged to supply them, in advance of the progress of their business, with a credit upon which they can draw at pleasure. The English doctrine is, that men must do all their business, in the first instance, upon their own credit; and the banks may then deal in the evidences or securities to which the business has given origin: the Scottish notion is, that aid should be extended to men of trade and industry in advance of their transactions, and as an element in their plans of business. In England, they think this will lead to over-trading, by the stimulus it affords to so large a class of dealers: in Scotland, long experience has taught them that this English apprehension is wholly groundless. They know that the dealers who enjoy these cash credits are so immediately brought under the supervision of the banks, and their own sureties, that they are, perhaps, the most prudent and safe men of business in the world.[1]

The system of banking in Scotland has, by a long and steady

[1] A witness before Parliament, in 1826, said:—"I literally have hardly ever heard of a bad debt by cash accounts. The Bank of Scotland, I am sure, lost hardly anything in an amount of receipts and payments of hundreds of millions. They may have lost a few hundred pounds in a century."

experience, vindicated itself against objections raised upon English theories; and its superiority in operation over the practice of English banking is so manifest, as to extort commendations of the strongest kind from Parliamentary Committees. When the necessity of reform in English banking was admitted, and measures of reform were adopted, it was determined that no change was needful in Scotland.[1]

We have shown, in the chapters on bank-notes and on deposits, that the fund by means of which nearly all the payments of commerce were effected, was derived from the proceeds of bills of exchange and promissory notes discounted by the banks. These proceeds take the shape of bank-notes or deposits, but chiefly the latter, and in that form become more available in payment than any other currency. We have shown how this took place: that the banks purchased the paper discounted by the issue of these credits, and that they could, therefore, receive the credits in payment of the securities: that these credits could circulate for the average time of the paper discounted, before they would be absorbed by the banks in payment of the paper as it matured: that, by means of this circulation, an immense amount of payments was effected, both in and out of the banks: that the demand for this currency, for payment of debts to the bank, gave it full employment, and fully maintained its nominal value: that this system of discounts and currency enabled men of business to employ the paper they take in paying the paper they give: and that, as the debts of trade are in a large degree mutual, this system is, to that extent, a plan of adjustment by which mutual debts are set-off, without being brought face to face in one account.

By this system, the basis of the bank-notes and deposits is the merchandise purchased with the discounted paper, and the punctuality and ability of the debtors; the banks having, at all times, a greater demand on the public than the public has on the banks, with this difference, however, that the claim of the

---

[1] Extracts from Parliamentary Reports of 1826 will be given, in this chapter, to prove this.

public on the banks is payable on demand, whilst the claim of the banks on the public is on paper, averaging a period of two or three months, which gives the public, in periods of financial difficulty, a crushing advantage over the banks. This advantage, however, is one which causes, in such times, a destructive reaction on the public. Banks and their customers are alike crushed by this system, in seasons of alarm or commercial revulsion.

The Scottish system of banking, so far as it rests upon cash credits, has some very different aspects from the system referred to above. If the banks of Scotland have granted five millions sterling in these credits, they are liable to be drawn upon for that amount, at the pleasure of the persons holding the credits; but to be drawn upon only for their bank-notes, for that is the agreement. If the holders were to demand gold, it could be refused, and the accounts could be closed. The banks, in fact, pay their notes only to those who draw upon these credits. If the notes were drawn, and the gold demanded for them, the banks could not refuse; but they can, at pleasure, close the credit accounts, and demand immediate payment of all that has been drawn out upon them. The banks of Scotland have, then, an actual practical demand upon the public for an amount as large as the public have on them, with the advantage to the banks, that their claim is all in their own hands, and can be made in a few hours, whilst the demand of the public on the banks is scattered over a wide surface, and cannot be concentrated upon them for many days. The holder of a cash credit in Scotland is at all times at the mercy of the bank, which can afford to be liberal, because it is never in danger.

To a considerable extent, banking in Scotland is conducted as elsewhere, and it is susceptible of employing, and does employ, every good device of English or American banking. In Scotland, the fund employed in payment of debts is not derived, chiefly as in England and the United States, from the proceeds of discounted paper, but, in a large measure, from the open cash credits. This fund is not based upon actual business transactions, or upon commodities which have actually changed hands in the channels of trade. It is a facility of payment granted in advance by the banks. The holders of these credits, in the progress of their business, have the choice of paying for what they purchase in bank-notes drawn out upon their credits, or of taking the longest credit they can obtain, and then paying in notes drawn from the banks upon their credits. Individual credits are as common in Scotland, and perhaps more so, than elsewhere. It is usual there to take acceptances for small amounts sold on credit, and to collect them through the banks. The facility of payment furnished by the cash credits makes renewals of credit less common, and greatly aids punctuality, especially in the lower branches of trade. They are a resource, and a means of payment, ever ready at the command of the holder. The notes issued upon them perform the same functions of payment in circulation which the notes of other banks do. If, in England, the customer of a bank is denied a discount, the proceeds of which would have been employed in paying a debt, and that debt remains unpaid, a circulation of notes is arrested or prevented, with very disastrous results for many individuals. One hundred pounds thus put in circulation in bank-notes or deposits may, in a few days, pay £1000; but, stopped at the beginning, it may cause to the persons interested in that circulation a loss of perhaps several hundred pounds. The bank in England acts, in refusing a discount, with especial reference to its own position and interests, and perhaps with necessary prudence. The banks of Scotland, anticipating the friction of this separate movement of business in the banks, and business out of the banks, have, as a preventive, advanced credits to their customers for a large sum, upon which they can rely, and for the use of which they have to make no special application to the banks. Thus a large fund, applicable for payments, and subject to be drawn as a deposit or paid out in bank-notes, is placed by the Scottish banks at the discretion of their customers, and through them at the service of the public, for which no application is required, and about the use of which there is no uncertainty. That these credits, thus employed, prevent a vast amount of currency friction, is demonstrated by the undeniable success of Scotch banking, and the great progress of that country in wealth. We have already adverted to the safety of the debts arising upon this practice of the banks: this safety does not rest wholly upon the special securities taken when the credits are granted.

If the banks of Scotland have granted five millions sterling of credits, from two to three millions would, according to the average of their use, be drawn from the banks all the time: that is, the average amount out of the banks would be about that proportion. For each sum drawn by any holder of a credit, we may assume that he either paid a debt incurred for property previously purchased, or made a purchase of commodities just received. Thus, the two or three millions sterling at any time actually drawn upon the amount of credits, have been just as much employed in actual business as if they were the proceeds of promissory notes or bills of exchange; commodities have been purchased or paid for by the amount thus drawn. The commodities thus obtained are the means which the holders of the credits rely upon to secure the amount of currency needful to make good their payments; for, though they are not bound to any day for restoring the amounts drawn upon their credits, they are required to keep the account active, as the evidence of a progressive and safe business. They enjoy this great advantage, that if they sell a commodity within a few days after the purchase and receive the cash, they can return the amount to the bank at once, and save all but one per cent. of the interest incurred. By the English mode there is a much greater expenditure of interest; for a note once discounted, the interest for the whole time of the paper is deducted, and is not to be recovered. For the amount upon the cash credits, the debtors are not under the strong necessity of paying at any particular day; but they are placed under incentives of interest and prudence, which, if they do not enforce payment upon a day fixed, are sufficient to secure prompt attention: the credit account must be active, and interest must be saved. These motives are found so powerful, that the credits are not abused by being converted into standing loans; the banks of Scotland are not forced to abolish cash credits, because both the day of drawing and the day of payment are at the discretion of their customers. They are fully secured from the abuse of this discretion by their power to close the account, and demand payment of the amounts drawn, at their pleasure.

The Scottish banks have ultimate security for their cash credits, in the bonds they take for that purpose with substantial names; but the real basis for the issues of notes made upon these credits, in the commercial or banking aspects of the subject, is the merchandise or commodities which the notes thus drawn have paid for or purchased: with these, the debtors can obtain currency to replace the amounts drawn. The two or three millions of notes thus drawn upon the credits, and for which the banks are liable to the public, have been exchanged for commodities, or something for which there is a demand, and these commodities in the hands of the debtors form a real and active means of repaying the banks. They form the true banking basis; for the bond with its sureties is but a precaution against dishonesty and abuse, which is but rarely resorted to for payment. If it were not rare that the sureties in these cash credit bonds were called upon for payment, the system would soon be discontinued. It is this real basis of commodities in trade, and movements in industry, which sustains the cash credits in their benefits both to the banks and their customers—which redeems the notes of the one, and pays the debts of the others.

The demand for bank-notes in Scotland, notwithstanding the discretion allowed in returning amounts drawn upon the credits, is still great enough, for reasons already stated, to maintain their value: this is proved by their usurping the entire circulation in Scotland.[1] The people seem to desire nothing better than the one-pound notes of their own banks; and all the attempts, on the part of Parliament, to reform their currency, and introduce

[1] A sovereign in Scotland, according to the remark of a recent writer, "is seldom seen, except in the card-purse of an old maid, or in the cabinet of some recluse virtuoso: and, in one instance, a bank was established, whose foundation was a large amount of guineas; but they remained in the bank undiminished, and were only taken out to be exchanged for sovereigns at the time of the new coinage." —*Lawson's History of Banking*, page 435.

sovereigns instead of their one-pound notes, has been resisted by the whole nation. The circulation of bank-notes in Scotland is, no doubt, quickened by the cash credit system, which is regarded by the banks as one of the most efficient means of enlarging and keeping up their circulation. The average amount of bank-notes in circulation in Scotland is about four millions of pounds sterling; the amount annually exchanged between the banks, at the semi-weekly clearing at Edinburgh, is one hundred millions; and as this does not include the exchanges of banks in the same city, or the movement of the notes in and out of the respective banks, and their branches, it indicates a very active circulation, involving a large aggregate in the whole movement.

In England, public men have spent much time in discussing the questions, whether banks should be governed, in the amount of their issues, by the foreign exchanges, or by the fluctuations in quantity of bullion and coin: leading men have long believed that the banks should establish, as a criterion of their circulation, one or the other. In Scotland, the principle has long since been adopted, that the issues of the banks should be governed by the course of domestic trade, and the legitimate business of the customers of the banks: the banks there look upon the movements of specie, and the fluctuations of the exchanges, as proceeding from causes too special and peculiar to be admitted as indications of what should determine their whole policy, or affect the whole business of a country. In regard to the rate of interest, the Scottish banks have, in some degree, been guided by the rates in London; and they have, therefore, raised the rates upon occasions of premium in the London money-market, and this for two reasons — one, because it was a time in which they could increase their profits; and another, that they might not be troubled with applications for loans from England. The rate of interest is not so much employed, as in England, to reduce their issues; for, in times of pressure, that never was the course pursued towards their regular customers. They continue their usual advances to their customers, through every commercial pressure and disturbance.

The superior working of the Scottish banking system, whether judged by its history or its present position, and however reluctantly the admission may be made, is incontestable. But few failures of banks take place in Scotland,[1] and these have, for the most part, been disastrous only to the stockholders. The banks of Scotland have never inflicted any heavy losses upon the people; they have never, directly nor indirectly, spread disaster and ruin over the whole community in which they are placed; they have never contracted their issues so rapidly, as seriously to injure their customers; they have never suffered any general discredit, by which their notes have been thrown back upon them, to the injury or the cessation of business from impeded circulation. When the Bank of England was obliged, in 1797, to throw itself upon the protection of the government, and accept from the Privy Council an order not to pay specie, the banks of Scotland asked no such order, and made no change in their mode of business. Yet there was no run for gold upon the Scotch banks. This is fully acknowledged in the Report of a Select Committee to the House of Lords, in 1826. "It is proved by the evidence, and by the documents, that the banks of Scotland, whether chartered joint-stock companies, or private establishments, have, for more than a century, exhibited a stability which the committee believe to be unexampled in the history of banking; that they supported themselves, from 1797 to 1812, without any protection from the restriction by which the Bank of England, and that of Ireland, were relieved from cash payments: that there was little demand for gold during the late embarrassments in the circulation [in 1825–6]; and that, in the whole period of their establishment, there are not more than two or three instances of bankruptcy. As, during the whole of this period, a large portion of their issues consisted almost entirely of notes not exceeding £1, or £1 1*s*., there is the strongest reason for concluding that, as far as respects the banks of Scotland, the issue of paper of that denomination has been found compatible with the highest degree of solidity; and that there is not,

---

[1] Only five or six in a century. Not more than two have failed to pay their deposits and their circulation. The one of 1857 may prove to be one of the worst.

therefore, while they are conducted on the present system, sufficient ground for proposing any alteration, with the view of adding to a solidity which has so long been sufficiently established."[1] The committee bear, in the same report, emphatic testimony to the advantage of cash credits, and also to the custom of receiving deposits of small sums, and paying on the same about one per cent. below the current rate of interest.

The testimony on which the report is founded is printed at length, and we look upon it as quite strong enough to extort this favorable opinion, even from those who regarded the Scottish system with no friendly eye. Equally strong and more fully detailed statements, favorable to the Scotch banks, were made in the same year by the witnesses called before the Select Committee of the House of Commons — testimony which drew from that committee an equally decided opinion, that the Scottish system needed no present reform. The latter committee, of which Sir Robert Peel was chairman, after stating that they regarded the chief inquiry submitted to them to be, whether Scotland should be permitted to retain her circulation of bank-notes between £1 and £5, in the face of the fact that England, after 1829, would have no bank-notes under £5, say that, upon the evidence submitted to them, they "cannot advise that a law should now be passed, prohibiting, from a period to be therein determined, the future issue in Scotland of notes under £5." They further say that they are "unwilling, without stronger proof of necessity, to incur the risk of deranging, from any cause whatever, a system admirably calculated, in their opinion, to economize the use of capital, to excite and cherish a spirit of useful enterprise, and even to promote the moral habits of the people, by the direct inducements it holds out to the maintenance of a character for industry, integrity and prudence."[2]

It is quite evident, however, that all these strong expressions in favor of the Scottish banking system are made, in England, with great mental reservation. They look upon it as unsound in theory, and practicable only in Scotland. Whilst

---

[1] See pages 3 and 4 of the Lords' Report, 1826.

[2] Commons' Report, same year, pp. 9–11.

they do not question the testimony of the witnesses, they remain unconvinced of the general merits of a system upon which they bestow such strong special commendation. Both committees betray great apprehension that the one-pound notes of Scotland will find their way into England, and, to some extent, displace the metallic circulation under five pounds, for which they had made provision there; and they both intimate that they would prefer the prohibition of the one-pound notes in Scotland, rather than permit them any circulation in England. They admit that the Bank of England suspended in 1797, after having, since 1777, issued nothing less than five-pound notes; whilst the Scottish banks did not suspend, upon a circulation of one-pound notes. They had reached the conclusion, in England, that the currency under five pounds should be gold; and from that conclusion Scottish experience could not drive them.[1] In Scotland, the views of the people are fully settled, on the subject of the currency: their system, which, by the admission of all, has worked wonders for the progress of Scotland, is one of which they only ask the undisturbed enjoyment. In England, on the topics of money, currency and banking, nothing is settled; and showers of books and pamphlets are poured out upon occasion of every commercial crisis, every renewal of the bank charter, and upon every public event, by which the attention of the people is strongly drawn to the subject. In Scotland, the topic is seldom the subject of agitation, unless as connected with some of the movements or projects of reform. In England, there is a prevailing prejudice against a paper currency, although it is largely employed; and a preference for a gold currency pervades all classes. In Scotland, the preference for a paper currency is as strongly marked, in all the channels of business. Neither the rebellion of 1715, nor 1745, nor the disturbances following upon the French Revolution of 1793 and 1797, which stopped the Bank of England, nor the grand crash among the English banks in 1825, could alarm the Scotch people, or produce a run upon their banks. No currency of modern times has

[1] English pride refused the lesson; English fairness let the Scotch banks alone.

been more effective, and less fluctuating in value and quantity, than that of Scotland. This is expressly admitted by committees of both Houses of the British Parliament; it is, in fact, undeniable, and yet is regarded in England as proving nothing — establishing nothing beyond this, that the people of Scotland ought to be allowed to enjoy it so long as the Scotch bank-notes can be kept on their own side of the Tweed. We refer to this, to show in what a narrow spirit the subject is considered in England.

There are two great lessons in currency, tendered by long experience and unquestioned facts, from which the English people have failed to draw the instruction they afford — the banking system of Scotland, and the history of the Bank of England from 1797 to 1822. A thorough, able, and honest examination of these great lessons is yet to come from the friends of the English system. We should not say English system; there is no system in England, unless it be that of the Bank of England; all else is unsettled, both in general policy and private opinion. There is a prevalent idea among statesmen and writers upon money, that there should be a broad basis of money or gold coin, under and as a support to the paper circulation; and it is this idea which banishes all bank-notes under five pounds. Upon this another opinion has more recently grown up, and become a law in the act of 1844, that a paper currency, to be perfect, should fluctuate as a gold currency would do, if it were the sole medium of payment. To the mind of a Scotch banker, a greater absurdity could not be presented in as many words. He would say:—"What! when a demand springs up for gold, in consequence of some foreign war, must we so regulate the issues of our banks, as to reduce the currency of notes in the same proportion that the currency of gold is carried off! Rather should we increase our issues, and supply the place of the currency that is exported." They know that bank-notes can fully discharge the functions of money, for they see it every day; and not only so, but they are certain that almost no business of Scotland is carried on by means of a currency of gold. The Scottish people can never be made to comprehend why their bank-notes, bank deposits, and cash credits, should fluctuate in amount as gold would fluctuate, if exclusively employed. These forms of currency do not come of gold; they are not founded upon it, and they have nothing to do with it. In Scotland they understand, as well as they do in England, the use of gold as money; they know its value as a commodity, but being a costly commodity, they do not incline to employ it as a currency, except so far as their bank currency fails of its object; nor do they wish to purchase or hold it as a commodity, except for such special purpose as may promise adequate advantage. Their system of banking enables them to dispense with it almost entirely. In this, they are far from thinking themselves behind their neighbors, in intelligence or financial skill. Sir Walter Scott, in the Letters already referred to, on the subject of the reform in Scotch banking projected in England in 1826, says, in referring to the oft-repeated metaphor, that gold, like water, will find its level: — "A metaphor is no argument in any instance; but I think I can contrive, in the present, to turn this water engine against those who employ it. Scotland, sir, is not *beneath* the level to which gold flows naturally. She is *above* that level, and she may perish for want of it ere she sees a guinea, without she, or the State for her, be at the perpetual expense of maintaining, by constant expenditure, that metallic currency which has a natural tendency to escape from a poor country back to a rich one." — "In countries where gold is indispensable, it must be obtained, whatever price is given for it while the means of paying such a price remains."[1] Scotland,

---

[1] See Third Letter of *Malachi Malagrowther* to the "Edinburgh Weekly Journal," page 16. The position of the writer is further illustrated as follows: —

"If my friend would consult the clerk of the Water Company, at his office in the Royal Exchange [Edinburgh], he would explain the matter at once. 'Let me have,' says Mr. Chrysal, 'a pipe of water to my house.'— 'Certainly, sir; it will cost you forty shillings yearly.' — 'The devil it will! Why, surely, the Lawnmarket is lower than the Reservoir on the Castlehill? It is the nature of water to come to a level. What title have you to charge me money, when the element is only obeying the laws of nature, and descending to its level?' — 'Very true sir,' replies the clerk;

according to the views of Sir Walter Scott, did not employ a gold currency, because it had to be purchased and paid for; and she had no inducement to make so expensive a purchase, in the face of a fact which long experience had taught her that she could do better without it; that her people preferred the bank currency to the gold. The views of Sir Walter Scott, in his celebrated pamphlet, were emphatically seconded by his countrymen of every class; and they retained their well-tried paper system, which, though convertible by law, as in England, is so wisely adjusted, that a run upon the banks for gold or silver is an event which has not occurred for a century in Scotland.

The position occupied by banks in England and Scotland, in the eyes of the people, is widely different. In England, the people are taught to look to the test of convertibility of liabilities into gold, or payment on demand, as the only right criterion of the solvency of banks; they well know, nevertheless, that this convertibility is not possible. Every bank is regarded as having undertaken what, if called upon, it could not perform; and every man is left to exercise his discretion about the degree of forbearance he can safely exercise. In times of commercial prosperity, the distrust which this view of the banks generates, in a greater or less degree, in all minds may be latent and unseen; but the moment any cause of alarm arises, this distrust is roused to fearful energy and action. Every man's apprehensions are multiplied by his estimate of other people's fears; and in England, as well as in the United States, a run upon the banks, to some extent, is inevitable in a time of commercial derangement or disturbance. When the banks sustain themselves upon such occasions, it is often regarded as a triumphant proof of their solidity and strength, though the merciless process by which the

'but then it was no law of nature brought it to the Reservoir, at a height which was necessary to enable us to disperse the supply over the city. On the contrary, it was an exertion of art, in despite of nature. It was forced hither by much labor and ingenuity. Lakes were formed, aqueducts constructed, rivers dammed up, and pipes laid for many miles. Without immense expense, the water could never have been brought here; and without your paying a rateable charge, you cannot have the benefit of it.'" —*Ibid.* page 17.

banks defend themselves, by contracting the currency, has inflicted losses upon individuals to many times the amount of all the coins in the banks. Under the English system, every attack upon the banks is inevitably attended by an attack of the banks upon their customers, and, through them, upon the whole community. To save a million of gold, lying unemployed in their vaults, the banks will diminish the active paper currency two or three, or even ten millions. The banks of England are looked upon, then, by the people, as institutions exposed to great risk, and as capable, in times of commercial trouble, of inflicting terrible losses upon the community in which they are placed; they are isolated, each one standing upon its own strength, and frequently as prompt to sacrifice each other, in averting the dreaded suspension, as to fall upon their customers by the process of contraction. In England and in the United States, an unappeasable jealousy of banks pervades a large portion of the people, which requires little special provocation to rouse into active enmity and opposition.

In Scotland there is no jealousy of the banks; they are not hated as monopolists, nor distrusted as unsafe. They stand together as one mass, prepared to uphold each other in every danger, and to sustain their customers in time of trial. The contractions of currency which, in England, prove such a severe scourge, the power of employing which the banks there regard as one of their most important privileges, are unknown in Scotland.

The Scottish banks have, from their commencement, received deposits as low as £10, and some even less, upon which they paid interest at about one per cent. less than the current rate. The deposits thus made for the sake of accumulation, ranging from £10 upwards, have for a long period exceeded ten millions sterling, perhaps they now exceed fifteen. This is the interest which the masses have in the banks of Scotland. The confidence of these depositors is so great, that, since the introduction of savings banks in Scotland, the poor commence their savings in them by shillings, and continue their economy, until they have succeeded in accumulating £10, which they carry to a bank for a regular deposit receipt. The Scotch banks are the pride of the people; all their spare money is at interest in them; and, never hearing the language of distrust or opposition, no fear or apprehension crosses their minds. No one has ever heard of a difficulty in collecting principal or interest, or in reinvesting them together. The people know that all the notes of all the banks are good over all Scotland; and that, if a suspicion were raised against any one bank, the others would make a point of giving their own notes for those suspected. It would be difficult to find a man in Scotland in whom a doubt existed, or could be planted, of the entire soundness of all their banks, now and hereafter. The system of redemption semi-weekly between all the banks, and their many local exchanges, give them such an oversight of their respective operations, that they have less fear of each other's solvency than the isolated banks of England. The banks of Scotland, consisting mainly of branches of a small number of banks situated in the chief towns, are governed by a policy which is uniform, and equally designed for the benefit of the whole people, and the safety of the banks. This esprit du corps which prevails among the banks in Scotland, has been strongly censured in England as likely to lead to over-issues, relying on mutual aid; but it must be noted that there is, among the banks there, not only a disposition to protect each other in danger, but an equally strong tendency to watch each other at all times. Their respective interests demand this, and their close association makes this watchfulness effective. Whilst all, therefore, are disposed to help each one that may need aid, all are equally interested to restrain the tendency of any one to go astray.

The complete success of the Scottish banking system, during a century and a half, while it commands the admiration of those who study it with proper attention, does not always convince them that it could, with equal advantage, be transplanted in another soil. It might be long before that confidence in banks, which exists in Scotland, could be inspired elsewhere. A popular writer, referring to this, says, — "The credit of one establishment might be doubted for the time — that of the general system was never brought in question. Even avarice, the most suspicious of passions, has, in no instance I ever heard of, desired to compose her hoards by an accumulation of the precious metals. The confidence in the credit of our ordinary medium has not been doubted, even in the dreams of the most irritable and jealous of human passions." If this extraordinary faith in bank currency is of long growth in Scotland, and therefore not readily transferable elsewhere, there must at least be something in the system which promoted that steady growth, and which warded off all those accidents and commercial troubles which elsewhere have not only destroyed confidence in banks, but, through them, inflicted incalculable mischiefs upon the people. It is in this aspect that the history, constitution and practice of the Scottish banks has not been properly studied out of Scotland, nor even in it. The value of the system is fully appreciated at home, but no Scottish writer has yet shown what elements in the system have given it such a large and firm growth. We are far from competent to this task, even if our space would admit of it.

We refer to one peculiarity in Scotland, without, however, looking for its origin: it is fixed in the minds of the Scottish people, that whatever will fully perform the functions of money, in purchase and payments, is as good as money for them; and, if cheaper and more convenient, it is to be preferred and employed. Such a substitute they find their bank currency to be. They see and know that it does not perform these functions in virtue of its being convertible, but that it answers the end designed, like a steam-engine, because it is properly devised for the purpose. They know that men pay their debts by balancing their books of account, and that the debts so paid are well and fully paid; and they know equally well, that the debts paid by the agency of their bank-notes are also fully and properly discharged. They know that, in all this, there is no intervention of money or the precious metals. In Scotland they look, therefore, upon coined money as a thing to be obtained and employed when there is need for it. They are so satisfied with their present modes of payment, that they have no more desire of replacing their one-pound notes with sovereigns, than a man of business has to wear buttons of gold, or to drink from vessels of gold, because it is a substance of real value. In Scotland the people have no fear of their banking system breaking down; they can see no possibility of that, so long as they continue their confidence. They do not regard it as resting upon gold; and if the directors of the Scottish banks were to send their whole stock of gold to London, reserving only what might be needful for change, and the supply of travellers to England, it would create no panic nor run. They know that their banking system is a device to effect payments in their business, not dependent upon gold for its power or validity. In the way of business, those who have bank-notes are sure that they can, at any time, buy as much gold as they may require; but they no more think of turning their bank-notes into gold, unless it is needed for a particular purpose, than of turning them into precious stones. Such is the long and deeply-settled feeling and opinion of the Scottish people; and it is no doubt due to some element in their system, the influence of which has not yet been sufficiently understood.

The feeling and opinion in England, on this subject, is, as we have already remarked, very different. They look upon the precious metals, but especially gold, as being the only legitimate medium of payment. All substitutes are not only to be subordinate to it, but convertible into it on demand. It is true that notes of the Bank of England are, by law, a legal tender — a relic of the long suspension, the retention of which has never been officially explained; but no doubt it is on the ground that the whole power and means of the government would be applied, if needful, in aiding the bank to pay specie. In England, the idea of convertibility is kept up in connection with all kinds of paper currency, and the people have learned to infer that the effectiveness of paper currency is dependent upon its being convertible. The real office of paper currency, its power and economy, are lost sight of in the absorbing feeling that it should be convertible; and that being the case, they attribute all the efficacy of paper currencies to the fact of its being payable on demand. All its powers, as it is regarded, are due to gold in the last analysis.[1] This is so fully contradicted by facts, past and

[1] We must remind the reader, that we are not arguing against the pro-

present, as to show that the subject, from some cause, has not received a candid consideration. The Clearing-house of London is a standing and unanswerable proof, that the great payments of commerce can be made with more economy and dispatch by the use of securities, books of account, and set-off, than by any possible use of gold. This prejudice against paper currency in England, to which the people are so much indebted in national, as well as in private affairs, and which they employ so largely, is detected in every glance we take at the condition of the country for the last century and a half. It is seen in the opposition to the Bank of England, from its origin, in the fact that the paper of the Bank of England is not received out of London with anything like the readiness with which the notes of the Scotch banks circulate. The local banks of England have but a very circumscribed circulation, whilst the notes of the Scotch banks circulate with equal facility over all the country. As early as 1777, £1 and £2 notes were prohibited in England. The extreme jealousy with which the Restriction of 1797 was regarded, was seen in the many contrivances which were resorted to, to keep it in force without appearing to give it too full a sanction. The feeling with which the measure was viewed may be gathered from the publication by Lord King, in 1803 and 1804, from the Report of the Earl of Liverpool to the King in 1805, from the speeches of the Opposition in Parliament, but more fully from the Bullion Report in 1810, and the discussions which followed, both in and out of Parliament. The jealousy of paper currency is seen in the interrogatories propounded to bankers and merchants by the Parliamentary committees which have, at various times during the last half century, had the subjects of money, banking and credit before them. The witnesses from Scotland before the Committee of Banks of Issue, in 1841, were pressed with questions in regard to their exclusive paper currency, in

---

priety or necessity of convertibility as a check upon banks, for that is a question which must be considered by itself; but we are insisting that convertibility is not the ground upon which the effectiveness and power of paper currency rests.

terms which clearly reveal the doubts of the interrogators.[1] After a very full defence and explanation of the system of currency had been given, they were asked, in every manner in which the question could be varied, whether the issue of paper did not in some way become a capital, and whether the abundance of the paper currency did not, as money or capital, affect prices. The witnesses all replied in the negative; they well knew that such was not the fact, for the whole circumstances and results were before them. They did not succeed in explaining why prices were not affected, in a manner to satisfy minds so prepossessed as their interrogators. As this question is often asked, without being properly answered, we offer an explanation which should never be omitted in that inquiry, whatever else may be brought to bear upon it. Whenever the paper currency issued by banks is, by their system of banking, in continual and effective demand, it has no undue effect upon prices, or, in other words, it has no tendency to depreciate, by which prices would seem to be increased. When all the issues of a bank are in demand, to pay debts to the bank maturing every day, thereby producing a daily current of the notes to the bank, they do not affect prices, because, being in constant demand to pay for purchases already made, they can have little influence upon current prices. Their functions are not to originate new business, but to adjust that which is past; they are subject to an imperative and absorbing demand, which prevents their free action on prices. Prices, as we shall explain in a chapter on that subject, are not so much made in reference to currency or money, as in reference to the feelings, opinions and estimates of men of business. The great purchases and sales of industry and trade are nearly all made upon the individual credit of the dealers, who are not governed, in fixing the price, by the quantity of money, so much as by the probable demand, the needs of consumption, and other like considerations; purchases and sales being made on the security of individual paper, are not dependent upon the quantity of money.

[1] Second Report on Banks of Issue, pp. 174–5.

But apprehensions about paper currency even find place in the minds of intelligent men in Scotland. In referring to an instance of this, we offer a word of explanation to that class of men, who, though intelligent and unprejudiced, look upon paper currency as something unsubstantial, dangerous, and only to be tolerated for a time, and until something better can be obtained. We find the following passages in the account of "The Scottish Banking Institutions," drawn up by William Chambers, for his "Book of Scotland." It is the best popular account of these banks we have found, and will repay the reader for a careful perusal.

"The remarkable fact of so many persons trading on borrowed capital, in such a limited country as Scotland, can give but an inadequate notion of the superficiality of wealth, and the hollowness of the apparent riches, and easy circumstances, of many individuals in this country. . . .

"So complicated is the curious mechanism of credit, which is interwoven throughout the whole fabric of society, that were the thick veil torn aside, which is at present thrown over its various workings, a scene of spectral pecuniary capacity would be exhibited, which, while it would alarm the political economist, would horrify and astonish those who usually look no deeper than the surface of affairs. But though paper money has been decidedly the moving cause of such a result, it must, nevertheless, not be viewed in the light of an instrument of evil; and we have no doubt that, by adhering to a certain mode of management, the banks will eventually be the means of instituting a solid for a specious wealth. . . .

"The Scotch notes were issued only as a succedaneum, until a certain quantity of solid wealth was generated; and the question thence arises, whether the nation has yet arrived at that precise epoch when their services can be dispensed with. This is an exceedingly nice point of inquiry; but we do not despair of answering it satisfactorily. Judging dispassionately of the present condition and prospects of the nation, we are satisfied that the time has *not* come when the Scotch could do without notes; but we are equally convinced, that the extension of their issues may be attended with great danger. The country now enjoys a sufficiency of real and representative capital fit for all useful purposes." . . .

"That an epoch is steadily and gradually advancing, when the money-broking operations of Scottish bankers will cease to be of moment, no one who is acquainted with the increasing accumulation of wealth will be able to deny. The banks have, in the course of years, been reducing the rate of interest they offer for money, just as it is becoming more plentiful; and such a procedure tells very explicitly, that ere long moneyed men will more frequently lay out their capital on speculations of their own, than lend it to others to do so through the intervention of banks. At present, the interest of two per cent. will gradually sink to one, then to a half per cent., and finally to nothing. When it reaches this point, it will be a pregnant proof that the wealth of Scotland is on a tolerably secure footing, and that the notes have nearly realized the intention of their creation."[1]

These extracts are taken from an account which places a very high estimate upon the banks and banking system of Scotland. In the midst of the highest appreciation appear these qualifying paragraphs, which show that the author did not fully understand the nature, power and necessity of paper currency; and that he could not, therefore, adequately appreciate its value to the industry, trade and progress of a country. As similar misgivings occupy other minds in Scotland, and prevail largely in England, we shall attempt to remove at least a part of the misapprehension on which these doubts are founded.

There is a plain distinction, universally understood, between a tract of land and the mortgage which is granted upon it. The one is the land, the other is a security. There is a like distinction between a hundred bales of cotton and the note of $4000 with which it is purchased; the note is merely a security. If the value of the mortgaged land is $5000, and the mortgage given is for that amount, it cannot be said that the capital involved is doubled, the land and the mortgage being each worth

[1] Chambers' Book of Scotland, pp. 346–7, 361, 363.

$5000. There is no increase of capital. So, when a hundred bales of cotton are sold, and a note for $4000 is received upon the delivery, no increase of wealth or capital has taken place. The cotton may be the subject of many subsequent sales, and each time for a larger sum, but no increase of capital results from these changes of ownership. The notes taken are all mere securities. The property for which they were given is not of sufficient value to pay them all at the same time; but, if properly managed, as it created all these securities, so it can be made to pay them all. The illustration is very simple, if we suppose the cotton to have passed through half a dozen or more hands, and to have come back to the original owner. It has created securities to the amount of $24,000, all which can be discharged by the last purchaser paying the first seller. The intermediate creditors will give up their securities, to be acquitted of their debts. If any of the notes thus given should be carried to a bank, and exchanged for its notes, they cannot properly be called either capital or money. The bank cannot make money out of paper; it cannot make of paper anything but securities. Their assumed convertibility may give them additional credit, but it cannot make them money. They are promises — undertakings to be paid in money, if not otherwise adjusted. It is the same with bank deposits, on which the depositor can draw at pleasure; they are, in every proper sense, securities, not money. If it were otherwise, money could be manufactured at pleasure by individuals and banks.

The yearly product of the industry of a country, when sent into channels of trade, foreign or domestic, is the annual contribution of labor and capital to its wealth; and is, in a large proportion, represented by the personal securities taken upon sales as they occur. The commodities are bought and sold, and by this means distributed; the payments accruing from these transactions are reserved for special management. The amounts to be paid are found in the securities which the parties took as the evidences of debt and credit, and as necessary for their safety. When property is sold more than once, there are motives and interests which ensure a good security upon every sale. It may be supposed that every man who parts with property for a security, will exercise that judgment and caution which may be expected of every one acting for his own interest. For the whole mass of securities extant at any one time, there is the basis of all the commodities for which they were given; and commodities, like money, will pay debts, if they circulate as often as they change hands. Every new security to which the resale of a commodity gives rise, will pay the debt created by the preceding sale. If A. sells to B., and B. to C., B. can use the security received from C., and through the bank pay his debt to A. The commodities then travel through the regular channels of trade, until they reach their final destination; the securities founded on them are employed to pay and extinguish each other by every way which the various devices of the credit system offers. The most effective of all the processes of the credit system, in this adjustment, is founded on the fact that, to a very large extent, the whole body of creditors are also debtors; that is, the holders of securities received in the course of business are indebted upon securities given by them in the course of business. The banks furnish in their notes, by their deposit system, and upon their books, in modes we have fully explained, a method of setting-off or fully discharging these mutual debts. Whatever opinions parties may form of each other's obligations, they are all on a par on the books of the bank; the securities are there all equalized, and one debt is made as good as another; that is, the deposits are equally available, however different the notes discounted. Every debtor, with this facility afforded him, can pay his own debts with the debts which others owe him. No currency in the world — none can be conceived safer and better than that which parties mutually indebted thus employ. It is paying debts with debts; it is exchanging credits for credits; and the whole proceeding is perfectly voluntary. Those between whom it takes place, are those most concerned; and they prefer this to any other mode of adjustment. It suits those not immediately concerned, because these mutual debtors are the holders of the chief articles of consumption, and their transactions throw into circulation a large amount of bank currency, which the people at large receive as money, and employ as money, not only in the discharge of debts, but in the purchase of any required article of consumption.

This is what is constantly going on in Scotland, in England, and in the United States, and in all other countries of active industry and trade, where commercial confidence and personal integrity exists in a degree sufficient to warrant it. Men who can make their purchases upon credit, can never be induced to keep on hand, or carry gold or silver to pay cash down. The interest on deferred payments is the same as the interest lost by keeping and employing coins. The substance of this mode of proceeding is, that men give their individual paper for commodities of trade; this individual paper is converted into bank-notes, or bank deposits, which pass into circulation, and become the very means or currency with which these commodities can be purchased, saving the use of money. Gold could not become so plentiful as to make it inexpedient to transact business in this way. The risk, trouble and expense of a gold currency is such, that it can never supplant the credit system. If the Bank of England, even now, were permitted to issue one-pound notes, they would rapidly take the place of sovereigns.

What, then, is the ground of the doubts and fears above expressed? When the "borrowed capital," the "superficiality of wealth," the "hollowness of apparent riches," is spoken of, the writer forgets that the paper money he sees in circulation was set in motion by some value of labor, or its products, and that there is an actual basis, not of gold and silver, but of something more needed, under that paper. When the man who holds a cash credit, takes from the bank £100, and purchases commodities with it, those commodities are the basis of that issue, and they will sell for enough, ordinarily, to redeem the notes, or their equivalent. In Scotland, the whole of the annual product of industry is purchased for consumption and export with the notes of individuals, convertible into bank-notes, or directly with the bank currency of the country; what is resold in Scotland, is resold for that currency; what is sent abroad, is sold for what will redeem an equivalent in that currency. There is no borrowing of capital in this, objectionable in theory or in practice; on the contrary, it is a mode of business that is likely to prevail in proportion to the integrity, intelligence and industry of the people. There is nothing superficial, nothing hollow in it. Like other good things, it may be abused; but what is right, and what is abuse, should be carefully distinguished. The advantages of this system are so great, that they are seized upon, to the full extent they are accessible, by all trading people.

This writer thinks that if the thick veil which covers the various workings of the complicated mechanism of credit were torn away, it would reveal a spectre which would horrify those who look no deeper than the surface of things. Doubtless, the rending of this veil would display some things which would horrify; but it would also reveal the power, beauty and efficacy of the credit system, and show what a mighty fabric is thus built upon human confidence and commercial honor; it would show that the losses and abuses by this system bear, after all, a very minute proportion to the vast amount of transactions effected by its means. The economy of the credit system covers, many times over, all the injuries suffered. The great effort should be, not to break it down, but to prevent its abuses, and improve its processes. The credit system will be as solid and reliable as anything human can be, when properly organized and protected. Nothing in Scotland has been more free from fluctuations, nothing connected with their institutions, political, social or religious, has been more firm, in every aspect, than their banking, the chief instrument of their credit system. It is because the working of the mechanism of the credit system is not seen, that it is not more fully confided in and appreciated. Its operations are so vast, that, to many who do not look below the surface, they appear inflated and hollow, because they cannot conceive how such immense sums can be paid without money. This apparent inflation and hollowness disappear, when it is considered that it is nothing else than making commodities pay for commodities — enabling men to use their credits in paying their debts. In their mutual dealings, men may have transactions to any amount; their business may require and adjust the whole on their books of account: these dealings might be regarded as imprudent, if all had to be paid in gold or silver: their transactions might appear inflated, hollow and dangerous, if brought to the criterion of their ability to pay in coin. But, in the simple mode of payment they adopt, their payments are as good as gold or silver could make them. There is no good reason, then, for the allegation, that the bank currency of Scotland is only a succedaneum — a preliminary step in the progress to more substantial wealth. The time can never come when Scotland will introduce a gold currency in place of paper, on account of her increased wealth. If her wealth were tenfold what it is now, it would still be the best mode of effecting the same objects: the Scottish people have now tenfold the wealth they possessed a century ago, yet they show no disposition to lay aside the simple, economical and sure processes of their banking system. It matters not to what low rate interest may fall, in the future abundance of accumulated means, so long as what is purchased must be paid for, so long as men give mutual credit for mutual convenience, so long as the payments of trade are as now mainly separated from the movement of the commodities, so long the Scottish men of business will find it for their advantage, and for the benefit of the whole country, to avail themselves of the facilities furnished by their banks, and of the working of the credit system. The wealth of Scotland is now as secure as that of any country; and this free use of credit, more than any other thing, has contributed to this result. Its advantages will neither be overlooked nor surrendered for any possible use of gold or silver coins — articles which the Scottish people will never purchase or retain largely, simply because they are very expensive; and they have learned to make their exchanges of commodities and mutual services without them.

NOTE TO CHAPTER XVI.

REGULATIONS FOR EXCHANGE OF SCOTCH BANKERS' NOTES.

The following is a copy of the regulations of the banks for exchanging each other's notes, dated Edinburgh, 29th June, 1835:—

"1. The exchange shall continue to be settled twice a week, on Tuesdays and Fridays, and for Glasgow on Wednesdays and Saturdays; the notice and amount of the description of notes held to be given by the respective banks at half-past nine o'clock, A. M., and the balances to be paid before one o'clock the same day.

"2. The payments shall be made in Exchequer bills, Bank of England notes of the value of £100 or upwards, or gold, at the option of the payer, it being understood that Bank of England notes shall only be employed to pay the fractional parts of £1000.

"3. The Exchequer bills shall be filled up in favor of the bank which may be the original holders, and shall bear the distinguishing mark of "Edinburgh Exchange Bill," showing that they belong to the Edinburgh exchanges, and are not intended to be used for any other purpose, and shall be received and paid at par, with the interest that may be due when the transfer takes place.

"4. The amount of Exchequer bills to be kept in the circle is fixed at £400,000, to be applied as follows:—

Bank of Scotland	£63,000
Royal Bank	62,000
British Linen Co.	50,000
Sir Wm. Forbes & Co.	50,000
Commercial Bank	50,000
National Bank	50,000
Leith Bank	15,000
Glasgow Union Bank	35,000
Western Bank	25,000

and each bank so to arrange their transactions as to maintain their quota in the circle at all times.

"5. The Exchequer bills to be of the value of £1000 each.

"6. The amount of Exchequer bills held by each bank shall be stated every exchange day, in the clearing-room.

"7. As the Exchequer bills may be expected to accumulate with some of the banks, and to be wanted at others, it shall be imperative on the parties so situated to sell or buy Exchequer bills; that is to say, the party holding the greater amount of Exchequer bills shall be bound to sell to the party in want of them what may be required for the legitimate purposes of the exchanges; but it shall not be imperative on that party to sell a greater amount than what will reduce their stock to the original quota.

"8. Interest shall be paid for eight days, equal at present to one shilling per cent. upon the purchase and sale of Exchequer bills from the banks, by a draft on London at five days' date, the purchaser also paying the stamp.

"9. The bills put in circulation are to be nearly of the same date, so far as is consistent with these regulations, and to be sent up for exchange before due, and new ones are to be provided, of a later day, so as to keep up the stock in the circle, and no advertised bills are to be used in the exchanges.

"10. The Exchequer bills, within a week after the government notice appears in the Gazette, are to be given up to the original holders, upon receiving other bills, not advertised, with a draft on London, Bank of England notes, or gold, at the option of the holders of the advertised bills.

"11. The seventh regulation will tend, in a great degree, to equalize the amount of Exchequer bills among the different banks; but if Exchequer bills should nevertheless accumulate in the hands of a party, so as to exceed their original quota by more than one-third, they shall have the power to call upon the party holding the smallest amount to purchase the excess; that is to say, the excess above their quota *plus* one-third. But it shall not be imperative on any party to take more than is required to bring up their stock to two-thirds of the original amount. In this way the fluctuation in the amount of Exchequer bills among the different banks, which is an essential part of this arrangement, need never permanently exceed one-third more and one-third less than the original quota of each. The terms of purchase to be the same as in the eighth article.

"12. The exchanges are to be made at the Bank of Scotland and Royal Bank alternately, who reciprocally undertake to pay to those banks who are creditors in the exchange the Exchequer bills, bills of exchange, Bank of England notes, or gold, received from those banks who are debtors in the exchange. But the Bank of Scotland, and the Royal Bank, shall not, nor shall either of them, be in any way responsible for the exchange transactions or otherwise soever.

"13. The statement of balances, after they are struck, to be sent to the respective banks, from the clearing-room, by their clerks, and the clerks of the bank creditors to be in waiting to receive the amount due to them at 12 o'clock. The British Linen Company shall send to the Bank of Scotland and Royal Bank alternately a statement of their exchange transactions, signed by the manager. The clerk to bring over Exchequer bills, Bank of England notes, or gold, for payment of any balance that may be due by them, and to receive Exchequer bills, Bank of England notes, or gold, for such balances as may be due to them on the day's transactions.

"14. Any bank party to this agreement to have the power of withdrawing from it, and receiving back their Exchequer bills at par, upon giving three months' notice." — *Lawson's History of Banking*, pp. 422–5.

CHAPTER XVII.

THE BANKS OF THE UNITED STATES.

§ 1. *Banks, agencies or instruments of payment — Discussions and difference of views — Banks are dealers in credits — General waiver of payment in specie — Fund for payment made by discounting notes — Banks absorb their own issues — Process exemplified — The demand for bank currency makes it good — Commodities of trade held by debtors to the banks — Are sold to pay the banks — Bank currency the medium — The commodities the basis; the individual and bank paper mere securities and means of adjustment — Circulation and deposits of New York banks in* 1857 *— Daily payments — Banks of the United States — Deposits, their agency — The banks pay and are paid in their own currency, and by this furnish, to a certain extent, a safe medium for circulation — Mutual debts.*

THE subject of banking has been one of growing interest for several centuries. When the Bank of Venice was the only institution of the kind in Europe, it was little known; its operations as an institution of credit, and an active agent in the payments of commerce, were understood by few out of the republic. The known fact, that the owners of the public debt transferred their claims on the public, in whole or in part, at pleasure, did not suggest the magnitude of the commercial payments effected at the bank by these transfers. While those who were uninitiated regarded these transfers at the bank as mere changes of investment, by which some sold and others purchased portions of the public debt — others knew that the fund thus transferred was the chief medium of commercial payments, very much the largest portion of which were thus effected. As it was then, so it is necessary now, to look deeper than the mere surface, to ascertain the real functions of banks. To very many, a bank is looked upon only as an institution enjoying, by charter, the privilege of issuing and lending bank-notes as a currency.

Nearly all the discussions upon banking, and nearly all the legislation upon that subject, proceeds from this point of view. And what subject has been more largely discussed in the United States — what more the subject of legislation than banking?

It is not from this point of view we now regard this topic. We intend merely to consider banks of circulation as agencies of payment. In their exercise of that agency, the bank-notes have but a small part. In the aspect just mentioned, in which the banks have been generally regarded, there are few subjects, the discussion of which has elicited wider differences of opinion. Language has been scarcely adequate to express the bitterness of opposition and dislike towards banks, on one side, and the admiration and eulogy of them, on the other. This discussion has scarcely paused, in this country, for the last half century. Our legislative halls, during that period, have seldom passed a year without devoting more or less time to this fruitful theme. Every order of talent has been applied to it, and every grade of practical knowledge has been employed upon it. That knowledge has been increased, and that opinions have been multiplied, is very true; but opinions are as conflicting as ever, and the main questions remain unsolved. Opposers of banks are found of every grade, from the mildest objectors to those who would banish every bank from the country, and allow no currency but gold or silver: and friends of banks, from those who think that the banks might be legislated into some shape or condition in which they would be endurable, to those who would make banking as free as farming or shoemaking. These parties view the subject from different points, and of course, never having the same facts before them, can never reach the same conclusions. But, as not unfrequently happens in such cases, there is much that is correct in the views of both.

We shall attempt neither to reconcile these opinions, nor to weigh the arguments of either party: but endeavor to show what the banks do, and how they do it. If we could do this as it should be done, it would not be difficult to find ample justification for the opposing opinions to which we have adverted. The banks of the United States are, properly speaking, dealers in credit. So far as their capital is paid up in gold or silver, it is reserved as a security for their circulation. It is a rare thing that a bank lends gold or silver. Their business consists mainly in purchasing commercial paper — that is, the evidences of debt taken by men of business in the ordinary course of their affairs; in paying for that paper with bank-notes, or with credits granted upon their books; in receiving upon deposit their own notes, and claims or transfers upon other banks; in allowing a constant transfer of deposits, in the way of payment, among their customers and those with whom they deal. The banks, then, are not lenders of money, though compelled to pay their obligations in money. They are founded on the idea that an association of men, with a paid-up capital, and a corporate existence, is entitled to a higher credit than individuals; and that the latter might find it greatly for their advantage, to avail themselves, in their business transactions, of this superior credit.

We have seen that the credit system rests upon the fact, that the business of purchasing and selling commodities is separated from the business of payments; and upon the further fact, that the commodities which men sell are made to pay for those they purchase. So far as credits and payments are concerned, it is a main object of every man to apply his credits to pay his debts; to employ what is due to him by others in discharging that which he owes to others. The main agency in this is the banks. It is well known that all the large transactions of business are made upon the credit of the parties concerned in them; that the great staples of the country, as well as foreign goods in large quantities, are bought and sold upon individual credit. The market value involved in every transaction is expressed in money of account, and appears on the face of the bills of exchange and promissory notes which the purchaser gives, and the seller takes, as evidence of the debt incurred and credit given in each case. These evidences of debt and credit, which represent, in various shapes, the market value of the commodities, foreign and domestic, as they move in the channels of trade, are the very articles in which it is the object and proper business of the banks to deal. The parties to these evidences of debt, or this commercial paper, having delivered and received the commodities upon which the credits and indebtedness are alike founded, have the remaining duty of payment to fulfil.

By the laws of the United States, every such creditor has the right to demand payment in gold or silver; and no State can, by the terms of the constitution, take away this right. But this right is waived in business to such an extent, that, out of the retail trade, not one per cent. of the payments are exacted or made in gold or silver coin. The reason is obvious and simple. Men extensively engaged in commercial and industrial pursuits are, by the very nature of their business, both buyers and sellers — both debtors and creditors. It is important to pay their debts, and realize their credits, with the least trouble, expense and waste of time possible. When any two of them have mutual accounts against each other on their books, they compare and balance them: of course debts so paid, and credits so realized, are as satisfactorily paid and realized as if gold had passed on each transaction. So each man of business indebted upon promissory notes and bills of exchange, and holding such paper of others for debts due to him, is only desirous of applying his credits to his debts. He never thinks of looking for gold or silver to effect a discharge of his debts, and as little does he think of exacting such payment from those who are indebted to him. This mode of payment is at once inconvenient, hazardous, expensive, and, if attempted by only one-tenth of the debtors, would be impossible. It does not enter, therefore, into the thoughts of business men; they perfectly understand the proper sphere of coins and bullion, and know that they are necessary only in the retail trade, and in payment of national or territorial balances. Nothing is better settled and acquiesced in, than this universal waiver of payment in the precious metals. No sane man of business is willing to exact that with which his debtors cannot possibly comply, and that with which it would be equally impossible for him to comply, if it were exacted of him. Debts, then, though all payable in lawful money of the United States, are very seldom so paid, because they cannot be so paid, and if they could, they would not be so paid. It is every way more advantageous for men to apply their credits to the payment of their debts, and that is what constitutes the crowning process of the credit system.

The banks of the United States are the chief agencies in this mode of payment. They offer the means and facilities of payment which the parties to this business-paper require. They receive this paper, having some months to run to maturity, and deducting interest for the time, give the parties bank-notes, or a credit on their books for the proceeds. This is not turning individual notes into money, it is simply turning them into promissory notes of the bank, or deposits; these being of higher credit, and fitted, from the manner in which they are issued, to be used as a currency or a medium of payment. The real basis of the individual notes discounted by the bank is the commodities which the persons giving the notes received. These persons contracted debts to the several amounts of their notes, and against these debts they hold the purchased commodities. They offer the goods thus purchased to the public, and expect, from their sale, to realize the means of paying the debts. The discounted paper, therefore, exhibits on its face the true market value of the commodities purchased by it; and the bank-notes, or bank credits, given for this individual paper have the same basis, with the added guarantee of the bank. All bank-notes and bank credits issued upon real business-paper are virtually issued for commodities actually moving in the regular channels of trade. The purchasers of these commodities expect to realize enough, by their sale, not only to pay for them, but a profit beside.

It is this process which is continually absorbing bank-notes, and returning them to the banks. The sellers of goods receive the paper of the purchasers, and dispose of it to the banks, taking therefor bank-notes and bank credits, the latter of which they employ in paying their debts, and the former pass into circulation in the retail business, and in this way soon reach the hands of the debtors of the banks, to whom they are always as valuable as the equivalent, or same nominal amount of gold or silver, and even more desirable, because they pay debts to the bank equally well, and with less trouble, expense and hazard. The debtors of the banks are, then, the special holders of the commodities, upon the sale of which their debts are founded; and they offer these same goods to the public for the same amount of bank-notes to which their sale gave origin: these goods should be adequate to redeem the bank-notes, or to bring as much money as will redeem them. A dealer who purchases from a miller 1000 barrels of flour, at $4.50, gives his note at three months for $4500; the miller carries this note to bank, and receives for it the promissory notes of the bank to the amount of $4430; if the dealer sells his flour at half a dollar per barrel profit, he will receive $5000, enough to pay the bank, and leave a profit for himself. He can have no better currency in which to pay the bank than its own notes, aud the bank can do no better than to receive payment in its own obligations. The people who consume flour need to look no further for a currency good enough to buy flour, than these promissory notes of the bank; for they are as readily received by the dealer in flour, as coins of gold or silver. What is true of flour, applies to every other article of general consumption. The business of the banks and their customers embraces the whole round of the articles of trade, and of the products of industry.

Let us suppose, for the purpose of illustration, that the dealer in flour, instead of giving his note for $4500 at three months, gives 900 promissory notes drawn by himself, payable in three months, each for $5; that the credit of the dealer, together with the endorsement of the miller, is sufficient to give these small notes free currency; that the miller pays them out to the farmers for wheat, and that these pay them to the mechanics, manufacturers and merchants with whom they deal; and that, finally, these classes pay them to the dealer for flour, an article of necessity for all. The dealer in flour can receive no better currency than his own notes for the amount of his debt. His profit of $500 will be realized in money, or in something equally satisfactory. The cases above supposed are similar in substance, the difference being that, in the first case, the bank issues the small notes, and in the latter, the drawer of the note for which the bank exchanges its issues.

We may employ the same parties for a further illustration. Suppose the dealer in flour, after giving his note in September at three months, for $4500, sells the flour to several parties in October, and receives their several notes at three months, for $2500, $1500, and for $1000. These notes, maturing a month later than the note for $4500, are not applicable to its payment, and without some special device or facility, afford no help towards that payment; but the bank furnishes the device and the facility. The bank holds the note for $4500, payable in December, and application being made, it discounts the three notes at the instance of the dealer in flour, and gives him credit on its books for the proceeds. Upon these proceeds standing to his credit, under the name of deposits, the flour dealer gives his check, in December, for $4500, and retires his note.

If the banks in any community have discounted notes to the amount of a million, averaging sixty days to maturity, granting therefor credits to the amount of $990,000, they will promptly give up any or all the notes going to make up the million, for a return of their credits to the amount. The banks give nothing for the notes discounted but credits on their books: what they gave for the notes they are willing to receive in kind for them. The profits of the bank, being the interest, for which they issued no credits, must of course be paid when the notes are retired. The main business of the banks consists, then, in purchasing commercial securities and evidences of debt, paying for them with their own notes and bank credits, and deducting the interest for their profit. In doing this, they not only furnish a medium of payment in which these commercial securities can be discharged, but a currency which may be employed in the interval, before it is applied to the extinction of these debts. What chiefly makes this currency available and effective is, that there is an active and urgent demand for it, to the whole amount due to the banks; that is, for more than all the banks have issued. This demand is active, urgent, daily, unremitting: the notes in bank are maturing daily, and the demand, therefore, never flags:

every day has its payments, which are to be effected with money or the issues of the banks. The latter, in any community where there are banks of circulation, being the chief medium of payment, is the medium most in demand.

We have shown that, in all cases where the notes discounted by the banks were given by the makers of them for commodities of daily use and consumption, these commodities are immediately offered to the public for bank-notes, or checks on bank deposits, as the proper fund with which to pay the discounted notes. The commodities, by their sale, give origin to promissory notes; the promissory notes give rise to the bank-notes and credits; these become, in their turn, a medium with which to purchase the commodities; and the bank-notes and bank credits coming thus, by circulation, into the hands of the debtors to the banks, are returned to the banks in payment of the discounted notes. This is a very simple and sound process of payment; the discounted notes are founded on the market value of actual commodities, and of course the same basis is beneath the bank-notes and bank credits; and the purchaser finally pays his debt by the sale of the commodities on account of which his liability was incurred. If a dealer issues 1000 five-dollar notes drawn by himself, for 1100 barrels of flour, and sells the flour for $5 a barrel, his own notes will make a good medium of payment, to the extent of 1000 barrels. The remaining 100 barrels are his profit, and must be paid for in money, or what is equally satisfactory. The transaction is the same, in substance, when the bank intervenes; the bank issues the small notes, or credits, and becomes the owner of the note given by the dealer. The latter sells the flour, and thus obtains the notes of the bank, with which he pays his own.

This process, or what is substantially the same, is the basis of a large proportion of the real business between the banks, their customers and the public. There are other processes by which payments are effected through the banks, equally legitimate and economical, some of which may not be equally safe for the public. Let us suppose that a miller sells to a dealer 1000 barrels of flour for $5000; that the latter sells the same flour to another dealer for $5250, and he to another for $5500; and that it is retailed by the latter at $6, or for a total of $6000: in this case, three promissory notes are issued, respectively for $5000, $5250, and for $5500, making, in all, $15,750 of wholesale transactions, besides the amount for which the flour was retailed, $6000. If these three notes, having an average of sixty days to run, were all discounted, bank-notes and bank credits to the amount of $15,593 would be issued on the basis of the 1000 barrels of flour. This, at first glance, may appear to be an over-issue. But each of these persons who parted with that quantity of flour for a mere promise to pay, must have deemed the purchaser to be good, and his promise reliable, and so must the bank which discounted the notes. Two parties besides the bank, deeply interested in being right and cautious, have adjudged these notes to be good. The process of payment is simple. The bank has issued notes or credits to the amount of $15,593, and holds three notes, amounting together to $15,750; the makers of these three notes must either return an equivalent in the issues of the bank, or the money. The debtor of the note for $5000 has the proceeds of his sale for $5250 to his credit, and with this he pays and takes up his note: so, also, the debtor of the $5250 has the proceeds of his sale for $5500 at his credit, and with this he retires his note: and, finally, the debtor of the note of $5500 gathers up the proceeds of sales at retail, in the shape of bank-notes or credits, and pays off the note remaining in the bank for $5500. Thus these notes provide the medium by which they may all be paid, for every note implies a debtor of sufficient credit to purchase property on the faith of his simple promise to pay; and every discount by a bank implies a confidence of the bank that the drawer or acceptor of the paper had ability to redeem the issues of the bank to the amount, or pay in money.

In cases where banks discount paper not given for property transferred at the time, it is, or should be, on well-grounded confidence that the maker of the paper has the power or means of redeeming from the hands of the public an equal amount of the issues of the bank. The banks being large holders of individual paper, either discounted or deposited with them for collection, they are of course constantly looked to for the means of payment; and a credit on the books of a bank, granted by the bank, or derived from another quarter, being all that is required, it is earnestly sought for that purpose. Where there are many banks, and large transactions in business and upon credit, the movement of these payments in banks, and the consequent movement of bank credits or deposits, become far too complicated to be followed up by any process of analysis. One great feature, however, must ever be prominent, and that the most effective of all in sustaining the present banking system; that is, that every debtor of a bank is an active agent in purchasing and returning to the bank its notes and credits; that the issues of the banks, whether notes or credits on their books, are more available, convenient and economical for these debtors, than the legal currency of coins. They are more abundant, more easily obtained, and equally effective. It is this which gives to bank-notes and bank credits their efficiency and rapidity of movement. The amount of the circulation of the New York banks averaged over $8,000,000 in 1857, and the deposits averaged over $87,000,000. These constitute the medium in which the payments of the City of New York are chiefly made. With these, there is a daily payment to be made of from $30,000,000 to $50,000,000, and they are quite capable of making that amount of payments each day, for both notes and deposits may be paid many times during the day. It is very safe to assume that over $30,000,000 of city bank-notes and deposits are paid each business day in New York. There is a demand, then, upon these notes and deposits in every week, for payments, to the amount of $200,000,000, and in every month for $800,000,000. This demand daily, weekly, monthly, constantly pressing upon a fund of bank-notes and deposits, which may at no time exceed $100,000,000, is certainly active and pressing enough to keep up the value of a fund so much used, and so indispensable to the men who have $200,000,000 to pay every week.

That these sums are far within the actual daily payments of New York is apparent from the operations of the Clearing-house. The amount cleared daily, in 1857, was over $20,000,000, and these clearings are but the balances on the transactions between the banks. A vast sum of payments is made every day in the business of such a city as New York, which is in no way embraced in the transactions of the Clearing-house. If we assume that the whole of the payments effected yearly through the agency of banks in the United States, is only ten times greater than the amount paid yearly in New York, we shall have an aggregate 400 times greater than the amount of the precious metals in the country; 500 times the amount of the bank-note circulation of the United States; 400 times the amount of the bank deposits; and 30 times the annual value of the whole productive industry of the country.[1] These estimates fall far short of the whole of the payments made in the country; for all payments made out of bank are expressly excluded, as well as all the transactions of the retail trade. In all this great adjustment of debt and credit, the office of the precious metals is that of payment, when adjustment fails. Where two banks have claims against each other, to the amount of hundreds of thousands, they only pay the balance in money: so between two cities, it is only the balance upon their mutual indebtedness that is paid in money: it is the same between two states or countries. The functions of the precious metals, then, in this great work of payment, is to pay balances, and to perform, as may be required, the office of a medium of exchange in the retail trade.

The great fund employed in this adjustment is created out of the promissory notes and bills of exchange given in the regular course of domestic commerce. In a statement of the condition of the banks of the United States for the year 1856, the discounts and loans are put down at $684,000,000. If these run off four times each year, it would make $2,736,000,000. These loans and discounts take the shape partly of deposits, and partly

---

[1] If the operations of the Clearing-house in New York were taken as an indication of the trade of the city, these figures would be increased. We suppose the amounts cleared daily in New York to be considerably swelled by the stock transactions which pass through the banks; and we make allowances accordingly.

of bank-notes; both of which are being constantly extinguished and redeemed by being returned to the bank in payment, at the rate of from nine to ten millions daily. But the fund thus constituted by the discounted paper of men in business is that which, by its transfer and circulation in the form of bank credits and bank-notes, effects the vast aggregate of payments we have noticed. The banks of the United States held, on the average, in the year 1856, the sum of $684,000,000; this amount would run off in ninety days, absorbing a proportionate amount every day of bank liabilities. But as this paper is discounted upon an average time of ninety days, the credits granted by the bank are applicable, during that time, to other service, and are used to effect a much larger amount of payments than is involved in lifting the securities discounted by the banks.

This fund, then, is subject to an additional demand beyond that which arises from the payment of nine or ten millions daily, in retiring the discounted paper — a demand of scarcely less than $300,000,000 daily. The indebtedness which produces this demand arises in many ways beside the sale of commodities, a very considerable proportion being the mere result of dealing in credit. Large amounts of bank credits and bank-notes are constantly lent by the holders, and notes of individuals taken therefor. Large transactions in stocks are continually occurring, giving occasion to notes and discounts. Although the sum of liabilities thus incurred is far beyond the amount of the discounts, a rapid movement of the deposits makes it practicable to effect payments every day, at least thirty times the amount required to discharge the discounted paper. The additional employment thus given to this fund, causing a demand for it every day nearly equal to its whole volume, keeps it at a value, for the purposes of payment, fully equal to the precious metals. It is observable that, when interest is at six, twelve or eighteen per cent. per annum, there is no increased price of the precious metals. When the price of this fund, which is that employed in the payment of debts, has risen three hundred per cent., gold and silver have not, as commodities, advanced at all. As a matter of fact, however, they are not the medium in which debts are paid, and therefore they do not increase in price under the most urgent demand for that medium or fund in which debts are usually paid.

The fund employed to effect the payment of these great sums is mainly that which is called deposits in the banks. For, however great the amount of payments effected by the circulation of bank-notes, it enters into our present estimate only to the amount of the bank-notes daily paid out and received at the counters of the banks. The payments by circulation of bank-notes are, therefore, left out in our approximation. The deposits are the chief agent in the work. They consist in credits given by the banks to those who have had notes or bills discounted: the banks become the purchasers and holders of this individual paper, and grant these credits in their place. According to returns of 1856, the banks of the United States had placed to the credit of their customers, in this way, $230,000,000, this being the average of the whole year. If this amount of deposits was moved 200 times in the year, it would pay $46,000,000,000. In many of the large cities, the deposits are, on the average, moved once each day.

We thus see that the credits of business and trade furnish, by the intervention of the banks, the very fund out of which the corresponding debts are paid. These debts are, in no proper sense of the word, paid in money: they are, it is true, payable in lawful money of the United States. Every creditor has a right to payment in gold or silver; and if debts be not so paid, it is because the creditor, whether bank or individual, is equally satisfied with some other mode. The legal right which every man has to demand payment of what is due to him in the precious metals, has no doubt a powerful effect in keeping other currencies up to the price of the precious metals. The law of legal tender, therefore, though of little practical application in the business of payments, exercises a beneficial and sustaining power, the benefits of which it would be difficult to estimate. When every creditor can exact payment from his debtor in gold or silver, it may be presumed he is satisfied with what he accepts instead; and no currency, in such circumstances, can remain long below its proper equivalent in coins, without being quoted and paid at a discount. Let it not be supposed, however, that the law of legal tender is the only, or even the chief, power which maintains the value of the great fund we have pointed out as the medium in which debts are chiefly paid. The main reason why this fund maintains its value is, that it is receivable in discharge of all debts payable at the banks; and being receivable by the banks, it is of course receivable by all the debtors of the banks, who will sell any article they have for this currency as readily as for money. The indebtedness to the banks is so great, the daily demand for this currency is so pressing, that it will purchase any commodity of trade, any product of industry, and pay wages or personal services equally as well, and with far more convenience, than any possible use of coins. It is, therefore, so far as it is employed, to all intents, as good and as effective as coin. Those who take it have their choice between currency and coin.

We have stated that this medium of payment created by the banks is as effective as gold or silver, because it is receivable for debts, and because it will purchase anything that gold or silver can purchase, and, it may be added, on as good terms. We have already explained why and how the banks can so receive it from year to year. If the banks have a special advantage in issuing this currency, the people enjoy an equal benefit in restoring it to them in payment of debts. The advantage of the banks in the business is too great to make it supposable they will ever voluntarily abandon it. They purchase with merely a credit on their books, or the issue of their paper, the very best and safest individual promissory notes which are made in business, and on these they have an ample profit. This power of purchasing individual paper with their own currency would cease if their customers did not enjoy the reciprocal favor of paying debts in the same medium.

If the amount of discounts and loans in 1856, reported at $684,000,000, were placed to the credit of 100,000 persons, it would be found that these persons were mutually indebted to within ten per cent., or perhaps less, of the whole amount. The banks might enter up a credit for the whole sum, interest deducted; but in less than ninety days the parties would have employed at least ninety per cent. of the whole amount in paying each other, and this ninety per cent. would be thus wholly extinguished. Nearly all men of business who give promissory notes in the course of their transactions, take them also. Whilst each individual obtains a credit for the notes he has taken, he finds that others have credit for the notes he has given. The effect is the same as if the bank had, at the instance of these parties, opened an account with each one, charging him with all the notes he had given, and giving him credit for all that he had taken. The balance would then have to be paid in money. By the actual process in bank, this result is obtained by allowing each customer to draw upon his credits to pay his debts as they mature. Each one who has a larger credit than is sufficient to pay his debts, may call on the bank to pay him that excess in money, which the bank can do, because some of its customers have balances in money to receive, and others have balances to pay; and as the amount of these differences would be the same, the banks would receive from the debtor balances the same amount they would have to pay upon the creditor balances.

It is this very large proportion of mutual indebtedness which makes the methods of payment adopted by the banks so efficient. No man should desire better payment than his own paper; and, in fact, the chief financial effort and object of every man in business is to apply the paper he has received in business to pay that which he has given. This operation proceeds through many a devious process, but with certain and complete success. Of the $684,000,000 of loans and discounts in 1856, at least $616,000,000 may be taken as the amount of indebtedness between the debtors. This large sum is thus extinguished at least four times every year by a virtual set-off; that is, every creditor gives up enough of his credits to pay his debts. The banks having issued credits to the amount of $616,000,000, for individual paper to that amount, surrender the individual paper to those who return the equivalent in bank credits. The complications of this process defy human scrutiny as to the details, but it is always making progress towards the proper result. A man of business may hold notes of persons residing in New Orleans, Cincinnati, Pittsburg, Chicago, and Buffalo, and his own may be held by persons as widely scattered. The banks give a present credit on their books for these wide-spread debts, and enable him to face his notes, as they are presented, by checks on his credits, so far as his credits may reach. This machinery of credit brings to every man's door the claims which others hold against him; and it furnishes every man with a medium of payment adequate to the purpose, and far more convenient than coins or bullion.

§ 2. *Bank-notes are not money — They are mere promissory notes of the banks — They are intended to perform the functions of money, and can be so employed — Bank deposits can be so employed, but are not money — Both are substituted by banks for the notes of individuals — Banks can make securities of paper, but cannot make money — The convertibility of bank-notes does not make them money, and is not so intended; it is a mere check on the banks — Gold and silver not the basis of bank issues: they are based on the paper discounted by the banks, and this paper is based on the commodities for which it is given — Convertibility a dangerous check — Employed with fatal effect against those who rely upon it — It abolishes time on commercial paper.*

In the ordinary language of trade, bank-notes and bank deposits are called money. Writers upon the subject of money too often class all kinds of currency under that general term. But this obliteration of needful distinctions should be discouraged, as unfavorable to clear views: the term money should be restricted to coins made a legal tender by law in payment of debts. If this definition is departed from, who can tell where to stop. There remains no longer any clear, defined boundary between that which is money and that which cannot, with any propriety, be so called. If bank-notes are money, at what rate of discount do they cease to be such? If bank deposits are money, are they such when the bank is in bad credit, or precisely how far must a bank be discredited before its credits cease to be money? Is a bill of exchange, or promissory note, which circulates freely, money? If it be said that all bank-notes and bank credits payable on demand are money, then do they cease to be money the moment the banks suspend, and whilst they are circulating as freely, and performing the same functions as before? If bank-notes payable on demand are money, are they made so by the promise to pay, or by the ability to pay? If by the former, all notes would be good; if by the latter, how is the ability to pay to be ascertained? It is well known to every one, that no banks of circulation and deposit can pay on demand all their liabilities; they may, nevertheless, be perfectly safe. Is their ultimate safety a sufficient ground for ranking them as money? Do bank-notes become money, in the strict sense of the word, when, like the notes of the Bank of England, they are made a legal tender? If so, could all bank-notes be made money in the same way? Questions like these are easily multiplied; and, if truly answered, must show that the term money has often received an application far too wide.

If names or proper designations were wanting, there would be more excuse for this confusion of terms. In Venice and Genoa, the term bank money was applied to the funds of the banks, which were for a long period at a high premium over money of gold or silver. In modern times, we have the terms bank-notes, bank deposits, currency, circulation, and cash. The term money properly means the legal coinage of gold or silver, or other coins, made a legal tender; the term currency may include all the various substitutes for money which circulate like money, and perform the same or similar functions. Where bank-notes are made a legal tender, they may be called paper-money. It may not be necessary to be always precise in maintaining these distinctions; but when precision is necessary, they should be kept clearly in view.

Bank-notes, deposits, checks, bills of exchange, promissory notes, and other things of like kind, which have been extensively and successfully used as substitutes for money, should not be confounded with money. Almost all these substitutes are really evidences of debt, the amount of which is clearly expressed on their face in money of account. They pass for an expressed amount, which is payable in money on demand, or at a future day, but which payment is not made, and never expected, as it is always adjusted in another way. They readily fulfil every function of money, by reason of the great demand, which makes them as desirable as money, and far more sought for. We may repeat here an illustration we have frequently before employed. If A. and B. have dealt with each other to the amount of $5000, A. having in his books charged B. with $400, with $1500, and $600; B. having charged A. with $600, with $1600, and $300. These several sums, as they stand on their respective books, are not in any sense money, although the several amounts are stated in money of account; yet A. and B. may, at any moment, pay each other in full, by balancing these accounts. As they stood on the books, they were but evidences of debt; and the accounts, when balanced, are but evidences of payment. If A. and B., instead of paying in that way, issue their notes to each other, payable at sixty days from each transaction, these notes, if negotiated in payment for goods, do not become money, but remain evidences of debt. If A. and B. carry these notes to bank, and have them discounted, receiving bank-notes in their place, they each remain debtor for the notes respectively given, and the bank becomes debtor for the bank-notes issued in the purchase of this paper. These bank-notes may perfectly perform every function of money, but they can be nothing more than the promises of the bank to pay. The bank holds a claim upon A. and B. for the full amount of the promises it has issued in this case; and it expects A. and B. to return an equivalent sum in these promises, or to pay their note in something that will enable the bank to redeem them. These bank-notes are but the issues of a promissory note of the bank in a convenient form for circulation, in place of the notes of A. and B.; and they are, in reality, no more money than the notes of A. and B., though far more suitable and effective substitutes. They may become as efficient in the purchase of all commodities as money, and far more efficient and convenient in the payment of debts; but this by no means converts them into money. They cannot be employed in paying balances of foreign trade, nor even in the discharge of balances between remote points at home.

It is no more the province of the banks to create money, than it is in their power, nor should their issues be treated or regarded as money. Their great function is that of effecting payments; they open accounts with men who are both debtors and creditors, and, by means of the facilities they afford these debtors and creditors, adjust their mutual claims, and pay and receive their balances, to the amount of thousands of millions yearly, without any use of money, or any need of it. The great fact, that nine-tenths of the payments of business in the United States, above the mere distribution effected by the retail trade, are made without any use of money, is one which should never be left out of view by statesmen and economists. If such payments are effective, correct in theory and practice, should not the principle be understood, and the practice promoted, protected and extended? If a million of men in the United States owe, on the average, $10,000 each upon notes maturing within three months, this would require, if paid in money, the sum of $10,000,000,000. The whole amount of specie in the banks being $60,000,000, the payments above would require this amount of specie to change hands nearly twice every day, and besides, to change its location from bank to bank, and state to state, hundreds of miles apart, with a rapidity equal to the despatch of the telegraph — a movement as impossible as it would be absurd, if it were possible. This great payment is effected with perfect facility by the processes of the banks, without any other movement of the $60,000,000 than paying the amount of some comparatively trifling balances. In the regular operation of banking, the sum of $60,000,000 in specie would not change hands once in a year.

In the great movements of industry and trade, goods and services pay for goods and services; the promissory notes, bank-notes, bank credits, or other currency, which intervene, are devices of adjustment, and not the very payment ultimately aimed at. Men give what they have to spare, to obtain what they desire. If they do not, in the first instance, sell for money, and with that purchase what they want, they take a security or evidence of debt; they make their purchases upon their individual credit, and give evidences of debt. The debt and credit extinguish each other in the banks, and the parties have, in substance, exchanged goods; all the rest is merely keeping and balancing accounts between them. These securities are issued, in this country, to an amount not less than $1,000,000,000 every three months, in which period this amount continually runs off and is renewed, making $4,000,000,000 in the year. Of this $1,000,000,000 of securities, the banks become the owners and collectors; and for half this amount, they are under a constant engagement to pay money on demand. To meet this engagement, the banks hold $600,000,000 against $500,000,000, or twelve per cent. of the amount. Of course, absolute convertibility of all this fund of securities into specie, on demand, is an impossibility. If all the gold and silver in the country, estimated at $250,000,000, were in the banks, it would be an impossibility. It must, therefore, continue to be impossible; and hence arises one of the gravest difficulties connected with banks of circulation.

If bank-notes, like checks upon banks, were confined in their use and circulation to those at whose special instance they are issued, and whose debts are to be adjusted by them, there would be less occasion for any public intervention or concern. For the public have little interest, whether men thus mutually indebted discharged their debts by balancing accounts, by bank-notes, or by checks on banks. But the experience of a century and a half has shown that, where bank-notes are offered as a currency, they are freely received, and soon become the chief medium of exchange. It is almost invariably true that, wherever bank-notes are offered as a currency, with even the slightest pretensions to regularity and security, they are accepted, and pass rapidly into general circulation. This facility of converting bank paper into a currency is a strong temptation to resort to it, and accounts in part for the multiplication of banks of circulation in this country, and elsewhere; but it has given rise, also, to that ceaseless jealousy with which this system of banking has been watched. There is, perhaps, more ground for this jealousy than many friends of the system have been willing to acknowledge. If the circulation of bank-notes had been confined to the payment of the debts in which they originate, no more mischief could ensue than now arises from the employment of checks upon banks, which the parties using them are interested to keep within legitimate and safe bounds. But as bank-notes, wherever offered, secure a wide circulation, it is not enough to say, let people take them at their risk, as they take them at their discretion. Every one who takes bank-notes for his goods may refuse them, if he will; and every one who takes them for a debt, takes them in place of gold or silver, which the law gives him the right to exact. The question then is, what security or protection should be provided for those who will receive bank-notes as a currency?

Public policy has determined that although the taking bank-notes is optional, yet the best security should be given for their safety as a medium of exchange, of which the nature of the case admits. The circulation of bank-notes is, no doubt, a mutual advantage to the bank and the public; but the bank acts as one body, while the public acts by its individual members, who are only occasionally and variably interested in bank-notes. The bank can, by one act, make all who shall become holders of their notes secure; and this tends not only to the confidence of the public, but to a more watchful management of the bank. It should not be the privilege of banks, or of individuals, to issue notes in small sums, to circulate widely as a currency, without first giving ample security. The banks can afford to do this, without injury to any legitimate business. In the United States, in more than a score of States, the utmost ingenuity of politicians has been taxed to provide adequate restraints upon banking. Two modes have been adopted, which are chiefly relied upon — one, simply the convertibility of all bank paper into specie on demand; and the other, in addition to convertibility, the deposit, with an officer charged by law with that duty, of some public security of the United States, or of one of the States, or of some other stock or bonds, for the notes issued to all the banks of the State. The latter is the best, and far the most successful yet adopted, and capable of being made still more effectual.

In regard to the convertibility of bank-notes on demand, there are difficulties so serious, that scarcely any approach has been made towards overcoming them. We have already, in the chapter on the Bank of England, shown how notes on demand came first to be issued, under the belief that the whole sum which might be thus issued would never be demanded at once, and that it would be practicable for the bank to pay in specie all that would be presented. That this was a shrewd guess, when it was made, is very true; and that it made the bank popular in its early career is also true; but it has opened some questions so difficult, that more than a century and a half of varied trial, and bitter experience, have failed to solve them. The question of convertibility has certainly labored under disadvantages which have been particularly unfriendly to the progress of truth. Ever since notes payable on demand, now called bank-notes, have come into constant use, there has been a numerous class, both in England and in the United States, who regard them with distrust, and yet scarcely endure any discussion which questions the advantage of immediate convertibility. This is a mistake, and its prevalence beclouds the whole subject. If convertibility, in the sense in which it is now understood, be a sound and desirable policy, it can be shown to be so both by fact and argument; at any rate, let the grounds upon which it rests be thoroughly understood.

If the question were simply, whether banks or bankers who receive the privilege of issuing promissory notes payable on demand, to circulate as a medium of exchange, should give ample security to the public that their notes should be safe and good, it would admit of no discussion. The readiness with which people generally receive paper currency makes this privilege of issuing bank-notes one of great importance, and requiring jealous care. If no other adequate security could be given, the question would be settled, for clearly some security should be given; not merely so, the best security should be given. The abuses to which this privilege of issuing bank-notes is subject, the temptation it involves, demands the best possible guarantees It is now generally acknowledged, that the promise to redeem bank-notes on demand, however desirable performance may be, and however numerous the legal enactments to secure and enforce it, has not proved an adequate protection to the public, either against abuses in the issue of notes, or in ensuring a circulation of bank-notes entirely safe and good. The security now required in many of the States by the deposit of stocks has, it is well-known, proved the most effectual safeguard against loss by the public yet tried. No doubt this mode of security could be carried to a point which would be beyond all ordinary hazard. Considered apart, safety and soundness in the circulation must be preferable to a mere promise of convertibility; for, after all, if the latter be relied upon, the security consists merely of a promise. Penalties cannot make the promise good. Hanging does not prevent murder.

If bank-notes were presented regularly for payment at some stated intervals, the ability of banks to pay would be regularly ascertained; but of the bank-notes issued in the United States, not one dollar in a thousand is ever presented for payment in specie. These notes perform all the functions expected of them, and scarce a thought is entertained of presenting them to the bank for payment. So long as they continue to circulate, their efficiency as a medium of exchange is complete: as to this, they are not dependent upon the promise to pay them in coin. It is not, then, that bank-notes may be useful, that they are payable on demand; it is, that they may be subjected to a constant test of their soundness. But as the incessant application of that test would take away all the convenience in their use, people decline applying it: and the circulation proceeds upon a tacit understanding between the banks and the people, to the effect that, if the notes are not presented for payment, specie payments shall be faithfully maintained: if the notes are presented, payment is impossible. The security of paper currency rests, in the opinion of many, upon this slender basis. They are so wedded to convertibility, that they prefer the pretence, or name, to substantial security in any other mode. The undeniable fact that convertibility is a mere pretence, that it is not now, and never has been, possible in England or in the United States, should have secured for the subject better treatment than it has yet received. That the banks, to whom this great privilege is conceded, of issuing bank-notes, should furnish the business public with such amount of the precious metals as the current wants of business demand, would be a reasonable requirement, and one with which they would be able, and could be forced, to comply. The banks have always been able to do this; for, in the large transactions of the domestic interchange of products, more than five per cent. of the payments is very seldom, if ever, required.

In July, 1857, the banks in the city of New York, where the proportion of specie is greatest and of bank-notes least, contained $13,000,000 of specie, and $104,000,000 of circulation and deposits; that is, they were subject to a demand for eight times as much specie as they had on hand. Of course, the banks of New York were badly insolvent, if ability to pay these demands in specie was a proper criterion. But it is indisputable, that these banks were then sound, and able to pay every cent they owed, for the public was then indebted to the banks the sum of $116,000,000. Between July, 1857, and January, 1858, the public reduced its debt to the banks to $97,000,000, and the banks increased their stock of specie to $29,000,000, whilst the circulation and deposits fell to $85,000,000. But, with all this great change in favor of the banks, the liabilities payable on demand were nearly three times greater than the amount of specie. Under such circumstances, it is surely forbearance that keeps the currency sound, and not convertibility.

By returns brought down to the close of the year 1856, the 1416 banks in the United States had in their vaults $58,000,000 in specie, against which there were bank-notes and deposits to the amount of $445,000,000; that is, the sums due by the banks, and payable on demand, were more than seven and one-half times greater than the amount they had to meet them. It scarce requires a glance at these figures to see that, if the solvency of these banks, or the goodness of their notes, and safety of the deposits, depended on their ability to pay their notes and deposits in specie, they were very unsound. But these banks were good and safe, because they held a claim on the public for $684,000,000, which absorbed every day from eight to ten millions of these bank-notes and deposits, and entirely pays them off, on an average, more than four times every year. The truth is, that men of business in the United States find it much more important to attend to the daily demand of the banks on them, than to give themselves any concern about their demand on the banks. The banks have a demand on the men of business for $684,000,000, accruing in the course of every two or three months, every dollar of which, although payable at maturity in gold or silver, they are willing to take, and do take, in their own notes and deposits. The banks waive a demand on the public, every three months, of $684,000,000 in specie, and ask forbearance for the sum of $445,000,000. The real advantage afforded by the banks is not that they furnish a safe place of deposit for gold and silver, for a very small portion of the deposits are made in coins or bullion, and of those which are so made the depositors receive them back in bank-notes, or pay them away by a check; it is not that the banks furnish notes payable on demand in gold or silver; but it is, that the banks furnish a medium of payment, to the amount of $445,000,000, far more effective in the payment of debts than gold itself, and so acceptable in form, as to be everywhere employed as the chief instrument of payment.

We have said, and the figures we have adduced show, that convertibility of the notes and deposits of our banks is impossible, even when the banks are in the best condition. And that this must continue to be the case, constituted as the banks of the United States are, is as certain. The main feature of the business of these banks is the discount of notes maturing at a future time: we have previously assumed that the average time to run, of the paper thus discounted, is ninety days, or one-fourth of a year. They issue to the parties at whose instance these discounts are made, their notes payable on demand, or give them credit on their books for the proceeds, payable in like manner on demand. The deposits of the banks are made up, almost altogether, from the notes thus issued, and the credits thus granted. The circulation and deposits of 1856 amounted to $445,000,000, for which the banks, by this mode of doing business, became liable on demand; that is, they received from their customers claims on the public maturing in three months, and they became liable to pay a certain amount on demand; in the year 1856, for instance, in every three months, $445,000,000, and in 1857, in every like period, $500,000,000. The paper discounted by the banks not being payable on demand would only be paid, and could only be demanded as it matured from day to day; whether the sums thus paid into the banks were eight or ten millions daily, it was all the banks could exact, and if the notes had not been discounted, the amount required to pay them would have been the same. But the banks became liable to the payment of from $445,000,000 to $500,000,000 in any one day in 1856 and 1857 — a position, stripped of the mists and prejudice which constantly surround it, which should be called, as it really is, stupendously absurd; and, in times of commercial revulsion, not less dangerous than absurd.

If the business men of the United States owe among themselves, at any one time, $700,000,000, payable in the course of three months, that payment can be required only as the paper matures. The time of maturity is that fixed by the parties to this paper; it is determined by the exigencies of the business in which they may be engaged, and it is a part of the contract. The question among the parties to such notes is not whether they will be paid at maturity in specie, but whether they will be paid according to the usages of trade, and to the satisfaction of the holders. The parties to this paper could not, as a body, anticipate the payment; by no possibility could they pay, on the 2d of May, the entire sum accruing between the 1st of May and the 1st of July. Their ability to pay depends on the gradual manner in which the notes mature — each month requiring the third of the whole, and each day only its share; the amounts paid one day assisting in the payments of the next, and so on.

The banks in 1856, however, issued credits and bank-notes to the amount of $445,000,000, payable on demand, in exchange for $684,000,000, maturing in the course of three months. They undertake what they cannot perform, and thenceforward exist from day to day on public forbearance.

The bank-notes and bank credits issued, in our system of banking, for discounted paper being merely substitutes for this matured individual or business-paper, the banks should not, in strictness, as we have often urged, undertake nor be bound to pay the notes or credits issued sooner than the maturity of the paper discounted. Whilst the banks have always a larger demand on the public than the public has on them, and whilst the banks are willing to take their own notes and checks upon deposit in payment of what is due to them, there can be neither risk nor inconvenience in allowing them the same time to pay specie which individuals accord to each other. This is all that the banks can be forced to do, simply because it is all that is possible. Under such a regulation, no suspension of payments could occur. The banks could safely keep up the supply of currency, even in the midst of a commercial crisis; as there is always more than enough due to the banks to absorb all their currency, and keep up a demand strong enough to maintain its value. When subjected to the test of instant convertibility, it may fail, but be perfectly good for the discharge of debts, which is the use to which nine-tenths of the bank currency is applied. A good bank may be destroyed by the test of instant convertibility, but remain a perfectly sound and useful institution, tried by the fitness of its issues to pay debts.

It is well known that bills of exchange and promissory notes are employed in some parts of England, and especially in Lancashire, as a currency, until within a few days of their maturity: so far as they are susceptible of being thus employed, they are none the less available because they are not due. So with bank-notes and deposits, they would perform every useful function to which they are applicable as well as they do now, if they were not payable in gold or silver for sixty days. It is only necessary for the banks to receive them in payment; this alone will make them good. The attempt to make them better, by making them convertible on demand, makes them worse, by subjecting the banks to a condition they cannot fulfil, and forcing them to defend themselves from sudden and needless attacks by a contraction of their issues, which spreads ruin and disaster far and wide. The people insist upon instant convertibility — a thing in itself impossible: the banks wait the day of onslaught, and then, in the struggle, cast the whole penalty of their failure, with tenfold more of evil, upon the shoulders of those who imposed upon them so absurd a liability. The people are guilty of an absurdity, but they arm the banks with full power to punish them with severity for the folly of insisting upon their own terms.

Independent of all other considerations, there is one circumstance which should control both legislation and practice in this matter. Individuals in their dealings, governed by the exigencies of trade and the progress of trade, give credits on their sales of from one to six months. In their estimation, the payments can be secured, or adjustments effected, within or at the maturity of that time. The banks step in and take the securities given, bearing that time, and receive the power of exacting payment accordingly. In doing so, they agree to become debtors to the public for nearly an equal amount, payable on demand. They destroy, in this way, the safe arrangement made between the original parties to the paper discounted; they change the time when payment in money could have been demanded between the parties to the paper, and they introduce an element of serious disturbance in what otherwise could have been settled without danger of trouble. The banks should neither lengthen nor shorten the credits of commerce, but aim only to effect the payments of their customers at the time fixed. Convertibility on demand abolishes time on paper discounted by the banks; for the banks undertake to pay on demand hundreds of millions, which men of trade only agreed to pay within the period of ninety days.

The expediency of making the issues of the banks payable on demand does not, then, arise from any necessity of making them so that they may be effective as a means of payment, but solely as a restraint upon the banks. But the imposition of a restriction upon the banks, in the shape of a condition which it is impossible for them to fulfil, has proved a security which of course always fails in the hour of trial. In times of confidence, the banks enjoy years of undisturbed quiet; when trouble comes, and confidence is lost, men realize that the banks cannot change paper into gold. People never demand payment of the bank-notes in circulation, unless they are alarmed; demand is then without avail, because it is general; and payment is stopped. Payment on demand is not necessary, in the regular progress of business; as a security, it is delusive and unavailable in the hour of need; and as a restraint, it is not sufficiently effective. The history of banks of circulation proves that they never restricted their issues to the amount they could pay on demand; their liabilities have ranged from two to ten times the amount of their specie.

Banks of circulation, however, here and elsewhere, are and continue to be placed under stringent legal obligations to pay their liabilities in coins. If any law could compel them to do this, and still leave them power sufficient to carry on the business of banking with the same advantage to their customers and the public as at present, the currency they would furnish would indeed be the best attainable for circulation. For a paper currency of sufficient amount, absolutely and at all times convertible, would combine almost every conceivable advantage. The obstacle is, that such a convertibility is impossible; no legislation can accomplish it; the omnipotence of the British Parliament could not achieve it. Even the unusual provision in the constitution of the State of New York, which denies the power to the Legislature of legalizing a suspension of specie payments, availed not in 1857, during the fearful panic of the hundred days. This precaution about the notes did not extend to the deposits. The banks suspended upon their deposits, which were ten times the amount of their notes. They have since resumed, and have now $31,000,000 of specie to $90,000,000 of notes and deposits. With this enormous and unusual accumulation of gold, payment on demand rests only on the forbearance of the people. The depositors could bring the banks to a state of suspension in two hours. Upon this state of facts, the common phrase that our bank circulation is based on gold and silver is absolutely untrue. If our paper currency had no other basis than this very uncertain, insecure, and ultimately impossible convertibility, it could not be upheld for a week, nor even a day. The real basis of our paper currency, that which does sustain it through extraordinary emergencies, is the individual promissory notes, and other evidences of debt, in exchange for which it is issued. These must all be paid, or the debtors must fail or suspend. The business men of the United States owed the banks, in 1856, the sum of $684,000,000; and the banks were indebted, for their circulation and deposits, $445,000,000. If we suppose that these debtors to the banks were 100,000 in number, owing an average of $6840 each, all this mass of business men would be active agents in redeeming the issues of the banks, of which the average burden of each would be $4450. The products of the industry of a country being sold, individual paper being given therefor, and the issues of the bank being given for that individual paper, it is evident not only that the issues are based upon that paper, but it is equally evident that the commodities for which the individuals issued their paper have come into their hands, that they have these commodities to offer to the public for the notes in circulation, and for checks on the banks, with which to pay their debts. The real strength of the banks is in this, that their business is founded on the trade and industry of the country; and all the business men, with the commodities of daily consumption in their hands, are under the strongest inducements to offer these commodities for the notes and deposits of the bank.

It must not, then, we repeat, be supposed that the basis of our paper currency is specie; the fact is, and must be, otherwise; that is no foundation to be relied upon, which must go with the first flood. No superstructure like our banking system should be reared upon a quicksand. We do not urge this as an argument against convertibility on demand, in the aspect of a check upon the banks. It may be necessary or expedient, but cannot be so on the ground of its being the basis, or adequate security, of bank issues. We should not make the concession even by implication, that $50,000,000 or $60,000,000 of gold and silver can be any proper basis for issues or liabilities of the banks to the amount of $445,000,000 to $500,000,000: it is a mere delusion, to regard the former amounts as sufficient to sustain a demand for the latter. If some of the European potentates who maintain armies of half a million, were to reduce their numbers to fifty thousand, upon the mere hope of forbearance on the part of those who could injure them, they would act as wisely, on the vital subject of public defence, as we do in regard to specie payments by the banks. France, with fifty thousand men in arms, would be overwhelmed in a day. The potentates of Europe are not so indifferent to the dictates of worldly wisdom. But our banking system disregarding alike common sense, worldly wisdom, and the lesson of Holy Writ, which teaches a ruler to consider beforehand whether he can overcome an enemy with a thousand who comes against him with ten thousand, undertakes, with fifty millions in its strong-holds, to meet five hundred millions always ready to come against the banks.

We object, then, to a phrase so likely to mislead, as that of calling gold or silver the basis of paper currency, under the present constitution of our banks. The obligation to pay on demand can be nothing more than a check on the abuse of banking, or a security to the public, and as such only should it be regarded and discussed. If it be indispensable, it is upon the ground that no other adequate security is attainable. We do not believe this, and regard this attempt to place the credit system on the back of our coinage system, as partaking of that caution and wisdom which would place a locomotive, for its best service, upon a one-horse cart.

§ 3. *Bank issues and agency the chief actual medium of payment — New York banks in* 1857 — *Contraction of the currency — Fund out of which debts are paid — Process of paying continuous — City banks and country banks — The former chief agents in payments — Demand for specie — Panics — Results — Banks increase, despite the abuses of banking — Progress and effects of rapid contractions of currency — That which is called specie payments — Banks at the mercy of the mob, and the men of business at the mercy of the banks.*

But whatever may be said in defence of the position, that paper currency is based upon the precious metals, it is very certain that, both in this country and England, paper currency is the chief medium of payment. In the first eight months of 1857, the clearings or payments at the New York Clearing-house fluctuated between $655,000,000 and $770,000,000 for each month. In addition to which, large payments occurred, not indicated at the Clearing-house. All payments made in any bank by a check on that bank are completed there, and do not go to the Clearing-house. The banks only resort to the Clearing-house for the adjustment of the checks they receive, and the claims they hold upon other banks. The monthly payments of New York were little less than $900,000,000, from January to August, 1857. During that time, the average amount of specie in the banks was under $12,000,000, the deposits averaged $95,000,000, and the circulation $8,000,000. It is apparent, then, that $103,000,000 of bank-notes and deposits effected, by aid of the books of the banks, payments of not less than $30,000,000 daily, whilst the $12,000,000 of specie in the banks scarcely moved at all.

The actual agency of the precious metals in these current daily payments is altogether too small to be either appreciated or noticed. It is only employed for the payment of occasional balances in the foreign and domestic trade. We have already adverted to the fact that, when the panic of 1857 set in, it cost the city of New York a contraction of bank facilities to the amount of $66,000,000 to retain $12,000,000 of gold. In August, 1857, the loans of the New York banks amounted to $122,000,000, and the deposits to $94,000,000; in the middle of October, the loans had fallen to $97,000,000, and the deposits to $52,000,000. Thus the banks were obliged to withdraw from the public $66,000,000 of paper currency, to keep $12,000,000 of gold in their vaults. This was withholding $1,000,000 daily, of the customary bank facilities, for sixty-six days. So long as the banks could, by this extraordinary contraction, keep their average of specie to nearly the amount of $12,000,000, they continued it. About the middle of October, even this terrible expedient failed. The patience of the public gave way; the people stepped into the banks and took out $4,000,000 of specie, and the banks stopped. But the consequences and operation of this contraction are not shown by the fact of the withdrawal of $66,000,000 of currency in as many days. The amount of currency at any particular time never exhibits the amount of payments which that currency can effect in a single day; its power or efficiency must be estimated by the sum of the payments which can be accomplished within a given time. The real contraction or diminution of payments would be shown by a comparison of the actual transactions of the banks for a day or week at the different periods compared. As it has not been customary to report the whole movement of the funds in the banks, we must resort to the Clearing-house for the best approximation. The average clearings in New York exceeded $700,000,000 each month, from January to August, 1857; in September they were $481,000,000; in October they were reduced to $308,000,000, much less than half the monthly average from January to August. Here is an actual falling off, in the monthly payments of the Clearing-house alone, of $350,000,000, or more than $12,000,000 daily: that is, the effort of the banks to keep less than $12,000,000 of specie, involved a diminution of the payments of the city of $12,000,000 daily. The whole sum of the payments made in the Clearing-house, in the months of September, October, November and December, 1857, were less, by $1,428,000,000, than the amount paid the preceding four months. The severity of this contraction was further shown by the advance of interest, from eight to ten per cent. in July, to twenty-four and thirty-six per cent. in October.

By whatever forms or complications it may be covered or obscured, the main business of the banks, especially in the chief places of trade and industry, consists in this payment of debts with credits, or by mutual set-off. The banks keep books for their customers, in which they are charged with the notes upon which they are indebted, and credited for the notes discounted or deposited. These notes are funded on the books of the banks, and every creditor of that fund can use it to pay his debts. It is obvious that, in this operation, there is no special virtue in the individual notes discounted or paid at the banks. These notes are merely evidences of debt. The debts are just as susceptible of being set-off without such evidences, as with them. Persons who are mutually indebted upon book account may set-off their debts, or balance their accounts, upon the evidence of their books. So a bank may keep the debt and credit account of a thousand persons, may set-off their debts so far as they are mutual, and collect the balances due to those who have more coming to them than they owe upon any evidence of indebtedness which the parties might deem sufficient. This adjustment may be effected by banks, or by any similar institutions; the mode of doing it, whether by bank-notes, bank deposits, or the books of the bank, is not of the essence of the operation; that consists in discharging or extinguishing debts by credits.

The extent to which this is done yearly, in the United States, may be approximated by reference to the movement of the New York banks. The returns of the Clearing-house, for the year 1857, give over $7,000,000,000[1] as the amount of the clearing between the banks. Taking the whole payments of the city at $8,000,000,000 yearly, and the aggregate of the whole country at tenfold this amount, and we have a total of $90,000,000,000. Of this sum, a close analysis of the business of the banks shows

---

[1] If the last half of 1857 had been equal to the first, the amount would have been $8,000,000,000.

that at least $85,000,000,000 are paid by set-off—a proportion which will not be very different, whether the real amount be more or less than the above. The banks have, then, a vast business of adjustment to accomplish among their customers, which is not dependent for its efficiency or success upon gold or silver, or coinage. This indebtedness is all expressed in a money of account perfectly understood by the parties who employ it. In this money of account, a thousand or a million of debt expresses precisely the same value as a thousand or a million of credit. The parties are dealing upon perfectly equal terms, so far as the figures go, and in a language they perfectly understand. To make these payments, they require neither gold, nor silver, nor coins, nor scales, nor weights, any more than they are required by those who are balancing their book accounts.

Another feature in the business of the banks should not be overlooked, in a strict analysis of their processes. If they were to close their operations strictly every year, their discounts of interest would not only have to be paid in money, but also all the debtor balances of their customers. The banks can only be paid in their own paper or credits, so far as their issues go; all further amounts payable to the banks must be discharged in money, or what is equally good to the banks. But the business of the banks is continuous; they are constantly receiving and reissuing their own notes and credits. In the year 1857, the loans of the banks averaged $728,000,000, which amount would run off, on the average, and be renewed at least every ninety days, making the sum of the loans or discounts, for the year, $2,912,000,000. To keep up the daily average of $728,000,000 would require, on every day, a payment of over $8,000,000, and a daily or weekly receipt of discounted paper large enough to restore the amount thus daily paid off and extinguished. The banks thus carry on a constant business of issuing new currency as the old is returned. Strictly speaking, a bank-note is only a medium to pay bank debts; so, also, with credits for proceeds of notes discounted in the shape of deposits. In practice, they are efficient substitutes for money, because the debtors to the banks must have them. The banks, therefore, can safely take their own issues for profit or interest, because it absorbs an equivalent portion of their liabilities; those of their customers who have balances in their favor can retain them in the shape of deposits, and carry them thus into the next year's account or business. Just as persons having mutual accounts settle their books, and ascertain the balances: but instead of paying them, carry them forward, and merge them in a new account.

The banks thus enable men to carry their accounts on continuously on their books, without regular payment of all balances in money; the process of setting-off debts going on without interruption, and without the intervention of any legal money, as men continue their mutual dealings for years, without any other payment than that which is effected by mutual accounts.

We have already intimated that the attention of those desirous of reforming our banking system has been too exclusively directed to the issue of bank-notes, as if the whole mischief of the system proceeded from the abuse of that power. Even if it were the fact, that the evils of the system belonged mainly to the power of issuing bank-notes, a distinction should be made between country and city banks. The former issue bank-notes more largely, in proportion to their capital and business, than the latter. The country banks, which rely for their business and profits upon their circulation, have more to answer for, in reference to the over-issue of bank-notes. The legislation proper to prevent abuses of the country banks might be very injurious to the system of banking in the great marts of industry and trade. It is upon these that depend mainly the steadiness of the currency, and the firmness of credit throughout the country. The failure of a country bank to redeem its issues, and its refusal to grant the usual facilities, have little effect beyond the limited circle of its business; but when the banks in the great money-markets in the large cities fail or refuse to grant the usual banking facilities, the effects are felt throughout the country. They are financial centres; their prosperity and their adversity both radiate to the circumference; they wield millions, where other banks wield thousands. It is to these powerful and influential institutions that we must look for some of the hazardous aspects of our banking system. They are the heart and lungs of the whole system, and any disorder in them sends dismay and danger through all the members. Passing by the special hazards of country banking for the present, we give our attention to the evils which specially beset the city banks, and through them inflict serious injuries upon the whole country.

The great commercial adjustments or payments of the United States are effected at the banks in the chief cities. At least one-tenth in amount of the whole occur at New York, and in proportion at New Orleans, Boston, and intermediate cities. The movements of the credit system tend strongly to a concentration of payments in these cities, but especially in New York. It is found to be economical, and otherwise advantageous, to effect payments at a point common to as many as possible. The men of large business, and the banks throughout the rest of the country, have their agents or correspondents in New York. A vast concentration of payments is accomplished: and where the payments are made, there, of course, the fund for payment is accumulated. Banks and individuals of the interior, North and South, East and West, make and receive payments in New York. Besides the great accumulation of funds, there is also, of course, a great concourse of borrowers. The banks of that city report a line of discounts exceeding $100,000,000. If this runs off every sixty days, the discounts in a year would amount to over $600,000,000 yearly. These discounts of individual paper yield an average daily deposit of from $75,000,000 to $100,000,000. We have, in speaking of the amount of the daily payments, shown with what great effect these deposits are wielded; with such success, that, with the aid of only $6,000,000 or $8,000,000 of circulation, payments to the daily amount of $30,000,000 are accomplished. These payments being made with a fund formed by the discount of individual paper not due, the circulation proceeds with a rapidity fully equal to any possible change of ownership. It could change hands, if the demands of business required it, every hour in the day, or more frequently, if needful; six times daily would, with $75,000,000 of deposits, pay $450,000,000. But whether the payments each day, in New York, are $30,000,000 or $100,000,000, they are made in the way we have designated. This fund, in the shape of deposits and circulation, is kept up by a line of discounts averaging say $2,000,000 each secular day; it is extinguished, also, at the average rate daily of $2,000,000; for the debtor in every note discounted at bank pays it by a check upon that fund; his payment absorbs and returns to the bank an equivalent amount of bank-notes or deposits. For this sum of $2,000,000 daily supplied by the banks to the paying fund, the banks engage to pay specie on demand: the notes discounted by them are payable at an average of sixty days; but the banks, so far as they and the public are concerned, make them due at once. This undertaking of the banks adds nothing to the efficiency of the fund, in its function of paying debts; for this medium of payment is always effective, so long as persons are willing to receive it. The banks in New York keep on hand, for the purpose of facing this obligation to pay $100,000,000 on demand, a sum of gold and silver averaging ordinarily from $10,000,000 to $15,000,000; they do not ever attempt to retain a sufficient amount to meet their liabilities, for, if they did, their business would not meet its expenses. They are, then, every day exposed to a demand for specie from three to ten times greater than they can meet.

In the ordinary course of the domestic trade they would seldom be called on for an amount of gold or silver great enough to cause an alarm, or seriously diminish their reserve. But New York is the point from which shipments are chiefly made to pay adverse balances, and the banks are especially exposed to a demand for all the gold required to pay unfavorable balances in the foreign trade. If over-trading has taken place, and heavy balances are to be paid, the proper penalty of over-trading, in the shape of high exchange, should fall upon the over-traders, who have to remit for their adverse balances; but our banks are required to ward off this penalty, and furnish, for the credits upon their books, the whole amount needed, and that without the privilege of charging any premium. The dealer in bullion can lawfully demand a premium for gold or silver, according to the nature of the demand, and the pressing necessities of the buyer. Every holder of a coin can ask for it any price the exigencies of the buyer may compel him to give; but the banks must part with their coin at the legal price, be the demand ever so pressing.

It is not difficult to see what abundant food for panic there is in such a condition of things. Persons in the United States have claims to the amount of $400,000,000 on the banks, payable on demand; these claimants know that the banks cannot pay in specie the fifth part of them, and often not the tenth part. And although the specie is not what they need, or would ever have asked, yet they know that the banks may stop payment in an hour; that they will then be branded as bankrupt; and that they may thereupon be subjected to injurious and damaging legal proceedings: panic becomes, therefore, inevitable. Men in such circumstances feel themselves to be involved in a wide-spread, complicated calamity. They fear the result, not only for the amount of their present deposits, and the bank-notes they hold, but they tremble for other debts due to them, and are in equal dread about what they owe. They know that if this machinery of the credit system is stopped, or seriously disturbed, debts cannot be paid. The banks, under the influence of a panic, knowing that they can neither trust one another, nor the unreasoning public, for an hour, adopt what seems to them the only safe course; they receive in payment all their issues as fast as current payments return them, without, however, as usual, keeping up the currency by fresh discounts. If the payments at the banks amount in the United States, for each day, to $300,000,000, the withdrawal of the usual facilities at the banks by contraction, to the extent of even one-half, would rapidly absorb the stock of bank-notes and deposits applicable to current payments, and of course make these payments daily more difficult, and finally, to a large extent, impossible. High interest, such as eighteen, twenty-four or thirty-six per cent. per annum, supervenes in this hour of trial to check still further the circulation of that portion of the bank-notes and deposits not absorbed by the banks.

In the fatal panic of a hundred days, which occurred in the last quarter of 1857, vast numbers of men in business failed in the United States, and hundreds of millions were lost in the wreck of credit, in the depreciation of securities and of property, real and personal, besides hundreds of millions lost by the check to industry, the stoppage of business, and the cessation of labor. Millions of idle laborers lose millions of dollars daily. The loss in a panic of a hundred days is a fearful thing to contemplate in figures! How much more so the reality, if it could be brought at one glance under the eye! The grave of many vast fortunes, the gulf which has swallowed the competency of thousands, the comforts, the homes, the food and raiment of millions who toil with their own hands for their daily bread!

It is calamity like this which opposes to the banking system of Great Britain and the United States a mass of prejudice, which nothing but its real utility and importance could withstand for a day; which brings down upon it, from time to time, a load of obloquy enough to crush or blot out any system or institution with which society can at all dispense. The Bank of England has, during the whole period of its existence, borne the blame and odium of most of the commercial revulsions and financial panics which have visited Great Britain. It has had to bear all sorts of Parliamentary intervention and restriction; and it has been the constant object of attack and vituperation on the part of journalists, authors and legislators. The bank has not only lived through all this, but in fact grows stronger from year to year. Whilst it is impossible to deny that there is some ground for all this enmity, and all these objections, the fact stands out obvious to all, that the advantages of the bank to the public are such, that it cannot be dispensed with.

It is the same with the banking system of the United States. It has borne enough of reproach, censure, and legislative restriction, to have wholly repressed, if not destroyed it, but for the evident fact that it was a system which the people could not surrender nor replace. The censure has been strong and well-founded; the objections to the system, and some of its workings, are well taken; the prejudices are the result of real mischief. The benefits of the system have outweighed all this, and the number of the banks in the United States is growing rapidly,[1] there being now more than four times as many public banks as there were in 1830. The great increase of private banking-houses of late years proves that the public banks had not transcended the demands of business. The public of the United States have decided unmistakably not only in favor of the continuance of our banking system, but in favor of its enlargement. This decision has been made against strong objection, great outcry, and persevering opposition. Upon the evidence of the past, we must conclude that our banking system cannot be put down, nor its progress wholly stopped. There is, therefore, the more reason that its faults should be understood, and the proper remedies applied.

Our banks are so constituted, that when the ignorant and alarmed multitude commence a run for coins, they have no resource but to withdraw the usual facilities of banking from the very men of business to whose custom they owe all their profits, and to whose forbearance they owe every day's existence. When this race begins, the banks, whilst they are daily receiving, in their own notes and credits (checks on deposits), the sums payable to them, withhold the customary facilities or discounts from their customers, and by this means create such a strong demand for bank-notes and credits for payment of debts, as checks their presentation for the specie. The stream of bank-notes and deposits sets steadily and strongly towards the banks, and returns to the public in a constantly decreasing volume. The demand of the banks upon the public may continue unabated for some sixty days, in which time, in a commercial community, the stringency may become such, that few, if any, can have bank-notes or credits upon which to make demand for specie; and those who have will be tempted by the debtors to the banks to accept

[1] The progress of banking in the United States may be seen in the decennial increase. In 1782 there was 1 bank; in 1790, 4; in 1800, 28; in 1810, 89; in 1820, 308; in 1830, 330; in 1840, 907; in 1850, 824; in 1857, 1400.

at the rate of twelve, eighteen, twenty, or thirty per cent. per annum; and thus these bank-notes and bank credits will be returned to the banks in payment of debts, in place of being presented for payment in specie. The contraction in New York, in the panic of 1857, is a specimen of what the banks are constrained to do, to save themselves. They can only protect their coffers by refusing to issue the usual supply of currency. The diminution of loans and deposits in the banks of New York stood thus in August and October, 1857: —

	Loans.	Deposits.
15th of August............	$121,241,472	$92,356,328
19th of September.........	108,777,421	75,772,774
17th of October...........	97,245,826	52,894,623

This exhibits a reduction of discounts, in one month, of $13,000,000, and in the succeeding month of $11,000,000; that is, $24,000,000 in sixty days: in one month deposits ran down, under this operation, $17,000,000; in the succeeding month, $23,000,000; making, in the two months, a reduction in the chief medium of payment of $40,000,000. The deposits were thus reduced nearly one-half. It cannot be surprising that, under such a process of contraction, interest went up to between fifteen and thirty-six per cent., and exchange down to nine or ten per cent. below par. What the banks did in New York was done, in a greater or less degree, in other cities; bankruptcy, ruin and destruction followed. It is estimated that from five to six thousand failures occurred, involving an indebtedness of from $280,000,000 to $300,000,000, with a loss to creditors of more than $150,000,000. But this loss bears no comparison with that arising from the depreciation of securities, and from the fall in price of real and personal property, which, judging from the results of estimates carefully made, cannot be less than $500,000,000, and may not improbably be twice that sum. The loss sustained by the men who labor for their living is even more severe in its consequences, if not equal in pecuniary amount. A million of men idle for six months involves a loss to the country of $150,000,000, besides the loss upon the machinery, shops, tools and factories, which stand idle when the workmen are unemployed.

The late panic has inflicted, in all its bearings and ramifications, a loss upon the country which may be variously estimated from $500,000,000 to $1,000,000,000. No doubt the ill effects of the panic were much enhanced by the previous abuse of credit, and that a considerable portion of this devastation should be set down to that account. With every allowance in that respect, we shall have a vast sum of loss to charge to the panic; and whether this sum be $400,000,000, or $800,000,000, matters not to our view. The loss was, to a great extent, unnecessary, cruel, terrible — a loss which has carried privation, distress and ruin to a million of homes. For a time, at least, not yet passed, it reduced hundreds of thousands of the best people to a state of entire dependence, if not beggary.

What was the occasion of these dire calamities? The banks of the United States had a reserve of specie for several years previous to 1857, and during the first half of that year, amounting to somewhat over $50,000,000; and of this, the banks in the city of New York held a little more than one-fifth. To save this amount of specie, the banks contracted the currency one-half, denied the usual facilities upon their books, put up the rate of interest from twelve to thirty-six per cent., put down exchange upon England to nine or ten per cent. below par, reduced the revenue from customs to less than half the usual amount, drew a surplus of $20,000,000 of gold out of the public treasury, and drove the government to an issue of paper promises to pay its current expenses, deprived hundreds of thousands, perhaps millions, of their customary employment, caused some five or six thousand failures among men of business, and finally inflicted a loss on the country, in the depreciation of securities, in the reduction of prices and by insolvency, of several hundred millions.—Not to save this sum of fifty millions from being lost, sunk in the ocean, or thrown away, were all these evils encountered, but merely to prevent it from passing into circulation among the people, or at the worst, to prevent it from being exported in payment of debts due in foreign countries. Nine-tenths of the debts of the country are paid, as we have seen, by the agency of discounts and deposits, with some aid from the circulation of the banks; but the banks have been placed under such heavy penalties to pay all their liabilities in specie on demand, that when they are threatened with a panic, a commercial revulsion, or a heavy export of specie to foreign countries, they are compelled, like Samson in the temple of the Philistines, to pull down the whole fabric of credit, public and private, about the ears of the people, to disturb and check the progress of industry in all its departments, to make bankrupts of their customers, and to sow pauperism broadcast in the field of labor.

This compelled policy of the banks, under the stringency of the laws which govern them, has been called paying specie. But with how little propriety. Instead of paying their liabilities with commercial promptness and the faithfulness of those who are discharging a legal and moral obligation, they resist it with all the power and weapons they can command. In the struggles incident to this resistance, they strike down friends as well as enemies, and deprive the public of an amount of currency necessary to business, ten times greater than the specie they are unwilling to pay out. And this is the convertibility so long aimed at, and to secure which so much legislation and so much thought has been expended! This is the triumph of banks which pass through a season of panic and revulsion without suspending! — a triumph like the victory which leaves 100,000 dead bodies on the field of battle, which makes 10,000 widows, 50,000 orphans, and 200,000 paupers!

We have spent half a century in heaping penalties upon the banks, to enforce an honest and full discharge of their promises; the performance consists in hurling back the penalties upon the heads of their customers, to disable them from asking a compliance with these engagements. Among individual merchants, that would be regarded as a very unsatisfactory kind of punctuality, which consisted in keeping creditors at bay, by depriving them of the power of asking for their dues, or by destroying them so effectually, as to prevent all possibility of their being troublesome. Such, thus far, is the achievement of legislation in reference to the banks. The penalties imposed are so heavy, and the consequences of suspending specie payments so much dreaded, that the banks do not hesitate to use all their power over their customers, and over the money-market, to save themselves: that power involves a sacrifice of greater amount than the whole capital of all the banks, with all their deposits and all their specie. This power of the banks has been not inaptly called the screw: when the banks become alarmed for their own safety, they apply the screw to the public, with such vigor, as to return with multiplied effect all the pressure and all the restrictions which the public has imposed upon them.

There is something absurdly and fatally preposterous in a policy which loads the banks with obligations they cannot fulfil, which imposes penalties they cannot escape, and then allows them to protect themselves by casting these burdens and penalties upon the very public for whose benefit they were imposed. Whatever may be the propriety of placing the banks under the most stringent regulations against abuses, and under the necessity, in all circumstances, of paying specie, it can neither be expedient nor wise to make it the interest of the banks to destroy credit, and paralyze industry, for their own protection. The people who force their banks to pay their issues on demand, under such imperfect regulations, do so, as we have seen in the panic of 1857, at a cost tenfold the amount of specie involved. Under such provisions, the banks at times must suspend, or the people must bear a pecuniary depletion fearful to contemplate.

In every struggle between the public and the banks, the public has had the worst of it. Banks may be destroyed; but, under their present constitution, their downfall involves greater mischiefs, and more destruction of capital, than many times the value of their corporate interests.

§ 4. *Banks intended to be a public benefit, not a public evil — Public right to the facilities afforded by banks — Contractions of the currency, and results — Remedies — Discounts, proceeds payable ot a future day in money, but receivable at all times for debts to the banks — Deposits legally payable at a future day, but receivable in bank at all times for debts — Bank-notes payable at a day future, but receivable for debts — — Long credits an element of disturbance in the credit system — Diversion of the funds of the credit system from their proper channel — Credit currency should be so marked as to be known — Country banks — Their business of a different nature — Present banking system not adapted to it.*

It cannot be doubted, in view of all this, that some change is needful in the very constitution of our banks; the payment of specie, in the mode in which it has been enjoined, cannot be enforced but at a cost which should never be encountered. If the banks are rightly placed under these obligations, their compliance should be full and free, without reservation or evasion, but especially should it be without any retaliatory measures against the public: if they are tolerated or encouraged as useful institutions, they should not be permitted to wield, for their protection, a power so irresistible, and a weapon so destructive. Having received their charters, in good part, upon public considerations; having offered to the public certain banking facilities and conveniences; having drawn from its previous channels certain portions of business, and the custom of large numbers of men in trade or manufactures, no sudden withdrawal of these facilities, no hasty desertion of their customers, should be endured, much less a policy more destructive than civil war, famine or conflagration.

The banks commenced their business, with the avowed purpose of serving the public, as well as making dividends for their stockholders. The business thus undertaken concentrates in the channels formed for it, and flows on with a steadiness proportioned to the regular progress of trade and industry. The facility afforded by the banks is very great, and their compensation is ample. Having assumed this position, they have given the public a title to the facilities of banking, for upon no other ground would their corporate existence have been conceded; the public have a right to their discreet and well-ordered continuance.

It could never have been within the contemplation of legislators, that banks might, at their pleasure, arbitrarily discontinue their functions, and refuse to be the medium of commercial payments; and while they were exacting fulfilment of every obligation, on the part of their customers, deny to them altogether the usual means of meeting their payments. It certainly never could have been intended, when the obligation to pay specie was imposed upon the banks, that this obligation should be accepted as a condition of their charters, but with the liberty of denying to the public the very facilities that banks can best furnish. The community in which banks are situated have a right to expect that they will continue the business of banking with a reasonable degree of consistency and steadiness. This function is too important to be the subject of starts and stops, or any unnecessary variations. Its progress should keep pace with the business of the time. The institution which obtains a charter to carry on the business of banking, which afterwards secures a large number of customers, with whom, of course, a still larger circle of business men are connected, and then, without sufficient reason, suddenly shuts its books and refuses to continue business in the regular and accustomed manner, commits an offence not less grave in its nature, and much worse in its results, than that of suspending specie payments.

In the regular progress of industry and trade, new business-paper is constantly made, and as constantly finds its way to the banks; while that which has been discounted matures and is paid, the new paper is offered for discount, by which the deposits, as they are paid to the banks, are replenished and kept up in amount. A contraction cuts off the supply of discounts and deposits; and whilst the notes of individuals are maturing, they are suddenly denied the usual, and indeed the only, means of paying them. They may be making their average sales, and receiving the usual paper; but the banks, in a state of contraction, refuse new issues, though they exact punctual payments. A firm doing business to the extent of $400,000 yearly, has payments to make, averaging over $1000 each day. A severe contraction by the banks may ruin such a firm in a month; that is, if the banks, during one month, withhold the usual facilities to the extent of only $15,000, it may stop the firm, and inflict upon it a loss of $100,000, or more, and other injuries wholly irreparable. When the bank screw is on, it bears upon all who have large payments to make; the scarcity is felt by all, and of course mutual assistance to any large extent is out of the question, and the resort to advanced rates of interest becomes inevitable. So, when the banks of the United States have a line of discounts amounting to $600,000,000, a contraction of $50,000,000, or $100,000,000, in a month, may cause thousands of men to stop payment, with a damage of hundreds of millions, besides accompanying mischiefs and evils, such as we have before indicated. A suspension on the part of the banks, however carefully it should be guarded against and avoided, and whatever inconveniences and losses it may involve, is an evil which cannot for a moment be weighed against the calamity of a contraction. A suspension may or may not be a serious evil: it may last for days, or weeks, or years, or even for a quarter of a century, as did that of the Bank of England from 1797 to 1822, with more or less damage to the banks, and injury to the currency. A contraction by the banks, if severe, or amounting to only fifty per cent. of their usual discounts, will in a week create distress and panic; in a fortnight, inflict bankruptcy and ruin upon multitudes; in a month, wide-spread insolvency, destruction of credit, a ruinous fall of prices, a paralysis of industry and trade, with all the train of starving multitudes, crowded almshouses, and overflowing prisons. But in dealing with the banks, our legislators have forsaken the old adage, "of two evils, choose the least;" they have spent their whole ingenuity in devising means to enforce the uninterrupted payment of specie, leaving the banks at full liberty to inflict upon the public all the evils of a contraction, as the only means of avoiding the disgrace of a suspension. No greater or more fatal mistake could have been committed; the results of this error in legislation can perhaps never be estimated. The history of banking proves, beyond question, that most of the mischiefs which have proceeded from the system have been caused by irregular action on the part of the banks, but more especially by rapid contraction in the face of a demand for specie. Experience has taught us, too, that all this legislation, and all these sufferings, are insufficient to secure the continued convertibility of bank liabilities.

We are forced to the conclusion, then, that there should be legal provisions against undue contraction, not less stringent than those against suspension. The former being, indeed, immeasurably the greater evil, demands proportionable care on the part of the public authorities. It may be thought that the evil is without remedy. The analysis of the processes of banking already presented, encourage us to believe that it is much less difficult to prevent needless contractions by the banks, than to secure the payment of $500,000,000 of liabilities with $50,000,000 of specie.

We know, by observation of the business of banks and their customers, that it is not specie these customers most need. The man who has $20,000 of his notes maturing in June, may in advance ask the bank which is the holder of these notes for a discount of notes held by him for that sum, payable in October. He does not ask for gold or silver, or for bank-notes; he merely wishes a credit on the books of the bank, upon which he can draw for the amount of his notes as they mature. He knows this is the business in which the bank is chiefly engaged, and that more than nine-tenths of the payments made to the bank are made by checks on it, or some other bank: he therefore neither needs nor thinks of specie in reference to his payment of $20,000. He may owe the banks $100,000 upon notes which will mature in three, four or six months, and hold the paper of others sufficient to pay the whole amount, provided he can have the needful facility for applying it. For this class of customers, who have to pay in bank from $5000 to $50,000 a month, it is proper that some legal provision should be made against the capricious use of power by the banks. It is against these that the power of contraction is exercised with such fatal results;

they are the chief business men of every community, and as such entitled to any protection wise foresight can provide.

The banks, therefore, should be authorized and required to open accounts with such of their customers as may desire it for the mere purposes of adjustment: that is, when a man offers a note, having four months to run, at a bank for discount, the proceeds in this new account to be placed on the books of the bank to his credit, payable in lawful money of the United States on the day when the discounted note matures, but receivable by the bank at all times in satisfaction of any debt payable at the bank. The bank would thus give for discounted paper, not money, but a credit on its books, payable in money as soon as the paper discounted is payable. The advantage to the customer is, that he receives at once funds to pay his debts in bank — funds divisible to the minutest fraction, convenient, safe and manageable. This is just what the man of business wants; his personal credit enables him to purchase on time, for his own paper, whatever his business requires. He gives the same advantage he enjoys to those who purchase from him; and the bank completes the transaction, by enabling its customer thus to pay his notes with the notes of others. In this part of their business, the banks would be dealing with their customers in credits, in a manner agreed upon beforehand, and mutually advantageous. They would then be authorized to open two accounts with every customer who desired it — one for money, and one for credit. The depositor of money would, upon a special book, and with a special form of check, be always able to draw money or transfer it. Upon a credit account, the depositor could only draw the same kind of funds he deposited; but his deposit would at all times be applicable to payment of any debt to the bank. Applications for discount would state whether the amount was needed in money, in bank-notes, or in a credit on the books of the bank. If granted in money, it would be paid in money; but if in credit, the proceeds of the discounted paper would be credited accordingly, and entered as a deposit applicable to all payments to the bank, but payable in specie only on the maturity of the paper discounted. The banks, by agreement, receive all deposits upon the condition of their being repayable in coins in sixty or ninety days, but receivable for any debt due the bank immediately, and at all times.

In this way a bank would only lend money when it had money to lend; and it could lend credit at all times, upon good notes, to any amount, because it would only become liable to pay in gold when the paper discounted matured. In this part of its business, a bank would have claims upon its customers for the same amount, and payable at the same time, as the claims of the public upon the bank. In other words, a bank would hold the notes of individuals for, say $100,000, payable on the average of two months, for which it gave credits on its books to the amount of $99,000, payable in specie *pari passu* with the maturity of the discounted paper. The debtors of the $100,000 must pay the bank, in the progress of the two months, $100,000, or $1000 in money, with $99,000 of bank credits. The latter is, of course, the currency in which the bank is paid; and it is this last process which it is important to separate from transactions in money, that it may not be interrupted or deranged by every fluctuation in the demand for money. It is one of the processes of the credit system, the magnitude and importance of which is far beyond any use of the precious metals.

But whilst it is quite practicable and proper that the banks should be bound to keep this process by special accounts with their customers open for the purpose of adjusting debts, it is evident that although bank-notes are employed in the same way, and are applicable to the same uses, yet their use cannot be left to any private management between the banks and their customers. The employment of bank deposits or credits is confined chiefly to the narrow circle of bank depositors and dealers in securities; but bank-notes take a wide range of circulation, in very subdivided amounts. Their proper tendency is always to the bank which issues them; its notes and deposits are the proper fund to pay debts to a bank, and are of course eagerly sought for by all its debtors. So wide is their track of movement, and so undoubted their usefulness, that every precaution should be taken to protect, not only the holders of the notes, but to uphold the confidence of the public in a security which, if wisely and skilfully managed, can be made to perform so successfully the functions of money. The economy of employing bank-notes, so far as they are applicable as substitutes for money, furnishes additional motives to guard against all practices or abuses which may bring discredit upon them.

In strictness, bank-notes should not be issued, payable on demand, in exchange for individual notes payable at a subsequent day, for the reason we have urged, that such a promise on the part of the banks is delusive; they cannot fulfil it, if required. It is made in the confidence, not of performance, but of forbearance. The public, in this respect, cannot rely upon the bank, nor the latter upon the forbearance of the public. Bank-notes issued in exchange for individual paper at four months, and the same with notes of shorter date, should in strictness be issued at four months, so far as it regards payment in specie; but *receivable immediately, and at all times, in discharge of any debts payable at the bank.* The banks might safely issue their notes in this form, and be ready to meet them when due, or at any time afterwards; in this form, with the security of public stocks, with ample margin, they would become as safe a currency as has ever been devised, and as free from fluctuation.

The inconvenience of making every bank-note payable in specie on a day corresponding with the maturity of the discounted paper on which it is issued, would involve some trouble and expense; but it is very certain the ingenuity of bankers and engravers could overcome this difficulty. Bank-notes payable on demand should never be issued, beyond the amount of specie actually in the bank. Bank-notes payable at a future day should only be received on deposit in the credit accounts, where they would be applicable to all the usual purposes of payment, without being convertible on demand. Deposits not actually made in coins or bullion, should by contract be legally payable say in sixty or ninety days from the date of the deposit, but be receivable, in the meantime, for debts in bank. With such regulations, the banks would never be under the necessity of enforcing any ruinous contraction of the currency, for their issues would return at the same rate as their liabilities to pay specie would accrue. They could continue to issue the average sum of currency, without hazard, as it would expose them to no instant demand; they could save their customers in a commercial crisis, and thereby stay the diasters of a contraction, which is one of the most direful evils of modern times.

The income of the banks would be in their own issues, or in money; that portion not received in their own issues would be received in money, or in some currency fully satisfactory. If the regular course of payment into the banks did not return their own issues in full, they would be subject to a demand for specie for all that might remain outstanding; and this should be a sufficient stimulus to watchfulness and caution in their business, both in the matter of issuing their own currency, and receiving that of others. They could then pay every demand for specie without any necessity for contraction, and they should be held to it by ample securities deposited for that purpose, with the penalty of a high rate of interest for any delay. Let the banks have ample opportunity to be useful to their stockholders and to the public; let their engagements be only such as, with proper care and skill, they can perform; and then let faithful performance be rigidly exacted. Let them have no power to oppress a whole country, in the mere effort to save themselves from a temporary suspension. Let not specie payments consist in making a famine, in place of offering a feast.

It is a frequent subject of remark and complaint, that in some departments of business the credits upon sales are too prolonged. There is, it is well known, much abuse of the credit system in that way. Industry, as well as climate, has its seasons and its yearly cycle. It counts its achievements and its gains by the year. The consumption of the annual products of industry has its regular stages, and its yearly completion. The distribution of trade is governed by the order of consumption. The time given upon sales should be controlled by the same rule; credits should not be prolonged for a year, but should be governed by the progress of consumption. That which is consumed should be paid for, and that which cannot be consumed should not be represented by paper in the processes of the credit system, in any of its agencies. The credit system is one of pure adjustment. It adjusts the accounts between labor and labor, commodities and commodities, capital and capital, and between all these as variously commingled and the persons who control them, where the circle of movement has been completed; commodities for which no debt has accrued, and no paper has been issued, are not yet items in the accounts of the credit system. Long credits do not fully change this condition, but only introduce complications and confusion.

To trace all the mischiefs of prolonged credits, given rather as a temptation to the purchaser than as any facility to the progress of consumption, would well repay the trouble, but might lead us out of our path. We can only make a remark in reference to their effects upon banking. We have seen that one of the chief advantages afforded by the banks is the facility they afford to men in business, of applying their credits to pay their debts; the paper which they take being discounted and applied to the payment of that which they give. In doing this, the banks act as agents of both parties, debtors and creditors, because collectively they are but one party — all are debtors, and all are creditor. The power of the banks in this agency depends, in no small degree, upon whether the maturity of the discounted paper does not fall too widely apart. As a general thing, persons who give notes in the progress of their transactions, payable at a future day, endeavor to take the notes of those with whom they deal, payable at times not too far off to be applicable, by aid of the banks, in discharge of their own paper. If a portion of the customers of a bank should give their notes at four months, and take the notes of others at eight or twelve months, the banks would properly hesitate to discount the long paper. When the notes given by a merchant mature within one, two or three months of those which he takes, the banks can. stand between the parties for this short time without risk; and allow the customer whose notes mature in March to pay them with the proceeds of notes payable in June. The notes of the bank issued in March, or the credit given on its books at that time, being payable in specie on demand, the bank is exposed, from March till June, to a demand for the amount of its notes or credits, at the pleasure of the holders. This is qualified, however, by the demand for the notes or credits on the part of the debtors who must be prepared, in June, to lift their notes, by returning in full the issues of the bank, or the money in their place. The shortness of the time between March and June begets an active demand for these issues, which not only sustains their value, but their circulation. In the case supposed, they are all required to pay the notes maturing in June; but being receivable for all debts due to the bank in the mean time, the demand is constant and efficient. But if we suppose the merchant whose notes mature in March, has taken notes payable in the following December, and that he pays the bank with the proceeds of these long notes, the bank must be exposed to a demand for specie for its issues upon this long paper for nine months: besides, the drawers of the notes payable in December are under no strong pressure to obtain the issues of the bank for a payment so remote. One of the chief elements which sustains and makes active a bank circulation is thus removed. A single instance of the discount of long paper is of course of little account; but if long credits become common, and the banks discount the paper to such an extent that a considerable portion of their issues or liabilities rests upon it whilst they are under obligation to pay on demand the very amounts thus issued, they must wait six or nine months to be reimbursed. The liability incurred by the banks is the same, whether the paper discounted is long or short, for it is immediate; whilst the liabilities of the debtors is only at the maturity of the long paper. This not only materially lessens the demand for the issues of the banks, but tends to diminish their value, power and usefulness as a substitute for money. Not being in brisk or urgent demand for the legitimate purpose of payment to the banks, they would run into other channels; and the banks would be compelled to pay them long before they could receive payment of the paper on which they were issued.

The banks being merely dealers in credit, cannot safely discount paper which soon results in a loan of money. They have not the money, and therefore the policy would be ruinous. That active demand for bank-notes, or bank funds, which best keeps them in good credit, and supports their circulation, can only be secured by a strong current setting towards the banks in payment of debts. The more rapidly the banks absorb their issues, the more confidence they inspire in the public. The banks, therefore, which are dealing in paper having an average time of three months, may prosper and be extremely efficient; whilst those which deal in paper averaging six months may not only fail of being useful, but be speedily and utterly ruined. When credits are short, the whole adjustment is soon completed: credits and debts meet on the books of the bank and extinguish each other: the debts are paid, the debtors are acquitted, the liabilities of the banks are absorbed, and the risk is over. When the credits are long, the process of absorption by the bank is slow, the circulation is languid, the parties to the paper remain longer liable, and the risk of the banks is greatly increased.

The mischiefs of long credits, even so far as banks are concerned, are not confined to the cases where such paper is discounted by them. The banks are so largely interested in the movements of credit, that any irregularity in the general system soon reaches them. The adjustments of the credit system contemplate not the evasion or postponement of payment, but actual set-off and final payment. If a hundred tons of iron are sold six times in a year, each time at a credit of two months, for $3000, the notes taken by the persons selling furnish, through the banks, the means of paying all without risk; for no one is liable longer than two months: but if one of the intermediate sales is at eight months, a link in this chain of credit is, if not broken, so drawn out, as to interrupt the progress of adjustment. With the short credits, the notes furnished the means of payment; but the long credit stops the process. The long note can furnish no facility for paying the note preceding it in order, and it must be paid in money, or from other resources. Long credits, therefore, interrupt the regular order of payment: and even if the proportion of these long credits do not exceed ten per cent. of the whole, the effects of the interruption may extend with bad results throughout the whole of the vast operations of the credit system, and be distinctly felt and perceived by the banks. Long credits are, then, not only violations of the proper laws of trade, but they are a dangerous interference with the safe working of the credit system.

Another abuse of the credit system deserves more attention than it has received — the misapplication of funds which specially belong to the regular processes of adjustment, by turning them aside to other channels of business, in which they are employed and treated as money. It is a very evident proposition, that all the debts and all the credits are equal, as they are but counterparts; whatever is the debt of one man, is the credit of another: it is equally evident, then, that, in a direct adjustment, it would require all the credits to pay all the debts. The only reason why the debts, in every mode of payment, do not absorb all the credits is, that the circulation given by the banks to a portion of the credits reduces the amount necessary to pay the debts. It is still true, however, that the proper application of the credits, in the working of the credit system, is to pay the debts, so far, at least, that every man shall have the opportunity and be held to avail himself of it, to apply what is payable to him in payment of what he owes to others. If credits are largely diverted from this, their legitimate channel, the result must be severe pressure in some quarter for means of payment. We have seen that the fund by means of which the chief payments of industry and trade are made, is formed by the discount of the securities created in that business. If, when this fund is formed by the action of the banks, it is used for other purposes — if it is employed in the purchase of real estate, in the erection of buildings, or in the construction of railroads — it is withdrawn from its proper channel, which was to follow in the track of the business out of which it originated, and to make the payments accruing upon those transactions.

If we could bring into one view all the debts to be paid, and see at the same time the position of the credits applicable to the payment, we should perceive at once the danger and the evil of perverting these credits from a disposition so appropriate for individuals, and so necessary in an industrial and commercial point of view. The whole public are deeply interested in the faithful progress of these payments. It is, however, mainly a work of individuals. Neither the public authorities, nor the banks, can apply the credits, or pay the debts. The whole process is one of individual effort; the banks are passive agents, and merely furnish the means of adjustment. If credits have been short, the paying of the discounted paper will create such a demand for the issues of the banks, that there will be little danger of any misapplication or perversion. Individual debtors find that all their means, and all their activity, are required, to keep pace with the rapidly maturing paper. If, however, motives more strong intervene, such as a rage of speculation; if debts are extensively incurred for building up towns, constructing railways, or other like works; if the debtors apply the whole or a portion of their credits to these purposes, which are wholly without the credit system, then they must either to that extent fail to pay the debts of trade and industry, or apply to the banks for accommodation loans, or renewals of their paper as it matures. These shifts are fatal to the sound working of the credit system; they show that the debtors have parted with the fund which should have been applied in payment, and that they are reduced to the necessity of asking the banks to carry the debt for them. This the banks cannot do without imminent risk. When the holder of a deposit draws his check upon a bank and pays a debt, a debt and credit have met, and both are extinguished. A debt is paid, and the bank is acquitted of a liability to the depositor to the same amount. But if the debt is continued by accommodation, or otherwise, the deposit or credit is not used, and the bank remains liable, and not merely so, but liable on demand — a risk which grows dangerous in proportion to the extent of such practices. The banks which discount new notes on time as they are offered, giving bank-notes or deposits in exchange, payable on demand, and which to any considerable extent renew or continue the discounted paper, giving further time, must very soon reach a point at which they and their customers will both collapse. If this wrong practice does not originate in a perversion of the funds applicable to the payment of the continued debts, it leads directly to it.

The instances of the misapplication of funds belonging strictly to the operation of the credit system, and the non-payment of debts in consequence, are numerous and flagrant; the results are full of admonitions. No severe and continued pressure in the chief marts of England and the United States, no commercial revulsion has occurred in these countries, no ruinous contraction of the currency, no general destruction of credit has happened, of which this misapplication of the funds of credit has not either been the chief, or at least a leading cause. It will not be denied, that our banking system is responsible for a large share of this mischief.

We have seen that all the funds thus perverted are the proceeds of commercial or business-paper discounted by the banks; these proceeds belong of right to the adjustments of the credit system, but, owing to special circumstances, are applied to other purposes. They are not money, but merely securities. The promissory notes and bills of exchange, before being discounted, would not be susceptible of such perversion, because they are not convenient nor efficient as currency; but when, by being exchanged for the notes or deposits of a bank, a currency is made, the danger of perversion begins. The power and functions of money being conferred upon the proceeds of this discounted paper, it begins to be regarded as money. It belongs, however, not the less to the channel of adjustment in which it originated. The character and functions of these issues of the bank make them very efficient, and add greatly to their usefulness; but with these advantages comes the danger of misapplication; for these issues are not merely a currency — they are a currency, supposed to be convertible, on demand, into money. If the entire issues of the banks were really so convertible, nothing could be said against any use of them which could be made of money; as they are not in fact, or by any possibility, convertible, the assumption is dangerous, by the facility it affords, and the temptation it offers, to employ bank issues as money.

Of the hundred million of deposits and circulation which the New York banks report, probably not five millions are at any one time applicable to any other purpose than to the current payment of the debts of industry and trade. These absorb over $30,000,000 daily. If, then, $50,000,000 of the hundred should be abstracted from this legitimate use, and diverted to other purposes, $50,000,000 of debt would remain unpaid; not only so, but the still larger sum which this $50,000,000 would have paid by the ordinary process of circulation would also remain unpaid. The withdrawal of such a large sum from the current payments of the day, and above all, the stoppage of the circulation of this sum, and the failure of payment involved in such stoppage, would be attended with results so disastrous, that it would be difficult to conjecture where they would end. The ruin of many fortunes might be in the path of this evil; the sacrifices to be made, the losses by fall of prices, the high rates of interest to be paid, and the manifold other mischiefs involved in this irregularity, show that the funds which belong to the payments of the credit system cannot be applied to other uses without consequences as lamentable as they are unjust. It may be true, that it is not possible to prevent such abuses; that they are, in some measure, incident to the use of credit. No doubt some abuses are incident to every form of credit, and that it is not possible to avoid all. We believe it would greatly lessen the abuse of credit, if the distinction between money and credit were more carefully studied and observed. If it were fully admitted that, of the $100,000,000 of deposits and circulation of the New York banks, not more than $5,000,000, or at most $10,000,000, could be spared at any one time from current payments for other purposes, banks and merchants would be more watchful to prevent or check such a perversion of credit as would inflict a public injury. It would no doubt greatly assist this repressive influence, if bank-notes and bank deposits were only payable in specie at sixty or ninety days. These funds would then be marked, and their proper destination would be known. They could not be so readily drawn off and applied to other purposes. The misapplication could be more readily detected and defeated. The banks are so much interested to prevent this abuse, that they would promptly avail themselves of any additional power or facilities they might employ against it.

We have regarded the banking system of the United States only in its general aspects. There is much that is special which should arrest the attention of those who would become familiar with all the details of the subject. Every part of the country has its peculiarities of business, which impress their special features on the local banking. Some care may be necessary in drawing very general conclusions; all which must be modified more or less by peculiar circumstances. The distinction between the business of city and country banks is one of those important circumstances that should not be forgotten in any effort towards improving our banking system, which, as we have explained, owes its power and success to its being one of the principal agents of the credit system. This agency, as we have seen, consists mainly in exchanging the credit of the banks, in the shape of bank-notes and deposits, for the securities or evidences of debt issued in the course of business. By the purchase of these securities, the banks become the general creditors of persons in business, and are enabled to receive their own issues in full discharge of all these debts — debts which, by law, are payable only in gold or silver. The power of the banks to furnish this great facility to the public depends upon the demand which the banks can create for their issues. If the demand for bank-notes and bank deposits is not constant and strong, they cannot long perform the functions of money; and no such demand can be created or exist, unless it come from the debtors of the bank who are under the necessity of providing the means of paying their debts as they mature from day to day. The concentration of payments involving vast sums makes the demand for bank funds peculiarly pressing and constant in the great cities and marts of trade. This is likewise proportionably the case in cities and towns of less importance. In the country towns, or in strictly agricultural localities, the banks find great difficulty in absorbing their issues fast enough to sustain the regular movement of their legitimate business. The proper destination of these issues is a return to the banks in payment of debts. This completes the circulation which gives them the title of banks of circulation. If the tendency of its issues is not directly and strongly back to the bank, in payment of debts due to it, there is good reason to fear that the bank will have difficulty in sustaining itself.

Such, in fact, is the case of the country banks. The circulation in their vicinity is not rapid enough, the debtors of the bank are not sufficiently numerous, and their transactions are not large enough to turn the current of the circulation towards the bank in payment of debts. If the issues of a bank are in such credit as to be employed as money, but not in demand enough to carry them back to the bank in payment, they leave the vicinity of the bank, or pass into other channels of circulation, and become liable to be returned, not in payments of debts due to the bank, but as a demand on the bank for specie. Whilst they circulate in the vicinity, they are a medium of payment to the bank, and prove, as such, a great facility to the debtors of the bank; but when they are carried out of the reach of the debtors, these are, to that extent, less able to pay the bank, and the bank is, to the same extent, exposed to a demand for specie. This is the chief practical obstacle to country banking under our system. The customers of the country banks are, for the most part, rather borrowers of money than credit; the banks cannot supply this demand for money, and issue bank-notes in place of it. The notes are carried to distant markets, and employed as money, whence they are immediately returned to the issuers with a demand for specie. This disturbs the operations of the banks, and unduly restricts their business. They do not profess to be lenders of specie, and they cannot turn their paper into gold or silver. The return of the notes, however, is perfectly proper and unavoidable. It is just as proper for the city banks to exact payment from the country banks for their notes, as it is proper for the latter to issue them. The truth is, that our system of banking is wholly unsuited to a mere country business. Banks of circulation require a rapid movement of their issues, short credits, and prompt payments. This is possible among mechanics, manufacturers and merchants, whose business is active throughout the year, but not among farmers and planters, whose cycle of industry and sales is completed once in a year. The country banks may safely deal with such of their customers as can pay in ninety days; but, not without great trouble and risk, with those who can only pay in a year. No mere modification of our banking system can remove this difficulty. Instead of bringing the practice of the city and country banks nearer together, by mutual concessions, they should each strive to accommodate more perfectly their respective customers — the city banks by dealing more exclusively in credit, and the country more exclusively in money. The complete success of the Scottish banks, in maintaining a paper currency in a small country like Scotland, does not prove that it could be done here with equal steadiness and safety, even upon their system. The semi-weekly exchanges of the banks in Scotland, which is an essential feature of their system, could not be applied to the whole United States. The difficulty of maintaining the exchanges of the banks in New England, by the agency of the Suffolk Bank, proves with what ill-grace the country banks there submit to this needful regulation. Whilst it is the essential condition of the soundness of the whole body, it is regarded by the country banks separately as a severe and unnecessary curb to their business; they deem it a hardship that they cannot employ their credit as largely and successfully as the banks of the cities. Their circumstances, however, are so different — the radical distinction in their business, which we have indicated, is so great — that they cannot, by any possibility, be placed on the same footing: the issues of the city banks are returned to them in payment of debts due to them by their customers; those of the country banks are brought to them by strangers, who demand the specie, or other payment equally difficult to make. So far as country banks receive from their debtors and customers funds which will redeem their notes when thus sent in upon them, their position is strong, and their business legitimate: and by this criterion the well-managed country banks are usually guided. Their business is largely done by the issue of bank-notes; it is to these issues, and the difficulty the banks have in providing for them when payment is demanded, that the attention of legislators and bank reformers has been chiefly directed. They have erred in their course by overlooking the distinction between the business of the city and country banks; all measures of reform should be skilfully adapted to the position of both classes of banks.

The people are deeply interested in the proper working of the banks; and when any unwise measures of change or reform are proposed or enforced, the public is more apt to suffer from the results than the banks. The power of the banks over all departments of business is sufficient to enable them to ward off danger and injury, but too often at an immense expense to their customers and the community at large. The true agency and utility of the banks, in their several positions, should be studied and promoted; the whole people being more interested in the proper working of the banks than even the stockholders or owners of the banks. The main point is to require of all banks of circulation ample security for their issues, in some form in which it can be made available upon short notice. Security being provided against all abuses, the business of banking should be promoted to the utmost, as a public advantage. There should be no monopoly, for all persons willing to comply with the prescribed conditions should be as free to engage in it as in any other business. The guaranty should, in strictness, cover the deposits as well as the notes, and should be of the highest kind attainable in the country. Such security being deposited with the public, the banks should be allowed to issue bank-notes payable in specie at not over four months, and to receive deposits payable in specie at not exceeding three months; both notes and deposits receivable at all times by the issuers for debts due to or at the banks. Holders of notes and deposits presenting them for payment before they are payable in specie, and not being paid to their satisfaction, should be entitled to double interest to the day when such notes and deposits become payable in specie; and for all delay of payment afterwards, four times the rate of lawful interest should be chargeable until payment be made. And to enforce such payment, proper summary remedies should be provided.

The issue of small notes, by which some mean notes under $20, some under $10, and some under $5, is regarded by many as the chief evil of our banking system. They hold that the paper currency should have a metallic basis in circulation to support it; and that, if the small notes are withdrawn, their place will be supplied by coins. This is a mistaken view; coins in circulation make no basis for paper currency; the withdrawal of the small notes in New England would not be followed by an equal circulation of coins. The small notes are issued for convenience; if they were withdrawn, two-thirds of the amount would be supplied by larger notes. If notes under $5 were now freely issued in Pennsylvania, a large proportion of the $5 notes now in circulation would be issued in $1, $2 and $3 notes. If New York and New England were to prohibit notes under $5, they might get from ten to twenty per cent. of the amount in coin. The people there would regard that coin as dearly bought by such an abstraction of paper currency. By law, every person may exact whatever is due to him in gold or silver, and make his payments in the same. Every person may, therefore, enjoy a hard money currency. No one does it; the usages of the country are opposed to it. The small note question is, in fact, without real importance; it does not reach the main problems of banking. The banks of Pennsylvania, with notes of $5 and upwards, stopped payment in the late crisis before those of New York and New England, circulating 1s, 2s and 3s. The commercial integrity, the intelligence and mutual confidence of a people determine the quantity of paper currency, be the notes large or small, which the people can employ with advantage.

But we must pause. It was not our intention, nor is it within our plan, to offer any projects of reform or improvement for our banking system. In making the suggestions at the close of this chapter, we offer them in part as mere illustrations of the subject, and do not, therefore, even attempt to follow these suggestions by proper details. We leave that to men of more experience, if any such shall deem these suggestions worthy of their consideration.

CHAPTER XVIII.

INTEREST.

Distinction between prices of precious metals and interest or the price payable for the use of them — The price of each fixed by the State — Evasion of such regulations — Fluctuations in the price of gold and silver not coincident with fluctuations in the rate of interest — Do not proceed from the same causes — Payments of the credit system — When interest is high, the demand is not for coins — Demand for facilities of the credit system determines rate of interest — High interest does not arise from scarcity of that for which interest is paid, but from the fears of banks and capitalists — The usual facilities withheld from real or apprehended danger — Usury laws should not apply to paper of the credit system — Amount paid yearly in the United States for interest — Objections — Interest a part of the expense of commercial adjustment — Not a question of money, but of dispensing with money — A saving of interest practicable in England and the United States greater than the national revenue.

THE price paid for the use of money has received the technical name of *interest*. It is a subject which has occupied no small portion of the attention of moralists, legislators and political economists; but, like most other topics in these departments of knowledge, it remains a disputed subject. It is not settled what is the proper rate of interest, or a just charge for the use of money; nor whether the rate should be fixed by law, or be the subject of contract, and be left to fluctuate like other prices. Many even cling to the ancient prejudice against any allowance of interest. The history of interest, or usury as it was long termed, is both curious and instructive; but in neither aspect does it come within our present inquiry.

There is a necessary distinction to be made between the price of the precious metals, whether as coins or as bullion, and the rate of interest which is the price of the use of money — as the annual rent of a building is a very different thing from the value or price of it. Governments have fixed the price of the precious metals, by virtue of their authority; in England, public authority has declared that an ounce of gold shall be worth £3 17*s.* 10½*d.*, and further has enjoined upon the Bank of England to purchase all the gold offered to it at £3 17*s.* 9*d.* In the United States, Congress has declared, by law, that 412½ grains of standard silver shall be worth one dollar, and that 258 grains of gold shall be worth ten dollars. And in this manner the price of other coins is fixed not only in the two countries named, but in other countries. This is only an attempt to fix the price of the precious metals, an attempt which is as futile as it is unnecessary. The precious metals have their fluctuations of price, as may be seen in the price-currents of the great money-markets of the world, just as other valuable commodities.

So the rate of interest, or the price paid for the use of money, has also been made the subject of public regulation, and is, in fact, fixed in most countries at rates determined by public authority. This intervention of public authority in matters so evidently within the range of private contract, is extensively disregarded. The price of gold and silver fluctuates, and merchants and bankers are governed in their large operations by these changes; interest rules high or low, according to circumstances, in defiance of the fixed rates. It is very plain, indeed, that no government has yet reached or discovered the true mode of applying authority to these subjects, if any intervention is needful or proper. But neither of these aspects of the subject is that we desire now to consider.

The fluctuations in the price of the precious metals are within a range of two or three per cent., seldom exceeding one per cent.; whilst the fluctuations in the rate of interest have a range of two or three hundred per cent.[1] It is evident, then, that the

---

[1] The average rate of interest in London is three per cent.; in the winter of 1857–8, it was as high as ten per cent., or over three hundred per cent. above the average. The market rate of interest in Philadelphia has, for the last ten years, ranged from six to twenty-four per cent., going up to three hundred per cent. above the legal rate of six per cent.

causes which govern the rate of interest are not the same which govern the price of gold and silver. It is well known that gold and silver, as such, are worth no more, when interest is at two per cent. a month, than when it is at the half of one per cent. per month; the price of gold, in coin or bullion, is no higher in London when interest is ten per cent. per annum, than when it is three per cent. When lands and houses bring increased rents, they rise in value; when stocks afford high dividends, the price of the stock corresponds; when freights rule high, ships rise in price; and so of most other kinds of property. Coins and bullion, or money, alone remain unaffected by the rate which is paid for their use, or the current rate of interest. If fluctuations in value of bullion and coins be closely observed, they will be found to arise from a special demand for exportation, or from some other similar causes, and not to correspond in time with changes in rates of interest.

It is evident that neither coins nor bullion are the specific things sought, when the demand for means of payment is so pressing as to raise the rate of interest. The demand in such cases is for the fund usually employed in making payments. This alone can be obtained in sufficient amount to make current payments, and it is, therefore, the real object of the demand. Commercial paper is very rarely purchased or discounted with coins. Where commerce is greatly developed, nearly all large transactions are upon credit; the payments are postponed, and evidences of debt are received instead. A single merchant may purchase to the extent of $100,000, giving his notes for that amount; he may sell to the extent of $105,000, and receive the paper of others. What this merchant wants is not $100,000 in coins, bullion, or bank-notes, to meet his engagements to that amount; he needs the means or facility of applying $100,000 of the paper he holds, in extinguishment of the $100,000 he owes. He never thinks of obtaining coins to make these large payments, and of course makes no application or demand for them, even though the rate of interest may have risen against him two or three hundred per cent., and the market price of gold and silver may not have changed at all. If our example be taken of a thousand persons instead of one, and those in the same vicinity, it will be found that the sum of their dealings with each other, represented by the paper they hold, amounts yearly to hundreds of millions — a sum which could not be discharged in coins as fast as it would mature, and which no one thinks of so paying. Each one of the mass is a creditor and debtor, and the desideratum is the readiest and least expensive mode of applying credits to debts. If each one had made all the paper upon which he is liable payable on the same day on which he had arranged to receive all that is owing to him, the whole payments could be quickly accomplished. But that is not practicable in business; and the debtors find that the paper they owe matures long before that which they hold. They are obliged to exchange their undue paper for something which is immediately applicable or receivable in payment. Every one knows what he has to pay, and when it is payable; preparation is to be made accordingly; the thing to be done is not to provide money, but to effect payment — not to purchase and pay coins, but to extinguish debts. The debtor enters a field of mighty competition; but his competitors, like himself, are all engaged in finding and securing the ways and means of payment.

We have seen that the price of coins and bullion does not vary with the rate of interest, and we say that they are not the articles specially sought when interest is high. They do not fluctuate in value with the greater or less amount of such payments; they are scarcely taken into the account for any agency they have, or can have, in such payment. By the law of legal tender at least $3,000,000,000 in coins could, every year, be demanded of debtors in the United States. Of this vast sum, not one dollar in $10,000 is so demanded. The precious metals, whether in the shape of coins or bullion, are not, then, the chief medium of payment employed in this country. Every creditor may demand such payment, if he prefers it; almost without exception, however, creditors do not elect to be so paid. Debts are paid by other ways and means.

The rate of interest must depend, of course, upon the supply of that fund or medium in which debts are usually paid. Debts are paid chiefly in three ways; by balancing accounts, by the delivery of bank-notes, and by checks on bank credits usually called bank deposits. Those who are indebted to each other upon mutual accounts, have the matter in their hands so fully, that they can pay or discharge their debts at their pleasure. Each party has the fund in which to pay, and their action can have no appreciable effect on the rate of interest. But the debts so paid are not considerable, in comparison with those which take the shape of promissory notes and bills of exchange. These are the evidences of debt chiefly employed in moving the great staples of trade. It is for payment of these that the demand for the means becomes so pressing and intense, as to affect the rate of interest to the extent of several hundred per cent. It is this demand for bank-notes and bank credits which governs the rate of interest or discount. In large commercial transactions upon paper drawn payable at a future day, interest takes almost exclusively the shape of a deduction of a certain rate per cent. from the amount of the security, according to the time it has to run.

He who has $100,000 to pay in June and December, who holds paper of his customers payable in October, must with that paper purchase bank-notes, or bank credits, applicable to his debts maturing in June; and to do this, he must submit to a deduction or discount, according to the current rate of interest, from the face of his paper maturing in October. He deducts four months' interest from the paper sold, and receives the proceeds in that which he knows to be available in the discharge of his debts. The rate of this discount depends mainly on the demand for such funds as are applicable to the payment of debts. We have heretofore remarked upon the intensity of this demand; no other urgency of trade can be compared with it. Ruin stares him in the face who permits his note to go unpaid. The penalty of failing to pay is fearful, indeed, and the rate of interest is affected accordingly in times of pressure. It is only in seasons of absolute famine that even food is sought with such avidity as the means of paying debts; and famine prices for food are much more rare than famine rates of interest. One, two and three hundred per cent. of an advance in the rates of interest is by no means uncommon.

It may, then, be considered as certain that interest is not a price paid for the use of gold or silver, in coins or bullion. No demand for the means of payment, however intense, increases the price of the precious metals. Interest is the price paid for that fund in which debts are usually paid, the origin and use of which we have fully explained.

As the credit system is at present regulated, a demand for gold and silver may undoubtedly affect the rate of interest, not because they may possibly advance in price one or two per cent., but because the demand disturbs our present banking system, on the regular working of which the supply of the fund employed in paying debts depends. So great may this disturbance be, that a demand for coins or bullion for exportation which only raises the price one per cent., may raise the rate of interest from one to three hundred per cent. But this arises from the circumstance that we try to make the whole fund out of which debts are paid, convertible on demand into gold or silver. The banks of New York, for instance, with a circulation of notes of only $8,000,000, are by law subject to a demand for over $100,000,000, the amount of their circulation and deposits, which is the fund by which a daily payment of over $30,000,000 is effected.

The manufacturing and commercial business of civilized nations proceeds chiefly on credit. The purchases and sales are made on credit. The great movement of production, distribution and consumption proceeds, in its regular course, upon the credit of the parties engaged in it. The payments corresponding to the large transactions which have taken place at prices and for amounts expressed in money of account, remain to be accomplished by the agencies we have indicated. These payments are often effected with far more difficulty, apart from the solvency of the debtors, under our present system, than was experienced in doing the business to which they correspond. The banks in this country are prohibited from taking more than a fixed legal rate of interest for a credit upon their books. Individual capitalists are able to exact their own rates upon securities which they purchase, by transferring merely a portion of their own credit on the books of a bank. The rate of interest, or the price paid for bank credits, is fixed by the dealings between the banks and capitalists, on the one hand, and those who have debts to pay, on the other. In a community where commercial punctuality is sustained at so high a point, that bankruptcy is the penalty of a failure to meet the payments of one day, the demand for the means of payment becomes, at times, by far the severest pressure to which men of business are exposed. In consequence of this dire necessity of punctuality, the rate of interest, where it is free to change, fluctuates with as wide a range as almost anything which is the subject of price. In the Bank of England, the rate of interest fluctuates between two and ten per cent.,[1] though this by no means marks the range in the London money-market, in which the rate is more variable than in the bank. In this country, where commercial and industrial activity is marked by greater boldness, if not recklessness, the range may be said to lie between five and thirty per cent.

These high rates do not arise from the scarcity of money, if by money is meant gold and silver, for they are not the medium employed nor demanded, and have no direct influence on the rate of interest. Neither do these high rates proceed from any scarcity of the credit fund employed in paying debts, or at least from any scarcity of the individual paper out of which these credits are made. High rates of interest are caused either by banks or capitalists holding credits at a high rate, in consequence of a great demand, or by their refusing, through some apprehension, to grant the usual credits or facilities. As there is no necessity of business so great as that of punctual payment, so there is no business in which monopoly is more sure to be rewarded, than that which deals in bank credits. Advanced rates are not caused, in any instance, by the actual scarcity of the means of payment, but always by the mode in which they

---

[1] The last half of 1852 it was two per cent. In 1855 and 1856 it frequently rose to seven; and in the panic of 1857, to ten.

are controlled, and sometimes from the want of proper control. The domestic debts and credits of every community correspond, being exact counterparts. The credits, properly managed, will pay the debts, leaving of course a great variety of balances to be adjusted among the parties, to go to new accounts, or to be paid in money or in goods. It is perfectly true, then, that it is never for want of the usual means that interest rules high; it is merely because the means of making payments are in the hands of those who can hold them at a high price, or who are afraid to part with them. This opportunity of asking and obtaining a high price is generally founded on some actual or apprehended event, which may make it unsafe to enlarge bank credits. It is not always the scarcity of a commodity which enables the holders of it to raise the price. There may be no scarcity of flour in May, yet the crops may look so very unpromising, as to cause a great advance of the price, in apprehension of a scarcity in August and for the rest of the year. The dealers in credits cannot be expected to forego the opportunity of increasing the price of their article, any more than the dealer in cotton or flour.

We abstain from such questions touching the rate of interest, as whether it should be left to find its own level, or be a rate fixed by law. These questions open a wide field of discussion, and deserve very full consideration. It seems to us, however, that a distinction should be taken between interest reserved on bonds, notes, and other instruments secured by mortgage, founded on the sale of real estate, or on the loan of money, where the day of payment is not fixed or long deferred, and those transactions which are merely a dealing in credit. It is certainly more proper for legislation to fix the rate on the first of these classes than on the second. The first is a limited class, and the result of any rate fixed could be observed and corrected as circumstances might dictate. But dealing in credit is so large a business, so complicated in its bearings, influences and results, and restraints so easily evaded, that it may be difficult, if not impossible, to detect the effect of a legal or fixed rate. There is a general belief that a legal or fixed rate of interest applied to mere dealings in credit has the effect of producing higher rates of interest, by lessening the competition among lenders and dealers in credit.

Whatever confines the business to fewer hands, tends to increase the rates, because it gives the greater power to those engaged. The fixed rate is no protection, except so far as the banks respect it. It is very well known that when interest is high, the banks are in such a state of alarm, that they reduce their business to the smallest possible circle. Individuals engaged in lending credit find some mode of evading any law which would restrict their charges. We cannot doubt that it would be greatly for the benefit of the commercial and business community, that all restrictions upon the rate of interest should be abolished upon paper not having over three or four months to run. Any policy which might tend to reduce the rate of interest on credits deserves serious attention.

The sum paid in the shape of interest, for the mere facility of applying credits to the payment of debts — that is, for furnishing the facility which enables a man to apply the debts which others owe him to the debts he himself owes — is a vast sum in any country; but in this country, and in England, it is far beyond the conjecture of any but those who have examined the subject.

The banks of the United States report, for the year 1856, a line of loans and discounts of $684,000,000; at the average rate of six per cent., they received upwards of $41,000,000 of interest on this sum. How much business is done out of the banks, it is difficult to conjecture. The transactions out of the banks are probably not less than in them, and at much higher rates. We may estimate the sum paid for discount and interest, out of the banks, at $68,000,000 for 1856, taking ten per cent. as the average rate of that year. The average rate of 1857 could scarcely have been less than fifteen per cent. So that, by this estimate, over $100,000,000 was, in 1856, paid for interest in the United States.

The clearings of the New York banks, in 1857, were about $7,196,000,000. These clearings accrue upon the payments of their customers. If we suppose that all this amount had cost the payers two months' interest, on the average, we have a sum of interest of over $71,000,000 paid in New York alone.

But another mode of estimating the sum of interest annually paid in the United States would make it much larger. We have, in the preceding chapter, estimated the payments of the city of New York at $30,000,000 daily, and have taken the whole payments of the United States at ten times this sum, or $300,000,000 each day, and of course at $90,000,000,000 for the year. Now, if this vast sum of annual payments under the credit system pays an average of sixty days' interest, or say one per cent. on the whole amount, it would make the sum of interest paid yearly no less than $900,000,000. But if the payments of the rest of the country are only five times greater than those of the city of New York, we should still have a total of $450,000,000. We do not say it is too much to pay for the advantages afforded; we think these facilities would be worth even a much larger sum, if they could not be obtained otherwise; but the amount, in any way it can be estimated, is so large, as to demand consideration whether some part of it could not be saved by more economical processes of adjustment.

It has been contended by some, that interest ought to be gratuitous; or, in other words, that as interest is a charge for the mere use of a credit, the government should furnish the needful supply of credits to the people without charge. This idea has been very elaborately repelled, but upon grounds no more sound than the position sought to be refuted. The proper and legitimate fund to meet deferred payments, in every country, is the credits, or exact counterpart of the debts. It is the proper fund, because it is the most available, the most economical, and the most rapid mode of payment. These credits being generally the proceeds of securities or evidences of debt of some kind, are always the property of individuals or corporations. For the use or loan of credits, the owners have as good a right to charge a commission, or interest, as to charge a profit on anything they have to sell, or to exact rent for the use of a house. Credits are constantly more in demand than any single thing in the marts of trade. There is nothing paid for more willingly, and no charge can be more legitimate. But this by no means obliterates the distinction between credits and money. The arguments advanced by some men of ability against gratuity of interest proceed wholly upon the ground that all interest is for money, and that it is absurd to expect a government to furnish the people with money for their business, or to pay them interest. It is true enough, that this would not only be absurd, but impossible; yet it is no more absurd than to assume that credits are money, and that interest is only paid for money. Nine-tenths of the so-called interest paid in commercial countries is paid for the privilege and facility of paying debts without money.

Commercially regarded, interest is one portion of the annual expense of adjusting commercial payments. By means of individual credit — personal confidence — the commodities of trade are permitted to go forth into the channels of trade, to be collected, transported, assorted, bought and sold, until they finally reach the hands of consumers; the payments which all these movements imply being all postponed, and finally concentrated as a separate and special business in the banks, and among brokers and dealers in commercial paper, who make this their particular occupation.

The great inquiry arising out of this business is not one of money or currency — it is merely one of adjustment. It is not how may banks be multiplied, or their issues increased, or how abuses of banking may be prevented, or guarantees increased, or convertibility insured, but how may men most promptly, and at the least expense, apply their credits in extinguishment of their debts. It is not a question how money can be obtained for this purpose; nor how far bank-notes can be substituted for money; nor is it, in fact, any question of currency or circulation, but simply a question of liquidation or set-off. It is so far from being a mere question of money, or any of its substitutes, that the problem is how to dispense to the utmost possible extent with all of them. Their use is what constitutes the greatest expense of adjustment; economy requires that the least possible resort should be had to them.

We are fully convinced that much of the friction of the credit system, now so much felt and lamented, and which results largely in that form of expense or charge which is called interest, might be prevented; and that a saving might, in this way, be effected of more than half of the whole amount thus expended. We do not doubt that the economy thus practicable in England and in the United States would, in each country, be double the public revenue. We do not say that such an economy is possible with the present machinery and methods; but with improved processes, which would inflict no shock upon existing institutions, and bring no risks with the gradual changes, the cost of carrying on the payments of the credit system might be reduced one-half, if not to one-quarter, of the present charge, with a proportionate reduction of the amount paid for interest; and that friction which is the cause of so many misfortunes, and so much distress, might be thus reduced to a point as low as human imperfections in matters of this kind would permit.

Human ingenuity on the one hand, and human patience on the other, has long been exhausted on the subject of taxation. It would be well for those who are deeply interested in the study of this subject, to inquire whether a door is not open, through the credit system, to a mode of raising the whole, or a large portion of thé revenue of a nation, by taking a burden off the national industry, instead of imposing one. The burden or tax of interest is now the heaviest which rests upon national industry in England and in the United States, and perhaps in several other nations; if half of that tax can be saved, the persons benefited could well afford to pay the whole of the national expenditure. The reduced friction would be a boon to industry and commerce almost beyond estimate. How gladly would those concerned pay the tax, if the friction of the machinery of credit, with all its uncertainties, its disappointments, its delays, its anxieties, and the dangers of its occasional crushing revulsions, and explosions could be prevented!

CHAPTER XIX.

PRICES.

§ 1. *Complexity of the subject—Market value expressed in money of account—Prices are not payments — Money a medium of payment — Prices, sales, and payments distinct things — Elements of prices — Influence of men's interests and passions — Necessity of purchasing — Necessity of selling — Fashion and fancy — Plenty and scarcity — Demand and supply — Monopolies — Commercial legislation — Duties — Speculation — Cost of production — Prices as affected in great marts of trade.*

THE subject of prices, always an absorbing one in commercial circles, has only recently engaged the attention of writers upon political economy. Few of these have brought to the task that practical knowledge of commerce which is indispensable to its adequate treatment; and many have brought only that love of theory and system which too often goes before, instead of following a full knowledge of facts. We fear that a long time must elapse before this subject will be cleared of the difficulties which environ it, and be reduced to that order and certainty desirable in so important a department of knowledge. Very few contributions have yet been published which go far to produce such a result.[1] It may be doubted, too, whether it be susceptible of

[1] Since the above was written, a work of eminent ability and great research has appeared in England, which is, beyond dispute, the most reliable and useful contribution which has yet been made to any department of political economy. We refer to "The History of Prices," by Thomas Tooke, two volumes of which appeared in London in 1838, a third in 1840, a fourth in 1848, and two more in 1858, in which last two Mr. Tooke had the assistance of William Newmarch. These six volumes are a history of prices from 1792 to 1858. This valuable production will be specially referred to in the course of this chapter.

reduction to any comprehensive theory, or of any scientific arrangement. Fortunately, it does not come within the scope of the present work to attempt any adequate treatise on prices.

It is our purpose chiefly to show that those who, in treating of banking, currency and money, have hastily drawn proofs, conclusions or illustrations from the state of prices, are exceedingly prone to mistake. Whatever intrinsic difficulties exist in those subjects, and they are many, they are neither so numerous nor so complex as those which belong to the subject of prices: it is, therefore, manifestly hazardous to explain what is best known by that which is least understood. There are so many conflicting opinions and contradictory theories respecting money and its substitutes, that it is as desirable to ascertain and avoid the sources of mistake as to strive after truth. It would be almost as unsafe to resolve difficulties in astronomy by the state of the weather, as questions about money by the state of prices.

The importance of the subject is derived from the fluctuations to which prices have been subject in modern times, and in all times of which any authentic record of prices exists. As fluctuations of prices are often vexatious, untimely and hurtful to all classes; as they often beget a gambling spirit in commerce, and thereby tend to increase and perpetuate the evil, it becomes important to anticipate or to prevent them, and to investigate the causes; and equally important to avoid attributing them to wrong causes, and thence to avoid introducing false doctrines, false management, and mistaken legislation.

The price of merchandise is its market value expressed in money of account. We have shown, in a previous chapter, that among civilized people prices are always expressed in the prevailing money of account, whatever that may be; that whatever coin or coinage, thing or commodity, men may for a time use as a medium of exchange, a money of account is soon formed upon the coin or thing so employed; the value of this as a unit becomes firmly fixed in the mind, and supersedes in practice the material article which may have given it origin. A unit of this kind may originate from the use of copper or iron, as well as from gold or silver.

This invariable and unconquerable mental habit of expressing prices only through the medium of a money of account, is a great feature of this subject, without a knowledge of which it is impossible to study it with advantage. Many persons are perfectly conversant with the money of account, who know little or nothing about coins, and are unable to detect the baldest counterfeit: they are skilled in the money of account, but unskilled in money of gold or silver. Coins are made to conform to the money of account to the minutest fraction, and are thus made a convenient medium of payment, but not a medium of prices. They are not employed as a measure, but are themselves measured by the money of account.

We have treated this at large in the chapter on money of account, but it is needful to bring the distinction fully to mind now, when we propose to speak directly of prices. Many persons entertain the notion that there is some proportion between the money of a country and the prices of its commodities; and that prices are high or low, in proportion as money is plenty or scarce. There is some truth in this, but it is not true as a proposition. Prices are not dependent on money; prices are not payments; and even payments are not dependent on money.

Money, and other means of payment, may be exceedingly scarce or hard to obtain, but there can be no scarcity in the language of prices. The prices of commodities may fall, because many must sell, and the means of payment may be scarce; but the facility of expressing prices is never thus lessened. The whole of the commodities of a country have their price, but it might not be possible to sell them all in a year. The naming of prices, the making of sales, and the making payments, are each distinct operations; and, as we have seen, neither of them is dependent for its validity on the presence or use of money. Gold and silver, whether in coins or in bullion, have their appropriate uses in commerce, and these are important enough, without attributing to them an agency in which they have no part. There is no strict or determinate relation between the quantity of money in a country, and its range of prices. They act and react upon each other in a way, and to an extent, that it is well to mark and study; but these influences are too undefinable, and too much blended with other causes, to be exactly appreciated. Of all the causes which materially affect the range of prices in a country, the changes in the quantity of money are, perhaps, the least influential. On this point more hereafter.

This may suggest to those who have not taken any extended view of the subject, the necessity of caution in solving questions of money and currency, by reference to fluctuations in prices; as whatever influence money or currency may actually have on prices, there are so many other ways in which prices may be changed, many of which are remote and unseen, and many not appreciable as to their force, that no more doubtful nor unsafe basis could be selected on which to rest conclusions. The danger of such conclusions is, however, much greater than anything we have yet said suggests. It must be borne in mind that many of the most operative of these elements of fluctuation in prices are under the full play of men's interests and passions. The most powerful springs which move the human heart are found at work in this game; scope is furnished for all good and all bad principles, for the highest financial abilities and the most unremitting industry. These, too, are often pitted against sloth, inertness, ignorance, dulness and indecision. The commerce of the world, in which the whole matter of prices is involved, is a great struggle for that power which accrues to wealth — a struggle constantly maintained, with varying success, over the whole world, the advantage being generally on the side of the shrewd and skilful, but with abundant occasional evidences that the fortunes of this contest are as capricious as the favors of fortune have ever been deemed. Supposing, even, that an accurate enumeration of the causes which operate to change prices were made, who then could measure their ever-varying intensity, who could estimate the operation of men's reason and passions upon these causes; who could foresee the effect of those which are accidental; who could discover those which are hidden; who could discern those which are remote, or weigh the effects of commercial alarm, or trace the result of commercial revulsion?

Yet all this, and more, should those be able to do who would settle questions of currency by the condition or fluctuation of prices.

These suggestions in relation to prices might suffice to put us upon our guard as to the influence of money or currency upon prices; but so accustomed are many to draw support for their theories of money and banking from this source, that we propose to refer distinctly to some of the causes which chiefly influence and determine the range of prices in the marts of commerce.

The necessity of purchasing is an element of prices of controlling force. Those who have the means of purchasing cannot postpone hunger and thirst. They must secure the means of subsistence, cheap if they can, but dear if they must. The matter does not admit of delay, nor of long negotiation. It is evident, therefore, that those articles termed necessaries of life are only kept, by the extent of the supply, and the corresponding wants of those who hold them, from going constantly to the highest prices. The necessity thus imposed is universal; none can escape its force; and yet such is the variety of substances which minister to animal life and comfort, that even this necessity, and the knowledge of what it requires to satisfy the cravings of these appetites, furnish little aid to those who would estimate the supply which will meet this demand. In fact, however, men no more agree in the quantity, quality or kind of articles deemed necessary for subsistence and comfort, even in the same circumstances, than they do in stature, in features, or in mind. This necessity, therefore, which acts continually and imperatively upon prices, furnishes no data by which its force can be measured, or by which it can be distinguished from other less powerful influences. It only appears in full view when famine or great scarcity begins to prevail, and then it shows how unimportant every other article becomes, in comparison with food. The necessity of eating is, nevertheless, equally great in times of plenty as in those of scarcity. Prices are then controlled by the supply in the face of a necessity to purchase. There is, however, a wide field of conjecture about the sufficiency of that supply, both in reference to the quantity really needed, and the quantity really on hand. It is upon conjectures and estimates of this kind that men of all sorts of minds, from the most astute and well-informed to the most dull and ignorant, from the boldest and most rash to the most timid and cautious, exercise their powers: as such men determine, prices are affected; and the operations of one man are often sufficient to affect prices over a wide extent of country.

The necessity of selling corresponds very nearly to that of purchasing; for, in general, men can only realize the means of purchase by the process of selling. The compulsion to sell must operate to depress prices as much as necessity to purchase enhances them. A necessity of selling equally affecting prices, and scarcely less imperative, arises in commerce from the obligation punctually to meet engagements. This is one of the most active and operating agencies which affect prices. Merchants and manufacturers would, but for this, and the new supplies which are coming on behind, be disposed to hold their commodities for the highest prices which could be exacted. They must, however, meet their payments, or become bankrupt; and to do this they must provide the means, by making sales. Those whose wealth would enable them to hold up their goods, are controlled by those who, from want of means, are compelled to make prompt sales upon small profits. The urgency of making sales for this purpose sometimes, doubtless, becomes excessive, and causes great sacrifices; but, in general, it operates to steady prices, by interfering with the speculations of heavy capitalists.

Who can conjecture the influence of fashion, of fancy, of taste, of extravagance, of inexperience, of hobby-riding, &c., &c., upon the prices of those articles which are subject to such caprices? The newest productions of the loom, of the needle, of the tailor's shears, of the milliner's taste, are sought for with an avidity, a perseverance, and a disregard of price, which bids defiance to all discretion. So it is with the first fruit and the first fish in the market: so with old wines, old books, old coins, old paintings, and old statuary. Let any one observe how large a portion of men in trade are employed in furnishing commodities to satisfy these and similar inordinate desires, and he will be convinced that the prices of no small portion of the articles of trade are dependent upon the mere caprice of the consumers, and the adroitness of the tradesmen. The observer will find that the dealer in these articles resorts, when the rage for purchase is up, to prices which will compensate him for the freaks of customers, who often so suddenly change their wants, as to leave a large stock of articles hopelessly on his hands. Here, then, is a rapid fluctuation of prices, caused by waywardness, and folly, and caprice; and this happens from year to year, under no more regular control than the most irregular wants of the most irregular people. The results of this are, however, felt throughout all the range of prices, but with what effect who can tell?

The terms plenty and scarcity are often used in regard to commodities of trade, and with sufficient precision, perhaps, to convey no false idea. It is certainly impossible, however, to ascertain with any exactness the quantity of any principal commodity; the attempt is constantly being made, and the approximation may be useful, though only measurably reliable. It is not seldom, that large mistakes are made in these estimates. They are not unfrequently made by interested persons, with a view to influence prices; and it is well known that many important commodities, such as cotton, wheat, coffee and tea, have their prices, to no small extent, influenced in that way.

In regard to many articles, it is often impossible to say when plenty exists, or even when scarcity has occurred. There are, to be sure, occasions when there can be no doubt as to either condition. In the former cases, prices take their course from men's conjectures; and in the latter, from the apathy produced by undoubted plenty, or the excessive alarm and eagerness produced by undoubted scarcity. It is well known that, in both extremes, the natural effects are increased beyond what would appear to be the proper result. In the case of plenty, the certainty of a steady and cheap supply, when needed, relieves the purchaser from any anxiety, and he abstains from purchasing until the moment of need. The necessities of the holders may be such, that they cannot wait this time; and they are obliged to urge their stock on a market in which there is little demand, and of course at reduced prices. On the contrary, when scarcity is apprehended, every one measures the danger by his fears, unwilling to wait coolly for results which may be so disastrous. All pecuniary considerations are sunk in the dread of want, and prices go rapidly to the highest rates. In England, a very deficient harvest of wheat has often sold for more money than a very abundant one; so in the United States, as to cotton.

In regard to quantity, prices generally transcend the apparently proper limit, on the occurrence of either extreme; whilst a medium opens a wide region of conjecture, and sometimes leads to very mistaken movements.

The commercial terms, demand and supply, do not correspond exactly with the more general and absolute terms, plenty and scarcity. The first relate merely to the operations of trade, while the latter refer to actual quantities. This distinction is, perhaps, frequently forgotten, or not observed. The demand which exists for articles of commerce, and the supply which is furnished in response to that demand, can never be placed beyond the reach of contingencies, so numerous and so varied, as to be out of the reach of any possible specification. If it were the business of government to furnish its subjects with all the commodities they need, it would be possible to make such an approximation of the quantity and kinds wanted as would enable its agents to order them with some precision. Even with such advantages, any attempt to meet the changing wants, desires and caprices of men must be unsuccessful. How much more so, where the course of trade commits this business to a host of merchants, all greedy of gain, or fearful of loss, all anxious for business, but consulting chiefly their own interest, acting without concert, and without that knowledge of each other's operations which could alone enable them to pursue their business with intelligence!

Men thus situated are left to act according to their various characters — boldly, timidly, irresolutely or rashly — and according to the best information they can obtain, which at the best must be always very imperfect. Success in the operations of one year encourages them into measures which end in disaster the next; and this, in its turn, produces over-caution in succeeding times. And these alternations must ever occur in trade, while commerce is carried on by the disconnected enterprise of individuals. And yet the operation of trade in regard to supply and demand, is subject to all the influences which create these alternations; and so far as prices are affected by quantities actually on hand, they are subject to corresponding variations. The supply of commodities which is offered to consumers is not only subject to the contingencies affecting the several branches of industry which produce them, but to all the varying opinions, wishes, estimates and dispositions of the merchants who carry on the business; and in addition, to all the accidents and delays of transportation by sea and land.

The chief stimulus of production is demand; but this demand proceeds from the masses, of whom some are prudent and foreseeing, some observing and cautious, some venturous and rash, some with experience, some without, and some utterly foolish and heedless: those upon whom the demand is made are of like character; and prices are in no small degree settled, and supplies regulated, by the action of such persons upon each other. Prices adjusted by such agencies can never be foretold, and must rest upon a complex combination of circumstances, such as cannot be fully unravelled nor analyzed.

Many of the great fluctuations and jerks which occur in prices arise from the schemes, the hopes, the mistakes, the enterprises, and the deceptions of those engaged in commerce, and have almost no relation with the actual quantities, or cost of production, of those articles, the prices of which are affected. There are so many insurmountable uncertainties hanging round all questions of supply and demand, that men, in a wilderness of doubts, but grope their way at best; and the results upon prices are as little to be conjectured as those which depend wholly upon chance.

Monopolies are the subject of much complaint. The hardship

and injustice imposed by them are so visible to every eye, that they have been constant objects for the hand of reform. Two centuries ago, nearly every department of commerce and industry was under the control of monopoly in almost every country of Europe. Many yet remain, to prove what must have been the injustice suffered by those who lived when they were more numerous. Their influence upon the prices of the monopolized articles is too well known to require much notice. The inhabitants of France know well enough that the price of tobacco is greatly enhanced to them by the government monopoly; but the producers and dealers in the article, in this country, do not so generally know that, if the French monopoly was abolished, the consumption there would be increased, and the price here would be enhanced. The heavy duties of England upon the same article are equivalent to the monopoly in France; to abandon them would have the same effect of raising the price in this country. The removal of the European monopolies of our products, or of heavy duties, would at once reduce the price there, and raise it here, upon the commodities thus set free. The amount before realized by monopolies and duties would fall fairly, if not equally, to the producer and consumer, by a double adjustment of prices. Monopolies, therefore, often react upon those who may not suppose themselves under their influence, and at such a distance, that those affected may neither perceive the effect, nor be aware of the cause. The power of the monopoly is chiefly felt in its direct effort to control prices, which its collected strength, and unity of action, enable it to attempt with advantage. The effects of these efforts are often made to extend to places where few can clearly detect them, or perhaps suspect their influence. They are yet sufficiently numerous, and efficiently managed, to produce a very undoubted effect upon certain prices; and yet there is no possibility of measuring that influence, or determining its comparative force and intensity.

Commercial legislation, protective and prohibitory duties, and public revenue, exercise a very important influence upon a large class of prices; of so wide a subject, we can only touch the threshold. The chief countries of Europe commenced a system of legislation upon industry and commerce, in modern times, which has been continued, with many changes and vicissitudes, for some two centuries. A similar policy was begun in this country, as soon as it could legislate for itself. The complication of this legislation in Europe is such, that very few can trace its results. The laws relating to navigation and tonnage, the prohibition to export the precious metals, the bounties, the prohibition of certain articles, the light duties on some, the heavy charges on others, the discriminating, the protective and the prohibitory duties, the drawbacks, &c., all operating together in each country, and in conflict with those of other countries, make a compound which no human ingenuity or astuteness can so analyze and explain, as to show their specific bearing upon prices. No one in the least conversant with the subject can overlook the important influence exercised in that respect by all this legislation; and in some instances no one can fail to perceive the particular effect; but the whole result of this combination defies explanation. When, however, to this complication is added the events of war, restrictive systems, embargoes, blockades, and such measures as the *Berlin and Milan Decrees*, and the *Orders in Council*, then the elements which influence prices, and their comparative power, baffle human scrutiny.

It is worthy of being noted here, as an illustration of the rashness with which men form opinions upon matters which they have not fully examined, and do not understand, that from the year 1800 to 1815, during which time a most animated discussion on the subject of banking and currency was maintained in Great Britain, one party drew its arguments and illustrations, and formed its conclusions, upon the condition of prices in that period. The same readiness to form and express opinions on similar grounds has been shown ever since, both there and in this country; all men seeming to think that currency and prices, money and banking, were subjects about which the most authoritative decisions might be pronounced, without special knowledge or hesitation. The newest demagogues, the most ignorant and presuming journalists, the experienced and the inexperienced, and in fine all classes of men, supposed themselves fully qualified to solve questions of this kind. It has happened, therefore, that no subject has ever been so bestridden and rode down, so abused by foolish, and so confused by contradictory opinions, emanating from the highest authority down, through every grade of respectability, to zero. The few who, in this time, have devoted prolonged attention to this subject, and proved themselves painful and anxious inquirers after truth, have scarcely been noticed in the mass.

It is, perhaps, impracticable, to draw a line between the ordinary processes of dealing and what is termed speculation. What, if done by one man, would be deemed speculative, may be perfectly within the legitimate scope of another's business. What, in times of great confidence and active business, would be deemed quite prudent and proper, would, in seasons of pressure and caution, be called reckless speculation. What a man of capital may do without exciting attention, a less rich man may not do but at the hazard of being called a speculator. Speculation cannot, therefore, be defined, although its prevalence is matter of much lamentation. Its influence in trade is constantly felt, and its operation on prices is very decided and notorious. Its chief design is undoubtedly to give undue, or at least unusual, excitement to prices. Its movements are as various as the conjunctures of commerce, and the men engaged in it. The very uncertainty of the events of trade, and the ever fluctuating condition of prices consequent upon it, furnish constant openings for the intervention of speculation. The observing, the well-informed, the experienced, and the bold, are those who are ever ready to avail themselves of those circumstances which are constantly occurring in some branch of trade, by which they anticipate an advance in prices, or produce one by their own management. There are, doubtless, certain limits within which this kind of action is deemed legitimate and honorable. It is too tempting a field, however, not to be occupied by many actuated by fraud, by a greedy spirit, by rashness, by the spirit of competition, and by sheer infatuation. This class, though more irregular in their movements, are not unfrequently as successful in their operations as the more deserving: and both frequently fail of their immediate object, even when their movements are felt in a change of prices. This multifarious body of speculators may be said to be continually operating upon the market values of the commodities which they touch, and through them upon various others. This influence, like many other elements of prices, can neither be measured nor estimated in its actual or comparative force; it can neither be anticipated, nor can its evil effects, to any considerable degree, be averted, without interfering with the freedom of trade to a most injurious extent. It must continue to be a disturbing element of commerce, and prices must hereafter, as heretofore, be subject to its manifold, incessant and active agencies.

The tendency of speculation is undoubtedly to widen the range of fluctuations, not only in the prices of the articles operated upon, but also of many others. This spirit is more rife and active in times of high confidence, when prices are, from that cause, looking up, than when any depressing cause operates to check the movements of trade. It suits the views of the speculator to urge upward prices that are tending to rise, rather than to attempt staying the downward course of a falling market. Dealers in stocks speculate on their fall, but merchants only on the expected advance of goods. The general effect of speculation, whilst moving within moderate bounds, is therefore to sustain and enhance prices; and this effect may be continued for many years, under the operation of favoring causes, such as a steady government and liberally-managed banking institutions, provided there be some restraining power of sufficient strength to repress that wild extravagance to which, otherwise, speculation always hastens. The periods of greatest commercial prosperity, in Europe and in the United States, have been those in which this state of things existed. Prices must be high, when commerce is active, when new-comers are constantly pressing into business, when those already engaged are seeking to enlarge their trade, when credit is high, when all are on the alert, when personal credit is sufficient to make all kinds of purchases without the use of money, or any of its substitutes. Such causes, so long as they continue, must operate on prices; and there is no question that, duly restrained, they promote general prosperity. So all experience proves; but experience proves, also, that if this restraining power does not exist, or be not efficiently exercised, the expansion of personal credit, and the advance of prices consequent upon incessant and uncontrolled speculative action, proceeds to a height at which they cannot remain, and the whole fabric of confidence falls at once. The reaction is rapid and complete, and prices descend below their wonted level.

All who are conversant in the walks of commerce can recall the signal effects of speculation on prices, not only in special instances, but in that state of restless activity and watchfulness which prompts men to be ever looking for advantageous purchases, and to secure the highest prices for what they sell. Yet what is more common than to attribute such results to an expansion of currency, without reserve or qualification. The reverse is very often the true state of the case; the expansion is the result of the speculation, and not the speculation the result of the expansion. In seasons of confidence, when men's notes are freely received for the commodities of trade, the first step towards the evils of undue expansion is a great issue of bills of exchange and promissory notes of merchants and dealers, who thus multiply their engagements, without immediately increasing the quantity of goods in the market; and these bills and notes being, for the convenience of the holders, converted into bank-notes, an increase of circulation takes place, which is called an expansion; many evils are referred to this which clearly belong to speculation, and not to expansion of currency. If the word expansion be proper in this case, it should be applied to the enlargement of individual credit. In most of these cases, the issue of bank-notes is an alleviation of the evil, and not an aggravation. The ability of the speculating parties to meet their engagements depends on their success in selling, for bank-notes, the goods purchased, or for something else which will be received in discharge of their liabilities. The issue of the bank-notes greatly facilitates such sale and payment. If it be said that this high confidence which enables parties to make such large purchases on the strength of their own bills or notes would not exist, but for the facility of converting them into bank paper, there is much force in the objection. The fault is, however, one of degree: the advantages of individual credits, and of bank-notes, within proper limits, are generally conceded; and the first fault is committed, in this case, in the community of men of business, and not by the banks. That an increased issue of bank-notes, consequent upon over-trading may stimulate prices, especially in the retail trade, is very probable, but not to the extent, nor in the way many suppose. For every bank-note issued by discount of commercial paper, an equivalent amount of debt is created to the bank; and the demand for bank-notes to pay these debts will be equivalent to the whole issue. The parties so indebted must sell their goods, to meet these payments, at an advanced price if they can, if not at the best price obtainable. The stringency of this necessity to meet engagements, which is the more felt as the advantage of maintaining credit in bank is appreciated, has oftentimes defeated the object of speculators, and compelled them to reduce the prices which they hoped to raise, and thus to counteract the very mischiefs apprehended from the increased circulation. Large issues do not, then, necessarily enhance prices, but may often be regarded as indications of a probable reduction. The particular action of men, or the course of trade, must always be taken into view by those who desire to attain just conclusions in regard to currency, as well as prices. The same causes, under different circumstances, do not always produce the same results: and their reasoning, in political economy, and upon questions of commerce, who overlook human nature, and its actual or probable action in any given circumstances, cannot be of much value. Whatever belongs to abstract science may be explained by exhibiting the immutable laws of nature, or the unfailing processes of mechanics, or the demonstrations of mathematics; but that which depends on the minds, temperaments and passions of men, and the casual occurrences of life, can never be reduced to laws like those which govern bees and ants; neither can problems arising thus be solved by algebraic formula, or any rule of proportion.

Actual value, the cost of production, and price, are by no means equivalent terms. Articles of trade are very often sold above or below their actual value, and they are often sold greatly above or below the cost of production; but whether one or the other, that estimation at which they are sold is their actual price, a term which belongs to commerce, and really has no absolute or necessary connection with either value or cost of production. The chief inquiry in the market is as to the price; neither buyer nor seller knowing, or caring to know, the cost of production. This, though not equivalent with price, is an universal and efficient element of prices. Other influences ceasing, prices must constantly tend to correspond with the cost of production, with the expenses of transportation and sale added. This centre about which prices revolve, is itself so changeable, that no advantage is gained by considering the subject in that aspect. In truth, the cost of production depends so much upon prices, that the inquirer into the cost is carried back into an inquiry about prices, and so the investigation turns in a circle.

Fluctuations of prices arise from such a variety of complex and hidden causes, that no human ingenuity can disentangle the web. The truth is, that even if an analysis could be completed at one time, a similar state of facts might never again exist, or, existing, might not be attended with the same results. The same men do not always act in the same way, under the same motives. Important changes of price are constantly occurring, which cannot safely be assigned to any one cause or to many; and he is most prudent, who least suffers himself to indulge in positive conclusions, without means of arriving at them or verifying them. We should avoid the path which leads to error, as sedulously as we seek that which leads to truth.

To the suggestions we have thus made on the subject of prices, we add one more. It is well known, that whatever influences may be operating on the prices of the chief commodities of both foreign and domestic trade, there is a constant tendency in these influences to yield to, and be overborne by, others emanating from the chief markets or points of distribution. Whatever may be operating on the price of cotton in Georgia or

Alabama, is likely to be overborne by other elements at work in New York. The city of New York is the arena in which more power is exerted over prices than in all the rest of the country. This is not always the result of design, or of any special movement among dealers in New York; it is more the result of the estimates made by men outside of New York, of what has taken place, or may take place there. Merchants and manufacturers throughout the country know that prices are mainly made there; and all turn their eyes thither for the elements on which to base their calculations. More sales take place there than at any other place; and when sales are forced, they generally occur there. These great markets are subject to so many contingencies, both powerful and sudden, that those who are interested, wherever they may reside, are obliged to watch these causes and results with great attention, that they may avail themselves of what is for their benefit, and avoid what may be for their injury. It may, therefore, and does happen, that the conclusions and movements of those residing out of the great marts of trade influence the markets within them, in reference to many important articles. The resident merchants of New York may, therefore, find prices in the city very much affected by causes and movements in which they have been passive.

The general range of prices, as it rests in the minds of the body of dealers, is one of the most sensitive things in the world. Like the ocean, the least breath of wind from any quarter will ruffle the surface; and it requires but a breeze of demand or speculation to set the whole in rapid movement, if not wild commotion, the result and termination of which none can for a time conjecture. One of the results often observed, in regard to prices, is the vast disproportion between causes and results. When harvests are abundant, even a little beyond the average, the price of the whole product may be diminished so as to reduce the sum received for the whole by an amount many times the value of the surplus. So, if harvests are short, the product often sells for more than if they were abundant. It is the same with supplies by foreign importation; a very little over-trading may affect the prices of a large stock of commodities so seriously, as to cause heavy losses. If we suppose, for instance, that the stock of iron in New York, and within the influence of its market, to be at any time worth $1,000,000, at prices upon which a regular business and consumption is proceeding, the sudden arrival from abroad of $50,000 worth, or only five per cent. of the quantity on hand, may so disturb the market, that purchasers may refrain from buying for a time, and sellers may become alarmed and desirous of realizing before an expected fall; a decline of prices to the extent of ten per cent. on the whole stock may occur, and a loss of $100,000 thus fall upon the holders of the iron, or double the amount of the importation. Every observer of the great markets can recall instances of a similar kind, which show how difficult it is to ascertain the causes which determine the range of prices. It is often, however, as easy to see that fluctuations are attributed to wrong sources, as it is difficult to assign the true causes.

§ 2. *The effect upon prices of the quantity of money — The theory of Montesquieu acceded to by Hume, Locke, and Harris; denied by Sir James Stewart, Adam Smith, Lauderdale, Malthus, Ricardo, Torrens, M'Culloch — James Mill — Prices are not coins, but expressions of money of account — Wholesale must mainly control retail prices; the former made upon credit — Propositions of Lauderdale — Malthus cited — Also Torrens — M'Culloch—Malthus — Confliction of opinions — Marquis Garnier cited — Adam Smith cited — Ganihl cited — Humboldt's proportion of gold to silver — Jacob on precious metals — Rise of prices not in proportion to the increase of money — Arthur Young's Inquiry into the Progressive Value of Money — Tables of prices in Spain — Beawes on Spain — Prices of wheat in France.*

If the reader bears in mind the vast variety and power of those elements which operate upon prices, to which we have in part referred, he will be prepared to consider the influences, in this respect, of an increase or diminution of money. Whatever the latter may be, the others are in full activity; their operation does not cease, though other forces are brought into conjunction or opposition. Whatever inherent difficulty there may be, therefore, in the subject, must be much increased by confining the view to money as the chief cause of fluctuations in prices. It is manifest that no one can ascertain to what extent fluctuation of prices is due to changes in the quantity of money, until he can measure the effect of other influences. If this cannot be done, no conclusions can be safely drawn; if it can be done only conjecturally, then conclusions resting upon such a basis must be subject to the contingencies of the conjecture. Whatever bears upon the subject of prices, whatever degree of uncertainty hangs over all branches of the inquiry, must be taken into account when the influence of money in these changes comes to be considered.

A prevailing inclination has long existed to establish a proportion between the quantity of money in the world and the quantity of all other commodities, and to make that proportion the rule of prices. This plausible idea is very likely to have occurred to such thinkers as had very little practical knowledge of commerce. Montesquieu very unhesitatingly gave it the sanction of his high authority, and it has had the circulation of his popular work[1] "Si l'on compare la masse de l'or et de l'argent qui est dans le monde, avec la somme des marchandises qui y sont, il est certain que chaque denree ou marchandise en particulier pourra être comparée à une certaine portione de la masse entière de l'or et de l'argent. Comme le total de l'une est au total de l'autre, la partie de l'une sera à la partie de l'autre." After an illustration drawn from the supposition of there being only one article of commerce, and one individual to purchase it, he concludes: "Les prix se fixeront en raison com-

---

[1] "If we compare the mass of gold and silver in the world with the whole of the commodities, it is certain that every commodity in particular may be compared with a certain portion of the entire mass of gold and silver. As the whole of the one is to the whole of the other, a portion of one will be to a portion of the other." . . .

. . . "Prices are fixed at a rate compounded of the whole of the commodities with the whole of the signs, and of that of the whole of the commodities in the channels of trade with the whole of the signs" (gold and silver) "employed as money."

"The establishment of prices depends always fundamentally upon the proportion of the total of the commodities to the total of the signs."—*Spirit of Laws*, book 22, chap. vii.

posée du total des choses avec le total des signes, et de celle du total des choses qui sont dans le commerce avec le total des signes qui y sont aussi. . . . L'etablissement du prix des choses dépend toujours fondamentalement de la raison du total des choses au total des signes."[1] This algebraic formula grappled the mind of Hume; but, though it hindered the progress of his investigation, did not prevent his obtaining glimpses of the truth. We find, in his "Essay on Money," many sound and original views. Locke had nearly the same impediments in his way on the subject of prices. So simple and complete does this theory of prices seem, and so plausibly has the idea been presented by Montesquieu, and many others since his day, that we find it cleaving to men's minds, in whole or in part, from that to the present time.

So much is it to be lamented, when men of that stamp lend their intellect and popularity to the propagation of error! It is in vain that others, less distinguished, point out errors of fact and doctrine; their works are forgotten, while those of such men flourish in constant vigor. The same sophism which, a century ago, misled the readers of the "Spirit of Laws," the papers of the "Spectator," and the "Essays" of Hume and Locke on money, commits the same mischiefs, with equal success, at the present time. Harris, in an "Essay upon Money and Coins," published only a few years after the "Spirit of Laws," a writer of far more practical knowledge than either of the distinguished men above mentioned, was wholly unable to surmount the theory of Montesquieu, and adopts it broadly, though evidently contradicted and disproved by many of his own positions.

But this fanciful proposition was not sent to the world without being early contradicted. It was very soon severely questioned and overthrown by a writer upon political economy, who will be hereafter, as we trust, better appreciated than has yet been his lot. Sir James Stewart, to whom we refer, sums up this false theory, as he found it in various authors, thus:—

"First. The prices of commodities are always proportioned

---

[1] L'Esprit du Lois, livre xxii. chap. vii.

to the plenty of money in a country. So that the augmentation of wealth even fictitious, such as paper, affects the state of prices in proportion to its quantity.

"Second. The coin and current money in a country is the representative of all the labor and commodities of it. So that, *in proportion* as there is more or less of this representation (money), there goes a greater or less quantity of the thing represented (commodities) to the same quantity of it. Thence it follows —

"Third. Increase commodities, they become cheaper; increase money, they rise in their value.

"Nothing," he says, "can be more beautiful than these ideas. But upon a close examination of these three propositions, I am forced to range this ingenious exposition of a most interesting subject among those general and superficial maxims which never fail to lead to error." [1]

The more celebrated political economists of Great Britain who came after Stewart entertained theories, on the subject of prices, quite at variance with the idea of an adjustment proportioned to the quantity of money. Adam Smith, Lauderdale, Malthus, Ricardo, Torrens, and M'Culloch, has each his own theory, or a peculiar mode of explaining the doctrines of others. Of the more known British economists, James Mill is the only one who has fallen into the errors above noted; and he felt himself obliged to add an explanation, which forcibly exhibits the absurdity of this summary method of adjusting prices. Unfortunately, however, for the truth, this inclination to algebraic propositions and illustrations clings to a whole class of political economists — a school of philosophers much more bent on *founding a science*, than on studying human nature, human institutions, or human happiness.

But the prevalent belief in the theory of Montesquieu was not the only ground for the common error on the subject of the relation between money and prices. It is taken for granted too generally, that prices are the naming of so many pieces of

---

[1] Inquiry into the Principles of Political Economy, book 2, chap. xxviii.

money, coins, or parts of coins; that the naming of a price is an occurrence always connected with a sale; that the seller is present with a commodity, and the buyer with the coins, and the question to be settled between them is how many of the coins are to go for the commodity; that a virtual barter is thus instituted of gold or silver, in the shape of coins, for some other commodity; and that the prices of commodities are the number of coins which are asked for a certain portion of each article. If this were the case, it would very probably come to pass that a relation or proportion would arise between the quantity of commodities and the quantity of coins, more or less definite. But as any approximation to such a mode of dealing only exists among uncivilized people; as every commodity is subject to fluctuations of price, depending upon causes and influences peculiar to itself; and as commodities in general are subject to changes in price, from causes in no respect connected with the quantity of money, there is no close nor invariable connection between prices and the quantity of coins. It is a great mistake to suppose that prices are chiefly made, discussed and settled in the cases of actual purchases. Prices are named, expressed and discussed a hundred-fold more than actual sales take place. They are the subject of a vast deal of conversation and conference, when no sale is contemplated. There is scarcely any topic among circles of business men, from the lowest range of the retail dealing to the largest transactions of trade, more discussed than prices, apart from any contracts or sales. Whatever influence the quantity of money in a country may have on prices, it is far less in the thoughts of those who fix prices, and far less influential than those causes which operate directly on the article of which the price is to be fixed.

Whilst the quantity of money in a country may be one of the most general causes operating on prices, because it must operate over the whole range of commodities, it is one of the least influential, one whose effects are the most difficult to detect and point out.

In civilized communities, where the credit system is in active operation, general prices are mainly governed by those which prevail in large transactions. For with all the complication of influences which bear upon them, the actual prices fixed in the wholesale operations, which always precede the lesser movements of retail, must control the latter. The retail dealer must be governed, in his selling prices, by his purchasing prices. The prices made by the larger transactions of trade become more extensively known, and thus exert a controlling influence. We have seen that the larger transactions of trade are almost exclusively carried on by means of credit; that is, the purchases and sales are made upon credit; the dealers purchase with their own paper upon time; they sell, and take the paper of others upon time; the payments accruing on this paper are, on both sides, adjusted through the banks, without any use of money or coins. Money, in these cases, has nothing to do with the prices, and nothing to do with the payments. The parties to this trade have very little occasion to think of the precious metals in any connection with their business, and perhaps not at all, unless a run upon the banks diminishes their usual facilities of adjustment.

In the large department of trade which is called wholesale, the quantity of money in a country has nothing to do with prices; it is not thought of; the parties are not dependent upon any considerations of that kind. The condition of the banks, or dealers in credit, is considered, but not the plenty or scarcity of money in the country. This view of the subject, when fully apprehended, disposes very effectually of the position taken by Montesquieu, and those who have embraced his views.

The persons who adopted these views always believed that prices were expressed in coins, and that naming a price was equivalent to holding up coins which would pay that price. We have seen, in the chapter on money of account, that this is not so; that, in civilized communities, prices are always expressed in the prevailing money of account; and that this is an invariable and unavoidable mental habit among a people conversant with the simplest rules of arithmetic. Such a people not only invariably form a money of account, by which they express all prices, but they carry in their minds, with equal facility, the quantities denoted by a great number of weights and measures, as tons, pounds, ounces, gallons, yards, feet, inches, acres, and miles; and they understand each other perfectly, in the use of these terms, although no mode of verification is at hand. As, when persons speak of pounds and ounces, they mean ascertained and understood quantities, and not pound or ounce weights merely: so, when they speak of francs, or shillings, or dollars, they mean ascertained and understood values, and not merely the material coin bearing those names. They express themselves as men did in England before the sovereign was introduced, when they spoke of pounds sterling. There was no such coin as a pound sterling; and yet they understood one another as well as men do now, when they speak of sovereigns. In our colonial times, prices were all expressed in the different colonial moneys of account; that is, in pounds, shillings and pence, as these terms were understood in the different colonies. There were no coins corresponding to these moneys of account, and there never had been. Yet there was no difficulty in expressing prices in moneys of account; and in the interior of Virginia and Massachusetts, the people cling, even now, to these old modes of expressing prices. This mode of naming prices, which is universal in civilized nations, also effectually disposes of the notion of Montesquieu. Prices are absolutely independent of coins, both for expression and payment. Coins are thus reduced to their true place of a commodity, bearing the stamp of the government as to quantity and quality — a commodity, also, which the law makes the standard of payment, where parties cannot agree upon any other mode. There is, then, so little occasion to think of or refer to coins in the matter of prices, that when there is no disturbance in the banking or credit system, there is no element of prices which exercises less influence than the quantity of money.

The idea, however, that the quantity of money and prices have some necessary and precise relation has prevailed so extensively, and still occupies so many minds, that we shall not leave the subject without reference to the positions taken by some of them. We cannot but think that the best refutation of some of these doctrines is to give the reader a few specimens. Their absurdity becomes more glaring, the closer they stand in array.

"When," says Lauderdale, "we express the value of any commodity, it may vary at one period from what it is at another, in consequence of eight different contingencies:—

"First. It would be subject to an increase of its value, from a diminution of its quantity.

"Second. To a diminution of its value, from an augmentation of its quantity.

"Third. It might suffer an augmentation in its value, from the circumstance of an increased demand.

"Fourth. Its value might be diminished, by a failure of demand.

"When, in common language, therefore, we express the value of any commodity, it may vary at one period from what it is at another," not only for the four reasons just mentioned, but for four corresponding reasons, "in relation to the commodity adopted as a measure of value:" that is:—

"Fifth. The commodity, money, will be increased in value if the quantity is diminished.

"Sixth. It will be diminished in value if increased in quantity.

"Seventh. It may be augmented in value by an increased demand. Or,

"Eighth. Diminished in value by failure of demand: and prices may be affected accordingly.

. . . "It follows that the variation of all value must depend upon the alteration of the proportion betwixt the demand for, and the quantity of, the commodity, occasioned by the occurrence of *one of the four circumstances* above stated; and that a variation in the expression of value may be occasioned by the occurrence of any of the *eight circumstances* we have alluded to."[1]

. . . "In every instance of bargain and sale," says Malthus, "it will be perfectly correct to say, that the prices of commodities will depend upon the relation of the demand to the

---

[1] Lauderdale on Public Wealth, chap. i. pp. 12, 59.

supply; or will vary as the demand (that is, the money ready to be offered) directly, and the supply inversely." And again: "In reality, prices are determined by the demand *in posse*, compared with the supply *in esse*."[1]

Col. Torrens resolves the whole question of prices into one of *effectual demand;* yet, in the course of an elaborate explanation, he uses the following language, which, by itself, would rank him as a believer in the theory of Montesquieu: —

"In all ordinary states of the market, prices will be determined by the proportion which exists between the quantity of commodities to be circulated and the amount of the currency with which their circulation is effected; and to occasion a general fall or rise of prices, the quantity of commodities must increase or diminish, while the amount of the currency remains the same, or the amount of the currency must increase or diminish, while the quantity of commodities remains the same."[2]

The *cost of production* is the guiding star of Ricardo and M'Culloch, the only clue on this mazy subject of prices. "If the cost of production be diminished, price will be equally diminished, though the demand should be increased to any considerable extent. If the cost of production be increased, price will be equally increased, though the demand should sink to the lowest possible limit."[3]

When such men mistake the boundaries of a subject in which they profess to be, and are deemed, specially skilled, the cursory reader should be on his guard. No department of political economy, and least of all that of prices, can be disposed of in this off-hand mode. Although Malthus indulges in it with the others, he was able sometimes to perceive its inappropriateness.

Mr. Malthus had previously, in the first paragraph of the Introduction to his "Political Economy," given his readers the following caution, than which nothing more wise is to be found in any work on that subject: — "Yet we should fall into serious

[1] Principles of Political Economy, chap. ii. § 2.

[2] Essay on Wealth, page 419.

[3] Principles of Political Economy, by M'Culloch, part ii. chap. ii. pp. 255, 333, edition of 1849.

error, if we were to suppose that any propositions, the practical result of which depends upon the agency of so variable a being as man, and the qualities of so variable a compound as the soil, can ever admit of the same kind of proofs, or lead to the same certain conclusions as those which relate to figure or number." "But even these (the great general principles of political economy) will be found to resemble, in most particulars, the great general rules in morals and politics founded on the known passions and propensities of human nature: and whether we advert to the qualities of men, or of the earth he is destined to cultivate, we shall be compelled to acknowledge that the science of political economy bears a nearer resemblance to the science of morals and politics, than to that of mathematics."[1]

It is because this mode of thinking, and this form of expression, has a specially misleading tendency, that we bring them thus prominently and fully before the reader: it should not require much reflection to conclude that current prices are not the subject of algebraic formulas. Almost all that regards prices must be deduced from careful observation; from careful comparison of the present with the past; and, after all, approximations may be all that is attainable. It is less in our power to reach arithmetical certainty in regard to fluctuation of prices in general, than it is for individuals to reach it in their own business. A wide and irreconcilable difference of opinion has long

---

[1] See also p. 134, chap. ii. § 7; Garnier de la Monnaie, tom. i. p. 39; Say on Political Economy, p. 295, 6th American edition.

This positive and arithmetical mode of expression, to which Malthus objects, prevailed extensively among the political economists on the continent, as well as in Great Britain; and examples might be cited at once curious and instructive. Its misleading tendencies were strongly denounced by Gioja,[1] who loses no opportunity, in his elaborate work, of placing his condemnation upon such opinions. One of the most flagrant instances we have met with occurs in "Principes d'Economie Politique, par N. F. Canard," crowned by the French Institute in the year 1801, in which the whole subject of prices is adjusted and settled by the most elaborate algebraic propositions, worked out at length, and the results given. See pages

---

[1] Nuovo Prospetto delle Scienze Economiche, vol. ii. p. 160.

prevailed between writers upon political economy, on the subject of prices. No real progress was made towards a proper treat-

---

28 to 61, and 161 to 165. We shall endeavor to abridge the problem at page 28.

"The sellers and purchasers having met in market, there will of course be a difference between the price asked and the price offered. This difference, from the highest to the lowest price, will form a range within which the struggle between the sellers and purchasers must take place. The first will avail themselves of all their advantages—that is, of the wants and the competition of the purchasers—and the purchasers will profit, on their part, by the wants of sellers and their competition; and each party will try to bring the other to that point in the range of most advantage to themselves.

"This being fixed, let R be that range, x that part of the range which sellers wish to add to the lowest price; $R—x$ will be the portion which purchasers wish to deduct. Let P be the wants of purchasers, C their competition; p the wants of sellers, c their competition.

"It is clear that the portion x, of the range paid by purchasers, will increase in proportion to their wants and their competition: x will then be at the compound rate of P and C, or will increase as $P\,C$; for the same reason, the other part, $R—x$ will increase as pc: this will give the proportion, $x : PC :: R—x : pc$, which gives the equation, $pcx = P\,C\,(R—x)$. In this equation, the quantity pc, the wants and the competition of the sellers, gives the power of the purchasers; and the quantity $P\,C$, the wants and competition of the purchasers, gives the power of the sellers. So the power of the purchasers multiplied by that portion of the range which the sellers make them pay, is equal to the power of the sellers multiplied by the other portion of the range which the purchasers throw back upon them.

"This equation, which I shall call the *equation of determination*, expresses the equality of *each momentum of the two opposed powers*, which make the equilibrium. It is to the principle of the equilibrium of these two powers that belongs the whole theory of political economy; as it is to the principle of the equilibrium of the lever that belongs all the theory of mechanics.

"From this equation it follows, $x = \frac{PC}{PC + pc} R$. If we make $pc = 0$, we have $x = R$; that is, if the competition of sellers is nothing, or if their necessity of selling is the smallest possible, the purchasers will pay all the range. If, on the contrary, we make $PC = 0$, we have $x = 0$; that is to say, if the competition or the necessities of purchasers is the smallest possible, they will pay none of the range: hence it follows, that the range is the difference between the highest and lowest price, which means between the monopoly of the sellers and the opposing monopoly of the purchasers."

ment of the subject, until the appearance of "Tooke's History of Prices."

If we supposed further exemplifications of algebraic political economy were necessary to nauseate the reader, we might furnish other specimens from the famed Beccaria, or the less known Aggazini and Schmalz. It cannot, however, surely be necessary to prove that such reasoning is inapplicable to the subject. As well might it be applied to the operations of the affections and passions, to the efforts of the intellect, to the exertion of bodily strength, and to the changing forms of disease. Moralists might tell us that love diminished in proportion to the squares of the distances; that our appetites were strong, directly as the demand, and inversely as the supply, of the gratifications desired; that mental efforts would be powerful, in exact proportion to the culture applied, and weak in exact proportion to the neglect of culture; that bodily strength would be manifested according to the length and breadth of the muscle exerted. We should not thus have dwelt upon this fallacious mode of reasoning, but that it is constantly repeated; it meets us, in this country, in nearly every summary of political economy which has appeared. It is repeated incessantly in the public journals; and some of the sweeping conclusions we have noticed are delivered from mouth to mouth, as if they no more admitted contradiction than that two and two make four. It is in vain they are refuted and shown to be false or deceptive; the disease prevails, and the remedy is forgotten. The following is from a popular treatise published in 1837, in New York:

"Other things, then, being equal —

"The greater the supply, the less the exchangeable value.

"The less the supply, the greater the exchangeable value.

"The greater the demand, the greater the exchangeable value.

"The less the demand, the less the exchangeable value.

"And, in general, cost being fixed, exchangeable value is inversely as the supply, and directly as the demand.

"And exchangeable value will be as the cost plus the effect produced by the variation in supply and demand."[1]

The qualification of *other things being equal* may save these propositions from being absolutely false, but it reduces them to absurdity, because *other things* never can be equal, while *every thing* that affects prices is eminently variable. It is strange that men of acute and well-disciplined minds can deal in dogmas, of which their own more detailed doctrines, if taken in their proper breadth, furnish ample refutation. In 1838, a treatise was published in Philadelphia, in which we find it broadly stated that —

"The effect on prices of the supply of money, or the demand for it becoming greater or less, is to cause them to rise or fall in the *same propor-*

---

[1] Wayland's Elements of Political Economy, page 13.

Some of their differing opinions have been exhibited in the preceding quotations. From Sir James Stewart, however, to M'Culloch, the leading authors advance theories, on the subject of prices, wholly at variance with the above cited opinions of Montesquieu, Locke and Hume. Whatever be their want of agreement among themselves, or of individual consistency, they generally admit that money or bullion is subject to similar variations in price with other articles of commerce, under the influence of the same causes. Adam Smith says: — "The occasional fluctuations in the market price of gold and silver arise from the same causes as the like fluctuations in that of all other commodities."[1] If this be correct, the price of these metals cannot be adjusted upon the single element of their quantity.

Even Harris[2] and James Mill, who maintain that the value of money is regulated by its quantity, advance opinions quite inconsistent with this notion. The former, in his first chapter, clearly recognizes the influence of labor, skill, &c., and of supply and demand, in determining prices. The latter thus sums up an elaborate argument on this topic: — "It thus appears, by the clearest evidence, that the quantity of labor, in the last resort, determines the proportion in which commodities exchange for one another."[3] The quantity of labor expended, the cost of production, the operation of supply and demand, with various modifications, explanations and additions, are the elements which nearly all the celebrated writers upon

---

tion. So long as the necessities and desires of men remain unaltered, will the money *actually circulating* be applied to the procuring of the very same commodities. If the circulating medium be doubled, the price of every thing will be doubled; and the like, in whatever other ratio that medium may be supposed to have increased, or in whatever ratio it be supposed to have diminished."[1]

This doctrine is nearly identical with that of Locke, Montesquieu and Hume; and shows, conclusively enough, the influence of false teaching, when wielded by men of such reputation and power.

[1] M'Culloch's edit. p. 21.

[2] Principles of Political Economy, by H. Vethake, LL.D., p. 47.

[3] Elements of Political Economy, by James Mill, p. 74; see also p. 95.

---

[1] Essay on Coins.

political economy, who have touched the subject of prices, have used to determine the value of the precious metals, and to account for their fluctuations. The quantity is, of course, one of these elements, and is allowed more or less influence in these various theories; but few attribute to it an exclusive, or even prevalent control.

The Marquis Garnier,[1] a disciple of Adam Smith, argues that no addition to the quantity of money can make any difference in its value, if it required the same proportion of labor to produce it: that if new mines be found, which yield a greatly increased quantity of the precious metals, even with a less proportion of labor, the value will not be reduced, unless the increased quantity satisfies the demands of commerce, so as to save the necessity of working the old mines, the value being fixed by the labor required to produce the metals at the poorest mines: that there cannot, in regard to the precious metals, be either scarcity or abundance, which are predicable only of commodities subject to be varied in their supply by causes beyond the control of man, such as the uncertainty of the seasons, or perishable goods, such as must be lost or sold for what they will bring: that, besides these, the only exceptions to the rule, that the quantity of an object of exchange has no influence upon its price, are the monuments of antiquity, or curiosities of natural history, sought by rich amateurs, and of which the rarity constitutes nearly all the price. A revolution in the value of gold and silver cannot, then," he concludes, "occur but in one way — by the discovery of new mines sufficiently fruitful to satisfy the whole demand, and to furnish to the consumption all it can absorb, upon terms more advantageous than before; that is, for less proportional labor than had, till then, been required in all the known mines."

As the Marquis Garnier occupies a high position among political economists, we offer here his views upon the influx of the precious metals consequent upon the discovery of the American mines: —

"The gold and silver of America, obtained with an amount

[1] Histoire de Monnaie, vol. i. chap. iv. p. 47.

of labor five or six times less than that hitherto required to produce them, and collected in such quantities as to satisfy the demand of all consumers, have cheapened the old gold and silver of Europe, and other parts of the world, and brought them to the level of the new product. . . .

"This gold and silver, obtained so cheaply from countries till then unknown, have attracted, by their low price, millions of consumers, who, but for this circumstance, had never thought of possessing them. The sphere of their consumption is prodigiously increased, and to fill it a corresponding quantity of gold and silver is required. After this revolution, no further superabundance has resulted in their production; they have taken, in the scale of values, the new place assigned them by the nature of the mines of which they are the product. This change took place in the first century after the discovery of these mines. The gold and silver of Mexico and Peru had not been sold more than fifty years in the markets of Europe and Asia, before this revolution in their value had been entirely accomplished. Since that epoch two centuries and a half have elapsed, during which time there have been imported into the old world more than $5,613,000,000 (*trente milliards de francs*); this vast importation has had, upon the price of the precious metals, no influence.

"In the sixteenth century, a half-mark of silver exchanged, in an average year, for a *setier* of wheat, Paris measure. At the present time (1819), the same *setier*, at the mean price of twenty years, will not bring certainly a greater quantity of silver. The prices of grain, as preserved in this country and in England, show in the most authentic manner that, for two hundred and fifty years, two *gros* of fine gold, or thirty *gros* of fine silver, have been the average price of a measure of grain, equal to from two hundred and forty to two hundred and fifty *livres*, or *pounds*. Thus, however great, during that time, may have been the product of these mines, the whole had been absorbed by the consumption, in which it is proper to include the amount employed in commerce with China and the Indies.

"The quantity produced at the mines is proportioned to the

demands of this consumption, and no superabundance could occur."[1]

Adam Smith seems to have been exceedingly puzzled with this subject, and his perplexity has produced a harvest of confusion. His difficulty was undoubtedly that of reconciling the facts, in the history of money, with his theory making labor the standard of value. "The quantity of labor," he says (book i. chapter v.) "which any particular quantity of gold or silver can purchase, or the quantity of other goods which it will exchange for, depends always upon the fertility or barrenness of the mines which happen to be known about the time when such exchanges are made." This is his opinion in chief. In a long digression placed at a good remove from the above, at the end of the eleventh chapter, the subject of the fluctuations in the value of the precious metals is treated at large. And here, compelled by the pressure of facts, he seems to allow some variation from his theory, and explicitly states that if the demand for silver "should increase, while at the same time the supply did not increase in the same proportion, the value would gradually rise:" that if the contrary happened, silver would become cheaper; and if the supply and demand were kept equal, its value would remain the same.[2] Again:—"But the supply had, it seems, so far exceeded the demand, that the value of that metal (silver) sunk considerably."[3] "Labor, *it must always be remembered*, and not any particular commodity, or set of commodities, is the real measure of the value, both of silver and of all other commodities." "Corn accordingly, *it has already been observed*, is, in all the different stages of wealth and improvement, a more accurate measure of value than any other commodity, or set of commodities. In all these different stages, *therefore*, we can judge better of the real value of silver by comparing it with corn, than by comparing it with any other commodity, or set of commodities." These two passages stand on the same page.[4] He is of opinion, that "about 1636, the effect of the

[1] Marquis Garnier, Histoire de Monnaie, tom. i. p. 55.

[2] M'Culloch's edit. p. 81.

[3] Ibid. p. 88.

[3] M'Culloch's edition of Smith, pp. 86–88.

discovery of the mines of America, in reducing the value of silver, was completed; it rather increased than diminished in value after that period." This digression in the eleventh chapter contains, in its confused form, nearly every idea so clearly stated in the above extract from Garnier.

Ganihl quotes another passage from Adam Smith, which contains a different opinion from any of those given above.[1] "When more abundant mines are discovered, a greater quantity of the precious metals is brought to market; and the quantity of necessaries and conveniences of life for which they must be exchanged being the same as before, equal quantities of the metals must be exchanged for smaller quantities of commodities. So far, therefore, as the increase of the quantity of the precious metals in any country arises from the increased abundance of the mines, it is *necessarily* connected with some diminution of their value."[2] This passage is regarded by Ganihl as supporting a doctrine similar to that of Montesquieu; and he goes into a refutation more elaborate than that of Garnier. He estimates the whole stock of the precious metals, when the supply from the American mines commenced, at a milliard of francs ($187,000,000), and the annual supply for three centuries at 120,000,000 of francs ($22,452,000), which has increased the mass to 35 milliards. This sum, after making every possible allowance for plate, for export to the Indies, &c., would still leave 20 milliards ($3,742,000,000), or an increase of twenty-fold as the then (1820) circulation of Europe. "If the doctrine of A. Smith was well founded," he proceeds, "it would follow that, as gold and silver have been augmented to twenty times the quantity which existed at the discovery of the American mines, their value must be diminished twenty times; so that what cost one franc then, would cost twenty francs now. In fact, however, though some agricultural products have increased in price three or four-fold, nearly every thing else, and especially the products of industry, have rather fallen than risen in price."

---

[1] Theorie de l'Economie Politique, tom. ii. p. 368.

[2] M'Culloch's edition, p. 86.

To disprove this doctrine, Ganihl relies further upon the fact that the importation of silver from America to Europe had been in the proportion of from 22 to 29 to 1 of gold (by Humboldt estimated at 45 to 1); "whence it follows, let the proportion of the amount brought from the mines be as 1 to 22, or 29, or 45, it has not had a corresponding influence upon the value in circulation, for that stands at 1 to $15\frac{1}{2}$; a new proof that the value of gold and silver, considered as products preferred, depends not upon their abundance or scarcity, but is subject to different laws."[1]

"For more than a century," proceeds Ganihl, "the mines of America have poured into Europe the annual sum of 120,000,000 to 140,000,000 of francs, without the smallest diminution of their value; and what is more to the point, nearly every country in Europe has devised a variety of substitutes, more or less ingenious, to save the use of gold and silver as money, which is equivalent to an increase of the quantity. It is impossible to tell the extent to which this process has been carried; but it is quite certain that this increase of money and its substitutes has not, according to the opinion of Adam Smith, experienced any diminution of its value. It is, then, evident that abundance has no influence upon their value."[2]

We have not space for a more extended examination of this subject. The main facts in the case are undeniable, however some may qualify, attempt to explain them away, or avoid the legitimate conclusions: and these are, that the depreciation of the precious metals, since the discovery of the American mines, has by no means corresponded with the increase of quantity, and, by consequence, that the general rise in prices of other commodities does not correspond with this increase. Our object is not to ascertain the exact increase in the amount of the precious metals, nor the precise influence which this increase had upon the prices of commodities in general, but merely to exhibit

---

[1] Tom. ii. p. 371.

[2] Ibid. tom. ii. p. 372. Ganihl proceeds with his argument at great length, and adduces many other considerations and facts in support of his position.

the fallacy of conclusions about prices drawn from the quantity of money. There can be no doubt that the increase of the precious metals has a tendency to depreciate their value; but the history of two hundred and fifty years of a constant increase shows that this tendency has not, during that time, entirely prevailed over other influences of a contrary tendency. The motive of self-interest leads men, by all the means which skill and ingenuity can devise, to resist the tendency of their possessions to depreciate; and this motive exerts its most powerful influence in regard to money. Hence new uses will be found for it when it is abundant, new avenues of commerce will be opened, new branches of industry will be essayed, until increased production finds employment for the increase of money. If money be increased, industry and trade are increased; and thus the tendency to depreciation is met, and strongly counteracted.

If the law which is supposed, by many, to govern the value of the precious metals, was not, as we have stated our belief, subject to opposing and prevailing tendencies, gold should have increased its value, as compared with silver, in the proportion of this increase in the quantity of silver; that is, fifty times.

Humboldt, who has, with the best lights, bestowed the fullest attention upon this subject, estimates the gold derived from the American mines, from their discovery down to the year 1803, at 9,915,000 Castilian marks; and that of silver obtained, in the same period, at 512,700,000, or more than 51 times as much silver as gold.[1]

The actual annual product of the two metals, at the commencement of the nineteenth century, is stated by the same as follows: —

	Marks.
Silver	3,860,840[2]
Gold	75,217

This exhibits the same disparity in the production, at that period, of 50 to 1 in favor of silver. The disproportion is not so great, when he includes in his estimate all the known mines

---

[1] Humboldt: Essai de Nouvelle Espagne, vol. ii. p. 645; an estimate at page 653 makes it 40 to 1. Bullion Report, 1810, Appendix No. 27.

[2] Ibid. p. 633.

of the world, being then as 45 to 1.[1] The change, however, which took place between the relative value of gold and silver, under the operation of this increased disproportion in the respective quantities, was only from 10 to 1, as it existed before the discovery of the American mines, to about 16 to 1, as it exists now. The whole addition to the stock of the precious metals in Europe made between 1492 and 1803, is estimated by Humboldt at $5,706,700,000, or more than thirty times the quantity existing at the date first mentioned, as stated by Jacob.[2] This immense sum was reduced, of course, by accident, by abrasion, by manufacturing, by hoarding, by exportation to the East Indies, and in other ways, so that the amount was greatly abridged. If this reduction, which is variously estimated, be taken at one-half, it left the stock, at the beginning of the present century, about fifteen times greater in Europe than that which existed at the beginning of the 16th century. Jacob, after much research, estimates the general rise in prices at 470 per cent.[3] Others have carried them higher; but a slight examination of the proper authorities shows that it is only in England, France, and a few others of the more prosperous commercial and manufacturing countries of Europe, that even such a rise as this has taken place. In most countries of Italy, the enhancement of prices is not considerable; and perhaps, on the average, no advance has taken place there. The whole depreciation of the precious metals produced by this increased quantity does not, measured by the rise of prices, exceed from 400 to 500 per cent., whilst their volume has swelled to 1500 per cent.

Among very many authorities we have consulted upon this subject, we prefer that of Arthur Young, so long and favorably known as a statistical writer, and as editor of the "Annals of

---

[1] Humboldt: Essai de Nouvelle Espagne, vol. ii. pp. 634, 644.

[2] Precious Metals, vol. ii. chap. xviii. p. 63.

[3] Ibid. vol. ii. chap. xix. p. 84. Bishop Fleetwood, writing at the beginning of the 18th century, estimates prices to have risen 600 per cent.; but shows that the pound sterling of the 15th century contained as much silver as two pounds of his day, which reduces the actual advance of prices to 300 per cent. — *Chronicon Preciosum*, p. 135.

Agriculture." His pursuits and inclinations, his high character, and his habits of accuracy, fitted him for such an investigation. He engaged in it deliberately, and pursued it with every advantage, and with all diligence; and, so far as we know, his conclusions are unimpeached and unimpeacheable. He has, probably, reached an approximation, where certainty was unattainable, as close as can ever be accomplished.

The following table contains a summary of the results wrought out by the elaborate investigations of Mr. Young. For the sake of clearness, he took the prices of the year 1810 as a unit or standard, and assuming them as represented by the number 20; the prices of previous periods covered by the table are represented by numbers showing the proportions of those prices to the number 20.[1]

---

[1] Before inserting this table, we place Mr. Young's own account of its origin, and the labor bestowed upon the subject. Arthur Young's name is familiar to those who are acquainted with the letters of General Washington, with whom he corresponded for a long period, chiefly upon agricultural topics.

"On going into the country, June, 1811, I entered particularly on the subject, and examined a multitude of authorities, from which I extracted a great variety of prices, carefully referring to every authority, quoting the volume and page, and combining them with all to be found in the books cited by Sir George Shuckburgh, as well as with the detail, more numerous than had before been published, given by Sir Frederick Eden, in his 'State of the Poor,' a work not referred to by Sir George: these prices I reduced, with much labor, to the standard of our present money. The investigation occupied myself, an amanuensis, and an accountant, with other occasional assistance, much the greater part of ten months, and at no inconsiderable expense. It was also necessary to form tables of population, taxes, with the imports and exports, and the bank circulation of the kingdom, for a period of above one hundred years. All these documents were regularly arranged in a manuscript on large paper, extending to above five hundred pages; and in order to gain, for the years 1810 and 1811, the prices of every sort of provision, labor, wool, timber, coal, and the year's purchase at which land sold, I despatched a circular letter to many respectable correspondents throughout England and Wales: the answers received were so numerous and satisfactory, as to leave little to wish for. The present publication will give a general idea of all the results; and I do not venture it to the public eye, without premising that the authorities collected are preserved for the inspection of those who may have curiosity enough to consult them: if

	13th century.	14th century.	15th century.	16th century.	17th century.	18th century.	1701 to 1766. 66 years.	1767 to 1789. 23 years.	1767 to 1800. 34 years.	1790 to 1803. 14 years.	1804 to 1810. 7 years.
Wheat	$5\frac{1}{2}$	$6\frac{1}{4}$	3	6	$9\frac{1}{4}$	$9\frac{1}{4}$	$7\frac{3}{4}$	11	12	13	20
Barley and Oats	$4\frac{3}{4}$	5	$2\frac{3}{4}$	$4\frac{3}{4}$	$8\frac{1}{4}$	$11\frac{1}{4}$	$7\frac{1}{4}$	11	$11\frac{1}{2}$	$16\frac{1}{4}$	20
Wheat, Barley and Oats, united	5	$5\frac{1}{2}$	3	5	$8\frac{3}{4}$	$10\frac{1}{4}$	$7\frac{1}{2}$	11	$11\frac{3}{4}$	$14\frac{1}{2}$	20
Provisions	......	......	......	......	......	10	$7\frac{1}{2}$	$11\frac{1}{2}$	$13\frac{1}{4}$	$16\frac{1}{2}$	20
Wheat and Provisions	......	......	......	$5\frac{1}{4}$	8	$9\frac{1}{4}$	$7\frac{1}{2}$	$11\frac{1}{4}$	$12\frac{1}{2}$	$14\frac{3}{4}$	20
Corn and Provisions, united	......	......	......	......	......	......	$7\frac{1}{2}$	$11\frac{1}{4}$	$12\frac{1}{4}$	$15\frac{1}{2}$	20
Victualling—Office Beef and Pork	......	......	......	......	......	......	$7\frac{1}{4}$	11	$12\frac{1}{3}$	17	20
Population	......	......	......	......	......	......	11	$15\frac{1}{2}$	$15\frac{3}{4}$	$16\frac{3}{4}$	20
Taxes	......	......	......	......	......	......	$2\frac{2}{3}$	$4\frac{3}{4}$	6	$10\frac{3}{4}$	20
Trade	......	......	......	......	......	......	$5\frac{1}{3}$	$8\frac{1}{4}$	11	$15\frac{1}{2}$	20
Taxes and Trade, united	......	......	......	......	......	$5\frac{3}{4}$	4	$6\frac{1}{2}$	$8\frac{1}{2}$	13	20
Labor	$3\frac{1}{2}$	$4\frac{3}{4}$	$5\frac{1}{2}$	$5\frac{1}{2}$	8	$12\frac{1}{2}$	10	$12\frac{1}{2}$	14	$16\frac{3}{4}$	20
Labor, Corn and Provisions, united.	......	......	......	......	......	......	$8\frac{1}{4}$	$11\frac{1}{2}$	13	16	20
Bank Circulation	......	......	......	......	......	......	5	$7\frac{1}{4}$	$11\frac{3}{4}$	$13\frac{3}{4}$	20
Artisans	......	$4\frac{1}{2}$	$5\frac{3}{4}$	$4\frac{1}{2}$	7	$11\frac{1}{2}$	......	......	......	......	20
Wool-combing	......	......	......	......	......	......	12	$15\frac{1}{3}$	12	$16\frac{1}{6}$	20
Horses	......	......	......	......	......	......	$15\frac{3}{4}$	$17\frac{1}{4}$	......	$19\frac{1}{2}$	20
Coals	......	......	......	......	......	......	$13\frac{1}{2}$	$14\frac{1}{3}$	$14\frac{1}{4}$	$15\frac{3}{4}$	20
Iron	$7\frac{1}{2}$	$12\frac{1}{2}$	6	......	15	$17\frac{1}{2}$	......	......	......	......	20
Manufactures at Greenw'h hospital.	......	......	......	......	......	......	$14\frac{1}{2}$	14	$15\frac{3}{4}$	$15\frac{1}{2}$	20
Post-office	......	......	......	......	......	......	$1\frac{1}{4}$	$2\frac{3}{4}$	$4\frac{1}{2}$	$9\frac{3}{4}$	20

From the foregoing table we deduce the one following, by taking all the averages for each period, and reducing them into one which stands as the proportion of the prices of that period to 20:—

PERIODS.	Proportion of the average prices to the number 20.	Advance of prices from last preceding period, per ct.	Fall of prices from last preceding period, per cent.	Whole advance, from average of 16th century, p.c.	Estimated stock of coins, in dollars.	Increase per ct. of the stock of coin upon the quantity of 15th century.	REMARKS.
13th century	$5\frac{1}{4}$	......	......	......	......	......	The stock of the precious metals employed as money is stated, upon the estimate of Jacob, in his work on the Precious Metals, v. ii. pages 63, 70, 131, 167, 214, 322.
14th "	$6\frac{5}{12}$	21	......	......	......	......	
15th "	$4\frac{1}{3}$	......	36	......	$163,000,000	......	
16th "	$5\frac{1}{6}$	24	......	......	624,000,000	380	
17th "	$9\frac{5}{28}$	80	......	80	1,425,600,006	875	
18th "	$10\frac{8}{9}$	11	......	108	1,824,000,000		
18 centuries in periods. 1701 to 1766	$8\frac{7}{38}$	......	20	......	......		
1767 to 1789	$10\frac{17}{19}$	25	......	108	......	1120	
1767 to 1800	$11\frac{7}{9}$	9	......	122	......		
1790 to 1803	15	27	......	190	......		
1804 to 1810	20	33	......	280	1,824,000,000	1120	

they do not prove the capacity of the collector, they will, at least, show such an extent of research, and industry of application, as shall exempt him from any idea of inattention to the means of rendering this work generally useful." — *Inquiry into the Progressive Value of Money in England, by Arthur Young; Introduction.*

To enable those who are desirous of making the comparison between the increase of gold and silver and the increase of prices, we annex a table from Humboldt and others:—

PERIODS.	Average annual importation from America into Europe, of gold and silver.
1492 to 1500	$250,000
1500 to 1545	3,000,000
1545 to 1600	11,000,000
1600 to 1700	16,000,000
1700 to 1760	22,500,000
1750 to 1803[1]	35,300,000
1803 to 1810[2]	39,900,000
1810 to 1823	17,000,000
1823 to 1847	34,000,000
1847 to 1851	64,000,000
1852	235,000,000

It appears, from these careful investigations of Arthur Young, that the whole average advance of prices did not exceed 280 per cent. from the 15th to the 19th century, or to the year 1810; that is, less than in the proportion of 1 to 3. In that same period, the increase of the precious metals employed as money was as 1 to 11. Humboldt estimates the receipts from American mines, up to the year 1500, at not over $250,000 yearly, but as having grown to nearly $40,000,000 in 1810; that is, as 1 to 160. In the period from the 15th to the 16th century, general prices were enhanced 24 per cent., while the whole stock of money had increased 380 per cent. In the 17th century, prices advanced 80 per cent., whilst the stock of coin increased 875 per cent. In the next, or 18th century, prices rose to 190 per cent., whilst the stock of money was increased 1120 per cent. So little do general prices appear, by this statement, to obey any influence arising from the increased stock of money, that it seems doubtful if we should allow any portion of the actual advance to go to that account. There were other influences operating on prices, for which allowance must be made; and, in fact, we shall not go far wrong, if we attribute the whole rise in prices to that increased activity in all kinds of business which increases de-

[1] Humboldt, Nouvelle Espagne, fol. edit. 1811, vol. ii. p. 611.

[2] The remaining figures are from Tegoborski des Gites Auriferes, p. 37.

mand. The increased stock of money proved, no doubt, a stimulus to industry and trade, and thus operated on prices. It is, at least, very clear, from this showing, that there is no necessary nor immediate connection between prices and the quantity of money. So far as the quantity of money is an element of prices, it seems to be one of the least influential; and it cannot be one of these causes to which great and sudden fluctuations of prices are ever due.[1]

If the influx of the precious metals from the American mines were calculated to have an immediate or strong effect upon prices, we might safely look to Spain for the most signal exemplification, as more than two-thirds of their products were shipped to that country, and thence distributed to the rest of the world. But we find no rise in prices there corresponding to the immense influx of the precious metals into the country.

In the following table, we furnish the average prices of wheat and barley in Spain for the five years ending 1680, and for every period of ten years after, to the year 1800, together with the coinage of the Mexican mint. One hundred fanegas are equal to 152 bushels. The real is equal to $\frac{1}{20}$ of a dollar.

Periods ending at the date annexed.	Average price of wheat per fanega, in reals.	Average price of barley per fanega, in reals.	Coinage of the mint at Mexico, in dollars.
1680, 5 years.........	37.6	14.0	....
1690, 10 "	16.2	9.3	....
1700, " "	17.0	8.4	$43,871,000
1710, " "	15.0	8.9	51,731,000
1720, " "	18.0	8.7	65,747,000
1730, " "	12.7	6.2	84,153,000
1740, " "	17.4	8.7	90,529,000
1750, " "	17.4	8.2	111,855,000
1760, " "	18.2	10.6	125,750,000
1770, " "	27.5	12.5	112,828,000
1780, " "	26.5	14.2	165,181,000
1790, " "	28.6	16.7	193,504,000
1800, " "	42.2	21.1	231,080,000
Total..................	....	......	$1,276,229,000

[1] Report on the High Price of Bullion, made to the House of Commons in 1810, Appendix, p. 182; Beawes on Spain, p. 272; Humboldt, Nouvelle Espagne, fol. edit. p. 580.

During the period embraced in this table, the mines of Spanish America were yielding an annual product of $33,000,000, a very large proportion of which were poured into Spain. Yet, in the face of this increase of money beyond any parallel in the world, the prices of wheat and barley, although extremely fluctuating, remained for eighty years under half the rates of 1680. The rise which took place towards the end of the 18th century, may be attributed, in part, to the neglect of agriculture consequent upon the emigration to the new world, and the immense wealth flowing from there. But the subject of prices in Spain present too wide a field for survey now; the only point presented is the influence on prices of this great influx of the precious metals.

We find the following passage in one of the most reliable works we have on Spain. The author, who investigated the subject of prices with special reference to the wages of labor and the price of grain, says: —

"We see daily that the price of grain is not ruled by the plenty or scarcity of gold or silver, but by its own superabundance or defect, as where we raise more than we can vent, or where we could vent more than we raise: so in laborers, where they are scarce, they command their wages; where plentiful, the wages command them. Hence it is evident that gold or silver is much balanced by the plenty or scarcity of other things, as those by gold and silver; and upon that balance depends the difference of prices."[1]

Although the intelligent and accurate author has the prices of England also in view, as he examined the subject partly in the light of Bishop Fleetwood's "Chronicon Preciosum," yet he expressly applies his conclusions to Spain, the country of which he was writing, and in which he had been thirty years a resident. He regarded the question of the influence of money upon prices as of the "last importance," and therefore gave the subject deliberate and earnest attention.

The following is a table of the price of wheat in France, taken

---

[1] The Civil, Commmercial, Political and Literary History of Spain and Portugal, by Wyndham Beawes, English Consul at Seville, folio, 1793, page 272.

at the average of various periods, from 1675 to 1800. The setier is equal to $2\frac{837}{1000}$ bushels. The price is carried out in money of the United States.[1]

Number of years of which average is taken.	Last year of the average.	Price of a setier of wheat.	REMARKS.
5 years......	1680	$6.10	The alterations of the French coins have been so
11 "	1691	4.27	frequent, that the periods have been taken between
7 "	1698	6.84	the dates of these alterations, as they show suffi-
9 "	1711	5.38	ciently the current of prices. Where the altera-
3 "	1714	6.29	tions have occurred several times in a year, and
4 "	1718	3.49	in two or three years, these are omitted, and so are
3 "	1723	2.37	years of famine. In 1740, the setier was at nearly
4 "	1730	2.89	$23; in 1841, it fell below $8; and the average
7 "	1733	3.17	of the following nine years was $3.19.
5 "	1739	3.33	Montveran estimates the quantity of money circu-
9 "	1750	3.19	lating in France, at various periods, to be as fol-
10 "	1760	3.97	lows:—
10 "	1770	4.32	1600... $109,600,000 | 1753... $259,432,000
10 "	1780	5.20	1684... 208,385,000 | 1797... 416,361,000
14 "	1797	5.77	1716... 240,601,000 | 1830... 523,366,000

It is equally clear, from the above statement, that during a period of more than a century, when the most extraordinary additions were making to the money of the world, no permanent advance in the price of wheat took place in France. According to the preceding tables, the productions of the mines, in the 18th century, more than doubled the stock previously existing. Yet it cannot be denied that the depreciation of the precious metals ceased at the end of the 17th century; or, in other words, no general and permanent rise in prices took place, corresponding with the increase of money.[2]

---

[1] This table is deduced from the very minute and extended one of Montveran, published in the "Bulletin de la Societé Française de Statistique Universelle," Nos. iii. et iv., 1830, p. 47.

[2] The following works may be consulted on this subject: — Wealth of Nations, book i. chap. xi. M'Culloch's edit. p. 111; Chronicon Preciosum, by Bishop Fleetwood; Jacob on the Precious Metals; Inquiry into the Prices of Wheat, Malt, &c., from the year 1000 to 1765, folio, London, 1768. Ruding's Annals of the Coinage, vol. i.; Seaman's Progress of Nations, New York, 1848, chap. xvii. xviii., a work we commend to every young American desirous of becoming a statesman; Dupre St. Maur Essai sur Monnaies, 4to; Chevalier; Economie Politique, vol. iii. sec. v. chap. xi.; Recherches sur d'Or et sur l'Argent, par Leon Faucher, Paris, 1843; Gites Auriferes, par Tegoboiski, Paris, 1853: De l'Or et de l'Argent, par Narces Tarassenko-Otreschkoff, Paris, 1856, 8vo.

§ 3. *Effects of bank currency upon prices — Increase of wealth in Great Britain in the eighteenth century — Advance in prices often increases currency — Power of purchasing does not depend upon money, but upon personal confidence — Seasons of high confidence lead to speculation — Lord Overstone — Tooke's History of Prices — His examination before the secret committee of* 1832 — *Evidence on prices before Parliamentary committees of* 1832 *and* 1840 — *Influx of gold from California and Australia — Comparison of all currencies in the United States in* 1848 *and* 1856 — *Prices the scale by which products of labor are exchanged — Justice to labor is determined by what men can purchase, and not by the price they pay.*

If the precious metals employed as money exercised so little influence on prices by their increase or decrease, we may safely infer that bank currency has no greater power in that respect. The economy of bank currency, as a medium of payment, being very great, it is important to discover whether there are countervailing disadvantages. It is chiefly in reference to this question that we have dwelt so minutely upon the influence of metallic money. The actual advantages or disadvantages of an increase of the precious metals is a different question from their influence upon prices; the latter may be enhanced by the depreciation of the metals, without other injury than increasing the weight and bulk of an equal value in money. But if the substitutes for money enhance prices in proportion to the extent they are employed, it becomes a question at once of grave import, whether such enhancement is not injurious, and whether the injury finds any adequate compensation in the economy of employing substitutes. This question can be best resolved by the operation of the paper currencies of Great Britain and the United States. We have anticipated this investigation by comparing the increase of the precious metals and the progress of prices in the 18th century. The use of paper currency in England commenced its great expansion with the beginning of that century; and the increase of prices, which we have examined only in connection with the increase of gold and silver, is in fact due, so far as that cause operated, to the joint influence of metallic money and paper currency, or the use of credit. We have seen, in the table deduced from Arthur Young's "Progressive Value of Money," that the average prices of the 16th century were only an advance of 24 per cent. over those of the 15th century, whilst an addition of 380 per cent. had been made to the stock of the precious metals; that the average prices of the 17th century were advanced 80 per cent. over those of the 16th century, and the addition to the stock of the precious metals 875 per cent.; that the average prices of the 18th century over those of the 17th were an advance of 11 per cent., and the addition to the stock of the precious metals 1120 per cent.; and to make the case more striking, that the prices of the 18th century over those of the 15th were an advance of 108 per cent., whilst the addition to the stock of the precious metals, in the three centuries, had been 1120 per cent. It is worthy of remark, that the average prices of the 17th century over those of the 15th, covering a period before the use of paper currency, exhibit an advance of 111 per cent.; whilst the average prices of the 18th century, in which there was a great use of paper currency, besides the immense increase of the precious metals just noticed, present an advance over those of the 17th of only 11 per cent.

The increase of wealth in Great Britain in the 18th century, by means of industry and commerce, had no previous parallel. This is familiar to all conversant with her history. A few facts will place it in a striking light. The united value of the imports and exports, for the years 1698 to 1701, is £12,000,000 sterling; in 1802, the united value had reached to nearly £73,000,000 sterling,[1] being an increase of over 600 per cent. In the year 1700, the tonnage of vessels clearing outwards was 317,328; in 1800, it amounted to 2,130,322, being an advance of over 600 per cent.[2] The public revenue of England, in the year 1701, from all sources, amounted to £3,895,205; in the year 1800, it amounted to £29,604,008,[3] being an increase of over 700 per cent. The increase of manufactures cannot easily be estimated, but its magnitude has long been the subject of

[1] M'Culloch's Dictionary of Commerce, Art. "Imports," &c.

[2] George Chalmers's estimate.

[3] Pablo Pebrer: Taxation, Revenue and Expenditures of Great Britain, page 156.

wonder. This increase of material wealth was not only aided by the influx of the precious metals then flowing into the commerce of the world, but by an increased use of substitutes for money to an extent constituting a principal feature in the commerce of that period. During the ten years ending 1710, the average circulation of the notes of the Bank of England was £758,000; this had increased, in the ten years ending 1800, to £11,470,000, or 1600 per cent. The Bank of Scotland is nearly coeval with that of England; and in addition to it, many other banks went into operation in Scotland during the 18th century, all of which contributed their portion to the paper circulation. Private bankers throughout the country added their paper to the mass of the paper currency — a mass which cannot be estimated, for want of proper data. The practice of circulating bills of exchange and promissory notes in payments, as a substitute for money, was greatly extended in this period.

During the whole of the 18th century, the balance of trade, with the exception of the year 1781, was in favor of Great Britain with the whole world; it must be clear, therefore, whatever doubts may rest upon the entire accuracy of these national balances, that Great Britain obtained her full share of the great accession which was then made to the previous stock of gold and silver. In addition to this was employed the vast accession of substitutes which banking and its various facilities produced. Yet, with all this, prices advanced only 11 per cent.; and to what one, or to how many, of the elements of prices, and in what degree to each one, this advance is to be attributed, no human knowledge or scrutiny can ever disclose. We find in these facts, surely, very little proof that prices are controlled by the quantity of money or currency in circulation, or that there is any regular proportion between them.

It is utterly unsafe, therefore, to infer that a currency is in excess, because prices have risen; or to conclude, if a currency is in excess, that prices must rise; or if they have risen, that the rise is in consequence of that excess, or that there can or will be any fixed proportion between them. It will be found not unfrequently, on close inspection, that a rise of prices has preceded and been the cause of an increase of money; but as the former is generally first known, and the latter slowly ascertained, the order of cause and effect is reversed in the minds of most observers. When the horizon of trade and politics is clear, when no pressure is felt, and no dreaded crisis is impending, when a few years of punctuality and fair dealing have blotted out the memory of frauds and losses, confidence between man and man rises, becomes strong and unsuspecting, grows into credit, and credit becomes even more efficient than money. When credit, therefore, furnishes to multitudes the power of purchasing at will with their own paper, the abuse of this power degenerates into speculation. The active competition which takes place in purchasing, between those who are thus unrestrained in their power of acquiring commodities, produces an immediate advance in prices, and that advance produces its usual effect of stimulating the movements of the speculators. It is deemed safe to purchase in a rising market. Prices must continue, while this spirit prevails, to advance, and the profits realized by first purchasers will tempt others to embark in the movement, which grows as it advances. All this enhancement of prices takes place without the use of currency, and is founded wholly upon personal confidence. It is true, that much of the individual paper issued in these purchases may be discounted, and the notes of the banks be thrown into circulation in place of them; and this may have a slight tendency to swell prices. Prices, however, as we have seen, generally begin and rise in the wholesale transactions, and these are almost altogether upon credit. The effect of the increased circulation is rather, in the first instance, to support the high prices than to create them. The holder of the goods is able more easily to make such sales as will enable him to acquit the liability incurred in their purchase, because his creditor, by having his note discounted at a bank, has added to the currency the amount of his debt; and thus he has only to exchange his goods for the equivalent amount of bank-notes which his purchase has added to the circulation.

It is in such seasons, and owing to this high confidence, that commercial dealings are pushed to an extent which results in an excessive issue of bank-notes; and surely no human sagacity could tell, in such case, what proportion of the advance of prices was owing to the spirit of speculation, and to the high state of individual credit, and what to the consequent excessive issue of currency. Any attempt thus to discriminate must be abandoned as useless by the careful inquirer. Yet what positive and unhesitating conclusions have been drawn from data as uncertain! How often, in such cases, have we been assured that the currency has been depreciated in the precise ratio of such an increase of prices!

The commercial events of the last fifty or sixty years must, if properly applied, be decisive of the relations between currency and prices; and more especially has the experience of this period been distinct in Great Britain and the United States. In regard to the former we are, fortunately for the patience as well as for the information of the reader, not without ample references.[1]

Among those who have recently written on the subject of cur-

[1] If it be thought that we are taking unnecessary pains in combating the position that currency regulates prices, let it be kept in mind that this false position is by many regarded as an axiom never to be doubted or called in question. It is the plausible and ready solution applied by multitudes to many difficulties and doubts in relation to the theory of money and banking. It is repeated on every side by pamphleteers and newspaper writers, and though often refuted, still reappears. As late as 1837, S. Jones Loyd, now Lord Overstone, in a pamphlet, expressed himself thus: — "If the currency be in excess, prices of all articles are affected in a corresponding degree." This opinion of Loyd is quoted by J. B. Smith, President of the Manchester Chamber of Commerce, in a pamphlet of 1840, addressed to Mr. Loyd; and Mr. Smith thus enforces the doctrine: — "Supposing the Bank of England to have a certain amount of paper in circulation, against a certain quantity of commodities of all kinds in the market, at a given period; then, supposing that the bank increased its issues by a million, the quantity of commodities remaining the same, it is quite evident that the natural tendency of such an operation would be to raise the money value of commodities. Either the price of commodities must rise, or the money must remain without employment. If the money remained for a time without employment, the necessary effect would be a reduction of the rate of interest, and so a rise in the price of commodities would be produced." — *J. B. Smith's Letter to S. J. Loyd*, page 10.

rency, in Great Britain, few, if any, have attained higher consideration than Samuel Jones Loyd (Lord Overstone), a London banker. His opinion on this subject is deemed none the less important, that he has changed his views since 1837. A letter of his, published in 1840, contains the following emphatic passage: — "Fluctuations in the amount of the currency are seldom, if ever, the original and exciting cause of fluctuations in prices, and in the state of trade. The buoyant and sanguine character of the human mind; miscalculations as to the relative extent of supply and demand; fluctuations of the seasons; changes of taste and fashion; legislative enactments and political events; excitement or depression in the condition of other countries connected with us by active trading intercourse; an endless variety of casualties acting upon those sympathies by which masses of men are often urged into a state of excitement or depression — these all, or some of them, are generally the originally exciting causes of great variations in the state of trade."[1]

To Thomas Tooke, Esq., of London, author of "A History of Prices, and of the State of Circulation, from 1793 to 1837,"[2] however, is the world indebted for the most thorough and searching examination of this subject. This work has no equal, in any department of political economy, for indefatigable research, for patient analysis, for the extent and variety of facts on which its conclusions are based, for fulness of illustration, and for lucid arrangement. It furnishes a model to which all investigations of this kind must in some degree be conformed, if destined to command eventually the public approval. What it fails in clearness of expression, is fully made up by other merits. This history has, from its appearance, received high commendation;[3] and we

[1] Letter to J. B. Smith, page 10.

[2] 2 vols. 8vo. 1833, with a continuation published in 1840, bringing down the history to the end of 1839; a fourth volume in 1848, and the fifth and sixth volumes in 1858.

[3] "A work equally distinguished for the soundness and comprehensiveness of its general views, and the extent and accuracy of its practical information." — *Edinburgh Review*, No. 86.

"Mr. Tooke's work on prices, in which details are given, accurate as to

are not aware that any respectable attempt has been made to refute its conclusions, or weaken its authority; although its main object and undeniable result has been to contradict many cherished positions of leading political economists and theorists of the present and past generation. In all that regards prices, and the state of circulation, in the period to which it refers, we deem this history as finally settling most of the questions with which it grapples: in regard to more general questions, in relation to money and banking, we think the author has shown himself unprepared to carry his analysis, and push his conclusions, to the extent to which his well-established facts would warrant. We cannot but think that if his patient search for truth, his strong powers of discrimination, and his long experience as a merchant, had been brought to bear specially upon the great questions involved in the subjects of banking and money, that equal light would have been shed upon them with that thrown upon prices. If we do not greatly mistake, he would have found himself, in that career, carried to conclusions as much opposed to commonly-received opinions as those which he established in his "History of Prices."[1]

The period embraced in the "History" of Mr. Tooke is considered under the following divisions of time: —

1..........	1793 to 1798	6..........	1819 to 1822
2..........	1709 to 1803	7..........	1823 to 1827
3..........	1804 to 1808	8..........	1828 to 1832
4..........	1809 to 1813	9..........	1833 to 1837
5..........	1814 to 1818	10..........	1838 to 1839

These periods are characterized by great and continual fluc-

time, and as nearly as possible accurate as to amount." — *S. J. Loyd's Minutes of Select Committee on Banks of Issue*, 1840, p. 260.

[1] A strong effort was made to break Mr. Tooke down, in his examination before the Committee of Secrecy of the House of Commons of 1832. He was called up many times, and finally put to the test of a severe cross-examination under the hands of some well-prepared opponent, who spared no ingenuity, and no effort, to involve him in contradiction. He passed through this ordeal with dignity and firmness, and without yielding his opinions, or suffering them to be seriously shaken. — *See Minutes of Committee, 12th July*, 1832; *Report*, p. 288, &c.; *Questions* 3962 *to* 4117.

tuations of prices, and by great changes in the quantity of paper currency; and yet the clearest proof is advanced that there was no close nor necessary correspondence between these fluctuations and the variations in the amount of the currency. The opinion of the author will be found in a summary at the end of each chapter, where it will be seen he very emphatically, in every case, denies that currency regulates prices. He avers "that the alterations of prices originated, and mainly proceeded, from alterations in circumstances distinctly affecting the commodities, and not in the quantity of money." "There is not," he remarks, "as far as I have been able to discover, any single commodity, in the whole range of articles embraced in the most extensive list of prices, the variations of which do not admit of being distinctly accounted for by circumstances peculiar to it;" and he therefore condemns, as wholly erroneous, the resort to the state of the currency for solution of the phenomena of prices. He does not deny that an increase of money may have, in many instances, a tendency to enhance prices, and that, all other things being equal, it would not in all instances have that tendency; but he maintains that the quantity of the currency is not a controlling regulator of prices, these being mainly determined by facts and circumstances peculiar to the various commodities whose prices are affected; and that these circumstances do frequently operate with such force as to reduce prices in the face of an expanding currency, and to advance prices when the currency is diminishing. In point of fact, the expansion of currency is frequently rather an effect than a cause of enhanced prices.

The expression of these opinions by Mr. Tooke before the Secret Committee of 1832 on Bank of England Charter, and the Select Committee on Banks of Issue of 1840, is very clear and emphatic, and is well worth consulting. The witnesses examined before those committees do not all coincide with him, and it is quite plain that certain members of those committees do not; yet an unprejudiced inquirer will find enough in their minutes to show that the relation between the quantity of currency and prices, for which so many contend, does not exist, and is nothing else than the old notion of a fixed proportion between the quantity of money and the quantity of commodities.[1]

It is worthy of notice that, in 1832, the greater number of the witnesses appeared to adhere to this old notion, and to dissent from Mr. Tooke; whilst, in 1840, the majority of voices is the other way, and the expression of opinion is strong and undoubting. In 1832, eight witnesses were examined specially on this subject. J. Horsley Pålmer, William Ward, and Samuel Gurney, Esquires, gave it as their opinion that an increase or diminution of bank issues might eventually, and in some way, operate upon prices; but they spoke with hesitation, and qualified their opinions by taking into the account other causes. Joseph C. Dyer and James Burt were clear in the opinion that prices were directly regulated by the issues of the bank: the latter gentleman was asked: "You mean to say, that the prices and the markets are not settled by the demand and supply, and by what may belong purely to the trade, but by the issues of the Bank of England? Yes, I do." George Grote was of

[1] It is strange that any one having such clear and well-defined views on the subject of prices and paper currency, should not see the little difference there is in the effect of metallic and paper money on prices. We find Mr. Tooke, in 1840, before the Select Committee on Banks of Issue, thus questioned, and thus answering: — "Suppose the supply of precious metals in the world to be increased, and to go on doubling and trebling, will not the prices of commodities estimated in the precious metals go on doubling and trebling, in proportion to the increase of the precious metals? Yes, they will, undoubtedly." *Question* 3300. "If the precious metals remain constant, and notes payable on demand be issued, will prices vary with the increase of such notes? Not if the notes are payable in gold on demand, except so far as gold may be affected by a substitution of paper for gold." *Question* 3001. If Mr. Tooke had examined the effect of metallic currency with the same attention which he had given to that of paper, he would not have made that distinction. His rule, with some modifications, is equally applicable to money and its substitutes.

George Grote was interrogated specially as to the difference, if any, of the effect of metallic and paper currencies on prices; and gave it as his opinion, that fluctuations in prices were as likely to take place with the one as the other. — *Committee on Bank of England Charter*, 1832, *Question* 4775, page 379.

opinion that fluctuations in prices were unavoidable, and as likely to take place under a metallic as a paper currency. Henry Burgess thought that, all other things being equal, an increase of bank issues had a tendency to enhance, and a diminution to reduce prices.

In 1840 and 1841, thirteen witnesses were specially examined by the Select Committee on Banks of Issue, on the subject of prices. J. B. Smith, R. Cobden, R. Page, and G. F. Muntz, express themselves, with more or less qualification, in favor of the opinion that bank issues have a direct and controlling influence upon prices. W. R. Wood attributes many of the fluctuations in prices to the mismanagement of the currency under what he deems a vicious banking system. G. W. Norman, S. J. Loyd, T. Tooke, H. W. Hobhouse, V. Stuckey, W. Rodwell, J. W. Gilbart (author of various treatises on banking), and A. Blair, are clearly of opinion with the general doctrine of Mr. Tooke, in his "History of Prices." This opinion gained much ground in the interval between 1832 and 1841. Can there be doubt that it will continue to gain ground, until it becomes the settled conviction of the public mind? For, after all, what is it but the doctrine, that whatever may be the tendencies of the expansion or contraction of paper currencies, there are other and more powerful causes continually operating upon prices which more than countervail such tendencies, and control the market value of all articles of commerce?

If any thing of fact or authority had been wanting to overthrow the doctrine of a proportion between the quantity of circulating medium and prices, it has been amply furnished in the addition which has been made to the metallic medium since the discovery of the gold-mines of California and Australia.[1]

[1] We again earnestly commend to every reader who may be still clinging to the position we combat, the study of "Tooke's History of Prices." It can scarce fail of carrying conviction to every candid mind. It furnishes, in the appendix to the second volume, tabular statements of the prices of forty different articles, four times a year, from 1782 to 1840; also tables of the circulation of bank-notes, the prices of bullion, and much other information bearing on the subject. No refutation of the doctrines of this work has ever been attempted, and no one has questioned the accuracy of its

The annual production of gold has, within the last ten years, increased five-fold. The first effect of this extraordinary influx was an increase of exports to the gold-producing countries. Commerce experienced a great impetus, and of course prices were affected by increased demand and greater activity; a considerable advance took place, but whether that advance would average 10 or 30 per cent., would require much investigation to ascertain. How much of this advance could be attributed to the mere increase of money, no one could pretend to say; but no observer could fail to see that the enhanced prices were to be ascribed chiefly to the increased activity of trade. Certain it is, that the rise in prices maintained no proportion with the increased production of gold. This is as true of the United States as of Europe. Something like such an advance occurred in California; but that rise was clearly owing to the condition of a new territory, in which the demand for labor was, for a time, far beyond the supply. Prices there were clearly not determined by the quantity of gold, but evidently by the quantity of the article which the holders of the gold wished to purchase. It is known that, as laborers and the commodities of consumption increased, the prices gradually fell, although the production of gold was increasing. It is probable that general prices, in California, fell 50 per cent. during a period in which the production of gold increased 100 per cent.

But leaving out of view the extreme case of California, and regarding results in the United States after business had subsided into its regular channels, the following figures furnish a comparison between the years 1848 and 1856, as to the amount of circulating medium in the United States: —

	1848.	1856.
Bank-notes	$128,506,091	$214,778,822
Bank deposits	103,226,177	230,351,352
Specie in the banks	46,369,765	58,349,838
Specie in circulation[1]	32,133,688	138,268,850
Total	$310,235,721	$641,748,862

statements. No person who wishes to be right on the subject of which it treats, is excusable for neglecting this valuable work.

[1] Estimated, not including the precious metals otherwise employed.

This exhibits an increase of the mixed currency of the country of over 100 per cent.—the increase being above that rate in both specie and bank currency.

It will not be pretended that the general prices of this country increased in this ratio between 1848 and 1856. In fact, no increase took place which has not since been lost, although at this moment (1858) the specie and paper currency of the United States are each double what they were in 1848.

We think ourselves authorized to leave this subject, by urging those who have adhered to the notion that there is a necessary connection and proportion between the quantity of the currency and general prices, to give up a fallacy disproved by the best authorities, and contradicted by the results of the influx of the precious metals from the mines of Spanish America, by the increase of paper currency in the 18th century and since, and still more emphatically by the late influx of gold from California and Australia.

There are many who believe that prices in this country are so inflated by a superabundant currency, as seriously to diminish our exports, by making it impossible to sell many products of our industry, in foreign countries, without loss. These persons contend that, if our paper currency were banished, prices would fall in proportion, and then we could manufacture against the world. They are mistaken in the supposition that prices would fall, upon that event, in any such proportion. Even if they should, the paper circulation being a device to facilitate the payment of debts arising upon an active industry and trade, the withdrawal of these facilities would check industry and trade; and the result would be not merely a decline of prices, but a decrease of production and of exports, instead of an increase.

If, however, our public banks were wholly discontinued, it is believed that the credit system could be worked by the aid of private bankers, to such an extent as to support the productive industry of the country, and sustain our present high prices, which are a public benefit, and not an evil, as many imagine. Prices are the scale by which labor is exchanged — the scale by which domestic products are valued and distributed; and there are very few consumers who do not receive as much benefit from a high range of prices as they would from a low range, especially if this high range enables the masses, the laborers, the actual producers, to purchase and enjoy more of the comforts of life than a lower range. It is not the nominal price, but what the masses are able to purchase with their labor, which determines whether the range of prices is just and advantageous. Those who find themselves paying, for some articles of their consumption, a higher price than the same could be purchased for abroad, should weigh that disadvantage against the advantage to the laborers, whose wages go to make up the increased cost. Well-paid laborers are, in return, liberal in their expenditure; and as they rise in the scale of comfort and knowledge, they impart firmness to all the institutions of society. When laborers are well compensated, the range of compensation is in like manner favorable to every other class and profession in the country they inhabit.

CHAPTER XX.

PUBLIC PAYMENTS.

§ 1. *Processes of receiving and paying — British Exchequer, its practice — Revenue of Great Britain five millions of dollars weekly — Exchequer bills introduced by Earl of Halifax — British revenue always anticipated — Floating debt a saving of interest — Exchequer bills suited to a certain class of lenders — The quantity carefully gauged to the demand — Wisely managed by the Bank of England — The great advantage of disbursing the revenue before its receipt, and of thus furnishing the currency in which the revenue is paid—Amount of Exchequer bills issued—Mode of reducing circulation by sale of Exchequer bills — Rate of interest — Printed in different colors — The Exchequer and the Bank — British system in contrast with that of the United States.*

THERE are some aspects in which payments by public treasuries come within the scope of our subject. We propose to consider neither the objects nor modes of taxation, nor the occasions of national expenditure; but as public treasuries receive and pay, it becomes with them, as with individuals, important to avail themselves of whatever facilities they can in the way of economy, of promoting expedition, and of preventing friction. The subjects of taxation, public revenue and expenditure, have engaged the attention of multitudes of public men; but whilst so much has been written and said upon these topics, the more mechanical or practical processes of receiving and paying have received much less notice than they deserve.

As the practice of the British Exchequer presents that aspect of the subject which we desire to bring before the reader, we shall first briefly advert to the system which prevails in Great Britain. The public income of that country exceeds that of all other nations, in proportion to the population. In 1801, the total amount of the annual taxes paid by the people of Great

Britain exceeded $200,000,000. In 1816, it had risen to upwards of $415,000,000; from that period to 1850, it maintained an average of over $250,000,000, or somewhat over $5,000,000 each week. It does not concern us now to notice from what sources, or by what means, this vast sum is levied, nor the various processes by which it is collected. Independent of the mode of collection, and of the particular interests affected by this heavy taxation, the mere act of receiving and paying $5,000,000 weekly is an important financial operation; and the mode of conducting such large receipts and payments may much enhance or diminish the burden of the payers. The withdrawal of $5,000,000 each week from the pockets of the people, and placing it in the public treasury, is an operation calculated to affect very seriously the movements of business. It should be done, then, other considerations not being overlooked, in the mode least likely to do injury. The business is unavoidable; but every palliative should be sought, for a process which must be hard enough under any circumstances.

As late as the beginning of the 18th century, deposits in the British Exchequer were certified by tallies, or sticks split and notched in the manner in which bakers and their customers keep their accounts of loaves delivered; these were the securities issued by the British Exchequer, until the present device of Exchequer bills was introduced by Montague, Earl of Halifax, at the time of the great financial difficulties attendant upon the recoinage, and the over-issues of the Bank of England to the government in the first years of its existence. From that time to the present, the Exchequer bills, then so useful, have been a prominent feature of the British system of finance. It may be safely asserted, indeed, that this system of Exchequer bills, as conducted between the Exchequer and the Bank of England, is one of the main props of British finance, without which its enormous burdens could not be borne, nor the income maintained. The history of British finance is interesting throughout; but the agency of Exchequer bills, and notes of the Bank of England, as employed from year to year, in aid of the treasury, is what we commend to the attention of the reader.

There is a great, and indeed unnecessary, complication, in Great Britain, in the management and appropriation of the various branches of income to the various items of public expenditure. This arises, in part, from ancient usages, and in part from the necessity of complying with many acts of Parliament, passed at different periods, and not always consistent or harmonious in their details. The following are, however, always prominent items of payment: the interest of the national or funded debt; the interest and principal of the unfunded debt; the annual expenditure upon the civil list for the army, navy, and other expenses of yearly occurrence. These together absorb the annual sum of $250,000,000, and upwards. For a very large proportion of this vast sum, the public treasury issues its notes, or Exchequer bills, in anticipation of the receipt of the revenue; and this, whether the income upon which the advance is made be applicable to the permanent debt or interest of the funded debt, or to the unfunded debt, or to the accruing expenses of every year, independent of interest or debt. It is the settled practice of the British Exchequer thus to anticipate the incoming taxes; that is, to borrow the amount, pay the demands upon the public treasury as they accrue and are payable, and return the borrowed funds out of the taxes as they come in. Two important advantages arise from this process; a large sum of floating debt is carried at a less rate of interest than that for which it could be funded as a part of the permanent debt; and the whole, or a large proportion, of the amount of the annual expenditures is actually paid by the government to the people before they are called upon to pay their taxes.

But the mere circumstance of carrying the floating debt at a lower rate of interest would not suffice to justify the plan. It is a great advantage, that the floating debt, thus managed, forms a perfectly safe reservoir into which to pour any temporary or occasional surplus of income. If the treasury should overflow, even for half a year, all this surplus would be at once applied to payment of so much of the floating or unfunded debt. This surplus would be applied to the payment of Exchequer bills, for which no corresponding amount would be issued until the money was wanted. The Exchequer carries, in this way, a floating debt of from £10,000,000 to £30,000,000 sterling, which is more or less, according to the productiveness of the annual revenue. This large sum is secured, at all times, by Exchequer bills, which are paid off quarterly, semi-annually, or annually; but so distributed as to be paid off a portion in each quarter of the year. After a specified time, a portion of them are receivable in payment of taxes or customs. They are issued in sums of £100, £500, and of £1000, and each bill bears a fixed daily rate of interest, which the government can increase by proclamation, as is done when there is danger of their being returned too rapidly to the treasury for payment. Exchequer bills have long, and deservedly, been a favorite security for temporary investment. The experience of more than a century has taught the people that they are faithfully managed; their credit has been so carefully maintained, that they are at all times saleable. The amount kept on the market is strictly gauged to the demand: if at any time it is found to be so great as to weigh upon the demand, or check their ready sale, a portion is immediately withdrawn or funded. The quantity of Exchequer bills in the hands of the people is large enough to keep them before the public as at all times an accessible security, and as safe as the nation itself. Thus managed, Exchequer bills become an important and sure resource for the government in every emergency, for every sudden demand upon the treasury, whether ordinary or extraordinary.

There is always, in a rich country like Great Britain, a vast amount of funds applicable to payments, public and private, of which the owners can dispose for a longer or shorter time, but which they cannot permanently invest. Every one who can spare £100, or £1000, for a week, or a month, or six months, or a year, is glad to avail himself of the facility of an Exchequer bill. They are almost always at a premium; and the only risk run is, that at the sale a less premium may be obtained than that which was paid at the purchase. It should be noted, that the class of lenders to which Exchequer bills appeal are such as would be less tempted by any other security. They would not lend the money they thus invest upon mortgages, nor upon commercial paper, nor upon public stocks, or private enterprises of any description. Upon all these, apart from other risks, there is greater hazard of fluctuation, which might absorb much more than all the profits of a short investment. The fluctuation of Exchequer bills has so narrow a range, that the most timid would never fear the loss of not only interest, but a part of the capital. The British Exchequer furnishes a security based upon the faith of the nation, under the careful management of the Bank of England, exactly suited to this class of lenders. Nothing could be devised, better suited to their position and wants. The funds they have to spare are cheerfully and promptly exchanged for Exchequer bills; and for every sum thus loaned, the lender obtains as many days' interest as it is out of his hands. There is, then, in Great Britain, a fund of some £20,000,000 to £30,000,000 sterling at all times subject to the call of the government and Bank of England, upon this form of security. Even in times of great commercial distress and pressure, Exchequer bills are in demand; because, the greater the distrust of individuals, the greater the disposition to resort to public securities. It is very true, however, that the success of this whole device of Exchequer bills has depended, from the beginning in 1696 down to the present day, upon the Bank of England, which has long had the actual management of the public debt of Great Britain. The delicacy and care necessary to regulate the issues of Exchequer bills could only be appreciated by a great bank, or similar institution, placed in intimate relations with the capitalists of a country; no mere public agents, or officers of a national treasury, could ever have managed such an issue of Exchequer bills as that which the Bank of England has controlled, from the very year in which it was founded.

This success has enabled the government of Great Britain not only to meet all the regular demands upon the Exchequer with complete promptitude, but to encounter great emergencies with wonderful ease and efficiency. It has not only met the extraordinary expenditure of the American Revolution, and the wars following upon the French Revolution, continuing through a period of forty years, but during that time it furnished immense sums in the way of loans and subsidies to other European Powers.[1] By the aid of this well-devised security, and the judicious management of the Bank of England, the government was never without available resources on the most trying occasions; it was often saved from such financial movements as cannot but create alarm. The Exchequer bills were always in circulation, and an extraordinary issue could be managed with little disturbance of the money-market. Not only so, but the facility thus enjoyed between capitalists and the government no doubt induced and enabled the government to extend special pecuniary assistance in cases of great emergency. In 57th of George III., an act was passed, establishing a board of loan commissioners, who were to have charge of the business of furnishing special relief out of public funds, or by the help of public credit. This act "authorized the issue of Exchequer bills, and the advance of money out of the consolidated fund, to a limited amount, for the carrying on public works and fisheries in the United Kingdom, and in affording employment to the laboring classes, under the then circumstances of the country." Under this and other provisions of law, vast sums, besides the ordinary taxation, were raised and applied to special purposes. Relief to Ireland, relief to the West Indies, as well as to those needing it at home, was largely afforded, to the amount of scores of millions of pounds sterling. Under the management of the bank, a very small advance in the rate of interest upon Exchequer bills sufficed to call forth large sums; but this store of capital was carefully husbanded by the Exchequer and the bank; if drawn upon too heavily, it might have been exhausted, or such a rise in the rate of interest might have occurred as could not easily have been reduced. This large fund, thus held at the disposal of the British Exchequer, is an affair altogether unique; it has no

[1] Between 1793 and 1814, loans and subsidies were granted to foreign Powers to the amount of over $230,000,000. The whole expenditures, between those periods, varied from $120,000,000 to $530,000,000 yearly.

parallel in any country.[1] It requires consummate management to sustain it, and a vast substratum of industrial and commercial wealth to serve for its foundation. We look upon it as a financial achievement of the highest order — as a facility and advantage beyond estimate. It may be objected, that it encourages extravagance, and facilitates going in debt: it may be so; being a machine of great power, it should only be in wise, skilful and virtuous hands. But it seems very certain that the public debt of Great Britain would have proved a burden too great to be endured, but for this facility; and it is still more certain that the annual income of that country could not, for many successive years, be collected without great oppression of the tax-payers, but for this well-fostered device of Exchequer bills.

The main advantage in employing Exchequer bills does not, however, arise from the ready access they give to a large amount of funds, which no other security can so readily command, nor from the fact that they can be always purchased by those who wish to have them, and always sold by those who wish to realize, nor because the fluctuations are confined to so narrow a range as to cause no apprehension among holders: the chief advantage lies in this, that as the collection of the British revenue involves a payment into the public coffers of £1,000,000 sterling weekly, or $5,000,000, the withdrawal of which, week after week, would be sensibly if not severely felt in the channels of business: all this is avoided by the use of Exchequer bills. They enable the government to borrow the entire sum required for the current payments of the treasury, and to disburse to the public creditors the whole amount of the incoming revenue, before its regular receipt into the Exchequer. The government, by this means, avoids even the temporary withdrawal of the currency employed in business; it draws the sums required for current payments from a vast mass of funds, which, for a time, would otherwise remain unemployed; and disburses the

[1] Some advantages of this kind have been, for the last twenty or thirty years, attained by the treasury of France, but by a very different process.

notes of the Bank of England, thus obtained, wherever the public money is payable. The expenditures come first; the payments into the treasury follow. The most effective mode of diminishing the burden of taxation is, no doubt, to secure a proper distribution of industry, and proper facilities for inland and foreign trade; but as an alleviation in the mere process of collecting revenue, we cannot conceive any thing greater than the mode of first distributing, and then subsequently collecting the public revenue. If the amount must first be collected, and then paid, it would involve a detention of money in the treasury of several weeks, or months, or even more; for money must, in that case, be kept in the treasury for emergencies, during the examination of accounts, and to meet drafts, the time of the presentation of which is uncertain. It is on record that the British Exchequer, previous to the introduction of Exchequer bills, was obliged, from time to time, to give notice when debts of a particular description could be paid; as, for instance, all between £10 and £50 after a day mentioned.[1] The present system ensures punctual and prompt payment of public dues, and secures that economy which prompt payment always brings with it, together with that high degree of credit which promptness and punctuality never fail to command.

Whatever complications and useless machinery may be connected with this feature of British finance, we think that it surpasses, in advantage to the government and to the people, any other known system. The British government thus avoids drawing money from the channels of business, and locking it up for months in the Exchequer; it avoids checking the circulation of money; it avoids disturbing the payments of trade; but, on the contrary, takes up weekly a million sterling from individual holders who would otherwise not employ it; it diffuses this large sum throughout the country, wherever the public payments carry it; it very wisely pays interest, for a few months, on the current expenditures, as a measure of relief to the public debtors, and of favor to public creditors, strengthening,

---

[1] Rolt's Dictionary of Trade, in folio, Art. "Exchequer."

at the same time, that public credit on which the measure is founded.[1]

The importance of avoiding the withdrawal, from the general circulation, of so large a sum as a million sterling each week, especially in a country in which debts are chiefly paid by the proceeds of discounted paper, is greater than some may imagine. To a certain extent, we know the fund created by discounted commercial paper can, with great advantage, be used as a substitute for money; but every use which diverts it long from its legitimate purpose of paying the debts created by its issue is at the hazard of creating pressure in the money-market. If the government should intervene, and take a million each week, and retain it for an average of only one or two months, it could not be attended with but damaging pressure. Every discounted note or bill must be paid, and it requires the amount issued for it to pay it and the amount of the discount beside: the fund created by these discounts may be employed as a substitute for

[1] The extent to which Exchequer bills are employed in Great Britain will appear from the following statement.* The amount outstanding on a particular day, in each of the years mentioned, with the whole interest paid on them that year, stands thus:—

Years.	Amounts outstanding.	Interest paid.
1836	£28,155,150	....
1838	24,026,050	£720,928
1840	21,626,350	642,947
1842	18,182,100	896,464
1844	18,404,500	531,843
1846	18,310,700	421,432
1847	17,946,500	436,298
1850	....	606,025
1854	....	490,461
1855	....	814,221
1856	....	818,403

The whole amounts issued in the following periods are as follows:—

Years.	Whole amounts.	Average yearly issue.	Whole interest.
1793 to 1802	£155,715,800	£15,571,580	£6,788,623
1803 to 1816	550,853,900	36,723,593	24,760,901
1817 to 1826	325,380,300	32,538,000	12,096,997

* Political Dictionary, vol. ii. p. 852; British Almanac, Finance Accounts; Marshall's Statistics, p. 192.

money, while the paper discounted is running to maturity; but if it is withdrawn by speculation, or by payment of taxes, from its ordinary channels of circulation, disturbance and pressure must ensue. The readiness with which the proceeds of discounted paper is received, in Great Britain, in place of money, furnishes many ways in which such funds may stray away, or be diverted from their proper uses. This perversion being, as we have shown, a principal evil of the credit system, it is a wise and provident feature of the British financial system, that it does not add the whole income of the nation to the other modes and occasions of drawing off the bank deposits, thus reducing the amount applicable to the current payments of business.

We have said that the sums borrowed by the government are drawn from a class of persons who would not otherwise have employed them. The government, therefore, avoids taking from a fund which is active, and needed where it is; and it draws forth, into active service, one which would not be used. It leaves £1,000,000 sterling every week in its proper channels, to do its proper work, and throws into circulation £1,000,000 which would otherwise do little or nothing. It is not difficult to divine how this policy not only renders the collection of the revenue less difficult and expensive, but how it increases the amount, and strengthens and fosters all the sources of revenue. Instead of drawing money from the business of the country, and locking it up for months unemployed, it is drawn from the recesses of capitalists, and cast into the current of trade and industry, months before the revenue is exacted.

It must not be supposed that the large deposits of the public in the Bank of England detracts from this view. These deposits are, for the most part, but credits given by the bank to the Exchequer, upon the credit of the bills. The Exchequer issues the bills, which are either discounted directly by the bank, or sold by the latter, and the proceeds carried to the credit of the government, in its various departments of public expenditure. It is not the money collected which figures, for the most part, as a credit to the public, but the fund which is borrowed. The bank itself being a continual lender to the government, by the purchase of Exchequer bills, the public deposits are, in fact, only a credit on the books of the bank. These credits appear, in the statements of the bank, as deposits of public money; when they are, for the most part, only a privilege of drawing at pleasure upon the bank for the amount of a credit.

We need not dwell upon these financial advantages; they are obvious, upon a little reflection. Grumblers are found in every country among tax-payers; and as the people of Great Britain are heavily burdened, the grumblers are not scarce. Tax-payers do not often appreciate the merits of their revenue system; what is wrong or disagreeable they are ever ready to specify and denounce, but seldom do full justice to that which is commendable. Men do not always, in Great Britain, measure the alleviation afforded by the system of Exchequer bills, nor perceive that, but for this relief, the burden of taxation might be not only heavier, but, perhaps, unendurable. The Bank of England has been steadily denounced, during its whole existence, by a large class of these tax-payers, who stand ready, with all the power and ingenuity they can bring to bear, to crush that institution. Whatever may be the faults in the constitution or management of the bank, and in the former respect the defects are important, it may be asserted that the public is more than repaid all it suffers in sustaining the bank, by this system of Exchequer bills, which the bank is mainly instrumental in upholding. The truth is, no national treasury has ever elsewhere established and maintained an issue of securities similar to the Exchequer bills, for a third of the time during which they have been successfully employed.

To employ them with success requires the two main conditions which sustain them in Great Britain — the ultimate security afforded by the public faith and national wealth, and the immediate security of a great institution of credit, having relations with the general business of the country, to insure punctuality and regular modes of proceeding. Where men are willing to make their bank deposits, they are willing to lend. Men of business will confide in the security of the nation, but they prefer the punctuality and processes of a bank when their money is in question. A bank can approach these lenders with perfect confidence; but the treasury, without this agency, can only go into the money-market for permanent loans. But even in this respect the floating debt, upon the security of Exchequer bills, affords a great facility when a permanent loan is contemplated. The Exchequer bills are, in due course, always paid off every year; the holders are compelled to present them, for that purpose, at the time appointed, or thereafter lose their interest. But when a loan is wanted, a certain portion of the holders of Exchequer bills are always found ready for permanent investment, and the loan is soon filled.

They are issued in sums of £100, £200, £500 and £1000. Each denomination is printed in different colored ink — the £100 in red, £200 in yellow, £500 in blue, and the £1000 in black. They bear interest at a certain rate per cent. per day, that rate continuing until the day of payment, which is fixed by public notice. They are generally paid off within the year in which they are issued; and as they are frequently issued, the process of payment also goes on by discharge of a certain portion every quarter. Lenders thus find a continual supply of new Exchequer bills in which to invest; and they are constantly assured, by notices to holders of a certain description of them to come forward and be paid, that the security is good, and the payment sure. Holders neglecting to present their bills at the time fixed in the notice, lose interest until new bills are issued, applicable to their case. Exchequer bills are transferable by delivery only. The usual rate of interest, for many years, has been from 2¼ to 3¾ per cent.; but the rate, at times, is much above this, and the Exchequer occasionally raises the interest upon bills already in circulation. As they are receivable, after a certain time expressed, in payment of taxes and dues to the government, the raising the interest prevents that use of them, and also prevents their being presented for payment.[1]

[1] At the usual rates of interest per day, the rate per year is as follows:

1½*d.*	per day is equal to	£2	5*s.*	7½*d.*	per year.
1¾	"	"	2	13	2¾	"
2	"	"	3	0	10	"
2½	"	"	3	16	0½	"
3	"	"	4	11	3	"

The bills are of various classes, well defined on their face, and understood by those among whom they circulate. Those given for the unfunded debt are not receivable in payment to the government until a year after they are issued; but they are, twice a year, advertised to be paid off, or rather exchanged, on certain days, after which interest ceases, if not presented.

The Bank of England is generally a large holder of Exchequer bills; no kind of security can be more acceptable to it, as a reserve of strength and protection in case of emergency. The government is deeply interested to maintain their credit, and the bank has no less interest, because the business of the Exchequer is as important to that institution as its management of financial matters is to the government. The bank advances, upon Exchequer bills every year, nearly the whole expenditure of the government; it is always ready to furnish the needful means, either directly, or by negotiation of these securities. The public revenue being receivable in bank-notes, at the rate of a million sterling weekly, the notes issued by the bank on the credit given to the government, are returned at about the same rate weekly at which they are issued; that is, if, upon any particular branch of the revenue, the bank at the beginning of a quarter grants to the government a credit of £5,000,000, to be drawn for as needed, the sums drawn upon this credit will be distributed over the whole quarter, and the revenue for the same period, upon the same branch, will be returning an equivalent amount of the bank-notes issued upon the drafts of the government. The bank, in making these advances, runs less risk of over-issue or overcharging the currency, than may be supposed; it is only issuing bank-notes to an amount required by the taxpayers, for the very purpose of immediate payment to the government. With the notes thus returned, the government takes up the Exchequer bills upon which the advance was made. In the mean time, the bank counts and charges interest on these bills to the stated day of payment.

The amount of bank-notes issued, in making these advances, may remain in circulation one week, or four, or eight; the more abundant the issue, the more rapidly will the public revenue be paid, for the money-market will be well supplied. The actual advance by the bank in notes, upon a credit of £5,000,000, may not exceed £1,000,000 or £2,000,000 at any one time; the interest, however, of the £5,000,000 will have run on steadily in favor of the bank. Of course this is a desirable kind of busisiness for the bank; we believe it is equally so for the people and the government. It affords the bank another advantage. In case of an unfavorable foreign exchange, or any other circumstance, making it desirable to reduce its circulation, the bank can so readily but cautiously put these Exchequer bills on the market, as very rapidly to absorb a large amount of deposits and circulation. And this is a mode of reducing a circulation, as unexceptionable as any that could be adopted. But for this, the bank could only adopt the plan so frequently used in this country, and in England, too, when the above remedy proves insufficient — that of refusing further discounts of commercial paper, whilst receiving payment of that which matures. When the bank, for the purpose of reducing its circulation, or of protecting its vaults, is obliged to withhold the usual facilities of discount from men of business, it withdraws so much of the medium of payment in daily use, as seriously to injure the progress of trade; to endanger the credit of individuals, if not worse; to enhance the rate of interest; to reduce the price of commodities; and thus to impair mutual confidence, and bring on all the other evils of a severe pressure. But the Bank of England can, to a large extent, avoid these mischiefs by withdrawing its circulation, and reducing its deposits, by the sale of Exchequer bills. The purchasers of these bills are not applying for discounts; they voluntarily pay over to the bank its notes, and give up their deposits for bills, without inconvenience or injury to any one; and so far the process saves the community generally from any hurtful diminution of the currency.

The mode of transacting the daily business between the Exchequer and the bank is by means of Exchequer bills. If the Exchequer has occasion for £5,000,000 for a particular service, during a certain quarter of the year, it delivers at once, or gradually, to the bank five thousand bills of £1000 each, and receives a credit on the books of the bank to that amount, upon which it can draw at pleasure. In the mean time, the revenue of the government, coming in daily, is deposited in the bank. As this deposit from such receipts accumulates, the bank, day by day, or week by week, delivers to the Exchequer so many of the Exchequer bills of £1000 as will cover the amount of the growing deposit. They are, however, only retained as a collateral security, and held until the quarterly day of adjustment, when they are returned to the bank. The Exchequer then pays off the bills and the interest by a check on the bank. Thus the government, on the security of Exchequer bills, obtains the facility and advantage of issuing Bank of England notes in payment of its various liabilities, as fast as they mature or accrue; the creditors of the government receive their dues with promptness; the public has the advantage of an increased volume of currency, for which the demand is so active that there is not the slightest danger of its being a superfluous issue; the bank has the advantage of making a large advance of its credits and notes upon the very best security, and with the least possible risk, in other respects, as it only enlarges its issues by an outgoing current, to the same extent it is diminished by the incoming current of the public revenue.

In all this movement of the British treasury, which involves a payment to the public of £1,000,000 sterling each week, and a payment by the public into the treasury of the same sum, very little or no coin is required. The government says to the public: "If you will receive these notes of the Bank of England in payment of what is due to you, the Exchequer will in return receive them in payment of what is due to the government."

At first sight, it might appear that the government could, with equal success and advantage, issue its own notes in payment of debts and and expenditures, receivable for all taxes and income payable into the public treasury. No doubt, if such notes were thus employed, the tax-payers and debtors to the government would gladly purchase them as a means of discharging debt to the public. But the actual system has the immense advantage of employing notes of the Bank of England, already the chief currency of the kingdom. These notes are always as acceptable and efficient as money, and the public creditor is neither compelled to sell the security he receives, nor to wait the demand of the tax-payer. The joint arrrangement between the Exchequer and the bank is, then, as beneficial to the debtors and creditors of the government as it is effective and convenient to the bank and the Exchequer.

Our design, in exhibiting this feature of British finance, has not been to recommend or approve all the details and accessories by which it is surrounded. Many of them are exceptionable. It is chiefly the feature of the government advancing to the public, by its expenditures, the very medium in which the public revenue can afterwards be paid, to which we would strongly draw the attention of the reader, as worthy of prolonged study in all its applications.

No other people in the world, we repeat, have a system of finance which, in this respect, so alleviates the burden of taxation. In the United States, the public revenue is only receivable in gold or silver. This medium of payment, which is only employed, in the transaction of business, in the payment of the balances of foreign trade, and in the merest matters of retail, is required to be produced and paid over for the whole amount of the gross revenue of the general government. This aggravates the hardship of taxation, and increases the burden. By the laws of the United States, every man is bound to pay every debt he owes in gold or silver; yet, in operations above the amount of mere retail, it is almost unheard of that any one is required, in the operations of industry or commerce, to pay a debt in gold or silver. The government, then, exacts from its debtors payment in specie, which the people, who have the same right by law, never exact as between themselves. If the people, as between themselves, should at any time attempt to enforce the practice of their government, a general suspension of payments, public and private, would ensue. The government enforces, therefore, against its debtors a mode of payment which would be disastrous, beyond all estimate, if enforced by the people against each other.

For several years previous to the year 1858, the treasury of the United States contained an average sum of $20,000,000 in gold and silver, unemployed, and of course wholly unproductive. That involved a loss of $1,500,000 of interest, and reckoning at the rates of interest prevailing, more than $2,500,000. By the British system, no gold or silver of any considerable amount comes into the public treasury, and of course none lies there unemployed; and instead of heaping up money in the public treasury, the British Exchequer pays interest to the bank and people for a temporary accommodation of credit every year, by which it is enabled to receive and disburse annually $250,000,000, without employing the precious metals at all, except for the purposes of change.

The English system withdraws no portion of coin or bullion from their appropriate sphere of usefulness. They may be employed by the banks as a reserve, as security for their issues, for the prompt redemption of notes and deposits, and to meet the emergencies of an unfavorable foreign exchange; but in none of these cases do the regular demands of the public treasury draw upon a fund so important to the steady progress of trade, and a safe condition of banks and money-market. If the whole income of the British treasury were receivable only in gold, as in the United States, it would empty the Bank of England at the rate of £1,000,000 sterling every week, and absorb its whole stock in three months. It would make it necessary for the Bank of England to keep in its vaults from £20,000,000 to £40,000,000 sterling, instead of from £5,000,000 to £20,000,000, as has been done since the resumption in 1822. This would take from the channels of business an average of £10,000,000 sterling in the precious metals, to remain unemployed, because the treasury, which only receives and disburses coins, should have an average sum on hand of not less than twenty per cent. of the year's revenue.

§ 2. *Financial system of France — Late Reforms — Count Mollien and Marquis D'Audiffret — The harmony and subordination of the system — Outline — Relations of the system with domestic exchange — Special functionary for distribution of public funds — Money to remain in treasury the shortest time possible — Economy of the new system — Commission on transfers — D'Audiffret quoted — Money always ready to be advanced on public account — Firmness of the system — Necessity of it — France first appreciates relations of public finance with trade and industry — Perils of credit lessened by this system — Want of details — Contrast with the system of the United States.*

The system of public finance in France, once so cumbrous and awkward, so expensive and otherwise disadvantageous to the nation, has, during the last half-century, under the able direction of Count Mollien, the Marquis D'Audiffret, and other eminent men, undergone such radical changes as have completely modified both its principles and its mode of operation. These reforms were resisted, in every stage and with every weapon, by the parties interested in maintaining old abuses. The persevering efforts of honest and enlightened men for thirty or forty years overcame all opposition, and France now enjoys a financial system, in not a few respects, superior to that of any other nation.

The great feature of the present system in France is the harmony of the whole, and the complete subordination of all its parts to the central administration, or Ministry of Finance, in Paris. Every officer connected with the receipt and disbursement of the public money is accountable to that ministry, and every officer is an officer of the treasury. The complications of this system of centralization are still very great, and perhaps susceptible of being somewhat simplified with a further economy in the administration. But if the complexity is great, the system, order and regularity are complete and admirable. The guards, securities and precautions against error, peculation and fraud, seem to be perfect; the whole movement of the public money, from its receipt to its disbursement, is so fully spread upon the public accounts, and the checks provided are so ample, that it appears as if nothing more could be effected in that respect. All this is worthy of study; but it is not the aspect of the system to which we now invite the attention of the reader.[1] We can only give the merest outline of the French treasury, before noticing that feature upon which we desire to dwell for a brief space. There are receivers-general in each of the eighty-six departments, into whose offices the public revenue of the respective districts flows. These offices are appendages of the general treasury, and money paid into them is in the treasury, and can only be paid or withdrawn by the regular processes of the treasury. The great books of the minister of finance at Paris contain a full exhibit of all the money in the various offices.

No money can be disbursed but in the regular order of proceeding: of course none can be paid but by virtue of, or under color of, some law; none can be paid without a credit opened under authority of the law permitting the payment; no payment can be made under that credit, unless a special order (mandat) is signed by a proper officer, and addressed to the special officer with whom the credit is opened; and finally, no payment can be made, unless the officer to whom the mandat is addressed finds every previous step in accordance with law and instructions; and when the disbursing officers make their return, it must appear that every formality has been observed, and that the whole proceedings are according to law, and in due form, or the credit will not be allowed.

The whole proceedings of the officers of the treasury in the processes of payment, and their mode of rendering their accounts

---

[1] The elaborate work edited by M. Maurice Block, published at Paris in 1856, "Dictionnaire de l'Administration Française," in super-royal 8vo. pp. 1630, contains ample details of the forms, processes and laws pertaining to the financial system of France. No other nation can boast a work upon internal administration to be compared with this volume; and yet France can boast another work, which, though not so abounding in details, is scarcely less important, and certainly more interesting to the general reader, the "Dictionnaire Politique: Encyclopedie du language et de la Science Politiques," super-royal 8vo. pp. 944, Paris, 1848. This volume, like the other, is the production of an association of distinguished and competent men, selecting respectively the topics of their contributions.

is subject to the scrutiny of a court of accounts, consisting of a president (premier), three presidents (de chambre), eighteen master counsellors, eighteen consulting counsellors of the first class, and sixty-two of the second class, and of a procureur-general. There is here abundant preparation for scrutiny and watchfulness. But although the forms are complete, the system perfect, the accountability strict and steadily enforced, and although nine-tenths and more of the officers may be thus held to strict official honesty, there must still be points of contact between the system and the outside world, at which frauds may enter and pass through all the forms which official care and experience have provided in the way of prevention. Extreme complication may, indeed, be the very hiding-place of peculation; and it may be more difficult to follow the traces of a systematic robber of the public, than if he had no such forms as a cloak to villany.

Our object now is to show that the French treasury, however complicated its machinery, and however numerous its official incumbents, is not without its proper relation and sympathies with those from whom it derives its supplies. It is not divorced from the business of the people. Among its numerous officials, is one in direct relations with the chief minister of finance, who has special charge of the locality of all money in the treasury. He can neither receive nor pay money; but he can transfer the public money from one office of the treasury to another, and place it wherever the exigencies of the government may require. It is in the office of this functionary that is established a direct and very important connection with the current business of the day. His duty requires of him a careful and timely study of the points of public expenditure; he must know not only where the money will be wanted, but he must have it ready when required. To accomplish this important object, it becomes his duty to study the domestic trade of the country, that he may avail himself of the internal exchanges in the necessary distribution of the money in the treasury. It is very rare, indeed, that the French treasury ever shifts the locality of gold or silver. It may require many circuitous transfers to move the excesses of revenue, in some departments, to the points of expenditure, and to supply the deficiency in other departments. To make these transfers, the officer who has special charge of that duty relies almost wholly on the domestic exchanges. He is well informed where funds are wanted for the purposes of industry or trade; he learns where and when those who reside in the vicinity of each office of the treasury desire to remit funds; and he learns whence and when they wish to draw them. His office becomes the depository of this information, because he intervenes in this business of giving drafts upon the treasury, payable at other points, and giving money at his own office for money received at other offices. His intervention in the transmission of funds assists in balancing the internal exchanges of the country; for, of course, the office is only applied to when the business of individuals requires such accommodation. But this business is not confined to receiving money at an office of the treasury in one place, and paying the amount as may be required at another office, in a different place; that is, to a mere exchange of money between the treasury and individuals at different places; it goes much further. At times and places where large transfers of funds become necessary, the proper officer of the treasury becomes the receiver of commercial or individual paper to a large amount.

The receivers-general of the eighty-six departments, and their subordinates, the receivers of the treasuries of the arrondissments and communes, maintain reciprocal business relations by frequent exchanges of money, by drafts upon each other, and by bills upon Paris and other places. The chief officers of the treasury become, by the constant report of this business to them, intimately acquainted with the whole industrial and commercial movement of the population. They regard it as extremely important to these interests, that the money which is necessarily withdrawn from private uses for public purposes, should be retained in the treasury as short a time as possible. Out of 300,000,000 or 400,000,000 of francs annually remitted from the country treasuries to Paris, not more than ten per cent., or 30,000,000 or 40,000,000 of francs, are ever at one time in the public treasuries. This shows that disbursement follows so rapidly upon receipt, that the money taken from the people for taxes does not remain, on the average, more than a month or two out of its proper channels, and that the government has carefully reduced the inconvenience and disadvantage of taxation to the lowest possible point. By this regular and constant communication with men of capital and business, by this constant association with them in the business of transferring funds, the officers of the treasury are able at all times to command, in advance of the regular receipts, large sums of money, which are freely placed in the public treasury at low rates of interest. Money is, in fact, frequently pressed upon the various receivers by those who desire short but safe investments, and by those who would secure, in good season, the aid of the treasury in placing money at particular points. The treasurers of the departments do not lend money, though they receive it in the way of short loans; they transfer money for individuals, and they purchase bills of exchange upon such points as the exigencies of the public may require. Upon one side, then, there are open relations between the public treasuries and the movements of trade, industry and currency; that is, upon the side of the domestic exchanges of the country; the transactions of the treasury, in relation to the distribution of its funds, are blended with the movements of the internal exchanges as conducted by the individuals concerned in it. This constitutes a very broad field of contact between the business of the country, from which the money is withdrawn by taxation, and the public treasury. The public money being retained for the shortest possible time, is so managed, nevertheless, as to render an important service in aiding and regulating the internal exchanges.

Taxation having reached, in France, a point beyond which it cannot be increased without passing the ability of the people to pay, an alleviation of the burden, like that we have just mentioned, is of signal advantage. According to the former revenue system of France, the money remained for many months in the hands of the receivers, who merely made advances, on interest, to the government from time to time, and settled their accounts once a year. Now, all money is held to be in the treasury from the moment it is received into the office of any department; and it is sent into the general circulation again with as little delay as possible. The assistance thus afforded to the adjustment of the domestic exchanges greatly promotes punctuality in commercial and industrial payments and remittances, by diminishing the expense and the disturbances occasioned by paying the balances of the internal trade. These features of the present financial system, by which it is so closely connected with the internal trade and exchanges, are regarded by an eminent French writer upon finance as rendering less necessary in France than in other countries, that development of credit in banking which is so prevalent and so dangerous elsewhere.[1]

The same author informs us that, under this system, the expenses of the negotiations or transfers of the treasury fell from 55,000,000 of francs to 2,000,000 or 3,000,000, upon the movement of four to five milliards of francs; and that the credit, or confidence, upon which this business proceeds has long been upon such a solid base, that it has survived uninjured many political revolutions; and that the people, thus brought into special relations with the treasury, have long since perceived the propriety of yielding, in all matters pertaining to public finance, to the formalities and precautions of the treasury.

No intermediary is permitted by the treasury in its financial operations. All that is done between the officers of the treasury and men of business must be done in the forms and methods of the treasury, which takes all the power, and assumes all the responsibility. Not even the Bank of France is exempt from this rule. It deals with the treasury only as individuals

---

[1] This is a remark of the Marquis D'Audiffret, one of the most distinguished of the French Ministers of Finance—a minister to whom, with Count Mollien, the French Government is chiefly indebted for that great financial reform, which, beginning half a century ago, has converted the French revenue system from one of the worst to one of the best, if not the very best, in the world. The Marquis D'Audiffret published in Paris, in 1854, in six volumes 8vo, "Systeme Financier de la France," a work to which we confidently refer the reader as among the best on national finance which has yet appeared in any country.

may do; there is no financial connection between the bank and the treasury. The treasury is enabled by law, through its officers, to perform all the acts necessary to its full operation, without any dependence on the bank; it would borrow from the Bank of France only as it would from individuals. The treasury is itself an institution having many of the features of a bank, of which the offices in the departments are branches. It absorbs a large portion of the business of the domestic exchange, because the distribution of the public funds is a business of the same nature; to keep the public exchange, or distribution of funds, wholly separate from the private, would be an injury to both. The receivers of the departments are authorized, under the direction of the minister having special charge of the distribution of the public moneys, to deal in the domestic exchanges so far as may be needful to effect the objects of the treasury. And for this they are allowed to charge a commission, when the rates of domestic exchange admit of it without expense to the government. It is obvious that the effect must be to facilitate remittances, promote punctuality, and lessen the rate of domestic exchange. The latter result is so obvious, that it has often been the subject of complaint, that this intervention of the treasury in the domestic exchange is an injury to bankers who are specially engaged in this business. To this it is replied that the treasury, in doing this, is only attending to its own business in the best way, and that all its exchange transactions in paper are but a branch, or a small fractiou, of its business. The profits made by the receivers are an economy to the treasury, because it is by this mode of proceeding that the expense of distributing the public funds is reduced to its minimum.

"The receivers-general, eighty-six in number, are the constant auxiliaries of the local officers, whose operations and acts they aid by timely provision of the ways and means applicable to the necessities of every day, and every locality. It is, in fact, through them that the treasury is enabled to meet every exigency, by its ready access to the capital of men throughout the country, who willingly commit their money to the public through the hands of these faithful depositories of the national funds. It is through the confidence they inspire, by their careful regard for private as well as public interests, that the idea of taking shares in the great book of the national debt is becoming daily more familiar and popular. It is upon the faith reposed in these treasuries of the departments, and upon the advances they can always command, so fully proportioned to the necessities of the moment, that a reserve of more than a hundred millions of francs is constantly at the disposition of the minister of finance.

"We may demand, then, what could replace, with such security and economy, a treasury system so well tried, and so much approved in France; so generally admired abroad, so favorable to all interests: a system which, subjected for more than thirty years to the perilous vicissitudes of so many political changes, has not ceased its regular operations for a single day; has not for one instant superseded the full use or due application of the public funds; has not suffered any deficit of the money in charge, nor any misapplication of resources, general or special; and has not promptly, in all circumstances, yielded to the requirements of law, and to the checks of that accountability needful to public security."[1]

"The task of a minister of finance would be incomplete, as a regulator of the movement of the national wealth, if he could not direct the distribution of the public funds derived from taxation and from credit; funds which, from this double source, are pouring into the treasury, and from the treasury into the channels of a circulation of paper and of coins; which funds are thus continually withdrawn for a short time from the employments of industry and trade, to be immediately restored. The local equilibrium of receipts and disbursements cannot be maintained properly and exclusively for the public treasury, if at the same time private interests, so far as they are concerned in the matter, are not assured by a wise and skilful management in the distribution of the public funds.

"France is the only nation which has fully appreciated the

---

[1] Système Financier de la France, par Le Marquis D'Audiffret, tom. i. p. 353.

intimate connection between the operations of finance and the general movement of individual transactions, and which has kept them in perfect harmony with each other, without disturbing the regular progress of either, by means of a mechanism skilfully adapted to the administration of the treasury.

"But that this incessant disposal of the means and daily exigencies of every locality be not deranged, in the hand which regulates it in all parts of the country, it is indispensable to leave to his direct and immediate disposition the numerous agents and functionaries who accumulate the funds to be distributed, who transmit them sometimes from the tax-payer to the public creditor, sometimes from the offices of the receivers into the channels of commerce, in exchange for credits in accounts current, or for bills of exchange payable on time at Paris and upon other places. These conversions of specie into commercial paper on time, these reciprocal advances of the agents of the treasury, and their private or unofficial correspondents, who accept from and render favors to the public treasury according to local necessities and the wants of the treasury, maintain at all points of the country the ways and means necessary to balance the exchanges, assure the punctual fulfilment of all engagements, and give a firm basis not only to private but to public credit. This beautiful financial organization gives great energy to the action of authority, by affording assistance to all interests, public and private, and thus aids the execution of its orders even in times of the greatest difficulty.

"The example of other nations has amply taught us how imprudent it is to abandon a prerogative involving such influence, to establishments directed by a special and, so to speak, individual interest, and which are not attached by strict ties to the direct and universal impulse of government. This powerful consideration counsels us, in France, never to extend the sphere of public banks and institutions of credit beyond a certain limit, distinctly and practically traced, by the power of the existing circulation. It is enough that banks and institutions of credit be permitted to supply that deficiency of the circulation which the present stock of money, the existing currency, and the operations of the treasury, with all its subordinate offices and functionaries, cannot furnish."[1]

Though alleged as a great fault in the financial system of the United States, that it is wholly secluded from the business of the country; that it manages the whole transactions of the public treasury without reference to any direct benefit which might be conferred upon the people at large, or any burden which might be lessened, or any regulating power which might be beneficially exerted, we are not yet sufficiently informed of the details and results of the French system, in regard to which the Marquis indulges so much complacency, to make a fair comparison between them. We have no reason to question his conclusions; but neither he nor any other writer that we have met with, furnishes full information in regard to the practical operation of that mode of dealing in domestic exchange carried on so extensively by the treasury of France, through its branches in the departments. Until this is known in detail, no satisfactory conclusions can be reached, and no reliable estimate can be formed of the true value of the system, and especially of its applicability elsewhere.

It is clear, from this and other passages in the works of the Marquis D'Audiffret, that the friends of the present admirable financial system of France sympathize with the friends of the Independent Treasury of the United States, in a jealousy of banks of circulation. It is remarkable, that whilst both partake of this feeling, they have taken opposite directions in their practical measures. In France, the public treasury has resolved itself, through its eighty-six branches, into a great institution for the management, aid and regulation of the domestic exchanges, having many of the characteristics of a vast national bank. In this country, all connection with the current business has been severed, the treasury performs no function of a bank, it recognises no persons but those from whom it receives money, and to whom it pays money — its debtors and creditors. What-

---

[1] Système Financier de la France, par Le Marquis D'Audiffret, tom. i. pp. 532–3–4.

ever has been done beyond this is against the spirit of the system, and the letter of the law. Like an individual who keeps no bank account, our public treasury merely receives, keeps and pays out its own money. The people of the United States make all their large payments through banks. The treasury wholly discards them: the people employ almost exclusively a paper currency — the treasury wholly discards it, and receives only gold or silver. The treasury of the United States discards all relations with banks, with paper currency, with industry, and with trade. It is a mere creature of income and disbursement. The French treasury associates itself, or blends its processes, with the general business of the country, so far as even to supply, to some extent, the place of banks or institutions of credit; the idea being that, so far as the treasury can afford the same facilities in regard to domestic exchange which banks give, it should do so to the exclusion of banks; that private institutions, wholly under the guidance of private interests, cannot so fully promote the general interests as the action of the treasury, when directed to the same end.

The prevailing opinion in the United States is, that neither banks, nor individuals, nor the officers of the treasury, can properly be allowed any discretion where the public funds are concerned. Our republic thus exhibits less confidence in official virtue than the monarchical government of France. Can it be that experience has generated this distrust?

§ 3. *The Treasury of the United States — Act of Congress,* 1846 — *Paper currency the usage of the country — Departure from usage — Effect upon the banks — Advance of interest — Increase of private banks — Economy of the system —Difficulty of execution — The remedy a step towards banking — Domestic exchange and the treasury — New York the centre of the operations of the treasury and the domestic exchanges — Transmission of funds to and from New York — Paper operations of the treasury — The present system seldom of advantage to public creditors — Indirect taxation and California gold have favored the Independent Treasury.*

The treasury of the United States is, by law, established in the buildings appropriated to that purpose in Washington: "and all moneys paid into the same shall be subject to the draft of the treasurer, drawn agreeably to appropriations made by law." There are seven sub-treasuries, or offices, for the safe keeping of money out of Washington, respectively at Philadelphia, New York, Boston, Charleston, New Orleans, St. Louis, and San Francisco. By the act of Congress of 1846, which established what has since been called the Independent Treasury, it is provided "that the treasurer of the United States, the treasurer of the mint of the United States, the treasurers and those acting as such of the various branch mints, all collectors of the customs, all surveyors of the customs acting also as collectors, all assistant treasurers, all receivers of public moneys at the several land offices, all postmasters, and all public officers of whatsoever character, be and they are hereby required to keep safely, without loaning, using, depositing in banks, or exchanging for other funds than as allowed by this act, all the public money collected by them, or otherwise at any time placed in their possession or custody, till the same is ordered by the proper department or officer of the government to be transferred or paid out:" "that all collectors and receivers of public money, of every character and description, shall, so frequently as they may be directed by the Secretary of the Treasury or the Postmaster-general, pay over to the treasurer of their respective districts all public money collected by them or in their hands; and it shall be the duty of the Secretary and Postmaster-general respectively to order such payments by the said collectors and receivers at all said places at least as often as once in each week, and as much more frequently in all cases as they in their discretion may think proper." It is further enacted in the same statute, "that, on and after the 1st of January, 1847, all sums payable to the United States shall be paid in gold or silver coin, or in treasury-notes issued under the authority of the United States: "that, on and after the 1st of April, 1847, all payments shall be made in gold or silver coin, or in treasury-notes, if the creditor agree to receive said notes in payment:" "that no exchange of funds shall be made by any disbursing officer or agents of the government, of any grade or denomination whatever, other than an exchange for gold or silver; and every such disbursing officer, when the means for his disbursements are furnished to him in gold and silver, shall make his payments in the money so furnished; or, when those means shall be furnished to him in drafts, shall cause those drafts to be presented at their place of payment, and properly paid according to the law, and shall make his payments in the money so received for the drafts, unless in either case he can exchange the means in his hands for gold and silver at par."

The Secretary of the Treasury is required, by the same act, to issue regulations to enforce the speedy presentation of government drafts for payment at the place where payable, and to prescribe the time within which, according to distance from Washington, all drafts upon the holders of public moneys shall be presented for payment: and these regulations so to be enforced are specially intended "to guard, as far as may be, against those drafts being used or thrown into circulation as a paper currency, or medium of exchange."[1]

The financial system established by this act of Congress is that which still governs the Treasury. Its main object was to restrict the receipts into the treasury and its payments to gold and silver coins. The very important privilege of paying in treasury-notes has had no practical effect: we shall refer to it, however, before we close the chapter. The result of this act

[1] Act of Congress, August 5th, 1846.

was to introduce a new and severe feature into public business. The usage of the people in this country has been to make all large payments in paper currency, or by the agency of banks. This usage has grown in strength, and spread more widely year by year, until it may be said that, for the last forty years, not one per cent. of the transactions of trade and industry within our borders have been effected by the medium of gold or silver coins. Although this usage has been the object of severe and continued attacks from a host of editors and authors, and although the people have had often before them the most lamentable specimens of the manner in which a paper currency may be abused, and of the sad effects of such abuses, they continue to multiply banks, and to employ them as the chief agents in effecting the payments accruing upon the annual domestic transactions of the country. In 1830, there were 330 banks in the United States; now there are over 1400. This is unanswerable evidence of the usage of the country — a usage which grows in the face of the constitutional provision, that every individual has a right, of which neither Congress nor the Legislature of any State can deprive him, to exact payment of what is due to him in gold or silver. Every man in the country may, at his pleasure, elect to do so, and no penalty can befall him, except what his fellow-citizens may inflict upon him by refusing to have dealings with one who thus departs from the customary modes of doing business. The government of the United States has, however, so administered the act of August, 1846, as to do what no man of large business has ever done in this country — it has broken through the usage of the people, and has for ten years refused to receive any thing but gold or silver coins into the public treasury. It has thus divorced itself in finance from the popular mode of effecting payments. The whole payments of the country, industrial and commercial, made through the banks, and by means of individual paper, exceed those of the treasury not less than a thousand-fold; and yet they are successfully accomplished by means which the national treasury disowns and rejects.

It is a striking feature of this measure, that whilst it is eminently anti-popular in its character, public payments being exacted in a mode which would not be tolerated in the walks of business, yet the government is not only sustained in a financial policy without parallel in the circumstances, but the measure is regarded with much complacency, and deemed by many a public benefit. The fact is, that this exclusive and severe policy which maintains a gold and silver currency for the government, whilst the people content themselves with one of paper or credit, is apparently successful. Its evil consequences, if great, are not visible; they are like that taxation which is imposed upon foreign products, not perceived nor directly felt by the consumer or sufferer. In many countries it might have produced an explosion which would have blown up the system. The people here, however, readily abandon to the government the hard currency they decline employing themselves. The experiment has shown that the government can pursue this financial policy, and collect its whole revenue in the precious metals, without direct or apparent evil results. It has turned out to be, on the surface, rather a question between the government and the banks, than between the people and the government.

In the United States, the banks are the only large holders of gold and silver coin. Being a costly commodity to keep, they limit the sum retained to an amount as low, or lower than is consistent with their safety. Their circulation and deposits being payable on demand, they restrict the amount to a sum sufficient to meet the probable demand. This adjustment, depending so much upon contingencies and conjecture, is one which is watched with great care and anxiety by the banks. It is, of course, a very sensitive line which the banks fix as the boundary of probable demand; it is easily disturbed, and apprehension sometimes shakes it as much as actual invasion. The banks being the only depositories of specie, being under the necessity of paying it when required, and without the privilege of asking a premium according to the intensity of the demand, become the source from which all the coins needed for payment into the treasury are obtained. But for this position of the banks, the revenue of the United States could not be collected without coins going to a high premium. Dealers in the precious metals would doubtless, in such case, purchase and hold coins for those who required them for payment to the government, but not without a full profit on their business. The actual result has been that, since 1847, the treasury of the United States has absorbed from $1,000,000 to $1,500,000 of coin weekly, nearly the whole of which has been derived from or through the banks. As, during the greater part of the time since 1847, the gold of California has been flowing into the country in a stream nearly equal to the public revenue, the banks have not suffered from this absorption of specie by the treasury so much as they might otherwise have done. They have, however, been continually reminded of the depleting power which the treasury held over them. The effect has been that, between the occasional large demands for specie to ship to Europe and the more constant but not regular demand for the treasury, the banks have been kept for the last ten years in a state of feverish excitement very unfavorable to a steady policy and the true interests of trade. The great activity of foreign commerce, and the vast movements of domestic industry and trade, seemed to demand and warrant a considerable expansion of credit and bank accommodation; when this began gradually to be conceded, the banks were, at short periods, checked by the outward current of specie to Europe, and the inward flow to the treasury. These checks, although felt by the banks, could not always be immediately understood. The blow might fall upon one or two banks only at a time, and through them upon others; the uncertainty as to the quarter from which demand came was accompanied by equal doubt as to its extent or continuance. These checks almost always induced some contraction of currency, or some hesitation in their discounts on the part of the banks; and this has led to one of the most striking results of our present treasury system. Banks may prudently hesitate; they may deem it necessary to contract their issues; but their customers cannot do this: their liabilities continue to mature, and must be met; and when the banks decline or hesitate, the needful facilities must be found elsewhere. A high rate of interest became the inevitable result; the rate of interest being determined, as we have explained, not by the abundance or scarcity of coins or specie, but by the demand and supply of those funds usually employed in paying debts. The banks being kept, by the general activity of trade, in a state of considerable expansion, and by the double demand for specie in a constant state of trepidation, often failed to meet the just expectations of their customers; and a demand for the means of payment sprung up in our chief cities, outside of the banks, which finally induced a large class of capitalists to enter into the business of discounting notes. There are, probably, now in the United States a score of private bankers for every one there was in 1847. But there were, probably, an hundred persons employing their means in discounting private securities in 1857, for one in 1847. The high rate of interest which had prevailed for so many years, proved a powerful temptation to capitalists; and the amount attracted to this business was, in many places, estimated to exceed many times the capital of the banks. This is believed to have been the case in Philadelphia. In New York, and other cities, it is known to have been very great. What the effect has been, of this large diversion of capital from its former applications, it is impossible to describe; but it must have been, and is now, disastrous. But with all this, the rate of interest continued high until the crash came, until importations fell off, and until the banks were wholly relieved from the foreign demand for specie, and the amount going into the treasury fell off one-half.

It is possible there may have been some advantage to the country in all this financial disturbance and complication. We cannot conjecture to what a state of expansion the banks would have gone, if they had not thus been held in check; it would be still more difficult to conjecture whether the evils of the crisis and the revulsion would have been more or less, if they had followed upon a greater expansion of the banks, or upon the mere extension of individual credit, as was the case in this instance. However that may be, the actual progress of this great financial movement has been to transfer from the pockets of the men of industry and trade in this country to the money-lenders, from

$50,000,000 to $100,000,000 more than the amount of interest which they would otherwise have paid. We regard this as a regular business transaction; and large as the sum which was thus levied upon industry and trade by men of capital, it was in the regular course of business; it might have proved far worse for those interested, if they could not have obtained this succor, heavily as they have paid for it. The solution of the difficulty lies in the inquiry, what caused and sustained this high rate of interest?

We are far from thinking that other causes have not intervened in this prolonged high rate of interest; but we are confident that the one we propound has been by far the most potent. The disturbances in our money-market, and the mysterious conduct of the banks, have been, during the last ten years, more than ever, subjects of wonder and speculation. Whoever reflects that, during this time, the banks were under the operation of a great double-action engine, which drew one stream of specie to the public treasury, and ejected another into Europe, will cease to wonder at the unsteady policy they pursued.

Much has been said, and much more might be said, about the economy of maintaining an exclusive currency of coin for the treasury of the United States. If the reasons in its favor were sufficiently strong, perhaps this consideration would be of little consequence to a national treasury. But these reasons may be, and are likely to be, the subject of question, so long as the people at large — every individual being entitled by law to the privilege of paying and receiving coin in all his dealings — shall choose, as they now do, to employ paper currency and the facilities of banking in preference. So long as this is the case, the cost of a currency of coin for the government will be regarded by many as a needless burden, and a want of economy without excuse. It will continue to be said, that what is good enough for the people is good enough for the government. The people are certainly free in their choice of a currency for themselves, and, therefore, that choice is the expression of actual public opinion. The real cost of keeping up this system as now administered would be estimated differently, according to the different modes of viewing the subject. Whatever the conclusions formed as to the actual cost, whether $500,000 or $2,000,000, the sum is too considerable to be beneath notice in itself, although insignificant in comparison of the indirect loss and injury to the industrial interests of the country.

The difficulty of carrying out strictly this plan of an exclusive metallic currency in all financial transactions of the government, was found from the first to be very great. It involved a vast and complicated distribution of coin from points where the revenue was chiefly received to the places of disbursement. To remove such masses of coin, imposed great expense and great risk. Disbursing officers could not be all supplied with places of safe deposit; and their embarrassments increased, until it became necessary to find a remedy, which was provided by allowing them to deposit their funds in the most convenient office of the treasury, and, upon the accounts thus opened, to draw in any amounts to suit the progress of their disbursement. The checks thus drawn were not only a convenience to the paymaster, but to the receiver, whether they went immediately into the hands of the public creditor, or whether they were received by some other person whom it suited to advance the specie for them. In either case, it was a step towards the usual mode of doing business. The office of the treasury, thus employed, became so far a bank, that it received public deposits and paid them out upon the check of the depositor. Whether these checks circulated or passed through several hands before payment, we are not informed; but it is quite probable.

It was soon perceived, under the operation of the act of 1847, that some further relaxation of its provisions was indispensable to effect the necessary distribution of the public funds. It was found that the transmission of coins by special messenger, or by private express, was not only very hazardous, but expensive, and that it required much time. It was natural to look to the domestic exchanges of the country for a remedy; but many obstacles rose in the way of transactions between the treasury, which received only coins, and the men of business, who only paid in paper. The treasury could only, at best, avail itself of occasions when there were balances to pay, and specie was to be remitted. It could only offer to receive specie in one place, and pay it in another. But, in the processes of domestic exchange, specie is rarely remitted, even when for a time there may be a balance between one locality and another, the operators keeping their accounts for another turn of the balance. The balance between the cities of New York and Philadelphia might change sides every month in the year, without any transmission of specie, and so between more remote points. Every day immense sums may be remitted between such places, at little or no expense, or with a premium to one side; yet the public treasury, under the present system, can only avail itself of domestic exchange to a very limited extent. The sums remitted are so vast in the aggregate, that even the large transactions of the government could be carried without being felt; and though the intervention of the treasury might be an advantage both to it and the public, no such step, by the terms of the law, can be taken.

Apart from some irregularities, which, by the novelty and perplexity of their position in conducting a business so foreign to the customs of the country, seemed to be forced upon the officers of the treasury, and which have been discontinued for several years, the processes of the distribution of the public money seem now to have found the best channels of which the system admits. Although it does not permit that broad and full contact with the domestic exchanges of the country, and make available all its facilities, as is the boast of the system of France; nor enjoy the aid of a great bank like the English Exchequer, which can pay any sum in Great Britain by checks on the Bank of England, or in its notes, with as good effect as it could pay in gold; yet for some years large sums have been moved, not only without expense, but with a profit. The profit, however, is probably due to remittances to California, as at San Francisco the Assistant Treasurer has been able to sell drafts of the government on New York at two and a half per cent. premium.[1]

[1] We give here, in connection, extracts from Reports of various Secretaries of the Treasury, and Treasurers of the United States, containing

The treasury of the United States, therefore, now looks beyond its circumscribed duty of receiving coin and paying coin; it notices the fact, that New York is not only the point of its

---

remarks upon the condition and progress of the Independent Treasury system. It would be very interesting to have from the Treasurer of the United States a detailed report of every movement of public funds, whence and whither, with the expense and profit of each operation, and how it was effected.

"Experience has demonstrated some of the requirements of the act to be productive of great inconvenience, if, indeed, there be not some which, under the influence of strong necessity, are often violated. Disbursing officers, to whom drafts for large sums are issued, are, by existing arrangements, obliged to receive the full amounts of said drafts at one payment from the proper assistant treasurer, while their expenditures must be made in small sums from time to time. The custody of the money is thus forced upon them, without any provision for its convenience, or even safety. If the money is to be disbursed at points distant from the place where it is received, the burden of transferring it is, in like manner, imposed on them. If they adopt the usual and customary mode of keeping and transferring money, they violate the law. If they undertake themselves its custody and carriage, they incur great risk and responsibility. The actual carriage of coin from place to place in the same town is burdensome, especially in those Southern ports where silver is the coin chiefly in use.

"To alleviate some of the inconveniences attending the system, if continued, I would suggest—

"First. That any person having a draft on an assistant treasurer be permitted to deposit his draft with the assistant treasurer, and draw for the amount, from time to time, in such sums as he may desire, upon his own orders, payable to any person or persons; provided that the whole amount of the draft should be actually drawn within a short period, say two weeks after the deposit of the draft.

"Second. That any disbursing officer having a draft on an assistant treasurer, be permitted to deposit such draft, and draw for the amount in like manner: provided that each order should be presented for payment within two weeks after its date. These provisions would, it is believed, effectually prevent the checks or orders being used as currency.

"The inconvenience arising from the accumulation of coin at points where it is not required for the public service, is very great; but it seems to be inseparable from the system itself. To pay a public creditor with a draft on a remote office, which he cannot sell but at a discount, or collect in person without a journey, would be unseemly; and the government has no means itself of making transfers, in such cases, other than the despatch of special messengers, at some expense, and much risk of loss."—*Mr. Meredith's Report, December 3d,* 1849.

largest receipts, but the financial centre of its operations, and the actual centre of the internal exchanges of the whole country. Funds flow from every State, and every district, to that city,

---

"The disbursing agents of the several departments of the government being without safe places of deposit for the public money entrusted to them, it was deemed right, and within the provisions and spirit of the law, to require the treasurer, and the assistant treasurers, and depositories designed by law, to receive deposits from the disbursing agents of the government, and to pay out the same on their checks. A regulation to that effect was issued, and is in operation, and accompanies this report. It is a great convenience to disbursing agents, and also secures the safety of the public money. The privilege of so depositing has not, as yet, been embraced by all the disbursing agents; and it has been suggested that some of them deposit with bank brokers, under an erroneous idea that the act does not apply to them. It is believed that such deposits are in contravention of the law." — *Mr. Guthrie's Report, December 6th*, 1853, page 14.

"The treasury receives money directly at its counter, and indirectly by its assistant treasurers and designated depositories at other points, and disburses through the same channels. It also issues drafts on the receiving officers of the treasury, not designated as depositories for the public money in their hands; and when paid, treats the amount of the transaction as at once a payment into and out of the treasury by the officers in question. When the disbursements of those officers are greater than their receipts, the government is saved the risk and expense of transporting the money to a depository, and the officer relieved from the risk of keeping it. . . .

"Prior to the 4th of March last, as I am informed, moneys were advanced in large sums to persons not officers of the government, for the ostensible purpose of purchasing United States stock, for paying interest on the public debt and coupons, and for other purposes of similar character.

"In like manner, the practice of issuing transfer drafts in favor of banks or brokers, to remain a considerable time on the books as an equivalent for the expenses of transportation, and occasionally renewed, instead of being paid at maturity, has entirely ceased. Instead thereof, in all cases, the transfer draft has issued only after the deposit of coin has actually been made, or when it was necessary to transport the specie, and then the money has been deposited at the desired point, as soon as the transportation could be effected, by an officer of the department." — *Report of Mr. Casey, Treasurer of the United States, to Mr. Guthrie, November 29th*, 1853, page 155.

"The Independent Treasury act still continues eminently successful in all its operations. The transfers for disbursement during the fiscal year, to the amount of $39,407,674 03, have been made at a cost of $19,762 35, whilst the premium on the sale of the treasury drafts has amounted to

not only to meet debts payable there, but for distribution thence to other places, and for all sorts of financial movements. Money in New York is so readily available at other points, that

---

$30,431 87. The receipts and expenditures during the fiscal year, amounting to $131,413,859 59, have all been in the constitutional currency of gold and silver, without any perceptible effects upon the currency, or on the healthy business operations of the country."—*Mr. Guthrie's Report, December 3d*, 1855, page 21.

"For facility and convenience of disbursements, and for greater security of the public money, you have caused to be issued, within the year, 1590 transfer drafts, in amount $41,319,054 18; and the transfers have been conducted and executed with commendable despatch, and satisfactory result.

"The operations of the money branch of this office continue to give great satisfaction, not to myself only, but to disbursing officers, government creditors, and to every class of persons having business to transact with it, especially the operations arising under the business extension of it, which you directed should go into effect on July 1st, 1853 (carrying out, in spirit and in fact, the Independent Treasury act of 1846); since which they have gradually increased to important magnitude, as will be seen by the following statement. The amount of coin received and paid during a year, ending the 30th of September, 1855, averaged, in and out, $1,261,792 66 per month.

"Treasury drafts paid, or passed to the credit of disbursing officers, number 1423.

"The accounts now kept with the disbursing officers are 57; and their checks paid and passed to the debit of their respective accounts, number 17,394, and amount to $7,093,208 85.

"The arrangement you were pleased to direct as a facility to the receipt of coin here in exchange for drafts on New York, without expense for transportation, by causing the issue of regular transfer drafts for $200,000 at a time in my favor, and the deposit thereof with the assistant treasurer of New York, subject to my check on 'transfer account,' as required, commenced on January 30th last, and has been highly appreciated by persons who desire to make such exchanges. Under it there has been received, in eight months, to the 30th of September last, $2,840,237 01; the money for which each check was drawn having been paid, as required, into the treasury here before the check was drawn." — *Report of Mr. Casey, Treasurer of the United States, to Mr. Guthrie, November 22d*, 1855, page 172.

"The Independent Treasury act has been carried into effect, the past year, as far as it has been practicable for the department to enforce it. Most of the disbursing officers of the government, where conveniently situated, have and continue to avail themselves of the convenience and security

it is kept there to be ready for use everywhere else. The treasury finds it easy to make its payments elsewhere, so long as it has funds in New York; the disbursing officers find persons in

---

of depositing in the vault of the treasurer, assistant treasurers, and public depositaries, as will be seen by statement No. 89 of this report. Those who have not deposited in the vaults of the government, although convenient, construe the act of 1846 as allowing the officer a discretion on the subject. This they sometimes exercise, by making what they term special deposits with chartered and unchartered banks. The security of the public money, and the prevention of its application to any other than public use, call for explicit legislation on this subject, and the extension of the penalties of the act of 1846 to those receiving public money from disbursing agents and others who have public money in their hands. The courts have found difficulty in applying the act to all cases within its spirit, because thought not to be technically within its terms.

"The amount transferred for disbursement, during the past fiscal year, was $38,088,113 92, at a cost of $12,945 87; whilst the premiums paid on sale of treasury drafts have been $54,924 16; leaving $41,978 29 over and above the expenses. It is believed that, with care and vigilance, the transfer of public money will hereafter be made through the agencies of the treasurer, assistant treasurers, and depositaries, without charge and without risk, except under extraordinary circumstances, and in peculiar times. The receipts and expenditures, during the past fiscal year, have amounted in the aggregate to $146,866,933 48, and have all been paid in the constitutional currency of gold and silver, without any disturbing effect upon the currency, the banks, or business of the country. However, the withdrawal and prohibition of the small-note circulation of the banks is still deemed essential to a sound and stable currency, and to be called for by the best interests of all the States." — *Mr. Guthrie's Report, December* 1*st*, 1856, page 42.

"The sum of $38,088,113 92, composed of coin and bullion, has been removed during the year.

"This operation has been effected, as a matter of account, by 737 transfer drafts issued singly, and 646 issued in duplicate; and, as a matter of fact, in part by actual transportation, and in the other part by using transfer drafts in sums suitable to and supplying the wants of the business community, so far as they came within the range of our own convenience or requirements.

"Accounts have been kept with 75 disbursing officers, whose credits have been drawn upon and paid to the amount of $6,695,410 56, on 17,003 checks.

"The sum of $4,544,129 44 has been transferred, during the year, from

every locality desirous of remitting to that city. Many of these officers, therefore, even at distant places, have their credits opened at New York. They can sell their checks upon that credit for large or small sums, and often at a premium, and thus draw from almost any place on New York, receiving coin for the draft. Neither is the treasury without some facility in transmitting funds from other places to New York; this is done by furnishing the assistant treasurer there with drafts on the place whence it is desired to draw funds, in such sums as may suit the convenience of merchants and bankers, who occasionally remit to the point at which the public funds have accumulated. The drafts furnished for this purpose lie until they find a purchaser, and if not used, they are cancelled.

In all this, the government holds relations with those who are concerned with the domestic exchanges. These relations, however, are imperfect, for the treasury can only operate by selling its own drafts; it cannot become a purchaser, and it cannot easily and promptly avail itself of circuitous exchange, or indirect remittances, by which at times a particular movement of funds could be effected quicker, and at less expense, than by any direct mode.

But, circumscribed as the operations of the treasury are, they bend to the customs of the country; the transfer drafts drawn by the Secretary of the Treasury, whether sold in the market, or whether the specie is removed, the checks given by disbursing officers on the treasury at New York, or on other officers, are

---

the assistant treasurer at New York to this office, by means of 2079 checks given in exchange for coin previously placed in my possession, and drawn in amounts placed to my credit by the assistant treasurer, in satisfaction of transfer drafts, and of drafts in my favor as agent for paying the compensation of the members of the House of Representatives.

"These operations, it is evident, have afforded favorable and very acceptable accommodation to our business community; while, at the same time, they have relieved the department from the onus of transporting that amount of specie, which it would otherwise have been compelled to encounter." — *Report of Mr. Casey, Treasurer of the United States, to Mr. Guthrie, November*, 1856, page 483.

paper operations. He who purchases a treasury draft takes the paper of the treasury; the government does not pay him in money, but gives him paper. It will be found, when all these transactions are followed out, that the actual metallic currency is departed from in various ways, and to a large extent. We regard these modifications of the original system as being made in the right direction; and believe that, as the system becomes more settled, a still larger discretion can be allowed to the officers, not only without danger to the treasury, but with positive advantage to the public.

It will be found, we believe, that however close the officers of the treasury keep to the letter and spirit of the law under which they act, in receiving and paying only coins, the public creditors either do not themselves receive the coins, or that they part with them for bank-notes, or a bank credit, at the earliest possible moment. They fall into the regular channel of business, as it is carried on outside of the treasury, as soon as they can. They do not receive coins to keep, but to pay away; and the government currency is exchanged at once for that which will pay debts and make purchases with equal advantage and less risk. The public creditors are not able to remain on the platform of a metallic currency which is occupied by the government. They are called up and paid, and then step off to mingle with their fellow-citizens in the use of the prevalent currency. Whether necessary to the government as a system, or not, it is seldom of any advantage to the public creditor. It is more than probable that inconveniences are unavoidably imposed upon public creditors by this obligation of the treasury to pay only in coins, which far outweigh all occasional advantages.

The apparent success of this experiment in the United States should not betray any one into the concession, without further investigation, that this is a wise or even expedient policy for other governments, or in other circumstances. Two things have favored this measure — one at its inception, and the other very soon afterwards. The revenue of the general government of the United States is paid upon indirect taxation. The burden is self-imposed. No man is bound, by law, to import foreign goods, nor is any man compelled to purchase public lands; those who engage in such transactions know the terms of payment before they begin, and they may refrain from the business, if they regard the terms as too hard. If the whole revenue of the United States were to be collected in gold and silver by direct taxation, the system would fall at the first congressional election after the attempt was made. We do not hesitate to say that the whole income of England could not be collected in gold and silver for two successive years. The people would never submit to it; and the doctrine, that what is good enough for the people is good enough for the government, would be proclaimed in tones loud enough to secure ample respect for the law of public usage.

The other circumstance which favored this experiment in the United States was the discovery and abundant product of the California gold-mines. Without this unexpected but immense accession to our stock of gold, this measure might have fared very differently, and might now be standing by no means favorably with the public. As it has turned out, the public treasury proved to be a reservoir of gold at the time of the commercial revulsion of 1857, and was the means of retaining $25,000,000 of gold in the country, which would probably have been exported, but for its safe position in the public vaults.

§ 4. *Independent Treasury a result of financial difficulties — State banks and a financial system — A mixed currency of government paper and specie — Opposition to banks and paper currency — Mr. Guthrie — Bank of France; luxury of severity — Banks not to be crushed, but replaced — A financial system founded on the act of* 1846 — *Treasury notes payable on demand without interest, and at six and twelve months with interest — French loans of* 1854–5 — *Whole loan offered by the people in France, out of Paris — Board of Treasurers proposed — Principles which restrict the issue of treasury notes — Lenders of money, their relations with the treasury — Offices in Washington and New York — Special duties in the proposed system — Necessary connection of the treasury with domestic exchange — Friction — A remedy required, and the co-operation of the treasury — A national institution to form the point of contact between the treasury and the domestic exchange.*

The chief feature of the Independent Treasury, as now administered, is, that it is contrary to the long-settled usages of the people of the United States. This is a more important fact than many seem to apprehend. Usages are stronger than laws; they may be suppressed for a time, but are sure to assert their dominion over governments, as well as people, in the end. The best writers on the elements of law tell us, that permanent laws are but the reflections of the settled customs and institutions of society, and that enactments which violate settled customs are generally short-lived; that they are either soon repealed by usage, or modified and bent to suit the customs. There cannot be any doubt that, in this country, the usage is, and has long been, to employ the credit system, and the aid of banks and paper currency, in all the large transactions of industry and trade. Although the constitution itself contains a provision which makes gold and silver the standard of payment, the people treat it as a standard to be used only in case of disagreement. They have arranged a mode of payment far more effective, and far more economical, and this they employ almost exclusively in large operations. This custom pervades and governs the whole country; and it is very rare indeed that any disagreement between parties compels a resort to the standard of payment. Taking the whole of the large payments of the country together, it may be safely assumed, leaving out the national treasury, that not one thousand dollars in a million are paid in gold or silver. The men of business make their purchases upon their own credit, and thus issue every year thousands of millions of dollars in amount of commercial paper; all that concerns the relations of debtor and creditor upon this paper is settled by the aid of the banks, and other devices of the credit system. The people deposit their money in the banks; they give and receive checks upon the banks; they pay and receive bank-notes. The government alone departs from this universal usage; it abjures credit, banks, deposits, and bank-notes, and insists upon an exclusive currency of gold and silver. We have already remarked upon some of the results. We now add, without judging by what has occurred, without dwelling further upon the evils or inconveniences already suffered from this measure, that, unless frittered away by the effects of the opposing customs of the country, it is certainly destined to be the cause of greater mischiefs. The experiment is to be tried in the State of Ohio, where it will have a much shorter life than it has had as a measure of the general government. Direct taxation and an exclusive currency of the precious metals cannot stand together in a government, the usual currency of whose people is paper.

It is indeed unfortunate, that a government and its people should differ so radically as has occurred in this measure of the government of the United States, enforcing an exclusive currency of the precious metals for its treasury; a timely modification may avert far worse evils than any yet anticipated. The least that can be looked for, if it be not modified by time, is that it may eventually crush the administration which endeavors to sustain it. The natural body may carry an unassimilated substance a long time without vital injury; but, soon or late, it finds a position in which it destroys life.

We have stated our objections to the present financial system of the United States thus strongly, not only because we regard them as important, but that we may be the better understood in our further remarks. We are far from being blind to the motives of those who projected the act of 1846, under which this financial system is carried out. The reasons which influenced them were of the strongest character. The wide extent of our territory; the numerous separate governments of the States, and their various systems of banking and credit; the flagrant, disastrous and continued abuses of banking — must have been obstacles of the most serious kind in the way of conducting successfully the finances of the United States previous to the act of 1846. We know, indeed, that the differences of opinion in all that concerned banks, previous to that time, as well as since, rendered it nearly impossible to harmonize the operations of the banks and the treasury. The perplexity arising from the number of the banks claiming a share of the public deposits — claims enforced by the various States in which the banks were situated, and by interested individuals of great political influence — justified the officers of the treasury, and members of Congress, in looking for some mode of escaping these troubles. Notwithstanding the objections urged against the present system, we do not hesitate to say that no system likely to be adopted in connection with the State banks would be preferable. A perfectly sound and well-arranged plan of national finance might be devised, but it would savor of partiality; and nothing of the kind could withstand the hostile influences which would be brought to bear upon it.

It is not surprising, in our view, then, that the idea of any close relations between the treasury of the United States and the State banks was given up as involving invincible difficulties. From considerations such as these sprung the act of the 6th of August, 1846. Some change was inevitable; escape from the financial troubles which had reigned for many years was indispensable. It was the duty of those who undertook to devise a new system to consider well the actual condition and the customs of the country. They might fairly desire to avoid all connection with the State banks; but they could, with no propriety, overlook the fact that the people of the United States employed the credit system, and the agency of banks, in all important business. It was their duty to make their new measure of finance consistent with the usages of the people. The tenor of the act of 1846 shows that its framers were not forgetful of this important consideration. The eighteenth and nineteenth sections provide "that all receipts into the treasury shall be in gold or silver coin, or in treasury notes, and that all payments shall be made in gold or silver coin, or in treasury notes, if the creditor agree to receive said notes in payment." This act did not, therefore, propose an abrupt departure from the customs of the country; it did not propose to enforce an exclusive specie currency for the government. It proposed that all payments to and from the treasury should be made in gold and silver coin, or in treasury notes issued under the authority of the United States. Now, this was offering to the creditors of the government their choice of specie or the very best paper currency which could be issued in the country. No medium of payment which could be devised would better accommodate the public creditors than treasury notes, issued in forms and denominations to suit the wants and convenience of the people.

We think our financial system should have been constructed in the true spirit of this statute. The receipts into the treasury should have been, since that time, only gold or silver coin, or treasury notes; and the public payments should only have been in gold or silver coin, or in treasury notes so issued as to be acceptable and convenient to the public creditors, and the people at large. The great defect of our present system of finance is not, then, due to the act of 1846, but to the manner in which it has been administered. Whether the manner of this administration was contemplated when the act was passed, we know not; but it is certain that this provision for treasury notes, which softened the harsh features of the measure, has been wholly inoperative. Whether the passage of the act was aided by this feature, we cannot tell; but it is to be lamented that the policy clearly indicated by the act, and necessary to place it in harmony with the institutions and usages of the country, should have been, ever since, neglected or purposely abjured.

It is not difficult, perhaps, to conjecture how and why this one-sided policy has been pursued under the act of 1846. The opposition to banks in the United States has been constant and vigorous for half a century. It has been stimulated, as well as justified, by the very great abuses of the system; but, great as these abuses have been, the censure and denunciations poured out upon the banks have been, for the most part, neither enlightened nor discriminating. The subject has not been well enough understood to give the banks due credit for the benefits they confer, nor to point out distinctly the mischiefs they commit. In proportion as the notions of the friends and enemies of banks have been indefinite on the whole subject, their imaginations have governed, and not their judgments. On few subjects has a wider difference of opinion existed; on few subjects have men been more ready to pronounce positive opinions, in direct conflict with each other, where the facts were all before them. So strong is the feeling against banks in many persons, that they cannot endure any thing that resembles banking. Paper currency is their abhorrence; they look upon every one as wronged or cheated, who takes a small note in place of gold or silver. Such persons shudder at the idea of treasury notes being issued in denominations small enough to make them a convenience to the people at large. They know that bank-notes, from one dollar upwards, are the general medium of exchange; they regard this currency with special dislike and distrust; but they would oppose, with all their might, the issue of treasury notes as low as ten dollars by the government, in payment of its debts.

Treasury notes, in denominations from five to one hundred dollars, payable upon demand, issued under proper regulations and checks, would constitute the safest possible currency for the people of the United States. A hundred millions of such a currency would be absorbed much more rapidly than it would be safe or proper to issue it; an issue only to be made in the gradual progress of a system well understood both by the officers of the treasury and the public at large. Yet the proposal to issue such a currency for the special benefit of the people, who are regarded as having suffered, and as still suffering, from the evils of banking, would be treated with disdain. Large treasury notes, for those who have money to lend, are deemed admissible and proper in national finance; but the subdivision of these notes, with the view to their becoming a general convenience and security, would be opposed with bitterness, as approaching one of the functions of banks of circulation. This morbid jealousy of banks is not merely absurd; it becomes a blunder, when carried to the extent of preventing even the consideration of measures of finance bearing some resemblance to the processes of banking. In France, they are jealous of banks, and desirous of restraining the development of credit in that form; the government there, in the administration of a newly-reformed financial system, exerts its power, shapes its processes, and employs all its opportunities to favor the operations of industry and trade, because it would, so far as it can, limit the power of banks, and remove the occasion of establishing them. Here the treasury merely provides for its own currency, its own receipts, and its own disbursements, leaving the whole field of industrial and commercial payments to the banks. The Bank of France is accused, by a late writer, of luxuriating in severity;[1] and the government therefore affords all the alleviation possible within the range of the operations of the treasury: here, where the banks are even objects of the severest attacks on the part of those in authority, we eschew, in doctrine and practice, all sympathy, and refuse all assistance.[2] The banks have multiplied

[1] "C'est in September et en October (1856) que la banque a déployé ce luxe de sévérité qui a si fort gêné le commerce." — *Annuaire D'Economie Politique*, 1857, page 584.

[2] The following extract from the Report of the Secretary of the Treasury, in 1855, will show that this opposition to banks is not confined to the ignorant and unthinking, but is shared by some of the ablest and best men who have been in the Treasury Department: —

"The Constitution of the United States was framed by the men who had felt all the evils thereof; and when provisions were inserted in that instrument, that no State should emit bills of credit, nor make anything but gold and silver a tender in payment of debts, and the coining of money was given to the general government, they believed they had provided for a hard money currency, and against the evils of a depreciated one; but these provisions were nullified, when the courts held that the States had power to charter banks, with authority to issue and circulate notes as money. It is now too late for the courts to retrace their steps, and give a broader construction to the prohibitions of the Federal Constitution, whilst it is hopeless to expect the States will refrain from granting bank charters with authority to issue small notes, or that the States will concur in enlarging the

here because there has been no effort to substitute any safer or better device of credit. The people have been offered their choice between a currency of the precious metals and a paper currency, and they have deliberately chosen the latter, in the face of innumerable warnings from the opponents of banks, both in and out of authority. The constant increase of banks proves, beyond question, that they are regarded by the people at large as an advantage, if not a necessity.

The only way to check the multiplication of banks in this country, or to check their operations, is to replace them by something better, or to furnish the facilities they afford, without the mischiefs or hazards. To propose a currency of the precious metals, which has been persistently rejected, as a remedy for the evils of banking, is not only inconsiderate, but absurd. The men of this day and country cannot be induced to go back two hundred years to a system long abandoned, and now impossible; they would endure quadruple the evils and vexations suffered from banks, before they could be brought to encounter the ex-

---

constitutional prohibition in respect to bills of credit, so as to prohibit this power to banks. The same local and individual interests that induce the granting of bank charters with this privilege, would induce the Legislatures of the States to refuse to Congress the power of prohibiting the use and circulation of bank-notes. The thirteen hundred banks now in existence under State charters, and the circulation of over $200,000,000 of bank-notes as money, in constant competition with the constitutional currency, attest the magnitude of the evil, and justify the worst apprehensions for the future. The gradual increase of banks, banking capital, and bank-note circulation, calls for repressive action under appropriate State legislation. When these thirteen hundred banks shall be increased to some two, three, four or five thousand, it may be feared their aggregate power will not be easily overcome until a suspension of specie payments, and universal bankruptcy, shall call for a suppression of the evil, and a restoration of the constitutional currency. If the States shall continue the charter and multiplication of banks with authority to issue and circulate notes as money, and fail to apply any adequate remedy to the increasing evil, and also fail to invest Congress with the necessary power to prohibit the same, Congress may be justified in the exercise of the power to levy an excise on them, and thus render the authority to issue and circulate them valueless. — *Report of Mr. Guthrie, Secretary of the Treasury, December 3d,* 1855, pages 22–3.

pense, the risks and slow movements of an exclusively metallic currency.

When the banking system of this country, the power and efficacy of which for public advantage cannot be denied, whatever may be its equally undeniable abuses and perversions, is to be superseded, whether for the special benefit of the public treasury, or from commercial considerations, the inquiry must be not how to introduce coins, but how to find a substitute for banks, or how to secure the facilities of banking without its mischiefs. The solution of this problem has made little progress, because the discussion has been too much confined to the arena of party politics. On the one hand, the effort has been to force the banks upon the public just as they are; and on the other, the effort has been to reject them altogether, without a substitute. The parties to this discussion have elicited no truth, and settled no principles. The people, however, have not stood still in the meantime, but, finding the immense power afforded by banks, they have multiplied them in a rapid ratio, although no progress was making in the solution of the problem involved.

We entertain no doubt that a sound financial system for the United States can be successfully constructed upon the act of August, 1846, establishing the Independent Treasury. The public creditors should be offered their choice of payment in coins or paper, as that act contemplates; and this offer should not be a mockery; the proffered treasury notes should be issued in such denominations as would make them a positive advantage and convenience to the public. They are issued, in Prussia, as low as five dollars, much to the satisfaction of the people not only of Prussia, but of other German States in which they circulate. There is no solid financial objection to issuing treasury notes, in the United States, as low as ten dollars, if such an issue were desired by the people, and of course none to the issue of other and higher denominations, to which they are accustomed. Treasury notes payable on demand should, doubtless, be issued with great precautions, and upon a system which would ensure their punctual redemption at all the offices of the treasury. They would not be payable with interest, because they would be issued for circulation and for public convenience; and all the advantage the government would derive from this circulation would go, in the first place, to meet the expense of the issue; and in the next, to the public benefit, and to the alleviation of the burdens of taxation.

The treasury, then, would receive only gold or silver coin, or its own notes, for all dues to the government; and would pay all creditors either in coins, or in notes, as they preferred. When the government issued a treasury note in payment, it would pay one debt by contracting another; when it received one of its notes for customs or lands into the treasury, a debt would be paid to it, and it would be acquitted of a debt. Treasury notes returned extinguish an equal amount of notes issued. The whole incoming revenue would be a fund constantly applied to the redemption of the treasury notes, a demand for which could not subside so long as there were debts due to the treasury. An issue of this kind should be kept strictly within the amount of probable available revenue; and then, if presented for the specie, the same amount of the revenue would become payable in specie. The treasury would be obliged skilfully to adjust its issues, and the distribution of its funds, so as to be prepared not only for the regular progress of its business, but for emergencies.

To enable such a system to work well, and attain its legitimate growth, it should have assistance like that furnished in England by the Exchequer bills. This would be furnished by treasury notes of $100, $500, and $1000, bearing daily interest, issued in an acceptable form, payable in six, eight or twelve months. These should be accessible, at all the offices of the treasury, in such sums as gradually to attract a class of lenders who would habitually depend on them for temporary investment. By punctual payment of these securities at maturity, by keeping up the supply, the number of competitors for them would constantly increase; and a regular as well as growing demand for them could be established, which would place at the disposition of the government, upon emergency, almost any desired sum. The constant supply of money which would thus be poured into the treasury in specie, would furnish an unfailing resource in every locality for the redemption of such of the small treasury notes as might be presented for payment in coin. The effect of thus opening a communication between the government and lenders of money, by a security adapted to their wishes, and constantly renewed, so as to give all an opportunity, can only be appreciated by those who have studied the English system of Exchequer bills in that aspect, or the French system as it is now connected with the domestic exchanges. The last French loans furnish an illustration:[1]—

	Loan of 1854. Francs.	Loan, Jan. 1855. Francs.	Loan, July, 1855. Francs.
Amount asked by government	250,000,000	500,000,000	750,000,000
" of the sums offered	467,000,000	2,175,000,000	3,653,000,000
" offered in Paris, and from other countries	214,000,000	1,398,000,000	2,534,000,000
" offered in the departments	253,000,000	777,000,000	1,119,000,000
Whole number of subscribers	98,000	177,000	317,000
Subscribers at Paris, and in other countries.	26,000	51,000	80,000
Subscribers in the departments	72,000	126,000	237,000

Upon the occasion of these three loans, the people out of Paris tendered more than the whole amount required by the government. The offering for these loans astonished all Europe. It was made abundantly clear, that the government of France was not dependent upon the capitalists of Paris, of England, of Holland, Belgium or Germany, for loans even of this great magnitude. The second loan of 1855, for over $100,000,000, attracted no less than 237,000 bidders in the heart of France, without including Paris. This extraordinary and prompt liberality was almost wholly owing to the relations maintained by the receivers-general of the departments with the men of business. More than 200,000 men were found ready to assist the treasury which had favored them. Those who had money to lend were generally known to these receivers and their officers. The ultimate power of a treasury, thus conducted, is beyond estimate; but it is a power which would vanish at once, if abused. It is a power which ought to exist in every nation, because it can be so exercised as greatly to alleviate the burdens of taxation, and prove a ready resource in cases of financial embarrassment.

---

[1] Annuaire de l'Economie Politique, 1856, page 471.

If it be objected, that all this involves dangerous abuses, great complications, and subsequent disasters, we reply that the present system involves greater mischiefs and disorders, and final disasters far greater, because the immediate causes are less visible. No system of national finance can be complete without some complication; but there is skill and ability enough in this country to surmount all this difficulty. It should not be overlooked, however, that our national system should be constructed with a view to the tendencies of the national mind, and the business habits of the people; it will then be not only more popular, but find the most skilful conductors. In the proposed system, there are special features which make wise provisions necessary, the administration of which would require special skill and experience in such matters; of these requisites, and the needful integrity, it is to be hoped the country is not deemed to be destitute. The Secretary of the Treasury, the Treasurer of the United States, the Directors of the mints, and all the assistant treasurers, might, *ex officio*, be formed into a board to which this whole system could, under a well-devised plan, be safely entrusted. To remove so important and delicate a task from the arena of politics, the members of this board should hold their offices for a fixed period, and be then ineligible; one-fourth of the board should go out every year.

It is very true that, as the people would prefer this currency not only to bank-notes, but to gold or silver, a much larger amount could be thrown at once into circulation than would be expedient. To determine the proper amount to be issued would, from the beginning, be a serious question; but, grave as the mistakes which have been committed in this respect, there are principles which would safely guide even governments in issuing notes payable on demand. The banks of circulation have been recommended to keep one-third of the amount of their issues in specie as a sufficient protection. This never deserved to be called a rule, or a principle. It is not even a reasonable conjecture. The true principle of such circulation is, that it should be returned by the debtors at a rate equal to that at which it is issued. The debtors of a nation, or a bank, are its proper agents of redemption. If a bank issues notes payable on demand, which the process of paying debts at the bank does not return as rapidly as they are sent forth, it must eventually be called upon to pay them in specie at a time when it may be inconvenient or impossible. The debts due to a bank should absorb all its circulation, or return some currency that would pay it; whenever this rule is violated, there is danger. The banks incur this danger habitually by discounting paper at the average time of two months, and giving their own notes payable on demand. They stand the hazard of the two months, even if the return current should finally be of the same volume as the one outward. Under this rule, they can never be safe, and people can never feel that they are safe.

The rule by which a government may issue paper, is the rate of the receipt of the revenue. The payments into the treasury should return all the notes issued, or the gold or silver that would redeem them. The amount issued should be kept so far within the receipt of the revenue, that no probable deficiency of the income can ever disturb the process of redemption. There will be no difficulty in providing specie to pay all that could be demanded under the exceptions to this rule.

In the case of a public treasury issuing notes payable on demand, it may occur that, being everywhere acceptable, and having a wide range of circulation, they would remain in the hands of the public, and thus leave the treasury to an increasing use of the precious metals, or to the issue of a larger proportion of treasury bills to meet the constantly increasing demand for them on the part of the public creditors. If this demand were complied with, the amount in circulation would soon run up to a large sum, and they might be thrown back on the treasury at a very inconvenient time. This difficulty would have to be met, for the issues of a treasury may circulate far too widely to be always within the reach of those who would pay duties, or pay for land. As a means of overcoming this, treasury notes might be issued payable within six months on demand, and after that time payable with interest on such days as the government might appoint, but receivable at all times for dues at the treasury. No accumulation beyond six months could then be brought suddenly upon the treasury, and no loss could accrue to the holder, for his note would bear interest from the time it ceased to be payable on demand; and both banks and individuals all over the country would gladly take them as an investment. These notes, however, should be all paid off within the year; of which payment, day and place, the holders should be duly notified in the public journals.

An issue of treasury notes would, upon this plan, in a few years reach the sum of at least $100,000,000, and displace nearly that amount of bank-notes, by furnishing a medium which would be equally good in every part of the country. This is the best mode of reducing the circulation of bank-notes, and limiting their power; it is only by furnishing something better — a currency more convenient, more acceptable throughout our whole territory, and more reliable — that people can be induced to forego the benefits of the banking system. The use of a bank currency is so rooted in the habits and usages of the people of the United States, that nothing can eradicate it but a better paper currency. They will give up their reliance on banks just in proportion as something else, as consonant with their modes of business, and more safe, is offered as a substitute.

The issue of treasury notes for circulation, and to be taken at the option of the public creditors, would be incomplete in another respect, as a measure of national finance, without an issue of larger denominatiens, bearing interest, for the advantage of those who desire to make investments in government securities. The people should not only have an opportunity of lending to the government — they should be accustomed to it. Financial skill and experience, and the combined knowledge of the various treasurers, could alone tell what amount of these treasury notes, bearing interest from date, should be issued. It should be large enough to attract special attention throughout the country, for they should be made accessible in as many places as practicable; it should also be great enough to supply all, or a considerable proportion, of those who desire this kind of security. This demand would be different from that which exists for

Exchequer bills in Great Britain; there it has a larger scope, because the amount required is greater, and because the government receives, in exchange for Exchequer bills, both notes and checks on the Bank of England; here the treasury would only receive its own notes, gold or silver coins, or bullion. Our treasury would become then, the reservoir of all the spare bullion and coins in the country. Now, as soon as the precious metals become abundant, they are shipped abroad, where there is always debt to pay. The banks, too, would promptly avail themselves of a facility affording them not only interest for specie they could spare, but giving them a security which would command the specie in case of emergency. Now, they lose interest on all their reserve of gold or silver, and are of course tempted to make that reserve small; the specie which is not immediately wanted now goes across the Atlantic, and cannot be recovered to meet an unexpected demand. If London, or Paris, or Hamburg, is in pressing need of a supply of the precious metals, a few days only are needed to furnish them; but we have no such convenient resource. The government here should keep that reserve, which neither banks nor individuals will be at the expense of maintaining. If the government here would but pay interest for the specie offered to it upon six or twelve months' treasury notes, an ample supply might be always on hand to aid the banks, or assist in regulating the currency. The issue of treasury notes upon interest here contemplated should be regarded as a purely financial operation, and be under the direction of the Board of Treasurers. The money thus advanced to the government should not be the subject of appropriation by Congress, or of draft by the Secretary of the Treasury, except under regulations, and to an extent, fixed by the Board. It should be an aid to the treasury, but should never be absorbed or broken down by it. No temporary wants of the treasury should ever disturb the punctual discharge of treasury notes made payable at a day named. So long as this punctuality was observed, they would be sought for and would absorb large amounts of the smaller denominations made payable on demand. These two modes of issue would, with careful attention, work together like the wheels of a clock, and ultimately give the treasury great power for useful financial regulation in all that concerns the currency of the country—a power which would be efficient in proportion as it could be skilfully and wisely exercised, and which would cease, if awkwardly or improperly employed.

The effect of this would be, that the people of the United States would sustain an issue of small notes by the government, not bearing interest, which would much more than pay the interest of a large amount of the precious metals kept in the treasury to support the currency, and strengthen the credit of the country and its institutions in those times of peril and difficulty which must be expected occasionally in the complicated movements of industry, trade and credit.

Two features should be prominent in the Independent Treasury, if amended in accordance with such or similar suggestions. The Assistant Treasurer of New York should have, under proper regulations and supervision, the charge of all the movements and distribution of the public moneys. This would be a responsible duty; but it can be best understood, and best executed, by the first officer of the treasury in New York. All needful facilities and information are most easily accessible there.

The other would be, that the office of the Treasurer in Washington should furnish a complete exhibit of all the funds in all the treasuries, not merely by an account with each sub-treasury, but by a complete summary of the books at each office. All financial agents, all disbursing officers, and others having charge of public money, should make report to the chief office at Washington, as well as to any other offices with which they might be in connection.

But whatever may be the system of national finance adopted by the United States, or indeed by any other nation, if it be sound and comprehensive, it must involve some relations with the domestic exchanges of the country. This is especially the case in our system of confederated States, covering so great a territory, each of which has its own laws and commercial customs. The home trade of the United States far exceeds the foreign trade between any of the countries of Europe, in proportion to the population. There the boundaries between the different nations makes that foreign trade which here is domestic trade; there that is foreign exchange which here is domestic exchange. That the internal exchanges of the United States are accomplished with as little movement of the precious metals as the same amount anywhere else, is probable; but that a vast amount of unnecessary friction exists, which might be saved, is very certain. It is not the friction of transmitting gold and silver, so much as the friction of credit; it is that which arises from want of concert, from want of information, and from the immense number of agencies employed in it. A system is needed, which only the power of the national government can give; a power certainly within the letter and spirit of the constitution.

Foreign exchange, which, like domestic exchange, is only a mode of setting-off debts against debts, by the mode of its operation becomes concentrated upon a few points, and in few hands. The foreign exchange of this country is chiefly carried on through New York, and by the agency of a few persons there, because it is scarcely the interest of many to form foreign connections, with a view to so limited a business. The friction of this exchange is therefore small, and the business is transacted with facility, because few are engaged in it. The domestic exchange, on the other hand, involving more than five times the amount, with less difficulty in forming the needful connections, becomes a favorite business with the public banks, a host of private bankers, brokers and merchants. From this ensues not only much friction and many complications in the movement, but a wide field is opened for fictitious operations in exchange. Undue competition of parties thus dealing in exchange induces them to offer, sometimes, more than legitimate facilities, and at other times to ask more than reasonable rates for their agency; at the best, it is productive of mischievous and embarrassing rivalry, and is the cover of not a few of the worst abuses of the credit system.

Domestic exchange involves the adjustment of the debts of those who, though of the same country, are yet so remote as to require correspondence, and the agency of third parties. As effected by the processes of the credit system, it is almost as simple as the mode of adjustment when the parties reside in the same city, for both are accomplished by means of banks, or those acting as bankers. But whilst three score of banks in New York may be engaged in making the adjustments of the men of business in that city, the vicinity of these banks to each other enables them, without great trouble, to make the daily settlements between themselves which inevitably accrue from the dealings of their customers. The business of these adjustments between the banks of New York became, however, at last so burdensome, as to require a special facility, which was found in a clearing-house. If the business done in all the banks of New York was confined to five or six of the number, they would need no clearing-house; it would be as convenient to settle with each other in the old way. So, if the domestic exchange in each city is controlled by a few banks or persons, it may work smoothly, where otherwise there would be friction. We refer to this, however, only by way of illustration; for, if the number of those in our chief cities dealing in exchange were ever so reduced, there would remain a necessity of providing a national system by national legislation. If the banks in many of our cities now find themselves compelled, from motives of economy and facility in business, to resort to the processes of a clearing-house, the same reasons apply, with far greater force, to the adjustments or settlements arising out of the domestic exchange. The daily clearing, or mutual balancing of accounts, between the fifty or sixty banks in the city of New York, amounts to over $20,000,000. But, large as this sum is, it must fall far below the amount paid each day, in the United States, in the operations of domestic exchange. If we take all the cities, towns or places of business in the United States, each one has its daily maturing claims on all, or a portion of the others; each place, leaving out of view individuals, may be said to have a certain claim upon all the others, and to be subject to claims from all.

New York has each day a claim upon other cities and places, and is subject to certain claims from other places. If the amounts were known, it could be stated whether, upon any particular day or week, the balances were in favor or against New York with all other places in the United States; and so with regard to Philadelphia, Boston, and other cities. All this vast business of payments between separate places, from Maine to Texas, and from California and New York, is adjusted every secular day through the agency of banks, or bankers. Who can conjecture the amount of payments involved in this adjustment? We know, generally, that these payments follow upon commercial transactions which have gone before; that commodities have been sent from the North to the South, and from the South to the North, and likewise from East to West, and from West to East, and that the paper securities which go into the banks exactly represent the amount of the transactions, and the market values involved; but the sum of all these we have no means of knowing. We know that, mainly, the commodities sold and transmitted pay for each other, and that the balances paid in coins are comparatively very small. A thousand persons in Pennsylvania may be dealing with a thousand in Louisiana, to the yearly amount of $10,000,000. They send money from neither side; the debtors in Pennsylvania pay the creditors in that State, and in Louisiana the same; and that is accomplished by the operations of domestic exchange, and the agency of the banks.

But this business, as now effected, involves needless expense, trouble and time. It must be evident that this adjustment between Pennsylvania and Louisiana, involving $10,000,000 on each side, can be made with more or less facility, according to the number engaged in it. If an hundred are engaged on each side, they would be claimants, on the average, of $100,000 each; two hundred persons would be corresponding on the subject, two hundred sets of books would contain the accounts, and quite a complicated adjustment would remain to be made on each side between these hundreds of agents, besides that which would have to be made by each one with his customers. If the number engaged were reduced from a hundred on each side to five or one, it is plain that the labor, complications and expense would be reduced in proportion. Our domestic exchange is now conducted on the cumbrous plan supposed; as banks and bankers increase, the confusion increases, and the expense and friction must also increase.

Not merely the individuals concerned in this domestic exchange need a new facility in these circumstances, the banks and bankers who are their agents need it still more; they need, in the business of the domestic exchange, an institution which should approximate to the operation of a clearing-house. If every bank or banker in New York, who discounts or purchases a bill or note payable at any other place, could at once send it to an office of exchange in that city, the books of that office would show each day the claims of New York upon all the rest of the country; and its correspondence would show the claims of all the rest of the country each day upon New York; and the same of such an office in every other city. The whole business of domestic exchange might be thus concentrated in every city at one office, in which would be exhibited daily the debts and credits of that city, and its dependencies to and with all others.

It is obvious that offices of domestic exchange thus representing whole cities or districts, and concentrating their debts and credits, could settle their mutual claims with a facility nearly equal to the operations of a clearing-house. Even the immense sums involved in the mutual claims between New York and Philadelphia, and daily paid off and settled by correspondence between hundreds of banks, bankers, brokers, and merchants, in which letters and remittances cross each other in an endless variety of ways, and with an amount of labor and friction beyond estimate, would be seen at a glance, their magnitude and importance appreciated, and the amount nearly paid off by the columns of a ledger. The aggregate indebtedness of the cities, each to the other, would be discharged as an aggregate liability. Each bank, or person concerned, would have only to account with their customers according to their relations with each other; amounts due by individuals in New York to persons in Philadelphia would be placed, in New York, to the credit of those to whom persons in Philadelphia were indebted; and so with individuals in Philadelphia creditors or debtors of persons in New York; both classes would make and receive their payments in their own city. The office proposed would, in a few hours, change the indebtedness between individuals residing in different States or cities into indebtedness between parties in the same vicinity, neighbors and customers of the same bank, and well known to each other.

By the agency of offices established for the express purpose of aiding domestic exchange, the government could distribute perfectly, promptly, at the least risk, and with the least expense, to every required point, all the public revenues; and at the same time the domestic exchange arising from commercial operations could be facilitated and economized to the utmost practicable degree. A public institution designed to regulate and assist the domestic exchanges of the country, with all the ramifications and branches to make it efficient, would be a boon to the industry, the trade, and the credit system of the country, the value of which would be almost beyond estimate. It would need to have a close and systematic connection with the financial system of the United States, that the offices of the public treasury, and the offices of domestic exchange, might operate together, so far as needful, and lend mutual support in every exigency, and that their information might be in common.

This can be done with great effect, without departing from the true limits of a proper system of national finance, and, on the other hand, without disturbing the regular processes of the credit system. This mode of facilitating the domestic exchanges, and of assisting the national treasury, might be ultimately enlarged, so as to curb or cure many evils of the credit system. It might, indeed, be so shaped and so managed, whilst promoting every legitimate interest of industry and trade, as to bring fairly and permanently within the power of the general government that control of the currency of the country which the present banking system has given to the separate States; a result attainable without any shock to credit, or any violence to the banks. The measures and financial policy directed to this important object might, we fully believe, be so shaped and so managed, as to secure the approval of all the best banks in the country, and still more certainly that of their customers.

An institution designed to regulate and aid the domestic exchanges of the United States, and to accomplish the transmission and distribution of the public revenues free of expense, would have to receive its shape and power from the general government.

For its general features, we make the following suggestions:

A capital of not less than $5,000,000 in coins or bullion, derived from residents of the United States. The subscription to remain permanently open to all persons applying by letter, by proxy, or in person, who pay the amount at the time of subscribing. No sum less than $100 received. Receipts to be given in sums of $100, negotiable and payable to bearer, or to order, as desired.

The depositories of the United States to be authorized to receive and keep this paid-up capital, but wholly apart from public money, until safe places of deposit can be provided.

To have as many offices as may be needful, one at least in every State, and one in every town of 10,000 inhabitants; no one of which to have power to lend money, to issue bank-notes, or keep deposit accounts, to discount or purchase commercial paper of any description, or any other security.

The capital to be strictly applicable to the payment of the balances of domestic exchange, and to afford the requisite facilities for the transmission and distribution of the public revenue.

To have power to receive, pay and purchase coins and bullion; to purchase at par treasury notes, or other securities of the general government; and to purchase its own scrip or shares at not less than par, payable in coins or treasury notes.

The office in New York to have the special direction as to payments of balances between the offices, and as to the transmission and distribution of the public revenue, in accordance with the requirements of the proper officers of the treasury. The affiliation of all the offices to be so complete as to make one body of the whole, all property and all liabilities being in common.

Each office to receive for collection, from banks or bankers, corporations or individuals, every description of paper security, payable at a different place from that at which it is received; and to make proper arrangements for all who desire to adjust and set-off debts without the use of money.

All collections to be made through the officers or agents of the institution, and in par currency of the place where the amounts collected are received.

The offices to make daily settlements with each other; where this is not practicable, to make them as often as the mails and the course of business will permit. The accounts of the offices, as against each other, to be first balanced, and the difference adjusted or paid. The proceeds of collections to be then distributed among those who had deposited claims for collection which had been duly paid at other offices. The charge for collection not to exceed half per cent., to which, at each settlement, is to be added at the creditor offices, and apportioned upon the whole, the cost of remitting specie to pay the balances.

To transmit, free of expense, any funds of the United States, at the instance of the proper officers of the treasury, to any office of the treasury designated; and to perform any other services for the treasury which may be within the scope of its action and organization; that is, any service pertaining to the payment or receipt of coins or bullion, or pertaining to treasury notes, or any other security of the United States.

To have power to correspond with institutions or individuals in foreign countries, in reference to the payment of balances, setting-off debts, and to the export or import of the precious metals; but not to have power to purchase or discount foreign bills of exchange, nor to draw bills, nor sell drafts upon any foreign correspondent or country.

The capital being paid, the organization being completed, the Secretary of the Treasury, the Treasurer of the United States, and all the Assistant Treasurers, the Directors of the various mints and assay offices, to be *ex officio* members of the Board of Directors.

Dividends to be declared half-yearly, payable in coins or treasury notes, as the parties entitled may request. No reserve of net profits to be retained, except what may be necessary to replace capital expended in building, or in the purchase of buildings, for the purposes of the institution.

Interest, at the rate of six per cent., to be paid to every new subscriber, from the time of his deposit until the end of the current half year.

An institution of this kind would rapidly commend itself to the whole country, by its usefulness and economy. It would be perfectly safe, because, with a large capital of the precious metals always in its vaults, it would incur no debt nor obligations which could sweep away, or even endanger its treasure. It would be a mere collector of the debts of others, never a purchaser of any. It would collect debts in current par funds, and pay in the same. Only balances between the offices would be payable in coin, which would be changing coin from one office to another. It could, therefore, never fail but from the dishonesty of its officers; and, the capital would be so subdivided, and the accountability so strict, and subject to the scrutiny of so many eyes, that no serious inroad upon it could occur from frauds or unfaithfulness.

It would be purely the servant of the public, and could only operate in proportion as the public patronized it. With it there could be no expansion nor contraction injurious to the public. No injurious competition between the offices could arise, for it would be one body through the whole country. It would be an instrument upon which the whole public could play, but which could not, like the banks, play upon the public.

It would be no monopoly, for the subscription book would be permanently open to all; and it would not grow too large, for, having the power to purchase its own stock at par, that process would always check its growth. It would grow at the convenience of the people, and diminish at their convenience.

It would have no feature of a bank, for it would circulate no notes, accept no deposits, and discount no paper. Neither would the specie in its vaults be idle, for the certificates of stock would circulate in large transactions. It would not only be open all the time for new subscriptions of stock, but the whole stock would be in motion as a medium of payment. It would be truly national, because an interest in it would be always open to every person who could pay $100.

It would sustain and strengthen the Independent Treasury, by bringing it into full contact with the internal exchanges and the capitalists of the country; and would remove, or greatly mitigate, every evil of that system unfavorable to the interests of trade and industry. It would always contain a large reserve of specie, of which a considerable portion could be spared upon any emergency. The holders of the stock could always find a purchaser at par in the institution itself, when occasion demanded.

The economy of thus clearing debts between cities, states and districts, cannot be computed at less than $5,000,000 annually; but, taking into account the friction and trouble to individuals and banks which would be prevented, the economy might be safely estimated at more than double the sum named.

Whatever advantage and saving of friction resulted from such a system would be clear gain, for there would be no power nor inducement to injure any of the great interests of the country, monetary, commercial, or industrial.

THE END.